THE ROUTLEDGE HANDBOOK OF POPULAR CULTURE AND TOURISM

T0341262

This handbook provides a comprehensive overview and holistic analysis of the intersection between tourism and popular culture. It examines current debates, questions and controversies of tourism in the wake of popular culture phenomena and explores the relationships between popular culture, globalization, tourism and mobility. In addition, it offers a cross-disciplinary, cutting edge review of the character of popular cultural production and consumption trends, analyzing their consequences for tourism, spatial strategies and destination competitiveness.

The scope of the volume encompasses various expressions of popular culture such as cinema, TV shows, music, literature, sports and heritage. Featuring a mix of theoretical and empirical chapters, the handbook problematizes and conceptualizes the ties and clusters of popular cultural actors, thereby positioning tourism within the wider context of creative economies, cultural planning and multimodal technologies.

Written by an international team of academics with expertise in a range of disciplines, this timely book will be of interest to researchers from a variety of subjects including tourism, events, geography, cultural studies, fandom research, political economy, business, media studies and technology.

Christine Lundberg is a Senior Lecturer at the University of Surrey, Associate Professor (Docent) in Sweden and the co-founder of POPCULTOUR, an international research network on Popular Culture and Tourism. POPCULTOUR is the leading research network on popular culture tourism and events and brings together cross-disciplinary researchers across the world with a shared interest in tourism and events in the wake of popular culture phenomena such as film, TV series, literature, music and fashion.

Vassilios Ziakas is Associate Professor at Plymouth Marjon University with a research interest in sport and leisure policy through the lens of an interdisciplinary approach that seeks to create linkages among the sectors of sport, recreation, leisure, tourism and events. His primary emphasis is on strategic planning for obtaining a range of sustainable community benefits. His research has been published in a range of leading journals and is widely cited. He is author of the book *Event Portfolio Planning and Management: A Holistic Approach* (Routledge, 2014).

THE ROUTLEDGE HANDBOOK OF POPULAR CULTURE AND TOURISM

Edited by Christine Lundberg and Vassilios Ziakas

Routledge
Taylor & Francis Group

LONDON AND NEW YORK

First published 2019 by Routledge

2 Park Square, Milton Park, Abingdon, Oxon OX14 4RN
605 Third Avenue, New York, NY 10017

Routledge is an imprint of the Taylor & Francis Group, an informa business

First issued in paperback 2022

British Library Cataloguing-in-Publication Data
A catalogue record for this book is available from the British Library

Library of Congress Cataloging-in-Publication Data
Names: Lundberg, Christine, 1972- editor. | Ziakas, Vassilios, editor.
Title: The Routledge handbook of popular culture and tourism /
    edited by Christine Lundberg and Vassilios Ziakas. Other titles:
    Handbook of popular culture and tourism
Description: Abingdon, Oxon ; New York, NY : Routledge, 2018. |
    Includes bibliographical references and index.
Identifiers: LCCN 2018002575 (print) | LCCN 2018017015
    (ebook) | ISBN 9781315559018 (Master ebook) | ISBN
    9781317193425 (Web PDF) | ISBN 9781317193418 (ePUB) |
    ISBN 9781317193401 (Mobipocket) | ISBN 9781138678354
    (hbk : alk. paper) | ISBN 9781315559018 (ebk)
Subjects: LCSH: Tourism–Social aspects. | Heritage tourism. |
    Popular culture.
Classification: LCC G156.5.S63 (ebook) | LCC G156.5.S63 R68
    2018 (print) | DDC 306.4/819—dc23
LC record available at https://lccn.loc.gov/2018002575

ISBN: 978-1-138-67835-4 (hbk)
ISBN: 978-1-03-233905-4 (pbk)
DOI: 10.4324/9781315559018

Typeset in Bembo
by Swales & Willis Ltd, Exeter, Devon, UK

CONTENTS

Contents

Contents

FIGURES

TABLES

CONTRIBUTORS

Ruxandra Ana received her MA from the Institute of Ethnology and Cultural Anthropology at the University of Warsaw and from 2015 onwards she has been a PhD candidate at the same Institute. From 2011 to 2014, she conducted field work in Cuba, focusing on Havana and Matanzas, looking at contemporary Cuban rumba. Her main research interests include dance anthropology and tourism anthropology, intangible cultural heritage, race and tourism in postcolonial contexts, especially in Latin America and the Caribbean. As of 2015 she has been conducting research focusing on cultural heritage in relation to work practices, entrepreneurship and social change in Cuba.

Ruth Barton is Associate Professor in Film Studies at Trinity College Dublin. She is the author of a number of publications on Irish cinema including *Irish National Cinema* (Routledge, 2004) and *Acting Irish in Hollywood* (Irish Academic Press, 2006). She has written critical biographies of the Hollywood star, Hedy Lamarr, *Hedy Lamarr, The Most Beautiful Woman in Film* (University Press of Kentucky, 2010) and the Irish silent era director, Rex Ingram, *Rex Ingram, Visionary Director of the Silent Screen* (University Press of Kentucky, 2014). She is currently preparing a new monograph on Irish cinema for Manchester University Press.

O. Hugo Benavides is Professor of Anthropology at Fordham University, as well as Chair of the Sociology/Anthropology Department. His initial interest in the past provided him an extensive archaeological practice excavating both Inca sites in the Andes and the Roman site of Pompeii in Italy. He has published three books: *Making Ecuadorian Histories: Four Centuries of Defining the Past* (University of Texas Press, 2004), *The Politics of Sentiment: Remembering and Imagining Guayaquil* (University of Texas Press, 2006) and *Drugs, Thugs and Divas: Latin American Telenovelas and Narco-Dramas* (University of Texas Press, 2008). He has written over 50 articles that have appeared in edited volumes and scholarly journals.

Melanie Ramdarshan Bold is a Lecturer in the Department of Information Studies at University College London, where she teaches and researches topics related to publishing and book cultures. Her main research interest centres around the changing nature of literary culture with a focus on digital developments in authorship, publishing and reading.

Leonieke Bolderman is finishing her PhD at the Department of Arts and Culture at Erasmus University Rotterdam. This research is part of the NWO-funded project Locating Imagination: An Interdisciplinary Perspective on Literary, Film and Music Tourism. As of September 2017, she will be Assistant Professor of Cultural Geography and Tourism Geography and Planning at the University of Groningen, The Netherlands. Her research focuses on the role and meaning of music tourism in contemporary media culture, and on the role of music in urban and regional development (www.locatingimagination.com).

Nikolaos Boukas holds a PhD in Management Studies from the University of Exeter, UK. He is currently an Assistant Professor of Tourism and Hospitality Management and the Director of the Center for Sustainable Management of Tourism, Sport & Events (CESMATSE) of the European University Cyprus. His research interests are focused on tourism policy, sustainable tourism, island tourism, cultural heritage tourism and youth tourism.

David Bowen is a Reader and Head of Doctoral Programmes at the Oxford School of Hospitality Management, Oxford Brookes University. His research interests focus on tourist consumer behaviour, tourism destination development and research methods. More recently he has completed research on the effect that visiting familiar places has on tourists and the tourism industry, and the politics of enclave and non-enclave tourism development.

Lluís Mundet i Cerdan has a Bachelor of Arts (Geography and History) from the Autonomous University of Barcelona, a master's degree in Leisure and Tourism Studies from the University of Ghent and a PhD in Geography from the University of Girona. He is an Associate Professor and member of the Multidisciplinary Research Laboratory in Tourism in the University of Girona, where he was the Dean from 2004 to 2012. He has taught at universities in Cuba, Costa Rica, Slovakia, Ethiopia, China and Brazil. He has published articles in leading academic journals on tourism. He is a co-editor of the *Revista Iberoamericana de Turismo* (RITUR).

W. Glen Croy is a Senior Lecturer in the Department of Management, Monash Business School, Monash University, and visiting researcher at the Oxford School of Hospitality Management, Oxford Brookes University. His teaching and research interests are in tourism and international business, with special research interests in the role of media in tourism, higher education and tourism in natural and protected areas.

Lena Eskilsson is a Senior Lecturer in Human Geography with a specialization in place marketing at Lund University, Sweden. Her research is directed towards place-marketing strategies and place development in a tourism and retail context. She took part as a researcher in the INTERREG IVC project, EuroScreen, focusing on the bridging of the film and tourism sectors between 2012 and 2014. Since 2016 she has been involved in a research project about the significance of the information sent that determines the success of an attraction, using Swedish places with a film and literature tourism connection as empirical examples.

Michael Fagence is first and foremost a geographer. All of the excursions made into town planning, tourism planning, history and heritage have used the toolkit of geography deeply ingrained from an undergraduate (BA) program at Nottingham University. Postgraduate study at Southampton (MPhil), Queensland (MA) and La Trobe (PhD), was accompanied by transitioning experience in teaching and research at Queensland, consulting with UNESCAP, to reach the current focus on geographical history and history-linked and heritage-based tourism. His present appointment is as an Honorary Research Fellow at the University of Queensland.

Shirley A. Fedorak taught Anthropology and Archaeology at the University of Saskatchewan in Canada from 1991–2006, and Social Sciences at Cairo American College in Egypt from 2008–2011. She is the author of *Windows on the World: Case Studies in Anthropology* (Thomas Nelson, 2006), *Pop Culture: The Culture of Everyday Life* (University of Toronto Press, 2009), *Anthropology Matters* (Broadview Press, 2007; University of Toronto Press, 2013, 2017), *Global Issues: A Cross-Cultural Perspective* (University of Toronto Press, 2014), and was the lead author from 2002–2008 for the Canadian edition of William Haviland's best-selling introductory text, *Cultural Anthropology* (Thomas Nelson, 2008). She now lives in Penang, Malaysia where she continues to write academic texts and genre fiction.

Joaquim Majó Fernández is a Computer Engineer and Doctor from the Polytechnic University of Catalonia, specialized in the use of Information and Communication Technologies (ICT) in the tourism sector. He has published articles in leading academic journals on tourism and ICT. He has participated and organized different national and international forums on tourism training. After being Coordinator of Studies and Vice President of Technological Development and Institutional Relations of the University of Girona, he is currently Dean of the Faculty of Tourism, where he has been teaching since 1993.

Sara Forgas-Serra is a PhD student at the University of Girona, developing a thesis on gastronomy and tourism. She has taught at Università degli Studi Milano, Bicocca. She is a member of the Multidisciplinary Research Laboratory in Tourism and participates in research studies on tourism in the framework of the Institute for Research in Tourism (INSETUR) of the University of Girona.

Warwick Frost is an Associate Professor in the Department of Management, Sport and Tourism at La Trobe University, Australia. His research interests include heritage, events, nature-based attractions and the interaction between media, popular culture and tourism. Warwick is a foundation co-editor of the Routledge Advances in Events Research series and a member of the editorial board of the *Journal of Heritage Tourism*. He has co-written five books with Jennifer Laing, including *Imagining the American West Through Film and Tourism* (Routledge, 2015) and co-edited five books to date.

Lincoln Geraghty is Reader in Popular Media Cultures in the School of Media and Performing Arts at the University of Portsmouth. He serves as editorial advisor for the *Journal of Popular Culture, Transformative Works and Culture, Journal of Fandom Studies* and *Journal of Popular Television* with interests in science fiction film and television, fandom and collecting in popular culture. He is Senior Editor for the online open access journal from Taylor & Francis, *Cogent Arts and Humanities*. Major publications include *Living with Star Trek: American Culture and the Star Trek Universe* (IB Tauris, 2007), *American Science Fiction Film and Television* (Berg, 2009) and *Cult Collectors: Nostalgia, Fandom and Collecting Popular Culture* (Routledge, 2014).

Michael J. Gross is a Lecturer with the School of Management at the University of South Australia in Adelaide. Michael holds a Bachelor of Science in Business Administration (BSBA) with a major in Hotel and Restaurant Management from the University of Denver, USA;

master's degrees in Education (MPET) and Business (MBA) from Deakin University, Australia; and a PhD from the University of South Australia. He has an extensive professional background in international hospitality management with some of the world's leading hotel firms. He teaches in hospitality and tourism programmes at the undergraduate and postgraduate levels, and his research and publishing focuses on hospitality management and tourism management areas.

Manuela Guerreiro is an Auxiliary Professor at the Faculty of Economics, University of Algarve (Portugal). She has a PhD in Economic and Management Sciences (University of Algarve), Msc in Cultural Management (University of Algarve and Université Paris VIII), and graduated in Communication Sciences (Technical University of Lisbon). She is Director of the Master in Marketing Management (University of Algarve). Current research interests includes marketing, brand management, consumer behaviour, e-marketing, cultural tourism and tourism experiences. She is also a researcher at the Research Centre for Spatial and Organizational Dynamics (CIEO).

Maria-Josep Mulet Gutiérrez is a Doctor of Art History, Senior Lecturer at the University of the Balearic Islands (UIB), Director of the MA in Cultural Heritage: Research and Management and specialist in contemporary art and audiovisual heritage. Responsible for the research group Audiovisual heritage, mass-media and illustration, she has published, among other books and papers: 'Fotografía y turismo. El registro de lo urbano a través de fotógrafos de proyección internacional por las Islas Baleares', in J. Calatrava et al. (eds), *La cultura y la ciudad* (Universidad de Granada, 2016, pp. 339–344); 'Fotógrafos de proyección internacional en Ibiza (1928–67). Sobre algunos motivos del viaje', in M. Olivera y A. Salvador (eds), *Del artefacto mágico al pixel. Estudios de fotografía* (Madrid: Universidad Complutense, 2014, 533–548); and *Fotografia i turisme a les Balears. Josep Planas i Montanyà* (Barcelona: Lunwerg, 2005).

Szilvia Gyimóthy is Associate Professor and Head of Research at the Tourism Research Unit, Department of Culture and Global Studies, Aalborg University in Denmark. Her primary research interest lies in strategic market communications in tourism, with a focus on place-making, commodification strategies and competitive differentiation of regions in the creative economy. Szilvia is particularly interested in the transformative impact of global and nonwestern popular culture on tourism places. In the past years, she has studied the narrative repositioning of European destinations along culinary inventions, outdoor adventures and Bollywood productions, as well as disruptive collaborative movements and platforms.

Azizul Hassan is a member of the Tourism Consultants Network of the UK Tourism Society, and is currently working towards a PhD at Cardiff Metropolitan University. His main areas of research are technology-supported marketing in tourism, innovative marketing dynamics, destination branding in tourism, cultural heritage tourism, heritage interpretation and sustainable management/marketing alternatives for cultural heritage industries. He is a regular reviewer of *Tourism Analysis*, the *International Journal of Human Resource Management*, the *International Journal of Ecotourism*, the *eReview of Tourism Research* (eRTR) and the *International Interdisciplinary Business-Economics Advancement Journal*.

Cláudia Henriques is Lecturer at the School of Management, Hospitality and Tourism (ESGHT), University of Algarve (Portugal). She has a PhD in Economics (Tourism Planning and Management) (University of Algarve), a master's degree in Social Policy and Economics (ISEG – Lisbon School of Economics and Management of Technical University of Lisbon) and graduated in Economics (ISEG – Technical University of Lisbon). She is Director of the Department of Economics at the School of Management, Hospitality and Tourism (ESGHT). Current research interests includes cultural tourism, tourism planning and management, tourism experiences and cultural economics. She is also a researcher at the Research Centre for Spatial and Organizational Dynamics (CIEO).

Myria Ioannou is an Assistant Professor in Marketing at the European University Cyprus and the coordinator of the BBA in Marketing Communications and Social Media. Dr Ioannou received her PhD from Manchester Business School and publishes in international journals and conferences on service quality, customer experience and engagement and relationship management. Before becoming an academic she worked in the industry as a business and financial analyst (Cyprus Development Bank) and as a training officer in the Human Resource Development Authority in Cyprus.

Burcu Kaya is PhD student and a Research Assistant in Tourism at Anadolu University. She has taken social anthropology courses from METU University in Ankara. She has conducted research about social memory and national identity and participated in an oral history project about tourism. She is currently conducting another research project that aims at modelling the relationship between places, narratives, commemoration and performances. Her research interests are heritage, space and place, rituals, social memory, narratives and performances.

Marieke Kersten graduated from the Department of Management, Monash University researching volunteer tourism. She has since changed focus, and is now an Occupational Therapist specializing in the area of adult psychiatry. Her role includes facilitating group therapy sessions and individual assessments for clients, assisting them to return to their activities of daily living.

Yuri Kork is Visiting Professor with LuxDev in Tourism Department, National Management Degree College, Yangon, Myanmar. He graduated from the University of Exeter Business School in 2014 with a PhD in Management Studies. Yuri specializes in culture tourism and its niche forms, such as film tourism, food tourism, dark tourism, as well as tourist behaviour and decision-making. More recently, his work expanded into the field of digital tourism, and prior to his current position, he spent a year working in IT and linguistics and exploring more technical aspects of digital and VR interactions.

Jennifer Laing is an Associate Professor in the Department of Management, Sport and Tourism at La Trobe University, Australia. Her research interests include travel narratives, the role of events in society, rural and regional development, tourism and the media and health and wellness tourism. Jennifer is a foundation co-editor of the Routledge Advances in Events Research series and a member of the editorial boards of *Journal of Travel Research, Tourism Analysis* and *Tourism Review International*. She has co-written five books with Warwick Frost, including *Gastronomy, Tourism and the Media* (Channel View, 2016) and co-edited three books to date.

Nicolle Lamerichs holds a PhD in Media Studies at Maastricht University. Her doctoral thesis *Productive Fandom* (2014) explores intermediality and reception in fan cultures. She currently works as a Senior Lecturer at International Communication and Media at HU University of Applied Sciences, Utrecht. Her research focuses on participatory culture and new media, specifically the nexus between popular culture, storytelling and play.

Linda Levitt teaches communication and media studies at Stephen F. Austin State University. Her primary research sits at the intersection of memory studies and media, considering media's role in shaping understandings of the past. She has published essays in *Participations, Radical History Review*, and *Velvet Light Trap*, along with book chapters in edited academic collections. Dr Levitt's book, *Hollywood Forever: Culture, Celebrity, and the Cemetery*, is forthcoming from Routledge.

Maria Lexhagen is an Associate Professor and Head of Tourism Studies at Mid Sweden University. She holds a PhD in Business Administration and Tourism from Gothenburg University, with a special interest in marketing and information technology. Her research covers both consumer behaviour and destination management and she has published internationally in both tourism and technology-focused journals and books. Her current research interests include implications of information technology and social media in the tourism industry, destination management and branding as well as pop culture tourism induced by film, music and literature, specifically fans and fan cultures.

Joakim Lind is a PhD student at the School of Business and Economics, Åbo Akademi University, Finland. Joakim has an academic background in economics and social anthropology, and extensive experience as consultant of marketing and communication from a number of cities, regional authorities and creative industries. Apart from other assignments, he has published various reports on value creation in connection with literary fiction and film, such as *Wallander* (Henning Mankell) and *Millennium* (Stieg Larsson). In his research Joakim is examining the value creation and capital that can be related to a popular culture narratives.

Henrik Linden is a Senior Lecturer in Tourism and Cultural Industries Management at the University of East London (UEL), where he is also the Programme Leader for the BA in Tourism Management. Before joining UEL in 2015, he was a Senior Lecturer in Creative Industries at London Metropolitan University. Henrik holds a PhD in Culture, Media and Creative Industries from King's College London, and he is the co-author of *Fans and Fan Cultures: Tourism, Consumerism and Social Media* (Palgrave Macmillan, 2017).

Sara Linden is a Lecturer in Events and Tourism at Goldsmiths, University of London. She is the Programme Leader for the MA in Events and Experience Management and also lectures in the areas of cultural tourism, arts management and regeneration. Sara is a PhD candidate at Birkbeck, University of London, and she is the co-author of *Fans and Fan Cultures: Tourism, Consumerism and Social Media* (Palgrave Macmillan, 2017).

Kristina N. Lindström received her PhD in Human Geography from the School of Business Economics and Law, University of Gothenburg, where she holds a position as a Senior Lecturer. She is currently involved in a three-year research project focusing on stakeholder collaboration for sustainable tourism. Her main research interest is the issue of transformation of local communities to spaces of production and consumption of tourist experiences, as well as collaboration between stakeholders and the role of policy in such societal transformation processes. Furthermore, Kristina's research interest covers the role of media, its conception and application in tourism development.

Philip Long is an Associate Professor in Tourism at Bournemouth University. His research interests include: festivals, cultural events and their tourism dimensions; connections between creative industries and tourism; diaspora communities, social exclusion and tourism. Philip is a Board member of the International Festivals and Events Association (Europe).

Christine Lundberg is a Senior Lecturer at the University of Surrey, Associate Professor (Docent) in Sweden, and the co-founder of POPCULTOUR, an international research network on Popular Culture and Tourism. POPCULTOUR is the leading research network on popular culture tourism and events and brings together cross-disciplinary researchers across the world with a shared interest in tourism and events in the wake of popular culture phenomena such as film, TV series, literature, music and fashion.

Maria Månsson is a Senior Lecturer in Tourism at Liverpool John Moores University, England. She has been researching film tourism since 2006, for example in her doctoral thesis *Mediatized Tourism: The Convergence of Media and Tourism Performances* (successfully defended at Lund University in Sweden 2015) and as a researcher in an INTERREG IVC project, EuroScreen, focusing on the bridging of the film and tourism sectors. She is particularly interested in place development and marketing and the influence of media on tourism and tourist behaviour in places visited by tourists.

Paul Mason teaches in the Department of Global English at Aichi Gakuin University, one of only two Zen Buddhist-sponsored universities in Japan. His research interests include both modern Japanese popular culture and fan studies. Before teaching in Japan, he worked in publishing and broadcasting in the UK, and wrote five gamebooks for Puffin's popular Fighting Fantasy series, as well as two based on the Robin of Sherwood TV show.

Audrey Mélinon graduated from her MSc in International Hospitality, Events and Tourism Management at the Oxford School of Hospitality Management, Oxford Brookes University. Her research focused on film tourism. Audrey is now working in the field of conferences and events.

Júlio Mendes holds a PhD in Management (Strategy and Organizational Behaviour) and is a Professor at the Faculty of Economics, University of Algarve, where he is also Director of the Master in Tourism Organizations Management and an active member of the board of the PhD program in Tourism. He is also a research member of the Centre for Spatial and Organizational Dynamics (CIEO) and author and co-author of numerous scientific articles, chapters and papers related to marketing management, tourism experiences, integrated quality management of tourism destinations, community-based tourism and sustainability.

Patrick Naef is a researcher at the Institute of Environmental Sciences of the University of Geneva. He is also a lecturer at the Institute of Geography of the University of Neuchâtel. He was previously a visiting scholar in the Department of Anthropology at the University of California, Berkeley. His main areas or research are associated with memory, violence, tourism, cultural heritage and mobility. His doctoral dissertation defended at the University of Geneva looks at conflicts of memory within the cultural heritage management and tourism sectors in Sarajevo, Srebrenica (Bosnia-Herzegovina) and Vukovar (Croatia). He is now conducting research on the case of Medellin in Colombia where he looks at memory construction in peripheral areas of the city.

Neil O'Boyle is Chair of the BA in Communication Studies Programme at Dublin City University. His work primarily examines the relationship between media, popular culture and collective identities, a topic he explored in his 2011 book, *New Vocabularies, Old Ideas: Culture, Irishness, and the Advertising Industry* (Verlag Peter Lang, 2011). Dr O'Boyle's work has been published in a wide range of academic journals, including *Cultural Sociology, Social Identities, Journalism Practice, European Journal of Communication, Nationalism and Ethnic Politics, Sport and Society* and *Communication Education.*

Kelly Palmer lectures and tutors in popular culture, literary studies, and creative and professional writing at the Queensland University of Technology. Her practice-led PhD looks to cultural and literary studies to explore how low-income locals practice belonging on the Gold Coast, Australia.

Nicola Palmer is Head of Research Programmes and Head of Doctoral Training at Sheffield Hallam University, with a first degree and PhD in Tourism Studies. Her academic research interests and consultancy include work on: the visitor economy; socio-economic and community dimensions of tourism development; representation, ideology and place; the politics of cultural tourism, heritage tourism and eco-tourism; and symbolic consumption. Nicola combines academic international tourism roles with regional business and community-based board memberships.

Rukmini Pande has recently finished her PhD on the intersections of identity in media fandom communities at the University of Western Australia. She is currently teaching as an Assistant Professor at Jindal Global University, India. Her thesis is under contract to be published as a monograph by the University of Iowa Press. She has been published in multiple edited collections on race in media fandom, including *Seeing Fans* (edited by Paul Booth and Lucy Bennett, Bloomsbury, 2016). She has also published in journals such as *Transformative Works and Cultures* and the *Journal of Feminist Scholarship.*

Charuwan Phongpanichanan is currently pursuing a PhD program in Hospitality, Tourism and Culinary Arts at Taylor's University, Malaysia. Her research background is related to the past work experience that she has gained as the project consultant. She has worked with a consulting firm specializing in the alignment of human resource management with strategic objectives in resolving HR-related and organizational issues.

Valeriya Radomskaya is a PhD candidate at James Cook University. Her work focuses on the popular culture tourism and its impact on the tourism market. Her current thesis explores how popular culture affects the contemporary events tourism market in general, and what effect it can have on Australia's events tourism in particular.

Célia M. Q. Ramos graduated in Computer Engineering from the University of Coimbra, obtained her Master in Electrical and Computers Engineering from the Higher Technical Institute, Lisbon University, and PhD in Econometrics in the University of the Algarve (UALG), Faculty of Economics, Portugal. Celia is Director of the Marketing course and her current research interests includes, tourism information systems, electronic tourism, business intelligence tools, digital marketing and panel data models. She is a researcher at the Center for Advanced Studies in Management and Economics of the Universidade de Évora (CEFAGE-UE).

Stijn Reijnders is Professor of Cultural Heritage, in particular in relation to tourism and popular culture, at Erasmus University Rotterdam. Furthermore, he serves as member of the Executive

Board of the Erasmus Research Center for Media, Communication and Culture, member of the Supervisory Board of Museum Rotterdam, and is Chair of the Popular Communication Division of the Netherlands Flanders Communication Association. His research focuses on the intersections of media, culture and tourism. Currently he supervises two large, international research projects and 11 PhD students.

Stefan Roesch is an internationally recognized film tourism expert, advising tourism managers and film commissioners on how to benefit from the exposure generated by movies and TV shows (www.filmquest.co/b2b). He is the author of the book *The Experiences of Film Location Tourists* (Channel View Publications, 2009), which is based on his PhD thesis that he completed at the University of Otago, New Zealand in 2007. In late 2016, Stefan founded FilmQuest (www.filmquest.co), a web-based B2C platform about all things film tourism, which combines an image-based location database with an inspirational story blog.

Gregory L. Rohe is an Associate Professor with the Department of Global English at Aichi Gakuin University in Nagoya, Japan, as well as the Associate Director of the university's Center of International Programs. He is a member of the Culture of Travel Research Group at the university's Institute of Cultural Studies, and recently curated the group's exhibit, 'Tabi: Rekishi to Bunka' (The History and Culture of Travel). In addition to the culture of travel, specific research interests include travel narratives of Western travellers in Japan, and representations by travellers of Japan and the Japanese during the late nineteenth and early twentieth centuries.

Carla Schriever is a Lecturer in Musicology, Philosophy and Media Studies at the universities of Marburg, Hamburg and Oldenburg in Germany. Her work focuses on fandom studies and diversity ethics. She has devoted further studies to the late musician Prince and his fan community, for example, 'The desire for the heel: Male fetishism and pop-fan culture around Prince' (*Clothing Cultures*, 2, no. 2 (2015), 157–165).

María Sebastián Sebastián is an Architect, Art Historian and PhD candidate at the University of the Balearic Islands (UIB). She holds a FPI fellowship from the Balearic Islands Government selected as part of the operational programme co-financed by the European Social Fund. Publications include 'Rul·lan y el hotel Bahía Palace de Palma. Los canales de difusión de la fotografía de arquitectura turística', in *Congreso internacional: Inter photo arch*, vol. II (Pamplona: Servicio de Publicaciones de la Universidad de Navarra, 2016, 202–211) and 'Un modelo turístico alternativo: el hotel Araxa de Francesc Mitjans en Palma de Mallorca', in *Actas del II Congreso Nacional Pioneros de la Arquitectura Moderna Española. Aprender de una obra* (Madrid: Fundación Alejandro de la Sota, 2015, 564–574).

Tina Šegota holds a PhD in Marketing Communications and will soon hold a PhD in Tourism, both from the University of Ljubljana, Slovenia. She was faculty at Faculty of Economics at University of Ljubljana, and is now a lecturer in the Department of Marketing, Events and Tourism at University of Greenwich. Tina's current research interest is on seasonality and sustainable tourism development, with a passionate focus on local residents. She is also interested in understanding this segment from a marketing perspective, and how residents participate in destination marketing activities. She has published in leading journals and has co-authored several book chapters.

Joan Carles Oliver Torelló is Doctor of Art History and Associate Lecturer at the University of the Balearic Islands (UIB). He is a member of the research groups Audiovisual heritage, mass media and illustration (UIB) and Drawing and Project (University of Granada). Some of his latest contributions related to the field of contemporary photographic representation are 'The appearances of the model: Staging and visual control in the photography of architectural models', in I. Bergera (ed.), *Modelling for the Camera: Photography of Architectural Models in Spain. 1925–1970* (Madrid: Fundación Ico, Ministerio de Fomento, La Fábrica, 2016) and 'La imagen del Crucificado en Salvador Dalí, José María Sert y Juan de la Cruz' (*Locus Amoenus*, 14(2016), 215–232).

Rhona Trauvitch received her PhD in Comparative Literature from the University of Massachusetts Amherst in 2013. She is an instructor at Florida International University, where she teaches courses in narrative theory, popular culture and science fiction, among other subjects. She has contributed chapters to several edited collections, including *Jim Henson and Philosophy: Imagination and the Magic of Mayhem* (Rowman & Littlefield, 2015), and *Literary Cartographies: Spatiality, Representation, and Narrative* (Palgrave Macmillan, 2014). Her research interests span narratology, popular culture, speculative fiction, and literature and science. Her current book project examines readers' interactions with fictional entities and the social experience of narrative.

Rodanthi Tzanelli is Associate Professor of Cultural Sociology at Leeds University, UK. Her research interests include globalization, cosmopolitanism and mobility theory. She is author of several academic articles and book chapters, as well as nine monographs, including *Thanatourism and Cinematic Representations of Risk: Screening the End of Tourism* (Routledge, 2016).

Bengt Kristensson Uggla is Amos Anderson Professor of Philosophy, Culture and Management at Åbo Akademi University. After defending his doctoral thesis on Paul Ricoeur at Lund University (Sweden) in 1994, he has been associated with a number of European and American universities, together with significant management positions, such as Dean at the IFL (Swedish Institute of Management: Stockholm-Brussels-Moscow). Between 2006 and 2010, he was Head of the Nomadic University for Art, Philosophy and Enterprise in Europe (www. nurope.eu). He is a frequently invited speaker and in a number of books and articles he has developed a kind of cross-disciplinary hermeneutics.

Maranke Wieringa obtained her MA in Media Studies (cum laude) at Utrecht University. She holds a BA (bene meritum) in Cultural Studies from the Radboud University in Nijmegen. During her BA, she participated in the Radboud Honours Academy. Maranke's recent work has been in the field of scholarly data analysis. She works as a researcher at Utrecht Data School.

Medet Yolal is an Associate Professor of Marketing at Faculty of Tourism at Anadolu University, Turkey, where he mainly teaches issues related to destination management and marketing, tourism marketing and consumer behaviour. In 2003, he received his PhD in Tourism Management from the Anadolu University, Turkey. He has worked on several research projects related to small and medium-sized enterprises and family businesses in tourism and has also worked as a visiting scholar at Washington State University, USA. His research interests mainly focus on tourism marketing, consumer behaviour, tourist experience, event management, tourism development and quality of life research in tourism.

Lisa Yong Yeu Moy is a Lecturer at the School of Hospitality, Tourism and Culinary Arts of Taylor's University, Malaysia. Lisa has over 13 years experience in international business having worked in Taipei, Taiwan. Prior to joining Taylor's University, she was teaching at SiChuan University, SiChuan, China.

Vassilios Ziakas is Associate Professor at Plymouth Marjon University with research interest in sport and leisure policy through the lens of an interdisciplinary approach that seeks to create linkages among the sectors of sport, recreation, leisure, tourism and events. His primary emphasis is on strategic planning for obtaining a range of sustainable community benefits. His research has been published in a range of leading journals and is widely cited. He is author of the book *Event Portfolio Planning and Management: A Holistic Approach* (Routledge, 2014).

PREFACE

Popular culture is the new Babylon, into which so much art and intellect now
flow. It is our imperial sex theater, supreme temple of the western eye. We live in
the age of idols. The pagan past, never dead, flames again in our mystic hierarchies
of stardom.

(Camille Paglia)

You played GOLF! You watched FOOTBALL! You drank BEER! We EVOLVED!

(Frank Zappa)

What is 'popular culture' within a globalized world and how do its different manifestations
traverse with practices of travel and tourism? Do they transform the world tapestry of various
socio-cultural, political and economic constituents and/or engender new phenomena that influence, in turn, the public sphere? At first, approaching the relationship between popular culture
and tourism as both a 'cause and effect' of wider change seemed to us to be very challenging
for its comprehensive treatment and the production of an edited volume. As disciplinary foci
that study different facets of popular culture place boundaries on them according to their own
agendas and priorities, thereby creating hybrid domains such as film tourism, arts and cultural
policy, event management, heritage or sport tourism and so on, the innate fragmentation of
popular culture and tourism is escalated. This obscures the common ground, shared among
different forms of popular culture upon which a comprehensive approach can be taken capable
of identifying interconnections and joint interests (but, at the same time, also appreciating their
distinctiveness). On the other hand, the obscurity over the nature and varieties of popular culture intermingling with tourism, and their subsequent fragmentation, make imperative the need
to study from an integrated perspective the relationship between popular culture and tourism.

In response, this Handbook aims at providing a comprehensive overview of the intersection
between popular culture and tourism. It defines the current state of theory and research in this
specialized field and creates a foundation for future scholarship and study. The scope of the
volume encompasses various expressions of popular culture such as cinema, TV shows, music,
literature, sports, heritage, etc. without, however, being exhaustive, due to the plethora of
expressions and space limitations of the book. We believe though that the Handbook provides

a representative delineation of this emerging area of study previously not addressed holistically in academic research. In doing so, the volume examines current debates, questions, and controversies of mobility and place-making in the wake of popular culture phenomena. Most importantly, the multi-disciplinary approach of the Handbook is intended to provide the reader with an inclusive coverage of areas ranging from cultural studies, fandom research, geography, political economy, business, media studies and technology. It consists of contributions in varying regions and disciplines, discursive and reflective pieces or discussions of original empirical work (cases). Overall, we have endeavoured to produce a Handbook with a global scope and outreach, and to explore less conspicuous aspects (non-Western popular culture phenomena, non-commercial and grassroots mobilities, etc.). Through this endeavour, we hope that we have made a start in building a common ground for the comprehensive study of popular culture tourism as an integrated field of scholarship and practice.

INTRODUCTION
Beneath the trivial façade of popular culture

People travel to attend or partake in popular culture activities and events that express particular worldviews, lifestyles and identifications. Culture in general embodies an inexhaustible accumulation of expressive practices that can widely appeal to fans and tourists. Up until now, research on popular culture and tourism has destination and tourist/fan perspectives. The destination perspective focuses on concepts such as commoditization (MacCannell, 1973), staged performance and authenticity (Cohen, 1988; Xie, Osumare & Ibrahim, 2007); these deal with the extent to which a tourism experience is organized for visitors and to what degree it can be regarded as 'genuine'. Other studies that originate in popular culture demonstrate how celebrities' associations with places can influence tourists' perceptions of the destinations (Lee, Scott & Kim, 2008). The area within which the majority of research has been focused is that of film tourism. This is where, according to Beeton's (2010) review, development has moved from confirming the phenomenon and calculating tourist flows (Riley, Baker & Van Doren, 1998; Riley & Van Doren, 1992; Tooke & Baker, 1996), to focusing on more complex factors such as tourists' motivations (Beeton, 2005; Riley & Van Doren, 1992) and the management of and impact on destinations (Mordue, 1999, 2001). Current research focuses on postmodern interpretations of concepts such as authenticity, hyperrealism and simulacra, which takes the discussion beyond simplified explanations of film as a marketer of places (Beeton, 2010). According to Baudrillard, hyperrealism means that the border between the simulated and the real is dissolved and that simulacra are simulated codes (substitutes for reality) that are communicated via consumption and the media (Baudrillard, 1994).

However, popular culture encompasses a broader range of expressive practices and aficionado pursuits that need to be studied and understood. So where can we draw the line among the multitude forms of cultural expression and activities as belonging or not to 'popular culture'? For example, is a classical music symphony orchestra or a folklore music concert, forms of popular culture when they appeal to a substantial (if not massive) number of fans and attendees? And what about physical cultures such as ballet, dancing and sport? Is popular culture correctly associated with less intellectually demanding activities, perhaps of trivial nature and substance? If so, is this area worthy of study?

Conventionally, the art forms of film, music, fashion and literature have been categorized as belonging to the field of popular culture based on the premise that they are consumed by the social majority (Lindgren, 2005). Popular culture has been defined as culture that is appreciated by many people, and is also called mass culture (Strinati, 2004). This is usually situated in contrast to 'fine culture', where a line is drawn between art (fine culture) and entertainment (popular culture) (Heilbrun, 1997). Another conventional characteristic of popular culture is that it is commercial. According to Lindgren (2005), it is when a popular culture tourism expression is placed to a market and financial considerations are made that it belongs to popular culture. Further, this type of culture is commonly described as easily accessible (not intellectually demanding) and linked to recreation and entertainment. Scholarly work into popular culture is often called 'studies of everyday life' and has its theoretical underpinnings on cultural studies such as sociology, ethnology, media studies, literary studies and anthropology. A core line of inquiry has been the concept of text, i.e. different cultural expressions as carriers of meaning (e.g. written texts, pictures, clothes) and how these are coded by a sender and decoded by a receiver (Lindgren, 2005; Traube, 1996). Lindgren (2005) believes that popular culture texts reflect and express many people's needs (aesthetic and otherwise), so the text says something about the audience.

Is the above conventional conceptualization of popular culture still current and profitable as its different forms increasingly intersect with tourism in various ways? To what extent do its production modes and consumption patterns deviate from standardized tourism structures, or engender unique meanings and allegiance for fans/tourists and foster representations that reinforce their cultural affiliations, while (re)shaping places as tourism destinations? To appreciate the dynamics of the intersection between popular culture and tourism and its implications for the changing conditions and business environments in which such activities take place, it is pivotal to re-conceptualize the nature and dimensions of popular culture in relation to pertinent tourism contexts, processes and outcomes. With this in mind, the current Handbook provides a framework for understanding the socio-cultural foundations of popular culture and tourism, their broader context of expressions and fandoms in line with processes and outcomes of tourism place-making and destination management. This conceptual origin constitutes the structure of the Handbook arranging it accordingly into five sections.

Rationale and structure of the Handbook

In arranging and structuring this edited volume, our guiding rationale was to capture the phenomenon that popular culture has become a destination commodification apparatus of multiple cultural significations and meanings, which are being marketed to foster tourism-related benefits for those destinations connected with them. This, in turn, raises questions of positive and negative consequences and how to incorporate popular culture associations into the overall destination product and service mix. To shed light on both the explicit and implicit intersections between popular culture production/consumption processes and the socio-economic and political conditions required for effective destination strategies, we adopted a broad interdisciplinary approach to develop a framework that can delineate the interplay and intertextuality of popular culture expressions and their media-driven construction of cultural signs into tourist products. This inter-disciplinary approach for scholarly work on popular culture tourism integrating, among others, cultural anthropology, sociology, geography, psychology, marketing and film and media and tourism studies, synthesized the Handbook composition with Part I providing the foundations of popular culture tourism, Part II delving into its plethora of expressions, Part III discussing fandom varieties, while Part IV analyzes processes of place-making, which, in turn, lead to an examination of pertinent destination management practices in Part V. To achieve a coherent hybrid neo-disciplinary synthesis throughout the volume, we also encouraged a common but flexible structure for all chapters; with the aim to keep internal cohesion of conceptual development due to the multi-disciplinary nature of contributions, different theoretical underpinnings and writing styles. Last, the concluding section outlines an inter-disciplinary comprehensive research agenda for the field of popular culture tourism. A description of the sections and chapters follows.

Part I Setting the stage: foundations of popular culture tourism

Part I of the Handbook outlines the different definitions of popular culture and how it is expressed in tourism practice. It further sets the scene for some of the main challenges arising in the wake of popular culture travels and their regional and national effects. For example, Chapter 1 by Fedorak explores the plethora of popular culture definitions presented in literature and creates a foundation for the understanding of tourism in the wake of popular culture expressions. Chapter 2 by Tzanelli explores the links between tourism and popular culture through scholarship, socialization and construction. The construction of synontological spaces in popular culture is explored in Chapter 3 by Trauvich, in which categories of such spaces are also presented. The differing notions of popular culture, history and heritage along with modern forms of capital (i.e. the tourism industry) are explored through the lens of Apocalypto and the Mayas in Chapter 4 by Benavides. The final chapter in Part I (Chapter 5) by Naef explores how popular culture and tourism participate in the commodification and memorialization of the violent heritage of narco drama in Medellin, Columbia.

Part II Broadening the scope: popular culture tourism expressions

Part II of the Handbook introduces the many different popular culture expressions that lead to tourism, such as films, TV shows, music, celebrities, dance and sports. It explores the demand, perceptions and behaviour showcased in popular culture tourism. As an example, the tourism demand of film tourists is explored in Chapter 6 by Kork. The chapter also presents the complex film tourist decision-making process. In Chapter 7, the Golden Age of television and tourism in the wake of this popular culture expression is explored by Roesch. Laing and Frost take a closer look at how the media has shaped modern views and understandings of the medieval period and influenced tourism in Chapter 8. The popular culture expression of contemporary music tourism and its connection to place is identified in Chapter 9 by Bolderman and Reijnders. In Chapter 10, Henriques et al. take a closer look at the Portuguese song form 'fado' and its identity and role in Lisbon tourist experiences. Dance and its relationship to tourism in Cuba is explored in Chapter 11 by Ana. In Chapter 12 by Wieringa, urban practices in the form of leisure time, tourism and of flânerie are investigated. Another form of sport – cricket in Bangladesh – and its relationship to tourism and technology is outlined in Chapter 13 by Hassan. In Chapter 14 by Lamerichs, video game tourism and augmented reality are examined. Chapter 15 by Palmer and Long investigates the concept of 'royal tourism' and how it can be used as a political and socio-cultural tool and context. In Chapter 16 by Palmer, the Gold Coast narrative fiction and its links to travel is under study. In the final chapter of Part II (Chapter 17) celebrity cemetery tourism, also known as dark tourism, is analyzed by Levitt.

Part III Performing fan cultures: popular culture tourism fandoms

Part III of the Handbook takes a closer look at the different fan groups – fandoms – that engage in popular culture travels. The section provides insights into a diverse range of fandoms and their travel-related behaviour. For example, in Chapter 18, Geraghty takes the reader through the pilgrimage and narratives of being a fan. Fan experiences linked to travel in the case of a Thai celebrity Sornram Theappitak is examined by Yong Yeu Moy and Phongpanichanan in Chapter 19. The Purple Army's (Prince fans) travel in the footsteps of their idol is in focus in Chapter 20 by Schriever. Two other music phenomena and their fans, the Irish band U2 and the Swedish band ABBA, are used to illustrate individual and social dimensions of music fan tourists, in Chapter 21 by Lexhagen. Chapter 22 by Linden and Linden provides insights into the Eurovision Song Content's fans and their travel motivations and experiences. The final chapter of Part III (Chapter 23) by Boyle investigates the (promotional) value of public-spiritedness in the case of Irish football fans at Euro 2016.

Part IV Getting on the map: popular culture tourism and place-making

In Part IV of the Handbook, the communicative power of popular culture tourism is explored, together with the transformative image processes that take place in the wake of popular culture tourism. For example, Chapter 24 by Ramdarshan Bold explores the characteristics of the literary village the Bloomsbury Group in London viewed by social media savvy tourists. In Chapter 25, Pande applies a post-colonial framework to India in the wake of popular culture tourism. Chapter 26 by Barton takes a critical look at the use of the protected area Skellig islands in the filming of Star Wars. In Chapter 27, Lind and Kristensson Uggla investigate the narrative capital of place in the case of Stockholm, Sweden and the *Millennium* trilogy. The 'touristed landscape' and its symbolic importance of place, space and text is outlined in Chapter 28 by Fagence. Chapter 29 by Mulet Gutiérrez et al. examines Spain's image as a tourist destination from an iconographic perspective, reflected on public photography, graphic guides, postcards and cinema. In Chapter 30, Mason and Rohe explore the relationship between place-making and 'play' in Japan. Displacement and representation of places in films in the case of the movie Troy in Turkey and Malta are in focus in Chapter 31 by Kaya and Yolal. The final chapter of Part IV (Chapter 32) by Gyimóthy addresses destination transformation in Switzerland in the footsteps of Bollywood films.

Part V Establishing a common ground: popular culture tourism and destination management

Part V of the Handbook pinpoints the complex stakeholder processes that take place when developing popular culture tourism at destinations. Furthermore, it explores the different destination development challenges and their impacts on popular culture tourism spaces. In Chapter 33, for example, Croy et al. review issues for film tourism stakeholders and provide indicative considerations to manage film impacts through the image generated. The stakeholder perspective is also used in Chapter 34 by Eskilsson and Månsson in which challenges in film tourism projects, in different parts of Europe, are critically analyzed. Chapter 35 by Radomskaya explores new marketing tools in the wake of technology development and popular culture. New marketing tools such as social media is also in focus in Chapter 36 by Šegota, in the case of the TV show *Game of Thrones*. In Chapter 37 by Forgas-Serra et al., the image of places following culinary films is under study. Chapter 38 by Boukas and Ioannou takes a management and policy approach to popular culture museums in Cyprus. In Chapter 39, Gross examines the viability and utility of a lifestyle strategy for the marketing of a destination. The final chapter of Part V (Chapter 40) by Lindström proposes a comprehensive analytical framework (evolutionary economic geography) for popular culture tourism development and management.

Building a research agenda for popular culture tourism

The final chapter of the Handbook summarizes the main areas to constitute the core of a comprehensive research agenda for popular culture tourism. Additionally, it provides guidance on issues and topics central for future research within this interdisciplinary field of study.

A final word

The need for broader conceptualization of popular culture as it intersects with tourism and the development of integrated perspectives in its study and management is pressing if it is to thoroughly understand this phenomenon and inform evidence-based destination policy. Popular culture is not necessarily, or always trivial, but can be perceived as such depending on how we define it, treat it and develop it. Certain forms and expressions can acquire or lose meaningful substance across time and socio-cultural, political and economic conditions. Yet, we should bear in mind that the attachment of tourists to destinations associated with popular culture expressions is closely linked to the symbolic meanings that popular culture performances obtain through their function as cultural significations. In other words, they project signs and images laden with symbolic meanings, which are constantly (re)interpreted by different actors/stakeholders, thereby rendering new meanings that foster emotional or ideological attachments. The connections between the cultural meanings of different actors in the tourism industry and popular culture signs create polysemic webs of significance (Geertz, 1973) that afford unexplored possibilities for understanding the contribution of popular culture tourism to social (re)ordering by offering opportunities for people to (re)interpret the world around them (Turner, 1974) and/or instigate social change.

References

Baudrillard, J. (1994). *Simulacra and Simulations*. Michigan, MI: University of Michigan Press.
Beeton, S. (2005). *Film-Induced Tourism*. Clevedon, UK: Channel View.
Beeton, S. (2010). The Advance of Film Tourism. *Tourism and Hospitality Planning & Development*, 7(1), 1–6.
Cohen, E. (1988). Authenticity and Commoditization in Tourism. *Annals of Tourism Research*, 15(3), 371–386.
Geertz, C. (1973). *The Interpretation of Cultures*. New York: Basic Books.
Heilbrun, J. (1997) The Competition Between High Culture and Popular Culture as Seen in the *New York Times*. *Journal of Cultural Economics*, 21, 29–40.
Lee, S., Scott, D. & Kim, H. (2008). Celebrity Fan Involvement and Destination Perceptions. *Annals of Tourism Research*, 35, 809–832.
Lindgren, S. (2005). *Populärkultur: Teorier, metoder och analyser*. Malmö, Sweden: Liber.
MacCannell, D. (1973). Staged Authenticity: Arrangements of Social Space in Tourist Settings. *American Journal of Sociology*, 79(3), 589–903.
Mordue, T. (1999). Heartbeat Country: Conflicting Values, Coinciding Visions. *Environment and Planning*, 31, 629–646.
Mordue, T. (2001). Performing and Directing Resident/Tourist Cultures in Heartbeat Country. *Tourist Studies* 1(3), 233–252.
Riley, R., Baker, D. & Van Doren, C. S. (1998). Movie Induced Tourism. *Annals of Tourism Research*, 25(4), 919–935.
Riley, R. & Van Doren, C. (1992). Movies as Tourism Promotion: A Push Factor in a Pull Location. *Tourism Management*, 13, 267–274.
Strinati, D. (2004). *An Introduction to Theories of Popular Culture*. New York: Routledge.
Tooke, N. & Baker, M. (1996). Seeing Is Believing: The Effect of Film on Visitor Numbers to Screened Locations. *Tourism Management*, 17(2), 87–94.

Traube, E. G. (1996). 'The Popular' in American Culture. *Annual Review of Antropology, 25*, 127–151.

Turner, V. (1974). *Dramas, Fields and Metaphors: Symbolic Action in Human Society*. Ithaca, NY: Cornell University Press.

Xie, P. F., Osumare, H. & Ibrahim, A. (2007). Gazing the Hood: Hip-Hop as Tourism Attraction. *Tourism Management, 28*, 452–460.

PART I

Setting the stage

Foundations of popular culture tourism

1

WHAT IS POPULAR CULTURE?

Shirley A. Fedorak

What is popular culture? Is it the latest vampire movie, the newest fashion trends, or the writing of Ukrainian Easter eggs? Or is it a European football game, Nubian face painting, or Mexican tamales? The meaning of popular culture, its roles and power structures, and its ideological and moral constructs has generated considerable debate within and outside academia.

Johann Gottfried Herder first coined the phrase popular culture in 1784 (Parker, 2011). Herder positioned popular culture against the culture of the learned, suggesting popular culture was different and inferior to the high culture of the elite. Thus, popular culture has become a contested concept that lends itself to several questions. How is popular culture different from other elements of culture and, in particular, so-called high culture? When did popular culture first arise and is folk culture also popular culture? What roles does popular culture play in human society? and, how and why should social scientists study popular culture?

Defining popular culture

Popular culture is the culture of our everyday lives (Fedorak, 2009). This straightforward, egalitarian definition rejects elitist characterizations of popular culture, and embraces diverse forms of symbolic expression and performance. Performance is a broad term referring to many, or even all, human activities and the ritualized behavior that influences people and involves everyday life (Turner, 1986; Bohannan, 1991). Popular culture is not limited to any one class, gender, ethnicity, or status group, and is embedded in "economic circumstances, nationalism, history and heritage, human migration and transnational cultural flow, political environment and cultural resistance, religious organization, and social relations" (Fedorak, 2009, p. 15). Popular culture reveals who we are as a society. As Browne and Browne (2001, p. 3) put it, "We have seen our popular culture and it is us." Popular culture, then, provides a window into human nature and behavior, and offers a medium for celebrating our lives and the world we live in.

Although far from an exhaustive list, the cultural artifacts and symbols of popular culture involve body art (e.g. tattoos, piercings), music (e.g. rock guitars, drums, wooden flutes), film (e.g. zombie movies, superhero movies), literature (e.g. graphic novels, genre fiction, oral stories), collectibles (e.g. car memorabilia, dolls), sports (e.g. baseball cards, jerseys), clothing (e.g. American torn jeans, Trobriander banana skirts), crafts (e.g. Doukhobor quilting, Malaysian batik painting), car culture (e.g. hood ornaments, classic models), mass media (e.g. television, cell phones), Internet (e.g. Facebook, gaming sites), and leisure (e.g. cruise ships, hiking boots). These cultural artifacts hold meaning and offer messages about the performers and the audience. They inform us about our culture and the culture of others, and how popular culture influences and impacts our society (Alvermann, Moon, & Hagood, 1999).

The difficulties with developing an inclusive, nonbiased, yet substantive definition of popular culture are legendary in academia. Oftentimes discourse on the nature of popular culture becomes caught up in dichotomies and etymology. Terms such as "highbrow" and "lowbrow" culture, "legitimate" and "illegitimate" culture, and "pure" and "mass" culture all create perceptions of popular culture's value, and what is worthy of academic study and what is not. Some definitions have focused on the folk or common aspects of popular culture, while in others the degree of popularity or lack of any qualities that authorities would consider high culture are the distinguishing factors. Mass-produced and consumed culture is also a distinction commonly made between popular culture and high culture (Bennett, 1980; Storey, 2006). More recent definitions assert that popular culture emerged in the Industrial Revolution as an outcome of urbanization and capitalism. None of these limited spatial and temporal views do justice to popular culture; they not only exclude eras before industrialization, they also exclude certain forms of popular culture, potential audiences, and the popular culture of small-scale societies.

Whether popular culture is labeled folk culture, common culture, public culture (Ortner, 1998), or the culture of the people (Delaney, 2007), and whether it is mass produced and consumed, or its origins, is not the point. Popular forms of expression hold meaning regardless of what they are called, and they play an important role in creating cultural identity and social solidarity. As Kidd (2007, p. 81) notes, popular culture is "an important element in the dynamics of contemporary social life," and can be as complex and worthy of study as great works of art or literature.

Popular culture is most often associated with urban, industrialized societies. However, it is not the exclusive domain of Western, capitalist countries, nor is it a recent phenomenon. All cultural groups are surrounded and immersed in their popular culture. Indeed, for most of human history, people have produced music, art, theater, and festivals to entertain and celebrate their world. Archaeological evidence verifies that humans as long ago as 40,000 years created musical instruments (e.g. flutes), made toys, and likely told stories and celebrated with gatherings and games.

Artistic or performance expressions before the Industrial Revolution are commonly referred to as folk culture. Here too, the distinction is vague. Roman circuses and plays in the Theater of Dionysus in Athens can hardly be called folk culture (Parker, 2011), yet they occurred before industrialization. The American Folklife Center maintains that folk culture "is part of everyone's life. It is as constant as a ballad, as changeable as fashion trends. It is as intimate as a lullaby, and as public as a parade" (DeGarmo, 2012, n.p.). Outsiders may call an artistic expression from a small-scale society folk culture, but to the locals, these performances are popular culture.

According to Parker (2011) artwork that is not recognized by authorities in the art world is popular culture, not high culture. The same goes for other forms of expression; they must be recognized by an authority to be legitimate. The philosophical argument that art produced for entertainment and profit is lowbrow popular culture and lacks artistic integrity if not fully authorized presents some challenges, most notably its elitism, by suggesting that the arts should be purifying and serious, and only available to the few who can appreciate them. The question of who is an authority also arises. A classic example is genre fiction, which is generally considered popular culture rather than literary fiction. Yet, until recently, most genre fiction was published by traditional publishing houses. Are these houses an authority? Or are the audience and the market the authority? If so, the value placed on genre or literary fiction originates with the audience rather than officials.

If the distinction between popular culture and high culture is based on class or the status of the audience, then the line between the two becomes even vaguer. Popular culture is increasingly accessed by those of high status, (e.g. football games). The elite, especially youth, partake of popular culture that might be considered pedestrian, such as youth raves. Cultural artifacts and performance that began as popular culture may over time become high culture. For example, Shakespearean plays were originally considered trashy and lowbrow. In the mid-nineteenth century, Shakespearean plays were "florid rhetoric, vivid characters, tempestuous gestures, and moral design" (Warner, 1990, p. 728) that appealed to the general population. As these plays became more restrained and refined, they lost their appeal with all but the elite. Today, Shakespeare is considered high culture, but is also popular with lower classes.

Wayne (2014) suggests that lower classes do not have as much access to high culture; however, this is not entirely accurate. The previous discussion of Shakespearean plays demonstrates that although upper classes have greater access to high culture because of financial means, today lower classes are also gaining greater access to some forms of high culture. The National Gallery in London, for example, welcomes people from all classes to view great works of art, as do most museums. Accessibility, then, cannot be used to distinguish popular from high culture as it is a fluid situation. Popular culture, then, is increasingly crossing social barriers, partly due to the transnational flow of popular culture via mass media. The futility of limiting popular culture to certain classes is particularly evident in tourism.

Tourism is a great equalizer in that tour groups take their middle-class charges to the opera or to the theater, and leisure activities that were formerly the sole domain of the elite, such as cruising, have now become accessible to people from lower status groups. Conversely, leisure activities formerly the domain of lower classes, such as hiking or attending crafts fairs, may be adopted by people in upper classes. Film-induced, mass media-induced, and literary-induced tourism commonly crosses social barriers. Youth from all classes loved the *Harry Potter* books and movies, and those able flock to visit *Harry Potter* film locations such as the site of Hogwarts at Alnwich Caste, Northumberland, England and ride the Jacobite steam train Harry Potter traveled on in Lochaber, Scotland. More recently, the hugely popular *Outlander* novels and television series have led to an increase in tourism to Scotland, particularly Scottish castles. Although popular culture may reflect social stratification to a certain extent, this is changing as the boundaries between low and high culture continue to blur and even disappear.

Popular culture is often associated with mass production and commercialization. Although Western popular culture tends to be mass produced, local popular culture, such as singing, dancing, painting, theater, and craft fairs, is likely not mass produced. In small, often rural communities in Ukraine and on the Canadian prairies, writing eggs with intricate designs during Easter is an age-old tradition that is popular among Ukrainians and non-Ukrainians alike. The eggs are handcrafted, not mass produced, yet production and performance of these cultural artifacts holds deeply embedded meaning and creates social bonding and community solidarity. Over-commercialization is also used to separate popular culture from high culture. Yet, virtually all cultural artifacts, whether high or popular, are sold in some kind of market. Beethoven's Fifth Symphony is mass produced and sold in the form of CDs, just as Rod Stewart's popular music is sold. The difference is popular culture is produced and consumed at a much higher rate than high culture.

Ultimately, any definition of popular culture that restricts the types of performance and expression to certain times, places, and audiences is too limiting, and has been influenced by the "politics of pleasure" (Alvermann et al., 1999). Although no definition is entirely inclusive, the Ministry of Foreign Affairs of Japan defines popular culture as "culture produced in the everyday lives of ordinary people" (Seaton & Yamamura, 2015, p. 5). This definition comes closest to recognizing popular culture in all forms, places, and times.

Why and how we study popular culture

The study of popular culture is most often the domain of cultural studies. Cultural studies is a critical approach to "how human subjects are formed and how they experienced cultural and social space" (Miller, 2001, p. 1). Body politics and power relations, including ethnic,[1] class, gender, national, and sexual identity, have become important themes in the study of the human condition, from the quest for women's body rights to self-expression, activism, and resistance.

Popular culture also plays a powerful role, whether on a local or global scale, in social and political commentary. As an example, the "Buffy studies" or Buffyology, investigate "moral philosophy, gender constructs, textual analysis, and linguistic culture" (Wayne, 2014, n.p.), through an exploration of the hugely popular *Buffy the Vampire* and *Angel* television series. Social commentary, the way our society is reflected in these television programs, and the fandom that emulates tribal or cult elements have all become areas of study. According to Joss Whedon, the creator of these shows,

> I think it's always important for academics to study popular culture, even if the thing they are studying is idiotic. . . . We think very carefully about what we're trying to say emotionally, politically, and even philosophically while we're writing it.
>
> *(*New York Times, *2003, n.p.)*

Two theoretical perspectives dominate discussions on popular culture: mass culture theory and populist theory. Mass culture theory suggests that high culture (e.g. opera) is more valuable and enlightening than popular culture that appeals to the masses who accept it without questioning its value. Populist theory, on the other hand, recognizes that popular culture is vibrant and offers both intrinsic and extrinsic rewards, and avenues for escape from everyday stresses.

One theoretical approach that seems particularly useful is performance theory. Humans, by their very nature, are performers, and performance is "the basic stuff of social life" (Turner, 1986, p. 81). Popular culture is performance, from wedding rituals, graffiti art, and rock concerts to cooking and eating a meal or chatting on Skype. Collecting car memorabilia is quite different from listening to rap music, and batik painting is different from making banana skirts, yet they are all performance, and they all present messages with multiple meanings for the performers and audience. Performance theorists analyze these meanings and address cultural concepts such as gender, ethnicity, sexuality, and nationalism. Popular culture is a lens through which we may gain understanding of the social, political, and intellectual components of a society. Performance theory, then, provides an avenue for studying human discourse and interaction in popular culture.

Popular culture has become a rich resource for anthropologists expanding their inquiry and analysis of the nature of human culture (Royce, 2001). They employ performance theory to study how performers and audiences are shaped and shape popular culture and what is revealed about both the audience and the performers through popular culture. For example, in Michael Taft's (2009) ethnographic study of mock wedding ceremonies on the Canadian prairies, he explored how performers and the audience used comedic, ritualized performances to communicate everyday farm life and address conflicting or dual gender roles. Taft's study demonstrates the potential for understanding human nature and the issues of everyday life through popular culture. Michelle Gilbert (1998) studied Ghanaian concert parties and plays that offer reflections on contemporary life in Ghana. The culmination of the concert parties is a dramatic play "that combines Vaudeville, morality drama and Christian revivalist sermons" (Gilbert, 2000, p. 1). These plays mirror the uneasy co-existence between Christians,

Muslims, and traditional religious practices. In historic times, the plays were also used for political commentary. They address jealousy and competition in polygynous marriages, fear of sorcery, ancestor worship, fragmenting extended families, youth unemployment, poverty, and religious conflicts (Malaquais, 2001). The concert parties, then, use morality plays, music, comedy, art, and acting to offer commentary and discourse on contemporary social, religious, and political issues in a form of collective reflection.

The study of popular culture embraces several methodologies, including quantitative content analysis, ethnographic research (participant observation, key informant interviews), oral histories, and archival research. However, these studies are best served through a multidisciplinary approach that embraces the learnings and theoretical and methodological perspectives of numerous disciplines. Researchers from gender studies, history, political science, media studies, anthropology, literary studies, sociology, art and art history, linguistics, and culture studies all contribute to the study of popular culture.

Characteristics and roles of popular culture

Generalizing about the characteristics of popular culture is challenging, given its complex and fluid nature. Some forms of popular culture, such as the World Cup, are consumed on a global scale, while other forms, such as quilting, may be popular on the local level and consumed and practiced in a more subtle way. Even this is changing; quilting is gaining global recognition and popularity through social media. This sharing of popular culture has facilitated the creation of social bonding and solidarity on a global scale, as well as at the community level.

Like the systems of culture, popular culture is holistic and integrated. Dining out involves fashion, music, food, and even the car culture, but this pastime also involves significant elements of social organization (e.g. gender roles, kinship and family, class and status, courtship) and economic systems (e.g. urbanization, consumer patterns, household dynamics). A love of sports likely also means collecting sports memorabilia, gathering at sports venues, body art, fashion, music, tourism, as well as elements of religious organization (e.g. rituals, values, and moral codes), social organization (e.g. kinship, ethnic and group identity, gender roles, class), economic systems (e.g. consumer consumption), and political organization (e.g. nationalism, international networks, and competition). The above examples of quilting and social media also demonstrate the interconnection of popular culture with the systems of culture. Popular culture, then, does not exist in isolation, and any discussion of popular culture must also address related systems of culture.

All cultural groups possess local forms of popular culture that shape and reflect their cultural identity. Wedding rituals, such as the bridal shower and wedding reception, are good examples of the commonality of popular culture across all classes and on a global scale, even though each cultural group maintains their own unique customs. Indian and Brazilian wedding customs are very different; nevertheless, both are expressions of popular culture and both symbolize the socio-economic importance of joining two people and two families.

Popular culture plays numerous roles in society, some positive, while others may be deleterious. Popular culture creates, sustains, and shapes community. Gatherings, festivals, and celebrations give meaning and offer identity, social bonds, and a sense of community to those who share in a popular expression of culture. Collective understanding of political statements and cultural references creates group solidarity. "We are what we watch and read and listen to, and we are political, so the culture we consume is, too" (Grady, 2017, n.p.). Popular culture's role as a community facilitator raises the question; does it perform the same role on a global scale? In other words, can popular culture assist in the formation of global communities and global citizens?

This question is best answered by examining virtual communities. Franklin (2001, p. 1) called going online "an emerging practice of everyday life" at the beginning of the twenty-first century. Nearly 20 years later, his prediction has become a reality. The Internet has facilitated the sharing of popular culture on a global level. People with common interests join virtual communities that provide a "place" for people to meet. An example of such a community is a virtual lesbian café where people engage in what Correll (1995) calls a surrogate community.

The Internet and social media platforms are a part of larger globalization processes. Globalization has increased the transnational flow of culture, including popular culture, across international borders. This free-flow of popular culture raises the spectre of localized popular culture being transformed through homogenization and hybridization processes. Homogenization results in forms of popular culture, such as ethnic music, being overwhelmed or deeply modified by other forms of music (e.g. rock 'n' roll). Fears of losing local popular culture are somewhat justified. McDonalds and Starbucks are everywhere. In Penang, Malaysia, for example, the elders are very concerned that youth are gathering at Starbucks to socialize rather than the traditional *kapitans* (coffeehouses). In hybridization, elements of popular culture are fused or blended to create a new form of popular culture (Heaven & Tubridy, 2002). For example, Chinese wedding clothes have been fused with the Western white wedding dress. A bride might still wear a traditional red wedding dress for part of the celebration, but she will also wear a Western-style white wedding dress for other parts of the ceremony.

Cultural flow is not a new phenomenon; ideas, customs, and cultural artifacts have always moved between cultures via trade networks, migration, and colonization (Strelitz, 2001). Popular culture is part of power relations (Fiske, 2003) and a symbol of the struggle to maintain distinct cultural and social identities. The difference today is the speed with which Western cultural artifacts and behavior are spreading globally, and the fact that only a few multinational companies control this flow (Tardieu, 2000). This new reality places local popular culture in danger of disappearing or being commoditized. Then again, in any community, the audience is selective in what new forms of popular culture it adopts, and people will continue to maintain traditional popular culture that they value.

Popular culture is often used to express opposition to political, religious, social, and economic repression. It provides a medium for generating political and social commentary, for challenging cultural norms, and for resistance and activism. Counter-cultural movements redefine cultural institutions (e.g. marriage laws) and challenge power relations, (e.g. civil rights for the LGBTQ communities). Rap music, body art, and body modification are artifacts of these movements. Marginalized groups, such as queer subcultures, use body modification (e.g. tattooing, piercing, and cutting) to express resistance to mainstream society (Kleese, 2007). For female body modifiers, modification is a way to contest patriarchy and reclaim control over their bodies. An historic example of resistance is the hippie counter-cultural movement of the 1960s and 1970s. Hippie philosophy and lifestyle changed and shaped popular culture, bringing blue jeans, sexual freedom, drug use, and environmental awareness into mainstream society. Their influence is still felt today. Counter-cultural movements, then, may challenge androcentric, racist, and classist ideals, as well as increase global awareness on issues that impact local communities.

Mass media is a powerful venue for increasing social awareness. Television shows, such as *Will and Grace* in the 1990s, brought the lives of gay people into North American homes. This television program both reflected changing attitudes toward gays and helped change perceptions of the gay community. The current television comedy *Modern Family* showcases the changing structure of the family, while also promoting acceptance of families outside the norm. On the Grammy Awards show in 2017, one of the trophy handlers on stage was a transgender person

(*CTV News*, 2017), again reflecting increasing acceptance of people previously marginalized. Popular culture, then, both reflects and influences societal values and practices, and influences worldview. In the coming years, mass media may serve to counter retrograde attitudes toward marginalized groups.

In the second decade of the twenty-first century social media has become a battleground against right-wing politicians and policies, and for countering marginalization, hatred, and racism (Romano, 2017). In January 2017 thousands of people took to the streets around the world to protest misogyny and demand equal rights for women. Posters of empowered women, such as Carrie Fisher, and quotes from popular movie lines and song lyrics on posters were used to get their messages across. These protests reflect the way popular culture and politics have become intertwined (Grady, 2017). The film industry has taken up the mantle with films such as *Arrival* (2016) presenting a strong female linguistic scientist, better able to meet the aliens than her male counterparts. In children's films, *Moana* is the female chief of her island, and in the most recent *Ghostbusters* film, women defend the city from supernatural fiends. These fearless women took on the establishment and established mindsets through popular culture (Romano, 2017).

The popular culture we consume and our association with others of similar tastes provides a distinct group identity. Adopting a particular kind of popular culture as one's own, and giving it personal meaning, often tells others something about a person. This is particularly true of youth, who create their own identities and social practices to resist existing hegemonies and racist and sexist inequalities. Indeed, social media has created social tribalism, at times at the global level, where no dissenting voices enter the group and identity is built through political choices (Grady, 2017). Daniel Miller (1995, 1998) even suggests that popular culture is replacing kinship as an identity marker. For example, Mexican American youth have accepted *Pachuca*—a distinctive dress—and loud behavior and lingo of Mexican actor Germán Valdez's character Tin Tan to separate their identity from that of Euro-American and African-American youth (Durán, 2002). Popular culture, then, creates gendered, ethnic, and class identity using various forms of popular culture.

Obviously, the most powerful form of popular culture is mass media. Mass media touches the lives of people around the world, and can have a profound effect on worldview, values, and behavior. This power has led to concerns regarding popular culture's damaging effects on the audience. The stereotyping and objectification of women via pornography and over-sexualization in films and literature, and the glorification of war and violence are commonly cited as negative influences of media popular culture. Critics also point out that the youth in many nations are enamored with American popular culture. I had only to open the windows in my apartment in Cairo to hear American rock 'n' roll blaring from passing car stereos to realize that the West's popular culture was invading Egypt's youth culture.

Peters (2003) believes youth controls popular culture. They determine what works and reject what does not work. An example of their power is the rise and fall of drive-in restaurants. Once the gathering place in the 1950s and 1960s, they were replaced by malls in the 1970s, and today malls face the same fate as young shoppers increasingly turn to online shopping, and gather in coffee shops and virtual communities for socialization (Underhill, 2004). If popular culture can shape as well as reflect our worldviews and cultural identities, then youth enamored with Western popular culture may turn away from their local popular culture, and the values and worldviews it encompasses. This is evident among Inuit, where the youth have embraced Western media culture and lost interest in quill work and bead work. "Kids everywhere want to be like Michael Jordan, sing like Madonna or eat at McDonalds" (Tardieu, 2000, n.p.). The power of American mass media is so all-encompassing that some critics have accused it of an insidious form of cultural imperialism.

Conclusion

Popular culture is the culture of our everyday lives. Whether it is a pair of ripped designer jeans or a virtual community, popular culture owns multiple meanings, symbols, and rituals. It is not the shallow end of human existence but rather the pulse of humankind and a window into the societal dynamics of our everyday lives. Popular culture is everywhere; it is embedded in every culture, and in every cultural institution. It surrounds us and defines us, and it reflects and influences our beliefs, values, and behavior.

Delaney (2007) suggests that urbanization, industrialization, mass media, and the rise in technology are responsible for the growth in popular culture. This is certainly a key factor; however, this discussion has maintained that popular culture can be found everywhere, and is not restricted to Western industrial societies.

Whether popular culture differs from folk culture depends on perspective; however, most of the arguments separating the two lack merit in our interconnected and global communities. The same is true of high and popular culture. Very few distinctions remain and the notion that high culture is more influential or enlightening than popular culture was repeatedly challenged in this discussion.

Critics of popular culture tend to label it frivolous and unworthy of academic study. However, popular culture is a vibrant and influential part of people's everyday lives and for that reason social scientists must familiarize themselves with the roles and influence of popular culture. Indeed, if we define culture as our whole way of life, then to ignore popular culture means ignoring a significant part of the human condition. In the twenty-first century, addressing the popular should not be avoided; if culture is the whole way of life, then the activities that enrich our lives and give meaning to human existence are also worthy of study.

Popular culture, in particular mass media, has received a great deal of criticism for being over-commercialized, presenting skewed values, and not having any cultural (elite) value. However, as you will see in the ensuing chapters, popular culture is an integral part of any culture and worthy of serious study. As Kidd (2007, p. 86) states, popular culture is "norm generation, boundary maintenance, ritual development, innovation, and social change."

The roles of popular culture are ever-changing. This is true of mass-produced popular culture as well as locally produced popular culture, partly due to the power and reach of social media in our globalized society. Popular culture can bring together people of similar values and lifestyle, especially among youth, and create virtual as well as physical groups. This discussion emphasized popular culture as performance that shapes and is shaped by performers and audiences. As we have seen in the mock wedding ceremonies and Ghanaian concert parties, popular culture provides insightful commentary on contemporary issues that are of significance to humans in all cultures and from all social strata.

Can local popular culture withstand the global flow of popular culture from powerful states? Globalization processes, such as telecommunications and transportation, have resulted in the rapid transnational flow of new ideas and behaviors, making it more difficult for cultural groups to adapt and absorb these forms of popular culture. Global investment and marketing by multinational corporations has also placed pressure on local popular culture. Hybridization of culture is a reality when cultural groups come into contact and this is true of popular culture as well. Yet, cultural groups are remarkably adaptable and selective. If they value their own popular culture, they will simply make room for more.

Ultimately, this brief examination of popular culture takes a postmodernist perspective in that popular culture and high culture are no longer distinctive entities, and that the performance and expression of popular culture is of equal value to that of high culture. The impact of popular culture on human society should not be ignored, nor should popular culture be labeled inferior to high culture. Simply put, popular culture is the things we do and make, the things we like, the things we believe, the things we learn, and the things we remember. It is who we are.

Note

1 The term race is disregarded given that it is based on political or social agendas and has no biological legitimacy.

References

Alvermann, D. E., Moon, J. S., & Hagood, M. C. (1999). *Popular culture in the classroom: Teaching and researching critical media literacy. Literary studies series.* Newark, DE: International Reading Association.

Bennett, T. (1980). Popular culture: A teaching object. *Screen Education*, 34(18), 20–36.

Bohannan, P. (1991). *We the alien: An introduction to cultural anthropology.* Long Grove, IL: Waveland Press.

Browne, R. B., & Browne, P. (2001). Introduction. In R. B. Browne & P. Browne (Eds.), *The guide to United States popular culture* (pp. 1–4). Bowling Green, OH: Bowling Green State University Popular Press.

Correll, S. (1995). The ethnography of an electronic bar: The lesbian café. *Journal of Contemporary Ethnography*, 24(3), 270–298.

CTV News (2017, February 12). *The latest from Grammy awards: Bowie's "Blackstar" wins best rock song.* Retrieved February 27, 2017 from www.ctvnews.ca/entertainment/the-latest-from-grammy-awards-bowie-s-blackstar-wins-best-rock-song-1.3282192.

DeGarmo, T. (2012). What is folklife. *Voices: The Journal of New York Folklore*, *38*, 1–2.

Delaney, T. (2007). Pop culture: An overview. *Philosophy Now*, 64. Retrieved February 27, 2017 from https://philosopynow.org/issues/64/Pop_Culture_An-Overview.

Duran, J. (2002). Nation and translation: The "Pachuco" in Mexican popular culture: Germán Valdez's Tin Tan. *Journal of the Midwest Modern Language Association*, 34(2): 41–49.

Fedorak, S. A. (2009). *Pop culture: The culture of everyday life.* Toronto, ON: University of Toronto Press.

Fiske, J. (2003). Understanding popular culture. In W. Brooker & D. Jeremyn (Eds.), *The audience studies reader* (pp. 112–116). London: Routledge.

Franklin, I. (2001). Abstract for *Inside out: Postcolonial subjectivities and everyday life online. International Feminist Journal of Politics*, 3(3), 387–422.

Gilbert, M. (1998). Concert parties: Paintings and performance. *Journal of Religion in Africa*, 28(1), 62–92.

Gilbert, M. (2000). *Hollywood icons, local demons: Ghanaian popular paintings by Mark Anthony.* Hartford, CT: Trinity College.

Grady, C. (2017, January 24). The women's march shows how intertwined pop culture and politics have become. *VOX Media.* Retrieved February 27, 2017 from www.vox.com/culture/2017/1/24/14358000/womens-march-washington-pop-culture-politics.

Heaven, C., & Tubridy M. (2002). Global youth culture and youth identity. UNESCO (pp. 149–160). Retrieved March 28, 2017 from www.tachbik.ma/documents/da619779-5-Global%20Youth%20Culture%20and%20Youth%20Identity.pdf.

Kidd, D. (2007). *Harry Potter* and the functions of popular culture. *Journal of Popular Culture*, 40(1): 69–89.

Kleese, C. (2007). Racializing the politics of transgression: Body modification queer culture. *Social Semiotics*, 17(3), 275–292. Retrieved February 27, 2017 from http://dx.doi.org/10.1080/10350330701448561.

Malaquais, D. (2001). Hollywood icons, local demons. *American Anthropologist*, 102(4), 870–882.

Miller, D. (1995). Consumption and commodities. *American Review of Anthropology* 24, 141–161.

Miller, D. (1998). *A theory of shopping.* Ithaca, NY: Cornell University Press.

Miller, T. (2001). *A companion to cultural studies.* New York: Blackwell.

New York Times (2003, May 16). *Ten questions for Joss Whedon.* Retrieved March 26, 2017 from www.nytimes.com/2003/05/16/readersopinions/joss-whedon-2003051692624509740.html.

Ortner, S. B. (1998). Generation X: Anthropology in a media-saturated world. *Cultural Anthropology*, 13(3), 414–440.

Parker, H. N. (2011, May). Toward a definition of popular culture. *History and Theory*, 50, 147–170.

Peters, B. (2003). Qu(e)erying comic book culture and representations of sexuality in Wonder Woman. *CLC Web: Comparative Literature and Culture*, 5(3), 6.

Romano, A. (2017, January 28). The Trump resistance is beating him on his own turf. *VOX Media*. Retrieved February 27, 2017 from www.vox.com/culture/2017/1/28/14407520/trump-social-media-backlash-protest.

Royce, A. P. (2001). Dancing the nation. *American Anthropologist*, 103(2), 539–541.

Seaton, P., & Yamamura, T. (2015). Japanese popular culture and contents tourism: Introduction. *Japan Forum*, 27(1), 1–11.

Storey, J. (2006). *Cultural theory and popular culture: An introduction* (4th ed.). Athens, GA: University of Georgia Press.

Strelitz, L. (2001). *Where the global meets the local: Media studies and the myth of cultural homogenization*. Transnational Broadcast Studies 6. Cairo, Egypt: American University of Cairo.

Taft, M. (2009). The mock wedding: Folk drama in the prairie provinces. In W. Haviland, S. Fedorak, & R. Lee, (Eds.), *Cultural anthropology* (3rd ed., pp. 373–376). Toronto, ON: Nelson Education.

Tardieu, J. (2000). Fear of US pop culture dominance drives anti-globalization sentiment. Retrieved June 26, 2007, from http://ksg.harvard.edu/citizen/07feb00/tardo207.html.

Turner, V. (1986). *The anthropology of performance*. New York: PAJ Publications.

Underhill, P. (2004). *Call of the mall*. New York: Simon & Schuster.

Warner, W. (1990, Winter). The resistance to popular culture. *American Literary History*, 2(4), 726–742.

Wayne, R. (2014, July 27). *Why it's important to study pop culture*. Retrieved March 18, 2017 from www.linkedin.com/pulse/20140727233003-19409547-why-it-s-important-to-study-pop-culture.

2

TOURISM AND POPULAR CULTURE

Socio-cultural considerations

Rodanthi Tzanelli

Introduction

'Popular culture' has become a ubiquitous term in contemporary social life in the greatest part of the socially organized world. The use of the term is especially prevalent where televised communication and digital networking became fully integrated into (cultural) industrial image management – where, in other words, creative and cultural industries became apparatuses that manufacture and/or disseminate global signs in various combinations with local cultural idioms. 'Popular' as an adjective commonly suggests an overlap of 'mass' and 'favourite', with 'culture' as reference to imagined (abstract) and material sites of collective reverie (tangible objects of consumption and the places in which these are consumed). This reverie is enacted through cinematic, televisual and digital engagement with such sites, objects and memories to which both are tied, as well as with the help of embodied technologies (through travel and tourism to such foreign sites). In what follows, I attempt to not only map distinctive modes of understanding what popular culture is and how it is experienced in contemporary societies, but also explain how such conceptual and experiential modes connect to the social and cultural activity of tourism.

In exploring links between tourism and popular culture one may divide the overall analysis into three 'modes' or manners of investigation:

1. The mode of *scholarship*: how this relational examination of tourism and popular culture entered academic debates and how these subsequently developed into institutionalized discourses.
2. The mode of *socialization*: how tourism can be, and is being considered as a self-contained form of popular culture, maintained through patterns of socialization.
3. The mode of *construction*: how a variety of socio-cultural practices and activities are now constructed, represented and marketed as 'tourism'.

Modes of investigation

Modes of scholarship: definitions and controversies

No scholarly analysis of popular culture can stand without specifying what 'culture' is and how it connects to the 'popular'. Here, commonsensical definitions have to give way to scholarly elaborations that we find in various disciplines across humanities and social sciences. Generally, the notions of culture that entered sociological and anthropological traditions and that, by turn, provided the most secure scaffolding for the production of links with tourism in interdisciplinary tourism theory over the last two centuries, favour an interchange between fluidity and mobility in collective custom and its interrelated individualized expressions. As a malleable and porous systems of beliefs, ideas and habits that order our everyday life and are communicated to others through signs and symbols, 'culture' allows for both the institutional and the informal public organization of society (Williams, 1958; Geertz, 1973, 1986). This open definition is contradicted or reinforced in postmodern studies of consumer globalization, in which an overarching 'Americanization', 'McDonaldization' or 'colonization' of culture suggests the pre-existence of 'authentic' or 'original' forms of culture and their erosion by supranational political and economic changes (Ritzer, 2006). Alternate Marxist analyzes considered the popular as 'folk' and informed early anthropological studies of ethno-cultures in the wake of Romantic nationalisms. In this disciplinary context, it was argued that cultures subjected to indiscriminate industrial modernization and tourismification are demoted to mere exchange objects in the global economy, sold 'by the pound' and endlessly reproduced as eroded commodities for tourists (Greenwood, 1997).

A more cultural approach to tourism brings to the fore the experiential dimension of engaging with other places and their people beyond any consumerist imperatives. Indeed, 'experience' and 'consumption' enabled scholars to align their work around two definitional axes in the field's central preoccupation with *who is a tourist*, how they are supposed to behave and regarded by others, including fellow travellers and researchers (see also Cohen, 1974). Experience and consumption work both as complementary and oppositional axes, with variables, such as class, age, gender or race as determinants in the provision of definitions. Put simply, 'being' and 'behaving' like a tourist was examined both in terms of self-definition (how tourists view their own subjectivity) and as an external attribute (how tourists are viewed by non-tourists, other tourists and even scholars). Scholars have identified the operation of various hierarchical mechanisms in such definitions, which often push tourism subjectivity to the categories of shallow, cheap or superficial engagement with culture, ultimately also associating all of them with notions of the 'kitsch' as an unreflexive 'popular' activity (McCabe, 2005).

It helps to stress that these debates placed tourism as popular culture within the *problématique* of Western and European modernity, a mode of experiencing, imagining and theorizing about society and culture in the context of industrialization, urbanization and hypermobility (Bauman, 2000). Considering 'popular culture' as both an extension and a creative modification of institutionalized custom in society, would eventually help such studies to elaborate on definitions of 'tourism'. A conventional definition of tourism as movement away from home (spatial dimension), for a relatively short period (temporal dimension) (Jafari, 1987) is embedded in the pivotal role of industrialization in the institution of tourism. State-centred understandings of holidays as productive relaxation period for labour, and the institution of paid holiday time as a universal right in the twentieth century, were related in academic scholarship to the consolidation of a tourist multi-industry dedicated to catering for such mass movements of humans across national borders (Urry, 2002; Dann & Parinello, 2009). This multi-industry of hotels, automobility complexes, entertainment parks, resorts and beaches partakes in manufacturing popular culture consumed by international audiences (tourists).

The initial definition of tourism was subsequently challenged. In the late twenty-first century globally networked communications further blended notions and experiences of taking time off work and being at work (Graburn, 2001, 2002; Urry, 2007). Automobile complexes that enable superfast connectivity to remote destinations (Edensor, 2004; Urry, 2004), new modes of consuming difference in venues not conventionally thought of as tourist destinations (see also section on modes of socialization below), and, finally, tourism as both an on-site activity and as cognitive praxis, suggest that we devise a more expansive understanding of tourism with/and popular culture. The notion of 'touring the screen' for example (Leotta, 2012), which has been coined, or laterally explored by film-induced and cinematic tourism scholars (Beeton, 2005, 2010; Tzanelli, 2007; Croy & Heitmann, 2011), suggests a special relationship between audio-visual and digital technologies and postmodern forms of tourism. Other emergent tourist trends, such as rock-climbing (Rickly, 2013), experimental tourism (strange activities as time 'off work'), airport tourism (visiting airports), mega-event and sports tourism (Getz, 2008; Tzanelli, 2015b), music tourism (Cohen, 2005; Spracklen, 2016) and even virtual/Internet tourism as an activity in its own right (Germann Molz, 2012), further connected contemporary popular cultural tools (computers, cinema, instrumental machines and the narratives these produce about culture) to the tourist experience. Today tourism researchers see contemporary tourism as a technologized, 'mass' and de-romanticized, rather than pure, cognitive intellectual experience. The archetype of the Grand Tourist, who traverses lands that hosted ancient civilizations to self-educate into humanity's allegedly shared pasts, has been replaced by a more blended one, according to which the tourist might pursue pleasure and/or education in various – not always neatly related – ways.

Such observations have raised questions concerning artificial distinctions made between the different forms of popular culture and tourism and their disciplinary study. There have been two prevalent trends in the debate since the early twentieth century:

(a) **The normative trend:** The original conception of the 'popular' in critical theory, which informed the 'culture industry' thesis (Adorno & Horkheimer, 1991), was predicated on the assumption that artistic and popular creativity form a Manichean structure of 'high' versus 'low', 'lofty' and individualized versus dangerous, collectivized (as mob) expressivity and resulting civic (non-) participation. The first Frankfurt School generation's fear that popular culture facilitated propaganda to control the masses entered subsequent academic definitions of tourism as an interwar (1930s) and a post-war (1950s) popular trend in Europe and then the United States (Dann & Parrinello, 2009). It was after the 1980s and well into the 1990s that radical Marxist approaches (see Enzensberger's (1974) tourism as a 'consciousness industry' in Europe, Boorstin's (1962) influential idea of image-saturated domination in tourism from the United States and MacCannell's (1989) organization of tourism into an industry of 'markers' and 'signs') slowly gave way to understandings of tourism as an interpretivist popular culture: an individualized but collective culture promoting the aesthetic appreciation of foreign cultures, landscapes and customs in their own right (see MacCannell's (2001) work on the intelligent tourist as an intermediary phase and, Urry and Larsen's (2011) revised 'tourist gaze'). The notion of aesthetic appreciation of other cultures and landscapes by tourists 'on the move', has now entered this trend, modifying the originally rigid argument.

(b) **The analytical trend:** A new 'paradigm' in the social sciences, moving away from unidisciplinarity and using science and technology in its methodological and epistemological tools, challenged the idea of 'tourism' as an activity disconnected from other types of mobility, such as migration, business travel, technological communication and the likes (Hannam et al., 2006). In this 'new mobilities paradigm', which draws on actor-network theory, tourism as a system with global connections to other systems of mobility, continues to consider tourism as a multi-industry but that is now maintained through blends of material (leisure complexes) and immaterial (virtual nodes) connections. Subsequently, tourism scholars began to consider experiential transformations in the tourist experience (Germann Molz, 2013) and how, by turns, such technology-modified experiences might also induce creative industrial changes (Tzanelli, 2013). For example, digital touring does not merely shape popular knowledge of destinations, it may also trigger their modification by tourists and articulate demands for modifications in the ways such places are represented or catered for, by tourist agencies. The new mobilities paradigm does not ignore the normative basis of these phenomena, but prioritizes the presentation of explanatory frameworks – for example, how the new moral economies of tourism work *en masse* (see Veijola et al., 2014 on new creative ontologies of tourism and mobility) or what problems new global economic environments in which popular tourism emerges generate (see Korstanje, 2009 on tourism and terrorism). Thus, in the new mobilities agenda, 'mass' and 'favourite' often supersede the conventional notion of tourism as a 'popular culture'. The new popular culture tourism has become a policy issue (how to deliver safe and just tourism) as much as it continues to be an ontological (who is a tourist) and an epistemological (how do we know it) category.

Within the analytical trend scholars explored the interconnectedness of different forms or expressions of popular culture and its hybridization more freely and creatively. With a clear focus on the development of audiovisual forms of technology, such studies have recently acquired scholarly venues in the annual International Tourism and Media Conference (ITAM), which includes several topics related to film and tourism and associated special issues in several leading tourism journals (Lundberg & Lexhagen, 2014). Focusing on conceptualizations of a 'popcultural placemaking loop' whereby representations and media convergences allow for endless transformations of leading narratives of place and culture (Gyimóthy et al., 2015, p. 18). Such studies are yet to identify patterns of hybridization at societal and cultural levels informing host–guest interactions and identity-making beyond consumption rituals and sites (Tzanelli, 2015a).

Modes of socialization: together we tour (but how?)

The mode of socialization prompts us to think of tourism as a popular culture in its own right, endorsing, or generating forms of sociality. Sociologically, this trend relates to the original study of tourism as a record of *Gemeinschaft* or *Gesselschaft* connectedness (Dann & Cohen, 1996), a shift from mechanical to organic and then nomadic forms of solidarity (Hannam, 2008). This mode of investigation considers associations between tourism and popular culture in terms of scales of interaction, commencing from the micro-level (interpersonal) and proceeding to the meso-level (family, small community/locality) and finally the macro-level (transnational communities and new post-national social formations). The meso- and macro-levels fit better in studies of tourism socialities, because tourism as an activity renders social networking and social solidarities possible (Larsen et al., 2006). For example, family and VFR (Visiting Friends and Relatives) tourism both comprise sub-fields in tourism studies and provide the organizing rationale of niche tourisms (Shani & Uriely, 2012; Janta et al., 2015). The same can be said about tourism-related migrations, which trigger new social formations abroad, with new expatriate tourist-like communities or second-home owner enclaves (Hall & Williams, 2013). These new social enclaves also alien transplant popular culture practices associated with the tourists' former home territories into the new host countries, triggering new processes of self-seclusion or transculturation and hybridity. Thus, studies have shown that among British tourist-migrants in Mediterranean countries, old bonding habits such as watching football or socializing in pubs while drinking and listening to popular music can reproduce ethno-national styles (e.g. 'bring a Brit') or hybridize them, with the inclusion of new styles (O'Reilly, 2000; Bott, 2004; Haug et al., 2007).

Studies of modes of socialization in tourist contexts were originally influenced by Victor Turner's (1974) *communitas* as a loose and ephemeral form of solidarity manifest in subcultural and counter-cultural mobilities and rituals from the 1960s and the 1970s onwards. The hippie movement and youth tourism in 'Third World' countries have been the most prevalent examples of tourism-generating popular cultures (Cohen, 1973). Studies produced in a similar vein looked at different forms of religious and secular pilgrimage as mass and popular culture phenomena respectively (Graburn, 1983, 1997, 2004; Coleman & Eade, 2004; Tzanelli, 2013, 2016b). Especially examinations of popular pilgrimages in film and music-induced tourism pointed, in a 'new mobilities' fashion, to new forms of sociality formed *en route*, or upon arrival at tourist destinations. These studies, which contextually feed into considerations of particular tourism niches, including lifestyle and backpack (Cohen, 2010, 2011), drug (D'Andrea, 2004, 2006) or even mega-event tourism (Tzanelli, 2015b), connect to the popular cultures of so-called neo-nomadism (Deleuze & Guattari, 1987) and neo-tribalism (Maffesoli, 1996), conveying new, non-organic forms of socialization in liquid modern contexts (Bauman, 2000). Neo-tribalism and neo-nomadism point to loose and liquid socialities formed precisely to facilitate or even stage experiential authenticity as a collective or individual autobiographical 'event', a change in the way reality appears to us or a radical transformation of reality for good or just for a day. Neo-tribal groups subvert or correct set 'scripts' and itineraries that industries and travel companies provide to tourists, turning the journey into a 'travel book' community subjects write as members of the enclave and/or as individuals. Such, now more often than not, digitized repositories of tourist mobilities revise scholarly conceptions of experience and authenticity through binary oppositions between 'reality' and 'non-reality', or even 'hyperreality', defining experiential authenticity as 'irreal': an endlessly and contextually produced emotional and cognitive conception of the destination, its cultural and natural artifacts.

Modes of socialization can be strengthened or formed through particular travelling rituals. From photographing landscapes next to tourists or video-recording landscapes and native performances, to purchasing souvenirs, especially travelling rituals related to image-making practices produce externally accessible (by others) records of internally formed experiences (aesthetic appreciation, emotional engagement) of the journey and the holiday. Families, for example, are known to produce collective memory records through photographed tourist experiences (Haldrup & Larsen, 2003; Larsen, 2005). These include all the external stimuli that will ultimately colour personal experiences of, and engagement with the destination. Other travelling rituals, such as consuming native foodstuff (Parasecolli & de Abreu e Lima, 2012) or purchasing souvenirs and items 'typically representative' of the tourist destination (Kohn & Love, 2001; Tzanelli, 2011), are often based on preconceptions, perceptions or impressions of the destination that may also be recorded (e.g. by creating individual or collective, written or audio-visual diaries of the experience of 'being there'). This dimension of socialization refers to internal/cognitive and inculcated ideas about the visiting cultures (by schooling, the family or the media), but also the changing perceptions of them via concrete encounters upon arrival at the destination (see Cohen's 1979 'phenomenology of tourist experiences'). Together, these modes of socialization (the first external, the second internal) are part of how ideas of domestic, folk cultures enter the world of global touristic interaction – how culture became 'tourismified' (Wang, 2000, p. 197; Salazar, 2009, p. 49) in a popular, 'democratized' way beyond the control of the nation-state.

Yet, popular culture can also be a priori reterritorialized – that is, it can exist as a global good or consumable. This is especially prevalent in the tourismified domains of sports (football and Olympics mega-events), where globally hypermobile subcultures of fans act as tourists.

Significantly, the disconnection of such tourismified popular cultures from national identity and territoriality triggers opposing practices of tight surveillance and control by the host city or nation-state. Collaborative initiatives between mega-event business and the hosting nation-state are known to streamline the traffic of such popular cultures into specific urban spaces, designated as 'fan zones', in an attempt to make the tourismified host city safer and to contain violence associated with hooliganism or even terrorist activities. Thus, practices of surveillance and policies of popular culture control during the Euro Football Cups is a well-researched area closely connected to the production of cultures of tourism in the host countries and cities (Klauser, 2008, 2011). Evidently, then, visited sites abroad and the very process of visitation as a mass socio-cultural phenomenon, contribute to constant redefinitions of what is popular and why it should be studied in the context of tourism.

Modes of construction

The third mode of associating tourism with popular culture looks into the development of novel popular culture environments in today's globalized world. Such environments enable the production and dissemination of representations or simulations of place, culture and human populations. The focus of the mode is both the representational conduits (machines and industrial complexes) and the representations or simulations they manufacture and broadcast.[1] One may distinguish two interconnected deliberations of construction in this vein:

(a) **Marketing popular culture tourism:** In more recent decades, a variety of new socio-cultural practices, as well as the emergence of new lifestyles and consumption rituals, products and experiences, have led to a radical redefinition of what comprises 'tourism'. Emphasis is placed on the audio-visual and digital environments manufactured by contingent, profitable collaborations between media (film, Internet) and tourist industries (hotel, entertainment venues, as well as aeromobile or automobile complexes catering for travel and consumption upon arrival at the tourist destination). For example, new processes of designing and marketing holidays online have led to the virtual consumption of distant cultures, landscapes and places. This practice has become commonly known as virtual, digital or Internet tourism (Tzanelli, 2007, 2015a). Likewise, the use of landscapes and heritage spots in the filming of movies, has generated fan cultures; this might or might not lead to embodied visits of the filmed sites by participants/members of these cultures, but it is certainly supported by tourist and mobility systems in terms of infrastructure. Examples of such tourismified fan cultural contexts include: *The Lord of the Rings* (2000–2003) (*LOTR*) cinematic trilogy, which generated new simulated heritage spots in New Zealand (the constructed stage of Hobbiton village in Matamata and the *LOTR*-dedicated museums in Auckland – see Beeton, 2005; Tzanelli, 2007; Peaslee, 2010, 2011); *The Da Vinci Code* (2006) tourism in London, Edinburgh, Rome and Paris, which reconstructs the cinematic drama for fans through tours to actual filmed sites (Tzanelli, 2013; Martin-Jones, 2014); the *Harry Potter* tours in London's tube to visit the famous 9¾ station; the *Game of Thrones* (2011–2016) visits to filmed Northern Irish landmarks (Tzanelli, 2016a); the Dracula movie-induced tourism (Reijnders, 2011b); and the *Breaking Bad* (2008–2013) tours to Albuquerque's spots in which the TV series filmed its criminal heroes' drug business (Tzanelli & Yar, 2016).

All these examples of tourismification find extensions in the cybersphere, in which various tourism agents and businesses generate virtual platforms of consumption, usually connected to cinematic paraphernalia (e.g. 'faux' crystal meth (candies) is sold online, with reference to the drug produced by *Breaking Bad*'s self-made entrepreneur, Walter White). Standing for (edible or not) tourist souvenirs, such tokens work as inducers of visits to filmed places and/or sensory stimulators substituting these embodied visits. Where conventional definitions of the 'popular' emphasized embodied performances, today's popular tourist experiences promote blends of virtuality and embodiment. Various combinations of digital, film-induced and cinematic tourisms challenge conventional understandings of what tourism is supposed to be about: an embodied experience produced through the relocation of people to unfamiliar socio-cultural settings, with referents to real histories, within a limited timeframe (Roesch, 2009). Such new tourisms are explicitly connected to 'places of the imagination' (Reijnders, 2011a) and to 'mind-walking' as symbolic/cognitive visits to actual or fantastic places (Ingold, 2010). Indeed, virtual visits to places have also been embraced by tourist designers and advertisers of holidays that induce in prospective tourists the desire to visit places through digital 'gamification', computer gaming that is based on real landscapes and topographies acting as prospective tourist destinations (Xu et al., 2015). In this respect, popular culture designs and products contribute to the emergence of the 'post-tourist' (Ritzer & Liska, 1997), the mobile subject that is not interested in accumulating experiences connected to alleged 'authentic' representations of culture or exclusively embodied visits to tourist destinations, but opts consciously for 'fake' (that is, manufactured) experiences or products fabricated by film and other digital industries (Strain, 2003). Perhaps more correctly, placing these fan cultures among new forms of socialization (see section above on modes of socialization), highlights the fragile and ever-changing relationship between the production (by industries *and* fans) and consumption of the touristic experience, as well as its claims to authenticity as an extension not of place-representation but of place-making. Such place-making suggests the slow but sure transformation of ethnonationally rooted land in terms of self-definition, thus granting places with new identities and new communicative possibilities: Auckland is now also Orcland for neo-tribal film-lovers; and the Pyramid of Louvre is also where Sarah was entombed, film fans are being photographed and Paris claims passage into global popular culture. Likewise, because several Scottish heritage destinations, such as the Callanish Stones, become enmeshed into the cinematic heroines' journeys in *Brave* (2012) as a rite of passage into adulthood, notions of Scottish national identity connected to these destinations are challenged as much as they can be reinforced (Tzanelli, 2014). Through this process, contemporary Scotland begins to view itself as a postmodern tourist destination that can even accommodate and domesticate film pilgrimages deviating from fixed notions of national identity.

(b) Representing popular culture tourism: All media are not mere industrial machines, but can also act as representational conduits. By this I refer to the ways cinematic and digital scripts, images and music or videos can proffer specific understandings of tourism as a self-contained popular culture. Hollinshead (2009) has stressed that popular culture representations are today managed by multiple 'agents' in the tourist business, with the state often working with, or following on, from individual pioneer mediators of culture, 'to institutionalize – sometimes wittingly and sometimes unwittingly – particular forms of identification . . . as it helps transform non-commercial entities and mythic symbols into items of economic exchange' (p. 533). Media scripts tend to stereotype tourism, the tourist and the tourist destination to produce 'accessible' notions of cultural practice and performance, so they are both vehicles and modes of construction. At the same time, individual representations of places and digital communications of the experience of 'being there' by tourists connected to home while 'on the move', also contribute to the dissemination of such scripts. New social media platforms, such as Tumbr, Facebook, Instagram, Flickr, Picasa and Google+ and devices such as laptops, tablets and mobile phones that facilitate new communicative practices such as blogging, texting and amateur video-recording, further pluralize and popularize representations of tourist destinations. Here, the idea of the 'popular' suggests a combined mass produced and democratized practice of generating and disseminating practices and experiences of terrestrial touring, which produces new cosmopolitan subjects (see Germann Molz, 2004; Tzanelli, 2013). Both individual and collective or institutionalized processes of tourismification in popular culture domains point to what Hollinshead (2007 in Hollinshead et al., 2009) terms 'worldmaking': a highly creative – 'and often "false" or "faux" imaginative [process]' – in which various mediating bodies engage, to purposely (or otherwise) 'privilege particular dominant/favored representations of people/places/pasts' (Hollinshead et al., 2009, p. 430).

The marketing and representation of tourism as a form of popular culture impacts on the formations and conditions under which worldmaking as a universalizing and essentializing process – what we often place under the rubric of 'cultural globalization' – takes place. Destination management as a form of image-making by experts is now also driven by the ways subcultural trends such as cinematic tourism, rock-climbing or even dance and food tourism are imagined and shaped by the fan groups, which may contribute to the generation of all forms of mobility of non-touristic nature (such as migrations and thus new ideological formations). Despite the constant control of such mobilities and subcultural formations by tourist industries or the fan groups themselves, on-site interactions between hosts and guests constantly produce new realities or world versions that can even modify or contest vested capitalist interests. This unstable relationship between tourism and popular culture enables the formation of strategic alliances between tourist destination hosts, guests-fans and industrial experts. Strategic alliances of this type can, under certain conditions, alter otherwise fixed forms of authority (who 'writes' consumption rules for the destination) and agency (who actually consumes, enjoys the benefits of visiting the destination).

Conclusion

The three modes of associating tourism with popular culture produce a socio-cultural 'template', a method of mapping tourism as part of everyday life and as a public culture. Their overlapping practices of representation and creative production or destruction and recreation of cultural universes suggest the presence of an experiential matrix in the apprehension of socio-cultural forms of otherness – what resides outside our frames of familiarity but begs to be defined, understood by us. Today understandings of tourism as part of common culture, accessible to the masses is inextricably connected to various systems of mobility of media, travel and representation. Such systemic connectivity has not rendered individuals (the tourist) and communities (touring groups and cultures) passive recipients of industrially produced ideas and practices at all times. On the contrary, these complex hypermobilities can, potentially, diversify and pluralize interpretations of the act and experience of travel in novel ways (Lash & Urry, 1994; Urry & Larsen, 2011). The practice of travelling and overall engaging with 'other' cultures, landscapes and people(s) produce repositories of knowledge no other activity can ritualize the same way in contemporary societies. Indeed, it has been suggested that because tourism as a *public culture* produces intelligent mobile subjects, not cultural dupes or disconnected humans, it is essential for the healthy function of contemporary societies (Hollinshead, 1999, p. 269). Thus, 'common', 'public' and 'popular' – the starting points of Frankfurt School criticisms of mass culture – can overlap fortuitously, to enrich the new knowledge economies of tourism. The link between tourism and popular culture is a programmatic statement on worldmaking that does not merely 'reproduce' or 'serve' ready-made worlds, but constantly makes new ones, hence stimulating human intelligence.

Note

1 For clarification, if 'representations' refer to real socio-cultural contexts, ideas and themes, 'simulations' are, to follow Baudrillard (1994), constructs with no real referent. Examples of such tourismified simulations include Disneyland, a 'hyperreal' fantastic 'land', which today attracts both group and family tourism. Disneyland theme parks are designed around the lives and stories of cartoon characters, with no anchor to social realities and in this respect, they are simulations. For a critique of these types of tourimification as an endorser of consumerist ideologies see Hollinshead (1998).

References

Adorno, T. & Horkheimer, M. (1991). *The dialectic of enlightenment*. New York: Continuum.

Baudrillard, J. (1994). *Simulacra and simulations*. Ann Arbour: University of Michigan Press.

Bauman, Z. (2000). *Liquid modernity*. Cambridge: Polity.

Beeton, S. (2005). *Film-induced tourism*. Toronto: Channel View.

Beeton, S. (2010). The advance of film tourism. *Tourism and Hospitality: Planning and Development*, 7, 1–6.

Boorstin, D. (1962). *The image*. Harmondsworth: Penguin.

Bott, E. (2004). Working on a working-class utopia: Marking young Britons in Tenerife on the new map of European migration. *Journal for Contemporary European Studies*, *12*, 57–70.

Cohen, E. (1973). Nomads from affluence: Notes on the phenomenon of drifter tourism. *International Journal of Comparative Sociology*, *14*, 89–103.

Cohen, E. (1974). Who is a tourist? A conceptual classification. *Sociological Review*, *22*, 527–555.

Cohen, E. (1979). A phenomenology of tourist experiences. *Sociology*, *13*, 179–201.

Cohen, S. A. (2005). Screaming at the moptops: Convergence between tourism and popular culture. In D. Crouch, R. Jackson & F. Thompson (Eds.) *The media and the tourist imagination: Converging cultures* (pp. 76–91). Aldershot: Ashgate.

Cohen, S. A. (2010). Personal identity (de)formation among lifestyle travellers: A double-edged sword? *Leisure Studies*, *29*, 289–301.

Cohen, S. A. (2011). Lifestyle travellers: Backpacking as a way of life. *Annals of Tourism Research*, *38*, 117–133.

Coleman, S. A. & Eade, J. (2004). Reframing pilgrimage. In S. Coleman & J. Eade, (Eds.) *Reframing pilgrimage* (pp. 1–26) London: Routledge.

Croy, G. W. & Heitmann, S. (2011). Tourism and film. In P. Robinson and P. U. C. Diecke (Eds.) *Research themes for tourism* (pp. 188–204). Wallingford: CABI.

D'Andrea, A. (2004). Global nomads: Techno and New Age as transnational countercultures in Ibiza and Goa. In G. Saint-John (Ed.) *Rave culture and religion* (pp. 256–272). New York: Routledge.

D'Andrea, A. (2006). Neo-nomadism: A theory of post-identarian mobility in the global age. *Mobilities*, *1*, 95–119.

Dann, G. M. S. & Cohen, E. (1996). Sociology and tourism. In Y. Apostolopoulos, S. Leivadi & A. Yannakis (Eds.) *The sociology of tourism: Theoretical and empirical investigations* (pp. 301–314). London: Routledge.

Dann, G. M. S. & Liebman Parrinello, G. (2009). Setting the scene. In G. M. S. Dann & G. Parrinello (Eds.) *The sociology of tourism: European origins and developments* (pp. 1–63). Bingley: Emerald.

Deleuze, G. & Guattari, F. (1987). *Thousand plateaus*, translated by B. Massumi. Minneapolis: University of Minnesota Press.

Edensor, T. (2004). Automobility and national identity: Representation, geography and driving practice. *Theory, Culture & Society*, *21*, 101–120.

Enzensberger, H. M. (1974). *The consciousness industry*. New York: Seabury.

Geertz, C. (1973). *The interpretation of culture*. New York: Basic Books.

Geertz, C. (1986). *Works and lives*. Cambridge: Polity Press.

Germann Molz, J. (2004). Playing online and between the lines. In M. Sheller & J. Urry (Eds.) *Tourism mobilities: Places to play, places in play* (pp. 167–169). London: Routledge.

Germann Molz, J. (2012). *Travel connections*. Abingdon: Routledge.

Germann Molz, J. (2013). Social networking technologies and the moral economy of alternative tourism: The case of couchsurfing.org. *Annals of Tourism Research, 43*, 210–230.

Getz, D. (2008). Event tourism: Definition, evolution, and research. *Tourism Management, 29*, 403–428.

Graburn, N. H. H. (1983). *To pray, pay and play*. Aix en-Provence: Centre des Hautes Etudes Touristiques.

Graburn, N. H. H. (1997). Tourism: The sacred journey. In V. Smith (Ed.) *Hosts and guests: An anthropology of tourism* (pp. 17–32). Philadelphia: University of Pennsylvania Press.

Graburn, N. H. H. (2001). Relocating the tourist. *International Sociology, 16*, 147–158.

Graburn, N. H. H. (2002). The ethnographic tourist. In G. M. S. Dann (Ed.) *The tourist as a metaphor of the social world* (pp. 19–40). Wallingford: CABI.

Graburn, N. H. H. (2004). The Kyoto tax strike: Buddism, shinto and tourism in Japan. In E. Badone & S. R. Roseman (Eds.) *Intersecting journeys: The anthropology of pilgrimage and tourism* (pp. 125–139). Chicago: University of Illinois Press.

Greenwood, D. J. (1997). Culture by the pound. In V. L. Smith (Ed.) *Hosts and guests: The anthropology of tourism* (pp. 171–185). Philadelphia: University of Pennsylvania Press.

Gyimóthy, S., Lundberg, C., Lindström, K. N., Lexhagen, M. & Larson, M. (2015). Popculture tourism: A research manifesto. In D. Chambers & T. Rakic (Eds.) *Tourism research frontiers: Beyond the boundaries of knowledge* (pp. 13–26). Bingley: Emerald.

Haldrup, M. & Larsen, J. (2003). The family gaze. *Tourist Studies, 3*, 23–46.

Hall, C. M. & Williams, A. (2013). *Tourism and migration: New relationships between production and consumption*. Netherlands: Springer Science & Business Media.

Hannam, K. (2008). The end of tourism? Nomadology and the mobilities paradigm. In J. Tribe (Ed.) *Philosophical issues in tourism* (pp. 101–113) Clevedon: Channel View.

Hannam, K., Sheller, M. & Urry, J. (2006). Mobilities, immobilites and moorings. *Mobilities, 1*, 1–22.

Haug, B., Dann, G. M. S. & Mehmetoglu, M. (2007). Little Norway in Spain: From tourism to migration. *Annals of Tourism Research, 34*, 202–222.

Hollinshead, K. (1998). Disney and commodity aesthetics: A critique of Fjellman's analysis of 'distory' and the 'historicide' of the past. *Current Issues in Tourism, 1*, 58–119.

Hollinshead, K. (1999). Tourism as public culture: Horne's ideological commentary on the legerdemain of tourism. *International Journal of Tourism Research, 1*, 267–292.

Hollinshead, K. (2009). The 'worldmaking' prodigy of tourism: The reach and power of tourism in the dynamics of change and transformation. *Tourism Analysis, 14*, 139–152.

Hollinshead, K., Ateljevic, I. & Ali, N. (2009). Worldmaking agency – worldmaking authority: The sovereign constitutive role of tourism. *Tourism Geographies*, 11, 427–443.

Ingold, T. (2010). Ways of mind-walking: Reading, writing, painting. *Visual Studies, 25*, 15–23.

Jafari, J. (1987). Tourism models: The sociocultural aspects. *Tourism Management, 8*, 151–159.

Janta, H., Cohen, S. A. & Williams, A. M. (2015). Rethinking visiting friends and relatives mobilities. *Population, Space & Culture, 21*, 585–598.

Klauser, F. (2008). Spatial articulations of surveillance at the FIFA World Cup 2006 in Germany. In K. F. Aas, H. O. Gundhus & H. M. Lomell (Eds.) *Technologies of insecurity* (pp. 61–80). London: Routledge.

Klauser, F. (2011). The exemplification of 'fan zones': Mediating mechanisms in the reproduction of best practices for security and branding at Euro 2008. *Urban Studies, 48*, 3203–3219.

Kohn, N. & Love, L. (2001). This, that and the other: Fraught possibilities of the souvenir. *Text and Performance Quarterly, 21*, 1–17.

Korstanje, M. E. (2009). Tourism and terrorism: Conflicts and commonalities. *Worldwide Hospitality and Tourism Themes, 4*, 8 – 25.

Larsen, J. (2005). Families seen photographing: The performativity of tourist photography. *Space & Culture, 8*, 416–434.

Larsen, J., Urry, J. & Axhausen, K. W. (2006). Networks and tourism: Mobile social life. *Annals of Tourism Research, 34*, 244–262.

Lash, S. & Urry, J. (1994). *Economies of signs and space*. London: Sage.

Leotta, A. (2012). *Touring the screen*. Chicago and Bristol: Intellect.

Lundberg, C. & Lexhagen, M. (2014). Pop culture tourism: A research model. In A. Chauvel, N. Lamerichs & J. Seymour (Eds.) *Fan studies: Researching popular audiences* (pp. 13–34). Freeland: Inter-Disciplinary Press.

McCabe, S. (2005). 'Who is a tourist?' A critical overview. *Tourist Studies*, *5*, 85–106.

MacCannell, D. (1989). *The tourist*. London: Macmillan.

MacCannell, D. (2001). Tourist agency. *Tourist Studies*, *1*, 23–37.

Maffesoli, M. (1996) *The time of the tribes*. London: Sage.

Martin-Jones, D. (2014). Film tourism as heritage tourism: Scotland, diaspora and *The Da Vinci Code* (2006). *New Review of Film & Television Studies*, *12*, 156–177.

O'Reilly, K. (2000). *The British on the Costa del Sol: Transnational identities and local communities*. London: Routledge.

Parasecoli, F. & de Abreu e Lima (2012). Eat your way through culture: Gastronomic tourism as performance and bodily experience. In S. Fullagar, K. Markwell & E. Wilson (Eds.) *Slow tourism: Experiences and mobilities* (pp. 69–83). Clevedon: Channel View.

Peaslee, R. M. (2010). 'The man from New Line knocked on the door': Tourism, media power, and Hobbiton/Matamata as boundaried space. *Tourist Studies*, *10*, 57–73.

Peaslee, R. M. (2011). One ring, many circles: The Hobbiton tour experience and a spatial approach to media power. *Tourist Studies*, *11*, 37–53.

Reijnders, S. (2011a). *Places of the imagination*. Aldershot: Ashgate.

Reijnders, S. (2011b). Stalking the Count: Dracula, fandom and tourism. *Annals of Tourism Research*, *38*, 231–248.

Rickly-Boyd, J. (2013). 'Dirtbags': Mobility, community and rick climbing as performative of identity. In T. Duncan, S. A. Cohen & M. Thulemark (Eds.) *Lifestyle mobilities* (pp. 51–64). Aldershot: Ashgate.

Ritzer, G. (2006). Globalization and McDonaldization. In G. Ritzer (Ed.) *McDonaldization: The reader* (pp. 395–410). London: Sage.

Ritzer, G. & Liska. A. (1997). 'McDisneyization' and 'post-tourism': Contemporary perspectives on contemporary tourism. In C. Rojek & J. Urry (Eds.) *Touring cultures: Transformations of travel and theory* (pp. 96–112). London and New York: Routledge.

Roesch, S. (2009). *The experiences of film location tourists*. Toronto: Channel View Publications.

Salazar, N. (2009). Imaged or imagined? Cultural representations and the 'tourismification' of peoples and places. *Cahiers d'Études Africaines*, *XLIX*, 49–71.

Shani, A. & Uriely, N. (2012). VFR tourism: The host experience. *Annals of Tourism Research*, *39*, 421–440.

Spracklen, K. (2016). Framing mobilities in heavy metal music festival events. In K. Hannam, M. Mostaphanezhad & J. M. Rickly (Eds.) *Event mobilities: Politics, place and performance* (pp. 40–51). Abingdon: Routledge.

Strain, E. (2003). *Public places, private journeys: Ethnography, entertainment and the tourist gaze*. Brunswick, NJ: Rutgers University Press

Turner, V. (1974). Liminal to liminoid, play flow and ritual. *Rice University Studies*, *50*, 53–92.

Tzanelli, R. (2007). *The cinematic tourist: Explorations in globalization, culture and resistance*. Abingdon: Routledge.

Tzanelli, R. (2011). *Cosmopolitan memory in Europe's 'backwaters': Rethinking civility*. Abingdon: Routledge.

Tzanelli, R. (2013). *Heritage in the digital era: Cinematic tourism and the activist cause*. Abingdon: Routledge.

Tzanelli, R. (2014). Heritage entropy and tourist pilgrimage in *Brave's* Scotland. *Hospitality & Society*, *4*, 155–177.

Tzanelli, R. (2015a). *Mobility, modernity and the slum: The real and virtual journeys of* Slumdog Millionaire. Abingdon: Routledge.

Tzanelli, R. (2015b). *Socio-cultural mobility and mega-events: Ethics and aesthetics in Brazil's 2014 World Cup*. Abingdon: Routledge.

Tzanelli, R. (2016a). *Game of Thrones* to games of sites/sights: Framing events through cinematic transformations in Northern Ireland. In K. Hannam, M. Mostafanezhad & J. M. Rickly-Boyd (Eds.) *Event mobilities: Politics, place and performance* (pp. 52–67). London: Routledge.

Tzanelli, R. (2016b). *Thanatourism and cinematic representations of risk: Screening the end of tourism*. Abingdon: Routledge.

Tzanelli, R., & Yar, M. (2016). *Breaking Bad*, making good: Notes on a televisual tourist industry. *Mobilities*, *11*, 2, 188–206.

Urry, J. (2002). *The tourist gaze*. London: Sage.

Urry, J. (2004). The 'system' of automobility. *Theory, Culture & Society*, *21*, 25–39.

Urry, J. (2007). *Mobilities*. Cambridge: Polity.

Urry, J. & Larsen, J. (2011). *The tourist gaze 3.0.* London: Sage.

Veijola, S., Molz, J. G., Pythtinen, O., Hockert, E., Grit, A., Germann Molz, J. & Höckert, E. (2014). *Disruptive tourism and its untidy guests: Alternative ontologies for future hospitalities.* Basingstoke: Palgrave Macmillan.

Wang, N. (2000). *Tourism and modernity.* Oxford: Pergamon.

Williams, R. (1958). *Culture and society.* London: Chatto and Windus.

Xu, F., Tian, F., Buhalis, D., Weber, J. & Zhang, H. (2015). Tourists as mobile gamers: Gamification for tourism marketing. *Journal of Travel & Tourism Marketing, 33,* 1124–1142.

3

SYNONTOLOGICAL SPACES

Rhona Trauvitch

Setting the scene: synontological spaces

As readers and text consumers, we have a propensity to actualize fiction. That is, we regularly interact with fictional entities as though they were non-fictional. Examples are myriad and multimodal: Quidditch is played on scores of college and university campuses and an annual world cup is organized by the International Quidditch Association (Williams, 2014); Wonka Bars are available for purchase in stores that are located outside of Roald Dahl's book's covers; Klingon and the Elvish language Sindarin are spoken by non-fictional people, and there are books about the grammar of Sindarin and Elvish vocabulary (Salo & Tolkien, 2004), as well as Klingon translations of *Hamlet* (Shakespeare et al., 2000) and the Bible. These are just a few instances of a phenomenon that has become widespread and commonplace.

When interacting with fictional entities in our non-fictional reality, we experience what I call synontology[1] – a convergence of ontological states. The prefix *syn* (with; together) denotes synchrony and combination. Synontology is characterized by the confluence of two ontological states: that which features the fictional entity, and that which features the fictional entity's non-fictional manifestation. Both ontological states are involved, for instance, when a player of Quidditch understands the nature of the game, as well as its [fictional] history. Readers[2] access synontology when they physically play a game of the originally fictional Quidditch, and draw on both ontological realms in order to comprehensively experience their interaction with fiction.

Here I focus on a particular grove within the vast forest of actualized fictions: locale-related entities that exist at ontological interstices, and thereby form synontological spaces. These entities are objects and events that are originally fictional, but now take up space and/or are commemorated in the non-fictional world. Synontological spaces manifest, for example, via monuments: there is an engraved stone in Riverside, Iowa, which indicates the future birthplace of *Star Trek*'s Captain James T. Kirk, a plaque at Reichenbach Falls, Switzerland, which commemorates – in three languages – the altercation between Sherlock Holmes and Professor James Moriarty, and statues of Yoda in San Francisco, Rocky in Philadelphia, and – sometime in the near future – RoboCop in Detroit (Letzer, 2016). Locales also exist synontologically: In 2007, a dozen North American 7-Eleven stores were reborn as Kwik-E-Marts as part of the promotion of *The Simpsons Movie* (Garfield, 2007), and Nickelodeon Hotels & Resorts in Punta Cana, the Dominican Republic, feature an above-sea villa that is a replica of SpongeBob

SquarePants' pineapple under the sea (Williams, 2016). Physical travel is not a prerequisite for finding such spaces where fictional entities and events are actualized. One need only find a particular police box on Earl's Court Road in London via Google Maps' Street View to click into Doctor Who's TARDIS (Kumparak, 2013). If one prefers the Batcave, one can explore it by Google mapping Bruce Wayne's residence (Renfro, 2016).

While the construction of synontological spaces involves actions that are simple – erecting plaques, building monuments, remodeling stores, and digitally representing locales are straightforward undertakings – the implications are complex, because they require reader interaction at the confluence of two ontological states. One ontological state is that of fiction. Readers become acquainted with a fictional entity by reading a narrative and getting to know the entity in its fictional setting: they watch the adventures of Captain Kirk on *Star Trek* and SpongeBob in *SpongeBob SquarePants*, they read about the mortal clash between Holmes and Moriarty in Arthur Conan Doyle's "The Final Problem," they become familiar with the Springfield Kwik-E-Mart by watching *The Simpsons* episodes, and they learn about the capabilities of the TARDIS on *Doctor Who*.

The other ontological state is that of actuality. In the town of Riverside there is an actual stone that celebrates the future birth of a fictional character, at Punta Cana there is an actual villa called the Pineapple, at the Bernese Oberland region of Switzerland there is an actual plaque that commemorates a clash between fictional characters, across North America stood actual convenience stores called Kwik-E-Marts, and the TARDIS is presented as a locale on Google Maps' Street View.

That which occurs or resides in fiction takes up physical or virtual space in actuality, and the people visiting these synontological spaces therefore take part in a special sort of popular culture tourism.[3] They are negotiating the fictional and the non-fictional in every visit, and delighting in the quirkiness of the juxtaposition. In what follows, I will turn to narratology to discuss boundary crossing, cognitive studies to shed light on how and to what end synontology is experienced, and geocriticism to formulate this investigation in spatial terms.

We know that in practice, the entities discussed in this chapter are often installed, built, and programmed for reasons of marketing, promotion, and entertainment. The Kwik-E-Marts, for example, served the double purpose of promoting *The Simpsons Movie* as well the products visitors could buy in the stores (some of them originally fictional – and suddenly available for actual consumption – such as Buzz Cola, Squishees, and KrustyO's). The present exploration, however, concerns itself not with how or for what purpose these spaces come into being, but rather with the narratological and cognitive maneuverings that synontology entails, and the ways in which we may conceptualize it spatially.

Theoretical underpinnings: narratology, cognitive studies, geocriticism

Narratology

Our focus here is on synontology that exists outside the borders of a given narrative. In other words, we are examining synontology that occurs beyond the readers' experiences of a text. A reader's purchase of a Wonka Bar, for instance, takes place outside his/her experience of reading Dahl's *Charlie and the Chocolate Factory* (1964), since his/her purchase is not described in the novel. A reader's visit to the monument that commemorates the future birth of Captain Kirk takes place outside his/her experience of watching *Star Trek*, as this visit is not featured in any *Star Trek* episode or movie.

Synontology regularly occurs within narratives as well – through the process of metalepsis. In her introduction to *Metalepsis in Popular Culture* (2011), Karin Kukkonen notes,

"Metalepsis means literally 'a jump across' and, when it occurs in literature, film or other media, the boundaries of a fictional world are glanced, travelled or transported across" (p. 1). Characterizing a jump across narrative ontological levels, metalepsis illuminates the machinations of the confluence of ontological states. However, metalepsis provides us with a springboard rather than a framework for understanding synontology that occurs beyond the reading process. Metalepsis is necessarily a text-bound device, which involves a paradoxical situation that cannot occur in actuality. For example, a character in a book might address the reader, but the character will not hear or be impacted by the reader's response. Moreover, fictional entities do not actually jump across into actuality, as what we see when we look at a Wonka Bar or do when we play Quidditch is a representation, copy, or reenactment of a fictional entity. If one were to re-paint in magenta a Kwik-E-Mart that exists in actuality, one would not whatsoever affect the walls of its fictional version, which continue to be orange in *The Simpsons* (S. Packard, personal communication, November 2015). Thus, while metalepsis and synontological spaces in actuality both pertain to the convergence or crossing of ontological states, they describe different negotiations of these states – one within the text and one beyond it.

Using metalepsis as a springboard, therefore, what can we learn, and what can we apply to synontological spaces in actuality? To best answer this, I suggest we consider ontological, rather than rhetorical metalepsis. Marie-Laure Ryan (2006, p. 207) explains the distinction between rhetorical and ontological metalepses as follows:

> Rhetorical metalepsis opens a small window that allows a quick glance across levels, but the window closes after a few sentences, and the operation ends up reasserting the existence of boundaries. This temporary breach of illusion does not threaten the basic structure of the narrative universe. In the rhetorical brand of metalepsis, the author may speak *about* her characters, presenting them as creations of her imagination . . . but she doesn't speak *to* them, because they belong to another level of reality. [. . .]
>
> Whereas rhetorical metalepsis maintains the levels . . . distinct from each other, ontological metalepsis opens a passage between levels that results in their interpenetration, or mutual contamination. [. . .] In a narrative work, ontological levels will become entangled when an existent belongs to two or more levels at the same time, or when an existent migrates from one level to the next, causing two separate environments to blend.

Ontological metalepses are those that engender truly paradoxical situations – ones that cannot occur beyond the narrative. While it is fun to ponder the destabilization of logic that ontological metalepses engender, the hinted implications of such destabilization can be quite unsettling. Understanding why the implications are unsettling will allow us to better characterize the cognitive processes that are at play in synontological spaces.

In *Postmodernist Fiction* (1994, p. 10), Brian McHale lists several typical postmodernist questions, among which are:

> What happens when different kinds of world are placed in confrontation, or when boundaries between worlds are violated?; What is the mode of existence of a text, and what is the mode of existence of the world (or worlds) it projects.

In the chapter "Chinese-Box Worlds," McHale notes, regarding the various types of recursive structures:

The consequence of all these disquieting puzzles and paradoxes is to foreground the ontological dimensions of the Chinese box of fiction. [. . .] Where a modernist text might pass over its recursive structures in silence, these postmodernist texts flaunt theirs. Our attention having thus been focused on recursiveness *for its own sake*, we begin, like Borges, to speculate: why stop the recursive operation of nesting worlds within worlds at any particular level of embedding? why stop at all, ever?

(1994, pp. 114–115)

McHale is referring to Jorge Luis Borges' famous hypothesis at the end of "Partial Magic in the *Quixote*," which runs as follows:

Why does it disturb us that the map be included in the map and the thousand and one nights in the book of the *Thousand and One Nights*? Why does it disturb us that Don Quixote be a reader of the *Quixote* and Hamlet a spectator of *Hamlet*? I believe I have found the reason: these inversions suggest that if the characters of a fictional work can be readers or spectators, we, its readers or spectators, can be fictitious.

(2007, p. 196)

In fact, in his essay in *Metalepsis in Popular Culture*, Keyvan Sarkhosh (2011, p. 90) notes that Gérard Genette "was the first to refer to [this conclusion by Borges] in the metaleptic context." Genette (1980, p. 236) writes the following:

All these games, by the intensity of their effects, demonstrate the importance of the boundary they tax their ingenuity to overstep, in defiance of verisimilitude – a boundary *that is precisely the narrating (or the performance) itself*: a shifting but sacred frontier between two worlds, the world in which one tells, the world of which one tells. Whence the uneasiness Borges so well put his finger on: "Such inversions suggest that if the characters in a story can be readers of spectators, then we, their readers or spectators, can be fictitious." The most troubling thing about metalepsis indeed lies in this unacceptable and insistent hypothesis, that the extradiegetic is perhaps always diegetic, and that the narrator and his narratees – you and I – perhaps belong to some narrative.

"The Man Who Created Woman" (1994), a short story by Svend Åge Madsen (in the course of which, incidentally, Borges is arguably evoked at least twice), perfectly captures this unsettling revelation. The primary narrator of this story conveys the terrifying claustrophobia of a book closing its covers around him:

Once more I felt her presence before I slowly closed the book and allowed her and her story to live on in her own world. For a time I thoughtfully contemplated the red book with the tattered binding into which she had disappeared. [. . .]
   Suddenly I am overwhelmed by a terrible shock. For a brief moment it is as though I can feel the eyes which are reading me, the hand turning over the pages in my story. I feel like a little word in a narrative, feel the story encompassing me. Am I smiling, or am I shouting as I feel the pages pressing close upon me as my book is closed?

(p. 51)

McHale (1994, p. 115) notes yet another instance of this disquieting conjecture:

the fictional author in Barth's "Life-Story" . . . who is writing about an author who is writing about an author, and so on, also suspects – quite rightly – that he himself is a character in someone else's fictional text. But why stop there? If there is a *meta*-author occupying a *higher* level than his own, just as there is a hypodiegetic author occupying a level below his, then why not a meta-meta-author on a meta-meta-level, and so on, to infinity?

Not so distant from these examples is Kim Newman's observation in his introduction to Win Scott Eckert's first volume of *Crossovers* (2010). Regarding Eckert's compilation of myriad fictional and fictionalized characters into one crossover universe, Newman provides a rationale for *his own* inclusion, which involves his great-great uncle, mother, and paternal grandmother: "Through some skewed logic rising from these connections, I can now write myself into the crossover universe" (p. 9). The appearances of his name "in other people's novels . . . further cement [his] phantasmal other self" (p. 9). Newman concludes, "This may be an area of worthwhile future research, since – as Farmer's *Riverworld* already proved – it means we all get to be inhabitants of the Land of Fiction eventually" (p. 9). The difference is that Newman's statement concerns the gathering of every entity into an eventual, fictional pan-cosmos, whereas Borges', Madsen's and Barth's are more ontologically spooky, implying that we might all be fictional to begin with. In each of these cases, however, we are presented with the ontological shift from actual to fictional.

In short, the above instances indicate that the permutation of narrative levels engenders ontological questioning because it raises the misgiving, What if *we* are fictional? As McHale proposes, recursive structures provide us with a vista to the next level – that of the real world. Otherwise put, they allow for the conceptual building of a staircase one level "up" from the diegesis (and, to repeat Genette's assertion, "the extradiegetic is perhaps always diegetic"). That there are levels *inside* the narrative propounds and even supports the existence of levels leading to the *outside* of the narrative as well.

That ontological metalepsis could contribute to spooky misgivings about our own ontological states may be instrumental in revealing why we are drawn to synontological spaces. If the "mutual contamination" of narrative levels steers us toward pondering our own possible fictionality, perhaps synontological spaces work in the opposite direction, and bring the fictional onto our ontological level; instead of our becoming fictional, the fictional takes on qualities of the non-fictional.

While this direction of [seeming] ontological transgression is less disquieting, it nonetheless retains the riveting scent of paradox. Synontological spaces are not paradoxical per se, and they do not involve any literal transgression, because nothing impossible takes place. However, the mind of a synontological space tourist is doing interesting things as he/she negotiates two ontological states. What happens in our minds that allows us to commemorate the occasion of a fictional birth – let alone one that is set in the future of our earthly, non-fictional timeline? With what mindset, and with which cognitive tools do we interact with fictional entities beyond our experience of reading about them? That we do so easily does not diminish the quirkiness of the situation; that we do so often indicates that there is something rewarding about this interaction. There is a fascinating cognitive puzzle here.

Cognitive studies

The cognitive underpinnings of synontology are flexibility and dissonance. Cognitive flexibility can explain how readers access multiple ontological states, and cognitive dissonance suggests that perhaps the tension evoked by the whimsical juxtaposition of the fictional and the non-fictional is experienced positively.

In their discussion of learning and knowledge acquisition, Spiro and Jehng (1990) define cognitive flexibility as "the ability to spontaneously restructure one's knowledge, in many ways, in adaptive response to radically changing situational demands" (p. 165). Cognitive flexibility is at play in synontological spaces, as one must almost simultaneously hold two ontological perspectives. Consider a Trekkie's visit to the monument that commemorates the future birth of Captain Kirk, which is located in the town of Riverside. The Trekkie must indeed display something comparable to "the ability to spontaneously restructure [his/her] knowledge . . . in adaptive response to radically changing situational demands." The situational demands are the demands made by fiction and the demands made by actuality. The demands do not so much rapidly change as they are merged and accessed simultaneously, but they are decidedly radically different. A reader approaches fiction with a mindset different from that with which he/she approaches non-fiction. For instance, when reading fiction one is typically ready to suspend one's disbelief. One is more willing to accept outrageous concepts and flex one's imagination. More fundamental, however, is the ability to *distinguish* fiction from non-fiction. This ability is central to the tourist's enjoyment of synontology: if he/she were lacking this ability, he/she would be incapable of consciously and joyfully shunning it.

The touring Trekkie accesses two ontological states – that of being in and perceiving the actual, non-fictional monument (Figure 3.1), and that of experiencing the fictional world of Captain Kirk – and he/she does so via cognitive flexibility. The Trekkie is able to concurrently co-inhabit both realms in touring a synontological space by rapidly switching mindsets or accessing both at the same time.

Elen, Stahl, Bromme, and Clarebout (2011, p. 2) describe cognitive flexibility as,

> the disposition to consider diverse context-specific information elements while deciding how to solve a problem or to execute a (learning) task in a variety of domains and to adapt one's problem solving or task execution in case the context changes or new information becomes present. [. . .]
>
> Given that context-specific information elements are taken into account, being cognitive flexible implies that one considers both the context and the information at hand.

Though Elen et al. (2011) are discussing cognitive flexibility in general terms and in reference to learning, problem solving, and task execution, we can apply their delineation to our purposes. In terms of synontological spaces, then, what is the information at hand, and what is the context? The information, to put it simply, is a given entity's ontological status. The Trekkie possesses information that Captain Kirk is fictional, and that the monument commemorating Captain Kirk's future birth is non-fictional – an actual stone that exists in an actual town. The context, on the other hand, is the synontological space itself, wherein the two ontological states are merged. The Trekkie operates within this context when he/she visits the monument.

Within the context of the synontological space, our information about one state must be reconciled with our information about the other state, and we appreciate the seemingly paradoxical juxtaposition. Essentially, the fictional must be conciliated with the non-fictional such that the two make sense contemporaneously and colocationally. Applying the definition provided by Elen et al. (2011) to our situation, we can determine that "being cognitive flexible implies that one considers both the synontological space ("context") and a given entity's ontological status ("information") "at hand." Tying this to Spiro and Jehng's definition and repositioning it for our purposes, we

Figure 3.1　Future birthplace of Captain James T. Kirk Monument in Riverside, Iowa.
Source: photo by Nana L. Kirk.

can further determine that cognitive flexibility "is the ability to spontaneously" reconcile pieces of information ("restructure one's knowledge"), "in many ways, in adaptive response to" seemingly incongruous ("radically changing") juxtapositions ("situational demands"). Synontological tourists, it would appear, are quite cognitive flexible.

So far we have noted the abilities of synontological tourists, but what of their motivations? What does one gain from visiting an actual place inhabited – in fiction – by a fictional character, or making a pilgrimage to commemorate a future, fictional event? I suggest that we interact with fictional entities beyond the borders of the narrative because we would like to perpetuate our connection to the entities' worlds. A good book does not have to end when we turn its back cover; we do not have to leave the side of a treasured character when his/her story concludes. The Trekkie ostensibly visits the monument to prolong his/her experience with beloved stories and come into contact with the world of characters he/she holds dear. Unable to reproduce something akin to Woody Allen's Kugelmass' journey to the novel *Madame Bovary*, the Trekkie superimposes the fictional onto the actual and visits – in actuality – a locale mentioned in fiction.

Additionally, we interact with fictional entities in our non-fictional reality because we seek novelty, and are beguiled by the peculiar confluence of fiction and non-fiction. I suspect a somewhat similar sentiment is at play when we encounter oxymorons, and perhaps even synaesthesia. We delight in seeing how two things that should not work together *do*.

The synontological tourist enjoys the jarring sensation of paradox, and this is where cognitive dissonance comes into play. Leon Festinger developed cognitive dissonance theory, and based it on the premise that "the individual strives toward consistency within himself" (1962, p. 1). Supplanting "inconsistency" with "dissonance" and "consistency" with "consonance," Festinger (1962, p. 3) described cognitive dissonance theory with two hypotheses:

1. The existence of dissonance, being psychologically uncomfortable, will motivate the person to try to reduce the dissonance and achieve consonance.
2. When dissonance is present, in addition to trying to reduce it, the person will actively avoid situations and information that would likely increase the dissonance.

Joel Cooper (2007, p. 2) writes that Festinger

> made a very basic observation about the lives of human beings: we do not like inconsistency. It upsets us and it drives us to action to reduce our inconsistency. The greater the inconsistency we face, the more agitated we will be and the more motivated we will be to reduce it.

Cooper notes that "a pair of cognitions is inconsistent if one cognition follows from the obverse (opposite) of the other" (p. 6). Thus, "[i]f a person holds cognitions A and B such that A follows from the opposite of B, then A and B are dissonant" (p. 6).

I characterize what synontological tourists experience as cognitive dissonance because they indeed hold "cognitions A and B such that A follows from the opposite of B," where "opposite" is broadly interpreted. For example,

- Let cognition A = the fact that you are visiting the site where Captain Kirk is to be born, and commemorating this future event.
- Let cognition B = the knowledge that Captain Kirk is a fictional character.

Cognition A follows from the converse of cognition B in that you would typically visit a site where something *non*-fictional happened and commemorate an *actual* event (moreover, one that occurred in the past). This is at odds with cognition B, according to which the event, like the character, is fictional. Given this formulation, any interaction with a fictional entity that takes place in our non-fictional world gives rise to cognitive dissonance. Of course, synontology does not usually produce the discomfort or vexation that Festinger and Cooper describe; even an accidental visitor to Google Street View's TARDIS is unlikely to feel distressed about this find. However, rather than indicating that synontological spaces do not involve cognitive dissonance, this actually suggests that cognitive dissonance – and inconsistency – are not always infelicitous. I am proposing that the contemporaneous and collocational confluence of ontological states gives rise to an inconsistency that is experienced *positively*.

Indeed, instead of striving to eliminate the inconsistency – their cognitive dissonance – visitors of synontological spaces actively seek it out. The tension produced by the curious juxtaposition of fiction and non-fiction is experienced favorably. The inconsistency is what makes it fun! Part – or perhaps most – of the thrill of shopping at Kwik-E-Mart emerges from the ability to purchase heretofore fictional products – something that, like a tourist suddenly finding him/herself in *The Simpsons'* Springfield, should not be possible. Instead of being avoided, this cognitive dissonance is sought, and cognitive flexibility sustains the delightful feeling of dissonance. In other words, happy synontological tourists are ones who have the flexibility to experience this dissonance.

Geocriticism

Since we are considering spaces – synontological or otherwise – it is also important to draw on geocriticism. How shall we map these synontological spaces – at least conceptually? How do we position synontological spaces with relation to typical spaces that are not conflated with fiction? It is true the Riverside monument, the Reichenbach Falls plaque, and the 12 Kwik-E-Marts exist/ed in physical space and that the TARDIS and Batcave exist in virtual space, but their essence is fundamentally different from that of objects whose meaning and history do not arise from fiction. Compare the statue of *Star War*'s Yoda with the statue of Mohandas K. Gandhi – both in San Francisco, California. Both statues exist in actuality, and both commemorate figures. Yet comprehending and appreciating each statue calls on different cognitive processes. Can this difference be expressed cartographically?

To explore these notions of differently conceptualized spaces, let us distinguish among categories of synontological space. There are various types of synontological space, which can be grouped into five broad categories:

1. A non-fictional locale that is described in fiction is used to commemorate a fictional event (e.g. Riverside, Iowa; Reichenbach Falls, Switzerland).
2. A non-fictional locale is repurposed to function as a place described in fiction (e.g. Kwik-E-Mart from *The Simpsons*, the pineapple from *SpongeBob SquarePants*).
3. A fictional locale is recreated in a non-fictional physical space (e.g. Warner Bros. Studio's Diagon Alley).
4. A fictional locale is recreated in non-fictional virtual space (e.g. Batman's Batcave; Doctor Who's TARDIS).
5. A fictional object is overlaid on a non-fictional space, as in augmented reality (e.g. *Pokémon Go*).

While spaces in categories 1, 2, and 3 exist on a physical terrain, spaces in categories 4 and 5 exist in virtual space. Spaces in all categories can be represented on a map, and in all cases we interact with fictional entities in non-fictional space.

Synontology does not affect the non-fictional space itself; it does not change the actual space in some fundamental manner. What changes is our perception of that space, now that it has been tinted not only by its entanglement with our imaginations, but also, crucially, by a marvelous ontological juxtaposition. In the Translator's Preface to Bertrand Westphal's *Geocriticism: Real and Fictional Spaces* (2011, p. x), Robert T. Tally Jr. notes,

> a *place* is only a place because of the ways in which we, individually and collectively, organize space in such a way as to mark the topos as special, to set it apart from the spaces

surrounding and infusing it. Our understanding of a particular place is determined by our personal experiences with it, but also by our reading about others' experiences, by our point of view, including our biases and our wishful thinking.

Any place can be imbued with meaning because of events that go on there. The big tree by the town library may be meaningful to one who, as a child, used it as a meeting place before setting off on adventures with friends. A synontological topos is different: it is unusually special in that it is set apart from other topoi by the ontological confluence that characterizes it.

One way to represent this topos is as a kind of palimpsest, where one ontological stratum is overlaid with another ontological stratum (or, in terms of cognitions A and B as above, one cognitive stratum is overlaid with another cognitive stratum) – both strata visible. This can be directly visually represented in synontological spaces that belong in category 5, where non-fictional space is overlaid with fictional objects, as in augmented reality.

While the palimpsest can be a useful approximation in terms of a representational structure, it does not capture the confluence that is the core of synontology. A better cartographic representation might rely on color, as when two colors are mixed to yield a third. One ontological space is thought of as red, the other ontological space is thought of as blue, and when mixed they produce purple – the synontological space. This conceptualization lacks [dimensional] structure, but it evokes conflux rather than overlay.

Navigating a fused space might conceivably call on a kind of combination of the cognitive processes used in each of the spaces in question. For instance, when in a purple, synontological space, visitors would draw on the blue cognitive process that pertains to the ontological state of fiction, and the red cognitive process that pertains to the ontological state of non-fiction. Cognitive flexibility and cognitive dissonance might be considered "purple cognitive processes," as they take into account at least two mental states.

Implications for popular culture tourism

The implications for popular culture tourism are theoretical rather than practical: this chapter does not propose changes to tourists' adventures of visiting or witnessing synontological spaces, but it does shed light on how these spaces are conceived, how they become viable, and how narratology, cognitive studies, and geocriticism come to bear on this type of experience. Understanding the multi-framework underpinnings of this phenomenon affords us a more comprehensive view of the popular culture tourism field.

Just as interesting as what is going on in the tourist's mind during a visit to a synontological space are the implications of such a visit for social behavior. Synontology that results from a reader's interaction with a fictional entity beyond the text wherein that entity originates requires action that is more often than not social in nature. One must behave socially in order to play Quidditch and speak Klingon. A visitor of Riverside – even if alone – is behaving socially because commemorating and celebrating famous fictional events immediately includes the visitor in communities of active fans. Synontology constitutes not only significant leaps in empathy, imagination, and abstract reasoning, but also a more public form of engagement.

Becoming absorbed in a good book or film, we are not content with merely transporting ourselves into its fiction. We take an additional step and interact with the fiction, going in the other direction and bringing it into our non-fictional world (invariably constricting it with the rules and conventions of reality), prolonging our enjoyment with pretend play. In actualizing fiction in experiences such as popular culture tourism, we re-access narrative in a markedly social way.[4]

Notes

1 The terms *synonty, synontology*, and variations thereof have been previously utilized in several fields. In *Whitehead's Ontology* (1972), John Lango uses *synonty* and *synontic* to discuss relations between entities. *Synontology* and *synontologie* are used in theology (e.g. ISPCK, 2001; Vagneux, 2015), sociology (e.g. Hermann, 2015), botany (e.g. Löschner et al., 1863), and conchology (e.g. Tryon, 1867) to denote various forms of coexistence. I am employing *synontology* here in a new context in order to express the convergence of ontological states.
2 I use *readers* to denote consumers of narratives in any medium, including that of book, moving image, etc. Similarly, when I write *texts*, I refer to the make-up of narrative in any medium.
3 I use the terms *tourist* and *visitor* broadly, to encompass those who access spaces via maps as well.
4 I dedicate this essay to my grandparents, Yona and Michael Traubici, and to the memory of my grand-aunt, Silvia "Coca" Landesberg. Their love, kindness, and warmth encourage me to pursue these journeys among fantastic locales.

References

7-Eleven becomes Kwik-E-Mart for "Simpsons Movie" promotion (2007, July 1). Retrieved from www.foxnews.com/story/2007/07/01/7-eleven-becomes-kwik-e-mart-for-simpsons-movie-promotion.html

Allen, W. (2007). The Kugelmass episode. In *The insanity defense: The complete prose* (pp. 245–260). New York: Random House Trade Paperbacks.

Borges, J. L. (2007). Partial magic in the *Quixote*. (J. E. Irby, Trans.). In J. E. Irby & D. A. Yates (Eds.), *Labyrinths: Selected stories & other writings* (pp. 193–196). New York: New Directions.

Brooks, J. L., Groening, M., Jean, A., Sakai, R., & Scully, M. (Producers), & Silverman, D. (Director). (2014). *The Simpsons movie* [Motion picture]. Los Angeles, CA: Twentieth Century Fox.

Cooper, J. (2007). *Cognitive dissonance: Fifty years of classic theory*. London: Sage.

Dahl, R. (1964). *Charlie and the chocolate factory*. New York: Knopf.

Doyle, A. C., & Paget, S. (1991). The adventure of the final problem. In *The original illustrated Sherlock Holmes: 37 short stories plus a complete novel comprising the adventures of Sherlock Holmes, the memoirs of Sherlock Holmes, the return of Sherlock Holmes and the hound of the Baskervilles* (pp. 327–339). Secaucus, NJ: Castle Books.

Elen, J., Stahl E., Bromme R., & Clarebout G. (2011). Chapter 1: Introduction. In J. Elen, E. Stahl, R. Bromme, & G. Clarebout (Eds.), *Links between beliefs and cognitive flexibility: Lessons learned* (pp. 1–5). Dordrecht: Springer.

Festinger, L. (1962). *A theory of cognitive dissonance*. Stanford, CA: Stanford University Press.

Flaubert, G. (2014). *Madame Bovary* (E. Aveling, Trans.). Leicester: Thorpe (Original work published 1856).

Garfield, B. (2007, July 9). 7-eleven's Simpsons Movie stunt: Brilliant cross-promotion. Retrieved from http://adage.com/article/ad-review/7-eleven-s-simpsons-movie-stunt-brilliant-cross-promotion/119062/

Genette, G. (1980). *Narrative discourse: An essay in method* (J. E. Lewin, Trans.). Ithaca, NY: Cornell University Press (Original work published 1972).

Herrmann, H. (2015). Synontologie. Retrieved from www.horstherrmann.com/index.php/forschungen/synontologie

Indian Society for Promoting Christian Knowledge (2001). *Jules Monchanin (1895–1957) as seen from east and west: Acts of the colloquium held in Lyon-Fleurie, France and in Shantivanam-Tannirpalli, India (April–July 1995)*. Delhi: Saccidananda Ashram/ISPCK.

Kukkonen, K. (2011). Metalepsis in popular culture: An introduction. In K. Kukkonen & S. Klimek (Eds.), *Metalepsis in popular culture* (pp. 1–21). New York: De Gruyter.

Kumparak, G. (2013, August 13). Google Maps Easter egg lets you explore the TARDIS. Retrieved from https://techcrunch.com/2013/08/13/google-maps-doctor-who-tardis-easter-egg/

Lango, J. W. (1972). *Whitehead's ontology*. Albany, NY: State University of New York Press.

Letzter, R. (2016, February 22). *A giant RoboCop statue will tower over Detroit thanks to a 5-year-old Kickstarter campaign*. Retrieved from www.businessinsider.com/robocop-statues-still-coming-to-detroit-2016-2

Löschner, J., & Gesellschaft Deutscher Naturforscher und Ärzte (1863). *Amtlicher bericht über die 37. versammlung deutscher naturforscher und aerzte in Karlsbad im September 1862*. Karlsba: Franieck.

McHale, B. (1994). *Postmodernist fiction*. London; New York: Routledge.

Madsen, S. A. (1994). The man who created woman. In C. Moseley (Ed.), *From Baltic shores: Short stories.* (pp. 37–51) Norwich, UK: Norvik Press.

Newman, K. (2010). Introduction. In W. S. Eckert, *Crossovers: A secret chronology of the world (Dawn of time–1939)* (pp. 7–10). Encino, CA: Black Coat Press. The Reichenbach Falls. Retrieved from www. atlasobscura.com/places/the-reichenbach-falls

Renfro, K. (2016, March 25). You can explore the Dark Knight's batcave from "Batman v Superman" on Google Maps. Retrieved from www.businessinsider.com/batman-bruce-wayne-house-google-maps-2016-3 The Rocky statue and the Rocky steps. Retrieved from www.visitphilly.com/museums-attractions/philadelphia/the-rocky-statue-and-the-rocky-steps/

Ryan, M. L. (2006). *Avatars of story.* Minneapolis, MN: University of Minnesota Press.

Salo, D., & Tolkien, J. R. R. (2004). *A gateway to Sindarin: A grammar of an elvish language from J.R.R. Tolkien's Lord of the Rings.* Salt Lake City, UT: University of Utah Press.

Sarkhosh, K. (2011). Metalepsis in popular comedy film. In K. Kukkonen & S. Klimek (Eds.), *Metalepsis in popular culture* (pp. 171–195). New York: De Gruyter.

Shakespeare, W., Nicholas, N., Strader, A., Shoulson, M., & Klingon Language Institute. (2000). *The Klingon Hamlet: The restored Klingon version.* New York: Pocket Books.

Spiro, R. J., & Jehng, J.-C. (1990). Cognitive flexibility and hypertext: Theory and technology for the non-linear and multidimensional traversal of complex subject matter. In D. Nix & R. J. Spiro (Eds.), *Cognition, education, and multimedia: Exploring ideas in high technology* (pp. 163–205). Hillsdale, NJ: L. Erlbaum.

Tally, R. T. (2011) Translator's preface. In B. Westphal, *Geocriticism: Real and fictional spaces* (pp. ix–xiii). New York: Palgrave Macmillan (Original work published 2007).

Tryon, G. W. (1867). *American Journal of Conchology: Vol. III.* Philadelphia: Conchological Section of the Academy of Natural Sciences.

Vagneux, Y. (2015). *Co-esse: Le mystère trinitaire dans la pensèe de Jules Monchanin-Swâmi Paramârûbyânanda:1895–1957.* Paris: Desclée de Brouwer.

Warner Bros. Studio Tour London begin a year of celebrations around the fifteenth anniversary of *Harry Potter*'s cinematic debut (2016, February 11). Retrieved from www.pottermore.com/news/warner-bros-studio-tour-welcomes-you-back-to-hogwarts

Williams, A. (2016, September 20). "SpongeBob" fans will love this pineapple-shaped villa in Punta Cana. Retrieved from www.huffingtonpost.com/entry/spongebob-squarepants-nickelodeon-resort-punta-cana_us_57e12687e4b0071a6e0953eb

Williams, O. (2014, November 21). Quidditch is real, and it wants to go pro. Retrieved from http://edition.cnn.com/2014/11/21/sport/quidditch-mudbloods/

Yoda fountain. Retrieved from www.atlasobscura.com/places/yoda-fountain

4

APOCALYPTO AND THE END OF DAYS

Basking in the Maya's shadow

O. Hugo Benavides

Setting the scene: entering and re-entering the Maya region

The Yucatan, which includes the famed Riviera Maya, has undoubtedly become one of the prime locations for international travel. Mixed with the high-end beach-seeking tourists are also many others interested in the Maya's esoteric enlightenment inherent in this culture's monumental archaeological remains. This exotic tourist destination that includes a prime Caribbean location, along with pyramids and a seductive mythical lore make the Yucatan an interesting lab of sorts.

In this manner, the article's main objective is to understand how differing notions of popular culture, history, and heritage, along with modern forms of capital (as represented by the powerful tourist industry) come together to produce contrasting forms of popular culture, including ideas of the local and the global, and Western and non-Western identities. This chapter also explores the West's, that is our own, fascination with the Mayas, and Maya cosmology, as it has been represented since the initial modern European depiction of the civilization's ruins in the late 1800s (see Stephens, 1987/1843, 1969/1841; Catherwood, 2013/1844).

Since John Lloyd Stephens' narrative and Frederick Catherwood's drawings in the 1840s, Maya images and cosmology has pervaded the West in unique and contradictory ways, both as a primeval context of noble savages and as the raw anti-thesis to Western civilization. Mayas have been portrayed and represented in popular culture by archaeologists, historians, filmmakers, politicians, artists, etc., in multiple manners. Each of these representations has also re-impacted on the contemporary Maya communities as well, all the while contributing to a flourishing tourism industry that ballooned towards the end of the twentieth century.

The chapter, even more specifically, also uses Mel Gibson's recent Maya epic, *Apocalypto*, to explore the manners in which notions of historical authenticity, popular culture, and notions of archaeological heritage have been used in recent Western representations. Particularly important in this regard is how these representations have contributed, and/or go hand-in-hand with the development of a trans-national modern multi-million tourist industry that is both supported by the Mexican nation-state, as well as, by the regional Yucatan local governments that look to usufruct from their ancient heritage.

Apocalypto has been seriously critiqued on multiple fronts by academics, local activists, and film critics as a neo-colonial representation of the Mayas; one that once again looks to benefit from the financial, as well as, the symbolic exploitation of this native-American population. However, my main concern in this regard, is less to validate or refute these claims as much to wonder and analyze why the Maya continue to fascinate people the world over, and are still an important object for cinematographic gaze and/or tourist consumption.

In other words, why, or even more specifically, how is the Maya's rich cultural and historical legacy turned into modern (and even post-modern) forms of popular cultural representations that are successfully digested by the West, including by citizens of the Mexican national-state. In this regard, the film *Apocalypto*, along with the state capital city of Merida and the Maya site of Chichen Itza, provide a succinct entry points into at least three different elements that continue to fascinate modern tourists in their travel to the Yucatan: (1) the haunting and mysterious archaeological images of pyramids and cenotes (large natural wells), (2) the pervasive image of the noble savage, and (3) the nostalgic ideal of a primeval paradise of pre- (and post-) Western civilization.

The fact is that since the nineteenth century Maya archaeological sites have contributed to the tourist industry of the region. And just as archaeology has contributed to the tourist imagination, the newly developed resort site of Cancun contributed to making Chichen Itza and Tulum two of the most visited archaeological sites in the Americas. Once again, this particular fascination is vivid in *Apocalypto*'s use of pyramids and the monumental Indigenous past as the visual seductive frame upon which the native story of the Yucatan unfolds.

In this same manner, this ideological backdrop of the noble savage is at the very core of *Apocalypto*'s plot, as well as, of the tourists' fantasy of the Yucatan region. Both promise a visual pleasure where the foreigner can enter a primeval moment where the trappings of Western civilized behavior is questioned, but most importantly, and contradictory, re-fueled. Because along with this backdrop of the noble savage is also present the alluring promise of indiscriminate violence (e.g. mass human sacrifices in the film and mass crime on the urban streets and rural towns of Mexico) helping to displace and project the foundational colonial violence of Europe upon the Americas.

Several scholars have critiqued *Apocalypto* as a neo-colonial attempt at doing visually what was historically done to the Maya population at the onset of the European conquest of the continent, and for some is still being done today (Ardren, 2006; see Stoll, 2007). The utilization of racial and linguistic authenticity (in terms of the actors for the film) belies a much more violent form of subjection that makes use of Maya history to reinforce the West's heterosexist and patriarchal ideology. To this effect the Mayas are presented in a primeval heterosexist and patriarchal world that the enlightened European is able to decenter and complement in its supposedly enlightened forms of global development and human rights discourses. Just as five centuries ago it pretended to do it through Christian religious proselytizing.

Ultimately, this chapter looks to engage the most significant elements present in Western tourism to the Yucatan: the archaeological imagery, an idea of pristine local natives and the nostalgia for a primeval state of human history. It is these exacting tropes that *Apocalypto* utilizes in its violent representation of the Maya past. The purpose of the analysis below is to use this visual object, as well as, the narratives at Merida and the site of Chichen Itza, as a way of reassessing the complex and pervasive elements that intertwine Western identity, desire, and pleasure, and are also exemplified in the tourist industry.

Disciplinary underpinnings: assessing the politics of popular culture in the Maya lands

The works of Stuart Hall (1997), Jamaica Kincaid (1988), Frantz Fanon (1967), James Baldwin (1984/1955; 1966), among several others (see Gilroy, 1991; Carby, 2000), allow for a particular fruitful re-reading of the cultural representation of the Mayas and the role this particular representation plays in the global tourism to the area. Beginning in the 1980s places like Cancun and the archaeological site of Chichen Itza have become routine destinations for tens of thousands of foreigners, most of them white North Americans and Europeans. Since its initial inception in the early 1970s Cancun became the model for what modern tourism would look like in the southern American tropics. Its success has relatedly made the Maya site of Chichen Itza the most visited archaeological site in the Americas, only rivaled by the Inca site of Macchu Pichu near Cuzco, Peru, in South America.

However, not only Cancun and Chichen Itza, but the island of Cozumel, the archaeological sites of Tulum, Uxmal, Ek Balam, among many others, and the towns of Valladolid, Izamal, and Merida, as well as, all the Riviera Maya itself, have become eponymous with the tourist's desire for the physical pleasures of sex, sun, and relaxation, along with some archaeological mystery and culinary delight. Independent of the impact on the local communities, and the power of transnational capital, the Yucatan has benefitted from a century-long Western fascination with the other that allows us to define and distinguish ourselves as Westerners, precisely through the desire of the body of the native other.

All of the above mentioned scholars provide insightful manners with which to assess how the Yucatan has been used and reconstructed within traditional Western narratives. Their scholarly contribution also enables us to see how these narratives allow us, in the West, to use the Yucatan imagery, to project ourselves into it, as one and the other, at one and the same time. Narratives as those developed in Mel Gibson's excruciatingly authentic (see below) blockbuster *Apocalypto*, by the tour guides at Chichen Itza, and the re-modeling of both the city of Merida and town of Izamal (see Benavides, 2013) make use of this "similar different" (see Hall, 1997) exoticization of the Yucatan peninsula. These Western narratives are useful to sell the local culture and territory to the tourist and bring in much needed revenue, but also to fuel a newly found Maya-Quiche identity that has multiple political outlets, implications and representations (see Arias, 2001; Stoll, 2007; Menchú, 2010).

Hall's (1997) particular insights into the nature of popular cultural representation prove useful in assessing the manner in which these historical narratives have been constructed, and why they have positively impacted a multi-million dollar tourism industry in the Yucatan peninsula. Hall's scholarly work, as part of the Cultural Studies approach, initially contributed to our understanding of the manner in which popular culture is always, already, a political venture.

Stuart Hall's (1997) work provides examples of how cultural elements such as race, ethnicity, gender, sexuality, migration, age, etc., as left-over colonial or neo-colonial markers are used to redefine the manner in which the modern is re-signified in the body of contemporary subjects. This initial racialized understanding, already present in Fanon's (1967) early work, also allows for a much more nuanced understanding of the manner in which modern capital and particularly cyber-capital negotiates forms of accumulation that re-trace the "new old ways" (Hall 1997) in which colonial legacies are re-inscribed in white, native, and dark bodies.

It is this particular insights into the foundational role of the native body, as that of the other, which allows the white Westerner to re-found its difference in hierarchical exclusive ways, re-signifying ancients forms of surplus extraction. The Yucatan, and the Mayas as the ancient inhabitants of the peninsula, provides the perfect backdrop upon which the Western white body has been re-inscribed. It is against these brown bodies (inferior yet creators of ancient cities with large pyramids), that the West has continuously, since the 1500s, been able to do two things: (1) exoticize the local population, and (2) hail itself as the measure of civilized behavior. What is most telling, in this regard, is the West's capacity to maintain this superior ideological arbitrator role despite the fact that its colonial conquest of the Yucatan carried out an indiscriminate genocide and ethnocide of the Maya population, for some present until today.

Hall's insights are particularly useful in assessing how *Apocalypto*, along with the other neo-colonial narratives, reify this representation of the native body, making us comfortable with attractive half-naked brown bodies running around the jungle butchering themselves to death. As I discuss below, this Hollywood representation works, as Hall would argue, because this particular narrative of inferior savages are essential in placing us above them in a hierarchical social order; an order that would allow us, as Westerners, to judge the civilizing values of ancient, and contemporary, Maya polities.

Of course, thinly disguised in this popular cultural expression is the fact that it is us, as representatives of the West, that butchered the Mayas indiscriminately, even a couple of million in the most conservative estimates, to exploit their natural and mineral resources, or just even a couple of decades ago that the global north supported the genocide of contemporary Mayas indigenous populations. It is precisely this representative double-standard, of us projecting ourselves upon the bodies of the others, but refusing to engage with this projection except through sexual desire and empathetic politics of development and humanitarian aid, that is at the core of the representative power of films like *Apocalypto*.

But it is this same representative power that makes the Yucatan, as well as, its adjoining Caribbean region, such a powerful center for tourist exploitation and development. As Jamaica Kincaid (1988) develops in several of her essays and memoirs, it is precisely the nostalgia of A Small Place (the title of one of her most powerful books), which allows for the region to be hailed as a primeval geographical space to be reimagined. In this fantasy, the Yucatan offers us a plausible space that looks like where our Western civilization might have originated.

And it is precisely the racialized native body, both in the imagined past and denigrated present, that enables us to recreate self-deluding and aggrandizing narratives of an ancient time; an ancient time that we desire but never existed, and a repressive exploitative present that exists but we deny. These primeval discourses are an important part of the narratives expressed at the site of Chichen Itza or in the tourism advertisements for places like Izamal, and above all Merida, especially as they are represented as the quaint colonial towns par excellence.

This racialized rendezvous is at the core of Kincaid's essays and fiction, where she explores how colonial histories have recreated these tropical spaces as primeval longings that then serve to redefine the local culture. This cultural remarking impacts everything, from political organization to familial relationships, and above all the varied ways in which good manners (*buenas costrumbes*) are used to police the racialized hierarchical order of things.

This racialized order is also essential in the work of both James Baldwin (1992/1963, 1984/1955), and Frantz Fanon (1967), and the manner in which they weaved their concerns with the power of history in re-defining the native subject, both in their fictional and scholarly contributions.

As Baldwin (1966, pp. 175–176) eloquently expresses:

> And it is with great pain and terror that one begins to realize this. In great pain and terror, one begins to assess the history which has placed one where one is, and formed ones point of view. In great pain and terror, because, thereafter, one enters into battle with that historical creation, oneself, and attempts to re-create oneself according to a principle more humane and more liberating, one begins the attempt to achieve a level of personal maturity and freedom which robs history of its tyrannical power, and also changes history.

[. . .]

But, obviously, I am speaking as an historical creation which has had bitterly to contest its history, to wrestle with it and finally accept it, in order to bring myself out of it. My point of view is certainly formed by my history and it is probable that only a creature despised by history finds history a questionable matter. On the other hand, people who imagine that history flatters them (as it does, indeed, since they wrote it) are impaled on their history like a butterfly on a pin and become incapable of seeing or changing themselves or the world.

It is not lost on all of these authors (e.g. Baldwin, 1984, 1992; Kincaid, 1988; Hall, 1997; and above all Fanon, 1967, as the precursor of much of their work), all of whom are part of the African diaspora, that their own livelihood depended very much on this historical colonial legacy and on the fact that they had been racialized as black subjects within the realm of modernity.

It is this same racial element that gets reconstructed in the Yucatacan region, as it is represented in popular cultural venues. This historical discourse, that of the racialized native other, is utilized, and many times, exploited to create new and fruitful ways to make the peninsula appealing to all, particularly national and international tourists.

In the following section I discuss three manners in which this development narrative has provoked new cultural arrangements and ideological formations within the area, but also among those tourist that visit the area. In this sense, creating a form of cultural production that goes beyond the individual tourist and development model employed by the national and transnational entrepreneurs that looked to simply make financial profit of the territorial and cultural resources available in the area.

Implication for popular culture tourism: colonial strolls (in Merida), climbing pyramids (at Chichen Itza), and seeing the Mayas (in *Apocalypto*)

The city of Merida, the capital of the state of Yucatan, is located on the northwest corner of the peninsula. Located just inland it is close to one of the major ports of the region, Progreso, as well as, conveniently located near major Maya sites (Uxmal, Ek Balam, Chichen Itza, etc.) and other Maya towns (Valladolid, Izamal, etc.). In the last couple of decades Merida has become a major tourist destination, particularly for those older tourists that are looking to get away from the Cancun "Spring Break" madness, and rather take in the more sedate and intellectual resources the region has to offer.

To some degree, Merida has become a prime destination for couples and families, and has also become an important place for scholarly conferences and professional meetings. The city is advertised as a colonial jewel, a throwback, in a way, to a much calmer, easy-going time, one not contaminated by the modern and fast-paced ways of today. Of course, in this particular advertising the city of Merida becomes a product unto itself, one that is to be experienced, lived in, and enjoyed. In these ways it makes use of kitsch folkloric cultural elements, particularly in the form of supposedly traditional dresses, dances, and more courteous forms of address and graceful body movements.

It is interesting to see how in the last three decades this small city has been translated to represent a picturesque colonial city that although still knows how to have fun (with lively bars and cafes), is able to do so in a much more adult-like and calm manner than the resorts in the neighboring Cancun. However, what becomes immediately transparent when one visits Merida is how disingenuous the colonial picture represented really is. Gone from this very modern representation of a colonial Merida is any reference to the historical violence that we know was an essential part of the colonial enterprise that is being nostalgically projected.

In this manner there is a necessity to sell the *mestizo/ladino* picture of a colonial landscape of genteel habits, soothing landscape and, above all, orderly social structure. However, gone and made invisible from these representations is the incredibly pervasive hierarchical nature of this social structure, and above all, the indigenous Maya community that is hailed as the builders of the impressive pyramids and architecture that surrounds the modern city of Merida.

The incredibly physical and cultural violence committed against the Maya communities is erased from the colonial landscape being sold to the tourist. This is a particular intriguing and complex device by which the historical reality of the region is represented in a benign manner, and in doing so further services the global capital that initially decimated the Maya communities. I would argue, that it is not a coincidence that the same West (sometimes even the same company, like Barclay's Bank) that initially exploited the native population now sells its pyramids and edifices for global tourist consumption. Yet, there is always the fact that tourist and locals alike, see more than is presented to them in pamphlets, ads and archaeological guides.

The town of Izamal, perhaps, presents the most disturbing reflection of this ideological break (see Benavides, 2013). As Merida, it is advertised as another quaint colonial town in the Yucatan, nostalgically referred to as the Yellow City (*La ciudad amarilla*). Because most of the city has been painted yellow (or off-sepia) to portray a nostalgic sense of time. However, Izamal still holds within its central urban perimeter two gigantic pyramids (see Figures 4.1 and 4.3). And you also slowly realize that the main church itself has been built on a gigantic pyramid, which was dismantled, and its stones used to build the colonial edifice we see today.

Figure 4.1   The main temple Kinich Kak Moo at Izamal.
Source: photo by Mathew Gartska.

Figure 4.2 Monument to Diego de Landa, infamous Bishop of the Yucatan during the colonial period.
Source: photo by Matt Gartska.

You also learn that Izamal was the physical center from where the Franciscan friar Diego de Landa, as Bishop of the Yucatan, carried out his genocidal enterprise against the Maya. A small plaque on his monument, at one side of the church, expresses this ambiguous legacy, celebrating a colonial genealogy marked by genocidal and ethnocidal practices (see Figure 4.2). And it is this same ambiguity that marks Merida's and Izamal's representation as the colonial jewels of the Yucatan, hiding under it the levels of violence, repression, and exploitation which still pervades the region today.

Similar narratives permeate the visitors at the site of Chichen Itza. The main pyramid at Chichen Itza is a central piece of the visit to the site, along with this central pyramid you have several other elements such as the sacred cenote, in which many artifacts along with human remains were found, the ball court, court yards, other minor pyramids, etc. In many ways visiting Chichen Itza is advertised as a full sensorial experience of being in an ancient Maya city, one where ritual, astronomy, and to some degree human sacrifice played an important role.

Most tourists, unless they pay or are part of a tour group, visit the site on their own and get to roam it freely, although following the site's outlined paths. Still the main pyramid occupies a central place since all visitors get to see and pass by it, although today nobody is allowed to climb it any longer. This is mainly due to the thousands of tourists that have climbed its stairs since the

Figure 4.3   Partial remains of the temple Itzamatul at Izamal.

Source: photo by Matt Gartska.

site has been an object of Western attraction, but ultimately the pyramid was declared off limits for the general tourist, fearing the wear and tear (plus the reigning pollution of the atmosphere) on the stairs and edifice in general.

However, I would argue that not being able to climb the central pyramid is part of that mysterious allure that adds to the tourist experience of visiting the Yucatan. This is what both the work of Quetzil Castañeda (1996) and Lisa Berglia (2006) highlights, the particular essential space that the site operates within the tourist logistics of the Yucatan. However, each scholar elaborates how different global historical and consumption processes have allowed Chichen Itza to be primed for transnational tourist consumption and representation.

For Castañeda (1996), Chichen Itza forms part of a long archaeological discourse in the Yucatacan area that started with the initial description of the sites at the hands of John Stephen Lloyd and Frederick Catherwood (see above). It was these particular artistic representations that caught the Western mind's imagination almost two centuries ago. However, this push to "develop" or "rescue" Chichen Itza was not at all a local idea, or even purely a national Mexican one, but rather was tied to the big capital of North American philanthropist families like the Mellon and Carnegie. In this way, this transnational capital related archaeological research to issues of global politics and Malthusian notions of social development.

This work would be continued over the last century throughout the Yucatan Peninsula, where the academic idea of the Maya as a peace-loving community with an egalitarian ethos proved to be far from what the evidence pointed to. The work done by myriad of scholars on

Maya writing/hieroglyphics, as well as, the finding of the violent murals at the site of Bonampak, painted a more conquering picture of a warring and conquering empire at the height of its territorial and political power by the ninth century AD.

This mysterious allure of a conquering polity with enigmatic rituals, as emblemized in their writing, murals, and ceramics, contributed to the Mayas becoming even more engrained in the popular imagination. Perhaps reaching the highest level at the turn of the last century where our knowledge of Maya astronomy and mathematics were interpreted in popular venues as signifying an ancient local knowledge of the apocalyptic end of days. Perhaps the popular Hollywood film *2012* (with John Cusack and Chiwetel Ejiofor) marked the most successful popular representation of this apocalyptic scenario to date.

It is precisely this racialized apocalyptic scenario that Mel Gibson's film captures, appropriately titled, *Apocalypto*. Most scholarly reviews markedly agree on the lack of historical authenticity of the film. This is interesting, and perhaps even shocking, because of the depth that the film production went to in terms of getting the facts about the Mayas right, including consulting with anthropologists and historians, using Maya-Quiche as the language for the film, hiring Native American actors, and using contemporary Mayas as film extras.

However, although the film represents many factual realities it completely misses the current general understanding of ancient Maya society, as it is expressed by most of the archaeological and anthropological evidence. More succinctly, the Mayas were far from the violent driven ethnic groups being represented in the film. Which is what makes one wonder what the use and popularity of such images belies? And how such a dominant violent representation of the Mayas may be used to ignore the colonial oppression and repression of Maya community that continues to this day.

Just like in the contemporary tourist representation for Merida, both at Chichen Itza and in *Apocalypto* the colonial genocide of millions and even the slaughter of thousands of indigenous Mayas-Quiche in the last three decades are belittled. Rather, the more popular image of naked male natives sacrificing each other on pyramids, that is, when they are not clubbing themselves to death in the jungle, is what captures the day.

However, I find it less useful to simply critique the film's lack of historical authenticity rather than to assess how and why these popular cultural representation of naked male Mayas are so vitally successful in the West's contemporary imagination. And ultimately, how these pornographic (as argued by Ardren 2006; see below) representations of the Mayas are exactly the ones used in popular cultural images for tourist development models in the region.

In her review of the film, "Is *Apocalypto* pornography?" Ardren (2006) argues quite convincingly that it is less about the nearly naked male and female bodies we see throughout the film but rather the sense of exploitation and utilitarianism that permeates our viewing of these Hollywood Mayas. Hollywood Mayas that are exactly what we want to see, native bodies put on the screen for our use and purpose. It is precisely in these savages, club-wielding patriarchal male natives, that we can contrast our own Western selves and congratulate us on how far we have come since those barbaric times before colonization.

The images on the screen, in one sweep, not only deny the horrors of colonialism but make us in the West the viewing protagonist of the story. The West's violent and patriarchal structures are completely denied in a favorable narrative (for us) in which half-naked brutes butcher each other to death, and for religious reasons to boot (any similarity with contemporary religious hostility is of course erased under the racialized difference).

However, these popular cultural images expressed in Merida, at the site at Chichen Itza and in the popular representation of the Mayas in *Apocalypto* are also, I argue, at the heart of the popular cultural imagination for the tourism in the Maya Lands of the Yucatan.

Albeit unconsciously at times, Spring Break revelers in Cancun, more sedate tourists at Merida and/or Tulum, or elite ones paying over $500 a night for cabañas along the Maya Riviera, all participate to some degree in these romantic pictures of the Maya region. A representation of a region once having been inhabited by enigmatic savages, that albeit violent were also capable, in some incoherent exceptional manner, of producing pyramids, pottery, and artwork of exceptional beauty.

The contradictions of such images are lost on us today, precisely because this Maya other is our own self-projections on the Yucatan screen. This is a projection of a group of Western natives, ourselves, that even more violently than the Mayas are capable of indiscriminate genocide and absolute denial of the violence we have perpetrated and continue to perpetrate. As James Baldwin (1992/1963, p. 67), again, so eloquently states, referring to the United State in particular and the West in general: "It is the innocence of the crime that constitutes the crime."

And it is in the placid waters off the Yucatan peninsula, in the archaeological remains, in the rural lifeways of contemporary Mayas that we look to wash away these colonial hauntings and the challenges of contemporary Western modernity. In this manner, the images offered to us of the Mayas by popular culture is big business and are at the core, consciously or not, of a multi-billion transnational touristy industry that is financially successful in terms of capital and resource accumulation and also in producing a changing cultural landscape, locally, nationally, and globally.

Conclusion

The Maya region and Yucatan peninsula, as all tourist landscape, are always a space of negotiation, conflict, and contradiction. As Kincaid (1988) poignantly elaborates, being a tourist is an ugly thing, and mainly because we all wish we could be tourist (and not all of us can). All of us wish we could leave our daily lives behind and go exploring others' landscapes, others' lives, when ours are too boring or too hard to bear. And it is precisely this freedom to move and travel, which is most hurtful to those natives that cannot do the same, and worse when this difference is racially expressed.

In the Yucatan this negotiation takes on different guises within images and representation offered by popular culture. As I have discussed, these popular images and discourses are essential in the tourist representation and appeal of the region but are also an important element for the livelihood of the different local rural and Maya communities. The locals live off this tourist exchange, and as such it permeates, how could it not, their own sense of self and identity.

This is adamantly expressed in the work carried out by Lisa Berglia (2006) in the Chichen Itza area. Berglia (2006) shows how local vendors have developed a very sophisticated identity, as the native inheritors of this ancient past, to sell their folk artifacts, archaeological replicas, and textiles. As such these local vendors maintain an ethnic power that rivals the local government and the larger national and transnational interests at the site. Not shockingly, precisely because of these power conflicts it has been attempted to physically remove the vendors from the site.

In this sense, I would argue, that it is this conflict over space and identity, as between the local national and regional governments and the vendors that we see over and over again throughout the Yucatan. As I have discussed above we see these conflicts and negotiations in Merida, at the archaeological sites, especially Chichen Itza, and in *Apocalypto*. What we are privy to are to what author Paul Sullivan (1991) calls some of the "unfinished conversations" of the region, and that allow us to realize we, as the locals, are part of a long discussion started centuries, if not over a millennia, ago.

References

Ardren, Traci. (2006). Is Apocalypto Pornography? *Archaeology Magazine*, December 5. archive.archaeology.org/online/reviews/apocalypto.html

Arias, Arturo. (2001). *The Rigoberta Menchú Controversy*. Minneapolis: University of Minnesota Press.

Baldwin, James. (1966). Unnameable Objects, Unspeakable Crimes. Special Issue on The White Problem in America. *Ebony Magazine*, pp. 170–180. Chicago: John Pub. Co.

———. (1984 [1955]). *Notes of a Native Son*. New York City: Beacon Press.

———. (1992 [1963]). *The Fire Next Time*. New York City: Vintage.

Benavides, O. Hugo. (2013). Working/Touring the Past: Latin American Identity and the Political Frustration of Heritage. M. Diaz-Andreu (Issue editor), *International Journal of Historical Archeology* 17 (2): 245–260.

Berglia, Lisa. (2006). *Monumental Ambivalence: The Politics of Heritage*. Austin: University of Texas Press.

Carby, Hazel. (2000). *Race Men (The W. E. B. Dubois Lectures)*. Cambridge: Harvard University Press.

Castañeda, Quetzil. (1996). *In the Museum of Maya Culture: Touring Chichen Itza*. Minneapolis: University of Minnesota Press.

Catherwood, Frederick. (2013 [1844]). *Views of Ancients Monuments in Central America, Chiapas and Yucatan*. Norwich, UK: Isha Books.

Emmerich, Roland (dir.). (2009). *2012*. Feature length film, 2h 38m.

Fanon, Frantz. (1967). *Black Skin, White Masks*. New York: Grove Press.

Gibson, Mel (dir.). (2006). *Apocalypto*. Feature length film, 2h 19m.

Gilroy, Paul. (1991). *"There Ain't no Black in the Union Jack": The Politics of Race and Nation*. Chicago: University of Chicago Press.

Hall, Stuart. (1997). The Local and the Global: Globalization and Ethnicity. In *Culture, Globalization and the World-System: Contemporary Conditions for the Representation of Identity*, edited by A. King, pp. 19–39. Minneapolis: University of Minnesota Press.

Kincaid, Jamaica. (1988). *A Small Place*. New York City: Farrar, Straus and Giroux.

Menchu, Rigoberta. (2010). *I, Rigorberta Menchu: An Indian Woman in Guatemala*, Elizabeth Burgos-Debray (Ed.). New York City: Verso.

Stephens, John Lloyd. (1969 [1841]). *Incidents of Travel in Central America, Chiapas and Yucatan*. New York City: Dover.

———. (1987 [1843]). *Incidents of Travel in Yucatan*. Panorama Editorial.

Stoll, David. (2007). *Rigoberta Menchú and the Story of all Poor Guatemalans*. Boulder, CO: Westview Press.

Sullivan, Paul. (1991). *Unfinished Conversations: Mayas and Foreigners Between Two Worlds*. Berkeley, CA: University of California Press.

5

THE COMMODIFICATION OF NARCO-VIOLENCE THROUGH POPULAR CULTURE AND TOURISM IN MEDELLIN, COLOMBIA

Patrick Naef

Although tourism is already flourishing in some regions of Colombia, the country is still struggling to achieve peace. On 2 October 2016, just over half of the Colombian population rejected the peace deal negotiated by President Juan Manuel Santos and the Revolutionary Armed Forces of Colombia (FARC). Two months later the nation's Congress finally ratified a renegotiated peace deal between the government and the largest guerrilla group of the country. After more than a half century of armed conflict, peace has never been so close, yet many Colombians are still reluctant to see former war actors such as the FARCs reintegrate civilian and political life.

In the context of this long-lasting war, violence is memorialized in diverse and fragmented ways. Since the establishment of a national law for victims and the displaced in 2011, various memorial projects related to the armed conflict involving the Colombian army, paramilitaries and guerrillas have been cropping up all over the country. This marks a change, as memorial issues were not previously prevalent; most of the victims still felt vulnerable and consequently did not want to participate in any memorial processes. The law for victims and the displaced thus provided a more secure and favourable context for the emergence of memorial initiatives.

The state has been active in the field of memory by supporting the construction of museums and documentary projects on the war, involving victims, academics and NGOs, the National Centre for Historical Memory being the principal example in this context. In parallel, alternative memorial productions relating to the war and the 'narcoheritage' (Naef, 2015) have started up. In Bogota and Medellin, both relatively tolerant environments regarding urban art, many murals flourish, illustrating themes associated with violence and social conflicts. These topics are also the focus of contemporary musical creations, from hip-hop to salsa, alternating between tributes to victims and narco-glorification. Moreover, while Mexico is famous for its *narcocorridos* (folk ballads focusing on the stories of drug smugglers), Colombia is also the cradle of many cultural productions, ranging from literature and *narco-novelas* (novels) to *narco-soaps* (soap operas). The cinema industry is similarly cashing in on this subject through the production of Colombian and international films, some of them – like *Blow*, featuring Johnny Depp and Penélope Cruz – reaching a worldwide audience.

This contribution aims to explore how popular culture and tourism participates in the memorialization of this dissonant (Ashworth et al., 2007) and violent heritage, and contributes to the commodification of violence. It is postulated that beyond public museums and memorials, popular culture and tourism represent an alternative and more organic way of memorializing violence. Some of these cultural productions are considered in the light of concepts related to the anthropology of tourism, such as trivialization, glamorization and commodification. Violence and memory are conceptualized as transversal objects featuring in an interdisciplinary perspective that covers fields such as history, anthropology and social geography.

Setting the scene: Medellin, from the most violent to the most innovative city

The exact setting of this analysis is the city of Medellin, the second largest town in Colombia. Often pictured as the most violent city in the world until recently, it is now rising from its ashes: an active promotion campaign is presenting it as the most innovative city in the world. Nevertheless, Medellin has been seriously affected by the war and the trauma is still vivid for many inhabitants. The surrounding slums have been experiencing first a significant number of street gangs and then the infiltration of guerrilla and paramilitary groups during the 1990s and the beginning of the current century.

Medellin is also notorious for being the capital of the cocaine business in the 1980s and 1990s, especially during the rule of the Medellin Cartel and its boss Pablo Escobar, who was killed on 2 December 1993. His ghost is now haunting the city, present in murals, clothing and tourism, but also on a more global scale through literature, TV shows and movies. *Narcos*, produced in 2015 by the US channel *Netflix*, looks back during its first season at the life of the drug king-pin and is already a worldwide success. Some tourist practices are also developing and presenting the history of violence in Medellin. 'Pablo Escobar tours' constitute one of the most popular offers of the emerging international tourism market (Giraldo et al., 2014; Naef, in press) and the small informal museum run by Roberto Escobar, his brother and former bookkeeper of the Medellin cartel, represents a star feature of the backpacker trail.

Reality and fiction in Medellin's mediascape

If the resonance of *narcocorridos* and narco-soaps is usually limited to a local audience, certain productions in other fields of popular culture definitely achieve worldwide success. The Spanish writer Arturo Pérez-Reverte undoubtedly contributed to the fame of *Narcos* when in 2004 he wrote his celebrated novel: *La reina del Sur* (*The Queen of the South*), portraying Teresa Mendoza, a Mexican-born woman who becomes a successful drug trafficker in Spain.

Nowadays, Pablo Escobar is also the focus of wide-reaching productions. In the cinema industry, Andrea Di Stefano directed his first movie in 2014, featuring Benedicto del Toro as Escobar in *Paradise Lost*. Furthermore, as these lines are written, Tom Cruise is preparing a new production called *Mena*, where the American actor plays a drug smuggler and a CIA informant who worked with the Medellin Cartel. According to the *New York Times*, 'Tom Cruise's arrival [in Medellin] was happily embraced by city officials, who decided to bend the Film Commission rule on narc films' (Londoño, 2015). Javier Bardem and Penélope Cruz are also filming another biopic scheduled for 2017, entitled *Escobar*, centred on his sentimental relationship with a journalist.

In Colombian cinema, some movies, usually adapted from popular novels, have also been successful beyond the national borders. *La Virgen de los sicarios* (*Our Lady of the Assassins*), produced in 2000 by Barbet Schroeder, and depicting the violence of the narcos in Medellin during the 1990s, was recognized as the best Latin American movie at the Venice International Film Festival. Likewise, the movie based on the well-known novel of Jorge Franco, *Rosario Tijeras*, was nominated for the Spanish Goya Award for the best foreign film. It is reportedly the sixth highest-grossing film in Colombian history, with more than 1 million tickets sold (Colprensa, 2015). The novel was also broadcast as a televised series in 2010, under the slogan 'It is harder to love than to kill'. The show sparked controversies in Colombia and beyond. The *Guardian* describes it in an article entitled: 'Colombians outraged by narco-soaps glamorising cartels` (Brodzinsky, 2010). According to the British newspaper, negative reactions were heard even in neighbouring Panama, where president Ricardo Martinelli officially declared that the show exalted drug trafficking, theft and mugging; damaging its own country and corrupting its moral values. Similarly, in *El Colombiano*, the former secretary of Education of Medellin, Ramiro Valencia Cossio (2010), harshly called into question the justification of the producers, when they stated that the show was no more than a reflection of Medellin's reality:

> Liars . . . Some search only for money and the others fame. [. . .] All of them are responsible for every young kid who, inspired by *el capo*, *Las muñecas de la mafia*, *El cartel de los sapos*, *Rosario Tijeras* . . . turns into a gangster. Yes, they are responsible for every new *sicario* [hit man].
>
> *(Translated from Spanish by the author)*

Popular culture and violence feed each other: fiction is significantly inspired by the violent context of narco-culture, while the Colombian mediascape is an important breeding ground for some of the violent aspirations of local youth. The 1998 movie *La vendedora de rosas* (*The Rose Seller*), directed by Victor Gaviria, nominated for the Cannes Festival 'Palme d'Or' and also part of the ten highest-grossing films in Colombia, is a sad illustration of this dynamic. Gaviria, in order to capture the reality of Medellin's slums, hired mostly street kids, imposing them only with few directions in their acting. As he recalls:

> It was one of the points where the limit between documentary and fiction was the closest. Some were acting while others were playing in an altered state, which was theirs anyway. It is by sniffing glue that they express their sadness.
>
> *(Rigoulet, 1998)*

Most of the actors met a tragic fate after the movie: some were assassinated while others finished in prison, like the main actor Leidy Tabares, due to her involvement in the murder of a taxi driver in Medellin (Cano, 2014).

If we look specifically at the Colombian mediascape of the last decade, the most successful production is without any doubt the televised series on Pablo Escobar, *El Patron del mal* (*The Boss of Evil*). In 2012, the national TV channel *Caracol Television* broadcast every weeknight one of the 113 one-hour episodes of this series retracing the life of Escobar. Although the show triggered criticism on the glorification of the infamous drug lord, it was enormously successful: the first episode was watched by 11 million Colombians, or 62.7 per cent of people watching television at this time (Edition of *Cosecha Roja*, 2012). The show won an international audience and was broadcast in 66 countries including North Korea; it is now considered as one of the biggest successes in the history of Colombian television (Wallace, 2013). An important feature in our context is the fact that it was produced and directed by close victims of Escobar. The producer, Camilo Cano, is one of the five sons of Guillermo Cano, who was the director of the newspaper *El Espectador* until his assassination by one of Escobar's hit men. The director, Juana Uribe, was the niece of one of the most fervent opponents of Escobar: Luis Carlos Galan, a presidential candidate who was also killed on the orders of the 'boss of evil' (Gómez, 2012).

Another television series related to Escobar that won a worldwide audience is the Netflix production, *Narcos*. While the principal sources for *El patron del mal* were Colombian victims, *Narcos* is partly based on the testimonies of two Drug Enforcement Agents (DEA), who served as consultants for the production. Former agents Steve Murphy and Javier Pena were operating in Medellin in the 1980s and are now the main characters of the show. Even though they agree that the real heroes were the Colombian National Police and that 'they were just doing their jobs and trying to have a good time' (Steve Murphy interviewed in *Men's Journal*, Throp, 2015), the international perspective on this traumatic memory is often criticized in Colombia.

Besides the recurrent complaint that the Brazilian actor Wagner Moura who portrays Escobar has a foreign accent, the simplification of the complex issues associated with narco-trafficking is widely criticized. As the blogger Bernardo Aparicio Garcva states: 'Watching *Narcos* seemed to me like grabbing a bag of popcorn and watching my country burn. [. . .] What bastardized idea of Colombia was about to spread through popular culture?' (Aparicio Garcia, 2015). Furthermore, the combination of documentary footage and fiction can be problematic, affecting people closely related to this violence, especially in a context where fiction and reality is often blurred. Another blogger, Pablo Medina Uribe, mentions for instance the footage of the murder of his grandmother's brother in law, used in falsified circumstances in the TV show (Medina Uribe, 2015). He adds that Colombians are robbed of their own history: 'which becomes a mere plot device, cut down too fine, shredded pieces for American audiences to digest without having to gnaw on the bones' (ibid.).

The former boss of the Medellin cartel is not the only one to be featured in Colombian *narco-soaps*. Many television series, most of them broadcast on the national channel Caracol Televisión, are closely linked to the country's history of drugs and violence. *La viuda negra* (*The Black Widow*) depicts the history of Griselda Blanco (also featured in *El patron del mal*), who was one of the pioneers in the cocaine business. *Las muñecas de la Mafia* (*The Mafia Dolls*) or *Sin tetas no hay paraíso* (*Without Tits There Is No Paradise*) are other examples describing Colombia's narco-history. Yet none of these shows achieved the huge success of *El Patron del mal*, which even included the creation of a 16-page children's sticker book. Until the authorities finally prohibited their distribution, stickers portraying Escobar were being sold in local grocery stores for 15 cents a packet (AFP, 2012). Additionally, many documentaries[1] re-examine the history of the capo and several biographies[2] have been written, by journalists and victims, as well as Escobar's relatives, including his sister and brother.

John 'Popeye' Velásquez, the former right hand of Escobar, also founded a YouTube channel – 'Remorseful Popeye' – now watched by more than 100,000 subscribers. 'Popeye' spent 22 years in jail after being convicted for the murder of the presidential candidate Luis Carlos Galán. However, he has also claimed responsibility for hundreds of other deaths, including many policemen. Even though the former hit man asserts that his objective is to warn young people away from crime, his channel is seen as deeply offensive by many victims. As Popeye claims: 'Everything Pablo Emilio Escobar Gaviria did was bad. It's important that new generations don't get fixated on the figure of Pablo Escobar and even less on mine. We should not be a model for anyone. We are bandits' (Brodzinsky, 2016). Colombia's Caracol Televisión is now producing a series based on his book *Surviving Pablo Escobar*, which will be broadcast by Netflix. This new series is equally considered as an apology of crime and an insult for the victims, as one of the son of Popeye's victim's states:

When I switch the Television on and the first thing I see is my persecutor, the less I can say is that it is not pleasant. [. . .] Why do they only make tributes to the bad guys and not to the good ones? Why don't they do that with all the good guys killed by Popeye?

(Semana.com, 2017)

In a context where reality and fiction often intertwine, popular culture and violence are closely related. Narco-history represents an important source of inspiration for every sector of the Colombian mediascape and popular culture: it appears in soap operas, documentaries, web-television, movies and literature, all elements contributing to the social fabric of Medellin.

Escobar, narco-aesthetic and tourism

The celebrated Colombian painter and sculptor Fernando Botero has also contributed to publicizing the image of Pablo Escobar. Even though he publicly expressed his disgust for the drug lord, Botero represented his death in two of his paintings: *The Death of Pablo Escobar* (1999) and *Pablo Escobar Dead* (2006). The work of Fernando Botero focuses on major aspects of Latin American society, such as religion, the circus, bullfighting and the family. In such a context, violence constitutes inevitably a major theme for the artist. *Bomb Car*, *Massacre* and *Massacre in Colombia* are among his paintings illustrating the violence in the country.

If popular culture is certainly an important vehicle, what could be labeled as 'high culture' is also contributing to the propagation of the Pablo Escobar legacy. Yet, Botero's work is familiar to many people in Colombia and it is accessible to everyone. Several of his sculptures are for instance exhibited in the 'plaza Botero' in Medellin's city centre. Additionally, his creations are closely related to people's everyday life. This brings into question the boundaries between 'popular' and 'high' or 'elite' culture. In any case, beyond these dichotomies, every domain of the arts contributes to diffuse the violent heritage of Colombia. The Medellin art student Ernesto Zapata won a grant in 2010 to craft a series of figurines representing Escobar with distinct identities: Robin Hood, paramilitary, politician, etc.[3] After being exhibited in the Antioquia Museum, also hosting numerous Botero paintings, the figurines were put on sale; in the end, buyers were mainly foreign tourists. Moreover, the artist offered several of his creations to families living in the popular neighbourhood commonly called 'barillo Pablo Escobar'.[4] Here again the distinction between 'popular' and 'elite' culture is very blurred.

Many shops and street vendors in Medellin propose goodies and clothes featuring the image of Escobar (Figure 5.1). Furthermore, Escobar's son, who changed his name to Santiago Marroquin (replacing his former name Juan Pablo Escobar Henao), after moving to Argentina, founded a clothing brand in 2010 called 'Escobar Henao'.[5] Under the slogan 'in peace we trust', t-shirts depicting mug shots of his father are sold on the Internet and in various boutiques around the world. These products are not available anywhere in Colombia.

Some local scholars and artists (Rincón, 2009; Henao, 2015) have introduced the notion of a 'narco-aesthetic', going so far as to link the current boom of plastic surgery in Medellin to the history of the drug trade and the tastes of the dealers, influenced by their trips in the United States, for blonde and buxom women. Henao (2015), in her photographic work 'Beauties', explores how these social factors modified the perception of the Colombian female body. According to her, the 1980s and 1990s changed the image of Medellin's women, from strong figures of 'mothers' and 'hard workers' to very materialistic representations:

Figure 5.1   Pablo Escobar t-shirts in Medellin's shopping centres.
Source: Naef (2015).

Drug lords would visit the US to conduct drug deals and return with images of beauty that they'd seen on prostitutes there: blonde and voluptuous, with thin noses. Back home, they had the money to transform any woman into that canon of beauty.

(Henao, 2015)

Moreover, this process is described in a famous novel that also generated a television series – *Sin tetas no hay paraíso* (*Without Tits There Is No Paradise*) – which documents what Rincón

(2009, p. 160) describes as follows: 'To be successful in Colombia, women have to be females and mothers [*mamacitas* in Spanish], use silicone and be fearless in bed' (translated from Spanish by the author). For this Colombian scholar, narco is not only a business, but an aesthetic embedded in Colombian history and culture, which manifests itself in music, television, language and architecture.

Violence and narcos are also significantly present in Medellin's tourism sector. Since 2007, an increasing number of guides have been offering what are often labeled as 'Pablo tours'. Guides generally bring tourists – almost all foreigners – to various sites associated with the capo: his grave in Montesacro Cemetery and abandoned buildings, like the one where he was killed. These tours are promoted by private entrepreneurs. Public bodies involved in tourism tend to distance themselves from the practice, which they consider harms the international image of the city (Giraldo, 2014; Naef, 2015). Tensions also arise from the fact that the most popular of these tours is based on a partnership between tourist guides and Roberto Escobar, the brother of Pablo Escobar and the former bookkeeper of the Medellin cartel. After his release from prison in 2003, Escobar's brother transformed the first floor of his house (a former Escobar hideout) into a museum for the memory of his brother (Figure 5.2). This museum is very popular within the emerging backpacker's scene; many young travellers are eager to take a souvenir picture with Roberto Escobar in front of a poster showing the two brothers as wanted and offering a $10 million reward.

Figure 5.2 The museum of Roberto Escobar.
Source: Naef (2015).

Furthermore, some peripheral neighbourhoods of Medellin, generally built by war-displaced people, are also becoming part of the tourist companies' proposed programs. 'Comuna tours' (Naef, 2016) referring to the common designation of these urban areas as *'comunas'*, explore specific parts of these neighbourhoods, looking at their violent past, but also at contemporary issues of violence, setting them against the creativity and resilience of their inhabitants. These tours generally offer a narrative closely associated with the urban transformation and social investments that can be seen in the city. They are thus an appropriate tool in relaying the public authorities' promotional discourse on the 'miracle' of Medellin: a place shifting from 'the most violent to the most innovative city in the world' (Naef, 2016, p. 1).

Theoretical underpinnings: violence, tourism and popular culture

The state certainly plays an important role in the memorialization of violence, by its implementation of institutions such as memorial museums and official commemorations, but many initiatives also flourish in civil society and popular culture. A clear-cut distinction between state and civil society-supported projects seems reductive, as does opposing a popular and an elite way of remembering. Some initiatives instigated by civil society may win the support of the public authorities. In this context, artistic and memorial projects born in popular neighbourhoods can end up in a state museum; private and small-scale tourism projects can become successful enterprises. Memory of violence in Colombia is thus fragmented, produced by various sources and represented in many different, and often conflicting, ways.

Violence and its fascinating aura significantly impacts popular culture, as well as the whole social fabric, and the tourism sector increasingly cashes in on it. Both tourism and popular culture are important vehicles of representations of this dissonant heritage. However, when a traumatic past is at issue, memory studies still tend to overlook this area, focusing instead on more legitimate institutions of memory, such as museums and official memorials. This analysis seeks to bridge the gap, and contribute to deconstructing the general opposition between 'popular' and 'official' (or elitist) memorialization.

Research related to violence and popular culture is growing in Latin America, especially relating to Mexico (Aguilera, 2002; Polit-Dueñas, 2013) Colombia (Cobo, 2008; Rincón, 2009; Polit-Dueñas, 2013; Naef, in press; 2015) and Brazil (Larkins, 2015). In Rio de Janeiro, Larkins (2015, p. 212), demonstrates how popular culture represents an effective vehicle for the diffusion of representations related to violence and drugs: 'virtual spaces of infotainment and leisure are increasingly militarized, one finds that violence circulates through all of us, as news, movies, games, photos, fashion and even smartphone applications'. It is first of all important to examine how popular culture is defined and what it encompasses. The notion of popular culture, often labelled 'pop culture', has been widely explored in various disciplines such as literature (Freccero, 1999), rhetoric (Brummett, 2014), sociology (Mouchtouris, 2007; Delaney & Madigan, 2016) and anthropology (Buhle, 1987; Danesi, 2007; Long & Robinson, 2009). Popular culture has various meanings and there is still a lack of consensus on what it does and does not include. (Long & Robinson, 2009) Scholars usually agree that it is largely determined by people's everyday activities, like food, sport or language, and it is disseminated and fed by the mass media, including vehicles such as television, radio, the Internet and printed materials (Brummett, 2014). As stated above, popular culture is often opposed to the notion of 'high culture' or 'elite culture': the fine arts, opera, theater and other elements not mass produced and primarily associated with the upper socio-economic classes.

Delaney (2007, p. 2) defines popular culture as 'the 'items (products) and forms of expression and identity that are frequently encountered or widely accepted, commonly liked or approved, and characteristic of a particular society at a given time.' Popular culture would thus participate in forging a collective identity and a place image. As in Assmann and Czaplicka's (1995) conceptualization of memory – a set of shared socialization patterns defining a collective identity – it can also create alternative ways of perceiving narco-cultures, rooted in real locations of violence as well as in imaginary places created in fiction (Polit-Dueñas, 2013). Yet, if popular culture enables large heterogeneous masses of people to identify collectively, some elements widely diffused by mass media can also clash strongly with other competing representations. Cultural productions closely associated with ambiguous figures such as the narcos, especially iconic ones like Pablo Escobar, certainly serve as an example of representations widely disseminated locally and internationally, but rejected by a large part of the population.

The narcos and the miracle of Medellin

The urban armed conflict in Medellin in the last decades profoundly marked its social fabric. For many Colombians, unfortunately, violence is part of everyday life. This violent heritage is significantly integrated in popular culture, determined, as Brummett (2014) states, by people's everyday life. Thus, many novels, movies, songs or soap operas focus on the gangs and cartels involved in drug trafficking. As Rincón (2009, p. 162) cynically claims:

> The truth is that in *Narco.lombia*, without tits, weapons and money, there is no happiness. The society enjoys the taste of mafia, the truth of silicone and the ethic of the gun. Therefore, our literary, artistic, musical and television fiction; our language, our architecture and our tastes; our politics and our president celebrate, without decency, the values of narco. And, most extraordinary of all, medias, journalists and Colombians, we do not see anything bad in it.
>
> *(Translated from Spanish by the author)*

Narco-culture is present in every segment of Colombian society: entertainment and tourism, but also architecture (Cobo, 2008), language (Salazar, 1990) and aesthetics (Rincón, 2009). The commodification process that accompanies tourism and popular culture significantly contributes to trivializing the violence described in these practices and productions. In the case of Colombian and Mexican *narco-novelas*, Polit-Dueñas (2013, p. 109) remarks that reality can often be stranger than fiction: 'Death is described in repetitive and shocking ways; it eventually becomes overly exaggerated. In the end, violence stands like a wry grin, provoking laughter, like in a Quentin Tarantino movie.' These narratives thus participate in the spreading of simplified and unverified facts about this violent history; propagating myths that often clash in a memorial arena where victims and perpetrators still closely cohabit.

In 2013, ProColombia, the public–private entity in charge of tourism promotion, launched an advertisement campaign depicting the country with the slogan: 'Colombia is magical realism.' Inspired partly by the work of the Colombian Nobel literature prizewinner, Gabriel García Márquez, magical realism encompasses diverse areas, such as literature, cinema and painting. It refers to the presence of irrational elements in a realistic historical and geographical setting. As demonstrated by the elements promoted, ProColombia associates magical realism with pristine beaches, wild jungle and mysterious indigenous traditions. The same representations occur in the field of popular culture with the release in 2015 of the film *Majia salvaje* (*Wild Magical*). Based on the exploration of the country's rich biodiversity, this documentary is now the highest-grossing cinematographic production in Colombian history, with more than 2 million tickets sold.

On the other hand, even if their history is certainly not promoted by tourism officials, former members of the Medellin Cartel were also frequently referred to as 'magicians', due to their ability to amass huge amounts of money in a very short time. Netflix introduces *Narcos* to the spectator like this: 'Magical realism is defined as what happens when a highly detailed, realistic setting is invaded by something too strange to believe. There is a reason magical realism was born in Colombia'. Two opposing versions of magical realism are confronted here, illustrating once again the dissonant heritage associated with Colombia's difficult past.

A similar dynamic can be observed in Medellin, when the violent history and the urban development of the city are the issues: On one side, public stakeholders promote the city through discourses praising its transformation and all the related social initiatives, looking toward the future, with a blind eye on its traumatic past. On the other side, private entrepreneurs propel foreigners in the footsteps of Pablo Escobar, presenting a sombre picture of the city, while acknowledging its difficult heritage. In the middle, inhabitants find themselves torn between memory and forgetting, between the narco-past and the bright future of the Medellin miracle, both narratives presenting a mythical and simplified vision of their city.

Implications for popular culture tourism: the commodification of violence

Popular culture and tourism significantly contribute to the commodification of violence and to the simplification of Medellin's history. Nuances are often screened out by the spectacular, romantic and glamorous vision of the narcos produced by the different sectors involved: cinema, television, literature, tourism, fashion, etc. Furthermore, this performative violence tends to divert public attention from the real-life social context that makes it possible (Larkins, 2015). As is often the case when a violent history is commodified, Manichean representations emerge in an arena where memories are still traumatic and disputed. The TV show, *Narcos*, despite its intention to portray the tortured minds and the mistakes of the heroes (for instance when agent Murphy beats up a business man in the airport due to a serious burn-out), situates its characters firmly in the categories of 'good guys' and 'bad guys'. In this dark representation of Colombia, locals are mainly hit men, compromised politicians and corrupt policemen or sexy and mischievous women, while the two American agents are represented as heroes struggling to remain sane in this savage context.

However, as it has already been underlined, because popular culture is about people's everyday life, people in Medellin talk about symbols of the narcos' violence as elements that constitute part of this everyday life (Polit Dueñas, 2013). Thus, daily life in a country still plagued with drug trafficking and violence represents an important source of inspiration for entrepreneurs in the fields of popular culture. This context contributes to create a mythical vision of narco-glamour and leads to the trivialization of violence. Colombia's violent history is simplified, notwithstanding the comment of agent Murphy in the trailer for the second season of *Narcos*: 'If there is something I learned in the narco world, it is that things are always more complicated that you think'.[6]

According to Long and Robinson (2009, p. 103), soap operas, like documentaries or sports broadcasts, 'contribute significantly in shaping daily and weekly leisure patterns and provide subjects for diversion, reflections and discussion'. Nevertheless, far from diffusing consensual representations, these elements trigger numerous conflicts and tensions in a memorial arena where victims, witnesses, journalists, politicians, actors and criminals cohabit. An important source of friction is related to the fact that many characters – Pablo Escobar, Griselda Blanco, Popeye, Don Berna,[7] etc. – are historical figures who left a traumatic imprint on Colombian society, especially in Medellin. Additionally, some of their victims are also occasionally incorporated into the series, played by actors or even appearing in documentary footage. Depending on how they portray these figures, some popular culture productions can spark harsh controversies. *Narcos, El patron del mal* and other large-scale productions represent key illustrations of the way dissonant representations and discourses clash in a society still traumatized by an unfinished armed conflict.

Moreover, some former criminals like Roberto Escobar and Popeye are now involved in the management of businesses in the tourism sector or in areas of popular culture. These can be financially profitable, while serving at the same time as a vehicle expressing a particular viewpoint. Roberto Escobar is not only a touristic resource; he is also a memorial entrepreneur (Naef, in press). In this context, victims can be even more uncomfortable with some of the representations of their heritage. Yet, on the other hand, the diversity of narco-productions in Medellin's mediascape and touristscape also reflects a form of pacification in the social tissue of the city. As the blogger Aparicio Garcia (2015) puts it: 'The mere fact that a show like this [*Narcos*] can exist is evidence of how much things have changed since that time, both in the United States and in Colombia.'

To conclude this analysis, it is stated that opposing popular culture to 'high' or 'elite' culture is more restrictive than productive. Projects and productions evolve in time and their status (and those of their producers) shifts from one context to another. Plus, the designation of 'popular' and 'high' can often imply a normative dimension, which can influence the public, as well as researchers. The study of narco-culture, far from being anecdotal and frivolous, provides important and concrete insights into contemporary Latin American society.

Notes

1 See, for instance, *The Two Escobars, The King of Coke, Hunting Escobar, Pablo Escobar: Angel or Demon?* and *Sins of My Father.*
2 See, for instance, *Killing Pablo, Pablo Escobar mi padre, Escobar: The Inside Story of Pablo Escobar, the World's Most Powerful Criminal, Memory of Pablo Escobar, El Verdadero Pablo.*
3 http://cargocollective.com/estebanzapataartista/Pablo-in-Commerce (accessed 26 October 2016).
4 A neighbourhood in Medellin financially supported by Escobar. It was built in the 1980s to host families living in deprived conditions.
5 www.escobarhenao.com/es/7-t-shirts-poder-poder (accessed 26 October 2016).
6 www.youtube.com/watch?v=U7elNhHwgBU&feature=youtu.be (accessed 27 October 2016).
7 Diego Bejarana, commonly known as 'Don Berna', started working for the Medellin Cartel and then became one of the leaders of United Self-Defense Forces of Colombia paramilitary group. He was finally extradited in 2008 to a jail in the United States. This historical figure has been included in different productions such as the second season of *Narcos*.

References

AFP (2012, 8 August). Pablo Escobar se impone de nuevo en Colombia en un álbum de cromos. *El Universal*. Retrieved from nhomepagewww.eluniversal.com.co/cartagena/actualidad/pablo-escobar-se-impone-de-nuevo-en-colombia-en-un-album-de-cromos-86842

Aguilera, M. (2002). El corrido de narcotrá co y la música popularesca en el norte de Mexico. Retrieved from homepagehttp://aplicaciones.colef.mx/investigadores/miguelolmos/narcocorrido/Corrido_del_narco.html

Aparicio Garcia, B. (2015). I grew up in Pablo Escobar's Colombia: Here's what it was really like. *Vox*. Retrieved from www.vox.com/2015/10/21/9571295/narcos-pablo-escobar-colombia

Ashworth, G. J., Graham, B. & Tunbridge, J. (2007). Place, identity and heritage. In B. Graham, G. J. Ashworth & J. E. Tunbridge (Eds.), *Pluralising pasts: Heritage, identity and place in multicultural societies* (pp. 54–67). London: Pluto Press.

Assmann, J. & Czaplicka, J. (1995). Collective memory and cultural identity. *New German Critique*, 65, 125–133.

Brodzinsky, S. (2010, 12 February). Colombians outraged by narco-soaps glamorizing cartels. *Guardian*. Retrieved from www.theguardian.com/world/2010/mar/12/columbians-outraged-by-soaps-glamorising-cartels

Brodzinsky, S. (2016, 8 June). Ex-Pablo Escobar enforcer who killed 300 seeks new career as YouTube star. *Guardian*. Retrieved from www.theguardian.com/world/2016/jun/08/pablo-escobar-popeye-enforcer-youtube-channel

Brummett, B. (2014). *Rhetoric in popular culture*. London: Sage.

Buhle, P. (1987). *Popular culture in America*. Minneapolis, MN: University of Minnesota Press.

Cano J. M. (2014, 10 May). No me siento feliz con que Lady Tabares esté en la casa. *El Tiempo*. Retrieved from www.eltiempo.com/archivo/documento/CMS-13968415

Cobo, A. (2008, 28 June). ¿Es el ornamento un delito? *Esferapública*. Retrieved from http://esferapublica.org/nfblog/?p=1305

Colprensa (2015, 8 October). Magia salvaje, la película colombiana mas taquillera de la historia. *El Colombiano*. Retrieved from www.elcolombiano.com/cultura/cine/colombia-magia-salvaje-se-convirtio-en-la-pelicula-colombiana-mas-taquillera-de-la-historia-DK2851207

Cossio, R., V. (2010, 16 April). Responsables por cada nuevo sicario. *El Colombiano*. Retrieved from www.elcolombiano.com/historico/responsables_por_cada_nuevo_sicario-DWEC_85996

Danesi, M. (2007). *Popular culture: Introductory perspectives*. Lanham, MD: Rowman and Littlefield.

Delanay, T. (2007). Pop culture: An overview. *Philosophy Now*, 64. Retrieved from https://philosophynow.org/issues/64/Pop_Culture_An_Overview

Delanay, T. & Madigan T. (2016). *Lessons learned from popular culture*. New York: State University of New York Press.

Edition of *Cosecha Roja*. (2012, 29 May). Pablo Escobar, capo del rating. *Cosecha Roja*. Retrieved from http://cosecharoja.org/pablo-escobar-capo-del-rating/

Freccero, C. (1999). *Popular culture: An introduction*. New York: New York University Press.

Giraldo C., Van Broeck A. M. & Posada L. (2014). El pasado polémico de los años ochenta como atractivo turístico en Medellín, Colombia, *Anuario Turismo y Sociedad*, 15, 101–114.

Gómez, V. (2012, 27 May). Viaje a las 'entrañas' de Pablo Escobar, el patrón del mal. *El Pais*. Retrieved from www.elpais.com.co/elpais/entretenimiento/noticias/viaje-entranas-pablo-escobar

Henao, M. (2015, 16 June). 'Beauties', o el rastro cultural de la estética femenina del narco. *Huffington Post*. Retrieved from www.huffingtonpost.es/manuela-henao/beauties_b_7604654.html

Larkins, E. M. (2015). *The spectacular favela: Violence in modern Brazil*. Berkeley, CA: University of California Press.

Londoño, R. (2015, 17 October). Watching 'Narcos' in a transformed Medellín. *New York Times*. Retrieved from www.nytimes.com/2015/10/18/opinion/sunday/watching-narcos-in-a-transformed-medellin.html?_r=0

Long, P. & Robinson, M. (2009). Tourism, popular culture and the media. In T. Jamal & M. Robinson (Eds.), *The sage handbook of tourism studies* (pp. 98–114). London: Sage.

Medina Uribe, P. (2015, 20 September). Netflix's Narcos cheapens Colombia and its history. *Fusion*. Retrieved from http://fusion.net/story/205405/netflixs-narcos-cheapens-colombia-and-its-history/

Mouchtouris, A. (2007). *Sociologie de la culture populaire*. Paris: L'Harmattan.

Naef, P. (2015, November). *Pablo and the hippos: 'narcoheritage' and tourism in Medellin, Colombia*. Paper presented at the American Anthropological Association annual meeting, Denver, CO.

Naef, P. (2016). Touring the 'comuna': Memory and transformation in Medellin, Colombia. *Journal of Tourism and Cultural Change*, 16(2), 173–190.

Naef, P. (in press). 'Narcoheritage' and the touristification of the drug lord Pablo Escobar in Medellin, Colombia. *Journal of Anthropological Research*.

Polit-Dueñas, G. (2013). *Narrating Narcos: Culiacán and Medellín*. Pittsburgh, PA: University of Pittsburgh Press.

Rigoulet, L. (1998, 15 May). Reptrages: Cadre. Victor Gaviria. Rtalisateur de 'la Vendeuse de roses' Sur les trottoirs de Medellin. *Libration*. Retrieved from http://next.liberation.fr/culture/1998/05/15/reperages-cadre-victor-gaviria-realisateur-de-la-vendeuse-de-roses-sur-les-trottoirs-de-medellin_236083

Rincón, O. (2009). Narco.estética y narco.cultura en Narco.lombia. *Nueva Sociedad*, 22, 147–163.

Salazar, A., J. (1990). *No nacimos pa' semilla: La cultura de las bandas juveniles de Medellín*. Bogota, Colombia: Centro de Investigación y Educación Popular.

Semana.com (2017, 7 July). Serie sobre 'Popeye' es un insulto para las víctimas. *Semana*. Retrieved from www. semana.com/nacion/articulo/victimas-de-pablo-escobar-en-desacuerdo-con-serie-de-television-de-popeye/514732

Throp, C. (2015). The true story behind Pablo Escobar and 'Narcos'. *Men's Journal*. Retrieved from www. mensjournal.com/adventure/collection/the-true-story-behind-pablo-escobar-and-narcos-20150908

Wallace, A. (2013, 2 December). Drug boss Pablo Escobar still divides Colombia. *BBC World*. Retrieved from www.bbc.com/news/world-latin-america-25183649

PART II

Broadening the scope

Popular culture tourism expressions

6

POPULAR CULTURE TOURISM
Films and tourist demand

Yuri Kork

Setting the scene

Fan consumption and demand for popular culture tourism can take a variety of forms, one of the most well known of which is, perhaps, film tourism. This is a relatively recently recognized form of tourism, but numerous examples illustrate the stimulating effect films can have on tourism development and demonstrate how films affect tourist demand and numbers. Through exposure in films, destinations get unique marketing opportunities to provide film tourism experiences not available at other destinations. The known examples include *The Lord of the Rings* and, later, *The Hobbit* trilogies attracting fans to New Zealand (Singh & Best, 2004; Jones & Smith, 2005; Buchmann, 2010), the increase in visitor numbers Gloucester Cathedral indicated after the exposure in *Harry Potter* films (Grihault, 2003; Lee, 2012), *The Sound of Music* film inducing travels to Salzburg (Hyunjung & Kaye 2008) and the *Pride and Prejudice* film stimulating tourists to visit the Netherfield Park, UK (Parry, 2008).

As film-exposed destinations are trying to capitalize on such new unique elements, it has become vital to explore the connections between films and tourist demand and to understand how films affect tourist consumption. However, film tourism is an increasingly complex phenomenon – it depends on a combination of personal characteristics of the viewer, such as emotional responsiveness, education, and cultural background, which makes film tourism a highly personalized experience (Connell, 2012). In addition, to date, film tourism has mainly been approached in case studies exclusive for a particular area or film, or more descriptive works focusing, for example, on the definition of film tourism (Busby & Klug, 2001), the relationship between the film and the destination image (Urry & Larsen, 2011), possible advantages and disadvantages films offer for the local tourism industry and community (Hyunjung & Kaye, 2008) and, more recently, the influence films may have on the emotions of tourists (Kim, 2012).

Despite existing research in this area, many researchers, notably, Couldry (1998), Riley and Van Doren (1992), Busby and Klug (2001), Beeton (2005) and Olsberg/SPI (2007) agree that there is still a lack of deeper theoretical understanding of this type of tourism. Contributing to the existing base of knowledge, this chapter examines the films influencing tourist demand. The empirical evidence suggests that the primary driving process for films to influence tourist behavior is the process of film-induced association construction and evaluation. Such associations develop familiarity with the destination, specifically, it's visual and atmospheric qualities, and form emotional connections with the portrayed images. Then such associations are evaluated as the empathy with the film, it's credibility, and strength of influence are assessed (Kork, 2016). Understanding the process of such evaluation and factors that affect it will contribute to the general understanding of film tourism and may help to predict and account for the changes it may cause in tourism product demand.

Theoretical underpinnings: film tourism

As suggested by Hudson and Ritchie (2006), film tourism is driven by both the increase in international travel and growth of the entertainment industry, which makes it a developing worldwide phenomenon. Frost (2004) noted the increasing interest in how films may shape tourism demand and resultant consumption of film-based tourism products and experiences.

Film tourism definition

The definition of film tourism was first suggested by Evans in 1997, but several subsequent studies in this area expanded and developed the initial definition resulting, as reported by Macionis (2004), in a range of terms to refer to film tourism: movie-induced tourism, media-induced tourism, cinematographic tourism, film-induced tourism, and media pilgrimage. Connell (2012) reported that such a diverse mixture of definitions was criticized by Olsberg/SPI (2007), Fernandez-Young and Young (2008) and Connell and Meyer (2009). Attempting to reduce potential misinterpretation, these researchers proposed to adopt an umbrella term "screen tourism," which would cover all forms of this tourism type.

Evans (1997), Busby and Klug (2001), Grihault (2003) and Macionis (2004) developed the definition of film tourism and, despite the variety of terms to address, it is possible to synthesize the general definition: Film tourism refers to post-modern experience of an attraction or destination that has been portrayed in some form of media representation, such as the cinema screen, television, or video. Macionis (2004) adds that this definition represents the most logical and straightforward approach.

Forms of film tourism

Busby and Klug (2001) analyzed the forms of film tourism present in the research literature at that time and attempted to summarize the characteristics of the identified forms of film tourism. They suggested that specific push and pull factors of the film-exposed destination affect the forms of film tourism. This led to the conclusion that different types of film tourists consume different forms of film tourism and are influenced by complex combinations of different factors, consequently, films can create a range of different film tourism consumers. Connell (2012) contributed to this theory by summarizing previous studies and concluding that film tourism consumers may be divided into groups depending on which form of film tourism they demand. In the context of this chapter, the form of film tourism where the viewer performs a "visit to portrayed location (real/substitute)" (Connell, 2012, p. 1010) is approached and examined.

Moreover, film tourism scholars agree that film tourism is a form of cultural tourism (Hudson & Ritchie, 2006; Iwashita, 2006). It can take the form of popular culture tourism, as films can communicate cultural meanings (Busby & Klug, 2001), but can additionally influence more specific culture tourists, for example, by creating a wish to visit heritage sites (Frost, 2004) or through connections to dark tourism locations, for example, concentration camps (*The Boy in the Striped Pyjamas*). The role of film tourism as a form of culture tourism was developed by Macionis (2004) as she adopted the cultural tourist classification model by McKercher (2002) and developed three types of film tourists: the *serendipitous film tourist* (this tourist just happens to be visiting a destination portrayed in a film, and the presence of this tourist is not related to film or media portrayal, this tourist may or may not participate in film tourism activities); the *general film tourist* (this tourist is not specifically drawn to a film location but participates in film tourism activities while visiting the destination); and the *specific film tourist* (this tourist actively seeks out places that they have been exposed to by the film). This chapter focuses mostly on general and specific film tourist types. However, this approach to divide film tourists was reported as simplified by Fernandez-Young and Young (2008) who argued that it does not comprise all possible degrees of this diverse phenomenon. It can be concluded that film tourism classification is a complex evolving process and no universally accepted system to classify film tourism exists.

Film tourist profile

It may be argued that film tourists have a number of profile characteristics that differentiate them from other tourist types. Specifically, Busby and Klug (2001) explored the demographical aspect of film tourists and suggested, presenting the evidence from Prentice (1996) and Kerstetter, Confer, and Bricker (1998) that cultural tourists tend to be affluent older professionals and senior managers from the ABC1 socio-economic groups. However, Busby and Klug (2001) additionally mention the research by Richards (1996), which argues that film tourists are younger, highly educated, and from higher socio-economic backgrounds. This suggestion gained additional support from the research by Kim, Agrusa, Chon, and Cho (2008), as they concluded that film tourists tend to be middle-aged, have a high income and a high education level.

The discussion of the film tourist profile was further developed by Connell (2012) who reported that the majority of research projects conducted in this area are case study based and focus on a specific film. As such film may be targeted at a specific demographic group and more efficiently increase the demand of that particular demographic, it may be less influential for other film tourists. From the case study perspective, this argument is supported in the research by Singh and Best (2004) (*The Lord of the Rings*) and Hyunjung and Kaye (2008) (*The Sound of Music*). The role of demographics in film tourist demand was further explored by Kim (2012) in a Korea-focused case study, which suggests that the nationality of the film tourist may influence film tourist demand and destination interactions.

Furthermore, despite the emerging research and discussion of this type of tourism, Connell and Meyer (2009) report that, currently, the understanding of how film tourists construct their demands is limited. This chapter, examining the results of a mixed method research of film tourist behavior and experiences (Kork, 2016), attempts to cover this gap by exploring the process of films creating tourist demand.

Implications for popular culture tourism

To explore and understand how films may affect tourist demand, this chapter adopts the results of a mixed methods (survey with subsequent series of interviews) exploratory research. The collected data and following analysis suggest that a connection between films and tourist demand may result from the process of association construction. Specifically, films create associations with the destination, which are then evaluated by the tourists and the evaluation establishes tourist demand. The stages and components of this process are summarized in Figure 6.1.

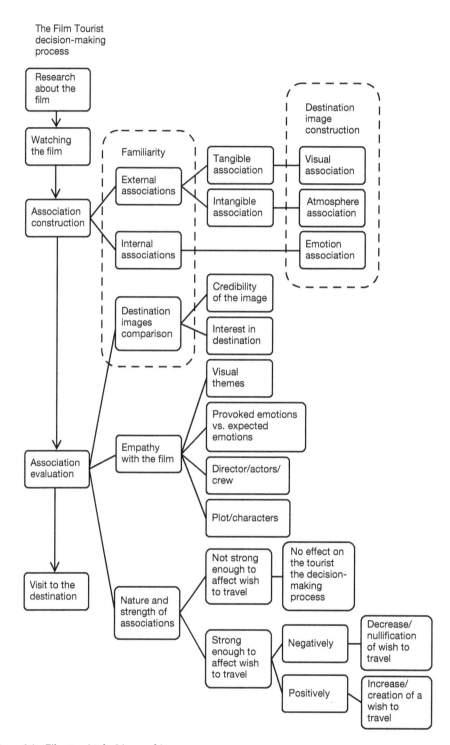

Figure 6.1 Film tourist decision–making process.

Source: Kork (2016). Developed from Faye and Crompton (1991), Macionis (2004), and Hudson, Wang, and Gil (2011).

As Figure 6.1 demonstrates, films begin to influence the possible demand of film tourists when they encounter the information about the film. This information may be presented in a variety of formats, most popular and widespread of which may be, perhaps, commercial description and word-of-mouth. Most often this information includes film genre, theme, director, and/or actors; and it can be intentionally researched in an attempt to ease the decision about possible film watching, or be incidentally acquired. During the decision about watching the film, this information is analyzed and the expectations from the film are constructed, one of the most important of which may be the emotional experience the film may cause. When such expectations are perceived as desirable, film watching occurs.

Association construction

First and foremost, the films construct visual association with a portrayed destination, connecting it to specific visual images, which can include scenic sights, memorable places, or heritage sites. Although relatively basic, this association is critical for the film influence on tourist demands. Some films, most famous of which may be *Avatar* or, more recently, *Alice in Wonderland*, have none or very limited destination exposure, and the major part of the film is featuring specially constructed sets or virtual environments. Therefore, although such films may cause strong responses from the viewer, their effect on tourist demand is severely decreased as they are not connected to a specific location.

From the demand construction perspective, by "offering a visual spectacle" (Lefebvre, 2006, p. 28) and offering visual information about the destination (Game, 1991), films may create a wish to physically engage with the destination, resulting in the demand for such tourist products (Connell, 2012). Reeves (2003) develops the argument by suggesting that, when developing such demand, film tourists may proceed to additional information sources to research the film-exposed location in greater detail which, consequently, may increase the desire to travel. In the context of analyzed data, the examples of films with strong visual association impact on tourist demand may be *Out of Africa*, *Australia*, and *The Best Exotic Marigold Hotel*.

Second, films construct atmosphere association, which is different from visual association as it belongs to the "intangible associations" group (see Figure 6.1). Indeed, the destination exposure in films is not limited to visual images, as this association creates connections between the destination and the intangible phenomena of culture, sensual characteristics and feeling. Weir (2002) adds that films can develop landscape into the "cultural property" by filling the filmed locations with symbolism and meaning (Bordwell & Thompson, 1993).

In addition, Urry and Larsen (2011) describe the phenomenon of "mediated gaze," which explores how media can develop tourism demand by engaging the destination with actions, perceptions, images, and texts. This results in films allowing viewers to visit the destinations in their own imagination (Connell, 2012), and the real location may be infused with fantasy elements. Furthermore, the visual and atmosphere associations are linked, as Debord (1983) noted that visual images are constantly inter-connected with cultural and social elements. The examples of films with strong atmosphere association may include *Lost in Translation* and, more recently, *Slumdog Millionaire*.

Lastly, films create emotional association with a destination, connecting it with specific emotional experiences. As films are designed to provoke emotions (Connell, 2012), this association may be the most developed association. Tooke and Baker (1996) suggest that strong associations between places and emotions increase the influence of the film on tourist demand, and Morgan (2006) adds that locations can be transformed into "emotional territory" when emotions are connected to places. Consequently, by connecting emotions and location, films may increase tourism demand as emotional attachments may induce the motivation to travel (Gnoth, Zins, Lengmueller, & Boshoff, 2000). However, the influence of emotion association is not limited to affecting tourist demand: Kim (2012) reports that satisfaction level from the trip may be affected by emotional connections.

Focusing on the development of emotions, a number of factors in the film affect this process. As suggested by Escher and Zimmerman (2001) and Olsberg/SPI (2007), emotional connections between the spectacle and the viewer may be induced by interrelation of plots and locations. Smith (2003) adds that the origin of the emotional response is more complex than interrelation between location and plot, and is also affected by soundtracks, narrative, and special effects. The examples of films that create strong emotional connections with the viewer include *Mamma Mia* and *Little Miss Sunshine*. The latter example is unusual because *Little Miss Sunshine* is a "road trip film" where the events unfold as characters are traveling through the United States in a van. In this case, the film infuses with emotions not a particular location, but rather a specific tourism activity.

Association evaluation

After associations are constructed, viewers evaluate them. This process, while being both conscious and unconscious, is critical in establishing the possible change in tourist demand the film can induce. In many cases, associations are not influential enough to have an impact on tourist demand, and the evaluation process determines their influence. In somewhat general terms, film needs to be trusted by the viewer, it needs to be liked by the viewer, and the combined associations need to be strong enough to influence tourist demand. These conditions will be explored in greater detail below.

Film and destination image

The fictional effects and locations from the films mix with and overlap the real location, which results in a process Rojek (1997, p. 54) describes as the intersection of cinematic events and the real physical landscape, resulting in the new interpretation of the physical landscape, stimulated by the cinematic events. Busby and Klug (2001) presented evidence of the difference between the location presented in the film and the actual filming location and Butler (2011) added that, because film-created destination image is fictional, the demand for the destinations conveyed through the film may be greater than for the actual location. As the associations are constructed, their combination results in film-created destination image. To assess credibility and authenticity of film-created image, viewers compare it to the image of the destination they had before watching the film, which can have three possible outcomes:

- *Reinforcing image*: The film-created image is similar to the pre-watching image of the viewer. In this situation, film reinforces the existing image, possibly adding new information to it. Such reinforcement can apply to both visual qualities of the portrayed locations, for example, *Midnight in Paris* showing various landmarks of the city, and to less tangible characteristics of the destination. For instance, *The Hangover* operates with the stereotypes about the destination of Las Vegas and reinforces these stereotypes. It may be suggested that such reinforcement may not necessarily have a stimulating effect, as both positive (fun, sex, money, fame) and negative (reckless consumption, irresponsibility, violence) stereotypes may be reinforced by the film.
- *Stimulating image*: The film-created image has tolerable differences with the pre-watching image of the viewer. In this situation, the difference between images is not major to the extent where the film is regarded as not credible, but high enough to indicate to

the viewer that the information he/she has about the destination needs to be updated and/or expanded, which may lead to additional information search and, possibly, affect tourist demand. The examples of this process may include such films as *Into The Wild*, which provoked interest towards hiking as a tourism activity; and *A Royal Affair*, which increased interest in a particular historical period in Denmark and, by extension, the locations where it was filmed.

- *False image*: The film-created image has high differences with the pre-watching image of the viewer to the extent where the credibility of the film is rejected. In this situation, particularly if the viewer has access to reliable information for comparison, the film is regarded as not credible. While it may be liked by the viewer and have a strong influence on tourist demand, when making travel decisions, the viewer may not perceive the film as a source of information about the destination. The example of this process may be *The Best Exotic Marigold Hotel*, which, while being pleasing to watch and increasing the tourist demand for India, was criticized for "sugar-coating" the destination and inaccurately portraying certain social elements of it.

Film and authenticity

If the film is evaluated as a trustworthy information source, the viewer examines the authenticity of the portrayed image, as Torchin (2002, p. 247) stresses the emphasis of authenticity in film tourism visits to the actual destinations. It can be suggested based on the case study of *Lord of the Rings* in New Zealand that, for some film tourists, a main demand-creating factor is not the actual location, but an artificial film-created vision of it (Tzanelli, 2004; Jones & Smith, 2005; Buchmann, 2010; Buchmann, Moor, & Fisher, 2010; Carl, Kindon & Smith, 2010). However, these findings may be case specific and less applicable to other film tourism locations.

When approaching the concept of authenticity, it is important to expand into the possibly more practical implication of it. In the context of film tourism (Connell, 2005), film tourists' demand is to experience the fictional reality – hyperreality, a "simulacra" in which "fantasy" and "reality" are confused in a world where access to unmediated reality is impossible, as the boundary between "actual" reality and "fantasy" reality is indistinct (Baudrillard, 1983; Schofield, 1996).

Couldry (1998) suggests that television and film locations are the perfect examples of the theory of hyperreality, and Connell (2005) adds that film locations can be destinations, recreated as the tourist sites, and having a constructed reality where visitors are not attracted to a real experience, rather to consume the mythology created by the interplay of fiction and environmental settings. Connell and Meyer (2009) suggest that some screen tourists specifically seek hyperreal experiences. Consequently, when evaluating authenticity and considering hyperreality, tourists may develop demand not only for the actual locations, but for a specific imaginary experience. Moreover, Connell (2012) argues that films can increase the familiarity with the destination because films affect the imagination of the viewers about the places they have never visited before.

Film and familiarity

In combination, association construction and subsequent destination image comparison and evaluation familiarize the viewer with the destination. The importance of familiarity in film tourism and its effect on the possible tourism demand have been approached in a number of case studies, most notably by Hyunjung and Kaye (2008), Iwashita (2008), and Tasci (2009).

Hyunjung and Kaye (2008) examined the influence of the movie *The Sound of Music* and established a correlation between frequency of watching the movie and possible tourist demand. Specifically, the researchers report that respondents who, during their life, were exposed to the movie more than six times, tended to be more heavily influenced by the movie than those who had seen the movie less than six times. Subsequently, the viewers who have seen the film more frequently were more strongly influenced to travel to Salzburg. Therefore, the degree of exposure to the film is an additional factor that has the power to influence tourist demand.

Iwashita (2008) conducted research about how films alter the perception of the UK for Japanese tourists and suggested that characters in films can alter the image of national identity. For example, the researcher reports that *James Bond* films show the polite and reserved perception of "Britishness," while *Mr Bean* portrays a more unconventional and peculiar image of British people. Moreover, the researcher stresses the possible negative consequence of this process: the familiarity with the destination may develop an inaccurate and/or stereotypical image. Tasci (2009) contributes to this argument by analyzing the relationships between movies, familiarity, and destination image, focusing on the case study of Turkey. It would appear that the lack of familiarity, prejudices, and stereotypes may act as increasers of social distance, distorting the image of the destination and reducing the possible tourist demand. Therefore, through the process of accurate familiarization, films can decrease the negative consequences of the lack of familiarity and increase tourist demand.

However, the development of familiarity may not necessarily have a positive effect on tourist demand. MacKay and Fesenmaier (1997) suggest that a high level of familiarity may have a negative effect on tourist demand as it can decrease the effect of the "novelty" factor. The "novelty" of the destination may positively affect tourist demand through the desire to visit new unknown places, so it is important that the film does not familiarize the viewers with the destination to the extent where the "novelty" factor loses positive effect on tourist demand. Furthermore, during or after the film consumption, credibility and authenticity are evaluated by the viewer and the degree of familiarity is established, the viewer assesses his/her empathy with the film.

Empathy with the film

The empathy with the film is increasingly complex to approach, as it would appear that the film production industry and scholars have no definite understanding about the qualities of a likable film. Indeed, film watching is, in most cases, a highly personal experience and depends heavily on the individual: different people like different films. In the context of this chapter, it may be suggested that the empathy with the film depends on four elements: visual themes, director/crew, plot/characters, and provoked emotions.

Visual themes depend on the locations in the film and whether the viewers would perceive them as beautiful, therefore, originate from the viewer's sense of beauty. Likewise, if the viewer prefers specific directors or actors, the film that features them may be more liked. The plot/characters quality is more complex, as it operates with representation of ideas and depends highly on the director's and/or screen writer's ability to convey and narrate, as well as viewers level of education and awareness. In addition, in some cases films are based on a pre-existing plot, such as a book series, comic series, or specific historical episode, which adds an additional dimension to the quality of the plot as viewers may compare the presentation of events in the original source and film.

Provoked emotions depend on how efficiently a film meets the expectations of the viewer. Specifically, during the research about the film (see Figure 6.1), viewers use genres, director, actors, and other information about the film to construct expectations. The ability of the film to meet such expectations, particularly the emotional element of it, affects the empathy with the film. An example of this process is *Slumdog Millionaire*, which, as described by one of its viewers, was advertised as a "fun family movie," but it begins with the scene where the main character is tortured as he is electrocuted in a bucket of water. The viewer was not prepared for such scene in a movie with that description, and did not like it as much as she would if she was expecting it. It may be concluded that not only the actual film, but also the marketing campaign of it may influence tourist demand.

Association strength

Finally, from the strength of associations perspective, in many cases, although the film may be trusted and liked by the viewer, it does not create associations strong enough to affect tourist demand. The combination of visual beauty, alluring atmosphere, and pleasing emotions conveyed through the film may affect film tourist demand. Moreover, in many cases, film tourists may not travel to the destination exclusively because of the film, but rather consider making film tourism experience a part of a longer and more complex visit. If the associations are strong enough to affect travel decisions, this process can have two possible outcomes: depending on whether the associations are perceived as positive or negative. The effect on travel decisions may be contributing or damaging (Kim & Richardson, 2003).

Strongly negative associations, for example, when films evoke strong undesired negative emotions, are less likely to affect tourist demand, and may even have a damaging effect on it. An example of this process is the film *In Bruges*, which, while portraying an attractive location, connected it with images of grotesqueness and gore, which, while appealing to some viewers, affected other viewers negatively. However, if the association is strong and positive, a film may create a demand for a tourism product or increase existing demand if it was present before watching the film. Films that are strong in increasing tourist demand may become the subjects of more detailed film tourism case studies. Examples of such films include *The Lord of the Rings*, *The Sound of Music*, and *Pride and Prejudice*.

Conclusion

In conclusion, this chapter reconfirms the complexity of film tourism, as it appears that it is highly dependent on personal characteristics of the viewer, which makes approaching and research it a challenging task. Despite such difficulties, it is possible to track the effect films may have on tourist demand by examining the elements of film tourist decision-making. It would appear that film can affect tourist demand as it constructs associations with the destination, and during the evaluation of such associations.

Visual association is a critical element in films affecting tourist demand as it is necessary for the film to portray an actual location to affect tourist demand, and positive effect on demand increases if the film includes images that viewers find aesthetically pleasing. Atmosphere association relates social and cultural aspects of the destination, fills it with symbolism, and may affect tourist demand as viewers may travel to experience the authentic "feeling" of the location, conveyed through the film. Finally, emotional association connects destinations with specific emotional experiences and may influence tourist demand as tourist may wish to travel to the location to recreate and re-experience positive emotions.

During and after their creation, associations are evaluated by the viewer and film credibility, empathy, and strength are determined. By comparing pre-existing destination images (if applicable) with film-created destination images, viewers attempt to assess the trustworthiness of the film.

Accordingly, if the film is not trusted by the viewer to be a credible source of information about the destination, the effect of the film on tourist demand may weaken. Moderate differences between pre-existing and film-created images may induce further interest in the location, possibly resulting in further information search, which may affect demand as new information is acquired. No difference between pre-existing and film-created images may reinforce the existing knowledge about the destination.

If the film is trusted by the viewer, the authenticity of the portrayed image is assessed. In some cases, viewers may be affected by hyperreal settings that films create and develop a demand to travel to experience these imaginary places. In addition, trusted associations develop familiarity with the destination, which may have a positive effect on tourist demand by reducing social distance. However, over-familiarizing the viewer with the destination may have negative consequences on the demand as it decreases the desirable "novelty" factor of the destination. In addition, the frequency of exposure to the film may have a positive effect on tourist demand.

Focusing on the empathy with the film, it may depend on four elements of the film: visual themes, director/crew, plot/characters, and provoked emotions. While the first three elements depend highly on the personal preferences and sense of beauty of the viewer, provoked emotions is more complex as it depends partially on the marketing campaign of the film. As viewers build expectations from the film and imagine what emotions the film will induce (based on the available information about the film), the ability of the film to meet such expectations affects empathy with the film, and, consequently, tourist demand. This makes film marketing an important factor when affecting the possible tourist demand that a film may result in.

Finally, summarizing the element of association strength, constructed associations may not be strong enough to affect tourist demand. Moreover, film may have negative effects on tourist demand if it develops negative emotions. It is the complex combination of visual beauty, engaging atmosphere, and pleasing emotions that transform films into a demand-creating factor for the viewers, and it would appear that the film industry does not have a definite understanding of the components of a good film. Despite this, films may induce tourist demand, and the elements that affect this process have been examined in this chapter. Furthermore, from the perspective of future research, it is important to approach film tourists outside a specific film-based case study setting and attempt to explore more generally the complex psychological process of film-induced demand formation.

References

Baudrillard, J. (1983). *Simulations*. Semiotexte. New York.

Beeton, S. (2005). *Film-induced tourism*. Channel View Publications. Clevedon.

Bordwell, D. and Thompson, K. (1993). *Film art: An introduction*. McGraw-Hill. New York.

Buchmann, A. (2010). Planning and development in film tourism: Insights into the experience of *Lord of the Rings* film guides. *Tourism and Hospitality Planning and Development*, 7 (1), 77–84.

Buchmann, A., Moor, K., and Fisher, D. (2010). Experience film tourism authenticity and fellowship. *Annals of Tourism Research*, 37 (1), 229–248.

Busby, G. and Klug, J. (2001). Movie induced tourism: The challenge of measurement and other issues. *Journal of Vacation Marketing*, 7 (4), 316–332.

Butler, R. (2011). It's only make believe: The implications of fictional and authentic locations in films. *Worldwide Hospitality and Tourism Themes*, 3 (2), 91–101.

Carl, D., Kindon, S., and Smith, K. (2007). Tourists' experiences of film locations: New Zealand as "Middle earth." *Tourism Geographies*, 9 (1), 49–63.

Connell, J. (2005). Toddlers, tourism and Tobermory: Destination marketing issues and television-induced tourism. *Tourism Management*, 26 (5), 763–776.

Connell, J. (2012). Film tourism: Evolution, progress and prospects. *Tourism Management*, 33 (5) 1007–1029.

Connell, J. and Meyer, D. (2009). Balamory revisited: An evaluation of the screen tourism destination-tourist nexus. *Tourism Management*, 30 (2), 194–207.

Couldry, N. (1998). The view from inside the simulacrum: Visitors' tales from the set of Coronation Street. *Leisure Studies*, 17 (2), 94–107.

Debord, G. (1983). *Society of the spectacle*. Black and Redition. Detroit.

Escher, A. and Zimmerman, S. (2001). Geography meets Hollywood: The role of landscape in feature films. *Geographische Zeitschrift*, 89 (4), 227–236.

Evans, M. (March 1997). *Plugging into TV tourism. Insights D35–D38*. English Tourist Board. London.

Faye, P. C. and Crompton, J. L. (1991). Image differences between prospective, first-time, and repeat visitors to the lower Rio Grande valley. *Journal of Travel Research*, 30, 10–16.

Fernandez-Young, A. and Young, R. (2008). Measuring the effects of film and television on tourism to screen locations: A theoretical and empirical perspective. *Journal of Travel and Tourism Marketing*, 24 (2–3), 195–212.

Frost, W. (2004). Braveheart-ed Ned Kelly: Historic films, heritage tourism and destination image. *Tourism Management*, 27 (2), 247–254.

Game, A. (1991). Undoing the social: Towards a deconstructive sociology. Open University Press. Buckingham.

Gnoth, J., Zins, A. H., Lengmueller, R., and Boshoff, C. (2000). Emotions, mood, flow and motivations to travel. *Journal of Travel and Tourism Marketing*, 9 (3), 23–34.

Grihault, N. (2003). Film tourism: The global picture. *Travel & Tourism Analyst*, October, 1–21.

Hudson, S. and Ritchie, J. R. B. (2006). Promoting destinations via film tourism: An empirical identification of supporting marketing initiatives. *Journal of Travel Research*, 44 (4), 387–396.

Hudson, S., Wang, Y., and Gil, S. M. (2011). The influence of a film on destination image and the desire to travel: A cross-cultural comparison. *International Journal of Tourism Research*, 13 (2), 177–190.

Hyunjung, I. H. and Kaye, C. (2008). An exploratory study of movie-induced tourism: A case of the movie *The Sound of Music* and its locations in Salzburg, Austria. *Journal of Travel and Tourism Marketing*, 24 (2), 229– 238.

Iwashita, C. (2006). Media representation of the UK as a destination for Japanese tourists. *Tourist Studies*, 6 (1), 59–77.

Iwashita, C. (2008). Roles of films and television dramas in international tourism: The Case of Japanese tourists to the UK. *Journal of Travel and Tourism Marketing*, 24 (2), 139–151.

Jones, D. and Smith, K. (2005). Middle-earth Meets New Zealand: Authenticity and location in the making of *The Lord of the Rings. Journal of Management Studies*, 42 (5), 923–945.

Kerstetter, D., Confer, J., and Bricker, K. (1998). Industrial heritage attractions: Types and tourists. *Journal of Travel and Tourism Marketing*, 7 (2), 91–104.

Kim, H. and Richardson, S. L. (2003). Motion picture impacts on destination images. *Annals of Tourism Research*, 30 (1), 216–237.

Kim, S. S. (2012). Audience involvement and film tourism experiences: emotional places, emotional experiences. *Tourism Management*, 33 (2), 387–396.

Kim, S. S., Agrusa, J., Chon, K., and Cho, Y. (2008). The effects of Korean pop culture on Hong Kong residents' perceptions of Korea as a potential tourist destination. *Journal of Travel and Tourism Marketing*, 24 (2–3) 163–183.

Kim, S. S., Agrusa, J., Lee, H., and Chon, K. (2007). Effects of Korean TV dramas on the flow of Japanese tourists. *Tourism Management*, 28 (5), 1340–1353.

Kork, Y. (2016). How film tourists experience destinations. In V. Katsoni and A. Stratigea (Eds.), *Tourism and culture in the age of innovation, second international conference IACuDiT proceedings, 21–24 May 2015* (pp. 145–156). Springer Proceedings in Business and Economics. Athens.

Lee, C. (2012). "Have magic, will travel": Tourism and Harry Potter's United (magical) Kingdom. *Tourist Studies*, 12 (1), 52–69.

Lefebvre, M. (2006). *Landscape and film*. Routledge. London.

Macionis, N. (2004). Understanding the film-induced tourist. In W. Frost, G. Croy, and S. Beeton (Eds.), *International tourism and media conference proceedings, 24–26 November 2004* (pp. 86–97). Tourism Research Unit, Monash University. Melbourne.

MacKay, K. J. and Fesenmaier, D. R. (1997). Pictorial element of destination in image formation. *Annals of Tourism Research*, 24 (3), 537–565.

McKercher, B. (2002). Towards a classification of cultural tourists. *International Journal of Tourism Research*, 4 (1), 29–38.

Morgan, J. A. (2006). Enchanted places, land and sea, and wilderness: Scottish Highland landscape and identity in cinema. In C. Fowler and G. Helfield (Eds.), *Representing the rural: Space, place, and identity in films about the land* (pp. 185–201), Wayne State University. Detroit.

Olsberg/SPI. (2007). How film and TV programmes promote tourism in the UK. Film Council. London.

Parry, S. (2008). The Pemberley effect: Austen's legacy to the historic house industry. *Persuasions*, 30, 113–122.

Prentice. R. (1996). *Tourism as experience, tourists as consumers.* Queen Margaret College. Edinburgh.

Reeves, T. (2003). *The worldwide guide to movie locations* (2nd ed.). Titan Books. London.

Richards, G. (1996). Production and consumption of European cultural tourism. *Annals of Tourism Research*, 23 (2), 261–283.

Riley, R. and Van Doren, C. (1992). Movies as tourism promotion: A pull factor in a push location. *Tourism Management*, 13 (3), 267–274.

Rojek, C. (1997). Touring cultures: Transformations of travel and theory. Routledge. London.

Schofield, P. (1996). Cinematographic images of a city. *Tourism Management*, 17 (5), 330–340.

Singh, K. and Best, G. (2004). Film-induced tourism: Motivations of visitors to the Hobbiton movie set as featured in *The Lord of The Rings*. In W. Frost, G. Croy, and S. Beeton (Ed.), *International Tourism and Media Conference Proceedings, 24th–26th November 2004* (pp. 98–111). Tourism Research Unit, Monash University. Melbourne.

Smith, G. M. (2003). *Film structure and the emotion system.* Cambridge University Press. Cambridge.

Tasci, A. D. A. (2009). Social distance the missing link in the loop of movies, destination image and tourist behavior? *Journal of Travel Research*, 47 (4), 494–507.

Tooke, N. and Baker, M. (1996). Seeing is believing: The effect of film on visitor numbers to screened locations. *Tourism Management*, 17 (2), 87–94.

Torchin, L. (2002). Location, location, location: The destination of the Manhattan TV tour. *Tourist Studies*, 2 (3), 247–266.

Tzanelli, R. (2004). Constructing the "cinematic tourist": The "sign industry" of *The Lord of the Rings*. *Tourist Studies*, 4 (1), 21–42.

Urry, J. and Larsen, J. (2011). *The tourist gaze 3.0* (3rd ed.). Sage. London.

Weir, D. T. H. (2002). Nevil Shute and the landscapes of England: An opportunity for literary tourism. In M. Robinson and H. Andersen (Eds.), *Literature and tourism: Essays in the reading and writing of tourism* (pp. 119–142). Continuum. London.

7

FILM TOURISM IN THE GOLDEN AGE OF TELEVISION

Stefan Roesch

Setting the scene: film tourism

Film as a tourism driver

A representative international survey conducted in 2010 suggests that around 5 per cent of the world's travellers are inspired by movies when selecting their holiday destination (Henry-Biabaud, 2015). The Irish National Tourism Development Authority commissioned a market research study in the same year, which revealed that 20 per cent of international travellers credit films as a source of information that had an impact on their decision to travel to Ireland (Millward Brown Lansdowne, 2010). Middle-earth-motivated tourism to New Zealand increased from 8 per cent in 2003 to 14 per cent in 2013 (Tourism New Zealand, 2003, 2014) while visitor numbers to the film set of Hobbiton rose from 11.500 in 2003 to 360.000 in 2015 (Tenbrock, 2005; Fletcher, 2015).

There are many other examples which prove that fictional film productions can put destinations on the map and increase tourism to screened locations. For instance, when the relatively unknown Rosslyn Chapel south of Edinburgh, Scotland played a major role in the movie *The Da Vinci Code* (2006), visitor numbers tripled (Finnigan, 2009). In saying that, the prior release of Dan Brown's literary precursor in 2003 certainly played a major part in this tourism surge. A recent report assessed the market share of film-induced visitors at six different tourist UK-based attractions (Olsberg/SPI, 2015). The authors conclude that 36 per cent of the surveyed international tourists and 12 per cent of all domestic tourists can be defined as film location tourists.

Despite the overwhelming evidence of how beneficial film productions can be for places seen on screen, in the author's experience, film tourism still seems to be regarded as the poor cousin by many destination marketers. This is surprising when taking into consideration that over the past ten years, we have seen a significant increase in the production of high-quality drama TV shows which has prompted the appropriate term 'The Golden Age of Television' (Renner, 2016).

The golden age of television

The growing competition in the US-American television market between traditional cable networks and streaming providers such as Netflix or Amazon has sparked a surge of innovation in the quality and format of television shows (Röscheisen, 2013). Within the last five years, the number of scripted original shows rose from 211 to 409 and consequently, there has been much debate of late as to how many different programs the market can absorb before reaching saturation, and whether we have already reached 'Peak TV' (Erlichman, 2016).

However, these developments have certainly pushed TV-based tourism to a new level. A study commissioned by HBO in 2015 with 2,000 participants illustrates that TV shows have definitely caught up with feature films when it comes to the market share distribution in film tourism. Amongst the ten most popular film locations, five are based on TV shows, namely New York as seen in *Sex and the City*, County Antrim in Northern Ireland as seen in *Game of Thrones*, West Bay in Dorset, England as showcased in *Broadchurch*, Iceland and Malta, which both featured in *Game of Thrones* (*Western Daily Press*, 2015). Other recent tourism-inducing TV shows include *Breaking Bad* (2008–2013), *Downton Abbey* (2010–2015) and *Outlander* (since 2014) (Kelly, 2013; Lennon, 2015; Millward Brown, 2015; Swan, 2016).

Apart from the increase in production quantity and quality, there are a number of additional factors that give TV shows some clear advantages over feature films in terms of their tourism-inducing properties. The strong point of serials is their periodic window of exhibition that enables the viewer to engage with the characters over a longer time frame. In addition, most TV shows portray the featured locations over an extended period, providing a longer exposure and a larger viewership. Consequently, destination marketers have the opportunity to assess the tourism-inducing potential of a TV show during the release of the first season, before investing into a marketing campaign accompanying the following seasons. As the example of *Game of Thrones* illustrates, TV shows also present the opportunity to showcase new locations with every new season, which also enhances the attractiveness of a film destination (Roesch, 2014a).

Disciplinary underpinnings: location placement through fictional film productions

Autonomous place imaging

Place imaging is an integral part of destination marketing (Croy, 2001). Bordelon and Dimanche (2003) distinguish between two different types of place imaging media: official and unofficial imaging media. Official imaging media are actively controlled and implemented by tourism marketers. Unofficial imaging media, on the other hand, are all sources of media that are instilled by an external agent, which Gartner (1993) refers to as autonomous image agents. Feature films and TV shows fall into this category of imaging media, as do novels.

The main challenge with autonomous images is that the affected community usually lacks control over the way the relevant place is portrayed. Should their portrayal be negative, destination marketers usually have very limited resources to counteract. On the other hand, autonomous images have certain advantages over marketer-controlled images. They are, first and foremost, 'free advertising' for the relevant destination, as it is the production company that has to invest in the creation and distribution of the message. Second, film-based autonomous imaging is indirect product placement, also referred to as location placement, and therefore not perceived as advertising. Audiences tend to be more receptive to below-the-line-advertising, which is why Gartner (1993) ascribes feature films and TV shows not only to be of medium to high market penetration, but also to have high credibility. Arguably, the ultimate type of location placement is any placement that connects the fictional places with the real names of the displayed location or destination, as is the case with *Notting Hill* (1999), *Vicky Cristina Barcelona* (2008) or *Midnight in Paris* (2011).

In addition, unofficial media can reach beyond the supposedly idyllic and protected space of the tourist bubble (Judd, 1999) through the use of images that would otherwise be regarded as negative or detrimental. For instance, the city of Bruges in Belgium has heavily marketed itself on the back of the thriller *In Bruges* (2008), which portrays the city as a dark, gritty place and a backdrop for brothels, shootouts and killings. A similar example occurred in the city of Albuquerque in New Mexico, which has been put on the tourist map due to its portrayal in the US hit show *Breaking Bad* (Kelly, 2013).

The evaluation of location placement values presents a significant challenge due to the complexity of the involved methodology. In a study of the regional spin-off effects of the three Swedish *Millennium* films (2009) shot in Stockholm, Lind and Sparre (2011) attempted to calculate the trilogy's direct location placement value by looking at how many times Stockholm is clearly portrayed as a location. Lind then looked at audience figures and multiplied the number of viewing contacts by contact costs. Lind estimates that by December 2011, the three films had generated exposure worth 106 million euros. However, the study does not hold up to scientific scrutiny due to the fact that it was the researcher himself who determined the location placement-relevant scenes, instead of involving neutral evaluators without prior knowledge of the films. In addition, when applying the research methodology of laboratory experiments, a control group has to be in place to validate the results, which was clearly not the case with Lind's evaluation model.

A different approach to quantifying location placement values was commissioned in 2014 by the INTERREG IVC initiative EuroScreen. Based purely on web data mining, the assigned researchers analyzed 238 social media channels and filtered out keywords relevant to locations from the nine feature films and three TV shows that were selected for this study (Human Digital, 2014). Then, the annual exposure value of each case was calculated using a specific formula. While the author agrees with the general conclusion that the examined productions generated millions of euros of exposure to some of the screened locations, there is a major flaw in this method. The analysis was based on a sample derived from social media channels, which excluded all the viewers who either refrain from posting on social media platforms, or simply do not engage with social media at all.

Controlled destination marketing

'If any of you ever make it to London, you can be sure of a very warm welcome'. This promotional tagline was not, as one might expect, created by a British destination marketer. It is one of the opening lines of the feature film *Paddington Bear* (2014) in which a British explorer meets a family of intelligent bears in the jungle of Peru and invites them to his home country. Roughly one year before the release of the movie, the national British destination marketing organization VisitBritain organized an initial meeting with the responsible film studio STUDIOCANAL in order to collaborate on a joint promotion. A few months later, VisitBritain contracted the author to assess the script for its tourism-inducing properties and to conduct a market potential analysis (Roesch, 2014b). VisitBritain then decided to invest into their first ever family-focused destination marketing campaign based on a film, which turned out to be their biggest film tourism social media campaign to date. The promotional activities included bespoke digital content, *Paddington* selfies at selected attractions throughout the UK (Figure 7.1), a global press trip, an international 'money can't buy competition' and, in cooperation with industry partners, the instalment of a *Paddington* trail through London (Croft, 2014). The campaign was rolled out to 31 markets and proved highly successful, not only in terms of exposure but also with regards to activating new visitors: 99.4 per cent of all competition entries were first-time contacts (Wilkinson, 2015).

Figure 7.1 Paddington selfies in front of Hadrian's Wall and Stonehenge.

Source: © P&Co. Ltd. 2017.

The entire process from the initial script assessment to the campaign launch took about a year. This proved to be an ideal time frame both for creating the campaign and also to establish a trusting relationship between VisitBritain and STUDIOCANAL. This in turn convinced the production company to transfer a number of intellectual property assets to VisitBritain, including the use of film stills, the use of the trailer and getting statements from cast and crew about London as a tourist destination.

A considerable wave of enthusiasm went through the Austrian state of Tyrol in 2014 when rumours were confirmed that a number of lengthy scenes for the Bond movie *Spectre* (2015) were to be filmed in the region. Filming started in the winter of 2014/2015, and spending on accommodation, catering, transport, equipment and employment of local talent amounted to 8.9 million euros. The shooting also generated a considerable amount of positive press for the region, with the highlight being an international photo shoot with some of the main actors, including Daniel Craig. The resulting pictures were disseminated around the world (Köck, 2015).

Although the responsible film commission Cine Tirol – which is a subdivision of Tyrol's destination marketing organization Tirol Werbung – was aware of the tourism-inducing opportunities presented by the movie, the production company's strict copyright regulations prohibited the use of any film-related intellectual property. The way forward was to implement a somewhat generic campaign headed by the slogan 'Tirol, a great cinematic landscape'.[1] The aim of the campaign was not so much to link Tyrol to James Bond but to showcase the grandeur of Tyrol's alpine setting as a cinematic winter wonderland (Egger, 2016). The overall advertising value equivalency (AVE) for the campaign amounted to 8.4 million euros, resulting in a return-on-investment AVE factor of 1 to 8.3 (Tirol Werbung GmbH, 2016). Interestingly enough, the regional tourism organization of Ötztal/Sölden, the main location of the Tyrol shoot, managed to secure the permission to use the Bond logo, a number of film stills and the trailer on a dedicated website[2] (Figure 7.2). For the responsible destination manager, the main impetus for investing in a Bond-focused tourism campaign was to generate destination awareness in China.[3]

Figure 7.2 Website dedicated to the shooting location of the James Bond film *Spectre* in Sölden, Tyrol.
Source: © Tourismusverband Ötztal Tourismus.

In an unprecedented move, Tyrol's Mexican counterparts offered a sum of 20 million US dollars to the filmmakers in order for them to make certain adjustments to the script and the casting decisions so that the film location of Mexico City would be portrayed in a more positive light than originally intended (Allen, 2015). The example of Bond and Mexico is extreme, yet it illustrates the worldwide competition by countries and regions for film productions and their subsequent PR effects.

Film locations as tourist attractions

In their function as tourist attractions, film locations can be categorized in different ways. Some locations represent natural or man-made features with a pre-existing attraction status. An example would be Kakadu National Park in Australia. The park profited enormously from its exposure in the feature film *Crocodile Dundee* (1986). Yet, it had already been an established major tourism site long before the film's release (Nelson, 2005).

Some places gain attraction status solely due to their representation in fictional film productions. Again, these places can be man-made or natural features. Arguably, no tourist would normally seek out the location of Mount Sunday, which is just a rocky outcrop in an alpine valley in central Canterbury on New Zealand's South Island. But since it featured in *The Lord of the Rings – The Two Towers* (2002), it has acquired meaning and status for tourists. Other film locations have become tourist attractions in their own right due to the remains of film sets or set parts, as the popular *Hobbiton* film set in New Zealand illustrates.

An alternative discussion of film locations is offered by Robinson's (2002) threefold spatial concept of literary places, which distinguishes fantasy lands, disguised places and real places. Adapted to the world of film locations, the term fantasy land describes a location that is portrayed as a non-existent, mythical land on screen. An example would be the fictional desert planet of Tatooine in the *Star Wars* movies. The film location tourist is 'invited' into the self-contained fantasy world of Tatooine instead of the real-world location of Tunisia. Film tourism can also occur with film productions that are entirely set in other-worldly settings, as was the case with Disney's animated film *Frozen* (2014). The fictional kingdom of Arendelle is loosely based on Norwegian landscapes, yet the locations are computer-generated. Despite this, international visitor arrivals to Norway were on the rise after its release (Beaumont-Thomas, 2014).

Disguised film locations come in two forms. One form is created when a location is used for the actual filming, but its geographic position is portrayed differently in the film. For instance, *The Last Samurai* (2003) was partly filmed at Mount Taranaki in New Zealand, which stands in for Mount Fujiyama in Japan. The second form comes into being when the location that attracts visitors is based on an existing place, but was in fact filmed elsewhere. This is the case with the production of *The Light Between Oceans* (2016), based on a novel by M. L. Stedman. Although the story is set in coastal Western Australia, most scenes were filmed in the South Island of New Zealand.

Finally, real places describe locations that are real-life settings in the storyline. Research shows that the role of places in film, meaning their importance for the storyline, as well as their connection to characters, can indeed impact on the attractiveness of the involved locations (Roesch, 2007, 2009). In saying that, the physical and visual properties of locations are equally important for tourists who need a focal point towards which they can direct their gaze. Furthermore, a high recognition value adds significantly to the on-site experience. Locations also need to be accessible, both in terms of physical and budget constraints.

In the experience of the author, the most attractive locations are places that feature a sacred sight – a place with a filmic cult status where the imaginary and the real morph into one. One *Star Wars* tourist at a Tunisian location put his experience of being at a sacred sight into words

(Roesch, 2007, p. 238): 'I did experience Luke Skywalker at the igloo with the sunset. I was living that moment.'

Methodology: case study inquiry – hotspots of television tourism

Breaking Bad – Albuquerque's dark tourism

With an IMDb rating of 9.5 out of 10, 120 awards and 197 award nominations, *Breaking Bad* (2008–2013) is one of the most critically acclaimed TV shows of all time.[4] The story is about the high school chemistry teacher Walter White who is diagnosed with terminal lung cancer. In a desperate move to provide financial security for his family, he starts to manufacture and sell methamphetamine, which ultimately leads to a lot of dead bodies around his home town of Albuquerque in New Mexico. Despite the brutality, fans loved the show and flocked to the locations in their hundreds in order to follow Walter's footsteps, making *Breaking Bad* location visits a prime example of dark tourism. Rojek (1993) refers to such places as 'black spots', which usually represent sites of atrocity, such as graves, massacre or accident sites.

Despite its gritty content, the tourism industry in Albuquerque has embraced the opportunity to showcase the city and the region on the back of the show. The Albuquerque Convention and Visitors Bureau set up a web page dedicated to the show that not only displays the most iconic locations but also showcases the entire range of film-related experiences on offer.[5] The pick of the bunch are the guided location tours with ABQ Trolley Co. who take visitors on a three-hour long tour to 13 different locations (Figure 7.3), including a lunch stop at the infamous money-laundering fast food diner 'Los Pollos Hermanos', aka the real-life 'Twisters Grill'. Themed culinary treats are also on offer, including 'Blue Sky' donuts from Rebel Donuts, film-inspired boutique beers at Marble Brewery, and a 'Breaking Blue' cocktail at Irish bar O'Niell's.

Figure 7.3   *Breaking Bad* film location guides, ABQ Trolley Company.
Source: ©Leigh Green.

You can buy look-a-like methamphetamine crystals from the Candy Lady, participate in 'cooking classes' with Urban Fresh Cosmetics to manufacture your own 'Bathing Bad' bath salt, or even book a *Breaking Bad*-inspired hotel package.

Breaking Bad features a number of locations predestined for tourism as there are strong focal points, such as Walter White's private residence. Many locations possess high recognition values and are closely tied to the storyline and the characters' actions. These are ideal prerequisites for

Figure 7.4   Scene framing at two *Breaking Bad* locations.
Source: © Tiia Öhman & Satu Walden/Fangirl Quest.

film tourism and allow for a wide range of on-site actions, in particular scene framing (Figure 7.4), costumed posing and scene re-enactments. The most popular scene recreation, whether in costume or not, is to pose for photos in front of the Los Pollos Hermanos location (Herron, 2016).

According to ABQ Trolley Company's co-founder and *Breaking Bad* location tour guide Jesse Herron, the majority of their clients come to Albuquerque because of the film locations. What is more, for many of the international participants, it's their first visit to the United States (Herron, 2016). Herron also told the author that '[l]ast season we even had a couple from China who were doing a *Breaking Bad*-themed honeymoon in Albuquerque' (ibid.).

Reportedly, this influx of visitors to certain locales have caused some minor problems, in particular at the location of Walter White's house where fans are now urged to keep a polite distance and respect the owners' privacy. Vince Gilligan, the mastermind behind the show himself, had to address fanatics asking them to stop throwing pizzas on top of the roof of the garage of the White residence – which they did because they wanted to recreate a particular scene (Dixon, 2015). Although the city's Convention and Visitors Bureau was initially relatively passive with regards to the growing success of the show, it has made the responsible destination managers aware of the opportunity to promote Albuquerque. However, despite the overwhelming success of *Breaking Bad* for Albuquerque's tourism industry, the numbers of film fans flocking to the city are now well and truly in decline (Herron, 2016).

Downton Abbey and Highclere Castle

In April 2016, the website of Highclere Castle, the main location of the British TV drama show *Downton Abbey* (2010–2015), advertised the castle's new mobile phone app with the tagline: 'Explore the real Downton Abbey'.[6] As in many other related cases, the ambivalent status of a film location as both a real and an imaginary place poses more of a challenge to the involved site managers, rather than to the tourists themselves. The tourists are generally very aware of the spatial and temporal attributes of film locations and are indeed capable of moving in and out of the two worlds (Roesch, 2007, 2009). Nevertheless, it requires a conscious effort to do so.

The management of Highclere Castle clearly emphasizes the real history of the estate wherever possible: 'There has been continued interest because of *Downton Abbey* and we are doing our best to convert the *Downton* audience worldwide into a Highclere audience' (Popplewell, 2016). Highclere Castle does not disclose visitor numbers but a documentary about the castle produced in 2012 states that Highclere had around 60,000 visitors that year (Pioneer Film & Television Productions Limited, 2012). According to Lewis Swan, the director of Brit Movie Tours, visitor numbers to the location skyrocketed after the release of the second season but in his opinion, current demand has plateaued and looks to be on the decline (Swan, 2016). However, with only a limited number of tickets available to view the castle every year, it's still likely that demand will outgrow supply for many more years to come. Val Blackburn, Brit Movie Tours' main film location guide for Downton Abbey tours estimates that between 75 per cent and 90 per cent of all visitors to Highclere are film-induced tourists (Blackburn, 2016).

As a general visitor attraction, Highclere castle offers a range of different visitor experiences and services. At the heart is the tour through a number of representative rooms, some of which house special exhibitions. London-based company Brit Movie Tours offers day tours to various *Downton Abbey* locations, including a visit to Highclere Castle. As the tickets issued by the castle management are very limited, the tour company only offered two bus tours in 2016. The majority of film tourists to Highclere Castle are affluent women between 40 and 60 years of age, generally hailing from the UK, USA, Canada, Australia and New Zealand. In terms of on-site performances, *Downton Abbey* location tourists are 'much more sober and conservative unlike other tours. People would just want a regular picture at the location' (Blackburn, 2016).

Regardless of the different expectations the location tourists have of their visit, the no-photo policy inside the state rooms of the castle poses a significant drawback for visitors. Film location tourists want to bring some of the magic back home and photographs are the most important mementos to record the essence of their experience (Roesch, 2007). Nor can film fans purchase film-related merchandise at Highclere Castle (Blackburn, 2016). However, the nearby town of Bampton, which prominently features in the show as Downton village, has truly made the most of its new claim to fame. Some locals offer guided location tours, Bampton's art gallery put on a temporary exhibition of costumes from the show and the community archive sells relevant memorabilia in its shop. All these efforts have resulted in an exponential increase in film-induced visitors to the village: In 2015, over 27,000 visitors came into the archive shop alone (Gottelier, 2016).

Northern Ireland is *Game of Thrones* territory

Surely, any destination promoting itself with the tagline 'Views to die horribly for' would lose its appeal in a matter of days. Not so in Northern Ireland where visitors are encouraged to 'invade with friends and family this summer'. The *Game of Thrones* social media campaign carried out by Tourism Ireland in 2014 and 2015 turned fact into fiction by selling Northern Ireland as the fantasy land of Westeros. Digital signposts were created and superimposed over selected locations, pointing the way to the fictional icons from the TV show. Over the course of 14 weeks in 2015, Tourism Ireland opened the curtain between the worlds by creating *Game of Thrones*-specific stunts at a number of public places throughout the country: the footprints of a giant appeared at the popular beach Portstewart Strand, a market stall in Belfast sold dragon eggs (which were remote-controlled and would move upon contact with customers) and in front of Belfast's city hall, two three-eyed animatronic ravens were perched on a bench. Tourism Ireland achieved over 4.5 million Facebook video views with these activities and an engagement rate of 40 per cent. The PR value of the entire campaign amounted to 13 million euros (Tourism Ireland, 2015). In mid-March 2016, Northern Ireland Screen launched the first official *Game of Thrones* location app, developed in conjunction with the film studio HBO.

Many of the TV show's fans are fanatics and Northern Ireland's tourism industry recognized the value in this. Between 2013 and 2015, 20 new businesses sprung up around *Game of Thrones*-based tourism products. Tourists can choose between various guided location tours, food banquets, horseback riding and archery (Lightbody & Webb, 2015). When the author travelled around the country to assess the tourism potential for Tourism Northern Ireland in November 2015, it became immediately evident that the essential pre-requisites for a long-lasting film tourism effect are in place. The country features over 20 locations, all of which have their own distinct natural or man-made focal points. The recognition value of most locations is very high and the majority are accessible to the public. There are plenty of scene-framing opportunities and the tourism industry is doing its part to enhance other on-site performances, in particular costumed posing (Roesch, 2015). For instance, many of the commercial location tour operators provide *Game of Thrones*-specific props and costumes for the participants to wear or use (Figure 7.5).

Film location tourists seek a highly emotional on-site experience. Being part of a group of like-minded people during a guided location tour provides a maximum of immersion and involvement, as opposed to self-guided options such as movie maps, guidebooks or apps

Figure 7.5 Costumed posing at *Game of Thrones* locations in Northern Ireland.
Source: © Game of Thrones Tours Ltd.

(Roesch, 2007, 2009). The tour guide is tasked with creating a cinematic sense of place, which can be achieved in a number of ways. First-hand interpretation describes the technique of leading tour participants through the film scenes by re-enactment where the guide actually acts out the different roles of the involved characters, cites the relevant dialogue lines and physically

Figure 7.6 The Dark Hedges – a sacred sight for *Game of Thrones* fans. Location photograph (left); illustration depicting the relevant film scene (right).

Source: © Courtesy of David Cleland (left); © Erich Roesch for the Northern Ireland Tourist Board (right).

imitates the action. The tour guide also needs to provide insider stories around the filming and assist with scene-framing opportunities. The latter is particularly important at locations that contain an iconic focal point, which is the case at the site of the so-called Dark Hedges. The location features only for a few seconds in the show, without any prolonged involvement of any of the main characters. Yet, it has become a pilgrimage site for *Game of Thrones* fans, due to its perfect recognition value and its attractive features (Figure 7.6).

In terms of the proposed longevity of the *Game of Thrones* effect, a survey among Northern Ireland-based tourism businesses affirmed that the TV show had a significant impact on revenue for 14 per cent of the interviewed stakeholders, and a slight impact on revenue for another 23 per cent. In addition, 86 per cent of businesses are of the opinion that the TV show presents a clear competitive advantage over other destinations (Millward Brown, 2015). With the right long-term strategy in place and an emphasis on the development of new location products and attractions, *Game of Thrones* might well be capable of increasing international visitor arrivals to Northern Ireland by 2 per cent to 3 per cent annually over the next five years.

Implications for popular culture tourism

The fierce competition in international tourism forces destinations to look for innovative marketing strategies. Popular culture tourism, and film tourism in particular, can provide unique opportunities to stand out from the crowd. No two films or TV shows are alike, which provides the portrayed destinations with a clear unique sales position. In particular, the growing number of high-quality TV productions enables a growing number of regions around the world to profit from film-induced spin-off effects.

In July 2016, the author conducted an online survey with international film commissioners on the current and future market potential of film tourism,[7] with the support of the Association of Film Commissioners International (AFCI). The survey link went out to the organization's 267 members out of which 47 valid responses were received. Some 85 per cent of film commissioners are of the opinion that film tourism will increase within the next ten years, either significantly (44 per cent) or slightly (41 per cent). Furthermore, 60 per cent of film commissioners estimate that TV shows will dominate the future market in film tourism. Accordingly, 56 per cent of film commissions state that they currently invest into film tourism opportunities, 58 per cent have done so in the past five years. Perhaps more importantly, 97 per cent intend to allocate funds to film tourism within the next five years, which seems surprising given the fact that the core business of film commissions is to increase screen production, not tourism. In the experience of the author, the reason for this is due to the fact that many tourism bodies are either not flexible enough to incorporate film tourism opportunities in their marketing portfolio, in particular on relative short notice, or they are simply not aware or interested.

We might move into the golden age of film tourism but destinations will have to professionalize themselves in this segment in order to fulfil the high expectations held by tourists. The tourism industry has to create high-quality location experiences so that film fans can experience the imaginary world of their beloved TV shows or movie whilst on location. The author urges the industry to fully recognize that TV shows and movies are expressions of popular culture with, quite literally, a global following.

Notes

1 In German, the original slogan is 'Tirol ist großes Kino'.
2 See http://andaction.soelden.com/de.

3 From personal communication, January 2016.
4 See www.imdb.com/title/tt0903747/.
5 See www.visitalbuquerque.org/albuquerque/film-tourism/breaking-bad.
6 See www.highclerecastle.co.uk.
7 Including movies and TV shows.

References

Allen, N. (2015). James Bond's $20 million reason to love Mexico. Retrieved 13 March 2016, from www.telegraph.co.uk/culture/film/jamesbond/11471324/James-Bonds-20-million-reason-to-love-Mexico.html

Beaumont-Thomas, B. (2014). Disney's Frozen gives boost to Norwegian tourism. Retrieved 11 April 2016, from www.theguardian.com/film/2014/jun/06/disney-frozen-boost-norwegian-Tourism

Blackburn, V. (2016). Brit movie tours and Downton Abbey. Skype communication. April 2016.

Bordelon, B. & Dimanche, F. (2003). The relationship between motion pictures and tourists' expectations of a travel destination. *Travel and Tourism Research Association, 34th Annual Conference Proceedings St. Louis*, n.p.

Croft, J. (2014). *Paddington is Great Britain* [PowerPoint slides]. Presentation at the 2014 EuroScreen conference in London, November 2014. Received via email.

Croy, G. (2001). The ideal spot: The appraisive component of destination image. In Holland, P., Stephenson, F. & Wearing, A. (Eds.), *Geography: A spatial odyssey* (pp. 412–418). Dunedin, New Zealand: Proceedings of the Third Joint Conference of the New Zealand Geographical Society and the Institute of Australian Geographers. Department of Geography, University of Otago.

Dixon, K. (2015). *Better call Saul insider podcast*. Retrieved 12 April 2016, from www.youtube.com/watch?v=flsGuajqkIY

Egger, K. (2016). Marketing campaign 'Tirol ist großes Kino'. Email communication.

Erlichman, J. (2016). The 'golden age of TV' has a lot of people worried – here's why. Retrieved 8 April 2016, from http://fortune.com/2016/01/18/golden-age-tv-peak

Finnigan, N. (2009). *Film tourism in Scotland* [PowerPoint slides]. Presentation at the 2009 Mixed Reality Conference in Ystad, Sweden. Received via email.

Fletcher, H. (2015). *Hobbit* films spur tourism surge. Retrieved 14 April 2016, from www.nzherald.co.nz/business/news/article.cfm?c_id=3&objectid=11543142

Gartner, W. (1993). Image formation process. *Journal of Travel and Tourism Marketing*, 2(2/3), 191–215.

Gottelier, N. (2016). *Downton Abbey* tourism in Bampton. Email communication.

Henry-Biabaud, O. (2015). *Keynote-panel: Film tourism: coincidence or strategy?* [PowerPoint slides]. Keynote presentation at the ITB Berlin 2015, Germany. Received via email.

Herron, J. (2016). Questions about *Breaking Bad* location tourism. Email communication.

Human Digital (2014). *Quantifying location placement value* [PowerPoint slides]. Presentation at the 2014 EuroScreen Conference held in London. Received via email.

Judd, D. R. (1999). Constructing the tourist bubble. In Judd, D. R. & Fainstein, S. S. (Eds.), *The tourist city* (pp. 35–53). New Haven and London: Yale University Press.

Kelly, S. (2013). The *Breaking Bad* tours driving a tourist boom in Albuquerque. Retrieved 19 November 2015, from www.theguardian.com/travel/2013/aug/11/breaking-bad-tour-albuquerque

Köck, J. (2015). *James Bond in Tirol*. Internal document. Innsbruck, Austria: Cine Tirol Film Commission.

Lennon, H. (2015). Scots tourism feels 'Outlander effect' of hit TV show. Retrieved 13 April 2016, from www.scotsman.com/heritage/people-places/scots-tourism-feels-outlander-effect-of-hit-tv-show-1-3933138

Lightbody, R. & Webb, J. (2015). *Screen tourism: Maximising the opportunity* [PowerPoint slides]. Unpublished presentation by Northern Ireland Tourism. Received via email.

Lind, J., & Sparre, M. (2011). *The Millennium Report: Economic impact and exposure value for the Stockholm Region in the Swedish Millennium features films*. Stockholm: Cloudberrry Communications.

Millward Brown (2010). Visitor attitudes survey main markets 2010. Retrieved 18 April 2015, from www.failteireland.ie/FailteIreland/media/WebsiteStructure/Documents/3_Research_Insights/3_General_SurveysReports/2010_Main_Markets.pdf?ext=.pdf

Millward Brown (2015). Tourism industry barometer: Additional questions – *Game of Thrones*. Received from Tourism Northern Ireland via email.

Nelson, M. (2005). Visitor numbers to Kakadu National Park, Australia. Received via email.

Olsberg/SPI (2015). *Quantifying Film and Television Tourism in England*. Report for Creative England in association with VisitEngland. London: Olsberg/SPI.

Pioneer Film & Television Productions Limited. (2012). *Secrets of Highclere Castle*. Documentary.

Popplewell, A. (2016). The case of Highclere and *Downton Abbey*. Email communication.

Renner, K.-H. (2016). Das goldene Zeitalter des globalen Fernsehens. Retrieved 19 March 2016, from www.handelsblatt.com/unternehmen/it-medien/berlinale-das-goldene-zeitalter-des-globalen-fernsehens/12961610.html

Robinson, M. (2002). Between and beyond the pages: Literature–tourism relationships. In Andersen, H.-C. & Robinson, M. (Eds.), *Literature and tourism: Reading and writing tourism texts* (pp. 39–79). New York: Continuum.

Roesch, S. (2007). *There and back again: Comparative case studies of film location tourists' on-site behaviour and experiences* (Doctoral dissertation, University of Otago, New Zealand).

Roesch, S. (2009). *The experiences of film location tourists*. London: Channel View Publications.

Roesch, S. (2014a). *The golden age of screen-based destination marketing* [PowerPoint slides]. Presentation at the AFCI Locations Show in Los Angeles, April 2014.

Roesch, S. (2014b). *Assessing the film tourism potential of the upcoming feature film Paddington Bear for Great Britain*. Assessment report commissioned by VisitBritain, March 2014.

Roesch, S. (2015). *Game of Thrones visitor experiences in Northern Ireland – Assessment Report*. Internal report for Tourism Northern Ireland.

Rojek, C. (1993). *Ways of escape: Modern transformations in leisure and travel*. Lanham, MA: Rowman & Littlefield.

Röscheisen, T. (2013). Das Goldene Zeitalter – Wie lange noch? Retrieved 19 March 2016, from http://drama-blog.de/das-goldene-Zeitalter

Swan, L. (2016). Brit movie tours and *Downton Abbey*. Email communication. April 2016.

Tenbrock N. (2005). *Film und Tourismus. Zusammenhänge zwischen Film und Tourismus unter besonderer Berücksichtigung der Auswirkungen der Herr der Ringe-Filme auf den Tourismus in Neuseeland* (Master's Thesis, Fachhochschule Gelsenkirchen, Germany).

Tirol Werbung GmbH. (2016). *Tirol ist großes Kino. Ein Drehort für Action, Drama, Abenteuer. Dokumentation*. Innsbruck: Tirol Werbung GmbH.

Tourism Ireland. (2015). Jump into Northern Ireland, *Game of Thrones* territory [video clip]. Unpublished campaign evaluation video, received via email.

Tourism New Zealand. (2003). *Lord of the Rings market research summary report*. Wellington, NZ: Tourism New Zealand.

Tourism New Zealand. (2014). *Growth and the impact of the Hobbit* [PowerPoint slides]. Received via email.

Western Daily Press. (2015). TV and film like *Game of Thrones* and *Broadchurch* see New Zealand and Dorset booming in popularity. Retrieved 19 March 2016, from www.westerndailypress.co.uk/TV-film-like-Game-Thrones-Broadchurch-New-</b>Zealand/story-26743011-detail/story.html

Wilkinson, E. (2015). *Planning the campaign* [PowerPoint slides]. Presentation at the AFCI Cineposium 2015 in Barcelona.

8

IMAGINING THE MEDIEVAL IN THE MODERN WORLD

Film, fantasy and heritage

Jennifer Laing and Warwick Frost

Setting the scene

In a 2014 episode of the BBC television series *Doctor Who*, the time-travelling Doctor (Peter Capaldi) asks his companion Clara (Jenna Coleman) where she would most like to go. 'Your choice,' he asks, 'Wherever. Whenever. Anywhere in time and space.' Clara thinks for a moment. 'There is someone that I've always wanted to meet . . . it's Robin Hood,' she responds. 'I love that story. I've always loved it. Ever since I was little.' The story of the medieval Robin Hood has been a part of her life since childhood.

Modern societies often imagine their heritage in terms of a past 'golden age'. This is a period not only valorized as shaping national identity, but one that is imagined as better than the present. While not as technologically advanced as today, this past golden age is lauded for having better values, morals, customs and traditions. Looking backwards at this seemingly utopian time, many see it as the antidote for the ills of modernity, if only – it is imagined – we could return to the past (Laing & Frost, 2012; Lowenthal, 1985, 1998). Of the many candidates for this golden age, it is the *medieval period* that has particularly captured the public's imagination; a historical epoch that has been reinterpreted and repackaged for modern audiences through media representations and tourism experiences.

As Lowenthal has observed, if the past is a foreign country, then it's 'a foreign country with a booming tourist trade' (1985, p. xvii). The vast array of medieval tourist experiences and attractions include:

- Medieval old towns with historic streetscapes, historic gems where economic change has preserved areas from development (Ashworth & Tunbridge, 2000). These include Toledo, Cordoba, Sighisoara, Bruges, Siena and York.
- Castles, such as the Tower of London, Warwick and Cardiff.
- Gothic cathedrals, including Notre Dame (Paris), Reims, Lincoln, Canterbury and York.
- Collections of preserved medieval buildings, including Spon End in Coventry and the Weald and Downland Open Air Museum in Kent.
- Themed visitor attractions such as the Canterbury Tales in Canterbury.
- Historical re-enactments, such as the annual re-enactment of the Battle of Hastings (Frost & Laing, 2013).

- Exhibitions, such as those for the 800th anniversary of the Magna Carta.
- Other medieval events, including Renaissance fairs and tournament re-enactments.
- Medieval dishes and banqueting (Mykletun & Gyimóthy, 2010; Robinson & Clifford, 2012).
- Faux medieval reconstructions. An intriguing example is the Castello di Amarosi in the Napa Valley of California. Advertised as an 'authentic' thirteenth-century Tuscan castle, it attracts in excess of 500,000 visitors per year.

We are engaged in a research project to examine how the media has shaped modern views and understandings of the medieval period and accordingly has influenced tourism. In this chapter, we consider two case studies of medieval myths as imagined through the media. These are King Arthur and Robin Hood. We have chosen these two case studies as they continue to be reinterpreted and repackaged in the twenty-first century, most notably through the BBC television series *Merlin* (2008–2013) and *Robin Hood* (2006–2009). The impact of these successful media productions was illustrated to us during fieldwork at the re-enactment of the Battle of Hastings in 2011. We spoke with a number of parents who explained that their young children were fans of *Merlin* and this was the key factor in attending this event. *Merlin* and *Robin Hood* are examples of a vast array of cultural productions over time; that constantly re-tell these stories, shaping them for modern concerns and rituals, while still referring to the tropes and archetypes developed in earlier versions. It is this inter-textual development of these stories and their meanings that we focus on in these case studies. The chapter then concludes with discussion of the implications of these findings for popular culture tourism.

Disciplinary underpinnings: media representations and meanings

King Arthur

The King Arthur story is so ingrained in Western culture, even though its origins are shrouded, that there are elements that we anticipate to be present in any retelling of the story (Orange & Laviolette, 2010). We expect an idealistic but ultimately doomed king (Arthur); his beautiful but fickle wife (Guinevere) and his trusted friend (Lancelot), who betray him by falling in love; their Edenic capital (Camelot); the wise old wizard who counsels the king (Merlin); the Round Table; a magical sword that symbolizes sovereignty over the kingdom (Excalibur); and a quest (the Holy Grail). This underlying narrative conforms to Campbell's (1949) *Hero's Journey*, with a call to adventure (taking up the sword); trials and temptations, often by women representing the archetype of a temptress (Morgan le Fay, Guinevere) and betrayal (Lancelot, Mordred); a supernatural guide (Merlin) and the services of Excalibur; the seeking of a boon or reward (the ideal of Camelot, the Grail); and an ending to the story where the hero cannot re-integrate into society, illustrated by Arthur's defeat in battle and the journey to Avalon. These various elements combine to make the story immensely satisfying, but are also flexible enough to be reinterpreted for a new generation.

While we have no conclusive proof that Arthur existed, several theories have been put forward to explain how the myth originally developed. Lucius Artorius Castus, an officer of the Roman army in Britain in the second century AD, is one contender. Others place Arthur in the Dark Ages, around the fifth and sixth centuries AD (Higham 2002; Matthews & Matthews, 2008). Regardless of the genealogy of Arthur, several seminal texts form the 'literary roots' of the myth (Orange & Laviolette, 2010, p. 89). The first is Geoffrey of Monmouth's *Historia Regum Britanniae* (*History of the Kings of Britain*), dating from around 1140, a chronicle of monarchy that includes Arthur, the son of Uther Pendragon, born at Tintagel in Cornwall and married to Guinevere. It provided the kings of England with 'a predecessor of heroic size, a great pan-British king' (Higham, 2002, p. 223).

The tales spread abroad, with French and German writers inspired by the Arthur narrative, notably Chrétien de Troyes, who may have heard the stories from travelling bards from Britain. Little is known about him, other than his five Arthurian romances, which brought to the fore themes such as chivalry and courtly love, and introduced Sir Lancelot and the Grail into the narrative (Matthews & Matthews, 2008). Another famous creator of Arthurian romances was Sir Thomas Malory, who wrote the poem *Le Morte D'Arthur* (The Death of Arthur) in 1485. It 'is still the source from which most of what we commonly know about Arthur has been derived' (Matthews & Matthews, 2008, p. 207). The timing of the poem was auspicious, given the rise of the Tudor dynasty to the English throne after the Battle of Bosworth Field and the importance they placed on establishing their bona fides to rule, including their genetic links to Arthur (Higham, 2002). Henry VII, the first Tudor king, even named his first-born Arthur, although the boy died before he could inherit the throne, which then fell to his younger brother, the infamous Henry VIII.

There was a revival of interest in King Arthur in the Victorian era, especially 'the figure of the knight in shining armour' (Bryden, 2011, p. 30). A notable example is the work of Alfred, Lord Tennyson, admired by both Queen Victoria and her husband Prince Albert, who wrote the poem *Morte D'Arthur* (1842) and a cycle of poems *Idylls of the King* (1859–1885) (Higham, 2002; Matthews & Matthews, 2008). The 1862 edition was dedicated to Albert, as 'my king's ideal knight' (Bryden, 2011, p. 31). The royal couple had earlier demonstrated their personal interest in the medieval period, when they dressed as the fourteenth-century King Edward III and Queen Phillippa in 1842 for a costume ball held at Buckingham Palace, commemorated in a painting by Landseer.

The Tennyson poems, along with the earlier work of Malory, further inspired the Pre-Raphaelites, a group of English artists and poets who were enamoured by all things medieval, including the fresco paintings, which they admired for their brilliant colour and lack of artifice. Arthurian-themed paintings by members of the Pre-Raphaelite Brotherhood include *Queen Guinevere* (1858) by William Morris and *The Lady of Shalott* (1888) by John William Waterhouse. This in turn had an impact on the 'iconography of Arthurian legends' (Matthews & Matthews, 2008, p. 247), conjuring up an image of willowy women with magnificent long tresses, often red-gold, and loosely flowing garments; the famous Pre-Raphaelite beauty (Bryden, 2011). The enthusiastic embracing of Arthurian chivalry was satirized by the American novelist Mark Twain in *A Connecticut Yankee in King Arthur's Court* (1889). In contemporary times, the *steampunk* sub-culture, based on an imaginary world where 'Victorian technology still holds sway' (Frost & Laing, 2014, p. 177) also plays with the nineteenth-century predilection for Arthur. For example, Jeter's novel *Morlock Night* (1979), with a plot that revolves around the peril faced by Victorian London from the Morlocks (a nod to H. G. Wells' *The Time Machine*) features Arthur and Merlin as key characters who regularly return to help Britain in its time of need.

In the 1960s, Arthurian myth was 'used to promote a particular cult of the White House' (Higham, 2002, p. 1). What higher praise could be bestowed on the handsome young President John F. Kennedy and his elegant wife Jacqueline, than to associate their administration with Camelot? It was actually Jacqueline who drew the famous comparison, in an interview with *LIFE* magazine after the assassination of her husband. Stratford (2013) argues that the mythical association is unhelpful, obscuring the real story 'of a weak and cuckolded leader'. Mrs Kennedy was apparently inspired by the Lerner and Loewe musical, *Camelot* (Stratford, 2013), which opened in 1960 on Broadway and was filmed in 1967. The Oscar-winning costumes for *Camelot* by John Truscott skilfully interpreted medieval dress for a modern generation, and influenced wedding dress design in particular.

Different directors and screenwriters have put their own stamp on the story, whether for television or the cinema, with just a few exemplars covered here. Hollywood's *Knights of the Round Table* (1953) depicts 'Modred' (*sic*), played by Stanley Baker, as Morgan Le Fay's lover, rather than her son, while Guinevere is played by a bombshell (Ava Gardner). Disney also came on board with *The Sword in the Stone* (1963), based on the book of the same name by T. H. White (1937). This tells the story of the young Arthur, then known as Wart, who pulls Excalibur out of a stone, thus fulfilling his destiny to be king. Much of the plot deals with the relationship with Merlin and his training of the king-to-be. The quirkiest version, poking fun at the knight in shining armour, is undoubtedly *Monty Python and the Holy Grail* (1975), with a famous fight scene featuring the Black Knight ending up with every one of his limbs cut off ('just a flesh wound!').

Recent versions are equally divergent in terms of how they deal with the myth. In John Boorman's *Excalibur* (1981), Nicol Williamson's Merlin and Helen Mirren's Morgana take centre stage. This is contrasted with *First Knight* (1995), which focuses on Lancelot (Richard Gere), complete with American accent, and his romance with Guinevere. It stars former James Bond star Sean Connery as the cuckolded Arthur, complete with a Scottish brogue. The TV miniseries *The Mists of Avalon* (2001), based on the 1983 novel written by Marion Zimmer Bradley, can perhaps be labelled a feminist version of the Arthur myth, in that it largely deals with Arthur's mother Igraine, his aunt Viviane, the Lady of the Lake and his half-sister Morgaine. In contrast, Jerry Bruckheimer's *King Arthur* (2004) sets the story in Ancient Britain at the time of the Roman occupation and women are largely sidelined or objectified in their clothing, including Keira Knightley as a warrior teenage Guinevere in leather with a bare midriff. She is not romantically interested in Lancelot, and her romance with Arthur is underplayed. The crescendo of the plot involves the battle scenes. A fifth, released in 2017, is *Knights of the Roundtable: King Arthur*, directed by Guy Ritchie, with a focus on the fight scenes, but also the comic potential of the plot.

The TV series *Merlin* deserves to be singled out for pitching the tale firmly at youth, yet providing nuances that can only be appreciated by those who understand 'Merlin's medieval antecedents' (Sherman, 2015, p. 82). Like *Smallville* (2001–2011) reinterpreting Superman, *Merlin* takes us back in time to the youthful days of a hero, in this case not only making Merlin a teenager but the same age as Arthur. Magic plays a big part in the story, with Merlin (Colin Morgan) forced to hide his powers to avoid the wrath of King Uther Pendragon (Anthony Head). Uther has outlawed the practice of magic from Camelot, and thus Merlin, like Clark Kent, must pretend to be a likeable bumbler, and hide his true self. Even Arthur is kept in the dark until the final episode.

The series is also notable for several innovations. It cast non Anglo-Saxon actors in leading roles, 'raising issues of race extradiegetically with the audience' (Sherman, 2015, p. 93). The most prominent example is the English bi-racial actress Angel Coulby as Guinevere (Gwen). This echoes the casting of Guy Ritchie's *Knights of the Roundtable: King Arthur* (2017), which has Beninese-American actor Djimon Hounsou as Sir Bedivere. Class is also explored through the story (Sherman, 2015) with Gwen as Morgana's serving maid rather than a noble-woman or princess. She ends up marrying Arthur by the end of the series, in a Cinderella-like twist. The ending is also memorable. After Arthur's death, we see Merlin as an old man, the familiar wizard with a grey beard. He is waiting for Arthur's return as prophesied by the dragon, but there is no hint as to when that might happen. Audiences are left with the fantasy that Arthur will come again in modern times when he is needed, just like Jeter's novel.

Robin Hood

Robin Hood epitomizes the outlaw myth. Found across many time periods and countries, stories of the good outlaw are another variant on the universal myth of the hero's journey (Campbell, 1949). As an early exemplar, Robin Hood sets up the outlaw archetype. Emerging when there is corruption and oppression and the rule of law has failed, the outlaw takes the paradoxical path of going outside the law to bring a return to justice and order (Frost, 2006; Frost & Laing, 2015; Kooistra, 1989; Seal, 1996). In doing so, the good outlaw is 'a symbol of social and political discontent, and this is what separates them from common robbers and murderers' (Kooistra, 1989, pp. 37–38). Features of the archetype include that the outlaw is initially a reluctant hero and that in fighting against superior odds he must resort to trickery to win. Such elements bring complexity and ambiguity to the outlaw persona. In Robin Hood's case, his stories are full of disguises and subterfuges.

Initially disseminated in medieval times through ballads and performance, his stories became the subject of plays and novels and in the twentieth century became popular in cinema and television. The different representations of the Robin Hood myth present different interpretations and meanings, reflecting the issues of the time they were produced. If we look at a few prominent examples, we see these variations in the key features of the story and their relevance.

Up until the nineteenth century, Robin Hood was placed vaguely somewhere in medieval times. Walter Scott changed that with his successful novel *Ivanhoe* (1819), which introduced a range of features that would be repeated in all later retellings. The action takes place against tensions between the Normans and the Saxons, Robin Hood is a loyal supporter of King Richard the Lionheart against the usurper Prince John and Scott's outlaw demonstrates his exceptional abilities through winning an archery tournament by splitting his competitor's arrow. The conservative Scott constructed his story as one of national reconciliation, particularly relevant in the period of unrest just after the Napoleonic Wars. England is divided, the rapacious Normans oppressing the stolid Saxons. As the country descends into chaos, the only resolution is for the Saxons (Ivanhoe and Robin Hood) to work with the Normans (Richard) and forge a new identity as English. Interestingly, this is the one version in which Robin realizes that Richard is flawed – being both brave and foolhardy – and his reign will only be effective if he is carefully guided by wise advisors. Again we can see that such advocacy of constitutional monarchy is a product of its time.

Over a century later, cinema took its cue from Scott for the story, but applied it to contemporary issues. *The Adventures of Robin Hood* (1938) was a big budget Warner Brothers epic, filmed with the new medium of technicolour. Starring Errol Flynn as the dashing Robin, it featured a perfect supporting cast with Olivia de Havilland as Marian, Claude Rains as Prince John, Basil Rathbone as the villainous Sir Guy and Alan Hale as Little John. While filmed in California by a major Hollywood studio, *The Adventures of Robin Hood* has a strong British flavour. Of the 11 main characters, 9 were played by British actors. Such casting was common in 1930s Hollywood and was due to the popularity of *Empire Films*. These were historical action films focusing on England and the British Empire. Due to their box office success, the studios recruited many British actors, though – for economic and logistical reasons – all these films were made in the USA.

Ostensibly a light action romance, *The Adventures of Robin Hood* had two strong sub-textual messages reflecting the political interests of Warner Brothers and aimed at the American public. The first is that the violent and oppressive regime instigated by Prince John and his henchmen is suggestive of the rise of the Nazis and other fascist groups in Europe. In resisting, Robin Hood provides a call to arms – particularly against isolationist sentiment in the USA. The second is that the dispossessed peasants who seek protection in Sherwood Forest are suggestive of mid-West farmers forced off their land during the Great Depression. That Robin provides aid calls to mind Roosevelt's New Deal. It is also important to note that it was only earlier in the same decade that real-life outlaws like Bonnie and Clyde and Pretty Boy Floyd had been active in rural USA.

The Adventures of Robin Hood and Errol Flynn's portrayal of the outlaw came to be seen as the definitive versions of the story. For the next 30 or so years, most media productions drew on it heavily (Knight, 2003). The British *Robin Hood Annual 1959*, for example, contained a 20-page cartoon version of the film and all the illustrations were modelled on Errol Flynn (Amalgamated Press, 1958). Indeed, there was a cross-generational influence at work, as the pre-war generation championed the Errol Flynn film of their youth to their Baby Boom children. That *The Adventures of Robin Hood* was in technicolour helped its longevity and it is still shown regularly on television.

In the twenty-first century, there has been a further re-invention of the outlaw myth. In *Robin Hood* (2010), the outlaw – played by Russell Crowe – is an ordinary soldier, rather than a knight. He returns after years abroad fighting in the Crusades and France, to find the country slipping into chaos. The trope of Robin as a returning soldier is also used in Kevin Costner's *Robin Hood: Prince of Thieves* (1991) and the 2006 television series. It is interesting to see a similar role with Doctor John Watson returning from Afghanistan in *Sherlock* (2010–). Such a background allows an exploration of modern concerns of soldiers reintegrating into society.

That villainous foreigners have infiltrated England in disguise and are attacking civilians suggests modern concerns with terrorism. As Haydock (2002) argues, modern cinema representations of the medieval have been firmly aimed at the lucrative US market and have incorporated American world views. Accordingly, villains are usually foreigners, who are working surreptitiously, have fooled or co-opted the authorities and can only be defeated by a vigilant everyman. Such historical epics are characterized by highly generalized calls for freedom and *Robin Hood* – with the star of *Gladiator* (2000) in the title role – is no exception. At 46 years of age when the movie was released, Crowe was one of the oldest Robin Hoods. In contrast, the television series cast actors in their twenties to play Robin and his band; a similar approach to *Merlin*. This trend has continued with the forthcoming film *Robin Hood: Origins* (scheduled for release in 2018) starring Taron Egerton as a young Robin. Once again, we will see the reinvention of Robin Hood.

The modern tourist geography

King Arthur

There are a number of destinations that are associated with the Arthurian myth. We focus here on Tintagel in Cornwall, where Arthur was supposed to have been born. The Castle at Tintagel was built by Richard, Earl of Cornwall, *c.*1230, 'possibly to capitalize on the popularity of Geoffrey's [of Monmouth] book and lend authority to his own power' (Earl, 2008, p. 401). Visitors to the Castle over the years include Tennyson, who wrote *Morte d'Arthur* there in 1842. As Cornwall's mining industry declined in the late nineteenth century, it looked to tourism to boost the local economy, and the region capitalized on its links with Arthur in its marketing. Tourists to Tintagel 'descended from trains named Merlin, Lyonesse and Pendragon' (Orange & Laviolette, 2010, p. 90) and could stay in King Arthur's Castle Hotel.

Tintagel is still a popular tourist destination, largely due to its associations with the Arthur myth. The streets of Tintagel contain various gift shops with items themed around Arthuriana (e.g. swords, knights in armor), alongside those connected to *Lord of the Rings* (perhaps based on the assumption that these products appeal to the same market) and Celtic style jewellery (Orange & Laviolette, 2010; Robb, 1998). Sadly, the medieval architecture of Tintagel has largely been demolished. Despite the modern streetscape and the often kitschy souvenirs, visitors on the whole appear to be satisfied with the experience: 'It appears that although the [town] was seen as commercialized it could be more so and crucially it appeared to fulfil visitors' expectations, it was what the majority of visitors wanted and expected' (Orange & Laviolette, 2010, p. 95). Work by Earl (2008) shines a spotlight on tour groups of literary fans who profess to have read texts such as Tennyson's *Idylls of the King*. A visit to Tintagel, complete with academic lectures, is thus a demonstration of their cultural capital.

There are interesting tensions with the way that the Tintagel site is interpreted to visitors. As Orange and Laviolette (2010, p. 94) observe of the people they studied: 'Almost all the visitors had a prior association of Tintagel with the legends of King Arthur.' While English Heritage's brochures of Tintagel make overt reference to King Arthur, a video in the interpretation centre focused on 'myth-busting' (Orange & Laviolette, 2010; Robb, 1998), which disappointed many of the visitors. There were few interpretation boards in and around the Castle, as English Heritage was keen to maintain the 'mystery' of the site. Visitors were not told what the site was used for or who had lived there, if not Arthur. This was the crux of the problem – visitors were 'left without replacement narratives and consequently appeared unengaged by the archaeology' (Orange & Laviolette, 2010, p. 102). The Celtic heritage of the site could be presented more strongly to visitors, given that it is 'the temporal context within which a person like Arthur may have lived' (Orange & Laviolette, 2010, p. 104). There might also be scope to consider 'competing theories of evidence' (Robb, 1998, p. 593) about the site, introducing an 'edgier' interpretation (Frost, 2005).

There are also tourist sites that specifically attract fans of the *Merlin* TV series. The first, Chateau de Pierrefonds in France, was used as the location for *Camelot* (Griffin, 2011). In contrast, Warwick Castle in England, while not directly connected with the production of *Merlin* or indeed Arthurian myth, has used it to enhance the experience of touring the site, targeting young visitors who watch or know about the show. The most notorious resident of the Castle was Richard Neville, 16th Earl of Warwick, colloquially known as the Kingmaker, who was defeated by King Edward VI at the Battle of Barnet in 1471. The Castle was bought by Madame Tussauds in 1978 (Westwood, 1989), which merged with Merlin Entertainments in 2007, still the current owners. In 2011, they opened *Merlin: The Dragon Tower*, where, according to their brochure: 'You'll be transported to the heart of Camelot to discover the secrets that are hidden deep inside the Tower before your ultimate encounter with the Great Dragon himself'. The day we visited the Castle, we saw an actor dressed to resemble Colin Morgan as Merlin from the TV series in front of what has been labelled the Dragon Tower (Figure 8.1). Another attraction was the Sword in the Stone daily event ('take the challenge; are you the truest and bravest of knights?'). Trading on the romantic notion of the medieval princess held captive, another tower was called 'The Princess Tower'. Warwick Castle thus styles itself: 'Britain's ultimate castle . . . where princesses are pampered and maidens are wooed, as winners become true heroes and losers are confined to dark, dank dungeons to be forgotten for eternity'.

Robin Hood

The medieval outlaw's adventures take place in Sherwood Forest and Nottingham. However, the mediatization of the story leads to an interesting paradox. As Shackley (2001, p. 315) observed, 'visitors to Nottingham have an image of place derived from Robin Hood feature films, which have always been shot elsewhere'. While the definitive cinema version, not only

Figure 8.1   Warwick Castle's Merlin and the Dragon Tower, with an actor impersonating the television star Merlin at its entrance.

Source: photo W. Frost.

wasn't *The Adventures of Robin Hood* filmed in Nottingham, it was entirely made in California. It was Bidwell Park in Chico in northern California that filled in for Sherwood Forest. This was primarily because of the number of mature trees, including the Hooker Oak, named after the naturalist and claimed to be the largest oak in the world at the time. To green the California landscape – and hide some of the eucalypts – green paint and fake vines leftover from a Tarzan movie were liberally utilized. The scenes in Nottingham were all filmed on the Warner Brothers backlot and studios.

The more recent films were shot in Wales and England. The television series was filmed in Hungary. As with *Braveheart* (1995) – set in Scotland, but shot in Ireland – it was simply cheaper to film elsewhere. Such strategies lead to *locational dissonance*, where the audience thinks they are seeing a certain place, but it is actually a completely different country. Does this affect tourism patterns? The evidence is: hardly ever. Tourists generally go to the places depicted on the screen (Frost, 2009).

Accordingly, tourists inspired by the media flock to Nottingham for their Robin Hood experiences. Place marketing tied to Robin Hood tends to be episodic and Nottingham provides an instructive example of campaigns that follow film production. In the 1990s, the release of Kevin Costner's *Robin Hood: Prince of Thieves* led to an increase in visitor numbers and a refreshing of visitor interpretation (Shackley, 2001). For the release of Russell Crowe's *Robin Hood* in 2010, the city's destination marketing organization produced a guide, trail and discount card for attractions on the trail (Experience Nottingham, 2010).

Tourism related to Robin Hood occurs in two nodes. The first is in the city around Nottingham Castle and a statue of Robin Hood (Figure 8.2). Between 1989 and 2009 there

Figure 8.2 Young tourists posing for photos at the Robin Hood Statue, Nottingham.
Source: photo J. Laing.

was also a tourist attraction called *The Tales of Robin Hood* (Henesey, 2009). Complementing this Robin Hood cluster is the historic pub *Ye Olde Trip to Jerusalem*, which claims to date from 1189. This concentration of attractions in Nottingham (and the associated souvenir shops) raises an interesting issue about the nature of heritage tourism. Robin Hood's home is Sherwood Forest. He is a rural outlaw, helping the peasants and robbing the rich on isolated roads. Nottingham is the base of his enemies – the Sheriff of Nottingham and his garrison. Yet, it is Nottingham, a growing regional city with transport connections, hotels and restaurants, which draws in the tourists. A similar situation occurs with the Australian outlaw Ned Kelly, with the main tourist attractions focused on the base of his adversaries in Melbourne (Frost, 2006).

The second node is at the village of Edwinstowe, 20 miles north of Nottingham. Here there is a statue and the church in which legend has Robin marrying Marian. Bordering the village is Sherwood Forest. The Sherwood Forest Visitor Centre hosts the permanent exhibition 'Robyn Hode's Sherwode'. When first visited in 1989, this was a very curious experience. The interpretation at that time firmly explained that Robin never existed and that popular media representations were romanticized rubbish. Instead – the interpretation narrative explained – it was important to focus on how oppressed medieval peasants were. This crude attempt at 'myth-busting' was similar to the video at Tintagel discussed above. Certainly, comments by Nottingham residents were that they found this display embarrassing. In the early 1990s, to coincide with the release of the Kevin Costner film, this interpretation was changed (Shackley, 2001).

The Visitor Centre exhibition provided an entertaining and insightful experience when we toured it in 2014. Rather than attempting to preach a master narrative, it provided historical evidence from the medieval period that the story was well known then and that an outlaw might

Figure 8.3   Visitor centre exhibition, Sherwood Forest.
Source: photo J. Laing.

have existed. These were juxtaposed with brightly coloured images of medieval castles and banners; traditional images that the public would associate with the period (Figure 8.3). There was also strong recognition that the story was heavily mediated from the nineteenth century onwards. One panel contained a large montage of film and television images of Robin Hood. Similarly, the visitor centre cafe was decorated with film posters.

Implications for popular culture tourism

In this chapter, we have considered how the media frames our understanding of the medieval world, focusing on the King Arthur and Robin Hood narratives, which have been endlessly re-invented through film and television and draw tourists to associated destinations. One of the key themes highlighted in this chapter has been the role of *authenticity* for visitors to these places. For some, it is not an issue in the objective sense. Previous studies suggest that many tourists are satisfied with sites that are over-commodified and even kitsch in their presentation of narratives, such as the main street of Tintagel, which intertwine the Arthur story with other popular culture narratives such as *Lord of the Rings*. Some tourists also find interpretation at tourist attractions that sets out to destroy myths about the existence of King Arthur, the Round Table and Robin Hood to be disappointing (Orange & Laviolette, 2010; Robb, 1998; Shackley, 2001). It may be that watching films and television shows bestows a certain authenticity on the story, which visitors subsequently do not wish to have disturbed or challenged through a tourist experience. Alternatively, the story is so beloved that disputing its origins is seen as disrespectful. Debunking one story and not replacing it with another is confusing, as it simply leaves a vacuum in its wake (Orange & Laviolette, 2010). Some attractions have acknowledged the myth but also showcased the latest thinking about its origin in historical truth, which lend the myth an element of veracity and appears to make the visit more compelling. Future research is required to tease these issues out further and to consider whether different aspects of authenticity are at play for tourists to these sites.

Another issue for popular culture tourism is the fact that some tourists seek out attractions and experiences that reinforce their cultural capital, and enjoy the links that are made between important literary or artistic works and what they are seeing (Earl, 2008). This might be extended to films or television shows in some instances, although empirical research is needed to explore this issue further. For example, it would be interesting to explore whether visitors to medieval-themed attractions or experiences are disappointed if there are no references made to media representations of the period or if they feel they have been 'dumbed down' for general audiences.

Tourist experiences linked to these narratives are consumed against a backdrop of these media-led imaginings and in turn help to reinvent medieval times for modern audiences; an example of *mediatization*. Attractions that are themed around medieval narratives must therefore understand the cultural frameworks of their visitors based on their media consumption, as this may affect their satisfaction with the experience. Research is needed to explore this issue further. The development and popularity of television series based on a fantasy medieval society such as *Game of Thrones* (2011–) might also be a fruitful area of future study, given they may also influence the tourist experience, with depictions of jousting, castles and sword fights between knights.

References

Amalgamated Press (1958). *Robin Hood Annual 1959*. London: Amalgamated Press.

Ashworth, G. J. & Tunbridge, J. E. (2000). *The tourist-historic city: Retrospect and prospect of managing the historic city*. Oxford: Pergamon.

Bryden, I. (2005). *Reinventing King Arthur: The Arthurian legends in Victorian culture*. Aldershot; Burlington, UK: Ashgate.

Bryden, I. (2011). All dressed up: Revivalism and the fashion for Arthur in Victorian culture. *Arthuriana*, *21*(2), 28–41. doi: 10.1353/art.2011.0018

Campbell, J. (1949). *The hero with a thousand faces*. 1993 reprint. London: Fontana.

Earl, B. (2008). Literary tourism: Constructions of value, celebrity and distinction. *International Journal of Cultural Studies*, *11*(4), 401–417. doi: 10.1177/1367877908096003

Experience Nottingham. (2010). *Experience the home of Robin Hood: Map & guide*. Retrieved from www.experiencenottinghamshire.com/xsdbimgs/in_the_footsteps_of_rh_web.pdf

Frost, W. (2005). Making an edgier interpretation of the Gold Rushes: Contrasting perspectives from Australia and New Zealand. *International Journal of Heritage Studies*, *11*(3), 235–250. doi: 10.1080/13527250500160526

Frost, W. (2006). Braveheart-ed Ned Kelly: Historic films, heritage tourism and destination image. *Tourism Management*, *27*(2), 247–254. doi: 10.1016/j.tourman.2004.09.006

Frost, W. (2009). From backlot to runaway production: Exploring location and authenticity in film-induced tourism. *Tourism Review International, 13*(2), 85–92. doi: 10.3727/154427209789604570

Frost, W. & Laing, J. (2013). *Commemorative events: Memory, identities, conflict*. London; New York: Routledge.

Frost, W. & Laing, J. (2014). The role of fashion in subculture events: Exploring steampunk events. In K. Williams, J. Laing & W. Frost (Eds.), *Fashion, design and events* (pp. 177–190). London; New York: Routledge.

Frost, W. & Laing, J. (2015). *Imagining the American West through film and tourism*. London; New York: Routledge.

Griffin, M. (2011). King of the castle. *The Age Travel* supplement, 21 May, pp. 16–17.

Haydock, N. (2002). Arthurian melodrama, Chaucerian spectacle and the waywardness of cinematic pastiche in *First Knight* and *A Knight's Tale*. In T. Shippey & M. Arnold (Eds.), *Film and fiction: Reviewing the Middle Ages* (pp. 5–38). Cambridge, UK: D. S. Brewer.

Henesey, B. (2009). Nottingham will 'fall off tourist map' after closure of Tales of Robin Hood. *Nottingham Post*, 15 January. Retrieved from www.nottinghampost.com/Nottingham-fall-tourist-map-closure-Tales-Robin-Hood/story-12271988-detail/story.html

Higham, N. (2002). *King Arthur: Myth-making and history*. London: Routledge.

Knight, S. (2003). *Robin Hood: A mythic biography*. Ithaca, NY: Cornell University Press.

Kooistra, P. (1989). *Criminals as heroes: Structure, power & identity*. Bowling Green, KY: Bowling Green State University Press.

Laing, J. & Frost, W. (2012). *Books and travel: Inspiration, quests and transformation*. Bristol, UK: Channel View.

Lowenthal, D. (1985). *The past is a foreign country*. Cambridge, UK: Cambridge University Press.

Lowenthal, D. (1998). *The heritage crusade and the spoils of history*. Cambridge, UK: Cambridge University Press.

Matthews, J. & Matthews, C. (2008). *King Arthur: History and legend*. London: The Folio Society.

Monmouth, G. of (1100?–1154). *The history of the kings of Britain*. Lewis, G. M. T. (ed.), 1976 edition. Harmondsworth, UK: Penguin.

Mykletun, R. & Gyimóthy, S. (2010). Beyond the renaissance of the traditional Voss sheep's-head meal: Tradition, culinary art, scariness and entrepreneurship. *Tourism Management, 31*(3), 434–446. doi: 10.1016/j.tourman.2009.04.002

Orange, H. & Laviolette, P. (2010). A disgruntled tourist in King Arthur's court: Archaeology and identity at Tintagel, Cornwall. *Public Archaeology, 9*(2), 85–107. doi: 10.1179/175355310X12780600917595

Robb, J. G. (1998). Tourism and legends: Archaeology of heritage. *Annals of Tourism Research, 25*(3), 579–596. doi: 10.1016/S0160-7383(98)00016-4

Robinson, R. N. S. & Clifford, C. (2012). Authenticity and festival foodservice experiences. *Annals of Tourism Research, 39*(2), 571–600. doi: 10.1016/j.annals.2011.06.007

Scott, W. (1819). *Ivanhoe*. 1965 reprint. London: Dent.

Seal, G. (1996). *The outlaw legend: A cultural tradition in Britain, America and Australia*. Cambridge, UK: Cambridge University Press.

Shackley, M. (2001). The legend of Robin Hood: Myth, inauthenticity, and tourism development in Nottingham England. In V. L. Smith & M. Brent (Eds.), *Hosts and guests revisited: Tourism issues in the 21st century* (pp. 315–322). New York: Cognizant.

Sherman, J. (2015). Source, authority and audience in the BBC's *Merlin*. *Arthuriana, 25*(1), 82–100. doi: 10.1353/art.2015.0004

Stratford, S.-J. (2013). Referring to JFK's presidency as 'Camelot' doesn't do him justice. *Guardian*, 21 November. Retrieved from www.theguardian.com/commentisfree/2013/nov/21/jfk-jackie-kennedy-camelot-myth

Twain, M. (1889). *A Connecticut yankee in King Arthur's court*. 1979 edition. Berkeley, CA: University of California Press for the Iowa Center for Textual Studies.

Westwood, M. (1989). Warwick Castle; Preparing for the future by building on the past. *Tourism Management, 10*(3), 235–239. doi: 10.1016/0261-5177(89)90082-4

White, T. H. (1937). *The sword in the stone*. 1998 edition. London: Collins Children's Books.

9
TUNING IN
Setting the scene for music tourism

Leonieke Bolderman and Stijn Reijnders

Setting the scene

At the end of the afternoon, tired but content with the impressions and observations of the day, I sat down on the terrace in front of a small café. The sun was shining abundantly, putting smiles on the faces of people walking by. I ordered a cup of tea to go along with the house special, which swiftly appeared on the table: Bach Torte. Looking up from the generous piece of mocha flavoured cake, across the street I saw a giant statue of the legendary composer, placed next to a church of impressive proportions. I found myself in Leipzig, Germany, a city known for its classical music heritage. Bach is its most well-known (former) inhabitant, having lived in the city for many years and composing his most famous works for the boys' choir of the Thomaskirche, the church that he is buried in and that I was currently looking at.

Walking around the statue and entering the church that afternoon, however, was not the kind of tourist you would expect taking an interest in Bach. Sipping my tea, I saw a young lady donning an intricate corset, toting a delicate lace umbrella. A bit further on, a group of men wearing long coats and heavy boots laughed about an apparent joke, while a group of boys and girls with neon dreadlocks and expressive makeup had started taking selfies with the Bach statue. The colour of choice uniting the outfits of all these tourists? Black.

Although not a typical classical music audience, the presence of these extravagantly dressed people in Leipzig was not all together surprising: one weekend per year, at Whitsun to be precise, Leipzig is home to one of the largest Goth festivals in the world, the Wave Gotik Treffen. During this weekend, the city is taken over by tens of thousands of Goth fans from all over the world who attend concerts, buy clothes and accessories at special fairs and take part in organized events such as the Victorian Picnic and a special tour of the city cemetery. While the Goth music lovers visit the city for the festival, fellow Goths, other tourists and locals alike feast their eyes on the many eye-catching outfits proudly paraded around.

As the example of Leipzig shows, music induces travel in many ways, involving widely different genres of music that sometimes coexist in the same city, attracting visitors of all ages and backgrounds. It is peculiar that mere vibrating air can accomplish tourism: 'In some respects this is remarkable since music is, strictly speaking, invisible, and often ephemeral, and the essence of tourism – 'the tourist gaze' – has only the most tenuous connection with music' (Connell & Gibson, 2003: 13). If music is hard to pin down geographically due to its intangibility, how do tourists know where to travel? Despite the abstract nature of music, examples such as Leipzig show that connections between music and place can be established and can become an integral part of a location's attraction for tourists.

Moreover, music tourism seems to be a phenomenon on the rise. Places such as Graceland and Liverpool have become popular destinations recognized for their popular music heritage, while music festivals such as Glastonbury in the UK, Coachella in the USA and Sziget in Hungary attract over 100,000 music lovers annually. Recognizing the potential pull of music, city and region marketers increasingly include music in their strategies.

In these various guises, music tourism raises both practical questions relating to tourism management and marketing, as well as more profound questions about contemporary culture, involving for instance the festivalization of culture (Bennett, Taylor & Woodward, 2014) and the meaning of intangible heritage (Brandellero & Janssen, 2013).

It is in this context that this chapter explores contemporary music tourism, first of all through tracing the particular connections between music and place that induce tourism. Second, we track the varied research disciplines engaging with the phenomenon. A growing amount of research is dedicated to exploring music and travel, from perspectives as wide ranging as tourism management, cultural geography and music sociology. In this chapter, the different branches of this research theme are discussed, while common issues and interests are identified. Last but not least, we point out the roads less travelled in current research on the topic, setting a research agenda for the years to come.

Disciplinary and theoretical underpinnings: understanding the connections between music and place

Because of its abstract nature, music differs from other art forms in the way it evokes ideas of place. Whereas a movie can show a clear and recognizable image of a particular place, music can be linked to place only indirectly. These linkages between music and place are what we call 'detours' (Bolderman, 2017): categories of associations between music and place that each in their own way are capable of inducing tourism. Four of these detours can be distinguished.

First of all, music can be connected to place through instrumentation or musical structure. The bagpipes signal the Highlands of Scotland like no other instrument, while the tango is associated with Argentina through its musical form and its sounds. This type of connection often revolves around myths of origin, in which music is seen as a natural local resource. Made from local materials, musical instruments especially contribute to the idea that music embodies the 'soul' of a landscape (Kaul, 2014).

Second, music can be connected to place through non-sonic aspects of music. As in the case of the enormously popular Psy song Gangnam Style, a song title, lyrics or video can put a city on the map. Abbey Road is as famous for its iconic crossing as much as for its recording studio. Tourists often recreate famous pictures and album covers, by posing on site in exactly the same way as their idol in the picture. This leads Podoshen (2013) to conclude that reenactment is a central element of music tourism activity, although it is more likely that recreating famous images occurs when this particular kind of music–place connection is present; it is not necessarily a central element to other kinds of music tourism.

A third category is formed through the biography of the composer or artist. Musical pilgrimages often belong in this category of place connections, such as the Elvis aficionado's in Graceland (Drummond, 2011), Queen fans visiting Montreux, trips to Macclesfield by Joy Division fans (Otter, 2013), and Beatlemaniacs visiting Strawberry Fields in New York (Kruse, 2003). Museums dedicated to artists or composers play into this kind of music tourism as well.

The Wagner Museum for instance, in Villa Wahnfried, Bayreuth, used to be the family home of the Wagner household.

Finally, specific places can become associated with music because they are the stage of its production, distribution or consumption. Famous recording studios such as the Hansa studios in Berlin belong to this category, as do famous venues such as Carnegie Hall. Record stores can also attract tourists (Bennett, 2002), for example to browse the racks for records they cannot find at home or online. Music festivals such as Glastonbury fit into this category as well, attracting perhaps the biggest crowds out of all the instances of music tourism mentioned.

Taken together, these four connections account for the varied forms of music tourism in practice. Musical places are also often a combination of these four connections, as is the case in for example music scenes. Moreover, research among music tourists in Europe suggests that the more types of detour are present in one place, the more successful that place will be as a music tourism location (Bolderman, 2017). This is one of the reasons why, for example, Hamburg is not successful in attracting Beatles tourism (Fremaux & Fremaux, 2013), while Liverpool is. The Beatles represent Merseybeat, the specific sound of the city they were from. The city features in their songs and in the pictures of the band circulating, and it is also where an infrastructure is present with recurring events such as the yearly Beatles week.

Combining music, place and travel: music tourism as a field of study

The interrelations between music and place have been on the scientific agenda for quite some time. Already in the late nineteenth century, ethnomusicological research has explored the role of music in geographically localized cultures. Focusing initially on the music of people in non-Western parts of the world, ethnomusicologists have increasingly included music in Western societies to their field of research. This is exemplified in the work of Steven Feld, who analyzes the ways different people across the globe experience and create a 'sense of place' through sound and through their unique musical cultures (for example in Feld & Basso, 1996). Although not directly dealing with music tourism, the idea of a musical sense of place and how this is experienced and differs across cultures chimes in with more recent work on how music appears in (embodied) touristic experiences of place (Bolderman & Reijnders, 2016; Saldanha, 2002).

With the spatial turn in the humanities and social sciences in the early 1990s, other disciplines have also started to pay attention to the relation between music and place. From a cultural geography perspective, music is studied for its role in the production and consumption of place. The early efforts focused on charting the geographical origins of music styles and analyzing lyrics for their representation of existing geographies. The criticism of Kong (1995) was one of the catalysts in cultural geographical research on music and place to start including the social and political contexts in which music is produced and consumed. This line of research has fruitfully continued, with work on the role of music in the social construction of space and place (Leyshon, Matless & Revill, 1998), attention for the importance of processes of consumption and distribution in light of globalization (Connell & Gibson, 2003) and the role of music in the construction of spatial identities (Krims, 2007).

A specific attention for music tourism as such coincides with the development of new research disciplines: popular music studies and tourist studies. The role and meaning of place in popular music genres has been approached predominantly from the perspective of scenes (Straw, 1991), neotribes (Bennett, 2004), or musicscapes (Cohen, 2014; Hesmondhalgh, 2005), inspired by Appadurai's work on mediascapes (1990). In the context of music scenes, tourists are a logical consequence of the popularity of the scene, an effect of its maturity. Despite the sociological underpinnings of this type of research, less attention is paid to the music tourist in the sense of their particular wants and needs and demographical background. There is also less attention to theory building in a comparative perspective, as this research is more focused on the theorizing of music scenes.

Finally, in the field of tourism studies, attention at the outset was paid mainly to music tourism from a management perspective, looking at the ways audiences could be managed during festivals and in popular destinations, and how specific sites and cities could become attractive sites for music pilgrimage (Henke, 2005). In the case of pilgrimage this research involved primarily eye-catching Anglo-Saxon examples of music tourism, such as Graceland and the Beatles. Next to management, cultural tourism-oriented research offers inroads into music tourism examples, taking up ethnomusicological topics from a different perspective. The politics of cultural tourism come into play, music being a manner in which boundaries between locals and tourists are created and perpetuated (Saldanha, 2002).

Having written the first full-length study dedicated to music tourism, Connell and Gibson (2003) have greatly contributed to putting music tourism on the map as a research topic in its own right. A central concern in their work is how music is embedded in certain places, while moving across geographical locations at the same time. In their book on music and travel, *On the Road* (Gibson & Connell, 2005), they offer many examples of music tourism from around the world, and discuss some central debates in music tourism pertaining to issues of authenticity, pilgrimage and nostalgia.

In relation to issues of authenticity, Connell and Gibson point out the central role authenticity plays in both tourism and music: the ways authenticity functions as denoting a core quality or a sense of originality – for example perceived as being true to the genre in music or the home of distinct cultures in tourism. Combined, this explains the prominence in music tourism on places known as 'authentic' sites of musical creativity (Gibson & Connell, 2007).

Through this focus on roots, music tourism is often related to heritage and memory. This leads Connell and Gibson to conclude that music tourism is primarily a form of nostalgia consumption: 'music tourism, like other elements of cultural tourism, might be thought simply to link nostalgia with some concern for heritage and authenticity' (Gibson & Connell, 2005, p. 15). Both the music industry and the tourism industry feed into the growing attention for nostalgia, positioning the commodification of culture as a central concern when dealing with music tourism.

Based on new research into nostalgia and its role in (Western) culture, in recent analyzes this focus on the nostalgia industry has been reframed, indicating new lines of research to be taken up.

The politics of music heritage

More than ten years on from Connell and Gibson, what characterizes the recent work on music tourism is its interdisciplinary nature. For instance, one of the most interesting strands of current research combines work from cultural geography and music sociology, studying the relationship between music and place as a mutually influential process transforming the postmodern metropolis. A central concern is the analysis of the tension between authenticity and commodification in times of rapid globalization. This research is frequently situated within a post-industrial context of urban regeneration and heritage politics, nuancing and refining arguments set forth by Connell and Gibson (Cohen, 2007; Cohen, Knifton, Leonard & Roberts, 2015; Lashua, Spracklen & Long, 2014; Roberts, 2014).

This tension is very much present in the popularity of popular music icons in city marketing (Cohen, 2007; Henke, 2005). As globalization has made the seemingly natural connection of music to particular regional cultures more diffuse, other places have become known for their 'sound' – a localized, musical atmosphere – that can be a hybrid of musical styles from all over the world. For example, Cohen (2007) has described how Liverpool's Merseybeat is an amalgam of styles not necessarily local to the region, including American rock and roll and Irish traditional music. Wagg, Spracklen and Lashua (2014) have described how Elvis has a cherished place in the culture of the Australian outback.

When a particular local 'sound' is sold as unique heritage of a city, a problem arises when all cities become tourist hotspots with similar ways of selling that popular music heritage: what happens when different cities claim globalized popular music as localized heritage? (Cohen, 2007). The efforts of the city of Hamburg to attract Beatles tourists is a case in point (Fremaux & Fremaux, 2013).

Another question that is put forward relates to exactly whose heritage is presented on site, and which voices are heard (Brandellero, Janssen, Cohen & Roberts, 2014). For example, many Beatles fans visit Penny Lane because of its reference to the song. In 2006, a debate ignited about the name of the street. James Penny, the person the lane was originally named after, was a slave trader, and therefore Liverpool councillor Barbara Mace developed a proposal to change the name of Penny Lane and six other streets in the area. After much protest, however, the plan was not put into effect.

Next to the politics of heritage, the commodification of music and tourism exposes another tension running through music tourism research: the question of its economic viability. As the numbers of tourists seem to be drawn primarily to live music events, some authors argue that music tourism is only sustainable when involving actual music (Lashua et al., 2014; Roberts, 2014), limiting the scope of inquiry to what can be called 'concert tourism'. This potentially shifts the focus of research from heritage-based tourism to, for example, music festivals and concert related travel.

These developments lead to the question of how the globalization of popular music influences and changes the relationship between (popular) music, place and locally grounded identities (Cohen, 2007; Wagg et al., 2014). Driven by the 'accelerating pace of globalization' (Cohen, 2007), music tourism brings questions of this complex relation between music and place to a confrontation. It is in this theme that the contribution of music tourism to the broader study of popular culture tourism can be found.

Implications for popular culture tourism: exposing a double bias

If there is one thing that music tourism shows, it is that popular culture attracts audiences from different ages, and its associated tourism and travel is also diverse in the profile of tourists attracted. This is relevant for popular culture tourism research more broadly, as popular culture in tourism practice is still frequently seen as a providence of the young.

To give one example: the ABBA walking tour in Stockholm is designed to attract tourists in their twenties and thirties. In reality, the tour attracts parents of around 40 years old and their tween children. This is because the parents were ABBA fans in their youth, and their children know ABBA from the *MAMMA MIA!* musical and movie (Bolderman & Reijnders, 2016). Presupposing a link between popular culture tourism and youthful age is a bias refuted by a look at music tourism examples.

Another contribution music tourism research has to offer, is a challenge to the visual bias that remains present in much popular culture research. Looking into music tourism and its peculiarities offers a way to analyze the affordances of other senses than the visual, in this instance sound. As the prominence of the tourist gaze continues to be challenged in tourism research (Chronis, 2015; Edensor & Falconer, 2011; Trandberg Jensen, Scarles & Cohen, 2015; Waitt & Duffy, 2009), it is perhaps time for popular culture tourism research to include its benefits.

One topic that might prove fruitful in this regard is to pay attention to the role of soundtracks in popular culture tourism. Whereas popular culture tourism research has focused primarily on the visual aspects of tv and film tourism, exploring comparisons between the location and print screens among other aspects, the role and meaning of the film or tv soundtrack remains rather unexamined. Roesch (2009), for example, describes the experience a *Star Wars* fan has in the Tunisian desert, listening to the soundtrack while gazing into the distance. The intensity of this experience is attributed to the fan's level of fandom, but the role of listening to the soundtrack remains out of focus.

Towards a research agenda for music tourism

Although music tourism remains one of the lesser-researched forms of popular culture tourism, the field is rapidly expanding and shows some interesting future directions for inquiry. This involves expanding both its empirical and theoretical boundaries.

Empirically, the scope of research could be evaluated through the kind of cases explored and by paying more attention to the music tourist. First of all, the focus has been predominantly on Anglo-Saxon, eye-catching examples involving popular music from the 1960s, casting the music tourist as so called 'snowbirds' and baby boomers who seek to re-live their youth and the emotions that this music evokes (Gibson & Connell, 2005, p. 264). In practice though, as we have seen in this chapter, music tourism consists of a variety of types of travel, attracting an even more varied range of audiences. Research is now diversifying to include different examples, such as 'blackpacking' (travel to Scandinavian destinations related to death metal, Podoshen 2013), and techno-tourism (Garcia, 2016). An empirical shift could mean moving beyond the prevailing focus on popular music, as for instance classical music is somewhat of a blind spot in current research.

Second, future empirical research has a lot to gain by focusing on the socio-cultural background of the music tourist, as well as his or her motivations and experiences on the spot. This will allow for an exploration of yet unknown differences in gender, class, ethnicity and age in the experiences of music tourists. A promising area to contribute to empirical music tourism research in this respect is the budding field of fan studies, which puts the fan-tourist firmly in the limelight.

An example of the possible contributions of a fan studies perspective is the analysis of fan travel as pilgrimage. In relation to music related travel, an important strand in music tourism research from the outset has been the focus on pilgrimage. Where research from a religion studies perspective favours musical pilgrimage as a modern form of secular pilgrimage (Margry, 2008), this view is challenged in fan studies, pointing out the analogies to pilgrimage are structural rather than functional (Whyton, 2014). Where traditional pilgrimage has at its core a belief in an all-encompassing story that somehow offers a shared cultural narrative representing an absolute truth, to fans the similarities to pilgrimage are of a more structural nature, as it is a deeply personal endeavour that represents personal truth.

Broadening the empirical horizon of music tourism research through including different kinds of music tourism cases and focusing more on the music tourist requires the further development of music tourism theory. This could be brought a step further by conducting more comparative research. The detours discussed in this chapter, for example, provide a categorization that could start of a theoretical debate concerning the ways music tourism contributes to connecting to places. This discussion is not only theoretically relevant, but also feeds back into the role of globalization: it concerns the way music tourism contributes to a sense of belonging.

If globalization is indeed such an important part of music tourism as a phenomenon, surely the borders of its research territory should likewise be globally expanded. As current studies are concerned primarily with Western examples of music tourism, a logical and also necessary next step is to involve non-Western regions and cities in comparative research. As already alluded to in the work by Krüger and Trandafoiu (2014), music tourism research is becoming relevant from the perspective of migration: how does music contribute to feelings of belonging, and a sense of (temporarily) feeling at home in different places?

Combining these empirical and theoretical new horizons, the different cultural contexts of this expanded empirical arena offer a critical perspective on current music tourism research. This leads us to conclude that there is a lot to gain from bringing music tourism research onto a global stage.

References

Appadurai, A. (1990). Disjuncture and difference in the global cultural economy. *Theory, Culture and Society* 7(2), 295–310.

Bennett, A. (2002). Music, media and urban mythscapes: a study of the 'Canterbury Sound'. *Media, Culture and Society* 24, 87–100.

Bennett, A. (2004). Subcultures or neotribes? Rethinking the relationship between youth, style and musical taste. *Sociology* 33(3), 599–617.

Bennett, A., Taylor, J. & Woodward, I. (2014). *The Festivalization of Culture*. London: Routledge.

Bolderman, S. L. (2017). *Musical Topophilia. Experiencing Music, Place and Travel*. (Doctoral Dissertation). Erasmus University Rotterdam Repub Repository.

Bolderman, S. L. & Reijnders, S. L. (2016). Have you found what you're looking for? Analyzing tourist experiences of Wagner's Bayreuth, ABBA's Stockholm and U2's Dublin. *Tourist Studies* 16 (4), 1–19.

Brandellero, A. & Janssen, S. (2013). Popular music as cultural heritage: scoping out the field of practice. *International Journal of Heritage Studies* 20 (3), 224–240.

Brandellero, A., Janssen, S., Cohen, S. & Roberts, L. (2014). Popular music heritage, cultural memory and cultural identity. *International Journal of Heritage Studies* 20 (3), 219–223.

Chronis, A. (2015). Moving bodies and the staging of the tourist experience. *Annals of Tourism Research* 55, 124–140.

Cohen, S. (2007). *Decline, Renewal and the City in Popular Music Culture: Beyond the Beatles*. Farnham: Ashgate.

Cohen, S. (2014). Urban musicscapes: mapping music-making in Liverpool. In L. Roberts (Ed.) *Mapping Cultures. Place, Practice, Performance* (123–143). Basingstoke: Palgrave Macmillan.

Cohen, S., Knifton, R., Leonard, M. & Roberts, L. (Eds.) (2015). *Sites of Popular Music Heritage: Memories, Histories, Places*. London: Routledge.

Connell, J. & Gibson, C. (2003). *Sound Tracks: Popular Music, Identity and Place*. London: Routledge.

Drummond, K. (2011). Shame, consumption, redemption: reflections on a tour of Graceland. *Consumption Markets and Culture* 14 (2), 203–213.

Edensor, T. & Falconer, E. (2011). Sensuous geographies of tourism. In J. Wilson (Ed.) *The Routledge Handbook of Tourism Geographies* (74–81). New York: Routledge.

Feld, S. & Basso, K. (1996). *Senses of Place*. Santa Fe: School of American Research Press.

Fremaux, S. & Fremaux, M. (2013). Remembering the Beatles' legacy in Hamburg's problematic tourism strategy. *Journal of Heritage Tourism* 22 (May), 1–17.

Garcia, L. M. (2016). Techno-tourism and post-industrial neo-romanticism in Berlin's electronic dance music scenes. *Tourist Studies* 16 (3), 276–295.

Gibson, C. & Connell, J. (2005). *Music and Tourism: On the Road Again*. Clevedon: Channel View Publications.

Gibson, C. & Connell, J. (2007). Music, tourism and the transformation of Memphis. *Tourism Geographies* 9 (2), 160–190.

Henke, L. (2005). Music induced tourism: strategic use of indigenous music as a tourist Icon. *Journal of Hospitality and Leisure Marketing* 13 (2), 3–18.

Hesmondhalgh, D. (2005). Subcultures, scenes or tribes? None of the above. *Journal of Youth Culture* 8 (1), 21–40.

Kaul, A. (2014). Music on the edge: busking at the Cliffs of Moher and the commodification of a musical landscape. *Tourist Studies* 14 (1), 30–47.

Kong, L. (1995). Popular music in geographical analysis. *Progress in Human Geography* 19, 183–198.

Krims, A. (2007). *Music and Urban Geography*. London: Routledge.

Krüger, S. & Trandafoiu, R. (Eds.) (2014). *The Globalization of Musics in Transit: Music, Migration and Tourism*. New York: Routledge.

Kruse, R. J. II (2003). Imagining Strawberry Fields as a place of pilgrimage. *Area* 35 (2), 154–162.

Lashua, B., Spracklen, K. & Long, R. (2014). Introduction to the special issue: music and Tourism. *Tourist Studies* 14 (1), 3–9.

Leyshon, A., Matless, D. & Revill, G. (1998). *The Place of Music*. New York: Guildford Press.

Margry, P. J. (2008). The pilgrimage to Jim Morrison's grave at Pere Lachaise cemetery: the social construction of sacred space. In P. J. Margry (Ed.) *Shrines and Pilgrimage in the Modern World: New Itineraries into the Sacred* (143 –172). Amsterdam: Amsterdam University Press.

Otter, J. K. (2013). *Joy Devotion: Adventures in Image and Authenticity Through the Lens of Kurt Cobain and Ian Curtis* (Unpublished doctoral dissertation). Goldsmiths University, London.

Podoshen, J. S. (2013). Dark tourism motivations: simulation, emotional contagion and topographic comparison. *Tourism Management* 35 (April), 263–271.

Roberts, L. (2014). Marketing musicscapes. Or, the political economy of contagious magic. *Tourist Studies* 14 (1), 10 –29.

Roesch, S. (2009). *The Experiences of Film Location Tourists*. Bristol: Channel View Publications.

Saldanha, A. (2002). Music tourism and factions of bodies in Goa. *Tourist Studies* 2 (1), 43–62.

Straw, W. (1991). Systems of articulation, logics of change: communities and scenes in popular music. *Cultural Studies* 5 (3), 368–388.

Trandberg Jensen, M., Scarles, C. & Cohen, S. A. (2015). A multisensory phenomenology of interrail mobilities. *Annals of Tourism Research* 53, 61–76.

Wagg, S., Spracklen, K. & Lashua, B. (2014). Afterword: reflections on popular music, place and globalization. In B. Lashua, K. Spracklen & S. Wagg (Eds.) *Sounds and the City: Popular Music, Place and Globalizaton* (317–319). Basingstoke: Palgrave Macmillan.

Waitt, G. & Duffy, M. (2009). Listening and tourism studies. *Annals of Tourism Research* 37 (2), 457–477.

Whyton, T. (2014). Song of praise: musicians, myth and the 'cult' of John Coltrane. In M. Duffett (Ed.) *Popular Music Fandom: Identities, Roles and Practices* (97–114). London: Routledge.

10

FADO AS A POPULAR CULTURE EXPRESSION IN THE CONTEXT OF A TOURIST CITY

Cláudia Henriques, Manuela Guerreiro, Júlio Mendes and Célia M. Q. Ramos

Setting the scene

The purpose of this chapter is to examine fado, a Portuguese song form, as a popular culture expression associated with the identity of the city of Lisbon, capital of Portugal. Simultaneously, we intend to present an exploratory research on the role of fado in the tourist experience in Lisbon, particularly of young Portuguese tourists. In order to achieve this purpose, we begin by presenting the theoretical framework mainly associated with the conceptualization of popular culture and the tourist experience of the city. In this context, we acknowledge culture as a very complex concept (Wendy, 2012) that encompasses different types of culture, such as 'high culture', 'popular culture' or 'everyday culture'. Particularly, we discuss the concept of 'popular culture' (Delaney, 2007; Shuker, 2016) and the importance of cultural tourism experiences in the context of the economy of experience (Pine & Gilmore, 1999). In terms of methodology, we adopt a case study approach that links fado as an expression of popular culture with Lisbon as a tourist city. Additionally, we conducted a survey among young people and the open-ended questions were analyzed using categorical content analysis, following Bardin (2015). Finally, we present and discuss the results and the concluding remarks.

Theoretical underpinnings

Conceptualization of popular culture

Culture is a complex and dynamic concept, and as such it has been a difficult concept to value (Wendy, 2012). More recently, it has become associated not only with 'high culture', but also with 'popular culture' and 'everyday culture' (Ashworth, 2015; Menger, 2013), where, beyond its more tangible expressions, intangible expressions and lifestyles gain an increasing importance (UNESCO, 2006).

It is important to point out that the distinctions between 'high culture' (elite) and 'low culture' (mass or 'pop' culture) have become fuzzier and fuzzier (Larsen, 2012). Consequently, 'popular culture' as a complex concept (Bennet in Storey, 2001; Delaney, 2007; Shuker, 2016) is difficult to define and many authors consider its definition as 'virtually useless' (Bennett in Storey, 2001, p. 1) or with 'confused and contradictory meanings' because it stems from the implied otherness that is always absent/present when we use the term 'popular culture'. Usually 'popular culture' is defined, implicitly or explicitly, in contrast to other conceptual categories: folk culture, mass culture, dominant culture, working-class culture, etc. Whichever conceptual category is deployed as popular culture's absent/present other, it will always powerfully affect the connotations brought into play when we use the term 'popular culture' (Storey, 2008).

Williams' (1983 in Storey, 2008, p. 5) conceptualization of the term 'popular' suggests four current meanings: 'well-liked by many people'; 'inferior kinds of work'; 'work deliberately setting out to win favour with the people'; 'culture actually made by the people for themselves. As Shuker (2016, p. 3) point outs, for some authors, the term popular means 'simply appealing to the people, whereas for others it means something [. . .] grounded in or "of" the people'. The former relates to commercially produced forms of popular culture while the latter is usually reserved for forms of 'folk' popular culture, associated with local community-based production and individual craftspeople.

Popular culture allows large heterogeneous masses of people to identify collectively. It consists also of the aspects, 'attitudes, behaviours, beliefs, customs, and tastes that define the people of any society. Popular culture is, in the historic use of term, the culture of the people' (Browne, 2005; Browne & Urish, 2014). In this context, the expressive practices of popular culture have the possibility to challenge and influence social values, norms of behaviour and sense of identity. This could lead some authors such as Storey (2001, p. 1) to argue that 'popular culture is in effect an empty conceptual category, one which can be filled in a wide variety of often conflicting ways, depending on the context of use'.

However, the attempt to define popular culture leads us to 'say that popular culture is simply culture that is widely favoured or well liked by many people' (Storey, 2008, p. 5). Following Storey (2008, pp. 5–13), there are six major theoretical frameworks of 'popular culture'.

The first associates popular culture with 'well liked by many people'; the second as 'a residual category', 'an inferior culture'; the third as 'mass culture' that is a hopelessly commercial culture; fourth, as a culture that originates from 'the people' (Storey, 2008, pp. 5–16). According to this definition, the term should only be used to indicate an 'authentic' culture of 'the people'. A fifth approach draws on the political analysis of Gramsci, particularly on his development of the concept of hegemony to refer to the way in which dominant groups in society, through a process of 'intellectual and moral leadership', seek to win the consent of subordinate groups in society. Finally, a sixth definition of popular culture is one informed by recent thinking around the debate on postmodernism. It is important to point out that a 'postmodern culture is a culture that no longer recognizes the distinction between high and popular culture' (Storey, 2008, pp. 5–16). In this last definition, we perceive that on one hand 'this is a reason to celebrate an end to an elitism constructed on arbitrary distinctions of culture', and on other hand, 'it is a reason to despair at the final victory of commerce over culture' (ibid.).

Regarding the relationship between popular culture and music, it could be contextualized in the assumption that 'popular culture is the accumulated store of cultural products such as music, art, literature, fashion, dance, film, television, and radio that are consumed primarily by non-elite groups such as the working, lower, and middle class' (Crossman, 2014, p. 1).

However, as Sardinha (2010, p. 21) points out 'there is no such thing as pure, genuine or timeless popular music (traditional) [. . .] the music of the people is constantly evolving and being influenced by other music genres, social classes, or other regions'. The author stresses that the manifestations that today are considered as belonging to the popular music tradition had an individual origin, often erudite or semi-erudite, only becoming collective as the people appropriated them and passed on to subsequent generations. For the ethnological study, the important point is the adoption by the people of materials that are then assimilated by the anonymous masses to their needs and subsequently transmitted to the next generation. Sardinha (2010, p. 35) states that if 'they endure over several generations, they will be considered traditional (*traditio*, Latin for transmission) and collective belonging to a community, i.e. an integral part of traditional popular culture'.

The geographical expansion of popular processes goes hand in hand with popularizing and traditionalizing mechanisms. 'The popular traditions are no islands and there is no way of preventing certain types of music from expanding into wider geographical areas'. And if we say that a tradition belongs to a place, parish or region, it is not because it 'had its cradle there, but rather because this community knew how or wanted to maintain and develop it over successive generations through the process of oral transmission, adapting tradition to their mode of existence and thus making it theirs' (Sardinha, 2010, p. 36).

The tourist experience of the city

The UNESCO *Global Report on Culture for Sustainable Urban Development* (2016b) sustains that culture is a key resource for sustainable urban development. The quality of urban life and the protection of urban identities, is a key priority to 'the valuing of local cultures, old and new, and the promotion of cultural expressions, the arts and heritage as pillars of sustainable social and economic development' (UNESCO, 2016b, p. 17).

Popular culture tourism refers to 'people visiting a destination featured in films or television shows (Iwashita, 2008) and it has received increasing attention over a relatively short time period (Connell, 2012)' (Lee & Bai, 2016, p. 163). Music is also important (creative music cities) namely when related to the concept of 'tourist experience'.

Consequently, culture is seen as 'key to what makes cities attractive, creative and sustainable' (UNESCO, 2016b, p. 17), and as such, music, particularly in the past 25 years, has been appropriated to varying degrees to revitalize and re-image the contemporary city through the nighttime economies and cultural industries. 'This of course is not a static picture, and the extent to which urban and musical heritage and change is reflected in city marketing, place promotion, "creative industries" and tourism agenda is variable' (Lashua, Cohen & Schofield, 2010, p. 105). Hudson (2001, p. 461) reinforces 'places' as complex entities, and consequently 'in the process of becoming, rather than essentialized and fixed, open and porous to a variety of flows in and out rather than closed and hermetically sealed'.

Therefore, tourism tends to be associated with a set of memories and emotions related to the visited places that are influenced by the tourist, the scenery (the destination) and the residents. The tourist experience, due to its subjective nature, leads to a close relationship between the individual (tourist), applicable at any given moment and existential/situational, and the territorial framework.

Keeling (2011, p. 113 in Long, 2014, p. 49) argues that 'popular songs reflect a particular geographic experience at a certain point in time, whereby both the producer and consumer of the songs engage with the landscape in ways that are reflected in the music and in our memory'. As Gibson and Connell (2007, p. 167) put it, 'music tourism constitutes evolving clusters of tourists, activities, locations, attractions, workers and events that utilize musical resources for tourist purposes'.

Many cities are associated with music and popular songs (Long, 2014, pp. 48–49), such as songs related to 'Senses of local and national "character"' that are conveyed through the compositions and instrumentation that 'evoke images and emotions stereotypically associated with such cities and nations'. For instance, the romantic compositions of Paris, Samba and Bossa Nova rhythms referring to Rio de Janeiro, and the jazz swing sounds of New York City, New

Orleans and jazz, Nashville and country and western music, Chicago and the blues, Memphis and rock and roll. 'An aural, "soundscape" of such cities thus exists in the popular imagination, conjured by recordings, broadcasts, films and television soundtracks' (Long, 2014, pp. 48–49).

However, the urban 'soundscapes' contribute to a 'sonic profile' and sense of place. Such musical associations may carry implications for some visitors' expectations; experiences and the places that they visit that may be at odds with 'official' city marketing imagery and the city centre locations that are typically promoted as places to visit (Lashua, Cohen & Schofield, 2010, p. 106). This leads to a production of narratives of the city through, for example, the work of artists mimicking the tropes of tourism mapping, text and promotion (Long, 2014, p. 48).

As far as the relationship between music, cities and tourism is getting stronger, we can refer to a 'commoditization' of popular culture and musical creativity. The fact is associated to 'tensions' between 'artistic, aesthetic, "authentic" musical sensibilities, fan cultures and commoditisation' (Henke, 2005; Pearce, Morrison & Moscardo, 2003). Regarding inner-city spaces, Gibson and Homan (2004) consider the use and promotion of popular music.

Eco (1986) mentions that tourists choose destinations associated with the 'hyperreal' where there is a connection between the fictional or mythical features and the activities that can be carried out in places. At the same time, concepts such as the 'production of space' (Lefebvre, 1991) and the 'poetics of space' (Bachelard, 1974, p. 354) where 'imagination is ceaselessly imagining and enriching itself with new images', illustrate that music helps tourists grasping the unutterable and the intangibility of places. In creative popular culture tourism, it is important to link the real and fictional features of places, allowing them to acquire meanings of worlds evoking emotion and engagement.

Methodology

Objectives

The main objective of this study is to investigate fado, urban popular song, as a popular culture expression associated with the identity of the city of Lisbon, capital of Portugal. From a tourism perspective, the major purpose is to investigate the role of fado in the Lisbon tourist experience of young Portuguese tourists.

Data collection instrument, study population and sample, data collection procedures, data analysis

In terms of methodology, we adopt a case study approach – fado as an expression of popular culture in a context of a tourist city, namely Lisbon and its historic quarters. Additionally, we conducted qualitative exploratory research using categorical content analysis (Bardin, 2015) of 37 interviews with Portuguese tourists, aged 18–25 years. This age segment was chosen to investigate young people's opinions about a traditional type of song of the people. The data collection occurred from February to April 2016.

We surveyed random young people that agreed to be interviewed in Alfama and Bairro Alto, historic quarters of Lisbon. The selection of the interview sites had to do with the proximity of the *casas de fado*, i.e. places (restaurants) where fado is sung and near the Fado Museum. The interviews took place at night because this type of music is associated with 'night-time' and the neighbourhoods' nightlife. It should be noted that the streets of these neighbourhoods are usually crowded with visitors. As for the interview script, the focus was on determining aspects such as: What are the attractions of Lisbon? What do you like most in Lisbon? Reason for visit?

Do you know fado? During the stay in Lisbon did you listen to fado? if so, where? Do you have any fado CDs? With whom did you go to a fado concert? What is your degree of knowledge about fado? To what extent do you like Fado? Do you want to know more? What themes and feelings do you associate with fado?

In the first step of the study, we conducted a literature review on the importance of tourism and fado, as a popular culture expression, in the city. The next step was designing the data collection instrument. Thus, we began by characterizing the relationship between the youngsters (using descriptive statistics), while staying in Lisbon, and fado. Subsequently, we tried to know what were the things they liked the most in Lisbon, and the themes and feelings they associate with fado, using categorical content analysis (Bardin, 2015). Additionally, in this research, data collected through the interviews was registered, organized and then analyzed through qualitative data analysis software (NVivo 9, QSR International).

Case study – Lisbon City: fado as popular culture expression

Lisbon, a cultural tourism city

The region of Lisbon was in 2015 the second largest Portuguese tourism region in terms of overnights (12.3 million) (the first is the Algarve) and the first in number of guests (5.2 million) (IMPACTUR, 2016). At the same time, there was a clear upward trend, between 2013 and 2015, of 22 per cent and 20.8 per cent in terms of overnights and guests, respectively (IMPACTUR, 2016).

Examining the case of the city of Lisbon the 'Global Destination Cities Index – 2016' (Mastercard, 2016) shows that Lisbon occupies (in a set of 132 cities) the 37th place in the ranking in terms of 'international overnight visitors' (3.63 million), of which more than 70 per cent are foreign visitors.

Lisbon is the fifth fastest-growing European city in terms of international tourists. 'Between 2009 and 2016, the number of international visitors staying in Lisbon grew by 7.4 per cent, placing the Portuguese capital in the top 5 of Europe's fastest growing cities after Hamburg, Berlin, Istanbul and Copenhagen' (Mastercard, 2016).

In terms of international overnight visitor spend ($1.43) (accommodation, restaurants, shopping, transportation, etc.), Lisbon is ranked 87th (Mastercard, 2016), which can be a clear factor of tourism competitiveness.

Accordingly, the 'Satisfaction and Image Survey 2015' (TL, 2015a, p. 21) shows the image of 'Lisbon – Lisbon region' as a 'capital city' (97.0 per cent), 'city of feelings/sensations' (93.9 per cent) 'ancient city with history' (92.9 per cent), 'creative and trendy city' (92.0 per cent), 'unique city' (88.0 per cent) (percentage of agreement: 'agree' and 'totally agree'), among others.

Regarding 'The differentiating image of Lisbon – what makes Lisbon different?' there are three main aspects that are highlighted: authenticity – 13.7 per cent (linked to gastronomy and culture); sensations – 12.5 per cent; and 'history' – 11 per cent (linked to heritage, 'historic centre', 'history') (TL, 2015a, p. 21).

The main 'motivational segments' are: 'city and short breaks' (44.9 per cent), 'MICE' (Meeting, Incentive, Conference and Exhibition) (15.3 per cent), 'touring Portugal' (14 per cent), 'visiting family and friends' (10 per cent), and 'private business' (7.6 per cent), 'sport events' (2.5 per cent) and 'cultural events' (2.5 per cent), among others (TL, 2014). These motivations are associated with the 'purpose of trip', which is mainly: 'visit monuments and museums' (50.1 per cent), 'to know the Portuguese culture' (38.5 per cent), 'rest/relax (31.6 per cent), 'gastronomy and wine' (31.1 per cent), 'to know different local customs' (30.9 per cent), among others (TL, 2014). These results reflect the underlying motivations for 'city breaks' and short stays, around two days (INE, 2016).

'As for the activities carried out in Lisbon city' (TL, 2015b, p. 26), the three most highlighted are: 'going out to dinner' (96.7 per cent), 'walking around' (90.9 per cent), 'museums and monuments' (86.9 per cent). The 'Visited Attractions and Places of Interest 2015' included in 'Places of Interest – Lisbon city' is the central area and its historic quarters, traditionally associated with fado: city centre (97.9 per cent), Bairro Alto (86.2 per cent) and Alfama (44.5 per cent) (TL, 2015b, p. 32).

Therefore, the interest of tourists in the 'cultural Lisbon' is evident, and it can indicate the tendency for an increasing popularity of fado as patrimony of the city and identity element. This is consistent with the geographic distribution of cultural activities and practices, which are either large concert venues/theater or *casas de fado* (restaurants where fado is sung) in the city's historic quarters. The city council (CML, 2009, p. 62) points out that many cultural activities reveal a geographical pattern generally marked by a high concentration of supply in the central part of the city, particularly, in the Chiado-Bairro Alto zone (with variations and extension to neighbouring areas, depending on the sectors, to Rato, Príncipe Real, Bica, Santos, Cais do Sodré, Baixa, Avenida da Liberdade or even Castelo, Graça, Alfama and Sé).

As for the 'Strategic Tourism Plan for the Lisbon region 2015–2019' (Roland Berger/ ERTRL/TL, 2014), Lisbon is presented as 'city/short breaks' and highlights its 'culture' as a transversal 'qualifier' of its offer. More recently, the 'Tourism Strategy 2027 Portugal' [Estratégia Turismo, 2027 – Portugal] (LET, 2016) considers Lisbon as being 'a multicultural destination with a strong international vocation'. It recognizes a set of assets of Lisbon to achieve it, namely 'active differentiators' (climate and light, history and culture, sea, nature and biodiversity, water), 'active qualifiers' (gastronomy and wines, artistic and cultural events, sports and business), 'emerging assets' (well-being, living in Portugal) and 'unique transversal asset' (people).

As such, we can see that fado is regarded as a cultural element that is important in the creation of routes wherein the *casas de fado* (mainly in historic quarters) and the city's festivals value it as an identity attribute.

Fado of Lisbon

Fado is a popular culture expression, a performance genre incorporating music and poetry (Instituto Camões [IC], 2014). It is an 'urban popular music' (Nery, 2012, p. 8), as well as an identity and symbolic element of the city of Lisbon and Portugal (Henriques, 2016; Nery, 2012; Pereira, 2015; Sardinha, 2010). In November 2011, 'Fado – an urban popular song of Portugal' was inscribed on the UNESCO's Representative List of the Intangible Cultural Heritage of Humanity, at the sixth session of the Intergovernmental Committee (UNESCO, 2016a).

The origins of fado is controversial, although Sardinha (2010) underlines what he calls 'the national origin of fado' associated with a story that can cause 'emotion' to all those involved, with roots in the troubadour tradition and Renaissance heritage and more recently in contemporary literary creation, conquering the territories of erudite poetry (Nery, 2012). The importance of the lyrics leads us to believe that the Portuguese tourist can better understand fado than foreigners, but they can also enjoy it because of the universal nature of the music and the fact that 'in their relationship with fado, each person (tourist or not) might consider fado as a "whole", but also each of its components or "parties", such as the music, lyrics, kinesis and participants' (IC, 2014). At the same time, the city is referred to as a city of 'feelings' evoked by the fado, such as 'longing' (*saudade*).

Therefore, Elliott (2010) mentions that fado appeals to a 'memory theater', wherein one explores the relationship between the poem (lyrics) put to music – listening to the 'echo' of the words throughout the city of Lisbon and its neighbourhoods. This fact leads Elliott (2014) to consider the connection between song and place (in Henriques, 2016).

Regarding the close association between fado and Lisbon, it takes us back to the nineteenth century (IC, 2014), when fado was a practice founded on a social basis 'widened within Lisbon's popular sociability network' (Nery, 2012, p. 67). This perspective is important if we link fado with the city's atmosphere perceived by tourists while experiencing the city of Lisbon and, specifically, its historic quarters.

Specifically, with respect to the themes, at the beginning of the twentieth century, Pimentel (1904 in Nery, 2012, p. 107) identifies: love; works and sufferings of social classes; aspects of the life of the people and social chronicle; jealousy, great disasters; death of celebrities; political or religious conflicts; popular nomenclature of working utensils in the arts and crafts or animals, trees, plants, flowers, etc.; the cities, the neighbourhoods and streets, the towns and villages of the country; Bible passages, religious subjects; expression of mischief and sauciness; flowery and complicated words.

The fado of sensations can be perceived in multiple fado lyrics, being able to provide the tourists in Lisbon a memorable experience, promoting elements associated with fado when delimiting the tours/itineraries. As Henriques (2017) emphasizes, fado evokes the sight,[1] between light and darkness; the smell, Lisbon is a set of smells of the river, the sea, but also of people and feelings;[2] the touch is also present in the hands on the edges of the shawl, in the fingers on the guitar, in kisses;[3] the hearing[4] is also expressed recurrently in the sonorities of the city; the taste,[5] associated with multiple flavours, takes us to wine, *aguardente* (brandy), chorizo but also to the taste of longing and sadness.

And the sixth sense (Pine & Gilmore, 1999) includes all the feelings that the poems convey in the intangible atmosphere of the lost and (re)found city of Lisbon: 'On the piers of yesteryear / There are empty ships . . . / And there are forgotten candles / From the high seas! / The rivers are of dark / remembrance! '(*'Cais de Outrora'* by Luis de Macedo). The sixth sense is also present in the various 'figures of fado' that animate and contribute to 'living' Lisbon, for example, the fado singer, the *varina* (the woman selling fish) the sailor, the *marialva* (ladies' man), the chestnuts man, among others, but also in remarkable elements such as boats (canoe, caravel, frigate, sail, trawler, mast, statue of bow, sailboat, black boat) (Henriques, 2017).

In terms of geography, fado is associated with the centre of Lisbon and especially to the historic quarters, namely Alfama. Today, it tends to be sung fundamentally in the so-called *casas de fado* (at dinner or supper accompanied by wine and traditional Portuguese food) located in the historic districts neighbourhoods, especially in Alfama and Bairro Alto.

Results

From the 37 interviews conducted for this study we verify that all Portuguese tourists, aged between 18 and 25 years, know fado. This fact shows the strong connection that exists between this type of music and the Portuguese and Lisbon identity. Moreover, 29.7 per cent of the respondents were visiting Lisbon for the first time, mainly for leisure purposes (94.5 per cent).

When asked to describe, in three words, what they liked most in their visit to Lisbon, the respondents referred 35 unique words, from a total of 81 words. Of these, the one that appeared most was 'unique atmosphere' (8.6 per cent) followed by 'shopping' (6.1 per cent) and 'monuments', 'gastronomy', 'culture', 'life' and 'night life' (each one with 4.9 per cent) (see Table 10.1).

Table 10.1 Most liked things in Lisbon

Categories					
People	3	Unique atmosphere	7	Life	4
Light	1	Weather	3	Night life	4
Restaurants	1	Gastronomy	4	Terreiro do paço	1
Life	2	Culture	4	Bairro alto	1
Monuments	4	Monument of the discoveries	1	Estadio luz	3
Tourism	2	Jerónimos Monastery	2	'Miradouros' (viewpoints)	1
Shopping	5	Monuments	2	Tejo	1
Colombo	1	Chiado	3	Leisure	1
Cityscape	5	Streets and squares	3	Belém	1
Oceanary	2	Traditional shops	1	Fado	1
St. George's Castle	1	Historic architecture	3	Alfama	2
Total: 80					

Of those interviewed 14.5 per cent during their visit to Lisbon attended a 'fado show', and 59.5 per cent had already attended one to three fado performances ('fado show'), of which 27.0 per cent in *casas de fado*, 13.5 per cent in the Fado Museum. 37.8 per cent attended these performances with family and the others went with friends.

With regard to the degree of knowledge about fado, 29.7 per cent of respondents replied that it was low, 37.8 per cent that it was sufficient and the others considered it good. In what refers to their degree of liking for fado, 24.3 per cent reported a low degree of liking, while the majority revealed that they like fado, of these 32.5 per cent indicated a high or very high degree of liking. When asked to what extent would they like to improve their knowledge about fado, most answers were positive (quite and very much); 13.5 per cent respondents said they had no interest in deepening their knowledge about this type of music.

As for the themes associated with fado, there were 30. Among those, the most popular were 'love' and 'sadness' (both with a share of 15.1 per cent), followed by 'broken heart' (9.7 per cent) and 'culture'. In addition, there were several themes related to feelings such as 'jealousy', 'melancholy/loneliness', 'passion', 'tenderness' (Tables 10.2 and 10.3).

Table 10.2 Themes of fado

Categories					
Love	14	Experience	1	Happiness/joy	2
Lisbon	3	Tradition	4	Melancholy/ loneliness	3
Broken heart	9	Anything	2	Emotions	3
Longing	3	Peace	1	Portugal	2
Sadness	14	Jealousy	4	HQ	2
Hapiness/joy	2	Alfama	1	History	2
Tenderness	2	People	1	Passion	2
Land	1	Wine	2	Relax	1
Life	1	Art	1	Beauty	1
Culture	6	Music	1	Portuguese soul	2
Total: 93					

Table 10.3 Feelings associated with fado

Categories					
Love	4	Calm	5	Welfare	1
Longing	6	Happiness/joy	5	Life	1
Patriotism	1	Patriotism	1	Freedom	1
Depression	1	Chagrin	1	Nostalgia	2
Peace	3	Sadness	15	Emotion	3
Anything	5	Proud	1	Passion	2
Total: 58					

The themes largely overlap with the 'feelings' associated with fado. This fact makes clear that the themes are wrapped in feelings, and vice versa. Regarding the 'feelings' 'sadness' stands out the most, followed by 'longing' and then 'calm', 'happiness/joy'. The feelings associated with fado are essentially 'sadness' (25.9 per cent) and 'longing' (10.3 per cent) (Table 10.3).

Implications for popular culture tourism

At present, and within the context of the growing valuation of local cultures, popular music, as a people's culture, has stood out. In terms of urban space, music is recognized as an element of attractiveness, creativity and sustainability. As a result, music as a cultural product contributes to improving city marketing, place promotion, creative industries, revitalizing and re-imaging the city, among other aspects.

As for the urban popular music, because of its symbolic character, it provides a tourist experience with a strong identity character, enhancing a greater 'knowledge' and 'sense' of the place. In the case of fado, the popular song of Portugal and Lisbon, it has come to capture the interest of the tourists, namely since it was listed as 'Intangible Heritage of Humanity' in 2011.

This exploratory study aimed at identifying the behaviour of young Portuguese tourists (18–25) during their visit to Lisbon, in relation to fado. We verified that about one-third attended a fado show in the city, mostly in *casas de fado* or even in street performances, accompanied by family and friends. Most considered that their knowledge about fado was sufficient or good, and they liked this musical genre and wanted to 'know more' about it. When asked about the themes and feelings associated with fado, the words that came up most frequently were 'love', 'sadness' and 'longing', which expresses the nature of fado.

The results highlight the popular nature of this type of music among the Portuguese, and the fact that Lisbon, whether associated with culture, its nightlife or gastronomy, can, through fado, appeal to images and emotions. Visiting the historic quarters of the city (especially Alfama and Bairro Alto) can lead to a greater perception of the 'unique atmosphere' or experience of the city and its culture, through the city soundscape. We should bear in mind that the cultural activities in the city reveal a geographical pattern with a strong concentration of supply in the central zone, which strengthens the connection between different cultural activities.

The connection between fado and the historic quarters is evidenced by the various 'senses' and 'feelings' inspired by the 'lyrics' that interpret the city and contribute to an emotional construction of it and can be an element of territorial competitiveness. However, we acknowledge some limitations of this study. Further research is needed to deepen the understanding of the subject, namely by increasing the number of interviews, and surveying both Portuguese and foreign visitors, in order to make international comparisons.

Acknowledgements

This research was funded by national funds through the FCT-Foundation for Science and Technology under the project UID/SOC/04020/2013.

Notes

1 'She lives in an attic / The highest of Alfama / That early morning sunlight sets on fire / When she gets up at dawn [...]' ('*Madrugada de Alfama*' ('Dawn in Alfama') by Mourão-Ferreira); or for instance: 'In Alfama, I rest my gaze/ Always unrolling the skein/ Of blue, of the sea. [...] In this light my eyes see you, so pure [...] A city embroidered in light' ('*Lisboa menina e moça*' ['Lisbon, Girl and Young Woman'] by Ary dos Santos).
2 'Alfama doesn't smell of Fado / Smells like people, like loneliness / Like a silent hurting' ('*Alfama*' by Ary dos Santos).
3 'Not even in Madragoa / Anybody competes with her, / when down from her window / she kisses Lisbon so early in the morning' ('*Madrugada de Alfama*' ('Dawn in Alfama') de Mourão Ferreira).
4 It is the cry of the *varinas* (women selling fish), the multiple sounds of the engines of the fishing boats, the ferries, the trams, the songs, the seagulls, the people in the taverns, as well as the very sound of silence or absence of sound – [...] And in her veins, has the bark / Of the engine of a *traineira* (traditional fishing boat). ('*Maria Lisboa*' by Mourão Ferreira).
5 'My love said I / my mouth tastes of longing' ('*Meu amor é marinheiro*' ('My Love Is a Sailor') de Manuel Alegre); 'Alfama [...] tastes like sadness with bread' ('Alfama' by Mourão Ferreira).

References

Ashworth, G. (2015). Railway heritage and tourism: a global perspective. *Tourism Management* 47, 240–240.
Bachelard, G. (1974). *A Poética do Espaço*. Trans. Franklin Leopoldo e Silva. São Paulo: Abril Cultural.
Bardin, L. (2015). *Análise de Conteúdo*. Editora: Edições 70, Extra Coleçao.
Browne, R. (2005). Folklore to popullore. In Browne, R. (ed.), *Popular culture consists of the popular culture studies across the curriculum: essays for educators*. Jefferson, NC: McFarland, pp. 24–27.
Browne, R. and Urish, B. (2014). Introduction. In Browne, R. and Urish, B. (eds), *The dynamics of interconnections in popular culture(s)*. Newcastle upon Tyne: Cambridge Scholars Press.
Câmara Municipal de Lisboa (CML) (2009). Estratégias para a cultura. www.cm-lisboa.pt/fileadmin/VIVER/Urbanismo/urbanismo/Documentos/estrategias_para_a_cultura.pd (accessed 5 March 2016).
Connell, J. (2012). Film tourism: evolution, progress and prospects. *Tourism Management* 33(5), 1007–1029.
Crossman, A. (2014). Popular culture. http://sociology.about.com (accessed 24 June 2016).
Delaney, T. (2007). Pop culture: an overview. https://philosophynow.org/issues/64/Pop_Culture_An_Overview (accessed 10 March 2015).
Eco, U. (1986). *Travels in hyperreality*. New York: Harcourt Brace.
Elliott, R. (2010). *Fado and the place of longing: loss, memory and the city*. Farnham: Ashgate.
Elliott, R. (2014). The choreography of longing: songs, screens and space in Carlos Saura's Fados [pre-publication draft of article published in *Quaderns de Cine* 9 (2014): 71–78.]. http://sro.sussex.ac.uk/50413/1/Elliott_2014_SaurasFados_article.pdf (accessed 20 January 2016).
Gibson, C. and Connell, J. (2007). Music, tourism and the transformation of Memphis. *Tourism Geographies* 9(2), 160–190.
Gibson, C. and Homan, S. (2004). Urban redevelopment, live music and public space. *Journal of Cultural Policy* 10, 67–84.
Henke, L. (2005). Music induced tourism: strategic use of indigenous music as a tourist icon. *Journal of Hospitality and Leisure Marketing* 13(2), 3–18.
Henriques, C. (2016). Lisbon fado as heritage of humanity: interconnections with tourism. In Henriques, C., Moreira, M. C. and César, P. A. B. (eds), *Tourism and history world heritage: case studies of Ibero-American Space*. Braga, Portugal: Interdisciplinary Centre of Social Sciences – University of Minho (CICS.NOVA. UMinho), pp. 381–407. www.lasics.uminho.pt/ojs/index.php/cics_ebooks/article/view/2516/2427
Henriques, C. (2017). O Património literário português e o Fado: sua valorização turística na cidade de Lisboa. In Lousada, M. A. and Ambrósio, V. (eds), *Literatura, viagens e turismo cultural no Brasil, em França e em Portugal*. Lisboa: Centro de Estudos Geográficos, Instituto de Geografia e Ordenamento do Território, Universidade de Lisboa, pp. 481–491.

Hudson, R. (2001). Making music work? Alternative regeneration strategies in a deindustrialized locality: the case of Derwentside. *Transactions of the Institute of British Geographers* 20(4), 460–473.

IC (Instituto Camões) (2014). Introduction of 'Exposições do Camões IP'. www.instituto-camoes.pt/exposicoes-para-itinerancia-pelas-redes/ (accessed 5 January 2015).

IMPACTUR (2016). Indicadores de Previsão e Monitorização da Actividade Turística. Informação estatística turística de Lisboa. www.ciit.ualg.pt/impactur (accessed 5 January 2016).

INE (2016). Estatísticas de Turismo. www.ine.pt (accessed 6 January 2016).

Iwashita, C. (2008). Roles of films and television dramas in international tourism: the case of Japanese tourists to the UK. *Journal of Travel and Tourism Marketing* 24(2/3), 139–151.

Laboratório Estratégico de Turismo (LET) (2016). Estratégia Turismo 2027: uma nova estratégia de turismo para a década. www.turismodeportugal.pt/Portugu%C3%AAs/turismodeportugal/newsletter/2016/Pages/EstrategiadeTurismo2027umanovaestrategiadeturismoparaadecada.aspx (accessed 5 March 2015).

Larsen, K. (2012). Why popular culture matters? Interview. *Journal of Fandom Studies* 4. www.intellectbooks.co.uk/MediaManager/File/popularculture(jan12)web.pdf.

Lashua, B., Cohen, S. and Sheffield, J. (2010). *Popular music, mapping, and the characterization of Liverpool*. London: Equinox.

Lee, S. J. and Bai, B. (2016). Influence of popular culture on special interest tourists' destination image. *Tourism Management* 52, 161–169. http://dx.doi.org/10.1016/j.tourman.2015.06.019.

Lefebvre, H. (1991). *The production of space*. Oxford: Blackwell.

Long, P. (2014). Popular music, psychogeography, place identity and tourism: the case of Sheffield. *Tourist Studies* 14(1), 48–65. doi: 10.1177/1468797613511685.

Mastercard (2016). *Global destination cities index – 2016*. https://newsroom.mastercard.com/wp-content/uploads/2016/09/FINAL-Global-Destination-Cities-Index-Report.pdf (accessed 7 June 2016).

Menger, P.-M. (2013). European cultural policies and the 'creative industries' turn. In Keery, T. and Chan, J. (eds), *Handbook of research on creativity*. Cheltenham, UK: Edward Elgar, pp. 1–20. www.researchgate.net/publication/303314894_European_cultural_policies_and_the_'creative_industries'_turn_Pierre-Michel_Menger (accessed 7 June 2016).

Nery, R. V. (2012). *Para Uma História do Fado*, 2nd edition. Lisboa: Imprensa Nacional-Casa da Moeda, S.A.

Pearce, P., Morrison, A. and Moscardo, G. (2003). Individuals as tourist icons: a developmental and marketing analysis. *Journal of Hospitality and Leisure Marketing* 10(1/2), 63–85.

Pereira, S. (2015). *Ecos do silêncio: para um estudo iconológico do fado*. Lisboa: Repositório da Universidade de Lisboa. FL - Teses de Doutoramento. http://hdl.handle.net/10451/17615 (accessed 10 January 2016).

Pine, B. J. II and Gilmore, J. H. (1999). *The experience economy*. Boston: Harvard Business School Press.

Roland Berger/ERTRL/TL (2014). *Strategic plan for tourism in the region of Lisbon 2015–2019*. Lisbon: Roland Berger/ERTRL/TL.

Sardinha, J. A. (2010). *As Origens do Fado*. Lisboa: Tradisom.

Shuker, R. (2016). *Understanding popular music culture*, 5th edition. Abingdon: Routledge.

Storey, J. (2001). *Cultural theory and popular culture*, London: Pearson/Prentice Hall.

Storey, J. (2008). *Cultural theory and popular culture*, 5th edition. London: Pearson.

TL (2014). Survey on the purpose of trip 2014. *Observatório de Turismo de Lisboa*. www.visitlisboa.com/sites/default/files/2016-10/Survey%20on%20the%20Purpose%20of%20Trip%202014%20-%20Lisbon%20City.pdf (accesesd 26 March 2016).

TL (2015a). Satisfaction and image survey – Lisbon region 2015. *Observatório de Turismo de Lisboa*. www.visitlisboa.com/sites/default/files/2016-10/SATISFACTION%20AND%20IMAGE%20SURVEY%202015.pdf (accessed 7 January 2016).

TL (2015b). Visitor activities and information survey – Lisbon region 2015. *Observatório de Turismo de Lisboa*. www.visitlisboa.com/sites/default/files/2016-10/VISITOR%20ACTIVITIES%20AND%20INFORMATION%20SURVEY%202015.pdf (accessed 7 January 2016).

UNESCO (2006). Tourism, culture and sustainable development (M. Robinson and D. Picard). http://unesdoc.unesco.org/images/0014/001475/147578e.pdf.

UNESCO (2016a). *Fado, urban popular song of Portugal: representative list of the intangible cultural heritage of humanity in 2011*. www.unesco.org/culture/ich/en/lists (accesesd 26 March 2016).

UNESCO (2016b) *Global report on culture for sustainable urban development*. www.unesco.org/new/en/culture/themes/culture-and-development/culture-for-sustainable-urban-development/ (accesesd 26 March 2016).

Wendy, G. (2012). *Cultures and societies in a changing world*. Thousand Oaks, CA: Pine Forge Press.

11

TRANSACTIONAL BODIES

Dance, tourism, and idea(l)s of Cubanness

Ruxandra Ana

Setting the scene

Shortly before noon, Isabel's mother welcomes me in their house in Old Havana, telling me the dance classes had already started early in the morning, but would carry on until late in the afternoon. That would give me the chance to talk to some of the instructors, even though their breaks were very short or sometimes even inexistent as the demand for dance classes was quite high due to the increased number of tourists (*la cantidad de turismo*). Isabel and her husband, Javier, my hosts ever since I first travelled to Havana, are running a rather successful business as owners of two *casas particulares* – Cuban houses for rent, also known among tourists and tourism organizers alike as the cheaper alternative to hotels, and advertised as an opportunity to glimpse at the daily realities of Cuban life. A few years ago, my hosts started renting the living room of their third house (in which they currently live, having kept the two other houses exclusively for renting out to tourists) for dance lessons, and Isabel's mother took charge of keeping the registry of the new business. '*No es facil*',[1] she tells me, a Cuban saying that can be heard very often all across the island, in order to describe shortly and accurately the hardships of everyday life.

> You know how it is, you come from a socialist country as well, you need to spend the entire day out in the street, looking for the things you need, and now with the dance classes I have even less time. But I have to be here, I have no choice.

Next to us, in the entrance hall, one couple is dancing casino,[2] and three other couples are dancing in the living room. The music is accompanied by short indications from the teachers: one-two-three/five-six-seven (counting out loud in order to help maintain the rhythm), *vuelta* (turn), *sombrero, setenta* (some of the most common figures in casino), high-fives, hugs and enthusiastic '*muy bien*', repeated every time a movement is executed correctly.

Six years ago, during my first research trip to Cuba, I used to take dance lessons with Isabel's son in the same living room, yet the policy was less restrictive. As the living room turned into a *salon de baile*, classes began to take place until 3 or 4 pm, bookings in advance were required, together with a strict evidence of the classes taught by each teacher. My first dance lessons at their house would take place even at 9 or 10 pm, and it was not uncommon for members of the family to gather around to watch, give indications, or interrupt the class in order to demonstrate the correct execution of a particular movement or combination, a rather new and, in the beginning, quite uncomfortable situation for someone used to train individually with a teacher, or during a group lesson, behind closed doors, in an organized setting. The living room was completely changed – six years ago, we used to move some of the furniture around, in order to make more room for dancing. Now the furniture was gone, there were big mirrors on one of the walls, one table in the back and one in the front, for the audio equipment.

While Isabel's mother and I were talking, three young women showed up for their lesson, looking forward to learn how to dance 'as Cubans do' and practice at night at parties, as they told me later, during a short break in their two-hour class. Halfway through their lesson, Sabine, the owner of one of the dance schools in Havana, who rents out rooms and rooftop terraces for conducting the lessons, stopped by to check how classes were going, and explained the idea behind her project:

> I could see that the people needed my help, especially after the state decided they could be self-employed. I talked to 4–5 dance teachers I knew, I told them I was going to help them, to make a website, to take all the steps in order to receive clients, so they would dance here and I would send clients. And the school here is doing really well, many people keep telling me they like it because it has a social aspect. The teachers make more money than in other schools. So the whole point was to help the people here. I didn't want to do the same thing that other schools do, I wanted something new.

The school Sabine runs is not an isolated example in Havana, especially in the old part of the city, which attracts the biggest influx of foreign visitors. Nor is this a phenomenon restricted solely to the capital, as dance schools are a common sight in most big cities across the island, rendering the experience of 'Cuban salsa as danced by Cubans and with Cubans' a possibility for dance aficionados and beginners alike.

This chapter looks at the processes related to the commodification of certain aspects of Cuban cultural heritage, and at the key role they play, as authenticating tools, in the development of the tourist sector. Given the increased demand for an alternative type of tourism (usually engaging more than just sight), body performances become central not only to institutions in charge of safeguarding and promoting heritage, but also to emerging small businesses as alternative forms of revenue. As embodied practices become available outside Cuba and inscribed in widely circulating imaginaries, tourist encounters create the premises for capitalizing on cultural heritage both in Cuba and outside of it.

Theoretical underpinnings: Cuban dance in light of international tourism

Dance classes in Cuba are not a novelty, and the tourism industry, especially in recent years, has been relying on aspects of Cuban cultural heritage (especially music and dance) that were transformed into key symbols of the island, being reshaped and becoming 'valuable' in very concrete ways. Performances became reference points for visitors, and as is the case of many other Caribbean countries, presented in such a way as to be recognized by the final targeted consumer – the foreign visitor (Scher, 2011). This has the potential of ensuring a continuous flow of foreign currency, which, in the complicated dual-currency Cuban economy, can make the difference between struggling for survival and having a slightly more comfortable life, despite all hardships. According to the statistics of the UNWTO (2015) and Caribbean Tourism Organization (2014), tourism is the most important industry to the majority of Caribbean countries. Furthermore, UNWTO predictions until 2020 indicate that tourist arrivals in emerging economy destinations in Latin America and the Caribbean are expected to exceed those in advanced economies. While being the economic lifeblood of the region, it is regarded by scholars, activists and locals alike as a double-edged sword or a necessary evil, as it provides the economy with significant revenue but at the same time may lead to cultural decline, deepening disparities and social tensions, and risk damaging almost all existing resources.

The emphasis on local goods and services, as a result of neoliberal economic policies in the Caribbean, generates what Scher describes as 'culturalist market', comprising of local agricultural products, spices, foods, artisanal crafts but also local accents manifested through dance, music and exotic bodies for sale:

> The structuring force of neoliberalism produces an emphasis on culture (a non-competitive market niche), yet also provides the hegemonic model of what counts as culture; that which is remembered and recalled by consumers as appropriate and legitimate to a region, is shaped by both global factors and local history or tradition.
>
> *(Scher, 2011, p. 8)*

Since the early 1920s, Cuba promoted itself as a tourist destination and became one of the most rapidly growing countries in the Caribbean in terms of foreign tourists, with the United States being one of the main markets generating tourist arrivals to the island. It was precisely this influx of tourists, associated mainly with capitalism, gambling, prostitution and bourgeois excess that came to be seen as harmful to the Cuban people in light of the Revolution of 1959.

The new regime brought about not only a series of political, social and economic changes, but also marked the beginning of a new era in terms of cultural policies as part of a larger political project. Nationwide, and especially in the capital, this new project was aimed primarily at erasing the memory of the United States and the image of Havana as a city of bourgeois excess, as pointed out by Lasansky (2004) in the case study of Cuban architecture exemplified by the reconstruction of Old Havana, focusing on colonial culture and bringing forward a romanticized image that lacked the traces of North American domination.

The collapse of the Soviet Bloc in 1991 determined a series of radical changes in Cuba. The country no longer had the help of the global power supplying gas and aliments in exchange for sugar. Eventually, Cuban sugar had to be sold on the global market, which meant a significant decrease in the country's income. GDP collapsed by more than 30 per cent in just three years (Gawrycki, 2010; Krohn and O'Donnell, 1999). The strengthening of the US trade embargo had direct consequences upon the everyday lives of Cubans, now confronted with dire lack of everyday products. Fidel Castro characterized this moment as a 'special period during times of peace'. Cubans faced extreme poverty and it seemed inevitable that changes to the political and economic system needed to be introduced. Among them were the new policies regarding tourism, which had as a direct consequence heavy investments in tourist facilities. As of 1994 the country reopened for tourists, a new Ministry of Tourism was formed and the majority of funds were devoted to the renovation and recreation of the tourist facilities in the country. Cuba experienced a significant increase in the number of foreign visitors, which resulted in the creation of special areas where only tourists or hotel employees were allowed access and the island shortly became denominated as a country of tourist apartheid. Given the rapid development of tourism and the increased demand for accommodation, the government allowed, as of 1997, the development of small businesses that aimed to rent rooms to foreign visitors looking for alternative accommodation. The tourist sector has been in the past two decades the one with the most dynamic expansion, depicted as a model industry for its ability to generate foreign currency and investment. When in 2006 Cuba's long-time president, Fidel Castro, was compelled by illness to step down, the country entered a new era of economic reforms that are slowly but definitively reshaping the relations between state, individual and society, without abandoning the socialist model. The rapid growth in international tourism was connected to a type of narrative disseminated by global media and tour operators worldwide, characterized by a sense of urgency to 'see Cuba before it changes'. While these narratives did not exclude the classical Caribbean trio of sun, sea and sand, they put forward a strong emphasis on Cuban culture, thus bringing aspects of cultural heritage to the attention of foreign visitors and placing a strong accent on its economic values. With rapid growth in international tourism and a very strong presence in the media, the island's official and unofficial promotion strategies came to rely on a limited set of symbols, often transforming Cubans into elements of the scenery and objects of 'the tourist gaze' (Urry, 2002): 'white Caribbean beaches', 'locals smiling and dancing to salsa rhythms', 'Havana's unique atmosphere', 'monuments inscribed on the UNESCO list' and 'the world's best cigars'. The 'beautiful people' of the island are usually presented as just another attraction, right next to the 'beautiful places' under the 'hot sun', accompanied by 'hot rhythms'. The nostalgia for 'the land frozen in time' mixed with pre-revolutionary extravagance and revolutionary culture appeared to be the main focus of most travel guides, organized tours and local businesses aimed at foreign visitors, doubled by the naturalization of the exotic and a rhetoric of light heartedness, sensuality and passion.

In fact, this vision of a country where time stood still was behind the notion that Cuban dance also had such a particular character – many dance aficionados travelling to Cuba for the specific purpose of improving their practice describe the dancing of Cubans as 'free', 'intuitive', 'authentic', 'sensual' and 'sincere', descriptions that were regularly intensified by oppositions and contrasts with European dances, both in their competitive and social forms. In this way, dance creates idealized versions of the practice and the practitioners, and thus privileges types of performances that coincide with romanticized Western perceptions. With the increasing popularity of Cuban style salsa on the international dance market, dance schools were also quick to respond to this opportunity. The increased number of dance schools and authorized dance teachers (*con licencia*) who offer their services mainly to tourists, is a phenomenon of somewhat recent date, as the government allowed Cubans to work '*por cuenta propia*'.[3] It is now almost impossible to walk through Old Havana without noticing a dance school, from those with an already established place on the market, with constant demand from both individual clients and tour organizers, to newer ones, some of them located in bars or restaurants that now also advertise themselves as dance schools. A very common sight at dance parties all around Havana are large groups of tourists and Cubans, the latter wearing t-shirts with the school logo and sometimes the information 'dance instructor' or 'dance teacher'. Business cards are passed around to those asking for dance lessons at parties, and it is quite common for tourists to be accompanied on a night out at one of the popular dancing venues or at a concert by professional dance teachers, as part of a constantly enriched and diversified offer put forward by dance schools, along with happy hours, discounts, promotional packages, additional percussion lessons, short dance trips to other parts of the island, Spanish lessons, massage or dance therapy.

The dance business and the maximization of bodily capital

The development of the dance business in the past few years is partly related to an increased demand for 'experiential tourism' (Salazar, 2011). Cultural practices and symbols that ensured recognition as well as revenue gained meaning both locally and internationally, making the island increasingly appealing for foreign consumption.

With the increasing popularity of salsa congresses and festivals in Europe and the globalization and increased commercialization of the dance and music (Skinner, 2007), situated between cultural heritage and leisure commodity (Pietrobruno, 2009), many dance aficionados outside Cuba become familiar with these dances through classes, workshops and constant participation in dance events, which most of the time include a Cuban section. Casino and 'Cuban style' classes are highly popular with dance schools all across Europe and travelling to Cuba in order to improve one's dancing 'at the source' becomes an important part in the training of many dance enthusiasts (hence the increased number of dance-oriented tours offered by travel agencies and tour operators). With salsa being one of the dances most commonly associated with Cuba in popular culture, it came to be synonymous with a more generalized concept of 'Latinidad', or a sense of Latino identity that facilitates a connection with a cultural 'Other'.

The availability of dance practices in an organized, institutionalized setting, was made possible, to a great extent, by the expansion of the small business sector. Self-employment in Cuba allows a shift from the state sector to the private sector, reshaping work relations and becoming a symbol of economic and political transformations. This is due to the meanings attached to the legalization of independent work, with '*cuentapropistas*' (self-employed workers), being regarded as facilitators of the transition from socialism to a free-market economy (Philllips, 2006). Self-employed workers, although they remain under strict regulations and taxation from the state, are characterized by a distinct position outside the state-regulated work, defining new market relations that place them between the state sector, the private sector and the black market, and creating new spaces and forms of economic activity and work practices, common for post-socialist transitions, in which the individual explores new spheres of decision-making and self-reliance.

> 'Cubans don't know how to get about this business. The first thing to do is teach them how to work', explained Sabine, owner of one of the dance schools in Havana, who runs her business from Germany and at the time of our interview employed almost 30 dance instructors in Cuba's biggest cities. Foreign ownership or partial ownership of dance schools in Havana is not uncommon, and many times even the schools that are owned by Cubans benefit from help offered by friends or relatives from abroad, especially in terms of promoting the school or keeping the website updated. Maximizing one's business is usually seen as a direct result of having a tour operator or travel agency from abroad, as explained by Mily, dance instructor and dance school owner in Havana:
>
> I am a professional teacher, and at times I can be a week without anyone. If you do not have someone, a foreigner, to send you students, your only option is to be out in the street all the time.

While the desired/targeted client is the tourism organizer who would ensure a constant flux of customers as well as steady and significantly higher income, in reality many schools rely on individual clients who find information on the Internet or simply happen to be passing by the school, asking for dance lessons on the spot or making appointments from one day to the next. Thus, worksites condition workers' time, activities, remuneration and social interactions, playing a formative role (Rose, 1999). Functioning outside the state regulated system, many of the self-employed dancers and dance school owners enjoy their new found independence and a sense of freedom that the state sector lacks. 'Under the mantle of legal legitimacy, *cuentapropistas* are not only breaking down traditional institutions and avenues of power, but they are also helping to create new social norm[s] characterized by increased individualism and autonomy' (Ewick & Silbey, 2003, pp. 1332–1333)

However, the private sector comes with new challenges of its own: 'This is not like working for the government, you work or not, but you still get the salary. Here, you take money when you work, when you have your clients' (China, dance school owner and dance instructor in Havana). Larger schools, with more clients and somewhat constant activity, usually have some teachers on site, all the time, ready to attend new potential customers, while others require previous bookings or reservations. Since appointments are usually made by the owner or need to be consulted and approved by the owner, this requires significant flexibility from the dancers. For example:

> [A] client says we will have classes tomorrow in the morning. But then something comes up, the client changes their mind, and says no, I will do the class in the after-noon. But maybe I also have plans, I have to do my own things, so change needs to happen in seconds. You always need to be ready to change your schedule for them, but it never goes the other way round. I am offering you a service, I would like some respect. Many times the owners of the schools only ask you to dance, dance, and smile.
>
> *(Adrian, dance instructor, Havana)*

Private businesses lead to a restructuring of labour routines and an overall change of temporal structures, bringing changes in work discipline and erasing the line between work time and free time (Chelcea, 2014). Time is rendered progressive and linear, facilitating not only production and consumption of services, but time–work discipline and initiating selves (Verdery, 1996). It is not unusual for a dance instructor to work with more than one dance school, as their *licencia* gives them the legal right to work for their own account, and so many of them are ready to work with anyone who requests their services, be it a dance school or an individual client, even though juggling with complicated schedules sometimes leads to misunderstandings: 'Sometimes the teachers don't show up, and then I have to do the class, because the client is waiting. I think it's because other schools pay more, so if the teacher has to choose, he will go there' (Oreste, dance school owner, Havana).

The price of a dance class is usually 12–16 CUC,[4] with the instructors being paid 4–10 CUC, depending on the school. As a means of increasing their earnings, instructors may choose to teach classes outside the organized setting of the school (usually at the *casa particular* where the client lives, or in another space that is available for renting), while dance school owners insist on developing the business:

> I always tell them you have to sell more. But this is sometimes problematic for them, because the class may have to be with another teacher, and they are afraid they may earn less, so I had to explain: not instead of your class, but as an addition. This is the way to sell more classes.
>
> *(Sabine, dance school owner, Havana)*

It is not just classes that bring revenue to both instructors and owners. After a certain number of classes, established by each school according to their own policy, but usually no less than five days, tourists get the chance to practice what they learned, outside the school, accompanied by their instructor: 'For five days of teaching you have the obligation to go out two times with the client. Of course if they want to go out more, independently, with their teacher, they can do it. And it is good pay' (Pascual, dance instructor, Havana).

In this way, enterprise relies on the 'self-steering' capacities of the individuals, designating rules for everyday life: initiative, ambition, personal responsibility. 'The enterprising self will make an enterprise of its life, seek to maximize its own human capital, project itself a future, and seek to shape itself in order to become that which it wishes to be' (Rose, 1996, p. 154). Going out to dance needs to pay off, as the tourists' leisure time is work time for the dancers, and bodily capital (Wacquant, 1995) needs to be converted into economic capital:

> For me to go to Casa de la Musica or 1830,[5] I need to have clients, because otherwise it is not convenient. Just go to these places to see what is happening . . . and if nothing is happening . . . I just wasted some money, I have a daughter, it's complicated.
>
> *(Pascual, dance instructor, Havana)*

> It has to make sense economically, as well. It's not that I am self-sufficient, but if you work with my talent . . . then I need to receive what I deserve. Financially, it has to be satisfying, because I am using my talent, my body. Why would I mistreat just to have the newest tablet or the newest iPhone?
>
> *(Luis, dance instructor, Havana)*

The discourse on ability is deeply rooted in the belief that once a dancer, always a dancer: many of my research participants repeatedly told me they did not need any special training, nor any other form of physical activity in order to be able to dance and teach. And while there appears to be no 'constant stewardship of key bodily functions [. . .] that affect, or are believed to affect, the fructification of corporeal capital' (Wacquant, 1995, p. 75), many of them described their work as constant compromising and making sacrifices:

> Sometimes people do not understand that if you want to achieve big things, you need to make some sacrifices. But I expect the same from you. If you do not respect my work, if you do not understand that I am not spending time with my daughter in order to teach you, then I will find someone else, there are many tourists right now.
>
> *(Adrian, dance instructor)*

Implications for popular culture tourism: 'I cannot tell my students I will teach them to dance like Cubans, because that would be a lie'

The growing demand for dance creates a differentiation between two groups of practitioners: those who learned the dance from family and friends, and those who acquired it through formal instruction (McMains, 2016). This, in turn, creates both employment opportunities and spaces for the institutionalization of the dance business, and creates the spaces for a constant performance not just of the dance itself, but of the profession of dance instructor, as was the case for Luis in his early career as a dance teacher for tourists:

> Back in the days I was selling CDs to tourists, to make a living. So one day I was in Obispo[6] and these girls showed up, with a Cuban guy, and of course I wanted to sell them my CDs. They said no, no, we are looking for a dance teacher. And in my mind, of course, I had to think fast (laughs) . . . there must have been something in my religion, in the energies that protect me, that closed my mouth, because normally I would have said yes, yes, I am a teacher. And at that moment, another guy who stopped

near us was like look, he is a dance teacher. And the girls said yes, but we are looking for someone who actually is a dance teacher, not someone who says they are a dance teacher. He also says he is a dance teacher (about the guy who was with them). Can you put on some music so we can dance, right here? This was my first experience with tourists. I kept dancing, and I felt I was ready to teach some classes. And I felt what the problem was with one of the girls. She didn't have many, but you know, I always look for problems, even if it is not there. You can be a perfect dancer, I will look for the problem. They talked, the two of them, and decided to stay with me. Of course I had to pay a comission to the other guy, every day, because obviously, these are the systems of the street, and I had to pay because I was teaching them, but he was the one who had found them. You know how the street is, one hand washes the other, and both hands wash the face. I come from the street, and I am very fair. Or at least I try to be as fair as possible. There is a difference between feeling and money, but in fact they are united, I will teach you because I need money, but when I am in class with you, there is feeling in what I do.

(Luis, dance instructor, Havana)

For many of the dance instructors, it is important to emphasize their opposition to amateur dancers (those who do not have formal training) and at the same time to point out that simply being immersed in the music and dance is not enough for tourists to actually learn how to dance. Especially since tourism reinforces the idea that in Cuba everyone dances, in order for both instructors and schools to be successful, claims at professionalism and authenticity become crucial. Parts of the tourist imaginary are adopted and adapted in Cuban narratives about Cubanness, attributes like 'blood', 'blackness', 'roots', 'tradition' become trademarks of quality, while for tourists dance appears to function as an embodied souvenir (Ana, 2017) that makes 'Cubanness' available and, in a way, portable, through the body that experienced it.

The ultimate declared purpose for many of the tourists attending dance classes is to dance 'as Cubans do', which is sometimes met with mixed feelings by some of the Cuban instructors:

It is actually an economic system. You have people in a dance school, you pass them through levels, even if they didn't get the basis right. And then people come here to improve that, saying that they want to dance like Cubans do. If you are going to tell me what to teach you, what do you need me for? I cannot tell my students I will teach them to dance like Cubans, because that would be a lie. I can teach you to dance as yourself, the way you are.

(Luis, dance instructor)

Dance teaching and the images of romantic love created and communicated through performances often lead to a fluid understanding of business and affection on both sides. The romantic theme becomes central to Western consumption, being inscribed in 'a complex pattern of hedonistic behavior, the majority of which occurs in the imagination of the consumer' (Campbell, 1987, p. 89), a pattern that frames touristic behaviour and constructs an exotic Other imagined as more passionate, more emotional, and more sexually tempting (Pruitt & LaFont, 1995).

Tourists come here to dance, but at the same time they want to know Cubans, there is much talk of Cuba right now, so they come to Cuba with this idea, I'm going to find myself a Cuban, it can be a dance teacher, a dancer, or someone you just met in Florida or Casa de la Musica. And now imagine, these girls come here with these ideas . . . if you find her attractive, you go for it, you are not going to deny yourself this.

(Pascual, dance instructor, Havana)

At the same time, Cubans themselves rely on an imagined understanding of what motivates tourists to take dance lessons, and the dynamic of these interactions is complicated by the assumptions made on both sides. Thus, dancing appears as merely a pretext, with different ultimate goals or intentions well hidden behind a declared desire to improve one's dancing: 'Some of the girls who come here to dance are good enough and really do not need any more classes. Most probably they are here for the teachers, there is no other explanation' (Jorge, dance instructor).

While dancers themselves tend to accept that interactions on the dance floor can lead to romantic involvement, dance school owners usually make it clear that they do not wish for their employees to be involved in any other way with their clients, as this can affect the image of the professional dancer and, subsequently, the school. In fact, the strong discourse of professionalization that characterizes many of these new businesses created around dance is built not so much around what a professional is, but rather around what a professional is not.

A professional dancer is not one of those guys from the street who always look for girls. You can't mix your intimate relationships with your work, because when the relationship starts, professionalism ends. This kills the image of the professional. I am also guilty of this, I did it, but I did it once, it's not the same as being out every night at La Gruta, or 1830, or Florida.[7]

(Luis, dance instructor, Havana)

Especially Cuban school owners tend to manifest a preference for 'trained dancers', coming from art schools or other recognized academic institutions, that guarantee proper training in the arts, a thorough understanding and knowledge of the dances taught (although in my experience unless specifically asked for, such information is not provided) and provide buffers from typical street interactions. In this way, not only does the school create a safe space for the tourists, where the school logo and name take responsibility for both the quality of the teaching, as well as for the personal safety of the tourist, but it creates a space for the affirmation and performance of a type of masculinity that is different from the one performed in the street:

There are people who live close to 1830 or La Gruta and visit them frequently, and they have various objectives: the first one, meeting someone who can get them out of the country, or someone to fall in love with, others are simply there to get money out of the tourist. And many dance with the purpose of getting some advantage, they are not there to dance.

(Pascual, dance instructor, Havana)

Given the daily struggles and the difficulties of living in a double currency economy, many of the interactions with tourists are commonly motivated economically, yet for dance school owners it is important to make sure that money is not the main reason for possible romantic involvements with clients:

Sometimes they go out with the clients, but I do not want anything more to happen, but it happens anyway because there are girls who come here and want more than just a dance class. I can't control and I can't change everything, but the important thing for me is that they don't do it because they want more money. They can do it because they like the girl, but not because they want more money.

(Sabine, dance school owner)

In this way, the emergence of small businesses centred around dance and practices related to dance instruction reveal how the transnational circulation of Cuban dance forms brings along not only the codification and commercialization of distinct units of steps, but also powerful ideas of gendered bodies that materialize in performance. At the same time, they reveal how economic realities and social inequalities that stem from contact with foreigners result in creative approaches for financial gain, perpetuating expectations about Cuban fantasies. Thus, performances and transmission of dance traditions become part of the touristic and political use of culture, strongly determined by economic factors and operating with essentialist concepts and definitions of identity.

Notes

1 'It is not easy' (translation from Spanish by the author. All interviews were conducted in Spanish and translated to English by the author, unless otherwise specified).
2 The dance marketed abroad as Cuban-style salsa is referred to in Cuba as 'casino'.
3 As part of the economic reforms implemented by Raul Castro on the island, self-employment was authorized in approximately 200 categories.
4 1 Cuban convertible peso (CUC) is roughly the equivalent of 1 euro, and the average monthly salary in the state sector is around 20 CUC.
5 Casa de la Musica and 1830 are popular dancing venues in Havana.
6 The main street in Old Havana.
7 La Gruta, 1830 and Florida are popular dancing venues in Havana.

References

Ana, R. (2017). Rumba: Heritage, Tourism and the 'Authentic' Afro-Cuban Experience. In E. Chrysagis & P. Karampampas (Eds.), *Collaborative Intimacies in Music and Dance: Anthropologies of Sound and Movement* (pp. 163–186). New York: Berghahn Books.

Campbell, C. (1987). *The Romantic Ethic and the Spirit of Modern Consumerism*. London: Blackwell.

Caribbean Tourism Organization (2014). Tourism Statistical Tables 2003–2015. www.onecaribbean.org/statistics/historical-data-1970-2015/. Retrieved 26 April 2018.

Chelcea, L. (2014). Work-Discipline and Temporal Structures in a Multinational Bank in Romania. In N. Makovicky (Ed.), *Neoliberalism, Personhood, and Postsocialism: Enterprising Selves in Changing Economies* (pp. 37–52). Farnham, UK: Ashgate.

Ewick, P. & S. Silbey (2003). Narrating Social Structure: Stories of Resistance to Legal Authority. *American Journal of Sociology* 108, pp. 1328–1372.

Gawrycki, M. & N. Bloch (2010). *Kuba*. Warsaw: Trio.

Krohn, F. B. & S. T. O'Donnell (1999). U.S. Tourism Potential in a New Cuba. *Journal of Travel & Tourism Marketing* 8(1), pp. 85–99.

Lasansky, D. M. (2004). Tourist Geographies: Remapping Old Havana. In D. M. Lasansky & B. McLaren (Eds.), *Architecture and Tourism* (pp. 165–186). Oxford, New York: Berg.

McMains, J. (2016). Hot Latin Dance: Ethnic Identity and Stereotype. In A. Shay (Ed.), *The Oxford Handbook of Dance and Ethnicity* (pp. 480–500). Oxford, New York: Oxford University Press.

Philllips, E. (2006). 'Cuentapropismo' in a Socialist State. In M. Font (Ed.), *Cuba: In Transition? Pathways to Renewal, Long-Term Development and Global Reintegration* (pp. 107–124). New York: Bildner Center for Western Hemisphere Studies.

Pietrobruno, S. (2009). Cultural Research and Intangible Heritage. *Culture Unbound* 1, pp. 227–247.

Pruitt, D. & S. LaFont (1995). For Love and Money: Romance Tourism in Jamaica. *Annals of Tourism Research* 22(2), pp. 422–440.

Rose, N. (1996). *Inventing Our Selves. Psychology, Power, and Personhood.* Cambridge: Cambridge University Press.

Rose, N. (1999). *Powers of Freedom: Reframing Political Thought.* Cambridge: Cambridge University Press.

Salazar, N. B. (2011). The Power of Imagination in Transnational Mobilities. *Identities: Global Studies in Culture and Power* 18, pp. 576–598.

Scher, P. W. (2011). Heritage Tourism in the Caribbean: The Politics of Culture After Neoliberalism. *Bulletin of Latin American Research* 30, pp. 7–20.

Skinner, J. (2007). The Salsa Class: A Complexity of Globalization, Cosmopolitans and Emotions. *Identities* 14, pp. 485–506.

UNWTO (2015). World Tourism Organization, UNWTO Annual Report 2014. Madrid: UNWTO.

Urry, J. (2002). *The Tourist Gaze.* 2nd edition. New York: Sage.

Verdery, K. (1996). *What Was Socialism and What Comes Next.* Princeton, NJ: Princeton University Press.

Wacquant, L. (1995). Pugs at Work: Bodily Capital and Bodily Labor among Professional Boxers. *Body & Society* 1(65), pp. 65–93.

12

THE VOYEUR AT LEISURE

Flânerie in a miniature city – the urban phenomena of Madurodam

Maranke Wieringa

Urban phenomena are not necessarily limited to actual cities, they can be situated in rural areas and perhaps even in non-places. My interest lies in the urban practices or phenomena that we partake in or can discern when leisurely strolling through the miniature city of Madurodam, a miniature theme park in The Hague, the Netherlands. Madurodam itself is an agglomeration of landmarks. The urban practices and phenomena that can be tied to this theme park are those of leisure time, tourism and flânerie.

Problematically, indices that are rooted in the 'real' mingle with fictitious indices. In Madurodam, the legendary Hansje Brinker, the 'real' windmills and delta works, and the fictional characters of the movie *Wiplala* are placed on the same premises, without distinction. Yet all of these sites, whether they exist(ed) in the actual world or not, are presented to the visitor-voyeur as ontologically equivalent. Madurodam functions as an institute that presents the canon of Dutch culture, yet it does not discriminate between fact and fiction.

In this chapter I will first briefly introduce the concept of miniature theme parks and in particular the Dutch park of Madurodam, before elaborating on the urban phenomena of leisure time. I will then discuss the models of the flâneur by Baudelaire (1964) and Benjamin (1993), and De Certeau's voyeur (2007). After introducing these theories, I will explain how these concepts function within the Madurodam theme park experience. My departing hypothesis is that tourism here is an escapist practice that allows the practitioner to temporally partake in the urban practice of flânerie – within the voyeuristically structured spatial environment of Madurodam. This structured environment functions as a 'museum without walls' (Malraux, 1949), and contributes to the aestheticization of everyday life (Featherstone, 1992). Furthermore, urban memory is fluid in Madurodam, in the sense that it can borrow memories from the places to which the miniature buildings indexically refer. Nevertheless, the park has an urban memory of its own as well (Crinson, 2005). Moreover, its buildings and inhabitants do not exclusively refer to actual scenes, but may also be rooted in the fictional – ontologically, the park does not seem to discriminate.

Setting the scene

Madurodam is a miniature theme park in The Hague, the Netherlands. It is one of the first parks of its kind in the world (Bulut & Yilmaz, 2006, p. 63), and opened its doors in 1952.[1] Miniature parks like these can now be found all over the world, and serve educational, recreational and touristic purposes.

So what does Madurodam look like? Once you have passed the entrance (Figure 12.1), which is very typically situated in a dike, you encounter all kinds of miniature buildings, landscapes and even 'Madurodammertjes', the inhabitants of Madurodam (Figure 12.2). All of these displays are scale 1:25, and are produced by the theme park itself. As the park (predominantly) displays landmark buildings and ordinary street life, it is very much an assembled space, in which time and space blur together. The obsolete, and abolished, telephone cell stands next to an electric car that is being charged (Figure 12.3) – a scene that can never be found in an actual Dutch city. Spatially, we see a similar phenomenon; the Kaaswaag of Gouda and the Frans Halsmuseum, which ordinarily stand 56 kilometres apart, are neighbours in Madurodam (Figure 12.4).

Bulut and Yilmaz (2006, p. 63) note that parks like these enable their visitors to come to an (albeit superficial) understanding of the national history and culture in a short period of time. Madurodam actively promotes itself in precisely this way: as a composite of cultural highlights and heritage of the Netherlands (Madurodam, 2017b). In the theme park's own words, it is there that you'll discover what makes a small country great (Madurodam, 2017a).

In Madurodam, the ordinary and the exceptional blend together, with no regard for spatial or temporal origins of their displays. As mentioned, the park isn't limited to the spectacular or unique urban landscapes, it also features the mundane. Little Madurodammertjes go about their business: the mundane urban activities we all take part in such as grocery shopping (Figure 12.5). Urban sights such as houses for sale or rent have also permeated Madurodam (Figure 12.6), and stand next to cultural highlights such as the Rijksmuseum in Amsterdam (Figure 12.7), or a DJ performance by Armin van Buuren (Figure 12.8).

Figure 12.1   Entrance of Madurodam. On the left Hansje Brinker has his finger in the dyke.

Figure 12.2   An overview of Madurodam showing the miniature Palace 'het Loo' (front).

This blurring allows the miniature theme park to serve as a physiognomy of the Dutch culture. Of old, physiognomy refers to the judgment or categorization of people based on their visual appearance, especially their faces (Pearl, 2010, p. 1). Pocket physiognomies were even published and drawn upon to help the urban residents to read their peers during modernity. Physiognomies were used to make sense of the new and urban reality, of industrialization and estrangement. Thus, they were a way to navigate the modern context (Pearl, 2010, pp. 26–27). In a way, contemporary miniature parks like Madurodam serve as pocket physiognomies of cultures, though they usually only highlight the best and beautiful, they still help us to categorize what characterizes a particular culture.

Theoretical underpinnings

Before we can delve deeper into the various urban phenomena, let us first look at their theoretical foundations. Below, I will first sketch a brief history of leisure time, and the rise of tourism. Then, I will discuss the notion of the flâneur, as formulated by Baudelaire (1964) and Benjamin (1993), and De Certeau's (2007) notions of the walker and the voyeur.

Leisure time and the rise of tourism

While it may feel as if free time is the most self-evident of things, leisure time was in fact only commoditized and professionalized in modernity. Thus, it is in fact quite a recent invention. Modernity proved to be the perfect breeding ground for tourism: a greater amount of leisure time, combined with increased technological abilities. The combination of both these developments gave people time to visit particular sites, and the means to do so. Thus, part

Figure 12.3   Streetscene of Madurodam showing the electric car being charged (front) and an obsolete public telephone cell (back).

of tourisms' success lies with technological inventions, which provided people with faster travelling options, such as railways. Yet, as said, it was not only technological innovations that stimulated the leisure 'industry'. The urban working class eventually negotiated that Saturday afternoons were to be free from work (Spracklen, 2011, pp. 148–149), for instance, thus paving the way for the weekends as we currently know them.

Enhanced mobility and the increase in leisure time for the working class were two of the main factors that spurred tourism. The world became 'smaller', because it would take less time to travel somewhere, and at the same time people had more time to explore this world. Over the years, regulated working hours were implemented in more areas of the industry, thus providing the working and middle classes with more spare time (Pangburn, 1922).

Through these developments, leisure time became something everyone could take part in. Yet this 'democratization' of leisure time, and tourism by extension, has not always been warmly

Figure 12.4   Haarlem's Frans Halsmuseum (front) and Gouda's Kaaswaag (back).

welcomed, and in fact has been criticized quite often. Due to mass transportation, less people were thought of as actively 'travelling' and more became passive 'tourists' that were being 'sent' somewhere by train (Boorstin, 1961, p. 85). This 'passive bunch of tourists' is united in their systematized knowledge of the world and their moral values. They all know what they ought to do in a particular country or city, yet they all wish that none of the other tourists were there (Culler, 1990; MacCannel, 1976).[2]

There is, however, also a more positive view on tourism. Tourism can be seen as an escapist move from ordinary life. In this chapter I follow Fussell (1972, p. 42), who states that "a tourist is best defined as a fantasist equipped temporarily with unaccustomed power". Thus, partaking in touristic practice deviates from ordinary life, and is temporally empowering. As the tourist breaks away from the ordinary practices they partake in at home, they are freed to take part in different ways. It is this empowering move that lies at the heart of the miniature park experience, as will be demonstrated shortly.

Figure 12.5 Madurodammertjes partaking in mundane urban activities.

The flâneur, the voyeur and the walker

With the rise of great metropolises in modernity, the urban experience markedly changed. A prominent urban figure of this modern period is the flâneur: the stroller, the anonymous walker who observes the city and its inhabitants. The flâneur is an urban type, or a state of mind that has been conceived in two different ways. As a state of mind the 'flâneur' is typically understood as having to do with the movement, rhythm and the urban experience in the mid-nineteenth century. As for the urban type, there is the Baudelairean conception and the Benjaminian one. I will elaborate on each of these in turn below.

In Baudelaire's interpretation of Edgar Allen Poe's *The Man of the Crowd* (1840), the flâneur is the narrator of the story. This character observes and classifies all the passing pedestrians, until he sees one that he cannot place. He follows this person in the crowd, because of his 'childlike curiosity' (Baudelaire, 1964, pp. 8–9). Though the flâneur is curious and passionate, he occupies a kind of meta-level within the urban crowds. He observes his fellow citizens from a distance: he is part of the crowd, but is able to observe the crowd as well, without being observed himself. But this distancing is not a characterization of the blasé attitude – for the flâneur is passionate about the environment and not numbed by it. The Baudelairean flâneur is a type that walks the borderline of the inside/outside of urban life, of seeing and being seen, of the public and the private as he feels at home in the public space of the crowd (Baudelaire, 1964, p. 9).

The Benjaminian concept of the flâneur is equated with the unknown 'man in the crowd' in Poe's story. This leads to a different interpretation of the flâneur. The flâneur could – in the Benjaminian sense – potentially be a criminal. He is someone who is there, in the crowd, to make a living. The Baudelairean passion of the flâneur is transformed into utility: the flâneur makes use of the crowd. Benjamin typically located the flâneur in the arcades, and states that the

Figure 12.6   House for sale in Madurodam.

Figure 12.7   The miniature Rijksmuseum.

Figure 12.8   Miniature performance by DJ Armin van Buuren.

type feels at home in the streets. This makes the flâneur again a type of 'border figure', for whom the interior/exterior, public/private binaries cease to exist. This conception of the flâneur is one that concerns itself with that what is to be gained from entering the crowd and navigating it. This 'profit' could perhaps be a collection of impressions that can be sold, or it can even be a pecuniary profit made from pick pocketing (Benjamin, 1993).

In the remainder of this chapter, I take the flâneur as a state of mind, which can be found in every gender, although I acknowledge how Benjamin and Baudelaire have informed this state of mind.[3] Thus, the flâneur, here, refers to an urban type that navigates an urban context, a figure that both classifies, yet is also a kind of border figure gleaning for impressions.

But the flâneur is not the only urban type of interest. Let us look at the two urban types that Michel de Certeau (2007) sees as a binary opposition: the walker and the voyeur. A walker follows "the thicks and thins of the urban 'text' they write without being able to read it" (p. 158). These walkers are the "ordinary practitioners", of the urban space (ibid.).

The voyeur, on the other hand, is able to read this urban text. Like the flâneur, this is a distanced figure. This distance allows the voyeur to 'read' the city, like the flâneur observes the crowd. But while the flâneur is within the crowd that it observes, the voyeur is placed outside of it. De Certeau (2007, p. 157) conceives of the voyeur as being elevated above the city, or, in a more poetic phrasing: as "[a]n Icarus flying above [the] waters". This bird's eye view allows the voyeur to see the city as it is, to read it like the proverbial book, to see its structure, its conception – like one cannot see from below.

Both the flâneur and the voyeur, are border figures. The (Baudelairean) flâneur occupies perhaps more mental borders, while the voyeur is literally placed on the high rises of the city – which grants him an overview, but excludes him from city life (Baudelaire, 1964; De Certeau, 2007). Moreover, both of these types are analytical in nature. Whereas the flâneur assesses the urban condition from within the crowd, the voyeur analyzes the urban context from above. Both these types are differentiated from the walker: the 'unknowing' pedestrian going about his business.

Walking in the miniature city

The touristic experience of Madurodam is an interesting one. It is an escapist move from the city to another, miniature, city, which is placed within the former. The Madurodam experience is inextricably bound to tourism and leisure. As a theme park it is meant to be visited by people, and cannot be entered unless one buys a ticket (or works there). With regards to the tourism, I take a positive stance, and regard it as an empowering practice. It is – as I will argue – this empowering deviation from ordinary life that allows the visitors of Madurodam to partake in the urban practices of flânerie and voyeurism. While at home they may go about their business as walkers, in this theme park the structured environment inescapably casts them as voyeurs.

The visitor of Madurodam can stroll through the park, and can observe both the 'Madurodammertjes', the plastic miniature citizens, and his fellow tourists – who are easily classified.[4] Yet the visitor is also a voyeur, one who is literally looking down on the city, who reads the city from a distance. Similar to the way in which the voyeur and the flâneur are border figures, the tourist too is both part of Madurodam, in the sense that he or she can walk through it, yet is forever excluded from it.

The visitors of Madurodam can never be the walkers that De Certeau describes, the voyeur-istic role is literally forced upon them, due to the way in which the miniature city is built. Thus, this voyeuristic flânerie is not reserved for a specific class, age or gender, but is practiced by every visitor that has paid the entry fee.

The city is conceived as a miniature agglomeration of Dutch landmarks and iconic buildings, which allows for easy classification of the Dutch culture as a whole: a kind of physiognomy of a whole country – where specific characteristics (landmarks), traits (practices) and notable events (history) are put on display for the flâneur to observe (Bulut & Yilmaz, 2006). Like the (pocket) physiognomies of Paris and London (among others), which taught its residents about the differ-ent urban types (Pearl, 2010), Madurodam is a physiognomy of an entire culture – its canonical architecture, cultural practices and touristic myths – and educates both natives and foreigners.

While strolling through the miniature city, then, the visitor takes on both the role of the voyeur and the flâneur. They are cast as analytical figures, distanced from the miniature, ordi-nary walkers. They are here to analyze the thicks and thins of the miniature city – and by exten-sion an entire nation's culture.

This analysis, or classification, inherent to the Madurodam experience is inseparable from the spatial environment. If Lefebvre's trialectics are taken into account (Merrifield, 1993), then it can be argued that this classification has to do with two things. First, the triumph of the conceived space over spatial practices, resulting in a 'museum without walls' (Malraux, 1949). The 'museum without walls' was a thought experiment by Malraux (1949), in which he tries to imagine a museum that contains all of the world's artworks. He sketches:

> the museum without walls, the imaginary museum which is filled by all the works of art of the world irrespective of their period, their location, their size or any of those fortuitous conditions which have in the past rendered them inaccessible.
>
> *(Lansner, 1950, p. 341)*

Second, the indexical and iconical nature of the representational space, which leads to fluid urban memories. Drawing from semiotics, the term index refers to a particular Peircean mode of a sign. An indexical sign demonstrates a relationship with a thing outside the sign itself (the sign's object). This relationship defines the indexical sign (e.g. cause and effect) (Chandler, 2007, p. 42). An iconical sign, on the other hand, resembles the object, as a portrait resembles a person (Chandler, 2007, p. 40). These two modalities of the miniature landmarks and urban sights, may invoke memories of the places these landmarks or sights represent – even though they are physically (far) removed from the premises of Madurodam.

Let us first discuss the way in which the conceived space results in a museum without walls. In the Madurodam themepark, one is not allowed to touch the buildings or the figurines. One can only observe them: among the crowd of plastic 'Madurodammertjes', yet never be allowed to interact with them. This not being allowed to touch the artifacts relates to what Lefebvre would term the 'conceived space', or 'representations of space'. This concept relates to the conceptual nature of a space, as it is conceived of by, for instance, urban planners. It is the abstract idea of what the space should be that heavily inscribes the created space. In Madurodam this prohibition of touching the figurines, of straying from the designated paths, leads to a certain classification of the Madurodammertjes and the miniature buildings. This, in turn, translates to the level of the spatial practices, that is, the way in which people use space. As people are not allowed to interact with the figurines, or walk among them, this creates a separation of 'us' and the miniature 'them'.[5] It grants the miniature city a kind of museological status, as in museums too we are not allowed to touch the objects on exhibit (Gombrich, 2002, p. 97).

In addition to this, the theme park functions, quite literally, as what André Malraux (1949) termed a 'museum without walls'. Lansner (1950, p. 341) describes this as "the imaginary museum which is filled by all the works of art of the world irrespective of their period, their location, their size or any of those fortuitous conditions which have in the past rendered them inaccessible". Problematically, however, this is a museum that does not discriminate between fact and fiction. In Madurodam, the legendary Hansje Brinker, the 'real' windmills, delta works, Schiphol airport, churches and fictional characters of the Dutch film *Wiplala* (2014) are or were placed on the same premises, without distinction (Den Haag Direct, 2014; Madurodam, 2017a).

While the statue of Hansje Brinker (Figure 12.9) is more or less life size, the airport, the other landmarks and the Wiplala characters (Figure 12.10) are all miniatures. Furthermore, they are all from different (legendary/fictional) times and the locations they refer to indexically could never co-exist in one and the same place. If this was not enough of an argument to vouch for the validity of applying Malraux's term to Madurodam, not even all of these sights originate in the Netherlands, as the legendary Hansje Brinker originally came from the book *Hansje Brinker or the Silver Skates* written by the American author Mary Mapes Dodge in 1865 – which renders it an imported legend (Meertens Instituut, 2013).

Yet all of these sites, whether they exist(ed) in the actual world or not are presented to the visitor-voyeur as equal to one another. Though Madurodam functions as an institute that serves the canonization of Dutch culture, it does not discriminate between, fact, fiction or legend. The miniatures that refer to the actual world are ontologically presented in the same way as their counterparts that refer to fictional worlds.

Thus, the boundaries between the 'real' and the 'imaginary' are blurred in the way that Madurodam presents itself. The 'everyday life' of the tourist experience – has become 'aestheticized'. According to Featherstone (1992, pp. 267, 286), this notion can be traced back to mid-nineteenth-century urban phenomena like carnivals, fairs and spectacles. These were sites of 'ordered disorder', where 'others' allowed the patron to construct their identity: to get a sense of who they were and who they were not (Featherstone, 1992, pp. 286–287). The miniature city of Madurodam is a pretty disorienting place that is structured around a few major 'landmarks' around several themes (i.e. inventions, water, the city) – even though most of the city

Figure 12.9   Statue of Hansje Brinker.

Figure 12.10   Wiplala characters on Dam Square.
Source: courtesy of Madurodam (2017).

itself is comprised out of dislocated miniature landmarks, forming a kind cognitive map (Lynch, 1960). Furthermore, the visitor, is not a 'Madurodammer', they are either foreigners or Dutch, but never one of these miniature people. For the foreigner the miniature folk may come to represent the Dutch Other, while for Dutch visitors they may represent a nostalgic, folkloristic Other, or perhaps just the miniature, plastic Other.

Tourists, like these patrons, aestheticized their everyday lives "by turning life 'into a work of art'" (Featherstone, 1992, p. 269; Harrison, 2001, p. 165). The democratization of these images, both those that refer to the actual world and those that refer to fictional worlds, efface "the distinctions between reality and image" – as Baudrillard puts it (Featherstone, 1992, p. 269). This museum then seems to familiarize its visitors with a physiognomy of Dutch culture in which myth, fiction and 'reality' seem to hold equal sway. It is a physiognomy that may hold true within the context of the theme park, but certainly not outside of it.

The second consequence of applying Lefebvre's trialectics to Madurodam has to do with the indexical nature of the representational space. As mentioned earlier, the miniature buildings and figurines are indices and icons of other urban places. Thus, when the visitor visits the miniature they may revisit memories of visiting the object of the indexical and iconical miniature. To clarify: when visiting the miniature Dom of Utrecht in Madurodam, the tourist that has visited its actual counterpart, may remember this visit – not the miniature one. The iconic miniature buildings serve to trigger urban memories that are not bound to the place they themselves occupy.

In the words of Crinson (2005, p. xii), urban memory indicates "the city as a physical landscape and collection of objects and practices that enable recollections of the past and that embody the past through traces of the city's sequential building and rebuilding". I have already mentioned how the indexical nature of the miniature buildings allows memories of other places to migrate to the miniature city, this would be the landscape and collection of objects that allows a recollection of the past. The latter notion can be applied as well. Over time new buildings may be added or updated, and there is thus a sense of building and re-building in the miniature city. For example: the miniature stage where once the figurines of the Dutch band Golden Earring stood, was updated and now features the Dutch DJ Armin van Buren (Den Haag FM, 2013). For visitors who were used to seeing Golden Earring figurines, this 'rebuilding' may allude to the past of Madurodam.

The hypothesis that I started out with is that tourism is an escapist practice that allows the practitioner to temporally partake in the urban practice of flânerie – within the voyeuristically structured environment of Madurodam. Moreover, this structured environment has several implications. We have seen that the miniature city of Madurodam allows for flânerie and voyeurism due to the way that it is built – it is a break with normal reality and empowers the person to partake in flânerie. As tourists, we are forced to watch the city from above when we stroll through the park. The theme park as a whole may serve as a physiognomy of Dutch culture: the agglomeration of miniature landmarks from throughout the country, as well as cultural practices that are on display allow the flâneur to classify the country it represents. The classification takes place as voyeuristic flânerie is strongly encouraged in Madurodam, and it is made to take place along two lines of classification, which are identified here with Lefebvre. First, the triumph of the conceived space over spatial practices, resulting in a 'museum without walls' – in which everything is democratized regardless of origin, size or 'truth'. Thus, the 'everyday' life of tourism in Madurodam is aestheticized. Second, there is the matter of the indexical and iconical nature of the representational space, which led me to the notion of urban memories. This notion is twofold. First there are the 'fluid' urban memories, this means that the miniature buildings (e.g. the Rijksmuseum miniature) can trigger memories of their actual counterparts (e.g. the Rijksmuseum in Amsterdam). Second, there are urban memories of Madurodam itself: the rebuilding and updating of the miniature sites within the theme park.

Implications for popular culture tourism

In a nutshell, there are two implications for popular culture tourism to be discerned. First, there is the matter of the flânerie and voyeurism that the structured environment of the theme park afford. Theme parks can thus be said to offer a touristic site in which visitors can practice particular behaviour they otherwise would not be able to exert, such as flânerie. In this sense, tourism can very much be employed in a (temporary) empowering or emancipating fashion.

Second, such parks can invoke memories of other times and places, not necessarily associated with the tourist attraction. Moreover, fact and fiction can blend together in these places. This ties in with the narratives such a theme park tells, and the way this connects with other aspects of (popular) culture.

Notes

1 The first being Bekonscot in England, which opened in 1929.
2 Illustrative of this sentiment is the so called 'picture spot' or 'Kodak moment' in various theme parks, in which this passive tourist is even provided with an ideal position from which to take the most picturesque picture (Doris, 1999) – which more often than not results in families taking identical pictures of the same places.
3 This flâneur was conceived of as being male. As Pollock (1988) and Wolff (1985) note, this was a privilege only reserved for the well-off males of that time, as women were often banned from this portion of the public sphere.
4 With regards to the latter, Culler (1990, pp. 157–158) writes – very vividly – that: "[t]ourists can always find someone more touristy than themselves to sneer at: the hitchhiker arriving in Paris with a knapsack for an undetermined stay feels superior to a compatriot who flies in on a jumbo jet to spend a week. The tourist whose package tour includes only air travel and a hotel feels superior, as he sits in a cafe, to the tour groups that pass by in buses. Americans on bus tours feel superior to groups of Japanese, who seem to be wearing uniforms and surely understand nothing of the culture they are photographing." Thus, there is very much a layering of identification and analysis at play. Visitors not only categorize the miniature, but also their fellow tourists. In the remainder of this chapter, I will, however ever interesting, not pay attention to this phenomenon. Nevertheless, it is paramount that we do acknowledge this parallel of categorization, of physiognomical analysis between the tourist and the flâneur. The Madurodam visitor not only categorizes the plastic miniatures, or Dutch culture, but also his peers.
5 One will note that throughout this chapter I practice a view that, indeed, 'things' can be thought of as having (a degree of) (inscribed) agency. With this, I mean that things or objects can influence humans and their actions. In this, I am very much indebted to the tradition of actor-network theory (ANT), the area of affordance analysis and material culture studies. For more information on ANT see, for instance, Latour (1996, 2005), Akrich (1992), Akrich and Latour (1992), Sismondo (2010), or Czarniawska and Hernes (2005). For more information on affordance analysis see, for instance, Norman (1988, 1998) and Gibson (1979, 1986). For more information on material culture studies see, for instance, Ingold (2008, 2012), Brown (2001, 2010) and Bennett (2010).

References

Akrich, M. (1992). The de-scription of technological objects. In W. E. Bijker & J. Law (Eds.), *Shaping technology/building society: studies in sociotechnical change* (pp. 205–224). Cambridge/London: MIT Press.

Akrich, M. & Latour, B. (1992). A summary of a convenient vocabulary for the semiotics of human and nonhuman assemblies. In W. E. Bijker & J. Law (Eds.), *Shaping technology/building society: studies in sociotechnical change* (pp. 259–264). Cambridge/London: MIT Press.

Baudelaire, C. (1964). The painter of modern life. In *Charles Baudelaire, The Painter of Modern Life and Other Essays* (pp. 1–41). New York: Da Capo Press.

Benjamin, W. (1993). The Paris of the Second Empire in Baudelaire. In *Charles Baudelaire: A lyric poet in the era of high capitalism* (pp. 35–66). London: Verso.

Bennett, J. (2010). *Vibrant matter: a political ecology of things*. Durham/London: Duke University Press.

Boorstin, D. J. (1961). *The image*. New York: Atheneum.

Brown, B. (2001). Thing theory. *Critical Inquiry, 28*(1), 1–22.

Brown, B. (2010). Objects, others, and us (the refabrication of things). *Critical Inquiry, 36*(2), 183–217.

Bulut, Z. & Yilmaz, H. (2006). Miniature parks and the sample of Miniatürk. *Journal of Applied Sciences, 6*(1), 62–65.

Chandler, D. (2007). *Semiotics: the basics* (2nd ed.). Abingdon: Routledge.

Crinson, M. (2005). Urban memory – an introduction. In M. Crinson (Ed.), *Urban memory history and amnesia in the modern city* (pp. xi–xx). London: Routledge.

Culler, J. (1990). The semiotics of tourism. In *Framing the sign: criticism and its institutions* (pp. 153–167). Norman, OK: University of Oklahoma Press.

Czarniawska, B. & Hernes, T. (Eds.). (2005). *Actor-network theory and organizing*. Abingdon: Marston book services.

De Certeau, M. (2007). Walking in the city. In S. During (Ed.), *The cultural studies reader* (pp. 156–163). London: Routledge.

Den Haag Direct. (2014). Personages bioscoopfilm Wiplala krijgen eigen poppetje in Madurodam. Retrieved 18 December 2014, from www.denhaagdirect.nl/personages-bioscoopfilm-wiplala-krijgen-eigen-poppetje-in-madurodam/

Den Haag FM. (2013). Armin van Buren verjaagt Golden Earring uit Madurodam. Retrieved 18 August 2018, from http://denhaagfm.nl/2013/06/18/armin-van-buuren-verjaagt-golden-earring-uit-madurodam/

Doris, D. (1999). It's the truth, it's actual: Kodak picture spots at Walt Disney World. *Visual Resources, 14*(3), 321–338.

Featherstone, M. (1992). Postmodernity and the aestheticization of everyday life. In S. Lash & J. Friedman (Eds.), *Modernity and identity* (pp. 265–290). Oxford: Blackwell.

Fussell, P. (1972). *Abroad*. New York: Oxford University Press.

Gibson, J. J. (1979). *The ecological approach to visual perception*. Boston: Houghton Mifflin.

Gibson, J. J. (1986). *The ecological approach to visual perception*. Hove: Psychology Press.

Gombrich, E. H. (2002). *Art & illusion*. London/New York: Phaidon Press.

Harrison, J. (2001). Thinking about tourists. *International Sociology, 16*(June), 159–172.

Ingold, T. (2008). Bringing things to life: creative entanglements in a world of materials (NCRM Working Paper Series).

Ingold, T. (2012). Toward an ecology of materials. *Annual Review of Anthropology, 41*(1), 427–442.

Lansner, K. (1950). Malraux's aesthetic. *Kenyon Review, 12*(2), 340–348.

Latour, B. (1996). On actor-network theory: a few Clarifications. *Soziale Welt, 47*(4), 369–381.

Latour, B. (2005). *Reassembling the social*. Oxford: Oxford University Press.

Lynch, K. (1960). *The image of the city* (2nd ed.). Cambridge/London: MIT Press.

MacCannel, D. (1976). *The tourist: a new theory of the leisure class*. London: Macmillan.

Madurodam (2017a). All attractions. Retrieved 17 August 2017, from www.madurodam.nl/en/the-park/all-attractions

Madurodam (2017b). Discover Holland's highlights and heritage. Retrieved 17 August 2017 from www.madurodam.nl/en/the-park

Malraux, A. (1949). *The psychology of art: a museum without walls*. New York: Pantheon Books.

Meertens Instituut (2013). Hans Brinker stak zijn vinger in de dijk. Retrieved 18 August 2017, from www.verhalenbank.nl/items/show/43368

Merrifield, A. (1993). Place and space: a Lefebvrian reconciliation. *Transactions of the Institute of British Geographers, 18*(4), 516–531.

Norman, D. A. (1988). *The psychology of everyday things*. New York: Basic Books.

Norman, D. A. (1998). *The design of everyday things*. London: MIT Press.

Pangburn, W. (1922). The worker's leisure and his individuality. *Journal of Sociology, 27*(4), 433–441.

Pearl, S. (2010). *About faces: physiognomies in nineteenth-century Britain*. Cambridge/London: Harvard University Press.

Poe, E. A. (1840, December). The man of the crowd. *Burton's Gentleman's Magazine*.

Pollock, G. (1988). Modernity and the spaces of femininity. In *Vision and difference: femininity, feminism and the histories of art* (pp. 50–90). London: Routledge.

Sismondo, S. (2010). *An introduction to science and technology studies* (2nd ed.). Chichester: John Wiley & Sons.

Spracklen, K. (2011). *Constructing leisure: historical and philosophical debates*. Hampshire: Palgrave Macmillan.

Wolff, J. (1985). The invisible flâneuse: women and the literature of modernity. *Theory, Culture & Society, 2*(3), 37–45.

13

TECHNOLOGY ADOPTION AND POPULAR CULTURE SPORT TOURISM

Azizul Hassan

Setting the scene

Sports have long been one of the key forms of entertainment. Sports as a form of popular culture, by their traditions, take different forms in accordance with different societies and cultures (Ivanovic, 2008) and sport in its traditional forms represents amusement within cultural diversities across the world. Sport as a tool of entertainment is said to contribute to the process of social well-being (Hinch & Higham, 2011) and in some countries, a sport can have unrivalled popularity among the locals and the enthusiasm and participation in such sports become very strong. In many societies, moreover, sports perform a role as one of the key opportunities for social and cultural progression.

In certain cases, a sport can become a valid and reliable element of the local culture, as evident from many parts of the world including Bangladesh. Cricket in this perspective is an instance of a sport that can have effects on the local population of a country. In the Indian subcontinent, including Bangladesh, cricket has become a very popular sport and seemingly a part of the local culture. Research studies also clearly support the view that a sport such as cricket has enormous acceptance and engagement from the mass of the population (Baum & Butler, 2014). In the particular cultural context of Bangladesh, cricket is integral in a way that creates a link between sports, cultures and innovation in technologies. The adoption of innovative technology in cricket has become common these days and has actually brought this sport to a broad spectrum of the population who previously never thought of watching a live telecast from their home. However, the adoption of technology in cricket has immense effects on its viewers as it facilitates the enhancement of popular culture. In this regard, the term 'popular culture' means the local culture and is nurtured and retained by the local population of an area.

This chapter pragmatically situates the application of technology in the process of popularizing cricket as a form of tourism. The study considers cricket as a form of popular culture tourism in Bangladesh. A good number of research studies have been carried out over the years, covering diverse aspects of cricket in the Indian subcontinent. However, a lack of research remains in examining cricket from a popular culture perspective. This research is one of the first to examine innovative technology adoption in tourism and its role in propelling cricket to its current position in local popular culture. Thus, this chapter offers an understanding of popular culture in the context of cricket. In this regard, the study incorporates the views and perceptions of cricket spectators as popular culture sport tourists to outline the reasons that cricket has become an element of popular culture in Bangladesh.

Theoretical underpinnings

Popular culture: the discourse

Popular culture is very often termed 'pop culture', offering comprehensive perspectives, ideas, attitudes, relevant phenomena and images within the scope of a cultural system. Popular culture is viewed as originating from Western culture during the very early to mid-twentieth century and accepted as the effective global mainstream until the very late twentieth and early twenty-first century (McGaha, 2015). Popular culture is taken as heavily influenced by the mass media, supported by ideas of daily livelihood and the society itself. Generic features of popular culture include: games, television, music, movies, politics, technology, slang, familiarity with places and persons, clothing or fashion and so on. Popular culture is seen as having the capacity to resist the boundaries of definition: this culture can be meaningful to different persons in different ways, while culture and ideology remain two basic aspects to generally understand popular culture. Popular culture expands to include diversions, mass media or even the truest form of entertainment.

Williams (1980) presents four distinct meanings of popular culture as: 'well-liked by many people'; 'inferior kinds of work'; 'work deliberately setting out to win favour with the people'; and 'culture actually made by the people for themselves'. According to Storey (2006), the first genre of defining popular culture is related to a quantitative definition of high culture. The second stream of popular culture definitions identifies it as a left-over culture after distinguishing the high culture. Thus, from this perspective, popular culture is a residual category. The third type of definition sees popular culture as a 'mass culture'. The fourth genre of definition states that popular culture originates from 'people'. The fifth stream shows that, popular culture draws on the political analysis of Antonio Gramsci, the Italian Marxist, for developing hegemony. The sixth definition explores the idea that popular culture, as defined by the neo Gramscian approach, is about the constitution of 'peoples'. Thus, complex meanings of both 'popular' and 'culture' are associated with popular culture.

Traditionally, popular culture is critically considered as insignificant because of seeking consensual approval within the mainstream. This is one of the key reasons that critiques of popular culture originating from diverse, non-mainstream sources (e.g. counterculture groups) label it to be corrupt, sensationalist, consumerist or superficial.

Cricket in Bangladesh

The origin and development of cricket cannot be traced back without the British. The British introduced cricket to Bangladesh as part of the Indian subcontinent during their colonial regime (Guha, 2001). Traditionally, the Bangladeshis were ruled, dominated and suppressed by different invading nationalities of the world. A long tradition of suppression created a kind of negative mindset of the locals against the rulers (Morgan, 2007). Cricket was spread and popularized rather quickly in Bangladesh, with the locals keenly ambitious to defeat the British, the colonial power. Traditionally, people used to watch cricket in person or follow the updates in printed media like newspapers. However, the recent forms of digital television broadcasts and the Internet have made cricket accessible to most of the people of Bangladesh. Also, policy interventions of the Bangladesh government, supported by the International Cricket Council's (ICC) global expansion strategies, pushed cricket to attain more popularity among the local

Bangladeshis (ESPNcricinfo, 2016). In recent years, Bangladesh offers a relatively favourable set of national tourism policies (Hassan & Burns, 2014; Hassan & Kokkranikal, in press). Traditionally, Bangladesh holds good prospects of nurturing tourism of different types with technological support (Hassan et al., 2015; Hassan & Rahimi, in press; Hassan & Ramkissoon, 2017; Hassan & Sharma, 2017). Cricket as a popular culture sport in Bangladesh has achieved an accepted position.

Cricket as a form of popular culture tourism

Unlike other sports, cricket can hardly be seen as purely a form of entertainment. Rather, it is more integrated with trade, global commercial activities and tourism and thus impacts the local economy and culture (Ritchie & Adair, 2004). Many purposes are served by cricket alone in recent years, resulting in increased cricket audiences that have grown to millions.

The origin of cricket is centuries old and rooted in Europe (Arnold & Wynne-Thomas, 2011), but over the decades, this sport expanded to other countries of the world, making it more popular than ever before. An oppressive mindset against the colonial regime and ready technological availability of broadcasting on television and radio are the most influential reasons. Cricket holds a strong position in Bangladesh in many separate areas, including especially culture, business and tourism. Although viewing cricket as the most common form of popular culture of Bangladesh is arguable, the unprecedented popularity of cricket has made this sport a key element of popular culture in Bangladesh.

Technology adoption by popular culture sport tourists

There is evidence that the most innovative technologies are adopted in broadcasting cricket (Southgate et al., 2016). Some years ago, general viewers had to struggle to follow cricket updates, but this dramatically changed as soon as they started enjoying live broadcasts of cricket matches on television and radio. One of the basic reasons for this trend is the involvement of global broadcasting agencies with updated technological support. This is a unique opportunity for seekers of commercial benefit and innovative technologies have been adopted for cricket on television and radio as well as for commercial operations. Moreover, innovative technology is commonly adopted by sport tourists these days to meet diverse demands (Bednarczyk & Gancarczyk, 2013). This also renders importance to the audience perspective as advertisement time during breaks of live broadcasting attract corporate houses to showcase their products and services (Batemand & Hill, 2011). The introduction of Global Positioning System (GPS) based technologies and satellite communication has further brought a revolution in cricket facilitating its development into an element of popular culture in some countries. The most recent innovative technology adoption in cricket appears in three broad categories (International Business Times, 2016; Quora, 2016):

1. *Television broadcasting*: Ultracam, StarCam360, Stump Camera, Umpire Cams and Spider Cam are some cameras that enhance cricket match broadcasting experience for television.
2. *Sport amenities support*: PitchVision, Ball Spin RPM/ Rev Counter, Bowling Machine and Speed Gun are technologies used during the cricketers' training session.
3. *Sport decision-making support*: There are some technologies adopted to support umpires in making their decisions: Hot Spot as an infra-red imaging system; Snick-o-Meter, a sensitive microphone technology or Hawk-Eye, a computer system to show the path of the ball; and LED stumps and bails, a technology that allows blinking of stumps and bails when the bails become dislodged from the stumps.

The recent rise of cricket broadcasting capacities through innovative technology adoption is an example of technology adoption in cricket. These technologies are getting updated day by day, creating a useful bridge between cricket, its spectators and popular culture. Thus, technology of an innovative nature clearly makes cricket a form of popular culture tourism; and innovative technologies are mostly adopted by popular culture sport tourists bringing them far closer to cricket as a popular sport. However, the extent of technology adoption varies from place to place and depends on different geographical aspects.

Sport as popular culture tourism and diffusion of innovation

Popular culture tourism is a relatively recent phenomenon whose relationship with sport has not been clearly defined. This is concerned with the process of linking a sport with the conventional cultural system of a nation or a country. The development of infrastructural and socio-economic settings of a society differs from one community to another in terms of their capacities and limitations, while popular culture tourism is more focused on a new form of cultural element. In recent years, people's activities relating to commercial, business and other purposes are significantly accelerated. Rapid and momentous advancements in communication, coupled with technological developments, have pushed the boundary of popular culture far ahead of its customary stage.

Sport always has appeal and acceptance to both domestic and internal audiences. Also, sport can apparently become an inseparable part of wider global cultural types. In recent years, the adoption of innovative technologies has accelerated the process of including newer elements into local popular cultures across the world. This process of inclusion is always obvious when the broadcasting facilities of events like cricket across the world remain powerful. This also becomes apparent in issues relating to popularity and universalization of a sport like cricket in many parts of the world including Bangladesh. The adoption of innovative technologies is the key facilitator in this context. In today's world, spectators from all over the globe can travel virtually to take part in sports events.

Thus, it is quite understandable that a sport like cricket in any part of the world can be widely accepted, regardless of any potential issues such as nationality, competitiveness and control of any form. Very often, sport can be connected with a new culture in its original form, yet any form of sport in the current world can attract audiences from all over the world and can connect them through the adoption of innovative technologies. A basic reason for this is that the transportation of people from one corner of the world to another has become virtual. This is made possible by an unbelievable progress in technological and communication networking systems.

Elements of local popular culture are attached to both interpretation and definition, in terms of trade, social issues, popular involvement and adoption of innovative technology. People's traditional games with balls made of stones, rocks, hair or feathers are modified and have started to take global shape in accordance with the international settings. Typically, popular culture is accompanied by facts and concerns like reaching the mass population through the adoption of innovative technologies. Parting from its most conventional application in innovative technology adoption research, the Diffusion of Innovations Theory by Rogers (2003) finds a unique call to this given perspective of cricket as an element of popular culture. By this theory, Rogers (2003) searches for explanation of at what rate, why and how new ideas or innovation spread in a society. According to this theory, diffusion is a process through which an innovation is accepted over time within the participants of a social system. This theory has a very particular focus on innovative technology adoption and thus can be the most relevant in this research context, justifying the adoption of innovative technologies in cricket to turn it into an element of popular culture.

Methodology

This study relies on primary data from qualitative research. Primary data were generated through face-to-face interviews with the target respondents. A total of 30 interviews were conducted with respondents selected purposefully for the sake of generating relevant and valid data. These respondents have prior knowledge of cricket in Bangladesh, its ongoing popularity and impacts on the local culture. The respondents are cricket spectators of both domestic and international cricket matches in Bangladesh, are seen as supporters of the view of cricket as a valid element of the local popular culture and have knowledge about the innovative technology adoption in cricket. These interviews were 15–20 minutes long. Three main themes of this research were covered in these interviews:

1. cricket;
2. popular culture;
3. innovative technology adoption.

Interviews were supported by informal and open-ended discussions. These interviews were conducted in Bangladesh at the main cricket stadium (i.e. Sher-e-Bangla National Cricket Stadium). Data used in this research follow critical and logical explanations from the available literature. A detailed review was carried out of existing literature about cricket in the Indian subcontinent, including Bangladesh, followed by literature relating to the recent trend of innovative technology adoption in cricket. Both published and unpublished reports, newspaper articles and editorials were reviewed. In addition, as useful and important secondary data, online resources were considered for secondary data generation. The most recent and updated statistical evidence regarding cricket, innovative technology adoption and popular culture were searched on relevant websites. Thus, both face-to-face interviews and the literature review are the main data sources for this research.

Findings and analysis

Popular culture: the discourse

Respondents do not seem to have critical knowledge of popular culture discourse or ideas related to it. However, all the respondents have a common understanding of their culture and associated artefacts. Popular culture is something very new and unique to them and, hence, requires further explanation. This explanation in general simplifies the meaning of popular culture with ideas generated from literature review discussions. After the explanation, in terms of understanding popular culture, the respondents are divided in their opinions. According to respondent 1, 'popular culture is the pattern of livelihood of peoples living in a specific society'. On the other hand, respondents 2, 13, 14, 25, 26, 27, 28, 29 believe that Bangladesh has a very visible popular culture that has been existing for a long time. Also, respondents 12, 15, 24 and 30 agree that popular culture is gaining importance in typical Bangladeshi society while its scope is rapidly expanding in many aspects of the local people's livelihood. Thus, popular culture is seen as an unavoidable feature of conventional Bangladeshi society, making it very common for the local population. Relating to Williams's (1980) view of 'well-liked by many people', respondents 6, 7, 8, 9, 11, 18, 19 and 20 believe that cricket in the Bangladesh culture is well liked by many people.

Cricket in Bangladesh

All respondents agree that cricket is the most popular sport in Bangladesh these days. The acceptability of cricket is enormous, meaning that this sport has obviously become an element of local popular culture of Bangladesh. Respondent 3 is straightforward in his claim that, 'Cricket as a popular sport of Bangladesh is now rather part of its culture'. Cricket has been brought to the country in the last couple of decades, making it a popular sport. From a different angle, respondent 5 believes that, 'Traditionally, cricket has a solid position in the Bangladesh sport because the society and the structure are aligned with the European sporting system'. The Indian subcontinent, including Bangladesh, can presumably be considered a strong base of cricket that has produced both cricket players and popular sport tourists. These cricketers and popular sport tourists very often travel to other cricket playing nations, mainly in Europe, upholding the identity of Bangladesh. Conversely, cricketers and popular sport tourists from those countries very often visit Bangladesh. Apart from entertainment, such inter-nation movement is related to better living standards, potential sources of earnings and financial gains. This is quite reciprocal, making cricket global and popular within sport-fanatic nations. Cricket has no geographical boundaries, making it enjoyable from any part of the world. In many cases, foreign players traditionally strengthen domestic cricket, creating a bridge to exchange their skills and experiences.

Cricket as a form of popular culture tourism

This association with the European sport system has resulted from the British colonial regime with its long years of ruling the country. Respondent 17 mentioned the mindset of local people as the basic factor to popularize cricket in this country and mentioned that, 'Actually, when we, the general people play cricket, we commonly believe that we are defeating the colonial rulers and their suppressions. This is because we have an enriched history of exploitation'. Cricket, now and in coming days, is expected to have more popularity among the mass of people of Bangladesh. A key finding of the study, as stated by respondent 4, clearly outlines that, 'Cricket remains one of the major sports in the country at least for the last few years mainly due to spectators' huge participation'. Cricket becomes a popular culture element because the living style, presentations and customization of cricketers and popular sport tourists in reality represent their own cultural influences.

In general, people engaged in sports or related activities can be identified as the consumers of both local and other culture. These people can have significant capacity in the onward advancements of society and cultural issues through sports. Findings explore an array of opinions related to cricket as an element of the popular culture of Bangladesh. Thus, in terms of these people's participation and involvement with cricket, this study clearly establishes that cricket is an element of the Bangladeshi popular culture. The availability of leisure time, free access to watch cricket on the television or on the Internet and relatively lower familiarity with other forms of sports can be influential reasons for cricket to be an element of popular culture in Bangladesh.

Technology adoption by popular culture sport tourists

Cricket is mainly supported by the effective implementation and interpretation of innovative technologies. The number of cricket tourists as popular culture sport tourists is relatively higher in the Indian subcontinent, including Bangladesh, in comparison to other nations of the world.

Table 13.1 Summary findings of face-to-face interviews

Respondent	Key factor
1	Cricket is akin to patterns of local people's livelihood
2	Bangladeshi culture is friendly and accepting of cricket
3	Cricket is a popular sport of Bangladesh
4	Cricket has huge participation by spectators
5	The society of Bangladesh aligns with the European sporting system for cricket
6	Cricket is liked by many people
7	Cricket is liked by many people
8	Cricket is liked by many people
9	Cricket is liked by many people
10	Bangladeshi local people's mindset is favourable for cricket
11	Cricket is liked by many people
12	The scope of cricket is rapidly expanding in many aspects of the local Bangladeshi people's livelihood
13	Bangladeshi culture is friendly and accepting of cricket
14	Bangladeshi culture is friendly and accepting of cricket
15	The scope of cricket is rapidly expanding in many aspects of the local Bangladeshi people's livelihood
16	Bangladesh has a strong follower base to track cricket
17	Bangladeshi local people's mindset is favourable for cricket
18	Cricket is liked by many people
19	Cricket is liked by many people
20	Cricket is liked by many people
21	Bangladesh has a strong follower base to track cricket
22	Bangladesh has a strong follower base to track cricket
23	Bangladesh has a strong follower base to track cricket
24	The scope of cricket is rapidly expanding in many aspects of the local Bangladeshi people's livelihood
25	Bangladeshi culture is friendly and accepting of cricket
26	Bangladeshi culture is friendly and accepting of cricket
27	Bangladeshi culture is friendly and accepting of cricket
28	Bangladeshi culture is friendly and accepting of cricket
29	Bangladeshi culture is friendly and accepting of cricket
30	The scope of cricket is rapidly expanding in many aspects of the local Bangladeshi people's livelihood

According to respondents 16, 21, 22 and 23, cricket, in its traditional form, is followed by millions of peoples from across the world, including both domestic and international matches. These followers are actually the basic reason for innovative technology adoption in cricket because their demands have to be met by live broadcasting. This number is increasing as more tourists follow the sport. Following globalization trends and better support of technologies, cricket is becoming border-free, with free access. Rapid commercialization of cricket benefits from adopting innovative technological excellence.

As this study relies on face-to-face interviews to identify influencing motives for cricket to be seen as an element of popular culture, the summary findings are outlined in Table 13.1. This presents a summary of findings from 30 face-to-face interviews that were conducted with target respondents. These interviews bring out the most common statement 'cricket is liked by many people'. The second most common statement is 'Bangladeshi culture is friendly and accepting of cricket'. Thus, the table above shows that cricket is a form of popular culture in Bangladesh.

Implications for popular culture tourism

This study was designed with the set objective to explore the reasons that the application of technology supports cricket in becoming an element of popular culture. In this research, cricket is seen as an element of local popular culture from the Bangladesh perspective. The research suggests that cricket has become very popular, mainly due to the adoption of innovative technologies. The rapid adoption of innovative technologies is responsible for cricket becoming an element of local popular culture. The best possible interaction between cricket and its spectators comes into effect through the adoption of innovative technologies. An equal balance between cricket and innovative technology is much desired, making it more enjoyable and ensuring acceptability. With the support of innovative technologies, cricket has reached many diverse areas of the world, making it easily accessible for both domestic and international spectators and audiences. A sport like cricket can possess major importance and the use of technological advancements can serve as a tool to reduce the gap between cricketers and popular culture tourists. As a common element of the popular culture of Bangladesh, cricket has been able to create a solid standpoint. In the Bangladesh context, this research explores amiable and harmonized interrelations between cricket and innovative technology adoption, when cricket stays as a useful element of popular culture. Drawing upon a theoretical analysis of the Rogers' (2003) Diffusion of Innovations Theory, it is shown that innovative technology adoption has allowed cricket to appear as an element of popular culture in Bangladesh. Findings of this research identify a number of reasons that enable innovative technology adoption in cricket to become an element of local culture in Bangladesh. The presence of the British in the Indian subcontinent, including Bangladesh, is a valid reason while the sport is also liked by many people. The conventional Bangladesh society and the people's mindset are also flexible enough to diffuse innovative technologies in cricket. Future research should encompass more innovative technology adoption in cricket and expand the study context beyond Bangladesh to the entire Indian subcontinent. The reason for this is that cricket has not only become an element of local popular culture in Bangladesh but arguably also in the entire Indian subcontinent.

References

Arnold, P. & Wynne-Thomas, P. (2011). *The complete encyclopaedia of cricket*. London: Carlton Books.

Batemand, A. & Hill, J. (2011) (Eds.). *The Cambridge companion to cricket*. Cambridge: Cambridge University Press.

Baum, T. & Butler, R. (2014) (Eds.). *Tourism and cricket: travels to the boundary*. Clevedon: Channel View Publications.

Bednarczyk, M. & Gancarczyk, J. (2013) (Eds.). Entrepreneurship in tourism and sport. Retrieved from: http://jemi.edu.pl/uploadedFiles/file/all-issues/vol9/issue1/JEMI_Vol_9_Issue_1_2013.pdf (accessed 1 September 2016).

ESPNcricinfo (2016). A brief history of Bangladesh domestic cricket. Retrieved from: www.espncricinfo.com/bangladesh/content/story/260114.html (accessed 1 October 2016).

Guha, R. (2001). *A corner of a foreign field: The Indian history of a British sport*. London: Picador.

Hassan, A., Ahmed, M. U. & Shoeb-Ur-Rahman, M. (2015). The development, nature, and impact of medical tourism in Bangladesh. In M. Cooper, K. Vafadari & M. Hieda (Eds.), *Current issues and emerging trends in medical tourism*. Pennsylvania: IGI Global, pp. 296–311.

Hassan, A. & Burns, P. (2014). Tourism policies of Bangladesh: a contextual analysis. *Tourism Planning & Development*, 11(4), pp. 463–466.

Hassan, A. & Rahimi, R. (in press). Addressing climate change effects on coastal tourism in St. Martin's Island of Bangladesh. In A. Jones & and M. Phillips (Eds.), *Disappearing destinations: climate change and future challenges for coastal tourism*. Oxfordshire: CABI.

Hassan, A. & Ramkissoon, H. (2017). Augmented reality for visitor experiences. In J. N. Albrecht (Ed.), *Visitor management*. Oxford: CABI, pp. 117–130.

Hassan, A. & Sharma, A. (2017). Wildlife tourism: technology adoption for marketing and conservation. In J. K. Fatima (Ed.), *Wilderness of wildlife tourism*. Waretown: Apple Academic Press, pp. 61–85.

Hinch, T. & Higham, J. (2011). *Sport tourism development*. Clevedon: Channel View Publications.

International Business Times. (2016). Top 10 technological advancements that changed cricket forever. Retrieved from: www.ibtimes.co.in/top-10-technological-advancements-that-changed-cricket-forever-62 4174 (accessed 1 October 2016).

Ivanovic, M. (2008). *Cultural tourism*. Kenwyn: Juta & Company.

McGaha, J. (2015). Popular culture & globalization. *Multicultural Education*, 23(1), pp. 32–37.

Morgan, R. (2007). *Encyclopaedia of world cricket*. London: SportsBooks.

Quora (2016). What are the technologies used during cricket matches? Retrieved from: www.quora.com/ What-are-the-technologies-used-during-cricket-matches (accessed 1 October 2016).

Ritchie, B. W. & Adair, D. (2004). *Sport tourism: interrelationships, impacts and issues*. Clevedon: Channel View Publications.

Rogers, E. M. (2003). *Diffusion of innovations* (5th ed.). New York: Free Press.

Southgate, D. F. L., Childs, P. R. N. & Bull, A. M. J. (2016) (Eds.). *Sports innovation, technology and research*. London: World Scientific Publishing Europe.

Storey, J. (2006). *Cultural theory and popular culture*. Harlow: Pearson Education.

Williams, R. (1980). Base and superstructure in Marxist cultural theory. Retrieved from: www.rlwclarke. net/courses/lits3303/2008-2009/04cwilliamsbaseandsuperstructureinmarxistculturaltheory.pdf (accessed 1 September 2016).

14

HUNTERS, CLIMBERS, FLÂNEURS

How video games create and design tourism

Nicolle Lamerichs

Setting the scene: tourism as a playful experience

In 2016, the augmented reality application *Pokémon Go* inspired people of all ages, all over the world, to go out and catch virtual creatures. Designed by Niantic, in collaboration with Nintendo, the game created a virtual map over our familiar surroundings, placing large "gyms" and "Pokéstops" on well-known spaces. As I traveled through Japan in 2017, *Pokémon Go* was still popular and included many new features. In the metro and on the streets, we ran into many Japanese people of all ages that were also playing the game. Though we did not speak their language, we could tell by their screens and the strategic ways in which they walked that these were our team members and, in some cases, our competitors in the game.

Gaming and tourism went hand in hand in our travel group, as we caught new Pokémon and engaged in gym battles together. Games allow us to immerse ourselves in new, virtual environments, but also to experience offline locations in new ways. Unlocking new areas and new Pokémon can be a great incentive to play *Pokémon Go* abroad. However, the game is also a helpful aid for any traveler, as it helps navigate an unknown town more easily. Since landmarks of the game correspond with real landmarks, players who walk to active spots in the game are treated to popular sightseeing spots in the town as well, such as beautiful statues, parks, and stores. Above all, most games give us a sense of wonderment and exploration, as we engage in new localities in meaningful ways.

This sense of exploration is an essential component in many modern games today, whether we think of majestic fauna in *The Elder Scrolls V: Skyrim* (Bethesda, 2011), or the ever-expanding forests, deserts, and river beds in *Zelda: Breath of the Wild* (Nintendo, 2016). Even shooters such as the *Call of the Duty* (Activision et al., 2003–ongoing) series, or minimalist games such as *Tetris*, produce a sense of space that players need to master, and operate within. Even in the independent game scene, where titles are produced by small teams, exploration and perspective has become essential. One of the most popular indie genres today is the "walking simulator," in which players explore and walk through an environment, but in which interaction is kept at a minimum. *Dear Esther* (The Chinese Lightroom, 2012) was one of the first and most well-known games in this genre, and is best described as a poetic game in which players navigate through an island and listen to a melancholic voice over to recover their identity. Later games in this genre, such as *The Stanley Parable* (Galactic Café, 2013) and *Firewatch* (Santo, 2011), offer similar experiences of walking, listening, and observing the environment. The gaze of the player is essential in these games, which have a first-person perspective, and allow for immersion in detailed spaces. These games are not about acting, but about exploring and above all, observing.

Now that we have reached an era of "media life" (Deuze, 2012), in which mobile and connected technologies affect all our practices, we need to rethink how tourism can be reconceptualized. John Urry (2001) already stated that the figure and gaze of the tourist have changed, due to globalization and mediation: "Tourist sites proliferate across the globe as tourism has become massively mediatized, while everyday sites of activity get re-designed in 'tourist' mode, as with many themed environments" (p. 7).

Since digital games rely heavily on virtual and offline spaces, it would not be odd to speak of tourism in games. How can we envision virtual tourism in games today? How are virtual environments experienced by their players? Can the virtual spaces of games be recreated in real life, and where might we find such sites of media tourism? This chapter examines the capacity of games to create new localities as virtual environments. Recent game successes, such as *Pokémon Go*, also demonstrate that games enhance bodily experiences and shape the environments that we are already familiar with through augmented technology. Games, then, do not only rely on our gaze to examine the new and virtual, but may force us to re-examine the offline and familiar as well.

In this chapter, I argue that video game tourism is fundamentally different from other types of media tourism, since tourism is actually heavily embedded within the structure of these media. This chapter introduces a conceptual and descriptive understanding of game tourism. It analyzes new spaces of tourism as they emerge in relation to new media, such as virtual reality, and to the particular medium of games and play.

Theoretical underpinnings: studies on media tourism

In this chapter, I rely on studies done on the mediation of tourism and narratives. Of particular interest is the field of media tourism, which points out the importance of traditional places in media and fandom.

These studies focus heavily on locality and media, and analyze *media places*, such as production spaces (e.g. film sets) and narrative spaces connected to media (e.g. theme parks). Media tourism is an important field that often shows the intensity and affect when fans visit a place that is integral to the cult text. *Twilight* fans, for instance, visit the film sets to re-experience the romance novel that shaped their youth (Lundberg & Lexhagen, 2012). That tourism helps audiences access, interpret, and actualize the beloved narrative anew explains how fiction is envisioned in these places by tourists (e.g. Cartmell, 1993). By traveling to certain locations, fans experience where authors wrote their famous novels (Watson 2010), discover film sites or the villages that star in their beloved fiction (Gordon, 2003; Waysdorf & Reijnders, 2017) and even retrace the steps of a character (Reijnders, 2009, 2011).

In media tourism, media scholars have argued that actual places are transformed by the narratives and the memories that we associate with them. Specifically, Nick Couldry (2000, 2003) investigated media tourism as a type of pilgrimage that involves an affective travel to get closer to the 'media centre'; the ritual heart of the media product. As other studies on fan and media pilgrimage show (Brooker, 2007; Norris, 2013), these pilgrimages are intimately related to the narrative associated with them, and the journey, to the place or event matters as much as experiencing the space itself.

My own studies on fan tourism focused on the pilgrimage of going to a fan convention, a large gathering of fans in hotels or other public venues to celebrate their love for certain (genre) fiction. By doing field research on large comic cons, anime conventions, and Japanese comic markets, I explored the role of belonging in fandom, and its relation to global fan identity (Lamerichs, 2014). By dressing up as fictional characters (engaging in *cosplay*), and by re-enacting scenes from specific media, fans created themed environments in which they could reconnect with their beloved series again. While spaces such as hotels are fairly neutral, and unrelated to the production of a narrative, the space gains interpretive meaning through the fan practices that are hosted there and its history of fan activity.

While the connection to virtual spaces (e.g. forums and fan sites) is often analyzed in the field of media tourism, the attention to games has been limited. This may be related to the fact that games are spaces of imagination. Games are fictional and virtual worlds that we inhabit and that have no real life counterpart, as is the case in the *Dragon Age* and *Zelda* series. In general, the idea of touring and revisiting spaces known from fiction is not that common in the case of video games, since they lack offline counterparts such as a film set.

However, the study of video games as touristic spaces could provide new insights. Both virtual and traditional games (e.g. board games) are different from media such as novels or film since they allow developers and players to create and experience new locations. Video game tourism is different from other forms of media tourism since games are performative media that rely on actions of the player as well as a sense of space. Game worlds themselves allow for touristic practices, especially virtual sightseeing, which is heavily connected to the control of the player, and his or her perspective through the playable character (the avatar).

While game tourism can be partly rooted in real life, as I will show in the next sections, I want to specifically unpack the relation with virtual. Furthermore, I will explore how this may fuel new understandings of tourism, which resonate with Urry's "touristic gaze" (2011).

Methodology

This chapter is a pilot, which may be followed up by a more exhaustive study on video game tourism. My method is a combination of close-reading, (ethnographic) participation in games and online forums. I rely on small-scale, recent data sets gathered through a combination of ethnography and online research or "netnography" (Kozinets, 2010; Markham, 1998).

In 2017, I searched *Assassin's Creed* fan tours on Tripadvisor and Reddit and read reviews, first exploratory, and then in detail. Moreover, to study virtual reality tours, and virtual reality as a way to market and gamify holiday destinations, I studied footage on platforms such as YouTube. Finally, I relied my own experiences as an active player, scholar, and reviewer of video games to conceptualize this framework.

My aim with this study is to draw attention to the production of locality in global media spaces, by using digital games as a case study. I reflect on the transnational spaces of online gaming, as well as the impact that games have on their players as affective spaces (Hills, 2001).

While this chapter focuses primarily on digital games, it is important to note that most games, even traditional ones, are rich spaces in which meaning is created. Paul Booth's *Game Play* (2015) encompasses a wide range of board games and reveals that traditional games are very apt at mediating existing fiction and narratives. Game designers can establish a new sense of place and ownership related to well-known universes and locations, such as *Game of Thrones'* Westeros or the wizarding school Hogwarts from *Harry Potter*. The study of game tourism, then, could even be applied to traditional games, but this is outside of the scope of this chapter.

Sightseeing inside and outside of games

While studies on media tourism often focused on official tours, as well as fan tours, the idea of "touring" to real-life locations is not that common in video game culture. Games do not have many production spaces that one can visit, since they are digitally created, and thus do not have a set life, such as movies. Though scholars have studied theme park rides inspired by films or the *Harry Potter* series (Waysdorf & Reijnders, 2017), there are hardly any real-life locations specifically inspired by games. In the case of films and fiction, fans can also go to the places and towns that inspired that fiction. They visit Abbey Road, or Forks, known from *Twilight*. Games, however, are often creative worlds, and are in some ways more similar to art and animation than to film. As simulations, games do not often offer real-world counterparts.

While video game tours are rare, some franchises have sparked this practice. A well-known example is the *Assassin's Creed* series. This action-adventure series has a strong historical component and relies primarily on stealth as players adopt the persona of an assassin. The series is praised for its aesthetic and complete recreation of historical cities. *Assassin's Creed* has remediated historical Palestine, Florence, Boston, and Paris, among others, and always with great attention to detail.

In many towns, unofficial fan tours are organized inspired by the series, which allow fans to walk through the towns together and see the spots that they know from the game. Moreover, fans give each other tips on forums such as Reddit, or share their experiences when they individually (without a guided tour) explored the town. The game is known for its climbing mechanic, which allows you to climb onto huge buildings and towers. In their reviews of tours, or forum posts of their experiences, fans often reflect on how beautiful it is to see these large buildings in real life.

One tour that is organized in Florence for *Assassin's Creed* fans is *Tatiana's Walking Tour*. This tour takes fans along the most famous spots that are featured in *Assassin's Creed II* (Ubisoft, 2009). One reviewer writes:

> Amazing! Tatiana was extremely well versed in both the history of Florence and the *Assassin's Creed* storyline. I found this tour to be very thorough. The historical information is plentiful making the tour enjoyable even for those unfamiliar with the game. Naturally the comparisons between reality and the game make the tour. If your [*sic*] a fan of the game, you must take this tour. Play the game one more time before going and you'll enjoy it even more!
>
> *(User 1 – Tripadvisor, 2013)*

As a metaphor for exploration and the leisurely enjoyment of games, the figure of the flâneur maps onto the figure of the player quite adequately. Players leisurely stroll through cyberspace, and enjoy the scenery. Benjamin's flâneur (1983) is an urban spectator, who is defined by his inquisitive gaze and appreciation. However, being a flâneur is not only about seeing but also about being seen. In many games, the player is not truly seen and part of the urban population, but part of a small team, or playing individually.

It is only in the gazing and observing that the parallel with flânerie works well. Games have a sense of space that is crucial to the experience of the player. This sense of topography and space is not new by any means. Decades ago, educational games such as *Where on Earth is Carmen Sandiego* (Broderbund, 1985) or *Oregon Trail* (Gameloft, 1971) created maps to teach topography and culture to children. Simulations may have become became more advanced, but a space has always been a factor in games.

In his article 'Beyond Cyberspatial Flaneurie: On the Analytical Potential of Living with Digital Games', Bart Simon (2006) examines the gamer as a *cyberflâneur*. Large games allow us to travel and experience new cultures, and this holds especially true for online games. Simon (2006, p. 62) elaborates:

It is in this sense that massively multiplayer online games like *Everquest, Star Wars Galaxies*, or even *The Sims Online* more so than Web sites, multiuser domains, or even spatially intensive virtual world games like *Myst* are commonly described in terms similar to how one might describe traveling to another country (Book, 2003). Indeed, it would seem that the more immersive the game, the greater this sense of transportation becomes. The age of virtual world tourism has arrived.

The semiotic and rhetorical way to analyze the game space has hitherto been dominated by the concept of the magic circle. In his anthropological study of play, *Homo Ludens* (1970 [1938]), Dutch scholar Huizinga envisions the game space as demarcated by rules that form a "magic circle" defining the context of the game. This concept has been picked up by Salen and Zimmerman (2004) in their influential handbook *Rules of Play*. They argue that, 'In a very basic sense, the magic circle of a game is where the game takes place. To play a game means entering into a magic circle, or perhaps creating one as a game begins' (p. 95).

While the circle can be understood as a semiotic domain or context, the concept is contested and interpreted differently throughout game studies. Scholars that use the term often point to fandom and game culture to show how games are not only within this circle, but often outside it a well. Games influence other contexts than the game itself, such as everyday life, identity, and belonging (Pearce, 2009). After all, fans extend the playful moment through their social and creative activities (Consalvo, 2007; Taylor, 2006). The circle, for starters, is a wide one since games spaces have become large virtual worlds over the years. Typically, video games create worlds that players can conquer or master, or even manipulate or create altogether. Games are about creating a journey. The magic circle is considered fluid in many recent game studies.

Moreover, the space of games has become a market space that we can often only master by buying some new downloadable content (e.g. new items) and that we pay to win. Immersive virtual reality spaces are practically available to just about anyone on demand, if they are willing to pay. Touring in *Pokémon Go*, for instance, often means paying to go ahead or spending hours and hours of tedious game play to level up one's team. In this sense, tourism in gaming should not only be seen as an artistic experience or an aesthetic endeavor, but as deeply commercial and marketed. In other words, like any type of tourism, game tourism is not only a type of leisure, but involves economic structures and labor.

Re-experiencing the city through a tourist gaze

At the heart of games lies exploration, and even the mastery of geography. In sociological terms, games allow us to transform a neutral place to a space, a site that is colonized, explored, and connected to our personal stories (Newman, 2004, p. 113). Creating spaces is an apt conceptualization of what it means to play recent games, such as *Pokémon Go*, which connect the game space to offline spaces. Augmented Reality games connect multiple technologies and interfaces, such as our mobile screens and templates from Google Maps, and use this to create mediated layers over our traditional environments. The predecessor of *Pokémon Go, Ingress* (Niantic, 2014) already successfully created a post-apocalyptic narrative across the world, which allowed two factions to compete. The game offered a new way of seeing the world and known monuments through a dystopic narrative.

Playing games such as *Pokémon Go* offers us a new way to see the world, and to traverse familiar streets. Playing the game often reminded me of De Certeau's famous essay *Walking the City* (1984). In this essay, De Certeau coins "strategies" and "tactics" as a way of analyzing the role of power and discourse in culture. In his essay, De Certeau shows that the city is produced by strategies (structures of power), which create a unified whole, but consumers can choose to act with or against these strategies. These tactics are captured by the pedestrian in Manhattan, who navigates the city in a tactical way, according to De Certeau. This walker may choose shortcuts, and may choose to ignore the grids of New York. The city is but one example of how strategies and tactics work in our culture. Consumers are always influenced by structures that are outlined by others, but never fully determined by them.

Pokémon Go brings these concepts to mind. The players of the game engage in tactics and look at the city in new ways. They take shortcuts to get to the next Pokéstop or Pokémon. As a result, they may behave in unexpected ways, which has also led to much critique of the game, and even led to some cities, such as The Hague, trying to ban the game. Walking has clearly become a tactic, a bottom-up practice. However, we should also be careful not to exaggerate what the game does. In their own way, consumers are led by strategies and rules of the game. They are, for instance, drawn to the newest "lure" that attracts Pokémon as a result, because this is the best reward in the game for now. Similarly, players may team up for a gym battle, because this is of use to them, but may disperse afterwards. In other words, we must not exaggerate what games do, since they create new structures in and of themselves, which affect consumers.

Pokémon Go creates new ways of interacting with our environment, similar to other location-based games. The app combines elements of traditional scavenge hunting with competitive aspects, such as gym battles. There have been other location-based games that achieved popularity, such as *geocaching*, a recreational activity that allows players to hunt for containers ("caches") at specific locations, based on GPS coordinates. Similar to *Pokémon Go*, geocaching shares aspects with traditional games such as treasure-hunting and letterboxing. However, *Pokémon Go* is undoubtedly the first mainstream success in this area of location-based games. It created its own unique story line, connected to a beloved franchise, and made full use of the functionality of the maps and mobile screen. The success may have to do with the fact that the rewards in this game are all virtual. The caches are all experience points, and new Pokémon, which means that the players do not actually have a physical object to engage with like they do in geocaching.

Touring new locations with *Pokémon Go* is a joy, and one way in which we could consider this game as virtual tourism. However, physical tourism also flourished as a result of the game. For instance, in my home town Utrecht, local shop owners clearly wanted to profit from the game, as they put up signs welcoming all Pokémon hunters, and sold special Pokémon cupcakes. It seemed that some shops, which permanently had lures on them to attract Pokémon, perhaps even bought in-game items to attract hunters. In Japan, there were special events offering double experience, as well as raids and unique Pokémon such as Farfetch'd, which can only be caught in Asia. This makes playing *Pokémon Go* abroad a very rewarding experience for players. When we traveled Japan with our group, for instance, catching Farfetch'd was an iconic moment for one high-level player, who immediately sent pictures of the Pokémon in Tokyo to her friends and family.

In this sense, tourism also flourished in real life, as many players spent the summer in towns and beaches abroad on their quest for Pokémon.

Virtual tourism

While entertainment games allow for a touristic gaze or play style, it is equally important to examine the virtual reality (VR) games and applications that are increasingly designed for touristic purposes. The primary point of these apps is to inform consumers about a destination, which may affect their decision-making process and customer journey when choosing a holiday destination.

A related function of these apps can even be to simulate threatened sites, or to create a virtual substitute for tourists who for physical, economical, or other reasons are not able to attend that holiday. In an extensive overview of VR applications in tourism, Daniel Guttentag (2010) writes that, based on existing studies, it is unlikely that virtual reality apps will function as substitutes to real-life holidays. VR, for instance, can still not simulate all sensory experiences that come with a holiday, such as the feeling of the sun, or the sand under your feet. Guttentag cites a study conducted by Sussman and Vanhegan (2000, cited in Guttentag, 2010) who surveyed 50 people in Britain and came to the conclusion that "virtual holidays cannot replace the real holiday experience, regardless of apparent inconveniences and environmental dangers to destinations" (p. 6, cited in Guttentag, 2010, p. 644). Guttentag summarizes various other studies which found that spontaneity, the lack of sensory experiences, the inability to buy souvenirs and other options make VR an unlikely substitute for real holidays in the near future.

In the past years virtual reality has developed rapidly with technologies such as Oculus Rift and Playstation VR. Low-key virtual reality headsets also allow consumers to easily play 360-degree films and small VR applications on their phones. Platforms such as YouTube have made it easy for everyone to upload their own 360-degree videos, which can be viewed on a headset. While the technology is still being experimented with, today most companies that design VR focus on digitally designed applications, created in software such as Unity, as well as 360-degree videos that are essentially shot as film footage. Virtual reality is not only applied to gaming at the moment, but also to architecture, health, and pornography. There has been a rapid development of content in these areas, which is still growing.

With the emergence of these technologies, we have seen many businesses, such as travel agencies, explore the use of VR. In 2016 Airway company Lufthansa created several 360-degree films on locations such as Hong Kong and Tokyo of 46 minutes, which fully allow you to fully immerse yourself in these destinations. Similarly, British Airways teamed up with Avios to launch a new virtual reality campaign that relies on 360-degree footage of various locations in Madrid, such as San Miguel Market and Retiro Park. Thomas Cook partnered with Samsung and VR company Visualize in 2015 to create short films about various destinations, which could be viewed on the Samsung Gear VR headset in stores. However, many of these films offer nothing but shots of locations, with a limited degree of storytelling. Some videos, such as those from Lufthansa, rely heavily on music rather than voice-overs or environmental sounds. This creates the ambience of a 360-degree music video rather than an informative or truly touristic experience of the site.

An exception is Marriott Hotels "Vroom Service," which allows hotel guests to borrow a VR device and experience short stories in Randa, Chile and Beijing. These "VR Postcards" give viewers the glimpse of a destination. Their mission statement is to "move beyond simply showing aspiration destinations towards a platform for delivering emphatic personal stories about exploring our world. A transportative call to action" (Frame Store VR Studio, 2017). Still, even their videos with a clearer focus on humans and culture rely heavily on depicting the scenery to create the sense of the traveling experience.

The quality of the videos, and their storytelling, is clearly still developing. At the moment VR is still being invented as a genre. Creative breakthroughs in VR are still scarce, though The Guardians *6x9* (2016) might be an achievement that can push the genre forward. In this app, the designers simulated solitary confinement, by relying not only on footage, but also on sound and the psychology of being alone in a tiny room. It creates awareness and empathy for solitary confinement, which is still a common practice today.

While touristic apps may still follow the route of advertisements and travel programs to showcase holiday destinations, other apps managed to generate empathy and to create a real story through place. In the future, we will undoubtedly see more applications of this in the area of tourism and marketing as well.

Implications for popular culture tourism

The current media landscape is one that goes beyond the boundaries of a medium. We live in times of transmediality in which virtual and actual spaces mingle, and the online and the offline are not clearly separate anymore. The notion of cyberspace, as one virtual space disconnected from reality, no longer holds true. Today, games are connected to actual locations or have become locations in and of themselves that we love to visit and live in.

In this chapter, I have shown that game tourism is fundamentally different from other types of media tourism. The medium of digital games relies heavily on its game spaces, which, unlike film and novels, often do not have a real life counterpart. However, games do offer us virtual sightseeing, and new ways to observe familiar environments. This trend will only increase in the coming years as game worlds become bigger, faster, and more detailed. More than ever, games offer us the physical, kinaesthetic pleasure of exploration. This sense of space is heavily connected to tourism, both as a practice of discovery and a way of seeing, as well as a commercial endeavor.

However, we must be wary of the fact that the virtual realities of gaming cannot yet replace real tourism. Its simulations are a poor substitute for what we see in real life. The near future, then, seems to rely more on the gamification of real places. We see this in both of the key cases in this chapter. *Assassin's Creed* is mediated in the form of tours to allow fans to re-experience the game in urban environments. In the case of *Pokémon Go*, however, which integrates gaming with real life, we see that gaming can motivate, and even supplement, real experiences. Mediation is key in this case, since the game shows us that familiar environments can be "themed" to create a touristic experience.

In the coming years, game spaces will advance even more. Tourism could take many forms: Will we in the future buy in-game and out-of-game souvenirs? Will we book trips to digitally designed spaces? Whatever the case, it is important to conceptualize game tourism, and this is a first step in that process. Game tourism can show us many things about identity, belonging, and location. It is an important point of comparison with other media, which create unique spaces of identity related to an existing narrative or point of production. Games, however, do show us that media themselves allow for flânerie and sightseeing. Media do not only open us up to new experiences, but also enhance our gaze, and make us see things that we were never aware of before. Within tourism studies, we need to reflect more on the playfulness of today's media, and its consumers.

References

Benjamin, W. (1983). *Charles Baudelaire: A Lyric Poet in the Era of High Capitalism.* Harry Zohn (trans.). London: Verso.

Booth, P. (2015). *Game Play: Paratextuality in Contemporary Board Games.* London: Bloomsbury.

Brooker, W. (2007). "Everywhere and nowhere: Vancouver, fan pilgrimage, and the urban imaginary." *International Journal of Cultural Studies* 10(4), pp. 423–444.

Cartmell, D. (1993). "Consuming *Middlemarch*: The construction and consumption of nostalgia in Stamford." In: D. Cartmell, I. Q. Hunter, H. Kaye, and I. Whelehan (Eds.). *Pulping Fictions. Consuming Culture Across the Literature/Media Divide.* London, Chicago: Pluto Press, pp. 85–98.

Couldry, N. (2000). *The Place of Media Power: Pilgrims and Witnesses of the Media Age.* London and New York: Routledge.

Couldry, N. (2003). *Media Rituals: A Critical Approach.* London and New York: Routledge.

De Certeau, M. (1984). *The Practice of Everyday Life*. Berkeley, CA: University of California Press.

Deuze, M. (2012). *Media Life*. Hoboken: Wiley.

Frame Store VR Studio (2017). *Marriot VR Postcards*. Available at: http://framestorevr.com/marriott-vr-postcards/

Gordon, I. (2003). "Superman on the set: The market, nostalgia and television audiences." In: M. Jancovich and J. Lyonseds (Eds.). *Quality Popular Television: Cult TV, the Industry and Fans*. Berkeley, CA: University of California Press, pp. 148–162.

Guttentag, D. (2010). "Virtual reality: Applications and implications for tourism." *Tourism Management* 31, pp. 637–651.

Hills, M. (2001). "Virtually out there: Strategies, tactics and affective spaces in on-line fandom." In S. Munt (Ed.). *Technospaces: Inside the New Media*. London, New York: Continuum, pp. 147–160.

Huizinga, J. (1970/1938). *Homo Ludens*. Boulder: Paladin.

Kozinets, R. (2010). *Netnography: Doing Ethnographic Research Online*. Los Angeles and London: Sage.

Lamerichs, N. (2014). "Embodied fantasy: The affective space of anime conventions." In: S. Reijnders, L. Duits, and K. De Zwaan (Eds.). *The Ashgate Research Companion to Fan Culture*. London and Lund: Ashgate, pp. 263–275.

Lundberg, C. and Lexhagen, M. (2012). "Bitten by the *Twilight Saga*: From pop culture consumer to pop culture tourist." In R. Sharpley and P. R. Stone (Eds.). *The Contemporary Tourist Experience: Concepts and Consequences*. Abingdon: Routledge.

Markham, A. (1998). *Life Online: Researching Real Experience in Virtual Space*. Walnut Creek, CA and London, New Delhi: Sage.

Newman, J. (2004). *Videogames*. London and New York: Routledge.

Norris, C. (2013). "A Japanese media pilgrimage to a Tasmanian bakery." *Transformative Works and Cultures* 14. http://dx.doi.org/10.3983/twc.2013.0470

Pearce, C. (2009). Communities of Play. London and Massachusetts: MIT Press.

Reijnders, S. (2009). "Watching the detectives: Inside the guilty landscapes of Inspector Morse, Baantjer and Wallander." *European Journal of Communication* 24, 165–181.

Reijnders, S. (2011). "Stalking the count: Dracula, fandom and tourism." *Annals of Tourism Research* 20, pp. 231–248.

Salen, K. and Zimmerman, E. (2004). *Rules of Play: Game Design Fundamentals*. London and Masachusetts: MIT Press.

Simon, B. (2006). "Beyond cyberspatial flaneurie: On the analytic potential of living with digital games." *Games and Culture* 1, pp. 62–67.

Taylor, T. L. (2006). *Play Between Worlds: Exploring Online Game Culture*. Cambridge, MA: MIT Press.

Watson, N. (2010). "Fandom mapped: Rousseau, Scott and Byron on the itinerary of Lady Frances Shelley." *Romantic Circles*, special issue "Romantic Fandom." Available at: www.rc.umd.edu/praxis/fandom/HTML/praxis.2010.watson.html (accessed June 2, 2017).

Urry, J. (2001). "Globalising the tourist gaze." *Cityscapes Conference Graz 2001*. Available at: www.comp.lancs.ac.uk/sociology/papers/Urry-Globalising-the-Tourist-Gaze.pdf (accessed June 2, 2017).

Urry, J. (2011). *The Touristic Gaze 3.0*. London, Thousand Oaks, New Delhi: Sage.

Waysdorf, A. and Reijnders, S. (2017). "The role of imagination in the film tourist experience: The case of *Game of Thrones*." *Participations* 14, 1, pp. 170–191.

15

THE PECULIAR ATTRACTION OF ROYALTY FOR TOURISM AND THE POPULAR CULTURE CONSTRUCTION OF 'ROYAL TOURISM'

Nicola Palmer and Philip Long

Setting the scene

In 2008, we explored both implicit and explicit relationships between royalty and tourism in contemporary and historic UK and some international contexts. In doing so, we provided an original, direct and specific focus on the hitherto neglected subject of 'royal tourism' (Long & Palmer, 2008). A range of historical, sociological and popular culture perspectives were included as a basis for examining the royal tourism phenomenon. There has to date, and surprisingly given the continuing relevance of the subject and enduring prominence of royalty, been no further academic studies of which we are aware that focus specifically on this royal tourism phenomenon. Nine years on, we revisit the peculiar attraction of royalty for tourism and specifically consider an enduring and persistent touristic focus on the monarchy, particularly in the UK.

This chapter re-investigates the concept of 'royal tourism' as a specific form of popular culture tourism and considers how royal tourism may be employed not solely for economic gain and commercial exploitation (one of the most enduring and publically contested aspects of the relationships between tourism and monarchy) but also as a political and socio-cultural tool and context. We consider royal tourism as a socially constructed concept (Berger & Luckman, 1966), whereby the entering into and playing out of roles and reciprocal actions by members of society as tourists are institutionalized. Thus, responses to royalty, in a tourism context, are embedded in the institutional fabric of society and popular culture. To explore this, we draw on our 2008 book though this material is adapted and updated to focus on popular culture dimensions of royal tourism.

The chapter considers, in turn: how there persists a focus on monarchy per se and in specific relation to royal events and tourism development and marketing activities; royal families and their prominent contribution to the reproduction of social mores and the establishment of tourist destinations through their patronage; the politics of royal tourism; and royal tourism's meeting of psychological and physiological needs for the tourist. It then attempts to make sense of these features collectively to consider how understanding of this specific form of tourism can inform and assist deeper understanding of tourism within a wider popular culture context.

Theoretical underpinnings

Monarchies are intriguing and persistent, if seemingly anachronistic and aberrant political, social, ritual and familial institutions that continue to exist and exercise actual and symbolic power to greater or lesser degrees and forms in many countries worldwide.[1] As institutions and as individuals, royalty attracts considerable public interest among the *subjects* of monarchies and the *citizens* of non-monarchical republics alike. Public and scholarly attention often is drawn to the extraordinary ritual, formal and ceremonial dimensions of royalty as played out in public life through the media, as well as to their more mundane quotidian activities.[2] Particular royal households and individual monarchs and their roles in a nation's historical and contemporary socio-political and cultural life are also subject to much scholarly research, popular publications, television series and public interest that, for some enthusiasts, verges on the obsessional.[3] Moreover, the life stories and daily activities of certain contemporary royal families and individuals, however seemingly mundane, attract huge media attention, with their routines, behaviours, relationships, finances and movements subject to detailed, even frenzied media scrutiny and, at times, controversy. Some individual members of royal households attain global mega-celebrity status and even mythical, iconic qualities.[4] Royal personages generally and more or less conspicuously travel a lot and tours, whether as official, state occasions or at leisure also attract considerable attention both at home and abroad.[5]

The idea of travelling royals as ambassadors and representatives of the nation (reinforcing and transmitting national social values) has been suggested through the work of historians such as Linda Colley (1984). Her analysis of loyalty, royalty and the British nation in the context of work on King George III not only highlights the reverential status of monarchy in certain societies at certain times but also illustrates the ability of monarchs to be socially positioned, in the case of George, as 'Father of his people' (Colley, 1984, p. 94). In contrast, more recent work by Burnstein (2015) questions the symbolic cultural functions of the British monarchy since King George, noting an arguable shift from 'symbol of a unified nation' to 'a kind of royal soap opera' (McKechnie, 2002 as cited in Burnstein, 2015, p. 162). This throws into question the extent to which royal families (at home or 'on tour') reinforce the institutional fabric of society in a modern context. It also demonstrates how, to hold relevance, royal families themselves have to be much more reflexive and adaptive to change in modern societies – at times, becoming followers rather than leaders of the institutional fabric of society and facing challenges to retain status as 'exemplary institutions' (Díaz, 1993).

Generally, if arguably in decline as political and constitutional institutions with extensive powers, monarchies continue to play important embodied and symbolic roles. However, while the travels of individual monarchs have been the subject of historical research and popular publications, there has been little work that has explored the broad and specific relationships between royalty, popular culture and tourism in contemporary contexts. A direct, specific focus on the subject of 'royal tourism' has thus been overlooked in the tourism literature (as well as in much other scholarly work on royalty).

It is possible to locate the concept of royal tourism within wider contemporary socio-political and popular culture contexts. It highlights the multi-faceted relationships between monarchy and tourism and identifies royal tourism as a complex form of (both) special interest (and mass) popular culture tourism, illustrating the ability of tourism to both reflect and perpetuate more fundamental social issues and class relationships. The links between royalty and tourism are played out or mediated both within public and private spheres. Contrasts between national, monarchy-endorsed events and celebrations (such as royal weddings, ceremonies, etc.) and private, family royal events (such as royal holidays and social occasions, etc.) must be noted.

The former legitimizes and formalizes royal tourism and the latter, with respect to socially embedded roles, suggests uninvited, almost deviant or at least intrusive public (tourist) attention. In this context, we are minded of many ongoing debates that exist around royalty and 'public interest', particularly in the context of the UK royal family and its constitutional position. Thus, royal tourism itself becomes something positioned in terms of public interest (with official royal tourism recognized to be institutionalized, scripted, stage-managed and malleable performances) versus an unofficial, illegitimate and intrusive royal tourism where boundaries set by the royal family are crossed. An emblematic example of the latter was demonstrated through the arrest of an intruder to Buckingham Palace in 2014 who was 'expecting a private audience with the Queen' (Corcoran, 2014).

For defenders of monarchy, there is a need for royalty to be seen in order to justify its existence and appeal to public support and funding. As the constitutional historian Walter Bagehot put it more than 120 years ago in the context of Queen Victoria's prolonged absence from the public gaze following the death of Prince Albert, there is a need to resolve the paradox of letting 'daylight in on the magic' of royalty while at the same time attempting to retain its 'divine, sacredly ordained mystique' (quoted in Hobsbawn & Ranger, 1983). Blom's (in Long & Palmer, 2008) distinction between 'visitors' and 'seekers' is useful here together with the proposition that royal tourists are seeking contrasts from everyday life in terms of exceptional or par excellence experiences. Butler's (in Long & Palmer, 2008) ideas also gain relevance here in terms of the associated linguistic (and commercial) value of the prefix 'Royal', indicating 'upper-class' acceptance and links to pre-eminence. If one of the key issues around heritage and cultural tourism is authenticity, then for royal tourism the potential tension between (accessible) extraordinary and memorable experiences in contrast to everyday mundane routines for the public appears to be a key issue.

With respect to this, it is possible to recognize how, in the context of royal tourism, the linguistic value and connotative meaning of 'Royal' can drive visitor demand even where the royal family has had both direct or indirect associations with locations, sites or scenes and this appears to hold true both in historical and contemporary contexts. For example, English Heritage has recently based a promotional campaign for the Isle of Wight, a favourite holiday destination of Britain's longest reigning monarch, Queen Victoria, around the Queen's favouring of the destination for her holidays. 'Holiday like Queen Victoria' not only focuses on the places patronized by Queen Victoria but also the private beach, dubbed 'Queen Victoria's Beach' (English Heritage, 2015), a 300-metre stretch of sand and shingle with no discernible remarkable qualities aside from its royal associative value (and hitherto, restricted access), has opened to the public for the first time. In 2014, it was reported that Prince Andrew had given his seal of approval for a London pub, 'The Duke of York' to include his picture on its sign. The landlady of the pub was quoted as saying, 'It is something I think Londoners will love but will of course be a pull for tourists too' (Bothwell, 2014). Even an incidental 'brush with royalty' it seems can affect visitor demand for a site or destination. The naked antics of the UK royal Prince Harry in Las Vegas in 2012 (well covered by international media) have, it is claimed, contributed to record-breaking annual visitor numbers for the resort in 2012 and have been dubbed the 'Prince Harry effect' (Saunders, 2013).

It must, however, be noted, in contrast, that a need to retain the mystique of royalty may perhaps explain the relative absence of images of contemporary royals in current induced tourism promotional literature. For example, both Yew Tree Farm in Borrowdale, UK and Klosters in Switzerland have regularly hosted visits from the current Prince of Wales but have refrained from claiming his royal patronage in their publicity materials. This restraint may be voluntary or perhaps required by the Prince's household in the interest of retaining his divine, sacredly ordained mystique, as well as his personal security.

Popular culture, royal tourism and destination image

The roles that monarchies play in societies are largely embodied and symbolic, not least in connection with tourism in countries where royalty continues to exist (or existed in the past and is now treated as part of a heritage tourism product), and in places that may lay claim to past royal associations or are favoured with recent or regular royal visits. Haid (in Long & Palmer, 2008) and Corak and Ateljevic (in Long & Palmer, 2008) consider this with respect to the imperial tourism associated with the Austro-Hungarian monarchy and the Habsburg (also known as Hapsburg) family. The way in which Austrian tourism policy was observed to be shaped around imperialistic memory, creating challenges around a lack of contemporary cultural contexts. Haid (in Long & Palmer, 2008) raises questions for visitor interpretation and sense-making. Coupled with observations from Nicola Palmer (in Long & Palmer, 2008) around the (cognitive) accessibility of providing meaning and significance to deceased characters and past events it is possible to support the notion of tourism marketing managers as 'cultural brokers' of tourism (Adams, 1984). The recent discovery of the remains of English King Richard III in Leicester and that city's exploitation of his re-internment and opening of a visitor centre is an excellent example of this. The specific implications of such memorialization in terms of shaping and manipulating the role and appeal of royal families for tourist consumption need to be considered.

As well as in the tourism packaging and consumption of royal ceremonials, there is a widespread selection and commodification of images, sites, memorabilia and the physical presence (whether historical, legendary, ghostly or contemporary) of royalty that is aimed at stimulating tourist interest. A material and corporeal as well as an imaginary and fantasized popular culture of royal tourism therefore exists. The nature of this culture has also been explored through the work of Nicola Palmer (in Long & Palmer, 2008). She reflects on fragmented national and regional identities in a (dis)United Kingdom, with arguably a privileging of England and London in royal associative place-making. She thus considers the appropriation of the British Royal Family and associated royal links in the tourism promotion of Britain by public sector tourism agencies. A key issue here is what this typically deferential emphasis on royal associations with particular places in the UK symbolizes both from the viewpoints of international tourists and British subjects.

The popular celebrity culture of royal tourism

Royal families are literally extraordinary people and institutions. They are also a declining breed in that there are now relatively few monarchies remaining in the world with explicit constitutional powers, as republican, liberal democratic models of governance and government have become arguably normative. The possession of an enduring monarchy therefore sets those nations in possession of a royal household apart as being different, distinctive and exotic – a valuable attribute by itself in appealing to tourist interest in the novel, anachronistic and unique. As far as the UK is concerned, the abnormal and archaic nature of the place of the monarchy culturally and constitutionally is a marker of difference and a tourist attraction in its own right, although this 'glamour of backwardness' and cultivated anachronism is a source of shame for some (Nairn, 1988). Perhaps more positively, as Brunt (1999, p. 290) puts it, 'the Royal Family form, by virtue of reproducing themselves, the only enduring category of Britishness. If they no longer existed, what would still be great about Britain?' While our 2008 book included contributions on monarchy and national identity in historic Austro-Hungarian and Spanish contexts, there is a need for research that addresses this in the context of tourism from other monarchical national contexts, such as Thailand, Saudi Arabia and Japan, for example.

For some habitual, loyal, dedicated and enthusiastic 'royal tourists' there may be a curious psychological need for royal narratives and for imagined participation in royal lives. This demonstrates the strange transnational obsession with and devotion to idealized, iconic celebrity individuals as evidenced by extensive mass media coverage of the 'royal soap opera' (at times played as tragedy, farce or fairy tale).[6] As Hitchins (1990) puts it, there is something rather hysterical and strange in the adulation afforded to royalty in the UK. There is also an enduring nature to royal celebrity compared with other more ephemeral media personalities, as Blain and O'Donnell (2003, p. 163) observe, 'royal celebrities are of a different substance from most other celebrities. They endure'. Meeting members of the royal family or even just 'being in the presence' of royalty is described as a life-affirming moment or transformational experience by some of those who have had such encounters and there is some evidence to suggest that dreaming about meeting royalty is commonplace (Masters, 1972).

The existence of 'real royalists' (Rowbottom, 2002a) throws up questions around a typology or continuum of royal tourism responses (ranging from fanatical through apathetic to antagonistic, though the latter seem likely to be a small minority in the UK at the time of writing). Issues of embodiment arise in relation to Blom's (in Long & Palmer, 2008) consideration of the 1997 funeral of Diana, Princess of Wales. The ways in which symbols are used as mental labels for experiences and expectations in relation to the assessment of tourist attractions and events using a scale of values is considered. This supports the idea of royal tourism as a socially constructed concept. Blom's work also raises deeper issues around self-identity, being able to feel 'nearness' and participation in another's misfortune. Similarly, Catherine Palmer's (in Long & Palmer, 2008) consideration of family as 'a state of mind' in relation to the royal family and Schama's (1986) domestication of monarchy raises issues around deeply embedded symbolic psychological and social meanings involved in the interpretation of royalty.

Catherine Palmer's (in Long & Palmer, 2008) consideration of the British royal household's image and identification as a family and how this pertains to tourism suggests that the royal familial image, including its, at times, displays of dysfunctionality, may be seen as representing British national 'character' and institutions for people in the countries that they tour. A further analytical issue arising here is the extent to which royalty personifies an 'ideal' version of family life as a model for emulation by other family tourists in the destinations that they visit and in the activities that they may aspire to pursue. The idea of monarchy as a transmitter (and social regulator) of values and social codes and the royal family as societal role models helps us to understand the emphasis on and dissonance surrounding royal acts of 'deviance' (divorce, drunkenness, sex scandals, etc.). There is a need for deeper analysis around the need for role models at all to maintain 'healthy societies'. Indeed, as Piper and Garratt (in Long & Palmer, 2008) argue, the discourses of tourism promotion and publicity that eulogize monarchy contribute significantly to underpinning a regressive state of affairs. Are claims for the 'moral excellence' of the royal family profoundly misplaced in that they leave the British as *subjects* of the Crown as opposed to *citizens* of the nation? Furthermore, is the early acculturation of children into the ritual and rites of royal events, performances and holidays a form of indoctrination into a highly inequitable status quo? (C. Palmer in Long & Palmer, 2008). Thus, royal tourism can be interpreted as a means of reproducing inequity and doing so in a way that promotes this as not only socially acceptable but where to desist or protest suggests deviance or 'anarchy'.

There are recorded historical reports that support this notion of 'anti-royal tourism' (albeit with few signs of sustained dissent and popular support for republicanism in recent years), although the Spanish royal family has been under critical scrutiny since the onset of the economic crisis in that country. Dissenting, anti-monarchist voices were suppressed during Victoria's Golden Jubilee, with outspoken republicans imprisoned as a precaution to avoid oppositional performances at jubilee events (Taylor, 1999). More recently, the BBC's banning of the Sex Pistols' version of 'God Save the Queen' during the 1977 Silver Jubilee provides a more contemporary example of such suppression (Back, 2002). However, there was little such public dissent to detract from the celebrations of Queen Elizabeth's Golden and Diamond Jubilees in 2002 and 2012. Indeed, taking a corporate heritage brand management perspective, Balmer (2011) argues that at the time of the royal wedding of Prince William in April 2011 and the celebration of Queen Elizabeth II's Diamond Jubilee (1952–2012), there was evidence of bilateral trust between the Crown (British monarchy) and the British public. In terms of the reproduction of social mores this highlights the centrality of 'trust' to the management and maintenance of the monarchy (Balmer, 2011) and, also, it might be observed that this relationship is fundamental to the underpinning of royal tourism, whereby endurance of royal events in particular requires public consent. This leads us to consider some of the political aspects of royal tourism.

The popular ceremonial culture of royal tourism

The pomp, pageantry and ceremonial performances that are associated with royalty provide exceptional and unique as well as predictable and scheduled events for tourist attention. The media hype that anticipates, reports and comments on some of these occasions and the images of crowds attending royal events may themselves stimulate the involvement of people wishing to be part of seemingly historical moments. However, their symbolic socio-cultural and political significance extends far beyond their touristic and economic values.

James' (in Long & Palmer, 2008) focus on discourses of nationality, loyalty and pageantry considers the Duke and Duchess of York's 1897 royal tour of Shannon, Ireland as a staged piece of political theater. In this context a royal visit to a region at that time 'undiluted to foreign influences' provoked contrasting responses amidst politically divided unionist and republican communities. The politics surrounding monarchy are explicitly considered by James and raise questions around the British royal family as *sovereign* celebrity endorsers of place, whether intended or otherwise. That this visit took place without major protests or disruptions again raises questions around the perceived status and interpretation of the royals as individuals and societal role models in particular times and places. It also raises some key questions around 'the mobilization of symbols of the Crown in tourist development schemes'. To what extent might such endorsements not only attract but repel or disenfranchise sections of a tourist population?

There is little research evidence on this beyond anecdotal reports and, indirectly, market research responses to the popularity of the monarchy reported via media polls. Where academic research has been undertaken it appears to imply that the British royal family at least has a positive effect on not only visitor numbers but can contribute additionally to tourism's ability to assist indirectly some wider and dominantly conservative political causes. For example, Haven-Tang and Jones (in Long & Palmer, 2008), discuss the employment of royal heritage themes in the development of a distinctive sense of place in a cultural tourism strategy devised for Monmouthshire, Wales, and raise the question of royal associations attracting tourist interest in the preservation of minority languages and regional/national identities.

In her examination of the responses of international tourists to royal encounters with the British royal family, Nicola Palmer (in Long & Palmer, 2008) notes how, regardless of royalist or republican persuasion, the experiences appear to be highly memorable and readily articulated events. Far from being manipulated, the general public emerges as an active and willing audience, conscious of the inter-dependent roles being played out between monarch/royal family member and audience in 'the royal performance'.

Royal performances and personalities as major media phenomena have been the subject of some theoretical discussion in relation to, for example: textual and visual representations of royalty past and present, the narratives of the monarchical 'soap-opera' and the development and portrayal of the celebrity/iconic characteristics of individual members of the royal family.[7] While these ideas may be extended and applied to royal tourism-related media, very little such research seems to have taken place. The motivations of royal tourists and the character portrayal of royal 'actors' suggest some deeply rooted factors to be at play. With respect to the latter, the work of Maddens and Vanden Berghe (in Long & Palmer, 2008) is illuminating. They discuss the changing interpretation over time of important heritage tourist sites in Spain with royal associations through a close, historically informed reading of official guide books and observe that 'the choice of the sites considered "royal" and the way these are discursively constructed in the rhetoric of tourism depends, amongst other considerations, on the prevailing ideological climate and the public and elite attitudes towards royalty' (Maddens & Vanden Berghe in Long & Palmer, 2008, pp. 102–103). This is an important comment that may be considered in respect to the interpretation of sites with royal associations in other former (post-colonial) and current monarchical states and the ways in which these may reflect official and public discourses about past and present royal regimes.

Implications for popular culture tourism

The direct, explicit and the indirect, implicit relationships between royalty, popular culture and tourism (and not just in relation to British royal tourism) are multifarious and have been little researched. This seems to reflect an apparent indifference from tourism social science researchers on the subject of royalty that may be explicable by possible perceptions of the anachronistic, dated and irrelevant notion of monarchical institutions and systems in an era of globalization and neo-liberal democracy. Alternatively, the subject may simply have been overlooked as having little to offer in developing theoretical and applied understandings of contemporary tourism. However, we suggest that researchers on tourism (and on royalty) may usefully explore this field, with reference, for example, to the work that has been produced by historians on royal biographies that include analysis of royal travels and tours as well as by commentators on royalty and social, political and constitutional matters, where their work may be related to issues of national identity and image as conveyed to tourists (Bogdanor, 1995; Broad, 1952; Coates, 2006; Pimlott, 1996; Prochaska, 2002; Thomas, 1989).

Re-examination of academic ideas around royal tourism identifies this specific form of tourism as a mechanism for reinforcing wider and more deeply embedded social norms, values and hierarchical power structures. It can be recognized that royal tourism acts as a structural enabler for royal tourists to perform as actors/agents in the mobilization and perpetuation of a status quo surrounding class structures, divine rule and power. Certainly in the context of the British royal family, some of the big issues around monarchy continue to be formed around republican versus monarchists and even anarchistic beliefs and viewpoints. In this context, royal tourism as a form of popular culture tourism needs to be recognized as a means of reinforcing rather than challenging dominant power structures. It places monarchy as a central attraction or nucleus whereby interpretations are framed by traditional, conservative social structures. Thus, it may be argued that this type of tourism serves as a tool for social continuity and the reinforcement, reproduction and maintenance of inequities, certainly in terms of power.

Deeply rooted notions of self- and social identity may also be recognized to be confronted in the performative aspects of being a royal tourist (or anti-royal tourist) whereby individuals do not simply appear to be consuming events or products. Rather, they are attempting to satisfy and confirm or disconfirm notions of self, linked to status and prestige. Tourism producers and marketers, through engagement with royal endorsement, are buying into an 'ideal' of superiority, aspirations and prestige grounded essentially through a class-based system (in a British context, at least). This suggests that far from merely being a niche form of tourism, royal tourism needs to be seen as a complex case – one that illustrates the ability of tourism to both reflect and perpetuate more fundamental social issues.

Our suggestions for directions for future research on royal tourism that we proposed in our 2008 book still stand. These include first, studying the roles performed by royal personages past and present in the conduct of their travels on official state tours and visits and as travellers at leisure, something that a number of royal individuals engage in to a large and more or less continuous and conspicuous extent (Reed, 2016). Popular, local histories of royal associations and their identifications with particular places may contribute to such research.

The powerful and controversial part that royalty plays in shaping historical and contemporary national, regional and local identities and the place of tourism promotional agencies in their use, interpretations and representations of royalty also warrants further study. In this context and conversely, what part may be played by apparently 'anti-royal' tourism that celebrates regicide and republicanism represented, for example, in the English town of Huntingdon's 'Cromwell Trail'? How may royal jubilees and other major events be subject to 'alternative' readings and performances by tourists that deviate from 'official' versions of events? Royalty as a tourism product and marketing opportunity may also be examined. What are the brand values of the House of Windsor and of individual royal family members, for example? Management and marketing perspectives may also be applied to royal tourism sites, locations, routes and events. What processes of consultation and negotiation take place between tourism interests and royal households in the designation, interpretation and sale of such 'products'? (Balmer, 2011; Ornes & Maclaran 2016)

Media representations of royalty, in mass print, broadcast and online forms and in specialized, celebrity-oriented media and the implications of these for potential tourist audiences may also be usefully examined in relation to the ways in which such media may be scripted and 'read' by audiences and potential tourists. There is scope to explore further the extent to which a growth in celebrity culture threatens to overshadow a more traditional role of royal families as national figureheads and role models. Perhaps also, in the case of Britain, the celebration of individual royal family members is open to further examination, with, for example, no apparent wane in media and tourist interest and press reporting in the 20 years since the death of Princess Diana, the anniversary of which was marked by extensive media coverage in the summer of 2017.

The motivations, behaviours and experiences of both casual and dedicated 'royal tourist' visitors to royal events and sites and in the presence of royalty would also bear analysis in seeking to understand how monarchy is consumed and interpreted by both domestic and international visitors. Consumption and the meanings of the material cultures and souvenir manifestations of royalty that are designed for tourists may also be explored in this context. What aesthetic considerations may be applied to these souvenir items and what meanings do they convey to the tourist?

A number of methodological considerations are also suggested. Accessing and analyzing archival documentary sources, ethnographic, observational studies and surveys of tourist information staff and royal enthusiasts/tourists and other approaches, such as critical discourse analysis and various approaches to visual/media analysis may also contribute to further research in this area. The extent to which the future of royal tourism is intertwined with the future of monarchy is contentious. In Britain, at least, the relative popularity of royal family members has been laid open to question, though the institution as a whole appears to be under no serious threat. For example, an abdication of Queen Elizabeth II, if highly unlikely, would generate some very real issues for British society, and, in turn, some would argue, British tourism (both in terms of the supply of and demand for that tourism).

There is little research on the tourism connections with monarchies past and present in Asian, Middle Eastern and African settings (Spellman, 2001). The formal, ritual dimension of royalty in diverse social, cultural and political contexts offers a potentially rich seam for anthropologists of tourism, for example. It is hoped that other researchers will come forward to address the numerous gaps in the literature that are suggested above. Hopefully, research on 'royal tourism' is far from dead.

Notes

1   There are three broad categories of monarchy: First, where the monarch is *de facto* and *de jure* head of state, for example in Morocco, Saudi Arabia and the Gulf States; second where the Crown is endowed with a quasi-religious, formal and highly ritualized status, for example in Japan, Thailand and Bhutan; and third, where the monarchy is symbolic of the secular state with very little political influence and no religious significance, though performing a symbolic role expressing national unity, for example in Scandinavia, the Benelux states and Spain. The British monarchy combines features of each of these categories (Hames and Leonard, 1998. See also Spellman, 2001).
2   See, for example: Cannadine and Price (1987), Edensor (2002), Handelman (1997), Hughes-Freeland (1998) and Palmer and Jankowiak (1996).
3   See Bramley (2002), Broad (1952), Couldry (1999), Prochaska (2002), Rowbottom (2002a).
4   The late Diana, Princess of Wales and Queen Elizabeth the Queen Mother are obvious examples from the British monarchy.
5   See Clarkson (2006), Garrett (1982), Maynard (1984), Pigott (2005), Price (1980) and Rowbottom (2002b).
6   A local example of dedicated royal tourists was contained in reporting in the Sheffield Star newspaper following a visit by the Queen and Duke of Edinburgh in May 2003 to open the city's new Winter Gardens. Here it was reported that the crowd gathered to witness this event included people who had travelled the 200 miles from London solely for the purpose of being in the Queen's presence, as well as a local man who calculated that he had travelled some 13,000 miles during a lifetime following royal tours.
7   See Blain and O'Donnell (2003), Boswell and Evans (1999), Dayan and Katz (1992), Hughes-Freeland (1998) and O'Toole (2002).

Bibliography

Adams, K. M. (1984) Come to Tana Toraja, 'Land of the Heavenly Kings': Travel Agents as Brokers In Ethnicity. *Annals of Tourism Research*, 11(3), 469–485.

Anderson, B. (1991) Imagined Communities: Reflections on the Origin and Spread of Nationalism. London: Verso.

Arnold, J., Davies, K. and Ditchfield, S. (1998) *History and Heritage: Consuming the Past in Contemporary Culture*. Shaftesbury: Donhead.

Ashworth, G. J. and Larkham, P. J. (Eds.) (1994) *Building a New Heritage: Tourism, Culture and Identity in the New Europe*. London: Routledge.

Auerbach, J. (2005) Imperial Boredom: Monotony and the British Empire. *Common Knowledge*, 11(2), 283–305.

Back, L. (2002) God Save the Queen: The Pistols' Jubilee. *Sociological Research Online*, 7(1).

Balmer, J. M. (2011) Corporate heritage Brands and the Precepts of Corporate Heritage Brand Management: Insights from the British Monarchy on the Eve of the Royal Wedding of Prince William (April 2011) and Queen Elizabeth II's Diamond Jubilee (1952–2012). *Journal of Brand Management*, 18(8), 517–544.

Bentley, T. and Wilsdon, J. (2002) *Monarchies*. London: Demos.

Berger, P. L. and Luckmann, T. (1966) *The Social Construction of Reality: A Treatise in the Sociology of Knowledge*. New York: Anchor Books.

Billig, M. (1992) *Talking of the Royal Family*. London: Routledge

Blain, N. and O'Donnell, H. (2003) *Media, Monarchy and Power*. Bristol: Intellect Books.

Blundall, N. and Blackhall, S. (1992) *Fall of the House of Windsor*. Chicago: Contemporary Books.

Bogdanor, V. (1995) *The Monarchy and the Constitution*. Oxford: Oxford University Press.

Boswell, D. and Evans, J. (1999) *Representing the Nation: A Reader*. London: Routledge.

Bothwell, E. (2014, 9 July) Prince Andrew Gives London Pub Sign Royal Seal of Approval. www.morning advertiser.co.uk/Article/2014/07/09/Prince-Andrew-gives-London-pub-sign-Royal-seal-of-approval.

Bourdieu, P. (1998) *On Television and Journalism*. London: Pluto Press.

Bramley, H. (2002) Diana, Princess of Wales: The Contemporary Goddess. *Sociological Research Online* 7(1).

Broad, L. (1952) *Queens, Crowns and Coronations*. London: Hutchinson.

Brunt, R. (1999) Conversations on the Diana Moment and its Politics. *Journal of Gender Studies*, 8(3), 285–293.

Burnstein, M. E. (2015) 'I Have Remembered How to Seem': The Symbolic Monarchy After King George. *Quarterly Review of Film and Video*, 32(2), 162–178.

Buzard, J. (2003) Culture for Export: Tourism and Auto-ethnography in Post-War Britain, in Baranowski, S. and Furlough, E. (Eds.), *Being Elsewhere: Tourism, Consumer Culture, and Identity in Modern Europe and North America* (pp. 299–319). Ann Arbor, MI: University of Michigan Press.

Cannadine, D. and Price, S. (Eds.) (1987) *Rituals of Royalty*. Cambridge: Cambridge University Press.

Chaney, D. (1993) *Fictions of Collective Life*. London: Routledge.

Chase, M. (1990) The Concept of Jubilee within British Radical Thought in Late Eighteenth- and Nineteenth-Century England. *Past and Present*, 107, 132–147.

Clarkson, A. (2006) Pomp, Circumstance, and Wild Arabs: The 1912 Royal Visit to Sudan. *Journal of Imperial and Commonwealth History*, 34(1), 71–85.

Coates, C. (Ed.) (2006) *Majesty in Canada: Essays on the Role of Royalty*. Toronto: Dundurn Press.

Colley, L. (1984) The Apotheosis of George III: Loyalty, Royalty and the British Nation 1760–1820. *Past and Present*, 102(1), 94–129.

Colthorpe, M. (1977) *Royal Cambridge*. Cambridge City Council.

Connerton, P. (1989) *How Societies Remember*. Cambridge: University Press.

Corcoran, K. (2014, 6 April) Moment Queen's Guard Pulled Bayonet on Would-Be Intruder Who Ranted at Police Before Marching Towards Buckingham Palace Gates. *Daily Mail*. www.dailymail. co.uk/news/article-2598044/Security-fears-Buckingham-Palace-Queens-Guard-pulls-rifle-intruder-ranted-police-marching-gates.html.

Couldry, N. (1999) Remembering Diana: The Geography of Celebrity and the Politics of Lack. *New Formations*, 36, 77–91.

Craig, D. (2003) The Crowned Republic? Monarchy and Anti-Monarchy in Britain, 1760–1901. *The Historical Journal* 46(1) 167–185.

Crang, M. (1998) *Cultural Geography*. London: Routledge.

Cubitt, G. (Ed.) (1998) *Imagining Nations*. Manchester University Press.

Davies, J. (2001) Diana: A Cultural History: Gender, Race, Nation and the People's Princess. London: Palgrave.

Davis, E. (2002) A Queen's Ransom: The Economics of Monarchy, in Bentley, T. and Wilsdon, J. *Monarchies* (pp. 75–82). London: Demos.

Dayan, D. and Katz, E. (1992) *Media Events: The Live Broadcasting of History*. Cambridge, MA: Harvard University Press.

Díaz, V. P. (1993) *The Return of Civil Society: The Emergence of Democratic Spain*. Cambridge, MA: Harvard University Press.

Easthope, A. (1998) *Englishness and National Culture*. London: Routledge.

Edensor, T. (2001) Performing Tourism, Staging Tourism. *Tourist Studies*, 1(1) 59–81.

Edensor, T. (2002) *National Identity, Popular Culture and Everyday Life*. Oxford: Berg.

English Heritage (2015) www.english-heritage.org.uk/visit/places/osborne/things-to-see-and-do/queen-victoria-beach/.

Farrell, T. (2002) Parks and Palaces: How Monarchy Reign over Public Space, in Bentley, T. and Wilsdon, J., *Monarchies* (pp. 90–98). London: Demos.

Finch, J. and Morgan, D. (2002) Generations and Heritage: Reflections on the Queen Mother's Funeral. *Sociological Research Online* 7(1).

Garratt, D. and Piper, H. (2003) Citizenship Education and the Monarchy: Examining the contradictions. *British Journal of Educational Studies*, 51(2) 128–148.

Garrett, R. (1982) *Royal Travel*. Poole: Blandford Press.

Geertz, C. (1993) *The Interpretation of Cultures*. London: Fontana.

Gillis, J. (Ed.) (1996) *Commemorations: The Politics of National Identity*. Princeton: Princeton University Press.

Gladdish, K. (2002) Decline or Fall? The Survival Threat to Twenty-First Century Monarchies, in Bentley, T. and Wilsdon, J., *Monarchies* (pp. 133–138). London: Demos.

Golby, J. M. and Purdue, A. W. (1988) *The Monarchy and The British People: 1760 to the Present*. London: B. T. Batsford.

Guss, D. (2000) The Festive State: Race, Ethnicity and Nationalism as Cultural Performance. University of California Press.

Hames, T. and Leonard, M. (1998) *Modernising the Monarchy*. London: Demos.

Handelman, D (1997) Rituals/Spectacles. *International Social Science Journal*, 15(September), 387–399.

Hebdidge, D. (1988) *Hiding in the Light*. London: Comedia.

Herbert, D. T. (Ed.) (1995) *Heritage, Tourism and Society*. London: Mansell.

Herzfeld, M. (1997) *Cultural Intimacy: Social Poetics in the Nation-State*. New York: Routledge.

Hewison, R. (1997) *Culture and Consensus: England, Art and Politics Since 1940*. London: Methuen.

Hitchens, C. (1990) *The Monarchy: A Critique of Britain's Favourite Fetish*. London: Chatto and Windus.

Hobsbawn, E. (1999) Mass-Producing Traditions: Europe 1870–1914, in Boswell, D. and Evans, J., *Representing the Nation: A Reader* (pp. 61–86). London: Routledge.

Hobsbawn, E. and Ranger, T. (1983) *The Invention of Tradition*. Cambridge University Press.

Hughes-Freeland, F. (Ed.) (1998) *Ritual, Performance, Media*. London; Routledge

Jenkins, R. (2002) Modern Monarchy: A Comparative View from Denmark. *Sociological Research Online*, 7(1).

Kumar, A. (1997) *Stately Progress: Royal Train Travel Since 1840*. York: National Railway Museum.

Lant, J. L. (1979) *Insubstantial Pageant. Ceremony and Confusion at Queen Victoria's Court*. London: Hamish Hamilton.

Law, A. (2002) Jubilee Mugs: The Monarchy and the Sex Pistols. *Sociological Research Online*, 7(1).

Lloyd, D. and Thomas, P. (1998) *Culture and the State*. London: Routledge.

Long, P. and Palmer, N. J. (2008) *Royal Tourism: Excursions Around Monarchy*. Vol. 14. Clevedon: Channel View Publications.

McGuigan, J. (2000) British Identity and 'The People's Princess' *Sociological Review*, 48(1), 1–18.

McGuigan, J. (1992) *Cultural Populism*. London: Routledge.

McKibbin, R. (1998) Mass Observation in the Mall, in Merck, M. (Ed.), *After Diana: Irreverent Elegies* (pp. 15–24). London: Verso.

Masters, B. (1972) *Dreams about HM the Queen*. London: Blond & Briggs.

Maynard, J. W. (Ed.) (1984) *The King and Queen at Craigwell 1929*. Pagham: Parochial Church Council.

Medhurst, A. (2002) Of Queens and Queers, in Bentley, T. and Wilsdon, J., *Monarchies* (pp. 124–132). London: Demos.

Merck, M. (Ed.) (1998) *After Diana: Irreverent Elegies*. London: Verso.

Montgomery-Massingberd, H. (2003) *A Guide to Britain's Royal Heritage*. London: Quantum Books

Nairn, T. (1988) *The Enchanted Glass*. London: Radius.

Nelson, M. (2001) *Queen Victoria and the Discovery of the Riviera*. London, I. B. Tauris.

O'Toole, F. (2002) Jubilee Girl in, Jack, I. (Ed.) *Celebrity*. London: Granta.

Ormand, R. (1977) *The Face of Monarchy: British Royalty Portrayed*. London: Phaidon.

Ornes, C. and Maclaran, P. (2016) *Royal Fever: The British Monarchy in Consumer Culture*. Berkeley: University of California Press.

Palmer, C. (2000) Heritage Tourism and English National Identity, in Robinson, M., Evans, N., Long, P., Sharpley, R. and Swarbrooke, J., *Tourism and Heritage Relationships: Global, National and Local Perspectives* (pp. 331–348). Sunderland: Business Education Publishers.

Palmer, G. and Jankowiak, W. (1996) Performance and Imagination: Toward an Anthropology of the Spectacular and the Mundane. *Cultural Anthropology*, 11(2): 225–258.

Parry, J. (2002) Family History: The Role of the British Monarchy in National Life Since 1750, in Bentley, T. and Wilsdon, J., *Monarchies* (pp. 67–74). London: Demos.

Paxman, J. (1998) *The English: A Portrait of a People*. London: Michael Joseph.

Peacock, M. (2002) A Lightly Locked Door: Australia and the Monarchy, in Bentley, T. and Wilsdon, J., *Monarchies* (pp. 160–165). London: Demos.

Philips, D. (2004) Stately Pleasure Domes – Nationhood, Monarchy and Industry: The Celebration Exhibition in Britain. *Leisure Studies*, 23(2), 95–108.

Pigott, P. (2005) Royal Transport: An Inside Look at the History of British Royal Travel. Toronto: Dundurn Press.

Pimlott, B. (1996) *The Queen: A Biography of Elizabeth II*. London: Harper Collins.

Plunkett, J. (2003) A Media Monarchy? Queen Victoria and the Radical Press 1837–1901. *Media History* 9(1) 3–18.

Price, H. (1980) *The Royal Tour 1901, Or the Cruise of H.M.S. Ophir, Being a Lower Deck Account of their Royal Highnesses the Duke and Duchess of Cornwall and York's Voyage around the British Empire*. Exeter: Webb and Bower.

Prochaska, F. (1995) *Royal Bounty: The Making of a Welfare Monarchy*. New Haven: Yale University Press.

Prochaska, F. (Ed.) (2002) *Royal Lives: Portraits of Past Royals by Those in the Know*. Oxford: Oxford University Press.

Reed, C. V. (2016) *Royal Tourists, Colonial Subjects and the Making of a British World, 1860–1911*. Manchester: Manchester University Press.

Rojek, C. (1999) Fatal Attractions, in Boswell, D. and Evans, J., *Representing the Nation: A Reader* (pp. 185–207). London: Routledge.

Rojek, C. (2002) Courting Fame: The Monarchy and Celebrity Culture, in Bentley, T. and Wilsdon, J., *Monarchies* (pp. 105–110). London: Demos.

Rowbottom, S. (2002a) Subject Positions and 'Real Royalists': Monarchy and Vernacular Civil Religion in Great Britain, in Rapport, N. (Ed.), *British Subjects: An Anthropology of Britain* (pp. 31–47). Oxford: Berg.

Rowbottom, S. (2002b) Following the Queen: The Place of the Royal Family in the Context of Royal Visits and Civil Religion. *Sociological Research Online*, 7(2).

Satoh, A. (2001) Constructing Imperial identity: How to Quote the Imperial Family and Those Who Address Them in the Japanese Press. *Discourse and Society*, 12(2), 169–194.

Saunders, R. (2013) 'Prince Harry effect' Sees Tourism Boom in Las Vegas. www.dialaflight.com/blog/prince-harry-effect-sees-tourism-boom-in-las-vegas_100168.html.

Schama, S. (1986) The Domestication of Majesty: Royal Family Portraiture, 1500–1850. *Journal of Interdisciplinary History*, XVII(1), 155–183.

Schechner, R. (1993) *The Future of Ritual*. London: Routledge.

Smith, A. D. (1991) *National Identity*. London: Penguin.

Spellman, W. M. (2001) *Monarchies 1000–2000*. London: Reaktion Books.

Spillman, L. (1997) *Nation and Commemoration: Creating National Identities in the United States and Australia*. Cambridge: Cambridge University Press.

Starkey, D. (2005) Does Monarchy Matter? *Arts and Humanities in Higher Education*, 4(2), 215–224.

Stevenson, N. (Ed.) (2001) *Culture and Citizenship*. London: Sage.

Steward, J. (2003) Tourism in Late Imperial Austria: the Development of Tourist Cultures and Their Associated Images of Place, in Baranowski, S. and Furlough, E. (Eds.), *Being Elsewhere: Tourism, Consumer Culture, and Identity in Modern Europe and North America* (pp. 108–136). Ann Arbor, MI: University of Michigan Press.

Storry, M. and Childs, P. (1997) *British Cultural Identities*. London: Routledge.

Strinati, D. and Wagg, S. (Eds.) (1992) *Come on Down? Popular Media Culture in Post-War Britain*. London: Routledge.

Taylor, A. (1999) *'Down with the Crown': British Anti-Monarchism and Debates About Royalty Since 1790*. London: Reaktion Books.

Thomas, P. (1989) *British Monarchy*. Oxford University Press.

Thompson, J. (1995) *The Media and Modernity*. Cambridge: Polity Press.

Tomlinson, R. (1994) *Divine Right: The Inglorious Survival of British Royalty*. New York: Little, Brown & Company.

Tulloch, J. (1999) *Performing Culture*. London: Sage.

Turnock, R. (2000) *Interpreting Diana*. London: BFI.

Vansittart, P. (1998) *In Memory of England*. London: John Murray.

Wardle, C. and West, E. (2004) The Press as Agents of Nationalism in the Queen's Golden Jubilee: How British Newspapers Celebrated a Media Event, *European Journal of Communication*, 19(2), 195–214.

Wilentz, S. (ed.) (1985) *Rites of Power: Symbolism, Ritual and Politics since the Middle Ages*. Philadelphia: University of Pennsylvania Press.

Williams, R. (1997) *The Contentious Crown: Public Discussion of the British Monarchy in the Reign of Queen Victoria*. Aldershot: Ashgate.

Yorke, J. (2002) Redeemed Characters: How the Nation Views the Monarchy as Soap Opera, in Bentley, T. and Wilsdon, J., *Monarchies* (pp. 117–123). London: Demos.

Young, R. (2002) Queen and Country Fifty Years On: Facts and Figures for the Golden Jubilee 2002. *House of Commons Library Research Paper* 02/28.

Ziegler, P. (1978) *Crown and People*. London: Collins.

16

SUN, SURF, SEX, AND THE EVERYDAY

Subverting the tourist gaze with Gold Coast narrative fiction

Kelly Palmer

Appearance—something that can be seen or heard by others as well as ourselves—constitutes reality. Compared with the reality which comes from being seen and heard, even the greatest forces of intimate life—the passions of the heart, the thoughts of the mind, the delights of the sense—lead an uncertain, shadowy kind of existence unless and until they are transformed, deprivatized and de-individualized, as it were, into a shape to fit them for public appearance.

(Arendt, 1958, p. 50)

As the Gold Coast approaches a population of half a million, it must find a broader role than just being a tourist resort.

(Jones, 1986, p. 8)

Setting the scene

As Australia's sixth largest city, set in the southeast of subtropical Queensland and along 57 kilometers of coastline, the Gold Coast enjoys its status as a "premier tourist destination" synonymous with "sun, surf, and sex" (Winchester & Everett, 2000, p. 59). For the last half-century, state and local governments' "supply-driven approach" to tourism in Queensland has certainly dressed the city for the tourist's gaze (Dredge, 2011, p. 154), though the Gold Coast has two faces. In tourist media and then across local texts—including television dramas, reality television, and literary fiction—images of the Gold Coast feed the tourist mecca stereotype: the Gold Coast is a "glitter strip" (Channel Ten, 2014) where locals can "feel young and not take life so seriously" (Gold Coast Tourism, 2014). These narratives stack in popular culture to portray the Gold Coast as an open-air hotel and characterize the local experience as liminal, where and when everyday is a holiday. Locals not affluent enough to afford a perpetual holiday are excluded from this narrative, while many low-income locals are further stereotyped as "dole bludgers"[1] or delinquents intruding on paradise. This class divide, manifesting in mainstream popular culture through binaries relaxed/orderly and delinquent/hopeless, is not irrelevant to the other stereotyped image of the Gold Coast: that of "the Crime Capital of Australia" (ABC, 2011). Like the image of tourist mecca, the Gold Coast as Crime Capital appears throughout popular culture, most prominently in mainstream media and journalism texts, and often alongside and reinforcing the glitz and glamour.

This chapter argues that the tourist-hungry image of a liminal Gold Coast, which on its own is shallow and largely enveloped in the cultural cringe of Australia, leaves much space for cultural imagination. With much history and culture of the Gold Coast erased or underrepresented, the loudest narratives come to define place, and the Crime Capital epithet fills the rest of the discussion. This chapter maps how the Gold Coast is represented through the tourist gaze as both celebrated tourist mecca and condemned underbelly, affecting its reading as a liminal space. I suggest that narrative fiction, specifically the mode of literary realism, can subvert the tourist gaze and instead illustrate the everyday lives of Gold Coast low-income locals. Cultural studies guide my understanding of how locals are represented or silenced in mainstream narratives of the Gold Coast, while humanist geographers and sociologists justify the role of literary fiction in place-making. Georgia Savage's *The House Tibet* (1992) is a local example of how voices concerned with the low socio-economic subvert the tourist gaze while evoking natural beauty, danger, work life, street culture, and domestic lives. I conduct close textual analysis of Savage's novel as a case study for how promoting the arts and literary tourism can generate an authentic sense of place beyond the glitz and glamour of mainstream media. Paying closer attention to Gold Coast narrative fiction may even enhance the image of the Gold Coast under the tourist's gaze, since the "tourist is a kind of pilgrim seeking authenticity in other 'times' and other 'places'" (Urry, 2005, p. 9). What Gold Coast literary fictions can offer, then, is a grounded view of the gold city—a view that creates and draws attention to existing histories, voices, and landscape features of a shared and contested home.

Theoretical underpinnings: gazing over the Gold Coast

Soft, sparkling surf. Lifeguards smiling as they run with an inflatable rescue boat. Mothers shopping in vintage boutiques. These are some of the first images in Gold Coast Tourism's "The New Surfers Paradise Lifestyle" video (2014)—a campaign that markets life on the Gold Coast as a perpetual holiday. According to "Local," Lou McGregor living in Surfers Paradise helps one to "feel young and not take life so seriously" (ibid.). Scenes feature undisturbed bliss, and showcase the Gold Coast as a beach paradise of leisure and luxury, where even lifeguards are decorative.

When looking at the Gold Coast through what John Urry conceives as the tourist gaze (2005), the city appears to be an open-air hotel. Local and state governments have fostered the tourist gaze for the last half-century in their deliberate attempts to build a tourist hotspot. The Gold Coast of 2017 has a population of 570,000[2] residents, but through "political intervention and vigorous promotion" (Craik, 1991, p. 172) and through their financial and bureaucratic support of hotels and high-end housing estate development (Dredge, 2012), the city attracts close to 12 million visitors per year (City of Gold Coast, 2017), including at least 7 million overnight international tourists recorded in 2015 (Queensland Treasury, 2017). The Gold Coast economy has been "heavily dependent on construction, retail trade" (Jones, 1986, p. 116), but mostly "tourism and residential development' (Dedekorut & Bosman, 2011, p. 9).

As "the leading Australian example of tourism urbanization" (Lawton, 2005, p. 189), the Gold Coast of today has undoubtedly been built around the tourist and the middle-class local, whose daily life flows through this place made for leisure. Robert J. Stimson and John Minnery recognize that the Gold Coast occupies a

> unique position . . . in Australia's urban system as the nation's first leisure and lifestyle consumption city . . . As well as being a place for people to recreate and live, part

of the lifestyle focuses on what may be termed hedonism, which both disturbs some existing residents and attracts new ones. The lifestyle and image of the Gold Coast as an area that is simultaneously brash, trendy, sophisticated, relaxed, overdeveloped and overurbanised, renders it a place of contrasts.

(1998, pp. 195–196)

Here, Stimson and Minnery capture the vision of the Gold Coast as an open-air hotel or perpetual holidayworld, which feeds the middle-to-upper-middle-class fantasy of uninhibited leisure and consumerism. This is why Jones surmises that "the Gold Coast is one of the few places in Australia where the moral and political values of capitalism are freely canvassed" (1986, p. 123), since the immense growth, or emergence, of the city in the last half-century has been built around leisure and luxury. Even if one cannot access the consumerism of the city off the beach, one will notice how the shopping centers and malls districts such as Surfers Paradise are "smothered with advertising" (Boyd, 2010, p. 43).

Laura J. Lawton maps that Surfers Paradise is where the "most intensive development occurs" (2005, p. 189). The coastal and central suburb of Surfers Paradise, whose skyscrapers are visible from most areas of the Gold Coast, is especially scrutinized as the epitome of Gold Coast's tourism obsession. For example, the Surfers Paradise Alliance—a tourism and marketing council body appointed especially to promoting Surfers Paradise—markets the suburb as the sixth Gold Coast theme park (Surfers Paradise Alliance, 2017). In Lawton's study of resident perceptions of the Gold Coast tourism, she found "most respondents strongly agreeing that [Surfers Paradise] is very touristy, very commercialized, very artificial, and very hectic/noisy" (2005, p. 193). Meanwhile, Robin Boyd notices how the place-names of suburbs, shops, and restaurants across the Gold Coast, and Surfers Paradise especially, evoke Las Vegas and other United States' destinations (2010, p. 88). Susan Ward and Tom O'Reagan also argue that the Gold Coast has much in common with Las Vegas and Orlando in Florida since the three cities' economies are "based on the delivery of themed entertainment" (2009, p. 221). For these reasons, as well as a distinct absence of an Australian aesthetic in Australian design, Boyd nicknames Surfers Paradise "Austerica" (2009, p. 86). Lawton's and Boyd's observations of Surfers Paradise illustrate not only that the city has been built and painted with the tourist rather than the local in mind, but also point to the cultural cringe of Australia, which recoils from contemporary Australia's imitation of US trends. In this sense, Boyd's derisive joke that the Gold Coast is a "musical comedy of modern Australia come to life" (2010, p. 87) highlights further the performative nature of the city, catering always to an audience so that it may expand itself.

This trend of gentrifying and commercializing the Gold Coast through tourist-centric infrastructure has not slowed in recent years, though there has been development that benefits locals in everyday life as well as tourists. For example, the new light rail system that began construction in 2011 cost US$1.2 billion and extensions pending for 2018 will cost another US$335 million (Burke, 2017). In addition, state governments are set to spend US$1.6 billion dollars for the 2018 Commonwealth Games held on the Gold Coast (Stolz, 2012), and the federal government plans to inject a further US$36 million into the Games (Potts & Skene, 2017). This new infrastructure is undoubtedly made for tourists, hence the connections. The finished tram (if there are no plans to extend the track again) will journey from the Gold Coast Airport, through Surfers Paradise, and then connect to the heavy rail, which runs express to the International Airport in Brisbane. Meanwhile, former Queensland Premier Peter Beattie heralds the 2018 Commonwealth Games as "the biggest opportunity to promote the Gold Coast that's ever existed" as he condemns council in-fighting over ticket reservations that threaten to detract from the potential egalitarianism of the Games (2017, para. 10). Thus, the local has started making an appearance as the city connects through infrastructure and marketing to the world, though the tourist is still at the forefront of these development projects. As Dianne Dredge interprets, "The growing activity in bidding for, and securing, major events (such as the 2018 Commonwealth Games) provides other examples" for how Queensland and the Gold Coast invest so much in tourism (2011, p. 168).

Between paradise and paradise lost

Because of the transient population and tourist-centric infrastructure, the Gold Coast is often dismissed as a stopover city, or as limbo, rather than as a city in its own right. Brendan Shanahan, in his book, *The Secret Life of the Gold Coast* (2004) reasons that the Gold Coast is not a city because a city is "a place with a subway, a natural history museum and a park downtown with a bronze statue of the founding father" (p. xiv), all of which the Gold Coast has none. Instead, it would seem, the Gold Coast has hotels and bars and beaches and ritualized celebrations, including the Gold Coast 600, a supercar race, and Schoolies week, a week-long festival of sorts that attracts approximately 40,000 high school graduates from across Australia (ABC, 2016). Citing Schoolies week, which is set predominantly in the beach suburb of hotels and bars, Surfers Paradise, Hilary Winchester and Kathryn Everett observe that such celebrations are one of many of the Gold Coast's liminal qualities. They argue that in addition to sitting at the state border and along the ocean, the Gold Coast is "a city of theme parks and leisure . . . a place to get away . . . where transitions are possible," and thus is a liminal space (2000, p. 61).

As a liminal city, the Gold Coast is conceived as separate from the everyday workweek. Urry identifies throughout his work that societies conceive the holidayworld and their own everyday life as separate from each other, but in the case of the Gold Coast, the everyday life of Gold Coast residents *is, apparently,* the holiday. These representations of the Gold Coast as a "beach resort" (Griffin, 2007, p. 289), rather than as a developed city, characterize locals as tourists in their home. In their study of migration to the Gold Coast, Robert Stimson and John Minnery find that "Migration within Australia is the major driver of population growth in the 'sun-belt' regions of the east coast," including Southeast Queensland in particular (1998, p. 198). That the Gold Coast is predominantly populated with visitors and new locals underscores the sense of the Gold Coast as being history-less, or without an authentic sense of self that emerged from within place. Although, the cultural landscape of Australia, which silences the Gold Coast's First Peoples, The Kombumerri, is also largely to blame for the Gold Coast's seeming isolation in history and space. Meanwhile, Shanahan characterizes the Gold Coast as "the city of the lost; a city where seemingly everyone had come from somewhere else and where 'running away' was a box you ticked on the emigration form" (2004, p. 2). This characterization of locals as "lost" rather than at home silences everyday narratives of the Gold Coast, denies the sovereignty of the Aboriginal Australians, and exacerbates representations of the city as a resort.

The tourist gaze pervades representations of the Gold Coast, highlighting its liminality and consequently upholding leisure and luxury—as a financial and environmental privilege—as the embodiment of belonging on the Gold Coast. Artifacts of popular culture sculpt the Gold Coast as limbo in the cultural imagination. A prime example is the reality show, *Big Brother,* which aired in Australia on and off from 2001 to 2011. The premise of the series is that a dozen or more strangers are isolated within one house, which is equipped with hidden cameras and microphones to document the daily and domestic lives of the strangers. Inevitably, the show often glorifies the mundane supposedly everyday lives of the housemates, and adds activities and games into their workless lives to enhance drama. In the case of the Australian version, the *Big Brother House* was located in one of the Gold Coast's largest theme parks, Dreamworld.

Jane Roscoe, drawing from network executive Tim Clucas, evaluates that the series "performs its Australian-ness and speaks to its local Australian audience," attempting to evoke a relaxed lifestyle and household (2001, pp. 475–476). What is problematic about the show's claim to explore Australian everyday life is its unyielding focus on leisure as the staple of local and national experience, thus characterizing the local again as floating in limbo. The distinctions between everyday life and cinema/attraction are blurry in the case of *Big Brother* since the voyeurism on screen promotes the everyday as an attraction, while the set is removed from, yet vaguely resembles, everyday life. Ward and O'Reagan note that because the set can be visited as part of the theme park, "the reality TV show becomes reconfigured as another attraction" (2009, p. 219). In this case, *Big Brother* on the Gold Coast is doubly an example of leisure and luxury standing in for the representation of everyday life on the Gold Coast.

Representations of the Gold Coast as a liminal space separate from the everyday workweek also underpins representations of the Gold Coast as the "Crime Capital of Australia" (ABC, 2011). What has become a stereotype or cliché throughout representations of the Gold Coast is not merely a literary conceit that exists only within the cultural imagination. Although the Gold Coast's crime rates are not the highest in the country, the transient population that forges to the Gold Coast's liminality "makes it difficult for the police to solve crimes" (Jones 1986, p. 101).[3] The Gold Coast often appears in mainstream journalism as a criminal hotspot, with some head-lines proclaiming: "Gold Coast underbelly: Sunny Days, Shady People" (Potts, 2016); "Gold Coast's Dark Underbelly" (Condon, 2008); "New Underbelly on Gold Coast" (Braithwaite, 2008); and "Australia's Crime Capital Looks Like a Paradise" (Hutton, 2014). Not surprisingly, many representations of the Gold Coast in popular culture explore the duality of this limbo where paradise is also paradise lost. Some examples in popular culture of the Gold Coast as a paradise where leisure and crime overlap include: the animated crime series, *Pacific Heat*, which premiered on the Comedy Channel in 2016; a police-detective drama, *The Strip*; and the reality show, *Gold Coast Cops*. Stephen Stockwell observes that "the vast majority of material set on the Gold Coast has criminal themes" (2011, p. 281). These representations of the Gold Coast do not subvert the tourist gaze, but rather unveil the underbelly of paradise, where the binary of para-dise and paradise lost simultaneously contrasts and highlights the "everyday is a holiday" myth.

At this nexus the local is characterized as a non-working tourist and also as a criminal, which fits the figure of the dole bludger. Kylar Loussikian (2017) of the *Courier Mail* reports that the suburb of Southport on the Gold Coast is one of Australia's "dole bludger" hotspots, after the federal government ranked suburbs by the number of welfare recipients failing to arrive to job interviews. The *Daily Telegraph* (quoted in Media Watch 2016) characterizes one type of welfare-dependent Australian, or "dole bludger," as "young, able and unwilling to work." Notably, this characterization overlaps with that of the Gold Coast local, who, according to the New Surfers Paradise Lifestyle marketing campaign, is "young," enjoys the Gold Coast as "an attraction itself," and does not "take life so seriously" (Gold Coast Tourism, 2014). The difference between the narrative of the dole bludger and the narrative of the Gold Coast local is marked only in their financial capital: the Gold Coast local shops and dines in high-end restaurants, while the dole bludger's time for leisure is mysterious, summarized only as "not work." These representations unfairly characterize welfare-dependent locals as thieves and frauds, while working-class and other low-income locals are otherwise underrepresented if not omitted entirely from popular narratives of the Gold Coast. In 2016, 35.7 percent of the Gold Coast population earned somewhere between negative income and up to US$400 per week (id.community 2017). This means that the third of the Gold Coast's population that receives an income less than that of the middle class is unseen in narratives that cater to the tourist gaze. Low-income residents appear rarely as delinquents in the narratives about crime, which serve only to reinforce the image of paradise through the contrived binary of paradise/paradise lost.

The dole bludger is a complicated figure in Australian culture. Sometimes, the dole bludger is a white local with poor personal hygiene, smiling cheekily or posing defiantly against a Holden or Ford sedan. Generally, the term is used to disparage welfare systems as a whole as well as those marginalized and disenfranchised, whether they are Aboriginal and Torres Strait Islanders, single parents, the mentally ill, addicts, the homeless, refugees, the unhealthy, among others. The term is always derogatory, and is associated with wastefulness, purposelessness, selfish behavior, immaturity, and even fraud and theft. These connotations overlap ceaselessly with representations of the Gold Coast as a superficial, liminal space for tourism and crime, but most of all, for leisure. The locals are so characterized as leisurely creatures, lazing on the edge of the country, between work, between realities.

These representations of the Gold Coast as a "hedonistic beach resort" (Lawton 2005, p. 189) are problematic because low-income locals are relatively silenced, and then depicted in the media as dole bludgers or welfare-dependent delinquents, as intruders in the tourist mecca. In this contrived binary where someone is either deserving or undeserving of the "everyday is a holiday" lifestyle, it is the low-income locals who are depicted as residents of the Crime Capital, who otherwise do not belong on the Gold Coast. Michel de Certeau recognizes how narratives about place define and shape place, and so motivate a cyclical process of place-making. De Certeau explains:

> Social life multiplies the gestures and modes of behavior *(im)printed* by narrative models; it ceasely reproduces and accumulates "copies" of stories. Our society has become a recited society, in three senses: it is defined by *stories* [. . .] by *citations* of stories, and by the interminable *recitation* of stories.
>
> *(2011, p. 186, emphasis in original)*

If narratives about place actively shape place in the cultural imagination, then storytelling is all the more important to develop local concepts of home and belonging. The Gold Coast is "often taken too lightly" (Dedekorut & Bosman, 2011, p. 1) and at the same time has created unattainable standards for itself as a consumable commodity in the form of a borderless theme park. Urry observes that tourists "are looking for the extraordinary and hence will be exceptionally critical of services provided that appear to undermine such a quality" (2005, p. 38). The vast mainstream criticism of the Gold Coast for being a beach resort rather than an authentic city demonstrates how the Gold Coast falls short of expectations.

I argue that narrative fiction offers a sense of low-income locals' everyday lives, and in doing so, has the potential to attract visitors through literary tourism. In this case, investment in the local arts is insidiously an investment in tourism—one that forges new identities of place that are more authentic than that of beach resort and underbelly.

Literary tourism and the everyday

The Gold Coast has an image problem that is off-putting to locals and mainstream media even if the city continues to attract millions of visitors each year. The vision of the Gold Coast as a beach resort is a tired and self-aggrandizing narrative that begs for authenticity, but instead makes way for representations of the city as having a criminal underbelly, all of which inaccurately characterize locals as leisurely creatures. Referring to local infrastructure that favors the tourist over local concerns, Dianne Dredge argues:

> If tourism is to maintain and assert its important role in Queensland's economy, and if it is to contribute to social, cultural and environmental well-being and regional sustainability, the industry's capture of the tourism policy space cannot continue. Vision, political leadership and commitment to a broader set of public interests will be needed in order to address this challenge.
>
> *(2011, p. 169)*

As Dredge notes, new approaches to tourism are required. New narratives about place, and new approaches to place need to complement and develop the tourist mecca features of the Gold Coast without alienating permanent residents. Distinctly absent from popular narratives of the Gold Coast is the everyday, and the everyday for low-income locals in particular. Everyday life is authentic, lived, endlessly reproduced, observable, and in the case of the Gold Coast, includes the experience of profound natural beauty.

Literary fiction, as a "material artefact" place, can express "the less tangible, experiential aspects of geographies" (Sharp, 2000, p. 327) that permeate everyday life. Kirin Narayan argues that fiction's power to capture society, place and locals, "points to a larger confusion about where ethnography ends and fiction begins" (2008, p. 136). In regards to capturing a sense of place that is communicable to others, Susan Carson, Lesley Hawkes, Kári Gislason, and Samuel Martin argue that the "best literary works tend to interrogate and add complexity to our understanding of everyday life, and in doing so encourage a diversity of views of the local landscape and its meaning" (2013, p. 47). Representing the Gold Coast through low socio-economic narratives subverts the tourist gaze and in doing so, may paradoxically offer tourists a more meaningful connection to the city. Literary realisms at once undermine tourist- and criminally concerned views of the Gold Coast and foreground alternative experiences of everyday living, which offer a place-based understanding of underrepresented Gold Coast communities with a unique stake in the development of the city.

I suggest that Gold Coast narrative fictions be interrogated and promoted for literary tourism so that an authentic sense of place can be shared between locals, artists, visitors, and onlookers. With literary tourism as part of the tourist's experience of the Gold Coast, new visions of place can emerge from the text as well as the tourist's experience of place in light of the text. With this in mind, literature does not necessarily define place, but opens a dialogue about place that values lived experience and subjectivities. Shelagh Squire argues:

> Influenced by such varied factors as gender, class, and ethnicity, textual meanings are incorporated into lived cultures or everyday life. These meanings foster new moments of production. An author's popularity may create interest in particular places and when a tourist business is developed, new textual forms (advertising, for example) are created in turn of the subject of new readings.
>
> *(1994, pp. 106–107)*

Squire (1994) thus counsels that not only can literary tourism validate experiences of place that are subjective and different to the place as it appears in tourism campaigns, but can also influence place-making in real life. Meanwhile, Squire deduces of literary tourism that "Linguistically and visually, the text becomes part of a wider symbolic system, read by different audiences who make sense of it in different ways" (1994, p. 106). Therefore, a work of literary fiction is not a manifesto for how to read and experience place, but rather illustrates features of a place that resonate with a particular viewer. As a result, "Authenticity becomes a subjective experience, a combination of the developers' intentions, the consumers' interpretation, and the interactions among them" (Herbert, 2001, p. 317).

There are few Gold Coast narratives that would serve well as inspiration for literary tourism, such as the fiction and non-fiction works of Matthew Condon, David Malouf, Amy Barker, and Sally Breen. However, in this essay, I have chosen to examine representations of the Gold Coast in Georgia Savage's novel, *The House Tibet* (1992) since it represents the Gold Coast through the eyes of a homeless child who is first a visitor, but becomes a local. The text is special in that it suggests ways to find beauty in the city despite the danger, artificiality of the holidayworld, and unfamiliarity. Moreover, the protagonist of Savage's novel, in becoming a local, does not simply utilize the Gold Coast as a place to escape and transition, but grounds herself, and makes a home. This grounding demonstrates that Australian locals "are not lost in space, unattached and freely floating" (O'Carroll, 1999, p. 32) and neither is the Gold Coast a city with "no past" (Shanahan, 2004, p. xiv).

The House Tibet follows a 12-year-old girl, who after her father rapes her runs away with her younger brother to the Gold Coast. While the Gold Coast is a setting to escape to, where the protagonist and her brother transform—even changing their names to Morgan and J-Max to shed their old life and create a new one—the Gold Coast of *The House Tibet* is not simply a liminal space for crime and escapism. Throughout the novel, Morgan and J-Max make a permanent home for themselves, which is built not only through adventure, but through work, friendship, new familial arrangements, and a connection to the natural landscape. The text makes room for representations of the Gold Coast as tacky tourist hub and criminal underbelly, but offers low socio-economic viewpoints that are hard-earned, and as a result, feel authentic. In these moments where expectations of and lived experiences of the Gold Coast clash and overlap, there is for the low-income local at least "the pleasure of recognition" (Midalia, 2012, p. 44) and for the tourist "there is a merging of the real and the imagined that gives places special meaning" (Herbert, 2001, p. 314).

Throughout Savage's novel, representations of the Gold Coast as a paradise or dangerous underbelly meet the characters' own perceptions of place as they, homeless, traverse the city. Meanwhile, Savage's exploration of homelessness complicates the myth of the Gold Coast local as floating in limbo. Morgan is first inspired to runaway to the Gold Coast when she sees an advertisement for the city in a Melbourne train station. The advertisement bejewels the beach and the skyscrapers, promising "Winter in Queensland—the Sunshine State" (Savage, 1992, p. 36).[4] Although Morgan is attracted to the perpetual summer that the Gold Coast offers as an escape, she in one breath associates this escape with work and domestic activities, musing, "I can get a job and find a little flat . . . it's even warm enough to sleep on the beach" (p. 36). As a homeless child searching for work, Morgan's characterization destabilizes the figure of the dole bludger and the myth of perpetual leisure, and instead complicates the experience of homelessness and financial insecurity/joblessness on the Gold Coast as a mental, emotional, and physical struggle for integrity and independence. Or, as Morgan succinctly states, "Running away *is* work" (p. 328).

As well as characterizing a low socio-economic experience of place as a constant effort for stability, Morgan's search for employment further defines home and belonging as related to work and routine. Early on in the text, after living with a group of other homeless teenagers, Morgan notices her brother stealing food from supermarkets, and this further propels her search for work. However, because the experience of homelessness and financial insecurity generally entails danger, Morgan cannot work until she also finds a permanent place to stay. As she begins work in the laundry of a hotel/brothel and stays with her brother in a room there, work and home become part of the same package, thus equating localism with the everyday workweek. Furthermore, the visibility of the workweek alongside the tourism industries at the hotel offers an authentic understanding of place-making, since the tourist-ready presentation of the Gold Coast is excavated as the work of locals. This idea is touched upon when Morgan complains to her employer that working in a brothel disturbs her, to which her employer replies, "if you were in the laundry of a big hotel up along the Strip, the same thing would be going on upstairs but you could pretend you didn't know. Does that make it any different?" (p. 231). In this scene, the text draws attention to how labor in the tourism industries is often ignored, and in making this labour visible in the narrative, the hotel feels not like a façade of the holidayworld, but as a real place supported in the everyday.

This equation between residence and work appears again when Morgan begins living in a decrepit house called "Tibet" and earns an income caring for an elderly neighbor. By the end of the novel, Morgan decides not to leave Tibet, "Not *permanently* anyway" (p. 344). Morgan thus suggests that she will always have a home on the Gold Coast to return to. Therefore, the Gold Coast for Savage's characters is not a stopover destination, or simply a liminal space for transitions, but is a permanent home, a place where she can learn that she is "at home everywhere" (p. 304). For Morgan, this home constitutes a permanent residence, stable employment, a supportive network of family and friends, and a connection to the landscape.

Throughout *The House Tibet* there are descriptions of the Gold Coast landscape and locals that are affectionate and critical, evoking paradise as well as the mundane, and often in one image. Morgan and J-Max find beauty in the landscape, though this beauty is not the result of a transcendent and extraordinary setting, but rather is the amalgamation of natural beauty of the landscape and the everyday intermingling. Morgan perceives the locals as "old" and enjoys seeing "them sitting in a row on the bus stop seat cackling away like a lot of water-birds" (pp. 109–110), and perceives the plain suburb of Southport as quite magical after the rain: "These sudden showers left the palms and things sparkling and that's how Southport looked to me" (p. 250). There are moments of beauty in the beach landscape such as Morgan's view of "the blue bulge of South Stradbroke Island and beyond it all, the glassy green of the ocean" (p. 274), as well as criticism for the contrived image of paradise that the Gold Coast devises through "lame [place-]names like Blue Waters and Golden Sands" (p. 129).

These descriptions of the Gold Coast that are simultaneously uninspiring and paradisal are consistent throughout the children's experience living there, from the moment they enter the city for the first time to Morgan's decision to call the Gold Coast her permanent home. As Morgan and J-Max enter the city on the bus, they notice the class distinctions in the suburbs as they pass "thirty kilometres" of houses that look "like holiday homes," "plain little places on stilts," and "new looking apartment blocks" (p. 59). In this instance, low socio-economic features of the Gold Coast, such as the old Queenslander houses, are not overshadowed by the glitz and glamour of the newer apartments and holiday homes. Savage's first descriptions of Surfers Paradise beyond the advertisement, too are not distracted with the grandeur of the skyscrapers, as Morgan finds herself fixated instead on how the skyscrapers throw "forest-shadows across the bus" (p. 59). Morgan's gaze focuses instead on the ground, the experience of moving through the city, rather than advancing a bird's eye view of the city as tourist mecca. Meanwhile, the locals in Surfers Paradise "rushed past city-style" (p. 60), thus stipulating that the Gold Coast is a place of work. By utilizing the point-of-view of a migrant, Savage's description of the Gold Coast defamiliarize the city in a way that a tourist could relate to, but does so without erasing the worklife of the locals. Similarly, Morgan's description of the Gold Coast as tacky and beautiful at the end of the novel accepts that the city is multi-faceted, never one thing at once:

Sometimes the moon comes up big red and glowing. Then the ocean and the wet sand turn red too. With the skyscrapers and everything making a *contrast*, it's pitsy but stunning at the same time. And I guess I won't be leaving here.

(p. 344)

These contrasts and contradictions inherent throughout Savage's portrayal of the Gold Coast "capture" what Douglas Pocock calls "the full flavour of the environment" (1981, p. 337). These representations suggest that the image of the Gold Coast as criminal hotspot or tourist mecca do not have to be replaced, but rather expanded with narrations of everyday life. As a sunny paradise, a shady crime hub, and a working city of varied social classes the Gold Coast is more than the edge (the edge of the state, the edge of the land, the edgy underbelly, reaching for the sky), but is (g)rounded, recognizably constructed. Since the Gold Coast is a city that is criticized for being fabricated, constructed for tourists, and therefore inauthentic, there is meaning to be made from the constructions themselves, in the contradictions and shortcomings of the liminal paradise.

Implications for popular culture tourism

In this chapter, I have suggested that those interested in (re)shaping conceptions of the Gold Coast look to and promote narrative fiction as material artifacts of place as a way of inviting literary tourism. Place-based fictions exploring everyday experiences of living in the city can capture the Gold Coast from working-class and welfare-receiving perspectives and undercut the figure of the dole bludger or Gold Coast criminal. Fiction is not compelled to portray place positively, though representations that feel authentic can help unearth and shape the identities of places in wider public discourse. Further, narratives that offer a sense of authenticity about the Gold Coast subvert the tourist gaze adopted by locals and visitors alike. Subverting the tourist gaze with everyday narratives does not necessarily dismantle the gaze, but complicates representations in the cultural imagination that may deepen mainstream conceptions of place. Paying closer attention to Gold Coast narrative fiction may even enhance the image of the Gold Coast under the tourist's gaze, since literary tourism offers alternative ways to understand and connect to place. A Gold Coast that knows why every person came, why people stayed, or why people left, and what the time in-between looks like, may offer travelers and locals a more immersive connection to the city.

Notes

1 "Dole bludger" is an Australian colloquialism referring to persons receiving welfare payments from the federal government, or "the dole." The term is derogatory, implying that the welfare recipient is undeserving or is criminally misleading the government, but can also express disdain for the welfare system generally.
2 The Australian Bureau of Statistics has the Gold Coast population at 569, 591 in 2015 (ABS, 2017), while Population Australia (2017) estimates that by June 2017 the local population reached 572, 722.
3 The epithet of Crime Capital, though, emerged across 2008–2011, when the Gold Coast experienced a spike of violent crimes and received substantial media coverage for what was being heralded as a problem with biker gangs in the region. However, crime as a whole on the Gold Coast was declining continuously after 2001, but then rose in 2016 (ABC, 2017).
4 All subsequent quotations from *The House Tibet* are from this edition and given in parentheses in the text.

References

ABC News. (2011). *Gold Coast the "Crime Capital of Australia."* Retrieved from www.abc.net.au/news/2011-07-21/gold-coast-becoming-crime-capital/2803830.
ABC News. (2016). *Schoolies Statistics: Sex, Drugs and Binge-Drinking.* Retrieved from www.abc.net.au/news/2016-11-18/schoolies-year-12-celebrate-end-of-year/8038182.

ABC News. (2017). *Reports Manipulated to Mask Rising Queensland Crime Rates, Police Sources Allege.* Retrieved from www.abc.net.au/news/2017-01-30/allegations-gold-coast-police-crime-managers-manipulating-stats/8217550.

ABS. (2017). *Gold Coast* (SA4). Retrieved from http://stat.abs.gov.au/itt/r.jsp?RegionSummary&region=309&dataset=ABS_REGIONAL_ASGS&geoconcept=REGION&datasetASGS=ABS_REGIONAL_ASGS&datasetLGA=ABS_REGIONAL_LGA&regionLGA=REGION&regionASGS=REGION

Arendt, Hanna. (1958). *The Human Condition.* Chicago: University of Chicago Press.

Beattie, Peter. (2017). *Commonwealth Games: Organisers Defend Gold Coast Council Buying Tickets Before Public Ballot.* Retrieved from www.abc.net.au/news/2017-07-10/commonwealth-games-organisers-defend-gold-coast-council-tickets/8692916.

Boyd, Robin. (2010). *The Australian Ugliness.* Melbourne: Text.

Braithwaite, Alyssa. (2008). *Channel Nine Drama The Strip—New Underbelly on Gold Coast.* Retrieved from www.dailytelegraph.com.au/entertainment/channel-nine-drama-the-strip-new-underbelly-on-gold-coast/news-story/0f9d804b8be6880b176fb80917be5927.

Burke, Matthew. (2017). *Why Gold Coast Light Rail Was Worth It (It's About More Than Patronage).* Retrieved from http://theconversation.com/why-gold-coast-light-rail-was-worth-it-its-about-more-than-patronage-78190.

Carson, Susan, Lesley Hawkes, Kari Gislason and Samuel Martin. (2013). Practices of Literary Tourism: An Australian Case Study. *International Journal of Culture, Tourism, and Hospitality Research,* 7(1), 42–50. www.emeraldinsight.com.ezp01.library.qut.edu.au/doi/pdfplus/10.1108/17506181311301345.

Channel Ten. (2014). *Gold Coast Cops.* Channel Ten video. Retrieved from www.tvcatchupaustralia.com/ten/gold-coast-cops/season-1-episode-1-61651.

City of Gold Coast. (2017). *Economic Development.* Retrieved from www.goldcoast.qld.gov.au/business/economic-development-288.html.

Condon, Matthew. (2008). *Gold Coast's Dark Underbelly.* Retrieved from www.couriermail.com.au/news/queensland/gold-coasts-dark-underbelly/news-story/3fd12f07f6588670c048721d8b48be8e?sv=c47644743139dc59fff4000019d4df8a.

Craik, Jennifer. (1991). *Resorting to Tourism: Cultural Policies for Tourism Development in Australia.* Sydney: Allen and Unwin.

de Certeau, Michel. (2011). *The Practice of Everyday Life.* Translated by Steven F. Rendall. Berkeley: University of California Press.

Dedekorkut, Aysin and Caryl Jane Bosman. (2011). *The Unbearable Lightness of Being Gold Coast.* Conference proceeding. State of Australian Cities National Conference.

Dredge, Dianne. (2011). Tourism Reform, Policy and Development in Queensland, 1989-2011. *Queensland Review 18*(2), 152–174. www-cambridge-org.ezp01.library.qut.edu.au/core/services/aop-cambridge-core/content/view/998EBFE2D0CBE81DC223779CD4A047E9/S1321816600000179a.pdf/tourism_reform_policy_and_development_in_queensland_19892011.pdf.

Gold Coast Tourism. (2014). *The New Surfers Paradise Lifestyle.* Retrieved from www.visitgoldcoast.com/.

Griffin, Grahame. (2007). The Good, the Bad and the Peculiar: Cultures and Policies of Urban Planning and Development on the Gold Coast. *Urban Policy and Research,* 16(4), 285–292. doi: 10.1080/08111149808727776.

Herbert, David. (2001). Literary Places, Tourism and The Heritage Experience. *Annals of Tourism Research 28*(2), 312–333. doi: 10.1016/S0160-7383(00)00048-7.

Hutton, Grey. (2014). *Australia's Crime Capital Looks like a Paradise.* Retrieved from www.vice.com/en_uk/article/mv5b38/ying-ang-photography-gold-coast

id.community. (2017). *Gold Coast City: Community Profile.* Retrieved from http://profile.id.com.au/gold-coast/individual-income.

Jones, Michael. (1986). *A Sunny Place for Shady People: The Real Gold Coast Story.* Sydney: Allen and Unwin.

Lawton, Laura J. (2005). Resident Perceptions of Tourist Attractions on the Gold Coast of Australia. *Journal of Travel Research 44*(2), 188–200. doi:10.1177/0047287505278981.

Loussikian, Kylar. (2017). *Southeast Queensland Town Is Nation's Dole Bludger Capital.* Retrieved from www.couriermail.com.au/news/queensland/southeast-queensland-town-is-nations-dole-bludger-capital/news-story/e1b2f0ef1634eaa1c65310d0ec0bf3a0.

Media Watch. 2016. *Neet or Not?* Retrieved from www.abc.net.au/mediawatch/transcripts/s4545977.htm.

Midalia, Susan. (2012). The Idea of Place: Reading for Pleasure and the Workings of Power. *English in Australia*, *47*(3), 44–51. http://search.informit.com.au.ezp01.library.qut.edu.au/fullText;res=AEIPT; dn=197345.

Narayan, Kirin. (2008). Ethnography and Fiction: Where Is the Border? *Anthropology and Humanism*, *24*(2), 134–147. doi: 10.1525/ahu.1999.24.2.134

O'Carroll, John. (1999). Upside-Down and Inside-Out: Notes on the Australian Cultural Unconscious. In Ruth Barcan and Ian Buchanan (Eds.), *Imagining Australian Space: Cultural Studies and Spatial Inquiry* (pp. 13–36). Nedlands, WA: University of Western Australia Press.

Pocock, Douglas. (1981). Place and the Novelist. *Transactions of the Institute of British Geographers*, *6*(3), 337–347. www.jstor.org/stable/622292.

Population Australia. (2017). *Gold Coast Population*. Retrieved from www.population.net.au/gold-coast-population/.

Potts, Andrew. (2016). *Gold Coast Underbelly: Sunny Days, Shady People*. Retrieved from www.goldcoast bulletin.com.au/lifestyle/gold-coast-130/gold-coast-underbelly-sunny-days-shady-people/news-story/ 229120d86a366b0c9cfe39082e1cd0db.

Potts, Andrew and Kathleen Skene. (2017). *Federal Budget 2017: Turnbull Government Unveils Millions for Gold Coast Commonwealth Games*. Retrieved from www.goldcoastbulletin.com.au/news/gold-coast/ federal-budget-2017-turnbull-government-unveils-millions-for-gold-coast-commonwealth-games/ news-story/845977c271296bfebcb8b96dc4f9b76a.

Queensland Treasury. (2017). *Queensland Economy*. Retrieved from www.treasury.qld.gov.au/economy-and-budget/queensland-economy.

Roscoe, Jane. (2001). *Big Brother* Australia: Performing the 'Real' Twenty-Four-Seven. *International Journal of Cultural Studies 4*(4), 473–488. doi: 10.1177/136787790100400407.

Savage, Georgia. (1992). *The House Tibet*. Vitoria: Penguin.

Shanahan, Brendan. (2004). *The Secret Life of the Gold Coast*. Camberwell, Victoria: Viking.

Sharp, Joanne. P. (2000). Towards a Critical Analysis of Fictive Geographies. *Area 32*(3), 327–334. http:// jstor.org/stable/20004085.

Squire, Shelagh J. (1994). The Cultural Values of Literary Tourism. *Annals of Tourism Research 21*(1), 103–120. https://doi.org/10.1016/0160-7383(94)90007-8.

Stimson, Robert J. and John Minnery. (1998). Why People Move to the "Sun-Belt": A Case Study of Long-Distance Migration to the Gold Coast, Australia. *Urban Studies 35*(2), 193–214. doi: 10. 1080/0042098984943.

Stockwell, Stephen Edward. (2012). Crime Capital of Australia: The Gold Coast on Screen. *Studies in Australasian Cinema 5*(3), 281–292. doi: 10.1386/sac.5.3.281_1.

Stolz, Greg. 2012. *2018 Gold Coast Commonwelath Games to Cost Queensland $2b—or About $300k per Athlete*. Retrieved from www.couriermail.com.au/news/queensland/taxpayers-to-foot-mammoth-games-bill/news-story/029b859f2ecea59d377320e5b42db539?sv=1741a79750b96632a02515eba9d 5bb54.

Surfers Paradise Alliance. (2017). *Surfers Paradise: Gold Coast*. Retrieved from www.surfersparadise.com/ things-to-do/attractions/surfers-paradise-the-6th-theme-park.

Urry, John. (2005). *The Tourist Gaze*. 2nd ed. London: Sage.

Ward, Susan and Tom O'Reagan. (2009). The Film Producer as the Long-Stay Business Tourist: Rethinking Film and Tourism from a Gold Coast Perspective. *Tourism Geographies 11*(2), 214–232. doi: 10.1080/14616680902827175.

Winchester, Hilary P. M. and Kathryn Everett. (2000). Schoolies Week as a Rite of Passage: A Study of Celebration and Control. In Elizabeth Kentworthy Teather (Ed.), *Embodied Geographies: Spaces, Bodies and Rites of Passage* (pp. 59–76). London: Routledge.

17

FANDOM AND ITS AFTERLIFE

Celebrity cemetery tourism

Linda Levitt

Setting the scene

Popular culture fans have long made pilgrimages to visit sites associated with celebrities: the popularity of Elvis Presley's home, Graceland, is an exemplar of a tourism destination designed to capitalize on the unique experience offered to fans and tourists. A highlight of Graceland tourism is the annual celebration of Elvis Week, which culminates with a candlelight vigil at the musician's grave (Elvis and his parents are buried on the grounds of his estate) on the anniversary of his death. Thousands of fans gather each August to mourn the rock and roll pioneer. Many see Elvis Week as a spectacle, epitomizing the excesses of fandom. Yet in recent years, public performances of fandom have rendered such celebrations more typical. As fandom communities become commonplace, so does the expansion for mediated grieving of celebrities and popular culture icons. Whether the death of a celebrity is sudden or media follows the illness and decline of a popular figure, digital media enables anyone with an online presence to participate in grieving. Participation is enhanced through the inclusion of still photos, movie clips, and music videos in social media posts that serve as parasocial eulogies.

Engagement with celebrity mourning facilitates cemetery tourism borne from the gravesite pilgrimage. The relatively recent acceptance of dark tourism sites as appropriate destinations, coupled with the death positive movement, has seen an increase in cemetery tourism. This chapter considers how cemetery tourism is encouraged and promoted through celebrity fandom that draws on existing practices in heritage tourism and dark tourism.

Theoretical underpinnings: cemetery tourism as dark tourism

In their seminal book *Dark Tourism: The Attraction of Death and Disaster*, John Lennon and Malcolm Foley (2004) note that through mediated experiences of both news and entertainment programming, millions of people witness death daily. The degree to which such incidents carry any emotional resonance is uncertain, yet these deaths are brought increasingly closer to one's immediate reality. This leads Lennon and Foley (2004, p. 9) to ask:

> Can it be surprising that, when the opportunity presents itself to validate that global-local connection that so many decide to visit the sites of these deaths and disasters? Where tourism destinations encompass such "celebrated" sites, should it be surprising

that national and regional tourism bodies, voluntary groups and commercial businesses see opportunities to pursue their objectives?

That tourists are drawn to sites of dark tourism is a motivating force for some instances of heritage tourism as well, as death and disaster are stitched into history-as-spectacle.

Yet cemeteries differ from sites where tragedy and public trauma have taken place. The aura of devastation that draws visitors emotionally to sites of dark tourism is seldom present at cemeteries, as the cemetery's character is typically aligned with creating a place of peaceful reflection. As the study of dark tourism has grown, Philip Stone (2006) offered a typology of dark tourism sites in an effort to categorize both visitor motivations and approaches to tourism destination management. Stone considers the darkest tourism sites as those which, as sites of disaster, are most significantly inflected ideologically and politically, therefore entailing education rather than entertainment. On a scale of 1–7, Stone places cemeteries at 4, dark shrines at 5, dark conflict sites at 6, and sites of genocide, the darkest, at 7. The typology is an effective system for understanding varied approaches to dark tourism, yet the categories cannot be understood as mutually exclusive because visitor motivations vary: a visitor to a site like the Viper Club in Los Angeles, where actor River Phoenix died on Halloween in 1993, may travel to the nightclub as a pilgrimage to pay respects and commemorate Phoenix, where another visitor may be a tourist who goes to the Viper Club simply to check off an item on a list of destinations or to bring the experience of death closer to them.

Although cemeteries might be considered only "moderately" morbid, popular culture establishes a sense of the graveyard as a foreboding and dangerous place. From Scooby Doo cartoons to feature films like *Night of the Living Dead* and *Carrie*, representations of the cemetery are more aligned with the macabre than the serene. Many cemeteries have worked to develop tourism programs that undo negative preconceptions and encourage a focus on heritage, architecture, or celebrity to draw visitors to their sites.

From Père Lachaise to Hollywood

Père Lachaise Cemetery in Paris is a model for drawing on celebrity to promote the cemetery as a tourist destination. The cemetery was established in 1804 at what was then a considerable distance from the central city. In order to make Père Lachaise a more prominent location in the public view, the remains of lovers Abelard and Heloise were moved to the cemetery in 1817 amidst great fanfare, attracting more visitors to stroll the grounds. Over the span of more than 200 years since its founding, Père Lachaise has added more than 1 million interments, including an array of famous actors, writers, musicians, and political figures. The grave of musician Jim Morrison remains among the most visited. Touissant and Decrop (2016) conducted ethnographic research at Père Lachaise, asking the visitors they interviewed if they left anything behind as a remembrance. Marco, who visited the cemetery with his girlfriend Georgia, said "A cigarette. With 'Marco e Georgia. Per Jim' written on it . . . We are leaving a sign, in order to let him know we were here" (p. 20). Although Morrison died in 1971, the music of the Doors and the iconic presence of their controversial frontman perpetuates the popularity of Morrison's music and persona. The earnest desire for a personal connection with Morrison draws visitors like Marco and Georgia to Père Lachaise, which serves as the most authentic place for that connection to occur.

While cemeteries like Père Lachaise draw tourists to famous gravesites, others deploy the artifacts of popular culture to attract visitors. Hollywood Forever Cemetery in Los Angeles is a forerunner in creating social events on the cemetery grounds. The Cinespia film series sees as many as 4,000 visitors each Saturday night during summer months. Visitors are invited to bring a picnic dinner and spread blankets on the lawn adjacent to the sarcophagus of Douglas Fairbanks and his son, Douglas Fairbanks, Jr. Feature films are projected on the exterior wall of the Cathedral Mausoleum, in which celebrities including Rudolph Valentino, Peter Lorre, and Peter Finch are interred. Hollywood Forever (formerly Hollywood Memorial Park) has long been a destination for celebrity cemetery tourism. The cemetery has hosted a memorial service in honor of Rudolph Valentino since the silent film star's death in 1926, an event that continues to attract fans, historians, and members of the entertainment industry. Like Père Lachaise, Hollywood Forever welcomes visitors to use the cemetery grounds as leisure space and to pay respects at the graves of popular culture figures. The flower shop, located beside the cemetery gates, sells a map of famous gravesites, much as street vendors in Hollywood would sell maps to celebrity homes. While encouraging tourism to the cemetery, Hollywood Forever's management also want the experience to be transformative. Jay Boileau, the cemetery's executive vice president, told *Los Angeles Magazine* that public events were intended toward the goal "to restore a forgotten gem and make the cemetery a place for the dead and the living" (Duelund, 2014, para. 1)

Although Hollywood Forever plays an active role in encouraging tourist visitation by focusing on celebrity graves, the cemetery has limited control of the discourse about its permanent residents in popular culture. In *Encounters with Popular Pasts*, Mike Robinson and Helaine Silverman (2015) note that tourism programs are no longer exclusively the domain of official organizations and government bodies. Heritage can be interpreted and circulated "not only by state-focused bureaucracies and ownership but by individuals, groups, and communities that have different and often challenging perspectives on what heritage is and who it is for" (p. 5). While some cemeteries work to prohibit practices of "celebrity graving," others welcome visitors who participate, intentionally or not, in this kind of upending of heritage-making. When there is a set narrative of tourism rhetoric on an established tour, those tours provide a ready-made heritage that does not leave space for tourists to discover their own paths. The increasingly popularity of dark tourism sites, and unofficial promotion of such sites in digital spaces including personal websites and social media, enables the circulation of heritage narratives that also draw visitors to cemeteries.

Heritage tourism depends on local and regional histories to attract visitors to experience a heritage site. Cemeteries readily become part of the heritage tourism landscape by offering an authentic location: what more powerful place to tell a life story than standing in front of the grave of a great politician, author, actor, or artist? Critics of heritage tourism have raised issues of cultural appropriation: whose heritage and where? Such questions might also come to bear regarding Hollywood heritage. Although Jean Baudrillard chose Disneyland as the site to map out the simulacra, Hollywood too is afloat in a sea of signs without grounding in reality. Disneyland is explicitly and deliberately an empty frame, designed to be filled by visitors' imaginative desires and nostalgia, supplied in part by the massive media empire of Disney. As a tourist attraction, Hollywood functions similarly. Tourists' familiarity with Hollywood is constructed through popular narratives, news stories, websites, previous experiences, novels, television, and film.

Popular culture can significantly influence the national ethos. Journalists, along with influential opinion leaders on social media, impact a celebrity's legacy in the immediate aftermath of his or her death (Kitch & Hume, 2008). Michael Jackson's death in 2009 offers a powerful example. Because Jackson's cause of death was officially declared involuntary manslaughter primarily due to an injection of the drug Propofol by an attending physician, the pop star was readily cast as a victim who suffered throughout his life with the difficulties of stardom. On the day of Jackson's death, as broadcast media worked to organize commemorative video segments, networks such as CNN shared Tweets, emails, and voicemail messages from viewers, enabling the fan community to have a voice in shaping the public view of Michael Jackson's life. As such, he was immortalized as the King of Pop. Cast as a tragic hero, the darker side of Jackson's history of child sexual abuse accusations and unconventional behavior fell to the background. Jackson is interred at Forest Lawn Cemetery in Glendale, California, the final resting place of many well-known celebrities with significant fandoms. Yet Forest Lawn famously discourages fans and admirers from visiting celebrity gravesites. Fans are prohibited from entering the Great Mausoleum, but the cemetery offered a compromise, allowing a fan-organized program to bring red roses for display outside the mausoleum. On the seventh anniversary of Jackson's death, more than 10,000 roses provided a substantial act of commemoration. Fans unable to travel to Los Angeles to pay tribute in person are still able to participate in this memorial at the cemetery, as the site of interment is considered the most authentic memory site. While Forest Lawn has forbidden an actual gravesite visit, the cemetery has made it possible for fans to create a spectacle of devotion for any visitors. Extending this relationship to the fan community also allows Forest Lawn to encourage cemetery tourism, even if the tourist experience is highly controlled, spatially and rhetorically.

Half an hour west of Forest Lawn, and a world away ideologically, is Pierce Bros. Westwood Cemetery, the final resting place of Marilyn Monroe and many other stars including Dean Martin, Roy Orbison, and Natalie Wood. Where a visitor needs a car to traverse Forest Lawn, one can park and easily walk the grounds at the small, intimate Westwood. Alongside Monroe's crypt is a white granite bench, donated by the Marilyn Remembered fan club, which is also responsible for organizing an annual memorial at Westwood. Marilyn Remembered streams the memorial service from its Facebook feed, with links available from the club's webpage and promotions on Twitter and Instagram, digitally bringing the cemetery to the rest of the world. The fan club works to keep Marilyn Monroe as a part of popular culture, although that work certainly does not occur in isolation. Monroe's image is ubiquitous in Hollywood, generating $17 million for Authentic Brands, the owner of her image, in 2015 (Greenburg, 2015). Some fan community members do see revenue related to their fandom, especially those who purchase and sell celebrity memorabilia. The benefits of fandom, however, also include a sense of community and belonging that results from engaging with others in a shared enthusiasm for a particular celebrity. Many fans maintain parasocial relationships with celebrities that enable a feeling of familiarity that is, although one-sided, often a sincere expression of affection and devotion. Parasocial relationships allow fans to psychologically transgress the boundaries of class and culture that separate them from their idols. Popular culture's role in making celebrities seem like everyday people enables not only parasocial relationships but also transgresses boundaries with regard to the gravesite visit. There are barriers that keep celebrities at a distance from their fans while they are alive, but when cemeteries facilitate access to celebrity gravesites, they help to enable a touristic pilgrimage for fans.

The death positive movement and cemetery tourism

The death positive movement is focused on changing attitudes toward death and dying. One of the founders and proponents of the movement is Caitlin Doughty, author of *Smoke Gets in Your Eyes & Other Lessons from the Crematory* (2014). She is also founder of the Order of the Good Death, an association of death professionals, academics, artists, and others devoted to making death an everyday part of life. Doughty's "Ask a Mortician" YouTube channel provides more than 80,000 subscribers (along with other occasional viewers who do not subscribe) with a lighthearted and sometimes humorous perspective on death, intended to answer questions in an effort to alleviate discomfort with death as an unknown, ominous force in life. The Order of the Good Death and the Death Café movement, started in London in 2011, create spaces for people to gather and talk openly about their concerns, fears, and experiences with death. Through the social construction of these discursive spaces, conversations about death and dying are more frequent and commonplace. A growing comfort with talking about death can also lead to a growing comfort with living with death. The death positive movement extends to a greater ease with cemeteries as well, keeping the dead as part of our communities in ways that are welcoming and not morbid.

Implications for popular culture tourism

Places evolve as tourist destinations not only through promotion and arrangement of space and experiences for tourist consumption but also through performance and repetition. When visitors to a cemetery recognize the behavior of others as tourists rather than mourners, they will observe and possibly emulate those behaviors. In an operating cemetery, the degree to which one carries and refers to a map, demonstrates enthusiasm, or discretely takes a few photographs will depend on whether those activities are aligned with the established social norms. Cemetery tourism drawn from popular culture sources and references will lead to additional cemetery tourism. This is especially true when the unusual phenomenon receives publicity that has a normalizing effect. John Urry and his collaborators (Baerenholdt, Haldrup, & Urry, 2004) note that tourism is a performance, and that for a destination to be thought of as a "tourist place" requires the integration of these places into our lifeways, expectations, and memories.

As Mike Robinson (2012) points out in his discussion of tourism and affect, "we do not go on holiday with the desire nor expectation to experience anger or sadness" (p. 34). Yet in addition to Robinson's "'doing nothing' of lying next to the hotel swimming pool" or seeing the Mona Lisa (p. 34) is a set of motivations that drives people to dark tourism sites. Referring again to Stone's spectrum of dark tourism experiences, the desire for an educational tourist experience need not be in opposition to experiences that are entertaining. With these polarities in mind, cemetery tourism can be seen as an opportunity for connecting with heritage and history, confronting discomfort and fear, and enjoying aesthetically pleasing architecture, statuary, and landscaping. As cemeteries are made more accessible and welcoming, tourists are more likely to consider including the cemetery on a travel itinerary. A more significant impact on cemetery tourism will be an ongoing focus on the relationships between popular culture and cemeteries, particularly when a tour or travel experience is connected to an opportunity to engage with the cemetery in the role of a fan. The death of singer Chris Cornell in May 2017 offers an example of the cemetery, along with the family of the deceased, facilitating celebrity fandom. A private ceremony, which was also a star-studded celebrity event, was held at Hollywood Forever, where Cornell's ashes were interred. The cemetery allowed public viewing shortly after, enabling fans to pay their respects personally and leave remembrances at the gravesite. Mainstream media and fans posted photographs and stories across digital media, making images of Hollywood Forever a focal point for commemoration. The cemetery garners publicity through these mediated channels, making a gentler dark tourism accessible to a vast audience of potential visitors.

References

Baerenholdt, J. O., Haldrup, M., and Urry, J. (2004). *Performing tourist places*. London: Routledge.
Doughty, C. (2014). *Smoke gets in your eyes & other lessons from the crematory*. New York: W.W. Norton & Company.

Duelund, T. (2014, January 21). Meet the man who curates the crazy cool events at Hollywood Forever Cemetery. *Los Angeles Magazine*. Retrieved from www.lamag.com/culturefiles/meet-the-man-who-curates-the-crazy-cool-events-at-hollywood-forever-cemetery/.

Greenburg, Z. O. (2015, October 27). The 13 top earning celebrities of 2015. *Forbes*. Retrieved from www.forbes.com/sites/zackomalleygreenburg/2015/10/27/the-13-top-earning-dead-celebrities-of-2015/#3bf4f9f744f6.

Kitch, C. and Hume, J. (2008). *Journalism in a culture of grief*. New York: Routledge.

Lennon, J. and Foley, M. (2004). *Dark tourism: The attraction of death and disaster*. London: Thomson.

Robinson, M. (2012). The emotional tourist. In M. Robinson and D. Picard (Eds.), *Emotions in motion: Tourism, affect and transformation* (21–46). New York: Routledge.

Robinson, M. and Silverman, H. (2015). Mass, modern, and mine: Heritage and popular culture. In M. Robinson and H. Silverman (Eds.), *Encounters with popular pasts: Cultural heritage and popular culture* (1–30). New York: Springer.

Stone, P. (2006). A dark tourism spectrum: Towards a typology of death and macabre related tourist sites, attractions and exhibitions. *Tourism: An Interdisciplinary International Journal* 54 (2), 145–160.

Touissant, S. and Decrop, A. (2016). The Pere-Lachaise Cemetery: Between dark tourism and heterotopic consumption. In L. White and E. Frew (Eds.), *Dark tourism and place identity: Managing and interpreting dark places* (13–27). New York: Routledge.

PART III

Performing fan cultures

Popular culture tourism fandoms

18

PASSING THROUGH

Popular media tourism, pilgrimage, and narratives of being a fan

Lincoln Geraghty

Setting the scene

With the rise of modernity in the early twentieth century and the growth of popular culture since the 1950s people have looked to their favorite sports teams, musicians, films, TV series, books, comics, games, and celebrities to build a sense of identity and form social relationships with others. As media fan texts diversify so too does the fan community, and notions of what makes you a fan change according to the financial value and cultural distinction people apply, and the social and economic contexts of the communities in which we live. At the same time, increases in the standard of living and leisure time have meant the tourist industry has also changed; growing exponentially as new technologies and methods of travel open up every corner of the globe at relatively low cost. While tourism based on texts and icons of popular culture is neither surprising nor new, it has become an important part of what it means to be a fan. From visiting the fictional home of Sherlock Holmes at 221b Baker Street to finding the birthplace of Charles Dickens in Portsmouth enthusiastic followers have been able to make connections to texts and people through travel since the Victorian era. Now, those interested in promoting such texts and people use tourism to reach out to new audiences and open up new ways of engagement. What has become apparent in contemporary tourism is that fans of popular texts are more visible, willing to spend the money, and able to travel further in order to get close to and interact with their favorite film, TV show, or book. Fans replicate the ephemeral and emotional experience of watching and reading by immersing themselves into familiar spaces and places they have only previously encountered through the screen or page. Fandom is now physical just as much as tourism is now mediated.

In the vein of tourists recording their holidays through pictures and reviews fans recount their travel experiences through the photographic recreation of popular texts, making vlogs and writing blogs. Processes of encountering mediated tourist sites, taking pictures, and seeing other fans in those spaces helps to create and tell a story. As the story is recounted through video and social media it contributes to the act of becoming a fan, staying a fan, and displaying a fan identity over time. Therefore, it is important to recognize the significance of narrative to the understanding of tourism and practices of fan pilgrimage. Through case studies of visits taken to various popular culture tourism sites related to sport, film, television, literature, and music, this chapter explores the variety of ways through which we might appreciate what it means to be a fan in contemporary popular culture when embarking on a fan pilgrimage. Taking into account the multitude of technologies, networks, texts, practices, and tourist sites with which fans build a sense of self, community, and cultural capital, I want to interrogate how important place is when identifying as a fan in the twenty-first century. By visiting such a diversity of geographic locations, valued by different fan communities, one is able to appreciate the importance of history and the affective connections offered when passing through those spaces. In studying this phenomenon, it is important to look beyond the intellectual boundaries of tourism, media, and cultural studies, and integrate methods and approaches across those disciplines. To do this, I want to revisit the figure of the flâneur, the passionate wanderer emblematic of nineteenth-century literary culture, to provide a conceptual framework through which to understand how fans relate to, interact with, and pass through spaces of popular culture. Tracking the fan as flâneur allows us to form a more intricate picture of how fans relate to their objects of fandom and understand the relationship between communities and individuals, texts and geographies, fan pilgrimage and tourism, memories and emotions.

Theoretical underpinnings of fan geographies: from typography to topography

Roger Aden uses the term "symbolic pilgrimage" to characterize the process fans go through when they watch television series repeatedly, getting closer to the text by shutting out the everyday distractions of life in their living rooms and other personal spaces. Will Brooker describes it as "a trip without drugs, a journey and return without leaving the easy chair" (2007b, p. 149). For Aden, the text itself becomes a sacred site, which fans travel to and return from when watching: "Symbolic pilgrimages feature individuals ritualistically revisiting powerful places that are symbolically envisioned through the interaction of story and individual imagination" (1999, p. 10). There is a preparation ritual to insure fans are not disturbed – getting snacks ready, locking the door, turning off the lights, taking the phone off the hook – that "removes the participant from the everyday and brings him/her closer to the fiction" (Brooker, 2007b, p. 155). Fans create a map of their favorite text that means something on a personal level, whether it is through the watching or rewatching of specific episodes or the emotive relationship created within a community of fans that share those experiences with others. The text, the story, becomes somewhere to go to, a "promised land," when fans want to escape the material world (Aden, 1999, p. 4). However, Matt Hills contests this metaphorical reading of pilgrimage offered by Aden; suggesting it does not take into account the desire for fans to travel to the places where their "promised lands" are filmed and thus suggests that "'inhabitation' of extra-textual spaces . . . forms an important part of cult fans' extensions and expressions of the fan-text relationship" and is "an affective-interpretive process which spills into and redefines material spaces" (Hills, 2002, p. 144).

Recognizing the contemporary importance of the "runaway" Hollywood production to Vancouver both Brooker and Hills have discussed how fans of television series made in the city treat visiting shooting locations as a form of actual pilgrimage. Traveling to sites once glimpsed or identified becomes a way of getting closer to the text and ascribing personal meaning to it. For example, making the intangible tangible by achieving a proximity to the "real" Kent Farm (a private dairy farm in the Fraser Valley outside the city) if you are *Smallville* fan or a "real" Caprican building (the Vancouver Public Library downtown) if you are fan of *Battlestar Galactica*. This liminal positioning of the fan is described by Brooker as offering an experience where they "hover on the borders between actual and fictional, holding both in a double-vision of alternate realities" (2005, p. 13). The allusion to the religious pilgrimage is clearly made; both

Hills and Aden ascribe some of the language of religious ritual and pilgrimage to the practices of traveling fans who must touch or be on the spot where their favorite character/actor once stood. But both Brooker and Hills emphasize the importance of being there – having a place to go to and feel at home. Similarly, Cornel Sandvoss asserts, "The Physical places of fandom clearly have an extraordinary importance for fans" (2005, p. 61). Popular tourist cities like Vancouver act as an "urban imaginary,"

> where a single point of geography – an alley, a building, a street – can, with an adjustment of "frequency" – a certain way of looking, a stretch of imagination and a leap of fan faith – transport the visitor to another, fictional world. One pilgrim sees this quad of Simon Fraser University as Earth-*X-Files*; the other sees it as Earth-Caprica; and the same pilgrim is quite capable of switching between the two, with a reprioritizing of investment, a different imaginary angle, a shifting of vision, a change in "vibration," a retuning.
>
> *(Brooker, 2007a, pp. 438–439)*

However, it is not simply being there that counts. What fans do or how they act in the space seems to make the travel unique and personally valuable. So, whether it is recreating the moment Scully was kidnapped in *The X-Files* on Grouse Mountain (just outside the Vancouver metropolitan area) by tying up someone, putting them in the boot of the rental car and taking a picture (see Hills, 2002, p. 149) or finding out where filming will happen on a certain night and standing in the freezing cold and rain just to get a picture of Tom Welling playing a young Superman on set (see Geraghty, 2011, pp. 142–143), the activity is of utmost importance. Most sites of pilgrimage are "*multiply* coded" (Brooker, 2007a, p. 430), and thus fandom connected to place differs for each fan. Locations that inspire fan pilgrimage have real-world uses, they are not just used or visited by fans, therefore they have to actively make these places special – either through physical transformation of the space (adding familiar objects) or performance in that space (costume and cosplay). According to Brooker, fan pilgrimage is about pretending, performance, and making the new from "the familiar and quotidian" and so fans traveling to a filming location or site of special interest are, borrowing Brooker's phrase, "approaching the location with their own agenda" and "are able to transform 'flatscape' into a place of wonder. They bring their own urban imaginary, their own maps of fiction and their own angles on the everyday" (Brooker, 2007a, p. 443). Stijn Reijnders has developed this idea of fans transforming real places through their imaginative engagement with space and text by applying Pierre Nora's concept of "*lieux d'imagination*" (places of the imagination). He argues that places of the imagination

> are not so much concerned with collective memory, as collective imagination. *Lieux d'imagination* are physical locations, which serve as a symbolic anchor for the collective imagination of society. By visiting these locations, tourists are able to construct and "validate" a symbolic distinction between imagination and reality.
>
> *(Reijnders, 2011, p. 8)*

Further, using their imagination, Reijnders outlines how fans seek physical and material references to their favorite media texts (2011, p. 114), for example: sitting in a particular seat at an Oxford pub made famous in *Inspector Morse* (p. 51); mimicking James Bond's actions in exotic filming locations around the world (p. 78); or bringing the story of Dracula to life by visiting Transylvania to experience sights, sounds, and smells described in the novel (p. 100).

Similarly, John Urry in describing different kinds of touristic gaze – the vision that occurs when traveling – refers specifically to the "mediatized gaze." Able to extend engagement with texts by inhabiting the world, tourists become part of the text: "Those gazing on the scene relive elements or aspects of the media event" (Urry, 2002, p. 151). Examples of such sites become venerated memorials to popular culture: "Traditional elite institutions build shrines to symbols of faith, patriotism, and knowledge. But popular shrines communicate the legitimacy of popular experience, even if it is lurid, frivolous, or downright kitsch" (Combs, 1989, p. 74). For Hills, being in a place matters more because it allows fans access to extratextual pleasures and affords them the opportunity to reinterpret the text since "the media cult cannot be entirely reduced to metaphors of textuality" (Hills, 2002, p. 145). Seeking out locations allows fans to extend their relationship with texts: "Cult geographies also sustain cult fans' fantasies of 'entering' into the cult text" (p. 151). These locations can be open to the public, made significant because of what media texts are associated with that space; or they can be private, made special by the rituals and performances in which fans participate. So, for the former, fans of *Withnail and I* make special trips to the Penrith Tea Rooms recreating a specific scene by ordering wine and cake; and for the latter, fans dress up and sing along to "The Time Warp" during midnight screenings of *The Rocky Horror Picture Show.*

Therefore, while this chapter seeks to understand the relationship fans create with their favorite texts, it focuses specifically on how notions of physical place and emotive space impact on the experiences fans have traveling through and within "venerable" tourist sites and everyday places, and also how this changes the geographic location that the site occupies. If communitas is defined as "intense bonding and sharing of the pilgrimage and the connection with the sacred place" (Brooker, 2005, p. 18), then I want to show that while tourist sites might control and limit the fan experience, fans also shape and define the physical surroundings that they inhabit. The interaction between people and site within a real space enhances both the emotional and physical relationship fans have with popular media texts. Traveling across borders, visiting mediated spaces, taking official and unofficial tours, make the site a secure place in which fans can play with notions of identity. Or, as Yi-Fu Tuan argues, "When space feels thoroughly familiar to us, it has become place" (1977, p. 73). Therefore, this chapter seeks to bring together ideas discussed so far about tourism, memory, and identity to offer a reassessment of popular culture tourism and fandom. How do fans create "deep and meaningful" connections with sites they have never been before? What role does memory have in making those unfamiliar sites seem more safe and familiar? Within the physical site of fan interaction how do landmarks, buildings, and the landscape bring fans closer to the fictional text and their geographical location? These questions inform the following analysis of specific case studies.

Narratives of becoming: memory and place

As Will Brooker (2007a, p. 429) describes fan pilgrimages to filming locations, they become "sites of play and carnival, poetry and magic." Fans use stored memories of their favorite texts to interpret and find their way around both the fictional and real space – "viewing the present through an archive of the past" (p. 433). Taking pictures of buildings, landscapes, and people on site and then comparing those images with shots drawn directly from the film or TV show allows fans a certain amount of control. They can see how it was made, how space was controlled and manipulated by the director or cinematographer; gaining such knowledge taps into a fan preoccupation for learning and developing their expertise. It also offers fans another more personal connection to the text; when watching and rewatching they can imagine themselves being there, they are now forever closer to the text. Memories of the visit continue to influence how they engage with their favorite text after the fact; as a result, the text is irrevocably transformed for and by them from that physical experience. I would call this a topography of becoming a fan, where memories of how being in that special and familiar space influence and enhance their relationship and emotional connection to the media text post return. In their work on geography and memory Owain Johnson and Joanne Garde-Hansen argue that the two are inextricably linked. Memory is defined by geography and geography defined by memory; actions that take place in a memorable space last longer and memories of the physical environment adds a level of detail to memories of events occurring in that space: "Memory is a fundamental (geographic) aspect of becoming, intimately entwined with space, effect, emotion, imagination and identity" (Jones & Garde-Hansen, 2012, p. 11). In terms of being a fan, memories of the tourist site (preserved in pictures) and what they did there (performance or rituals) strengthen the connection to the media text and form the basis for their fan story after the event.

While the importance of the fan collective, groups of fans and specific communities is not in dispute, more recent fan scholarship has centered on fandom as a form of temporal identity, an extension of the self as they age. This aligns with Anthony Giddens' concept that modern identity formation is individualistic and subjective, creating a "narrative of the self" (Giddens, 1991). It follows that fandom too should be considered individual and subjective – not all fans attend conventions with others, socialize online, or welcome/agree with newcomers. Likewise, Hills (2014) has studied what he calls "becoming-a-fan" stories, which articulate the emotional connections created between text and individual fan, when they can first remember this happening and how it has developed over time. He identifies that fans often describe their first memory of watching and liking a film, book, or TV show in terms of a "conversion" and during the course of life this narrative of becoming a fan turns to "transference" as they talk about sharing their love with other fans, take pleasure in seeing others become fans, and even how they stopped being a fan. Fandom is therefore transformative, transforming, and transformational; texts can shift in and out of favor with fans, fans can like and dislike multiple texts at the same time, and fan attitudes towards texts might change significantly over long periods: "Retuning to discourses of becoming-a-fan enables a focus on transformational moments, as well as on the gradual mediations, prefigurations and transfers of fandom" (Hills, 2014, pp. 17–18). While I agree a focus on such stories can help scholars understand individual fan motivations and identities I would also stress the importance of place and space in those narratives of becoming. As Jones and Garde-Hansen argue above, memory and geography are linked and therefore stories that articulate a fan identity will have a specific geographic anchor (more physical than Reijnders' concept of the symbolic anchor discussed earlier) upon which memories of becoming, conversion, and transference are inscribed. Whether memories of a fan tourism site are individual (finding a filming location on the street), communal (fans traveling together as a group on a movie tour for example), or commodified (the site being created specifically to attract particular fans such as the Warner Bros. Harry Potter Studio Tour at Leavesden) through their retelling we can draw connections between fans, groups, practices, texts, places, and spaces.

What I have surveyed so far helps to contextualize the movement and practices of fans in geographical spaces and relates to Hills' discussion of "affective play." The term "deals with the emotional attachment of the fan" and "suggests that play is not always caught up in a pre-established 'boundedness' or set of cultural boundaries, but may instead imaginatively create its own set of boundaries and its own auto-'context'" (Hills, 2002, p. 112). In terms of media, memory and geography meaning, attachment, and a sense of belonging are created through physically being in the city where a television series or film was filmed, recreating moments of viewing, and sharing the experience with other fans after the event. Thus we might be able to understand fan tourism and memories of becoming a fan after entering specific fan spaces through the lens of phenomenological geography. This concerns the study of place and space, taking into account "practical and emotional aspects of day-to-day existence . . . habitual movements and unselfconscious senses of place" (Moores, 2006, para. 1). For David Seamon (2006, note 1), phenomenology is:

> the description and interpretation of human experience. A major effort of phenomenology is to identify and describe broader, underlying patterns – e.g. the lived expressions of environmental embodiment – that give order and coherence to the richness and "chaos" of human experience as it is lived as everyday life.

The way we react and interact with our natural and built environment helps define a sense of identity through place. The media we use in those spaces also contributes to this sense of place, whether it is talking on one's mobile phone walking through town or taking pictures of famous landmarks.

The flâneur and fan tourism

The flâneur is personified by the act of "passing by" – walking, wandering, window shopping in the city (de Certeau, 1984, p. 97). This act of urban exploration has a triple "enunciative" function: the pedestrian appropriates the "topographical system" through the process of walking and learning the city; they act out the city by following routes in and around the multiple spaces; and through this movement the pedestrian creates relations between different spaces, connecting the city in multiple ways. Thus, the flâneur by walking "enunciates" or "speaks" the city, articulating the space through the route they take and what they visually take in (de Certeau, 1984, pp. 97–98). For John Urry, the nineteenth-century flâneur was the forerunner to the twentieth-century tourist: once "able to travel, to arrive, to gaze, to move on, to be anonymous, to be in a liminal zone," now by taking photographs they are about "being seen and recorded, and of seeing others and recording them" (Urry, 2002, pp. 126–127). Similarly, when fans pass through mediated spaces, taking photos to preserve the moment and celebrate their fandom, they are "enunciating" or "speaking" their fan identity. Fans perform, communicate, and remember meditated spaces of popular culture.

The contemporary movie tour offered in so many cities around the world personifies this aspect of the fan as flâneur, enunciating their fandom through movement around spaces and taking photographs. The Original New Orleans Movie Tour takes advantage of the Crescent City's long-standing popularity as tourist destination, with sites such as the French Quarter being a particular draw, and combines this with New Orleans' growing reputation as a Hollywood filming location. Multiple television series and blockbuster movies have made New Orleans their home, using purpose built studios and state tax breaks to film in and around the city. The Original New Orleans Movie Tour maps a route through this mediated city, driving groups of film and TV fans in a bus to and between filming locations both old and new. While on board the driver reminds fans of specific scenes, using DVD clips and music to help them visualize mediated space. So, for example, after showing a clip from television series *American Horror Story: Coven* the driver pulls up in front of the Buckner Mansion, one of the oldest in the neighborhood of City Park, and reminds people that it was used as the coven house in the series. Fans get out, walk up to the gates and have pictures taken. Spaces familiar from *Coven* suddenly become real as fans witness and pass through this New Orleans neighborhood. It becomes a liminal space, making the series more tangible for fans able to situate themselves in the text when posing and photographing their experience. Back on board the tour motorizes the movement of the fan flâneur as focus shifts from *Coven* to a completely different media text: the James Bond film *Live and Let Die*. Partly filmed in the French Quarter the driver reminds people of the plot, describes the stakeout scene of the Fillet of Soul nightclub on Chartres St. and informs them that when filming cars had to travel the wrong way down the one-way street. Fan appreciation is therefore enhanced through the sharing of information about the location, the film's production, and local knowledge. The movie tour again blurs fantasy and reality, this time Bond's investigation of a drug cartel and the historic French Quarter. The Original New Orleans Movie Tour, like many others, remaps the city through media tourism. Fans become modern day flâneurs as they pass through locations, enunciating their fandom by discussing their favorite texts, remembering specific scenes, and taking photographic records of their journey.

For the flâneur the journey is important, exploring and making connections, but so too also is the notion of place; the search for a place to rest: "To walk is to lack a place. It is the indefinite process of being absent and in search of a proper" (de Certeau, 1984, p. 103). Fans of popular culture, both sport and media texts, are similarly in search of a special location where they can connect to what they enjoy. These locations become sites of popular veneration as outlined earlier; strange and familiar they become home to fans looking for a physical connection to what is usually ephemeral, temporal and unreal. Just as scholars have argued that the flâneur walks through unfamiliar spaces they have also argued that walking masters those spaces, making them familiar and permanent. Rob Shields describes the flâneur being in a constant state of appropriation, mapping and remapping the city through repeated touring. This transforms the streets from the unknown to the mastered, the city becomes the flâneur's to control and manipulate:

> The gaze of the flâneur is thus part of a tactic to appropriate not only the local, physical spaces of the city as one's own "turf" . . . but also to participate in the popular sense of empire, to master and even revel in the "emporium."
>
> *(Shields, 1994, p. 74)*

Further to this Stefan Morawski says the flâneur is "a kind of tourist at home" (1994, p. 184), someone who is both homeless and at home when traveling through space – occupying spaces not of their own yet made so through imitation and being present. This description of the flâneur mirrors earlier discussions of television fans who feel a sense of familiarity and home (or *heimat*) when visiting Vancouver, filming location of series like *Smallville* and *The X-Files*. Yet, this homecoming may only be temporary and a one-off. Those fans who seek repeated pleasure in revisiting familiar spaces not only create a sense of home; they create a sense of ownership. The space is theirs and thus what takes place in it is highly emotive and personal.

Sports arenas represent familiar and personal spaces for fans. Football (American, Australian, Canadian, and soccer), baseball, cricket, basketball, ice hockey, rugby, and all popular team sports that have mass followings are played in physical surroundings that encourage familiarity and loyalty. Over long periods of time during a playing season and spanning several decades and generations, sports arenas become like second homes to fans to regularly turn up to watch, cheer on, and celebrate their favorite local team. Take, for example, the Chicago Cubs who have played baseball at Wrigley Field in Chicago's North Side neighborhood since 1916. The stadium has been dubbed "the friendly confines" and the team, successful or not, has attracted a devoted and large fanbase. Visiting Wrigley Field, even for non-fans of the Cubs who just love baseball, is a venerable act – the environs are historic, the ballpark traditional, and the team has a certain quality being one of the oldest in the league. Indeed, Wrigley Field is the second oldest ballpark after the Boston Red Sox's Fenway Park. The stadium is not only home to the present-day team but areas of the ballpark are highlighted as historic, important, and hallowed. Statues to past players and memorial to days of glory long gone remind fans that they are walking through and connecting with a special space; a space that is still in use and modern, but at the same always time looking back on the past. It is not hard to see the intense loyalty created within long-standing fans who go to Wrigley Field many dozens of times in a season – cheering on their team, commiserating with other fans and celebrating a win – but the site also attracts sports fans from across the globe; those who want to see a game at the second oldest ballpark and sit in the historic bleachers. Attending alongside Cubs fans these fans also want to take in the experience; like the flâneur they want to master the space. Indeed, in his study of soccer fandom Richard Giulianotti (2002) creates a taxonomy of spectatorship. Identifying "supporters, fans, followers, flâneurs" in a descending order of loyalty and connection to the team, the flâneur represents the most commoditized and least identified spectator; using media like television and the Internet to follow the team. However, in traveling to the stadium and passing through the site I would argue they are able to achieve a physical connection to the team, its history, and what draws millions to the ballpark. Also, buying merchandise and wearing Cubs hats and shirts, allows those non-fans the opportunity to pass as real fans. As they respond to and cheer on the home team they replicate the rituals of Cubs fans who have done the same for generations. The stadium, a site of fan interaction, encourages all those who enter it to partake in the rituals of support. It becomes a temporary home and continues as a shared fan pilgrimage site.

Discussions of fan pilgrimage so far have suggested that a specific media tourism site is made special when fans believe there to be an intrinsic value in visiting it; fans are drawn to physical sites that make their fandom more real whereas to non-fans those sites are ordinary and everyday. For example, only *Star Trek* fans will recognize the value in visiting Riverside, a small farm town in Iowa, because it has been designated as the future birthplace of Captain James T. Kirk (with birthstone and museum to visit), however, for most people, Riverside is just another Midwest town you pass by on the freeway (en route to larger cities or the University of Iowa campus in Iowa City). Of course, *Star Trek* was never filmed in Riverside. It has a connection to the series because of Gene Roddenberry's choice to make Kirk an Iowan. Similar can be said of 221b Baker Street, it is special to fans of Sherlock Holmes because it is in the stories (Holmes lives there) but of course with Holmes not being real the site takes on extra significance as it is one of the few places that can be seen, visited, or explored. While filming locations such as those on the Original New Orleans Movie Tour are familiar to fans and non-fans, they appear both on screen and can be visited, the act of fan pilgrimage makes them extra special to fans who follow specific media texts. For example, Dubrovnik is a popular cruise ship stop and historic city but further significance is brought to it through the fact it is an important filming location for the HBO series *Game of Thrones*: therefore, it is both a traditional tourist destination and newly formed fan pilgrimage site. Whether multiply coded or known only by a specific fan community the fan as flâneur makes a space important through the act of walking around and passing through it. For Michel de Certeau spaces become liberated, broken free of meaning when explored by the flâneur (de Certeau, 1984, p. 105). Riverside, Baker Street, New Orleans, and Dubrovnik are all familiar spaces to local residents and tourists but they are also special to specific fan communities for distinct reasons: a fictional character is born or lives there; a film or TV series was filmed there. Original meaning and significance of a place is transformed when fans recognize and enter into those spaces.

Music fans, more specifically country music fans, consider Nashville an important city to visit: it is home to the Country Music Hall of Fame, recording studios where iconic artists like Elvis Presley made their name, and the Grand Ole Opry is *the* venue for live musical performances. With such an array of tourist sites to visit fans are able to achieve a tangible and comprehensive mastery of the city: like the flâneur of old. But what of tourists who grow to become fans through the act of passing through such important spaces? Being in such an important site for some has an inevitable effect on those who weren't necessarily fans of country music or a particular artist. Visiting provides a foundation for new fans to learn about country music and encourages existing fans to learn more and reaffirm their fandom. Similarly, as a multiply coded site, the Grand Ole Opry attracts both fans of the music, fans of stars such as Dolly Parton, and fans of the popular TV series *Nashville* (which is all about the country music industry). As a non-fan of country music myself, visiting the Opry meant little in terms of any long-term fandom but recognizing its significance as a live music venue and current filming location for a series with which I am familiar increases the significance of being there. Standing on stage where famous artists have performed, the "x" upon which Parton, Johnny Cash, Hank Williams, and others have stood have stood, makes the visit more special – with photographs to prove it. I would argue this phenomenon corresponds to Leon Davis' analysis of football fandom and authenticity, where proving one's fan identity when supporting a particular team relies on a number of factors including attending games and going to the stadium. This engagement with the team ignites and proves one's fandom over time; it is part of "a continuum of fandom" (Davis, 2014, p. 434). For both fans and non-fans visiting the Grand Ole Opry, a continuum of fandom is seen in how significant the site already is for some fans and how it becomes significant for others after being in that space. Media fans change the meaning of places and spaces through the act of passing through and between them but they also become fans of specific media texts because they had the physical experience of being there and participating in the rituals of performance and pilgrimage associated with those spaces.

Implications for popular culture tourism: fans passing through, as, and from

In this chapter I have outlined how media fan tourism is about passing through different tourist spaces and finding meaning in the act of being present, taking photos, and performing as a fan within those spaces. As this happens multiple identities are revealed, fan identities are transformed over time, and memories of geographic landmarks become important signifiers of fandom. As I have argued elsewhere, fan spaces are imagined, real and unreal, constructed and natural, subverted and official, consumed and constructed, creative and hierarchical (Geraghty, 2014). They can be known through traditional tourism, such as visiting a city like Vancouver, but made more personal for fans aware of what's filmed there and what they can also do in particular locations. Spaces can also become fan spaces because they are designated as such, like Riverside Iowa, or they can be constructed specifically to attract a fan audience, as in the Harry Potter Studio tour. What fans do in these media tourism sites contributes to their fan identity; it can reaffirm their fandom and make them fans of new media texts after exploring the site in more detail. Applying the concept of the flâneur to short case studies of a movie tour, sports stadium, and music city, I have argued that media fans both construct and are constructed by the physical environment in which they travel.

Like the flâneur walks through the city, taking in the sights, sounds, and people, the fan travels to media tourism sites to view, take in, and interact with landmarks and other fans. Fan tourism is therefore an act of *passing through* space; the fan pilgrimage is characterized by physical movement between familiar spaces and venerated places of popular culture. We see this happening in the phenomenon of the city movie tour where fans travel around and between local neighborhoods that are familiar to them because of the media texts they follow and consume. But also fan tourism is about *passing as* a fan, as in the case of the Chicago Cubs and a pilgrimage to Wrigley Field. In sports fandom we see how the stadium or arena where a team plays becomes a physical location where fans can engage with them and other fans. At the same time they can connect with the history of that space via statues and memorials; assuming the characteristics of a fan by dressing in appropriate attire. Just as the flâneur masters the city through walking, the media fan can master sites of popular culture through the appropriation and exploration of a particular fan identity. Lastly, the example of Nashville shows us that media fandom is also about *passing from* one fandom to another: transitioning from country music fandom, to television, and back again as in the case of visiting the Grand Ole Opry. In walking through the city the flâneur fractures space and creates new meanings within it. Likewise, those fans that travel to locations that have multiple meanings for different people can move between levels of fandom as they pass through. A non-fan of country music can gain an appreciation of the genre, its personalities, and cultural significance, and at the same time celebrate on a meta-level their fandom of a television series based on the industry. Fans and non-fans perform and take on aspects of fandom related to that specific place and doing so helps the shift between contrasting fan identities.

References

Aden, Roger C. (1999), *Popular Stories and Promised Lands: Fan Cultures and Symbolic Pilgrimages*, Tuscaloosa: University of Alabama Press.

Brooker, Will (2005), "The *Blade Runner* Experience: Pilgrimage and Liminal Space," in *The Blade Runner Experience: The Legacy of a Science Fiction Classic*, Will Brooker, Ed., London: Wallflower, 11–30.

———. (2007a), "Everywhere and Nowhere: Vancouver, Fan Pilgrimage and the Urban Imaginary," *International Journal of Cultural Studies* 10(4), 423–444.

———. (2007b), "A Sort of Homecoming: Fan Viewing and Symbolic Pilgrimage," in *Fandom: Identities and Communities in a Mediated World*, Jonathan Gray, Cornel Sandvoss, and C. Lee Harrington, Eds., New York: New York University Press, 149–164.

Combs, James (1989), "Celebrations: Rituals of Popular Veneration," *Journal of Popular Culture* 22(4), 71–77.

Davis, Leon (2014), "Football Fandom and Authenticity: A Critical Discussion of Historical and Contemporary Perspectives," *Soccer & Society* 16(2–3): 422–436.

De Certeau, Michel (1984), *The Practice of Everyday Life*, Berkeley: University of California Press.

Geraghty, Lincoln (2011), "'I've a Feeling We're Not in Kansas Anymore': Examining *Smallville*'s Canadian Cult Geography," in *The Smallville Chronicles: Critical Essays on the Television Series*, Lincoln Geraghty, Ed., Lanham, MD: Scarecrow Press, 2011, 129–152.

———. (2014), *Cult Collectors: Nostalgia, Fandom and Collecting Popular Culture*, London: Routledge.

Giddens, Anthony (1991), *Modernity and Self-Identity: Self and Society in the Late Modern Age*, Cambridge: Polity Press.

Giulianotti, Richard (2002), "Supports, Followers, Fans and Flâneurs: A Taxonomy of Spectator Identities in Football," *Journal of Sport and Social Issues* 26(1): 25–46.

Hills, Matt (2002), *Fan Cultures*, London: Routledge.

———. (2014), "Returning to 'Becoming-a-Fan' Stories: Theorising Transformational Objects and the Emergence/Extension of Fandom," in *The Ashgate Research Companion to Fan Cultures*, L. Duits, K. Zwaan, and S. Reijnders, Eds., Farnham: Ashgate, 9–21.

Jones, Owain and Garde-Hansen, Joanne (2012), "Introduction," in *Geography and Memory: Explorations in Identity, Place and Becoming*, O. Jones and J. Garde-Hansen, Eds., Basingstoke: Palgrave, 1–18.

Moores, Shaun (2006), "Media Uses & Everyday Environmental Experiences: A Positive Critique of Phenomenological Geography," *Particip@tions* 3(2), November.

Morawski, Stefan (1994), "The Hopeless Game of Flânerie," in *The Flâneur*, K. Tester, Ed., London: Routledge, 181–197.

Reijnders, Stijn (2011), *Places of the Imagination: Media, Tourism, Culture*, Farnham: Ashgate.

Sandvoss, Cornel (2005), *Fans: The Mirror of Consumption*, Cambridge: Polity Press.

Seamon, David (2006), "*A Geography of Lifeworld* in Retrospect: A Response to Shaun Moores," *Particip@tions* 3(2), November.

Shields, Rob (1994), "Fancy Footwork: Walter Benjamin's Notes on *Flânerie*," in *The Flâneur*, K. Tester, Ed., London: Routledge, 61–80.

Tuan, Yi-Fu (1977), *Space and Place: The Perspective of Experience*, Minneapolis: University of Minnesota Press.

Urry, John (2002), *The Tourist Gaze*, London: Sage.

19

A THAI STAR'S APPEAL TO CHINESE FANS AND ITS IMPACT ON THAILAND POPULAR CULTURE TOURISM

Lisa Yong Yeu Moy and Charuwan Phongpanichanan

Setting the scene: Thai wave

Several years ago, Thai TV drama was rather new in China; its popularity was below that of Thai fragrant rice and Tom Yam Soup. However, since 2009, following the downturn in the popularity in TV dramas/films of the "Hong Kong and Taiwan" waves and the "Japanese and Korean" waves, is the rising popularity of "Kaka" and "Krupkrup" TV dramas from Thailand. These Thai TV dramas were first aired by China Central Television (CCTV) in 2003, which was the first exposure of Thai drama in China. As of 2010, China has had the world's largest television audience, with a 97 percent household penetration for TV coverage. On average, CCTV programs are seen by about 73 million viewers daily, and a typical viewer spends about two hours a day watching CCTV programs (Italian Trade Commission, 2011). Thai TV dramas have gained more popularity since then. During 2009, CCTV released eight Thai TV dramas to air with the slogan "The First Thai TV Drama TV station in China" (China Forum, 2011).

In addition, iQIYI, being China's leading advertisement supported online television and movie portal, focuses on fully licensed, high-definition, professionally produced contents videos. iQIYI obtained the exclusive rights to air six Thai TV dramas within a six-month period. It "blew" the first ever "Thai wave" into the Internet world, with more than 40 million viewing times within a month's airing of one single Thai drama "Ruk Nai Marn Mek" on the Internet (Yuegu, 2011). It also outnumbered the Korean drama that aired at the same time. Subsequently, Thai TV dramas entered into the golden hours on various Chinese TV stations. In 2009, Anhui China TV station aired "Battle in Angels" at 10 pm; it hit the top 10 provincial TV viewing rates within a week, and ranked second place in China TV viewing rates. This brought the first hit from Thai TV drama into China. The purchases of Thai TV dramas to air in China TV stations rose from 1–2 dramas in 2009 to over 10 dramas in 2011, especially TV stations such as Zhejiang Huace Firm & TV Co. Ltd., when it purchased 6 dramas at one time. In other words, with Thailand's total annual TV productions estimated to be only about 50 dramas, one-fourth of the yearly TV productions of Thailand TV dramas were purchased and brought into the China market (*Chongqing Evening Newspaper*, 2011). Currently, besides the China TV stations that air Thai TV dramas, Internet video sites are the main channels of entertainments where Mainland Chinese viewers watch the Thai TV dramas and movies. Based

Table 19.1 The top 10 online video websites in China by daily reach (million visitors)

Rating	Website	Visitors (millions)
1	Youku.com	26.449
2	Tudou.com	16.484
3	Xunlei.com	9.89
4	Qiyi.com (Baidu)	7.914
5	Ku6.com	6.749
6	56.com	6.734
7	Cnti.cn	4.734
8	Pps.tv	3.073
9	Pptv.com	3.051
10	joy.cn	2.501

Note: adapted Incitez (2011).

on the list provided by Icitez (2011), the existing top 10 online video websites in China are shown in Table 19.1.

With the rise of Thai TV drama on the top video platform in China, Chinese viewers are able to watch Thai dramas on a daily basis using the Internet. The free video platform is becoming increasingly popular in Thai popular culture. The trend indicates that Thai popular culture is gaining popularity in China particularly via mass-entertainment products such as MV, songs, movies, or TV dramas. Chinese fans have now become more active in visiting Thailand, learning the Thai language, tasting Thai food, and experiencing the Thai lifestyle.

Existing tourism and leisure literature suggest that mass media serves as a powerful tool in stimulating a tourism/leisure demand by which the viewers form certain images and anticipation for what they have watched in the films or television (Connell, 2005; Kim & Richardson, 2003; Riley, Baker & Van Doren, 1998; Riley & Van Doren, 1992; Tooke & Baker, 1996). However, these studies contributed only to the understanding of the impact of mass media on the tourism/leisure phenomena. The detailed linkage between the diverse components of mass media and tourism/leisure perceptions and behaviors of Chinese fans toward Thai TV drama and their idols has been rarely researched.

Fans' attachment to the celebrities may play an important role in developing perceptions and attitudes. As such, the concept of celebrity fandom is introduced and examined in this article. Fandom means "fanaticism," a derivative of the word fanum, which means "temple or sacred place" (*American Heritage Dictionary*, 1985, p. 489). Fan, an abbreviation of *fanatic*, is a follower of different professional and amateur sports teams (Jenkins, 1992). The non-sport, commercial entertainment use refers to female theatergoers, known for their admiration for particular actors rather than the films. Media fans and sports fans have become popular characters of scholarly investigation because of the high visibility and familiarity to many individuals (Gibson, 2000; Smith, 2004). Media fans are the ones who are more devoted to their favorite star in their everyday life and with more intensity, not only devoting their time and money to a star, but also become emotionally attached. For them, fandom becomes a part of everyday life to the point at which it is included as a major part of their self-identity. Thus, it can be said that the level of leisure involvement significantly influences fans' behavior and attitudes particularly in relation to the particular star. Furthermore, being a fan provides individuals with risk-free topics of conversation that can help establish social interaction and cohesion (Smith, Patterson, Williams, & Hogg, 1981). The attachment to Thai celebrities seems to create an actual demand for popular culture tourism in Thailand. The increased number of Chinese tourists to Thailand

(Department of Tourism, Ministry of Tourism and Sports, Thailand, 2014) can be attributed to the heightened interest in and affection for Thai celebrities, which points toward the possible linkage between celebrity fandom and popular culture tourism. As Morgan and Pritchard (1998) indicated, celebrities not only operate as supporters of popular culture tourism, but also become icons of tourism themselves.

The objective of this study is to examine the under-researched power of Thai celebrities in shaping Chinese fans' tourism/leisure related perceptions and behaviors and how they may impact the popular culture tourism in Thailand. The Thai star who has been researched is Sornram Theappitak (nickname Noom or Num), a celebrity who has been in the entertainment industry since 1992. The results and the significance of this study will explore the potential development of popular culture tourism in the hospitality and tourism industry in Thailand.

Disciplinary underpinnings: popular culture tourism

Tourism potential of icons

Famous individuals were first coined as "icons" by Pearce, Morrison, and Moscardo (2003) due to their human achievements. Their discussions focused on the tourism potential of icons. Examples of famous icons and their related tourist attractions include: William J. Clinton in the Presidential Center and Park in Little Rock, Arkansas in the United States; Alexandre Dumas in File Island, Marseille in France; and Mao Zedong in Shaoshan, Hunan in China. Celebrities have been employed or involved in special tourist resources and potential attractions worldwide. As such, the famous person researched in this chapter (who has not been the subject of any previous academic research), is Thai celebrity, Num Sornram Theappitak.

The study by McCarney and Pinto (2014) examined the influence of advertising on Chinese outbound travelers and celebrity endorsement strategy in decision-making with Macao as a destination and indicated that the celebrities' endorsement tactics have influences on younger and middle-income tourists, whereas the high-income tourists were the most influenced when it came to actual destination selection and purchase. The findings also suggested that resources assigned to celebrity endorsement should be taken into account along with the revenues that will be induced from the younger tourists, middle-income tourists, and high-income tourists to Macao. The study further suggested that the impact of celebrity endorsement should be tested in each Asian market and ethnic regions, given the many provinces within Asian countries such as China, Thailand, Malaysia, Philippines, or Indonesia.

The celebrity endorsement in media-induced tourism has generally impacted television programs such as drama series or soap operas that have been studied with regards to their influence on tourism (Han & Lee, 2008; Iwashita, 2006; Kim, Agrusa, Lee, & Chon, 2007; Young & Young, 2008). Yen & Teng (2013) in their study suggested that celebrity involvement may be translated into celebrity worship, and the transfer process of constructing significant personal meanings will enhance tourists' intention to visit a travel destination; as such, the tourist will perceive that the benefits are higher than costs, which will result in future behavioral intentions. However, media exposure is also increasingly gaining attention. In a suggestion by Mowen and Brown (1981) and Trippet, Jensen, and Carlson (1994), it is implied that paid celebrity endorsement may not be as effective as expected.

Film-induced tourism is when fans visit a destination due to the influence of television, video, and DVD (Beeton, 2005), and has received increasing attention over the past decade (Beeton, 2004; Iwashita, 2006; Macionis & Sparks, 2006; Riley et al., 1998). In general, destinations such as Korea, the USA, New Zealand, the UK, and Australia are popular for film tourism.

While there have been extensive studies on film-induced tourism focusing on Western films and Korean films, there has been limited research investigating the effects of Thai drama series via television, DVD, and the Internet on the tourism industry although Thai celebrities have gained popularity in Asia. Table 19.1 below shows the growth in visitor numbers at TV and film locations worldwide (Table 19.2).

Table 19.2 The growth in visitor numbers at TV and film locations worldwide

Film/TV drama	Location	Impact on tourism
Braveheart	Wallace Monument, Scotland	300% increase in visitors year after release
Bull Durham	Durham, North Carolina, USA	25% increase year after release
Captain Corelli's Mandolin	Cephalonia, Greece	50% increase over 3 years
Close Encounters of the Third Kind	Devils Tower, Wyoming, USA	75% increase in 1975 20% visit now because of the film
Crocodile Dundee	Australia	21% increase every year 1991–1998 from US
Dances with Wolves	Fort Hayes, Kansas, USA	25% increase compared with 7% for previous 4 years
Dallas	Southfork Ranch, Dallas, USA	500,000 visitor per year
Deliverance	Raybun Country, Georgia, USA	20,000 film tourist a year
Field of Dreams	Dyersville, Iowa, USA	35,000 visits in 1991 Steady increase every year
Forrest Gump	Savannah, Georgia, USA	7% increase in tourism
Four Weddings and a Funeral	The Crown Hotel, Amersham, UK	Fully booked for at least 3 years
Gorillas in the Mist	Rwanda	20% increase in 1998
Harry Potter	Various locations in UK	50% or more increase
Heartbeat	Goathland, North Yorkshire, UK	3 times the number of normal visitors in 1991
Steel Magnolias	Louisiana, USA	48% increase year after release
Last of the Mohicans	Chimney Rock Park, North Carolina, USA	25% increase year after release
Little Women	Orchard House, Concord, Massachusetts, USA	65% increase year after release
Mission Impossible 2	National Parks, Sydney, Australia	200% increase in 2000
Miami Vice	Miami, Florida, USA	150% increase 1985–1988 from Germany
Middlemarch	Stamford, Lincolnshire, UK	27% increase in 1994
Mrs. Brown	Osborne House, UK	25% increase
Notting Hill	Kenwood House, England	10% increase in one month
Pride and Prejudice	Lyme Park in Cheshire, UK	150% increase
Saving Private Ryan	Normandy, France	40% increase from US
Sense and Sensibility	Saltram House, UK	39% increase
The Beach	Thailand	22% increase in youth market in 2000
The Fugitive	Dillsboro, North Carolina, USA	11% increase year after release

(continued)

217

Table 19.2 (continued)

Film/TV drama	Location	Impact on tourism
The Lord of the Rings	New Zealand	10% increase every year 1998–2003 from UK
Thelma and Louise	Arches National Monument in Moab, Utah, USA	19.1% increase in 1991
To the Manor Born	Cricket St Thomas Leisure Park, Somerset, UK	37% increase 1978–1980
Troy	Canakkale, Turkey	73% increase in tourism
Winter Sonata	Nami Island, Korea	2,600% increase in 2004 from Japan
James Bond 007 Man with the Golden Gun	Phuket's Phang Nga Bay, Thailand	n/a
Star Wars Episode III	Krabi Province, Thailand	n/a
The Hangover, Part II	Bangkok, Thailand	n/a

Note: adapted from Busby, Brunt, and Lund (2003); Croy and Walker (2003); Riley et al. (1998); Riley and Van Doren (1992); Tooke and Baker (1996).

Thai popular culture tourism

What is the role of the Thai government in the tourism industry? In 2012, Thailand achieved 22 million tourist arrivals marked for the first time from two markets, China and Malaysia, which generated more than 2 million annual arrivals each (Svetasreni, 2013). According to a Thailand visitor arrival report from January to May 2013, Thailand received a total of 1.9 million Mainland Chinese arrivals (+93 percent). The number of Chinese tourists crossed the 1 million mark back in March 2013. This shows that the number of Chinese tourists have sharply increased since 2012, an increase of 93 percent in total tourist arrivals. As such, what are the tourism plans that Thai tourism sectors have planned for themselves?

In a speech given by the Thai Governor, Mr Svetasreni of The Tourism Authority of Thailand (TAT), at the British Chamber of Thailand Special Luncheon Meeting (Svetasreni, 2013), Svetasreni stated that the TAT strategies in 2013 included the introduction of the DISCO plan, which comprises of five components, namely:

D for digital marketing

I for image building

S for sustainability

C for crystallization and crisis communication

O for organization management

The Governor further emphasized image building in which Thailand is working with Thai celebrities to promote Thailand cultural tourism:

> Image building is not confined only to colorful ads, but also involves in essence taking Thainess to the world at every high-profile opportunity. In this regard, we go to great length to maintain consistency when we work with celebrities to promote Thailand.
>
> *(Svetasreni, 2013)*

The speech showed the awareness of the Thailand Tourism Authority in using celebrities in their promotion of strategic planning. The Department of Tourism Thailand (2014) indicated that its new cultural tourism promotion measures included a 30-day extension of stay for visitors from 48 countries and one territory, in addition to the free visa for Chinese tourists, although tourists from many other countries do not need holiday visas.

Celebrity involvement

The term "celebrity involvement" is used to describe the affection and attachment of fans toward a celebrity. Havitz and Dimanche (1997, p. 246) referred to the concept of involvement as an "unobservable state of motivation, arousal or interest toward a recreational activity or associated product." They further argued that it is evoked by a particular stimulus or situation and has drive properties. In other words, a celebrity is an object of leisure involvement for fans, whereas involvement is about the length and frequency of activity participation (Park, 1996; Schuett, 1995; Venkatraman, 1988), expenditure associated with a chosen leisure activity (Bloch, 1993; Siegenthaler & Lam, 1992), and a future intention to participate in a chosen leisure activity (McCarville, Crompton, & Sell, 1993; Norman, 1991). Although there were research findings relating to the influence of celebrities on diverse aspects of society, few studies have been conducted to explore the celebrity fan experiences, particularly as a part of leisure activity in Thailand. The celebrity does have influence over his/her fans' attitude toward and intention to visit Thailand, which this research aims to study.

Num Sornram Theappitak

Num, born on August 22, 1973 in Bangkok, Thailand, is a Thai actor, model, singer, football player, court mediator, TV program producer, and TV drama/film director. He earned his Bachelor of Political Science degree from Ramkhamhaeing University (RU) at age 32 (Baike, 2013). At the age of 18, he started his career as a model in 1991, and began his acting career in 1992. He has a record of 75 movies/TV dramas and is still active in the Thai entertainment industry. Among his most famous TV dramas, which established his popularity and top the history of Thailand TV, were his first TV drama *Good Morning* on Channel 3 Thailand (for which he won the "Mekhala Best New Actor Award" in 1992) and *The Junction Is Still Young*. In 1994, his drama *Daoprasook* hit 38 percent of TV viewers' ratings and ranked in the top 2 in the history of Thailand TV and to date remains in the top 10. Subsequently in 1995, the TV drama *Sailohid* was specially appointed by Her Majesty Queen Regent Sirikit, Thailand, for him to act in the main role. Again, with a record high of 34 percent of viewers' ratings, it hit the top 4 in the history of Thailand TV drama viewers' ratings, where it remains to date, unbreakable (Postjung, 2014). The TV drama *Sailohid*, which was filmed at Phra Nakhon Si Ayutthaya, is a must-go site for Chinese tourists. Furthermore, the film *First Flight* (2008), which was directed by a French director, was the largest budget film in the history of filming in Thailand. It was nominated in France for the Cannes Film Festival in 2007 to celebrate the cultural and trade relations between Thailand and France, and it also marked the 100th anniversary of Thai aviation in 2008 (Baike, 2013). Num Sornram Theappitak has also won a long list of awards in the Thailand entertainment industry and is recognized as the most popular celebrity since 1992 (Baike, 2013).

Methodology

This study aims to examine the extent to which Num Sornram Theappitak influences the perceptions of Chinese fans in considering Thailand as a popular culture tourism destination.

The pilot test

The pilot test, conducted in September 2014, consisted of Chinese fans who are over 18 years old and reside in China. Data for the sample group of this study was collected from Baidu Tieba Num Bar (SFCC) in China (hereafter referred to as Num Bar), an online forum established in 2008 where Sornram's fans blog worldwide. Num Bar provides an alternative context to contact a reasonably diverse range of fans in terms of social demographic characteristics.

Instrument translation and questionnaire design

Based on an extensive literature review, a preliminary self-administered questionnaire was developed. The target respondents were Mainland Chinese, hence, the questionnaires were using the back translated method as explained by Brislin (1976), whereby two experienced interpreters were chosen to translate the questionnaire from English to Chinese. The two translators were fluent in both English and Chinese and had good working experience in translation. This process was to ensure the accuracy of the multilingual survey instrument (Soriano & Foxall, 2002).

The questionnaire in this study consisted of two sets of questions: (1) demographic characteristics and (2) attitudes and behaviors of popular culture tourism in relation to the Thai star Num Sornram Theappitak. The questionnaire was designed for open-ended text responses and the data analysis was collected from the Survey Monkey website. Prior to data collection, the questionnaire was checked by a senior fan of Sornram who is one of the pioneers in the Num Bar forum in order to verify the validity of the questions asked. A pretest of the revised questionnaire was conducted by one of the fans to determine the system's ability to answer all the survey questions prior to the questionnaires being distributed for data collection.

The sample size for the study consisted of 42 respondents. The questionnaires were combined into two sections: the demographic characteristics and attitudes and behaviors of popular culture tourism in Thailand in relation to Num Sornram Theappitak. The first section was to explain the differences in fan's attributes and knowledge about Thailand. This part included the respondent's profile and traveling experience in Thailand and popular culture, which included (1) age group; (2) marital status; (3) education; (4) occupation; (5) monthly income before tax; (6) views and image of Thailand; (7) familiarity with Thailand as a travel destination, how much the respondent had seen or heard of Thailand and through which channel; (8) familiarity with Thai culture; (9) past experience with Thailand; and (10) intention to visit Thailand.

Findings

Based on the Chinese fans' perception of Thailand as the travel destination, what can Thailand offer to them? In this question, rating scales were used to measure and compare sets of variables from 1–5 (strongly disagree, disagree, neutral, agree, and strongly agree). Respondents strongly agreed on good values for travel expenditure (43 percent), while slightly more (57 percent) were interested in history and culture.

The majority of respondents (64 percent) were interested in nature attractions and scenery, with less interest given to local Thai food cuisine (8 percent), good night life entertainment (4 percent), good quality of transportation (5 percent), standard hygiene and cleanliness (4 percent), suitable accommodations (4 percent), and lastly friendliness of Thai people (5 percent). In the category of familiarity with Thailand in terms of information sources on how much the respondent had seen or heard about Thailand and through which information channel, there was a considerably high presence on the Internet, followed by film/TV drama and other media

Table 19.3 The demographic characteristics and attitudes of the respondents (N = 42) and result shown by percentage (%)

Status	Profile	Respondents (%)
Age	Below 20 years old	2.4
	21–30	33.3
	31–40	33.3
	41–50	31
Marital status	Single	36
	Married	64
Education level	Below secondary school	14
	Secondary school	19
	University level	62
	Post-graduate	5
Occupation	Student	2
	Full-time employee	81
	Housewife	14
	Self-employed	10
	Retired	2
Monthly income before tax	RMB 1,000–2,000	7
	RMB 2,000–4,000	21
	RMB 4,000–6,000	36
	RMB 6,000–10,000	24
	Above 10,000	12

products, word of mouth information from friends and relatives, articles from newspapers/magazines, advertisements in magazines or TV, travel books, travel agency brochures, and Thailand tourist maps. With regard to familiarity with Thai culture, respondents were mostly familiar with the history of Thailand, followed by popular culture in Thailand, Thai lifestyle, Thai food, and lastly Thai language.

Past experience with Thailand from respondents showed a high percentage of respondents who had never been to Thailand (62 percent), a considerable proportion having traveled once (21 percent), and some having traveled more than twice (17 percent). With regard to the purpose of their trip to Thailand, less than half (about 40 percent) came to tour Thailand, followed by to experience popular culture tourism (26 percent), fan meeting (10 percent), because of a particular idol (10 percent), tour and work (5 percent), the chances to go to see a particular idol and join in popular culture tourism (3 percent), and about 1 percent came for other reasons. Most of the respondents (about 83 percent) had never experienced popular culture tourism and fan meetings, while a small proportion (17 percent) had been to a fan meeting. Most respondents (93 percent) were willing to meet Sornram at a fan meeting and visit popular culture tourism destinations, whereas very few (5 percent) were not sure, and even fewer (2 percent) were not interested in meeting him. As for a budget to tour Thailand, over half of the respondents (53 percent) would spend RMB 10,000–20,000, while considerably fewer respondents would spend below RMB 10,000 (21 percent), have no plan or it depends on needs (19 percent), would spend RMB 30,000 and above (5 percent), or have no set limit (2 percent). With regard to their intention to visit Thailand, most of the respondents agreed that their interest in the Thai star Sornram impacts their interests towards Thailand (96 percent) and also impacts their desire to travel to Thailand (98 percent). Since becoming fans of popular culture tourism, most of the respondents have contributed to Thailand popular culture tourism

(79 percent) and they indicated their intention to continue contributing to Thailand popular culture tourism (100 percent).

The second section of the question was to explain the attitudes and behaviors of the respondents in relation to Sornram. This part focused mainly on leisure involvements and how the respondents' attitudes relating to Sornram raised interest towards recreational activities or associated products (Havitz & Dimanche, 1997; Rothschild, 1984). In this category, the researcher wanted to learn about respondents' behaviors and attitudes toward Sornram over the past 12 months. A high percentage (about 77 percent) were involved on a daily or almost everyday basis by watching movies/TV dramas related to Sornram; most (over 90 percent) of respondents often obtained news related to Sornram through social media and the Internet, the Num Bar forum, news articles, and magazines. Less than half (47 percent) talked and shared information about Sornram with others. One category focused on the most watched media productions related to Sornram according to percentage: TV drama presence (72 percent), movies (8 percent), TV entertainment program/interviews (8 percent), music video (4 percent), Sornram's production company's Ritthiram TV programmes (3 percent), songs from albums (3 percent), Thai TV programs, and with Sornram as the host in TV programs (2 percent). Most of the respondents learned entertainment news through the following sources: Baidu Tieba Num Bar (53 percent) forum, followed by Instagram (13 percent), Baidu Tieba ThaiLakorn Bar (10 percent), Youku Video (10 percent), PPS (6 percent), Tianya Forum (4 percent), Tudou Video (2 percent), Youtube (1 percent) and others (1 percent). Furthermore, the result showed that about a high proportion of respondents (84 percent) are currently members of Num Bar devoted to Sornram, while very few (16 percent) are not yet members.

Implications for cultural tourism in Thailand

This study aims to examine the under-researched power of Thai celebrity Num Sornram Theappitak in shaping Chinese fans' tourism/leisure involvement in terms of influencing their perceptions and behaviors and how they may impact the popular culture tourism in Thailand. A pilot study methodology was used and a survey was conducted at Sornram Fan Club China (SFCC) of Baidu Tieba Num Bar, China to examine intentions of Chinese fans to go on tour to Thailand in relation to their leisure involvements with Thai celebrities. Three conclusions were drawn from the findings.

The results indicated that Sornram, the celebrity icon, had a direct impact on his fans' intention to visit Thailand. Furthermore, most of the respondents indicated that they have contributed to Thailand popular culture tourism and all of them will continue to do so. This study provides evidence about the popular culture tourism in Thailand delineated in three conclusions as follows.

Attachment to Thai celebrity Sornram

The first conclusion is that Chinese fans' level of attachment towards Thai star Sornram impacts their intention to tour Thailand. From the findings, it is concluded that the Chinese fans' level of celebrity involvements positively affected destination familiarity and visitation intention. It was the high frequency of their viewing of Sornram's TV dramas/films that created the desire to know more about Thailand, thus eventually leading to the intention to visit the destination. From viewing the Thai TV drama/films, it is possible that the Mainland Chinese fans came to know about Sornram, and subsequently because of the high attachment to him, this created the intention to visit Thailand.

This study makes a significant contribution to the existing popular culture tourism literature. First of all, it introduces the concept of celebrity fandom that impacts popular culture tourism studies and therefore contributes to a theoretical understanding of how fans' frequency of participation in mass media influences popular culture tourism attitudes and behaviors. Second, although leisure involvement has received extensive research over the last two decades (Guttmann, 1986; Jenkins, 1992; Leerhsen, 1986), its application to celebrity fandom from the Mainland Chinese fans toward Thai stars has been under-researched. This study helps expand the applicability of the concept of leisure involvement by researching it within the context of media celebrity fandom. It suggests that fans' attachment to a celebrity can be analyzed as a privileged kind of leisure activity, which has been under-researched by leisure scholars. For Sornram's Mainland Chinese fans in this research, an attachment to a celebrity is a means of attaining pleasure, expressing self-identity, and developing social networks among the fans that have the same preference for Sornram. Future research could be focused more on the differences between the celebrity fandom and conventional leisure activities.

Fandom Forum of Thai Star Sornram – Baidu Tieba Num Bar

The second conclusion is the online Baidu Num Bar Chinese fandom forum (Num Bar) that Chinese fans sign in to share their views and critiques on the TV dramas/films and other information related to Thai star Sornram. About 53 percent of the respondents use Num Bar as an Internet channel of entertainment to follow their favorite Thai star. Num Bar acts as the most powerful source that bonds Chinese fans throughout China and worldwide. Some 90 percent of the Chinese fans sign in to Num Bar on a daily basis. In addition, 84 percent of the respondents are devoted members of Num Bar. It provides a home for Sornram's Chinese fans to comment freely on topics related to Sornram, which helps to establish social interaction and cohesion. They tend to develop feelings of solidarity with fans who support the same Thai star in Num Bar.

This chapter seeks to expand the applicability of leisure involvement, which has been tested in North American contexts, but this conclusion has not been tested in Asian settings, especially in Thailand. This study confirms the validity of the fandom involvement in diverse popular culture tourism settings.

Motivation to visit Thailand

The third conclusion of the study is the "motivation" from fandom of a Thai star that leads to their intention to tour Thailand. Based on the interview results, there are three types of fandom attitudes toward their favorite Thai star Sornram. More than 65 percent of the 42 respondents wanted to meet Sornram in person and tour Thailand at the same time. On the other hand, about 35 percent of the fans chose not to meet Sornram in person, but chose instead to see him from a distance and keep him in their memory although they still intended to visit Thailand. None of the respondents said that they have no intention to meet Sornram or that they have no intention to visit Thailand. In other words, even when the Chinese fans have no intention to meet Sornram for their own reasons, the intention to make a popular culture tour to Thailand remains, therefore reflecting the influence of a Thai celebrity on popular culture tourism in Thailand. As such, the Chinese fans' motivation to tour Thailand is derived from Thai star Sornram and they will continue to contribute to Thailand popular culture tourism. The findings also reflect that fans' familiarity with Thailand have the most powerful influence on travel intention. In other words, respondents like to travel to Thailand when they are familiar with Thailand information and culture, and their familiarity with Thailand comes from their attachment to Sornram.

Acknowledgment

This study has been granted full permission from Thai star Num Sornram Theappitak to research on the topic and distribute questionnaires related to him. The authors would like to thank Mr. Sornram for his kindness and support for the completion of this study.

References

American heritage dictionary (1985). Berube, S. M. (Ed.). Boston: Houghton Mifflin.

Baike (2013). Sornram Theappitak. Retrieved from http://baike.baidu.com/view/12991928.htm?fromtit le=Sornram+Theappitakfromid=7605726type=syn.

Beeton, S. (2004). Rural tourism in Australia – has the gaze altered? Tracking rural images through film and tourism promotion. *International Journal of Tourism Research*, 6(3), 125–135. doi:10.1002/jtr.479.

Beeton, S. (2005). *Film-induced tourism*. Clevedon: Channel View Publications.

Bloch, P. H. (1993). Involvement with adornments as leisure behavior: An exploratory study. *Journal of Leisure Research*, 25, 245–262.

Brislin, R. W. (1976). Comparative research methodology: Cross-cultural studies. *International Journal of Psychology*, 11(3), 215.

Busby, G., Brunt, P., & Lund, J. (2003). In Agatha Christie country: Resident perception of special interest tourism. *Journal of Tourism*, 51(3), 287–300. doi:10.1107/s0108768107031758/bs5044supl.cif.

China Forum. (2011, June 12). Retrieved from http://forum.china.com.cn/thread-1058131-1-1.html.

Chongqing Evening Newspaper. (2011, July 6). Thai TV drama. Retrieved from http://ent.jschina.com.cn/system/2011/07/06/011163815.shtml.

Connell, J. (2005). Toddlers, tourism and Tobermory: Destination marketing issues and television-induced tourism. *Tourism Management*, 26(5), 763–776. doi:10.1016/j.tourman.2004.04.010.

Croy, W. G. and Walker, R. (2003). Rural tourism and film: Issues for strategic regional development, In Hall, D., Roberts, L., and Mitchell, M. (Eds.), *New directions in rural tourism* (pp. 115–133). Aldershot, UK: Ashgate.

Department of Tourism, Ministry of Tourism and Sports, Thailand. (2014). *Thailand Tourism Statistics*. Bangkok: Ministry of Tourism and Sports.

Gibson, M. L. (2000). *The mediated self: An exploration of the subjective experience of mass media celebrity fanship*. (Unpublished Doctoral Dissertation). Simon Fraser University, British Columbia, Canada.

Guttmann, A. (1986). *Sport spectators*. New York: Columbia University Press.

Han, H., & Lee, J. (2008). A study on the KBS TV drama *Winter Sonata* and its impacts on Korea's hallyu tourism development. *Journal of Travel & Tourism Marketing*, 24(2–3), 115–126. doi:10.1080/10548400802092593.

Havitz, M. E., & F. Dimanche (1997). Leisure involvement revisited: Conceptual conundrums and measurement advances. *Journal of Leisure Research*, 29(3), 245–278.

Incitez (2011, August 11). Chart: China's top 10 online video sites in Q2. Retrieved from www.china internetwatch.com/1228/chart-chinas-top-10-online-video-sites-in-q2-2011/.

Italian Trade Commission (2011). *China television industry market report*. Retrieved from www.ice.gov.it/paesi/asia/cina/upload/174/CHINA%20TELEVISION%20INDUSTRY%20MARKET%20REPORT%202011.pdf.

Iwashita, C. (2006). Media representation of the UK as a destination for Japanese tourists: Popular culture and tourism. *Tourist Studies*, 6(1), 59–77. doi:10.1177/1468797606071477.

Jenkins, H. (1992). Strangers no more, we sing: Filking and the social construction of the science fiction fan community. In Lewis, L. A. (Eds.), *The adoring audience: Fan culture and popular media* (pp. 208–236). New York: Routledge.

Kim, H., & S. L. Richardson (2003). Motion picture impacts on destination images. *Annals of Tourism Research*, 30(1), 216–237. doi:10.1016/s0160-7383(02)00062-2.

Kim, S. S., Agrusa, J., Lee, H., & Chon, K. (2007). Effects of Korean television dramas on the flow of Japanese tourists. *Tourism Management*, 28(5), 1340–1353. doi:10.1016/j.tourman.2007.01.005.

Leerhsen, C. (1986, August 4). Aging playboy. *Newsweek*, *108*, 50–56.

McCartney, G., & Pinto J. F. (2014, March 5). Influencing Chinese travel decisions: The impact of celebrity endorsement advertising on the Chinese traveler to Macao. *Journal of Vacation Marketing*, *20*(3), 253–266. Retrieved from http://jvm.sagepub.com/content/20/3/253.

McCarville, R. E., Crompton, J. L., & J. A. Sell (1993). The influence of outcome messages on reference prices. *Leisure Sciences*, *15*, 115–130.

Macionis, N., & Sparks, B. (Eds.). (2006). *Proceedings from ITAM '06: The 2nd International Tourism and Media (ITAM) Conference*. Melbourne, AU.

Morgan, N., & A. Pritchard (1998). *Tourism promotion and power: Creating images, creating identities*. Chichester, UK: Wiley.

Moven, J. C., & Brown, S. W. (1981). On explaining and predicting the effectiveness of celebrity endorsers. *Advances in Consumer Research*, *8*(1), 437–445.

Norman, W. C. (1991). *The influence of perceived constraints on the generic decision of whether or not to take a summer vacation*. Symposium on Leisure Research, Arlington, VA: National Recreation and Park Association.

Park, S. H. (1996). Relationships between involvement and attitudinal loyalty construct in adult fitness programs. *Journal of Leisure Research*, *28*, 233–250.

Pearce, P. L., Morrison, A. M., & Moscardo, G. M. (2003). Individuals as tourist icons: A development and marketing analysis. *Journal of Hospitality Leisure Marketing*, *10*(1–2), 63–85. doi:10.1300/ j150v10n01_05.

PostJung (2014). Retrieved from http://board.postjung.com/676812.html.

Riley, R. W., D. Baker, & C. S. Van Doren (1998). Movie induced tourism. *Annals of Tourism Research*, *25*(4), 919–935.doi:10.1016/s0160-7383(98)00045-0.

Riley, R. W., & C. S. Van Doren (1992). Movies as tourism promotion: A "pull" factor in a "push" location. *Tourism Management*, *13*(3), 267–274. doi:10.1016/0261-5177(92)90098-r.

Rothschild, L. (1984). Perspectives on involvement: Current problems and future direction. *Advances in Consumer Research*, *11*, 217–227.

Schuett, M. A. (1995). A critique of leisure constraints: Comparative analyses and understandings. *Journal Leisure Research*, *29*(4), 430–452.

Siegenthaler, K. L., & T. C. M. Lam (1992). Commitment and ego-involvement in recreational tennis. *Leisure Sciences*, *14*, 303–315.

Smith, G. J., B. Patterson, T. Williams, & J. Hogg (1981). A profile of the deeply committed male sports fan. *Arena Review*, *5*, 26–44.

Smith, S. (2004). *Fanatic consumption? Reconsidering fanaticism and fandom in consumer research*. Unpublished Doctoral Dissertation. Fayetteville, AR: University of Arkansas.

Soriano, M. Y., & Foxall, G. R. (2002). A Spanish translation of Mehrabian and Russell's emotionality scales for environmental consumer psychology. *Journal of Consumer Behaviour*, *2*(1), 23–36. doi: 10.1002/cb.87.

Svetasreni, S. (2013, June 28). *Speech by the Governor, Tourism Authority of Thailand, on the occasion of the British Chamber of Commerce Thailand Special Luncheon Meeting at Swiss hotel Nai Lert Park Bangkok*. Retrieved from www.tatnews.org/thailands-tourism-sector-for-the-future/#sthash. M5LymYh8.dpuf.

Tooke, N., & Baker, M. (1996). Seeing is believing: The effect of film on visitor numbers in screened locations. *Tourism Management*, *17*(2), 87–94. doi:10.1016/0261-5177(95)00111-5.

Trippet, C., Jensen, T. D., & Carlson, L. (1994). The effects of multiple product endorsements by celebrities on consumer's attitudes and intentions. *Journal of Consumer Research*, *20*(4), 535. doi:10.1086/209368.

Venkatraman, M. P. (1988). Investigating differences in the roles of enduring and instrumentally involved consumers in the diffusion process. *Advances in Consumer Research*, *15*, 299–303.

Yen, C., & Teng, H. (2013). Celebrity involvement, perceived value, and behavioral intentions in popular media-induced tourism. *Journal of Hospitality & Tourism Research*, *39*(2), 225–244. doi: 10.1177/1096348012471382.

Young, A. F., & Young, R. (2008). Measuring the effects of film and television on tourism to screen location: A theoretical and empirical perspective. *Journal of Travel & Tourism Marketing*, *24*(2–3), 195–212. doi: 10.1080/10548400802092742.

Yuegu (2011). Tencent technology weibo. Retrieved from http://tech.qq.com/a/20110728/000456.htm.

20

ON THE ROAD—AGAIN

Revisiting pop music concert tourism

Carla Schriever

Setting the scene: defining ad hoc tourism in pop music fan cultures

Considering tourism as a phenomenon of distinctive directions, tourism devoted to fandom leads to different perspectives. Regardless of these differences, fandom tourism and general tourism feature multiple and interlocking dimensions: economic, social, cultural, political, institutional, as well as personal abilities. Jayapalan (2001) argues that the main reason for tourism is rooted in individual curiosity. New technologies made it easier for people to satisfy this curiosity by traveling across long distances. With the introduction of travel frequency on diverse means of transportation people "seem to enjoy the prospect of moving from one continent to another in a matter of hours" (Jayapalan, 2001, p. 1). This also affects the motivation and options of fandom travel, which I will focus on in more detail later. Jayapalan argues that experiences that are gained by traveling "have [a] profound effect upon the life of the individual as well as upon society as a whole" (2001, p. 8). In dimensions of fandom tourism this can be applied to the diversity of individual reasons and the effect on the concert travel within the micro and macro fan cultures concerning each artist's fan culture. This chapter foregrounds the motifs and dynamics of fandom travel within the fan culture around the late singer Prince over the course of 35 years. The majority of fans, who are life-course fans, a term introduced by Paul Booth (2010), have followed the artist's career since adolescence, which means they became fans during the early 1980s. Within this time their travel practices changed, caused by the alterations in the artist's tour scheduling and general approach. This needs to be considered as influencing the fandom tourism within the thematized fan culture. Being used to a structured approach, with annual concert schedules, the artist's practice was transformed by the lack of concert management. To keep track of the artist's career, fans had to adjust to ad hoc concerts. Concerts announced between half a week and two hours before the event require a lot of energy, commitment, as well as economical and personal flexibility. Focusing on the perception of these concerts shines a light on popular culture tourism within the study of fandom tourism. The performative change of the fan culture will, in the last instance, be reflected by introducing tourism that followed the artist's death in April 2016.

Theoretical underpinnings

Fandom tourism

"Travel exercises a very healthy influence on international understanding and appreciation of other people's life styles" (Jayapalan, 2001, p. 10). In comparison to an earlier use of the term "tourism," tourism nowadays features far more individual aspects. The definition adopted by International Association of Scientific Experts in tourism (AIEST) clarifies the key elements of tourism as: (1) involvement of travel by non-residents, (2) stay in the area visited in temporary nature, and (3) stay not connected to any activity involving earnings. Jayapalan argues that "tourism is therefore a composite phenomenon which embraces the incidence of a mobile population of travelers who are strangers to the places they visit" (2001, p. 6). A distinction seems to occur between pleasure-oriented tourism and non-pleasure-oriented tourism, which is undertaken in connection with financial earnings or any kind of business or educational matters. Jayapalan's study includes a distinction of reasons for tourism, which are considered as follows: spending holidays, recreation, cultural contact, relaxation, seasonal tours, social tours, or group tours.

Since I position fandom travel between the aspects of pleasure as well as status and prestige in matters of international group tours, I will focus on these aspects according to Jayapalan (2001). One of the main aspects of various forms of tourism has to be the definition of pleasure. An individual longs to escape his/her everyday life in order to gain some distance; this stance is often combined with a desire for relaxation. In the context of fandom travel, the connection between relaxation and pleasure can be suspended, and a connection between pleasure and excitement can be challenged instead.

Excitement highlights the potential pleasure and reinforces the repetition of fandom travel. Considering the effects of status and prestige-associated travel within fan culture, it becomes apparent that individual fans, for example, undertake concert travel because they consider it to be important for their status in fandom hierarchy. The community exists on the basis of shared reminiscence of concerts and other fandom associated with travel occasions. Important aspects like prestige and status are being emphasized by the financial dimension of the matter, which Jayapalan (2001) explains as a statement of wealth made to friends and family by talking about travel undertaken. The same functions are relevant within the fandom community. The most important social dimensions focusing on fandom are the international tour and the group tour. International tours are very prominent in tourism nowadays. Since the development of frequent airfare people can change their residence easily. International tours feature a high significance of fandom travel, since far distance travels are undertaken, a fact that offers a combined understanding under the aspect of prestige and status. The farther the distance, the more important the occasion and the elevation of status within the community.

The last aspect I would like to focus is the group tour. According to Jayapalan (2001), this travel exists in the area of workers or students. This definition is not sufficient enough for a focus on fandom tourism, since, for example, concert travel implies a different and interchangeable group of fans who organize a concert visit together using digital networks or personal contacts. In different music fandoms, certain travel groups are formed over the course of a certain time. They grow close by shared experiences, and some even establish groups with certain names and stable group memberships. In any target-oriented form of travel, such as fandom travel, people "mediate their identities in their individual worlds" (Church, 2007, p. 3).

The creation of the individual world could be understood as the core to fan tourism. The desire to visit fictional and non-fictional places leads to various kinds of fan tourism. Reijnders

(2011, p. 231), for example, formulates a possible motivation for fan travel considering the topic of movie fan travel, in particular for Bram Stoker's version of the movie *Dracula*. Reijnders (2011) explains the fans' desire for the comparison between the imagined and the actual space of the movie scene. Due to Stoker's detailed description, fans are able to organize tours around the landscape to combine the physical and the imagined reality. Reijnders (2011) exemplifies that the significance of place identity (e.g. as seen on a trip to the area) is constructed by the visitors (Frost, 2009, p. 86) and is not contained by the object (or area) itself. These dimensions of the comparison between the imagined and the physical realm seem very important in considering the different aspects and motivations of fan tourism in a broader genre overlapping sense. Beeton (2005) takes into account that film tourism differs from the traditional perspective on the push–pull motives of general tourism. Besides connecting the imagined to the physical existence of the place, people could also expect to spot celebrities, which could be another motive for the travel, and that connects the considerations of film-induced fandom by Beeton (2005)and the fandom tourism as examined by the fan scholar Mark Duffett (2013).

According to Duffett (2013, p. 227), "the discussion of fan tourism is framed by the metaphor of 'pilgrimage.'" This understanding reflects the emotional and spiritual reasons for fandom travel. Matt Hills extends this distinctive connection by stating: "Sacred places do not simply reproduce sacred/profane oppositions, neither are they merely 'containers' for the purity of the sacred, as these forms of behavioral legislation emerge after the fact" (Hills, 2002, p. 154). Even though Duffet differentiates fandom tourism in traveling to object-related places without the opportunity of physical co-existence with the fan object, I would like to put emphasis on concert tourism, which enables shared experiences and even traditions. This sometimes leads into the creation of certain inter-fan groups (travel groups) who develop new practices, self-designations and symbolic devices of their own (Gibson, 2005, p. 189). The concert as such offers various places for fans to meet and to exchange their experiences. McCray (2000, p. 2) notes "the culture outside the concerts became a ritual, a home-coming, almost a religion" (p. 3). These cultural traditions connect to tourism in the form of group developments, common planning and transportation, community support, and shared accommodations. Supporting one another is the key element concerning fandom travel. Whereas other popular music fandoms offer continuity by tour planning, due to marketing tour schedules and ticket sales up to half a year in advance and allow fans to organize their personal travel routes between the concerts, this was not given within the reception of concerts by the late musician Prince. Additionally, popular music fandom tourism features planned gatherings, permanent group formations, and offers compatibility to the individual work–life balance of the fans, due to their exact predictability, which was not given in the ad hoc concert organization within the cultural space and the fan community around Prince.

Methodology: redefining flexibility in popular music fandom tourism and the Purple Army (Prince Fans)

To understand the nature of this specific fandom tourism, it seems to be gainful to have a closer look at the fan community, the self-entitled "Purple Army." To evaluate my findings I conducted interviews with 30 European Prince Fans. The majority of European Prince fans are male and aged between 35 to 65.[1] Most of them became fans during their adolescence in the 1980s, which coincides with the artist's mainstream success.

The participants of my case study had to fill out a questionnaire prior to the second part of data collection, which featured a detailed interview with open-ended questions. The interviews allowed the participants to reveal more detail about their concert experiences and their fandom travels. This study derives from participant observation. I have been part of the fandom for over 10 years, but the participants were different from my identification, by age, gender, and sexual identity. The interviewees were selected on the basis of their amount of fandom-associated travel experience, which varied between 20 to 40 different occasions, mostly concerts over the course of the last 30 years. The interview focused on the questions of predictability of ad hoc concerts (in comparison to earlier times, between the 1980s and the late 1990s), the compatibility with a personal work–life balance, and the definition of priority considering concert attendance, the meaning of group travel, and the pleasure and pain relation considering the spontaneity of the artist and the nature of ad hoc concert attendance.

A majority of interviewees could agree on the fact that concert planning, including organizing travel routes, groups, and ticket scoring had been easier in the analog times, between the 1980s and the late 1990s. Many of them shared stories that included factors like buying physical tickets in store and having the chance to prepare for months in advance. This opportunity enabled many of them to organize their personal life around their fandom activities, a practice they felt "being ripped off" (Mary, 45) when Prince changed marketing and concert techniques. Due to his name-change in the 1990s and his aversion of mainstream media, ticket scoring and concert attending became an "almost underground-ish activity" (Paul, 54). Before the prevalence of digital channels, it became "highly difficult, sometimes even impossible" (Frank, 48) to follow the artist's career. The fandom restructured itself during this phase, leaving it up to hard-core fans having enough time capacity to keep track on the artist's "encrypted ways and plans" (Timo, 45).

Within the last 10 years the majority of concerts was planned on an ad hoc basis, which required the fandom to enhance its flexibility to fit the artist's demand. "I had a love hate relationship to the last phase of concert experiences, I loved it when I was able to go and I hated it when it was impossible for me" (Markus, 41). The experience of these ad hoc-concert was highly different from the strategically planned and organized tours of the 1980s and 1990s. Giving the artist the possibility to perform whenever he wanted and to support him in "being on call" (Mary, 45) allowed a different experience of artistry, which was viewed as more experimentally oriented and featured the possibility to see the artist in small venues, up close, and in a more personal setting compared to the big arenas of the past: "I enjoyed all of them, the latest ones are gigs he really enjoyed himself. In the beginning there was a whole tour planned out, in the end it was more like he wanted one, he did one" (Hans, 42). Traveling to concerts on an ad hoc basis had specific implications on economic dimensions, since it was nearly impossible to save money to go to the concert; many fans owned Prince-designated saving boxes and accounts having enough economic flexibility to act without having to think twice. In these years concert tourism was ranked as a high priority for the participants. In some cases it even gained the highest position. "There is nothing I would not call off, if he was there" (Florence, 51). "Going there" was a flexible term for most Prince fans. It could imply the next city but also a city within a distance of 1,000 kilometers from their location. This implies that all forms of transportation, public and private, were used to get to the concert venue.

The high flexibility transformed the fan culture and separated the fans in different groups: those being able to set their fandom and commute tourism as highest priority and those who were excluded due to family or job responsibilities. This can be understood as a reason for less stable traveling groups of fans, since dates were published a week or even a day before the concert was taking place. Even those who focused on attending any concert faced problems realizing it. Compared to fan cultures in which traveling together and the development of micro-groups within the fandom are important parts of fandom experience, in the Prince community this was replaced by enjoying the community in the queue. This the fans described this coming together as really supportive regarding the group identity. Sometimes concerts were organized just days after the last one, so that fans went home after the concert not knowing when and where the next concert would be, only to meet in another European city for the next one two days later. The artist made extended use of the digital platforms and networks to announce his concerts, which enhanced the need to be "On Prince Watch," a practice assigned by the community in continuously checking social networks like Facebook or Twitter for updates on the next scheduled concert.

This climaxed, for example, in Prince's ad hoc concerts in London in the spring of 2014, when he played about 20 surprise concerts within the time frame of two weeks. Attending these concerts highly affects prestige and status, combined with traveling. In the first case being able to depose work and social life for an unknown time duration like in London as the duration of the artist's stay and with such an amount of surprise concerts remained unclear until the last minute. Joining the Purple Army under the worst weather condition affects the individual fans' prestige within the fan hierarchy. The attended ad hoc concerts are of higher value, as, for example, a concert in the Netherlands, when tickets are sold just three days beforehand. Expressing commitment in fan cultures is equally as important as in religious concepts. To undertake this kind of extreme travel without knowing the possible outcome reflects the priority stance of the fan. This shows that concerts are differentiated by the size of the venue, set lists, difficulties in ticket scoring and duration—all aspects that effect each other. In this way concerts in average venues can become reevaluated in the community by, for example, having a different set list consisting of unreleased songs. Since the fan community around Prince is well informed about his catalogue, it has a strong focus on rarities. Bootlegs from concerts or of unreleased material function as a high-class exchange value within this culture. They implicate the dimension of collection, which is of high importance for the community. Besides average releases, this fan culture collected the immaterial aspects of the concert. "The more concerts you witness, the luckier you are" (Bethan, 38). In storytelling, these moments gain high significance for the identification of the individual fan. Having undertaken long-distance travel with no advance planning means gaining recognition by the surrounding fan culture. When asked if they undertook these frequent forms of travel to impress others or to gain status within the community hierarchy, all of the participants of the study argued that they only focused on "feeding the desire to see him perform" (Amy, 46). This practice can be understood as the main reason for the performative adjustment to the artist's techniques.

Considering the statement by Jayapalan (2001), that a main incitement for travel was caused by excitement, fandom tourism seems to qualify on all levels. The repetition seems to be an important factor for people returning to their favorite holiday places over the course of their lifetime. The same is true for fandom tourism, where fans return to their fan object to regain a certain feeling of excitement, which is linked to previous experiences in some cases and also with memories of their youth. These positively connoted stories seem to need an extension. A matter that can challenge an understanding for people undertaking exhausting trips through countries, sleeping in their cars or even on the street, driving thousands of kilometers for just a few hours of escapism and excitement.

In attending an ad hoc concert the community fulfills different tasks for the individual fan. It becomes the source of information. Hills (2002, p. 236) states that "the internet transformed and further facilitated the whole phenomenon of fandom." In the 1990s ad hoc concert tourism was to some extent impossible compared to the mid-2010s. "Sometime I talked to a friend, and she asked me, why I was here and not at the Prince concert, which happened in the next town—I froze immediately—I hadn't heard anything about it" (Amanda, 46). These and comparable stories were rooted in the 1990s when Prince had already turned to use digital media, but fans weren't equipped with it, which led to communication problems between fans and fan object. With the boom of digital media and the introduction of social networks fans more easily gain access to suitable information, which turned out as a sufficient form in announcing concerts on an ad hoc basis and led to another key task of this fan culture, community support. Not all fans were able to continuously keep themselves up to date, which was even more difficult because the artist chose a diversity of media platforms to announce concerts: different Twitter accounts, YouTube, personal websites (which he used to close after a couple of weeks), Facebook, and even Instagram (while referring to it as Princestagram). Links to ticket sales were sometimes posted on only one of these channels. Fans had to check all channels frequently to keep track of the artist's plans and concert schedules. "It was a kind of nightmare, I could rarely sleep well when he was on tour (which felt like always). I had to keep a constant eye on him" (Paul, 49). These factors of this certain form of fandom tourism do not solemnly reflect the difficulties in attending the concerts but also on a psychological dimension that many fans carried over the last ten years: "It felt like on-call duty, a 24/7 job—besides everything else. There was always a packed bag in my drawer, a shirt, passport, medication and my credit cards—I was always ready to leave any minute" (Frank, 41). It is not presumptuous to claim that this kind of ad hoc concert tourism restructured the whole fandom over the course of ten years. A change that effected the European fans massively. Even though these kinds of travel were undertaken by the interviewees and many other fans as frequently as possible, the financial and emotional encumbrances have to be considered while focusing on the touristic behavior within this fan community.

A new dimension of travel: post-artist fandom travel

Since Prince's death on April 21, 2016, enormous changes have affected the fan community and the dimension of fandom and tourism. This change can be visualized best in the dimension of proceedings in the American fan community since April 21.

Since October 6, 2016, fans are able to visit Paisley Park, Prince's residence for some time, including a studio complex featuring various connections to the work corpora of Prince. Paisley Park has a transcendental connection to every Prince Fan, since the artist wrote a song entitled Paisley Park in the beginning of the 1980s. It became the hymn of the Purple Army. Over the course of almost 30 years, many fans (even half of the European study participants) have visited Paisley Park. Many of them shared stories of the beginning of the 1990s when the artist used to organize CD-release celebrations including workshops and get-togethers for his fans. Some of them had the chance to get there during the last decade, when he organized after-parties on an almost regular basis. Paisley Park has always been both a real destination and a fictional place. This understanding can be proven by a competition Unsie Zuege published on the website of half-pricebooks.com in the beginning of April 2016, in which she asked readers to choose their favorite fictional place in the 2016 tournament of fictional places. The result was choosing Paisley Park as a fictional place. The creators of the poll explain: "It is a fictional place that became real" (with reference to the song featured on the 1985 album *Around the World in a Day*) (Zuege, 2016). This leads to an understanding of Paisley Park as a distant and as such desirable travel destination. By turning it into a museum this dream came true for many American fans. For this reason I changed the scope of my study to include the changing process and meaning of tourism for the fan community. I interviewed 15 American fans who have been to Paisley Park after it became a museum. My questions focused on the dimension of travel activities regarding Paisley Park. Many of them had previously been engaged in ad hoc concert travel and described traveling to Paisley Park as "more planable" and "without risk" (Ada, 44), which had made it easier to enjoy the travel as such and to connect it more easily with other aspects.

This also simplifies the planning of group activities around the visit. It connects pleasure and group travel and challenges a different approach to the subject of travel, which experienced a form of transformation.

Fans who consider traveling to Paisley Park pointed out that they had been doing it for merely the same reason as the concert travel—to seek closure with the artist. This closure evolves on a different basis compared to the physical dimension and aims to compensate for the lack of physical approachability. By visiting Paisley Park, additional travel motivations seem to be fulfilled. Since the building was transformed into a museum, visiting it evokes educational dimensions. Fans and other visitors can expand their knowledge about Prince and even gain a taste of his life at the Park, for example eating Prince's favorite dishes prepared by his private cook. Additionally, there is an exhibition of clothes, instruments, and awards, and also a shop for memorabilia, which connects it to merchandise consumption known from concerts.

Comparing the fandom tourism post-April 21, 2016, it should be noted that fans who had less ability to attend concerts because of their ad hoc nature are now in charge of planning their trips and saving money for it. Even though the distance between the destination within the United States and the location of the majority of the study's participants in Europe expands costs, and the necessity of structured planning was mentioned by many of them. On the one hand, traveling to Paisley Park is said to be equal with reaching a dream destination and having the ability to visit the artist's associated places. On the other hand, ad hoc concert travel was fueled by extreme excitement and surprise, which many people felt was an important part of their fan culture.

Implications for popular culture tourism

Transforming Paisley Park into a museum features implications that are important for different forms and motifs of popular culture tourism. The sacred dimension of visiting a place associated with an artist features a meta-connection between the artist and the fan. Additionally, it affects the positioning of the individual fan concerning fandom hierarchy. Being financially able and, in the demonstrated case, emotionally stable enough to take this kind of trip, divides fans in groups just as the quantity of attended concerts and the quality (considering length, venue size, and set list) of these events are important to the fan culture. Focusing on the implications of popular culture tourism, this kind of ad hoc fandom tourism allows a focus on the adjustment between fans and fan objects over time. Even though Williams (2015, p. 28) argues that "fans may gain comfort from the routine of their fandom (for example by anticipating a regular scheduling)" in concerts like, for example, the regular tour scheduling of Madonna or Bruce Springsteen. Furthermore, Williams notes that fans were capable and "can deal with the unexpected and adjust to changes in routine" (p. 28). In the case of the Purple Army, routine always meant expecting the unexpected, this dimension led to the creation of a fandom self-narrative highlighting spontaneity and prioritization of fandom activities. In consideration of the diverse adjustment between fan community and artist the conducted research emphasizes on revisiting fandom tourism as a form of individual and collaborative adjustment processes that allow artists and fans to participate in a shared venture within the modes and practices of popular culture.

Note

1 The age of participants are given in parentheses for all subsequent quotations.

References

Beeton, S. (2005), *Film induced tourism*, Clevedon: Channel View Publications.

Booth, P. (2010), *Digital fandom: New media studies*, New York: Peter Lang.

Church, A. (2007), *Tourism, power and space*, London and New York: Routledge.

Duffett, M. (2013), *Understanding fandom: Introduction to the study of media fan cultures*, London and New York: Bloomsbury.

Frost, W. (2009), From backlot to runaway production: Exploring location and authenticity in film-induced tourism, *Tourism Review International*, 13 (2), 85–92.

Gibson, C. (2005), *Music and tourism: On the road again*, Clevedon: Channel View Publications.

Hills, M. (2002), *Fan cultures*, London and New York: Routledge.

Jayapalan, N. (2001), *Introduction to tourism*, New Delhi: Atlantic.

McCray-Pattacini, M. (2000), Deadheads yesterday & today: An audience study, *Journal of Popular Music and Society*, 24 (1), 1–24.

Reijnders, S. (2011), *Places of the imagination: Media, tourism, culture*, Farnham: Ashgate.

Williams, R. (2015), *Post object fandom: Television, identity and self-narrative*, London and New York: Bloomsbury.

Zuege, U. (2016), *Paisley Park, where fiction becomes reality*, www.swnewsmedia.com/eden_prairie_news/news/opinion/columnists/zuege_unsie/paisley-park-where-fiction-becomes-reality/article_448e0533-b7e3-5684-9c0f-53857146d51d.html/ (accessed October 14, 2016).

21

MUSIC FANS AS TOURISTS

The mysterious ways of individual and social dimensions

Maria Lexhagen

Setting the scene

In popular culture tourism people travel to and visit places associated with various popular culture phenomena. Following seminal work and state of the art research defining fans and fandoms (Ford, De Kosnik, & Harrington, 2011; Gray, Sandvoss, & Harrington, 2007; Jenkins, 2012; Lewis, 1992), popular culture tourists can to varying degrees be considered as fans. Studying popular culture tourism as a type of fan practice or fan activity is based on focusing on what fans pursue in everyday life if fandom is defined as a role in relation to popular culture (Duffett, 2015). Specifically, music tourism "can be seen as a range of practices where sites of music production and expression become the points of attraction for tourists" (Gibson & Connell, 2005, p. 16). It is an act of consumption that involves complex rituals and suggests the powerful emotive role of music in contemporary society (Gibson & Connell, 2005). People travel to music events and attractions as well as places associated with music either as fans, pilgrims, concert goers, festival attendees, or perhaps to places where the sound of music is closely associated to the experience of place (Lashua, Spracklen, & Long, 2014). Research that uses various perspectives of place and geography has described music tourism in previous literature (c.f. Carney, 1997; Cohen, 1991, 2007; Cohen, Knifton, & Leonard, 2013; Connell & Gibson, 2003; Gibson & Connell, 2012; Krims, 2007; Leaver & Schmidt, 2009; Watson, Hoyler, & Mager, 2009; Xie, Osumare & Ibrahim, 2007). However, it should be noted that for popular culture tourism, and in general, it is important to acknowledge that fan practices or fan activities are only indicative of fandom as a role. People can do things for any number of other reasons outside the role of fandom, such as for the pure pleasure of listening to a piece of music or as part of a musician's working life (Duffett, 2015).

From the perspective of the fan and the tourist "Music provides an important and emotive narrative for tourists, as an expression of culture, a form of heritage, a signifier of place and a marker of moments" (Lashua et al., 2014, p. 5). However, the concept of fans as tourists is often studied in the context of sport tourism and sports fans (Gibson, Willming, & Holdnak, 2003; Hoye & Lillis, 2008; Jones, 2008; Smith & Stewart, 2007; Weed, 2010; Yu, 2010). Whereby studies of identity, motives, and fandoms have found that this influences their likelihood of travelling to places associated with their interest. Furthermore, in popular culture tourism research and research on fans as tourists, motives, experiences, practices, involvement, identity, and community-related social behavior or fan culture is in focus (Lundberg & Lexhagen, 2012, 2014; Lundberg, Lexhagen, & Mattsson, 2012). Yet, there is limited research that brings together knowledge on popular culture fans and fandoms, sports fans and tourism, and music fans and tourism, for the purpose of understanding how and why music fans choose to travel and how the concepts of identity, involvement, motives, and social behavior are interrelated in the context of music tourism. Understanding the potentially complex interrelationships between individual and social dimensions of fan practice related to music tourism can help to further our knowledge and explain fan motives as well as behavior. This in turn, can benefit stakeholders in both the creative and tourism industries as well as provide a general understanding of societal changes where popular culture phenomena influence different aspects of society.

Two internationally well-known examples of popular culture music enjoying lasting careers, a global audience, and fandom are ABBA and U2. Both these examples are also clearly linked to a number of places across the world that can act as destinations for popular culture fan travels (see Figure 21.2). For example, Ireland, Dublin, America, and southern France are linked to U2. Sweden, Brighton, UK, and Australia are associated with ABBA. These are places where members of the bands lived, recorded, performed, had photo shootings, places where attractions such as museums associated to their music are located, or perhaps even places where fans have created an association to their music.

Sweden's most successful music export, ABBA, have sold more than 400 million records (ABBA official site, 2012) and in May 2013 ABBA the Museum located in Stockholm, Sweden, opened its doors to the world. Visitors to the museum are part of the experience as many interactive elements, such as singing with an ABBA hologram and singing in a replica of the Polar Studio, are available alongside exhibitions of costumes, gold records, original items, and memorabilia. The museum has attracted a large number of visitors and is often ranked as a top attraction for visitors to Stockholm and Sweden.

U2 started out as a band in 1976 in Dublin, Ireland, and has since gained a massive global audience through their album releases, live tours, and other musical productions. U2 have sold almost 200 million records and are highly ranked in the *Rolling Stone* magazine's list of the 100 greatest artists of all time. They have toured the world for more than four decades and are strongly associated with Dublin and Ireland as well as being well known for their campaigning in human rights and various philanthropic causes.

These two examples are used in this chapter as empirical cases to illustrate individual and social dimensions of music fans as tourists.

Theoretical underpinnings

Tourists' motives have traditionally been described as continuums of seeking–escaping, push–pull, and personal rewards–interpersonal rewards. On one side of the first spectrum seeking–escaping, we find intrinsic motives where the tourist aims at satisfying internal needs. On the other side of the continuum, the tourist attempts to find release from everyday life by engaging in touristic activities. The second well-documented travel motives continuum is push–pull. The former entails psychological and social tourist characteristics that drive the tourist to partake in travel while the latter refers to destination-specific characteristics that steer tourists' destination choice (Crompton, 1979; Dann, 1977; Uysal, Gahan, & Martin, 1993). The personal rewards–interpersonal rewards continuum focuses on rest, relaxation, and ego enhancement (personal rewards) on the one hand, and social interaction with family and friends (interpersonal rewards) on the other (Uysal et al., 1993).

To complement this, fan motivations have been divided into three dimensions: psychological, socio-cultural, and social belonging. Examples of psychological motives are eustress (positive stress or arousal or stress release), escapism (diversion from daily life), aesthetic pleasure (enjoyment of the beauty of the activity), and drama and entertainment (intense enjoyment) (Crawford, 2004; Fink, Trail, & Anderson, 2002; Smith & Stewart, 2007; Trail & James, 2001; Wann, 1995; Wann, Melnick, Russel, & Pease, 2001; Weed & Bull, 2004). Socio-cultural motives include spending time with family, friends, and like-minded (social interaction) and cultural connections such as "mythical images," icons, and symbols (Segrave & Chu, 1996; Smith & Stewart, 2007; Trail & James, 2001). Social belongingness motives consist of tribal connections and vicarious achievement and self-esteem. The former entails being a part of a "tribe" with norms, routines, symbols, rituals, and language. Vicarious achievements are reached by being associated to a success(ful) person/team and by this attain some form of empowerment (Morris, 1981; Sutton, McDonald, Milne, & Cimperman, 1997; Trail, Anderson, & Fink, 2000). Lundberg and Lexhagen (2012) found that indeed travelling fans were motivated by their interest in a popular culture phenomenon to a larger extent than merely by the destination itself, which indicates the need for studying fan motives in order to fully understand popular culture tourism.

The extent of consumers' involvement with an object is said to impact behavioral decisions (Zaichkowsky, 1985, 1986). Involvement is defined by Park, Lee, and Han (2007) as "the perceived personal relevance of a product based on the individual consumer's needs, interests, and values" (p. 129). According to Andrews, Durvasula, and Akhter (1990) the level of intensity in involvement varies by product types, situations, and individual conditions, or as with Huang, Chou and Lin (2010), involvement can be understood based on personal involvement, product involvement, and situation involvement. This model has been applied to popular culture fans and their use of social media by Lexhagen, Larson, and Lundberg (2013), showing that the inner needs, interests, and values of fans, as well as perceptions about the popular culture phenomenon are important for explaining tourism behavior.

From a psychology point of view, fan identity is an important concept that also relates to the "self" (the individual component of identity) and that in fact an individual possesses more than one "self" (Markus & Nurius, 1986). Wlodarczyk (2014) shows that active and passive music fans differ significantly in establishing their personality profiles but also that fans and non-fans do not differ a lot in terms of personality, values, plans, and selves. Research on sport spectators has shown that the more fans identify themselves with the object of their fascination, the more likely it is that they will travel: "Fans with stronger identification have sport more deeply embedded in their self-concept, and are more likely to attend games and travel greater distances to do so, purchase merchandise, spend more on tickets and products, and remain loyal" (Smith & Stewart, 2007, p. 162) (see Figure 21.1).

This idea may be further studied by the sociological concept of serious leisure, which has both an individual and a group component. Robert Stebbins (1979, 1992, 2005, 2006) found that some individuals are committed to free time sport or hobby activities to an extent that it may be regarded as a lifelong leisure vocation. Serious leisure therefore entails a long-term, systematic engagement with any recreational activity (jazz playing, charity work, film interest, or mountaineering), resulting in developing specific skills, knowledge, and experience. Serious leisure and regularly exercised recreational activities are intertwined with one's self-image, and may mark social status or belonging to a subculture.

In popular culture tourism the dimension of social behavior and group-related social identity is believed to be important. Social identity and a sense of belonging are important for our understanding of any social community. Social identity is widely used to explain group and collective behavior (Bagozzi & Lee, 2002). Dholakia, Bagozzi, and Klein Pearo (2004)

Figure 21.1 Fan event – New York Rangers first home game for season 15/16.

Source: author's own photo.

conceptualized social identity as having cognitive, affective, and evaluative components. The cognitive component concerns how the individual forms a self-awareness of virtual community membership, the affective component implies that social identity includes a sense of emotional involvement with the group, and evaluative social identity is focused on the evaluation of self-worth on the basis of belonging to the community. Lexhagen et al. (2013) studied the importance of social identity in relation to popular culture fans and tourists and their use of online communities, and found that social identity was not as important as involvement but that affective social identity was relatively important.

An important aspect of the fandom is the shared collective experience with other fans. Fan communities may be real or virtual, converging on digital platforms to exchange information to build clusters of social affiliations with like-minded peers across geographical or temporal divides. Accordingly, popular culture tourism research may benefit from theoretical approaches highlighting the role and social dynamics of consumer tribes (Cova and Cova, 2002; Maffesoli 1996). Consumer culture theorists (Arnould, 2006; Arnould & Thompson, 2005; Firat & Venkatesh, 1995) suggest that citizens in the twenty-first century are more interested in social links and the identities that come with them, than the pure consumption of objects. Tribes are heterogeneous networks of individuals, who are linked by a shared passion or emotion towards a brand or a product. People sharing cultural or subcultural traits are today gathering in virtual communities and the emergence of these "tribes" is often accountable to brand fandom or other consumption interests (Cova, Kozinets, & Shankar, 2007). Popular culture tourism often manifests itself in tribal gatherings where the sense of community is as important as the fancied story or characters. Social media augments non-digital tribal practices and ceremonies and redefines the communicative practices of traditional communication channels (Gyimóthy, Lundberg, Lindström, Lexhagen, & Larson, 2015).

Studying music fans, Nuttall et al. (2011) found segments that can help explain social identity and behavior towards furthering knowledge on individual and group dimensions of fans and discuss the impact on tourism and experiences. For instance, one segment is described as *the loyalists*, which is a tribe that demonstrates a deep affection and loyalty towards bands or artists. This shares many similar characteristics to "cult fans," which in turn Hills (2002) describes as committed, knowledgeable, and fan-community orientated. Alternatively, another segment labeled *the experience seeker*, which is a tribe that shares certain traits with *the loyalists*, such as their high passion for music. They also consider physical ownership important, but they do so for different reasons, namely a desire for memorabilia and nostalgia and a greater need for satisfaction through experiential consumption. Furthermore, they place a high emphasis on mood enhancement and socializing through music consumption and are heavy consumers of concerts and live music events.

Methodology

Primary data for studying individual and social dimensions of music tourism was collected in 2013 through a quantitative online survey, of the ABBA fandom (see Table 21.1). The survey was implemented through non-probabilistic snowball sampling (often used in hidden populations) by advertising the link to the survey on the official ABBA fan club website, other ABBA fan club websites, ABBA-related Facebook groups, Twitter, and on ABBA the Museums Facebook page. A total of 1,315 responses were collected with varying number of respondents for each question (1,004 completed the entire survey).

Table 21.1 Sample descriptives: ABBA fan online survey

Item	Percentage/age/country
Male	58%
Average age	46 years
Family status single household	41%
Family status married/partner with children	15%
Family status married/partner without children	26%
University degree (2 years or more)	60%
Country of residence (in order of number of respondents)	UK
	Netherlands
	Germany
	Sweden
	Australia
	Belgium

A survey on U2 fans

Secondary data for studying music tourism was obtained from the worldwide fan survey conducted in April 2012 by the fan website @U2 (www.atu2.com). The goal of the survey was to learn what U2 fans think about a variety of topics and questions related to U2 and U2 fandom. The survey included 116 questions in 9 categories, and the survey was open from April 5 through April 3. U2 fans in 79 countries around the world participated and 3,530 fans completed the whole survey and 4,069 finished at least the first section (atu2.com, 2016) (see Table 21.2).

In addition, the empirical account in this chapter of my personal experiences as a U2 fan can be said to follow the basic principles of participant observation often used in ethnographic research (Jorgensen, 2015). More specifically, inspiration was drawn from key features, such as complete member research status, analytic reflexivity, narrative visibility of researcher's self, and commitment to theoretical analysis of analytic auto-ethnography introduced by Anderson (2006). In participant observation the researcher studies the life of a group by sharing its activities. Similarly, being a researcher with a personal interest in a specific popular culture phenomenon is sometimes referred to as being an aca-fan. As an aca-fan you are supposed to have the opportunity to minimize the distance between the researcher and what is actually studied in that you can get intimate and capture your own subjective responses to popular culture and thereby gain knowledge on how popular culture works our emotions (Jenkins, 2006). For the purpose of this chapter the empirical account is limited to a reflection, by way of interviewing myself, of my own motivations, and behavior rather than that of the U2 fandom as a group.

ABBA fans

The results of the online survey clearly show that there is a phenomenon, which could be labeled as ABBA tourism (see Table 21.3).

Furthermore, 85 percent of the visitors to the ABBA museum had ABBA as their primary motive for the trip. The results also indicate the importance of fandom for choosing to go to the destination since more than 70 percent of the respondents state that they would not have visited the destination of their most recent trip if it wasn't for their interest in ABBA.

Table 21.2 Sample descriptives: U2 fan survey

Item	Percentage/age/country
Male	68%
Average age	30–39 years
Country of residence (in order of number of respondents)	United States
	Italy
	England
	Canada
	Australia
	Ireland
	Netherlands
	France

Table 21.3 Online survey results: ABBA fans' travel behavior

Item	Percentage (%)
Visited Sweden because of ABBA	50
Visited the ABBA museum	32
Travelled "in the footsteps of" ABBA (not including a visit to the museum)	60
Travelled more than 10 times with ABBA as primary motive	40
Likely or very likely to do another ABBA-related trip or participate in event in the future	72
Likely or very likely to visit Stockholm again	88
Likely or very likely to visit other parts of Sweden in the future	76

Interestingly, the study also illustrates the importance of both individual and social aspects of motivation for the trip. On a Likert-type scale (1 = not important, 7 = very important) the respondents stated that the five most important motives (ranging from 5.3 to 5.9) for their trip was "to experience an ABBA atmosphere," "to participate in activities that are fun," "to experience excitement," "to experience new and different things," and "to have fun with friends and/or family."

Some examples of the degree of involvement between the respondents and their interest in ABBA can be seen in Table 21.4.

However, other results are inconclusive such as the degree to which travelling in the footsteps of ABBA is important for the self-identity of fans. Instead, the majority of the respondents strongly disagree that participation in an event or trip helps them to feel acceptable, improves the way they are perceived by others, helps them obtain social approval, helps them make a good impression on other people, or enables them to interact and communicate with other people.

Regarding the importance of Internet activity by fans, 40 percent state that they use the Internet once or several times a day for visiting ABBA-related websites, blogs, or communities. They look mostly for general information about ABBA or the members of the band as well as read or watch ABBA-related content. Also, the results show that 42 percent thought the Internet was the most important source of information for their most recent trip. A majority state that they strongly agree that they have used information in blogs and communities, to plan their trip, that the information was helpful, and that they have shared their experiences on blogs or in communities after their trip or participation in an event.

The study also demonstrates what Internet activity represents to them in terms of involvement. For example, the majority of respondents state that they strongly agree that they are

Table 21.4 Online survey results: ABBA fans' involvement

Item	Percentage (%)
Perceive themselves as ABBA fans	72
Listen to ABBA every day	34
Strongly agree[a] that they are interested in ABBA	78
Strongly agree[a] that ABBA is essential to them	24
Strongly agree[a] that they purchase ABBA products to reward themselves	27
Strongly agree[a] that purchased products symbolize their personality and character	22

[a] Likert-type scale, 1 = strongly disagree, 7 = strongly agree

Figure 21.2　Famous photo of ABBA as a backdrop for photo opportunity for fans, from ABBA the Museum.

Source: author's own photo.

interested in information and photos of ABBA in blogs or communities, that they feel this information or these photos are appealing, and that when reading information or watching photos or videos they feel ABBA is relevant in their lives. Additionally, results show that users, when using the Internet, feel that ABBA means a lot to them and that using the Internet generates a perceived efficiency when searching for information in blogs and communities. The results also support the importance of individual dimensions in that respondents strongly agree that they feel happy, pleased, contented, and stimulated when using blogs and communities.

However, again other results of the study do not fully support the importance of creating self-identity through the use of blogs and communities. Instead, the results suggest that a majority of the respondents strongly disagree that their self-image fits with the identity of the group, that their personal identity is strengthened when they interact in the community, that they are very attached to the user group or that they have a strong feeling of belonging toward the user group, and that they are a valuable and/or important member of the group.

U2 fans

The fan survey by @u2 provides some interesting and informative results in relation to individual and social dimensions of music fans. Most of the fans, 33 percent, became a fan of U2 between 1984 and 1990, but some as late as 2009 or later. Approximately 27 percent have travelled to Ireland because of U2 and/or Irelands' connection to U2 and about 5 percent have stayed at a hotel in Dublin owned by members of the band. The results also show that slightly more than 28 percent of the fans have seen 3–6 concerts live in person, 49 percent have travelled within their own country, 26 percent have travelled to another country, and 15 percent have travelled to another continent to see a live concert.

Approximately 80 percent own all U2 albums and 72 percent of the respondents say they have a collection of memorabilia or merchandise besides albums and singles. Also, 58 percent state that they have been inspired by U2 to join an organization or become active in some cause or campaign. As an example of results that indicate a link between fandom and individual dimensions such as identity, the results show that approximately equal shares (20–29 percent) of respondents feel that one of the band member's personality is closest to their own.

The majority of fans, 26 percent, say that they discovered the U2 online fan community between 2002 and 2005, but some as early as 1994. On a typical day 74 percent of the respondents state that they spend 30 minutes or less visiting U2-related websites, blogs, message boards/ forums, etc.

Inspired by analytic auto-ethnography, below I introduce my own personal reflections as a music aca-fan.

Almost 30 years ago a friend first introduced me to the music of U2, and since then I have considered myself a fan of U2. I have all their records in various formats and listen to their music daily. I have been to six live concerts in Sweden, both at indoor and outdoor arenas and venues. Furthermore, for more than 10 years, I have been a paying member of the official U2 fan club and I own several merchandise items such as t-shirts, books and photos, or graphical designs. Buying items such as t-shirts, albums, dvds, and books is rewarding and makes me feel happy and proud. I regularly visit general news websites or U2-related websites such as u2.com or atu2.com, with varying frequency. Most often depending on upcoming tours or new releases of albums or songs. Mostly I'm interested in general information and news about U2 but I also listen to their music on u2.com or via Spotify, watch videos on u2.com or on Youtube, read comic strips by other fans, look for information about band members and personal news about band members, or U2-related projects such as the RED campaign. Also, I have bought and read documentary magazines and books about the band and individual band members. Keeping up to date and digging in to details of the band and their history makes me feel good and is something I like to do to relax and reward myself. My interest also extends to other artists associated in some way or another with U2 such as music producers and DJs, downloading remixes of U2 songs, or listening to other things they have done, and the famous photographer Anton Corbijn in the form of buying his books or visiting exhibitions.

Members of the fan club get a newsletter that I always read and if there are invitations to submit comments or answer questions I most often respond. Also, I follow the band's official Instagram account and I sometimes post U2-related content or my own photos and comments on my social media profiles on Facebook, Twitter, and Instagram. For instance, I would post photos of when I have purchased tickets to a concert or got a package of a new record in my mail box.

I have never creatively contributed to the fan community of U2 by designing art, recording new versions of songs, or in any other way created something of my own as a tribute to U2. However, I often tell people I'm a U2 fan (and will frequently fall into referencing U2 lyrics when I tell stories or talk to people) and my children are well aware of my interest in and knowledge on U2's music. One example is that one late Thursday evening in the fall a few years ago, I drove 1.5 hours with my children to a movie theater in a small village that was showing U23D. I thought this would be a great opportunity to introduce them to U2 live performances since I have so far not been able to take them to a real live concert.

In trying to express my feelings towards U2 and being a fan of U2, I would say that their music really resonates with me and I feel somehow connected to their sound and lyrics as well as performances. I'm proud to be a fan and I have great respect for their work and often look forward to their next release whatever that might be. Also, I feel akin to other fans and I appreciate the atmosphere created by fans in concerts and in online communities and communication. Being a U2 fan is important to me. One example of how important is that on one occasion when I was celebrating an important personal event I invited a band to play U2 music live. Another example is that I still carry around an old concert ticket from 1994 in my wallet.

Furthermore, not only have I travelled to cities in my home country to attend concerts, I have also travelled to several destinations related to my interest in U2. I have travelled to Dublin, Ireland, for a business conference but chose to extend my stay so that I could take the opportunity to also experience U2-related sites in Dublin such as the old and new recording studios, pubs, and exhibitions as well as hotels, restaurants, and neighborhoods (see Figure 21.3). I used mostly information from the Internet to plan my trip to Dublin using for instance the Guide to U2's Dublin on the atu2.com website. Twice I was in southern France in a village east of Nice that plays a significant role in both the personal and professional lives of the band and individual members. On both occasions I shared this experience with different groups of friends who didn't identify themselves as U2 fans. However, both visits made a profound impression on me that lasted long after I left and still represents strong, vivid, and important memories for me. Another time I was in Barcelona, Spain, with a group of friends and we went to visit the football arena Camp Nou. While they enjoyed experiencing the arena for its significance in the history of football, I was enjoying an imaginary experience of the first concert of the U2360 tour in 2009, which was at the Camp Nou arena. Furthermore, I recently had the opportunity to travel to Berlin for work and of course I instantly planned to extend my stay to explore U2's Berlin where I, for example, took a guided tour of Hansa Studios.

I expect that travelling to destinations associated to U2 and exploring significant places related to their music and history will continue to be an important motive for me when making travel plans in the future. For instance, in 2017 I will finally get to experience a live U2 concert at Croke Park in Dublin, Ireland.

Figure 21.3 U2 exhibition at the Little Museum, Dublin, Ireland.
Source: author's own photo.

Implications for popular culture tourism

Music fans as tourists are characterized by many different motives and behaviors with both individual and social dimensions. Previously established categories of motives, such as the push and pull continuum, in tourism research prove not to be sufficient for a comprehensive understanding of music fans as tourists. Instead, a more complex set of motives need to be considered where greater emphasis is put on a variety of elements of psychological, socio-cultural, and social belonging. Specifically, the empirical results presented in this chapter suggest that individual dimensions of fandom, such as the elicited emotions from being involved, are important aspects of motivation to travel to places associated with the music/band. Furthermore, social dimensions are also important factors to consider and further explore both in an online and offline context. Therefore, it is suggested that elements such as atmosphere or belongingness need to be considered especially in the context of Internet activity, such as interaction in social media. Also, group-related dimensions, such as emotional involvement with a group, are important in explaining motives and behavior, which is particularly evident from the importance of Internet activity and online interaction with other fans. Little is also known about how individual and social dimensions of music fans as tourists contribute to expectations, experiencing as well as value and satisfaction in the pre-, during and post-trip phases. For instance, how does intrinsic motivation to engage with the phenomenon, such as listening to music, when planning the trip influence the experience of emotional and social involvement at a concert or in a museum? Moreover, what influence does that have on the creation of motives to travel more or engage in tribal communication and practice? Or, how does the evolving interest in a popular culture phenomenon transform into a life time of fan-related travel? Concepts such as learning and adding new experiences and knowledge most likely influence the extent to which travelling fans lose or gain interest and pursue or abandon popular culture travel.

Like the title of the ABBA song, "Slipping Through My Fingers," establishing valid and reliable knowledge on music fans' identity formation from an individual and social aspect and its importance in explaining fan activity, such as popular culture tourism, remains to be further studied. Research is inconclusive in regards to what role the concept of identity and self actually play in individual and social dimensions of motivation and behavior of music fans and tourists. It seems as if passive and active fans have different profiles but not necessarily fans and non-fans. Therefore, the notion that there is a certain profile or personality of people that make them fans and that they are hence different to other people, is not supported by research.

The practical implications of research on music fans as tourists are related to both marketing and management of destinations and popular culture tourism events and attractions. A more in-depth understanding, *knowing me knowing you*, of the complex interrelationships between individual and social dimensions of fan activities, can facilitate new marketing strategies as well as innovation in destinations, events, and attractions. For example, if music tourists are mostly influenced by individual dimensions in forming their motive for travel then these aspects need to be considered when designing the experience or tourism service as well as in marketing communication. Yet, on the other hand, since social and group-related dimensions are important, for example, for searching and finding information in order to plan a trip, this then needs to be reflected in the marketing and communication strategies of tourism stakeholders by considering how and where to distribute information and offers.

On a *Beautiful Day*, it is proposed that, in line with the research by Nuttall et al. (2011) on segments of music fans, an interesting future agenda for research in music tourism is to link the concept of fan and fandom with the central concept of customer loyalty in tourism research on destination development and management. It is believed that fan studies can provide new aspects and inform scholars as well as practitioners into a re-conceptualization of customer loyalty in destinations where social and emotional aspects can take center stage.

References

ABBA the Official Site (2012). *Stardom*. Retrieved from www.abbasite.com/stardom

Anderson, L. (2006). Analytic autoethnography. *Journal of Contemporary Ethnography*, *35*(4), 373–395.

Andrews, J. C., Durvasula, S., & Akhter, S. H. (1990). A framework for conceptualizing and measuring the involvement construct in advertising research. *Journal of Advertising*, *19*(4), 27–40.

Arnould, E. J. (2006). Service-dominant logic and consumer culture theory: natural alliances in an emerging paradigm. *Marketing theory*, *6*(3), 293–298.

Arnould, E. J. & Thompson, C. J. (2005). Consumer culture theory: twenty years of research. *Journal of Consumer Research*, *31*(March), 868–882.

Atu2.com (2016). *2012 U2 Fan Survey*. Retrieved from www.atu2.com

Bagozzi, R. P. & Lee, K.-H. (2002). Multiple routes for social influence: the role of compliance, internalization and social identity. *Social Psychology Quarterly*, *65*(3), 226–247.

Carney, G. (1997). *The sounds of people and places: readings in geography of American folk and popular music*. Lanham, MD: University Press of America.

Cohen, S. (1991). *Rock culture in Liverpool: popular music in the making*. Oxford: Oxford University Press.

Cohen, S. (2007). *Decline, renewal and the city in popular music culture: beyond the Beatles*. Aldershot, UK: Ashgate.

Cohen, S., Knifton, R., & Leonard, M. (Eds.) (2013). *Sites of popular music heritage: memories, histories, places*. London: Routledge.

Connell, J. & C. Gibson (2003). *Sound tracks: popular music, identity and place*. London: Routledge.

Cova, B. & Cova, V. (2002). Tribal marketing: the tribalisation of society and its impact on the conduct of marketing. *European Journal of Marketing*, *36*(5/6), 595–620.

Cova, B., Kozinets, R. V., & Shankar, A. (2007). *Consumer tribes*. Abingdon, UK: Routledge.

Crawford, G. (2004). *Consuming sport: fans, sport and culture*. London: Routledge.

Crompton, J. L. (1979). Motivations for pleasure vacation. *Annals of Tourism Research*, *6*, 408–24.

Dann, G. M. S. (1977). Anomi, ego-enhancement and tourism. *Annals of Tourism Research*, *4*, 184–194.

Dholakia, U. M., Bagozzi, R. P., & Klein Pearo, L. (2004). A social influence model of consumer participation in network- and small-group-based virtual communities. *International Journal of Research in Marketing*, *21*, 241–263.

Duffett, M. (2015). Introduction: fan practices. *Popular Music and Society*, *38*(1), 1–6.

Fink, J. S., Trail, G. S., & Anderson, D. F. (2002). An examination of team identification: which motives are most salient to its existence? *International Sports Journal*, *6*(2), 195–207.

Firat, A. F. & Venkatesh, A. (1995). Liberatory postmodernism and the re-enchantment of consumption. *Journal of Consumer Research*, *22* (December), 239–267.

Ford, S., De Kosnik, A., & Harrington, C. L. (2011). *The survival of soap opera: transformations for a new media era*. Jackson, MI: University Press of Mississippi.

Gibson, C. & Connell, J. (2005). *Music and tourism: on the road again*. Aspects of Tourism. Clevedon, UK: Channel View.

Gibson, C. & Connell, J. (2012). *Music festivals and regional development in Australia*. Farnham, UK: Ashgate.

Gibson, H. J., Willming, C., & Holdnak, A. (2003). Small-scale event sport tourism: fans as tourists. *Tourism Management*, *24*(2), 181–190.

Gray, J. A., Sandvoss, C., & Harrington, C. L. (2007). *Fandom: identities and communities in a mediated world*. New York: New York University Press.

Gyimóthy, S., Lundberg, C., Lindström, K. N., Lexhagen, M., & Larson, M. (2015). Popculture tourism: a research manifesto. In D. Chambers & T. Rakić (Eds.), *Tourism research frontiers: beyond the boundaries of knowledge*. Tourism Social Science Series, Vol. 20. Bingley, UK: Emerald Group, pp. 13–26.

Hills, M. (2002). *Fan cultures*. London: Routledge.

Hoye, R. & Lillis, K. (2008). Travel motivations of Australian football league fans: an exploratory study. *Managing Leisure*, *13*(1), 13–22.

Huang, C. Y., Chou, C. J., & Lin, P.C. (2010). Involvement theory in constructing bloggers' intention to purchase travel products. *Tourism Management*, *31*(4), 513–526.

Jenkins, H. (2006). *Convergence culture: where old and new media collide*. New York: New York University Press.

Jenkins, H. (2012). *Fan studies*. Retrieved from Oxford Bibliographies. doi: 10.1093/obo/978019 9791286-0027

Jones, I. (2008). Sport fans and spectators as sport tourists. *Journal of Sport & Tourism, 13*(3), 161–164.

Jorgensen, D. L. (2015). *Participant observation: emerging trends in the social and behavioral sciences: an interdisciplinary searchable and linkable source*. Retrieved from Wiley Online Library. doi: 10.1002/9781118900772. etrds0247

Krims, A. (2007). *Music and urban geography*. New York: Routledge.

Lashua, B., Spracklen, K., & Long, P. (2014). Introduction to the special issue: music and tourism. *Tourist Studies, 14*(1), 3–9.

Leaver, D. & Schmidt, R. A. (2009). Before they were famous: music-based tourism and a musician's hometown roots. *Journal of Place Management and Development, 2*(3), 220–229.

Lewis, L. A. (1992). *The adoring audience: fan culture and popular media*. London: Routledge.

Lexhagen, M., Larson, M., & Lundberg, C. (2013). The virtual fan(g) community: social media and pop culture tourism. In S. Gyimóthy, A. M. Munar, & L. Cai (Eds.), *Tourism social media: transformations in identity, community and culture*. Tourism Social Science Series, Vol. *18*. Bingley, UK: Emerald, pp. 133–157.

Lundberg, C. & Lexhagen, M. (2012). Bitten by the *Twilight Saga*: from pop culture consumer to pop culture tourist. In R. Sharpley & P. Stone (Eds.), *Contemporary tourist experience: concepts and consequences*. Abingdon, UK: Routledge, pp. 147–164.

Lundberg, C. & Lexhagen, M. (2014). Pop culture tourism: a research model. In A. Chauvel, N. Lamerichs, & J. Seymour (Eds.), *Fan studies: researching popular audiences*. Oxford: Inter-Disciplinary Press. pp. 13–34.

Lundberg, C., Lexhagen, M., & Mattsson, S. (2012). *Twication: The Twilight Saga travel experience*. Östersund, Sweden: Jengel Förlag AB.

Maffesoli, M. (1996). *The time of the tribes: the decline of individualism in mass society*. London: Sage.

Markus, H. & Nurius, P. (1986). Possible selves. *American Psychologist, 9*, 954–969.

Morris, D. (1981). *The soccer tribe*. London: Jonathan Cape Co.

Nuttall, P., Arnold, S., Carless, L, Crockford, L., Finnamore, K., Frazier, R., & Hill, A. (2011). Understanding music consumption through a tribal lens. *Journal of Retailing and Consumer Services, 18*(2), 152–159.

Park, D.-H., Lee, J., & Han, I. (2007). The effect of on-line consumer reviews on consumer purchasing intention: the moderating role of involvement. *International Journal of Electronic Commerce, 11*(4), 125–148.

Segrave, J. & Chu, D. (1996). The modern Olympic Games: an access to ontology. *Quest, 48*, 57–66.

Smith, A. & Stewart, B. (2007). The travelling fan: understanding the mechanisms of sport fan consumption in a sport tourism setting. *Journal of Sport and Tourism, 12*(3–4), 155–181.

Stebbins, R. A. (1979). *Amateurs: on the margin between work and leisure*. Beverly Hills, CA: Sage.

Stebbins, R. A. (1992). *Amateurs, professionals and serious leisure*. Montreal, QC: McGill-Queen's.

Stebbins, R. A. (2005). *Challenging mountain nature: risk, motive, and lifestyle in three hobbyist sports*. Calgary, AB: Detselig.

Stebbins, R. A. (2006). *Serious leisure: a perspective for our time*. New Brunswick, NJ: Aldine Transaction.

Sutton, W. A., McDonald, M. A., Milne, G. R., & Cimperman, A. J. (1997). Creating and fostering fan identification in professional sport. *Sport Marketing Quarterly, 6*, 15–29.

Trail, G., Anderson, D. F., & Fink, J. S. (2000). A theoretical model of sport spectator consumption behavior. *International Journal of Sport Management, 1*, 154–180.

Trail, G. T. & James, J. D. (2001). The motivation scale for sport consumption: assessment of the scale's psychometric properties. *Journal of Sport Behaviour, 24*, 108–27.

Uysal, M., Gahan, L., & Martin, B. (1993). An examination of event motivations. *Festival Management and Event Tourism, 1*, 5–10.

Wann, D. L. (1995). Preliminary validation of the sport fan motivation scale. *Journal of Sport and Social Issues, 19*, 377–396.

Wann, D., Melnick, M., Russel, G., & Pease, D. (2001). *Sport fans: the psychology and social impact of spectators*. New York: Routledge.

Watson, A., M. Hoyler, & C. Mager (2009). Spaces and networks of musical creativity in the city. *Geography Compass, 3*(2): 856–78.

Weed, M. (2010). Sport fans and travel: is "being there" always important. *Journal of Sport & Tourism, 15*(2), 103–109.

Weed, M. & Bull, C. (2004). *Sports tourism: participants, policy and providers*. Oxford: Elsevier.

Wlodarczyk, A. (2014). Is there a "fan identity"? In A. Chauvel, N. Lamerichs, & J. Seymour (Eds.), *Fan studies: researching popular audiences*. Oxford: Inter-Disciplinary Press, pp. 3–12.

Xie, P. F., Osumare, H., & Ibrahim, A. (2007). Gazing the hood: Hip-hop as tourism attraction. *Tourism Management, 28*(2), 452–460.

Yu, C. C. (2010). Factors that influence international fans'intention to travel to the United States for sport tourism. *Journal of Sport & Tourism, 15*(2), 111–137.

Zaichkowsky, J. L. (1985). Measuring the involvement construct. *Journal of Consumer Research, 12*(December), 341–352.

Zaichkowsky, J. L. (1986). Conceptualizing involvement. *Journal of Advertising, 15*(2), 4–14.

22

"THERE WERE ONLY FRIENDLY PEOPLE AND LOVE IN THE AIR"

Fans, tourism and the Eurovision Song Contest

Henrik Linden and Sara Linden

Setting the scene

This chapter will give some insight into the Eurovision Song Contest (ESC) as an event that attracts a particular group of tourists – fans. Fan tourism is a growing field and the travel industries are increasingly viewing fans as a key market segment. Visit London, for example, has built a whole marketing campaign around fans and fan tourism – "Fans of London" (Visit London, 2017) – and VisitBritain encourages fans of Britain to post pictures and comments on social media as part of the global #OMGB ("Oh My GREAT Britain") campaign (VisitBritain, 2017). As the concept of the fan has become more inclusive it has also entered into the mainstream consciousness – we can now be fans of "almost anything" (Guerrier, 2015). Although being a fan may still be "fraught with baggage from historical and contemporary media representations" (Stanfill, 2013, p. 17) – and fans are sometimes viewed as a threat to the dominant social order (Jensen, 1992; Hills, 2002; Sandvoss, 2005; Jenkins, 2008; Duffett, 2013) – the broadening of the fan concept has placed particular emphasis on fans as customers and, as such, they are attractive for businesses (Linden & Linden, 2017). In fact, in the experience economy, or consumer society, where subcultures are increasingly difficult to identify, it is instead *normal* to be a fan. So, while fans were previously viewed with suspicion, being a fan can now enhance one's status and increase one's social and cultural capital not only within the fandom, but beyond it too. Fans *experience* things, and after all, experiences are what we are all after.

Fan tourism traditionally often takes the form of a secular pilgrimage (Hall, 2002; Digance, 2006), as a location or site that has a meaning in the "text" surrounding a popular culture figure may be regarded as "sacred" within the fandom (Linden & Linden, 2017). A well-known example is Graceland in Memphis, the former home of Elvis Presley, which is one of the most popular tourism destinations in Tennessee (Graceland, 2017). Another common form of fan tourism is linked to events – such as travelling to attend a fan convention, a football match or a concert. In this sense, a travelling fan can also be viewed as an event tourist. Donald Getz (2013) divides event tourists into two categories: spectators and participants. However, in terms of the ESC it is increasingly difficult to draw the line between these two categories, as a large group of fans are not only directly involved in planning, organizing and delivering the event – they also sometimes perform at sub-events such as EuroClub nights. Fans thus play a particularly important role in the staging of and experiences surrounding the ESC (Linden & Linden, 2017). Swedish fans also expressed the civic pride they felt when Stockholm hosted the event in 2016 and data suggest that both locals and visitors have a more positive attitude towards the city after the event (Stockholms stad, 2016). According to Stockholms stad (2016) 70 per cent of the visitors who came just for the ESC plan to return within five years, and a report on the 2017 ESC in Kyiv (Institute of World Policy 2017) suggests that 92 per cent of the visitors want to return – a remarkable number considering the reluctance of some fans (as we will see below) to go to Ukraine for security and safety reasons.

Event-led place and destination branding is a popular strategy for cities to seek global attention (see, for example, Landry, 2000; Evans, 2003; Pike, 2016; Gold & Gold, 2017), and to ensure a positive event legacy it is important that the objectives of the host city are in alignment with the values of the event. In Stockholm in 2016, the ESC slogan "Come Together" connected well with the "openness, technology and music" themes (Malhotra, 2017) of the host organization, which in turn are closely linked to Richard Florida's (2002) three Ts for a successful creative city: talent, technology and tolerance.

In the following pages we will present an overview of the ESC in relation to fandom and tourism, covering aspects such as hosting the ESC, the fan experience, LGBT travel and what it means to be an ESC tourist. As we believe that it is important to give the fans a voice, we have included some quotations from an online qualitative survey that we conducted in early May 2017, where 18 members of the official Swedish ESC fan club, Melodifestivalklubben, answered (in addition to two demographic questions) the following five questions about Eurovision fandom and travel:

> "Why did you become a Eurovision fan – and what does it mean to you to be a Eurovision fan?"

> "Have you ever travelled to the Eurovision Song Contest? If the answer is YES, how many times and to what destinations – and what motivates you to travel to Eurovision?"

> "Did you go to Stockholm during Eurovision 2016? If the answer is YES, please tell in your own words about the experience."

> "Are you planning on going to Kiev for Eurovision 2017? If the answer is YES, what is your reason for going and what expectations do you have? If the answer is NO, what is your reason for not going?"

> "What country do you hope will win the 2017 contest – and why?"[1]

Theoretical underpinnings and empirical insights: hosting the Eurovision Song Contest – and being a fan of it

The ESC has produced few lasting superstars, at least on a global scale. The exception to the rule is of course ABBA (who won for Sweden in 1974) and to some extent Celine Dion (the Canadian, who won for Switzerland in 1988), although she did perhaps not become a "mega star" until later. This does not matter, however, as the lure of the competition goes far beyond the competing artists and acts. A unique aspect surrounding the ESC – an event that has both been described as "American Idol meets the Olympics" (SVT, 2016) and termed the "Gay Christmas" (Rehberg, 2007) – is also that it has spawned fans of the *competition itself*, rather than fans of specific acts.

A European invention, the contest is also largely a European affair – although it has increasingly transcended beyond Europe, both in terms of its audience and the countries that are taking part in the competition. Morocco took part in 1980, and Israel – due to the Israeli Broadcasting Authority (IBA) being a member of the European Broadcasting Union (EBU) – have participated most years since 1973 (even winning it three times in 1978, 1979 and 1998). The ESC has been popular in Australia since at least the 1980s, and to mark the 60th ESC in 2015 Australia was allowed to enter a contestant for the first time. They are now – after having participated three times already – an established ESC participant. The event is also broadcasted in China and the USA, further cementing the global nature of the event – and confirming that there are large groups of fans outside of Europe. In the USA, the official ESC broadcaster is Logo, an LGBT themed cable network that reaches around 50 million homes (Jordan, 2016). Chris McCarthy, the network's general manager, told the *Guardian* in 2016 that "Eurovision is a cultural phenomenon we have admired from afar for years [and] we are thrilled to bring the event to US audiences and cheer alongside the rest of the world" (Qvist, 2016).

Initially, the ESC was created to try out transnational broadcasting links in Europe, and to provide content to the EBU (Fricker, 2013, p. 75) – thus not for any explicit European unification purposes. However, the contest and broadcast have developed into "an occasion for the performance of European unity, and its recurrent and ritualistic character add to the sense of cultural import and gravity around it" (Fricker, 2013, p. 76).

The ESC is the longest running pan-European media event (Sandvoss, 2008). It is also an event that has grown both in size and importance – in its inaugural year, in 1956 in Lugano (Switzerland), only 7 countries took part, while in 2017 in Kiev (Ukraine) 42 countries entered the competition. It is now the largest non-sporting live media event in the world, with viewing numbers far exceeding those of the Academy Awards (Szalai & Roxborough, 2016; Carniel, 2017). Therefore, it is not surprising that it has become seen as a nation branding tool, and – after the fall of the Soviet Union – as an opportunity for Eastern European countries to "return" to Europe (Iglesias, 2015, p. 233). Paul Jordan (2014, p. 11) states that "participating countries have used the contest to project certain images of themselves on the European stage, and shape how they are perceived by their European others and by themselves".

A fan, quoted by Cornel Sandvoss (2008, p. 193) recounts that Eurovision was an early source of information about Europe: "as a child it informed me about Europe, made me interested in languages, travel, etc." As a pan-European event, it has the scope to give the audience across Europe a shared experience of what it means to be European. Jessica Carniel (2017, p. 14), in a paper about Australia's participation in the ESC – a participation that in itself makes the "Europeanness" aspect more complex – also compares the "opportunity to showcase national cultural industries in a state-based competition with nationalistic implications" to those offered through "sporting events such as the Olympics and the FIFA World Cup". Thus, the contestant competes *on behalf* of their country, and may also represent a particular culture *within* that country.

We need to be careful not to generalize too much – the ESC means different things in different countries, and some countries take it more seriously than others (as they are aware of the public relations benefits) – the contrast between the United Kingdom and many other countries, in terms of the attitude of the media for example, is significant (Georgiou, 2008). The British comments about the ESC are often steeped in irony (Coleman, 2008), but other nations have a non-ironic approach as Julien Danero Iglesias (2015, p. 234) points out: "the contest is seen in Moldova as something very important and journalists take seriously all developments around the contest".

In many ways, the ESC resembles a sporting event – particularly as it is a competition where, in the end, there is a winner. The winning nation also gets to host the following year's ESC.

This ensures a spread of host countries and cities, but it also means that there is little time for preparation (Stockholm, for example, only had ten months to prepare for the 2016 ESC – as they first needed to win a bidding competition against Gothenburg). It affects host cities and organizers as well as the fans – meaning that there is less time to prepare, compared with, for example, a big sporting event. It gives nations less control too, as they cannot put in a bid – they need to *win* the competition to be able to host it. However, this does not stop countries from actively working towards hosting the ESC. Many countries put in a lot of time and effort to find a winning formula, like Azerbaijan, for example, did in the years running up to their victory in 2011 (Ismayilov, 2012) – when they also hired a Swedish team to pen the winning song. Sweden have won the competition twice in the last five years, and this may be partly due to having the most advanced national selection procedure, as confirmed by the official website of the ESC: "The most successful televised national selection format is Melodifestivalen in Sweden, which features four live shows in different cities across the country, a second-chance show and a spectacular final" (Eurovision, 2017, para. 2). While the ESC as a broadcasting event sometimes reinforces cultural stereotypes, the corporal city event adds other dimensions. Watching from the sofa and following social media may thus fuel old-fashioned dichotomies (see Coleman, 2008; Georgiou, 2008). However, travelling to attend the event and mixing with fans from other countries may instead foster a deeper sense of understanding for other cultures.

Michael Morgan (2006, p. 305) has stated that the word "experience" is used by the leisure industries to "describe the essence of what customers are seeking and paying for" (cited in Cohen, 2010, p. 27). So, what does the Eurovision "experience" consist of, from a holistic point of view? To be precise, the Eurovision Song Contest is, in essence, a broadcasting event – created and designed for a television audience. However, it is also a *city event*, encompassing a number of sub-events, which is an event strategy that we have come to associate with most large-scale events and festivals. As such, it involves a big organization, and the whole city – whether its population like it or not – is affected.

In Stockholm in 2016, the stage for the broadcasting event was the Globe Arena where the actual competition took place. The city event took place throughout Stockholm and its suburbs, but the focal point for the "two-week musical extravaganza" (Stockholms stad, 2016) was Kungsträdgården and Skeppsbron in front of the Royal castle in Old Town:

> Eurovision Village in Kungsträdgården Park became the official party venue for the public, boasting two stages, food, and activities. The 81-meter-high City Skyliner attraction was located in the center of the park. The pavilion at Skeppsbron in front of the Royal Palace was home to the official party venues EuroClub and Euro Fan Café.
>
> *(Stockholms stad, 2016, p. 14)*

One fan who took part in our survey refers to how the event has grown since the last time he attended in 2000, thus confirming the festivalization of the city through the event:

> A fantastic experience in all different kinds of ways. Eurovision evening in Kungsan [Kungsträdgården, the location for Eurovision Village] with Carola and Herreys [former Swedish ESC winners] among others, and a Ted Gärdestad [former Swedish ESC contestant] celebration at Euroclub – my first visit to Euroclub. An awesome experience. In 2000 this didn't exist in Stockholm as far as I know. In those days you just booked the hotel and ticket and took the train to Stockholm, entered the arena and then out again. There was no Euroclub back then and it wasn't as enormous as it is now!

The ESC is increasingly regarded as a mega event – a term usually associated with the Olympic Games and the FIFA World Cup – and Annika Malhotra (2017), Project Manager for Events at Stockholms stad (the City of Stockholm), referred to it as such when we spoke to her. This is not surprising, seeing that the television audience was 204 million in Stockholm in 2016 (EBU, 2017) and 182 million in Baku in 2017 (Jordan, 2017). Also, according to Stockholms stad's (2016) *Host City Summary Report*, the direct tourism revenues for Stockholm 2016 is estimated at approximately £33 million. Each visitor spent on average five days in Stockholm, spending around £200 every day, while media representatives spent an average of £330 per day and stayed 9–10 days on average (Stockholms stad, 2016).

There are a number of reasons for why someone becomes a fan of something, but it is often linked to a "milestone" event occurring in one's life (Harrington & Bielby, 2010). For the ESC fans a common factor is that of a "milestone" event occurring in childhood or adolescence (see, for example, Sandvoss, 2008), such as one's own country winning or doing well (indicating a communal national experience) or that the fan has been moved by or identified with a particular performance on a more private level (indicating a more individual experience). However, for the travelling fans, the private needs and wants become shared experiences. From the event tourist's point of view there is thus room for individualization and self-development (Richards, 2011, 2013), co-creation (Lugosi, 2014) and a communal experience fostering a sense of belonging (Ferdinand & Shaw, 2012; Taylor & Woodward, 2014) – and the ESC could be viewed as a form of safe haven where the individual and collective needs and wants meet.

Despite its status as a mega event, the ESC has maintained a certain intimacy that is rare for such big events. This is largely a consequence of the central role played by the fans – and the close relationship that exists between the fans, the artists and the competition itself. In Stockholm in 2016, fans were given greater access to the event than ever before, and Stockholms stad (the City of Stockholm, the organizers of the events programme) immediately involved Melodifestivalklubben (the official Swedish OGAE fan club) in the planning and design of the EuroClub and Euro Fan Café. Linnea Rosén (2017), Events Manager at Stockholms stad and the Project Manager for EuroClub and Euro Fan Café at the 2016 ESC, told us in an interview that the fans possessed invaluable knowledge and insight into what makes the event work – both from the artists' and audience's point of view. Thus, the fans can be seen as co-creators of the event – and their expertise ensured that the *fan experience* was at the heart of the event organization. For example, for the fans attending the ESC, digital connectivity is important – and many of the press-accredited journalists and bloggers are also fans. Therefore, when planning the functional aspects of the Euro Fan Café and the EuroClub, it was important to have plenty of power sockets available (as well as extra chargers) and to give fans the opportunity to stash away their equipment (such as cameras and laptops) safely within the premises, so that they did not have to return to their hotel between the rehearsals and performances at the Globe Arena and arriving at the EuroClub.

Social media has played a major role in enhancing the ESC experience for the television audience, and particularly Twitter has proved to be an effective platform for engaging live ESC audiences in conversations, often of an ironic or humoristic nature, to enhance the sense of fan community and belonging (Highfield, Harrington & Bruns, 2013). It could be argued that social media enhances the travel experience too, as it gives fans the opportunity to share their corporal experiences with not only their travel companions, but with a much wider group of friends and "connections" who are not there physically (Linden & Linden, 2017). In addition, they will also be able to access other travellers' photographs and comments (for example, via Instagram or Twitter), thus *augmenting* the experience – and prolonging it, as they will be able to look back on these images and reminisce once the event is over.

Although the event is the main draw, event tourists and fans do care about the destination. Some destinations are viewed as more attractive by the ESC audience, for several different reasons. From the LGBT aspect, safety and tolerance are often brought up as central components, and the fan reactions to Austria winning in 2014 – Vienna is described by UNWTO as "an iconic destination for LGBT travellers" (Rahbar, 2017, p. 92) – and Ukraine in 2016 were thus quite different. The British fan site EUROfiasco (2016, para. 8) wrote the following when it was confirmed that Ukraine would host the 2017 ESC:

> So for the first time since 2011 [when Azerbaijan won], a country has won that, on balance, we are unlikely to go to. (I am assured that Kiev has many charms, but Ukraine's not going through the best of times at the moment – and their attitudes to The Gays are a bit, well, mixed).

A motivator for travelling can be to experience a stronger sense of self, and to reinforce one's perceived identity and create a sense of belonging (Pearce, 2005; Cohen, 2010). This may be extra prominent in fan travel, as the object of the fandom draws people together through a deep common denominator. Although many Eurovision travellers may be driven by escapism as a push factor, the pull factors are more obvious: the contest itself, the opportunity to mix with like-minded people and the chance to experience the destination itself (if viewed as an attractive one). Immersion is important in relation to escapism (see, for example, Pine & Gilmore, 1999) and the fans are often completely immersed in the series of ESC events and experiences that form part of a separate, or parallel, universe. For the fans, the ESC and its related events is seen as a more tolerant universe. A Swedish fan that took part in our survey, confirmed this aspect: "I am in a wheelchair and I stood right at the front by the stage at Euroclub; I never dare to do that otherwise but here there were only friendly people and love in the air."

When Baku hosted the ESC in 2012, the theme was "Light Your Fire," reflecting that Azerbaijan was promoted more widely as "The Land of Fire" – further indicating that hosting the Eurovision Song Contest was part of a broader destination marketing project for Azerbaijan. As ESC hosts, Visa regulations may be less strict for ESC tourists, as was the case with Azerbaijan in 2012:

> In an effort to encourage an ever greater number of tourists to visit the country during the Eurovision week in May 2012, the Azerbaijani authorities moved to simplify the country's visa regime for those intent on attending the ESC (Eurovision ticket holders, accredited individuals, and invited guests, that is), making it possible for the latter group to obtain a visa on the border and do so at a lower than usual rate.
>
> *(Ismayilov, 2012, p. 845, note 12)*

There are of course other issues involved in restricting the fans' travel patterns too. One of our respondents, a fan from the south of Sweden who has attended the ESC five times since 2000, has mainly visited ESCs in the neighbouring countries due to his fear of flying. However, a trip by train to Baku was planned, but in that particular case other circumstances stood in the way:

> I was planning on going to Baku in 2012 and a train journey had been drawn up for me since I don't fly if I can avoid it. The train journey included a transfer in Dagestan and since UD [the Swedish Ministry of Foreign Affairs] advice against traveling to Dagestan it was UD that had to make the decision for me.

Murad Ismayilov noted in 2012 that that the ESC sparked "the first wave of open discussion in national online media as to the overall situation with, and the society's attitudes towards, the country's sexual minorities" (p. 846). Also, following the Azerbaijan victory in 2011, an LGBT website was launched, "the first of its kind in Azerbaijan and indeed the entire Caucasus" (p. 846). Taylor and Woodward (2014) state that festivals – and we can certainly regard the ESC as a festival – are often sites of cultural critique. Thus, given the history of the ESC and its large LGBT following, it is not surprising that hosting the ESC creates discussion and puts the host country under political scrutiny but, as Catherine Baker (2014) has pointed out, this is not always reflected in policy-making and actual improvements of LGBT rights.

From 2013 onwards, the Eurovision themes have been directly linked to the wider values of the ESC – such as inclusion, diversity and acceptance. In Malmö in 2013, the slogan was "We Are One". In Copenhagen in 2014, it was the more modern but similarly inclusive "#JoinUs". In 2015, in Vienna, the theme was "Building Bridges". In Stockholm 2016, the slogan was "Come Together" and in Kyiv in 2017 it was "Celebrate Diversity". These overarching themes correlate well with the views of the fans, and the "coming together" component is put forward as a key aspect of their fandom. The themes go well with what is often put forward as a positive effect of travel and tourism more generally, in that it helps fostering tolerance (see e.g. Scott, 2015; Crotti & Misrahi, 2017).

In an article for the magazine *Vice*, freelance journalist Weronica Perez Borjas (2016) admits that Swedes have a special relationship with Eurovision:

> I've never really been a fan of the Eurovision Song Contest but I have to admit that I've found myself falling for it over the years. It shouldn't come as a surprise that living in Sweden can do that to a person – Swedish people have a collective perpetual obsession with the ESC.

In her article, she interviews some travelling fans who have gathered at the Eurovision Village in Kungsträdgården in central Stockholm, where the final was shown on big screen:

> It's our third time attending Eurovision, after Copenhagen and our own city, Vienna. We decided that every time the ESC is in a city we'd like to get to know better, we'll travel for the event and for the sights.
>
> *(Paul and four Austrian friends, cited in Borjas, 2016)*

> Eurovision is like nothing else in the world. If you go to football, rugby or any other sport, there's always rivalry. Here, no one is aggressive or high on power, there are no barriers.
>
> *(Matt from the UK, cited in Borjas, 2016)*

Borjas (2016) also notes the friendly atmosphere surrounding the event and writes: "Halfway through the results, it struck me that the Eurovision Song Contest is one of the few large scale events, where people get piss drunk, wave their national flags and peacefully hug it out together." This statement confirms what Linnea Rosén (the Project Manager for EuroClub and Euro Fan Café in 2016) told us – that the atmosphere was friendly throughout the Eurovision week and that, despite high levels of alcohol consumption, there were hardly any incidents involving the police (Rosén, 2017). This, of course, is in stark contrast to many sport events where atmosphere can sometimes be violent and hostile (see e.g. Crawford, 2004; Jamieson & Orr, 2009). Another reason for the friendly atmosphere at ESC may be the closeness of the fans, and the community aspect (as many fans visit again and again – for example, the majority of the Swedish fans who took part in our survey had attended several ESCs).

LGBT travel – and Eurovision fans as tourists

The ESC is regarded to be a safe space for LGBT travellers. According to Baker (2014), already in the 1980s there was a transnational fandom based around Eurovision – largely consisting of gay men. As Peter Rehberg (2007, p. 60) has pointed out, Eurovision "provides a rare occasion for simultaneously celebrating *both* queerness *and* national identity". However, some destinations are viewed as safer than others, and no former Soviet Union states are listed as gay friendly destinations by IGLTA (the International Gay and Lesbian Travel Association). IGLTA was formed in 1983 and is "the world's leading global travel network dedicated to connecting and educating LGBT travellers and the businesses that welcome and support them along the way" (IGLTA, n.d.) and provides tourists with travel advice. They are also involved in UNWTO's (2017) new report on LGBT tourism.

Ahead of the ESC in Kyiv, the British Government advised UK visitors to be aware of some differences between Britain and Ukraine – particularly with regard to attitudes towards the LGBT community and risks involved in being open about one's sexuality:

> although homosexuality isn't prohibited by law, public attitudes are less tolerant than in the UK and public displays of affection may attract negative attention. There's no provision under Ukrainian legislation guaranteeing freedom from discrimination on the grounds of sexual orientation.
>
> *(British Embassy Kyiv, 2017)*

Here we can see a contrast between Kyiv and Stockholm, where the former is regarded as less of a safe place to go for LGBT travellers. This did not discourage Jonathan Koo, a 39-year-old programmer from San Francisco (cited in Gander, 2017) to look forward to going to Kyiv for Eurovision 2017:

> Everyone by now knows Eurovision has turned into "gay Christmas" and there's no reason for it to stop being such. I know I'm being naive but in my head I imagine a Footloose scenario where we convince the town to loosen up and have fun, but as is evident in Kiev with the controversy over the rainbow arch, that would probably never happen.

The fandom has certain subcultural elements, in that it provides fans with the opportunity to pursue an alternative lifestyle without being judged: "Eurovision has always meant, for many of its LGBT fans, a way to rewrite heterosexual community and ritual into something special to them" (Baker, 2017, para. 2). As we saw above, the ESC has been referred to as a form of "gay Christmas" – a "national holiday for queers" (Elmar Kraushaar, cited in Rehberg, 2007). The OGAE, the international fan club of the Eurovision Song Contest, has also been described as a form of support group, and according to Rehberg (2007, p. 60) Eurovision fandom "has in itself been read as a metonymical secret code for being gay". Most researchers and commentators agree that gay men make up the international core of the fandom, and it is evident that the connection to LGBT culture is strong – although the fans are made up of a wide demographic (the Swedish fan club, for example, has a significant female membership – and 8 of our 18 respondents were women). We did not specifically ask our survey respondents to account for their sexual orientation, although one of them did answer the question "state your age and gender" by writing "gay guy of 46".

Although attending the Eurovision events and partaking in Eurovision-related activities are the main focus for the fans, we must not forget that they are also tourists – and, as we saw above, many of them are staying several days. There is therefore at least some room for sightseeing and experiencing the host city in a broader sense. Leading up to each Eurovision Song Contest, fans exchange information about what to do, and the fan websites – such as *ESC Insight* – as well as general travel magazines and newspapers post tourist advice and travel tips. It is clear that the number of articles, blog posts, tweets, etc. about a destination increases when they are set to arrange any major event – and particularly when it is a global media event such as the Olympic Games, the FIFA World Cup or the ESC. The online behaviour among people also changes – according to Ismayilov (2012), in the first month after Azerbaijan's Eurovision victory in 2011 the Google searches on the country increased eightfold, while the interest on TripAdvisor went up by 4,000 per cent. Writing for *ESC Insight*, Alison Wren (2017, para. 2) urges fans who are planning on visiting Kyiv to explore the destination beyond Eurovision:

> As tempting as it is to totally immerse yourself in the Eurovision bubble, Kyiv is a city which is well-worth getting out and exploring. With three million inhabitants this large city has a wealth of interesting architecture, tourist attractions and tasty food options.

There are various ways for locals and tourists to engage with the event, and like most larger festivals or sporting events there are multiple event locations – as we have seen the ESC is not only about the broadcasting events, it is also about the *city* events and established experiences such as EuroClub, Euro Fan Café and Eurovision Village. In Stockholm 2016, the EuroClub and Euro Fan Café were brought together for the first time, thus giving access to a wider group of fans and facilitating deeper interaction between the superfans and the curious public. EuroClub (the Eurovision night club) were only for participants, delegates and members of the OAGE fan clubs, but accreditation was open to a larger number than previous years.

As we saw above – Kyiv is regarded by fans as less of a "natural" ESC destination than the previous host cities Stockholm (2016) and Vienna (2015). Of the 18 fans participating in our survey, only 2 were going to Kyiv for the 2017 ESC. Some respondents explained that the reasons for not going included logistical and financial aspects such as time constraints, high travel costs and difficulty to get time off work. One fan wrote: "I don't have time to go and it is cosier to lie on the sofa with a bowl of candy and watch it on TV", while another one simply stated: "No, I can't afford it." However, other key reasons for not attending were uncertainty about the safety, accessibility and political value discrepancy. Here follows a sample of responses that gives some further insight:

"No, as a wheelchair user it doesn't feel accessible to go there."

"It is mainly because I wasn't ready to go abroad alone, especially not to a country like Ukraine that feels a bit unsafe. It was also partly due to my finances."

"I am not going, as Ukraine feels a bit messy with the Russia situation and I also feel that it would be expensive to bring the children there. It is not a country that I generally want to go to either, so therefore I will stay at home."

"No. On the one hand it is the safety situation in Ukraine that keeps me from going, and in addition it is too expensive to go there."

"I wasn't a fan of the winning song and I don't want to go to a country that is in conflict with Russia [. . .] The fear of ending up in an eventual war zone is big. When it was confirmed that Ukraine had won, I was so disappointed (as I wanted Australia to win) that I went straight home without partying with my friends."

"No, I feel that Ukraine is not a country for me. They are so far removed from my values that I don't want to give them anything."

"Niet! No! I only go when the ESC is in Sweden, that's enough for me!"

"No! Me and my husband felt that if we were to take a break it would be 2017. We planned another vacation. I don't feel 100 per cent confident about the security in Ukraine."

"No, it's a bit far away and it's too unsafe in Ukraine. But it is fun to be at home and watch Eurovision too."

Two of the fans, however, were planning on going, and very much looked forward to it:

"Yes, to visit a new country. I expect it to be as good as the other shows."

"Yes. I think it will be slightly less well organized compared to Stockholm but it will be good anyway. I appreciate seeing ESC live on location, it is something special."

These answers indicate that the event itself holds a strong attraction and that, despite some concerns regarding organization and safety, it is a "must" for some fans to see the event "live on location". The draw, as we have seen above, is not only the live event but also the surrounding spectacle and being part of the ESC travel community – which involves fans as well as artists and other delegates.

Implications for popular culture tourism: so, who should win – the song or the destination?

When asked about what country they wanted to win the 2017 ESC, many of our respondents clearly indicated that the destination was of greater importance than the song. For example, one respondent who favoured the entries from Bulgaria and Portugal hoped Italy would win: "if I think of what country I want to go to next year I would vote for Italy". Another one, who liked Estonia, FYROM (Former Yugoslav Republic of Macedonia) and France best, wanted Portugal, Cyprus, Malta or Iceland to win, as "they have competed a long time but never won" – and "it would be nice with a week by the Mediterranean: sunbathing, swimming and partying". One respondent, who preferred Romania's song, stated: "but for me it would be more suitable if e.g. Italy, who is the favourite, won, as it would make it easier to dare to travel to Eurovision". Another respondent stated:

I don't think there is a standout winner, but the others have convinced me that Italy is best, so I suppose they are the country I will support. It is also a country that I would not mind taking the children to, what with the pasta, pizza and ice cream and sun :)

Here follows four other examples, further emphasizing the importance of the destination – and also showing that one's own country is not necessarily the favourite (which is a different approach compared to sport fans):

"Italy – to get the chance to go to a warm country on vacation in May. Would be nice. Otherwise I look forward to Sweden winning . . . if only to equal Ireland's record of seven victories."

"Italy or Iceland. I really want to go to these countries."

"Italy, Estonia, France or Finland because I like the songs I would really like to go to one of those countries. Because a fan also thinks about what country one would like to go to."

"My favourites in this year's competition are Estonia and Israel. So I would probably rather go to Tallinn next year. Israel is too far away."

All the answers above, together with some of the respondents' reluctance to go to Kyiv for security reasons, shows that there are a number of components contributing to what motivates fans to travel. The tourism experience is central and cannot be discounted, but even for determined fans more mundane aspects such as time, cost and distance are key obstacles. Even the small sample here shows that the Eurovision audience, at least the members of OGAE Sweden (Melodifestivalklubben) is diverse, and that there are different motivators involved. It also shows that the tourism experience aspect cannot be discounted – instead it would be fruitful to further explore the ESC from an event and fan tourism perspective.

What makes the Eurovision Song Contest quite unique both as an event (or, rather, a set of events) and a fandom – is that the fans are first fans of the *competition*, and not of a particular artist. With a television audience of 204 million in 2016 (EBU, 2017) and 182 million in 2017 (Jordan, 2017) the ESC can be regarded as a mega event, but despite its size it has maintained a certain intimacy – which may be partly due to the friendly atmosphere among the travelling fans (many of whom are regular ESC attendees). The ESC as a media event is sometimes prone to stereotyping, and perhaps constructing simplified European identities, but the corporal event experience adds other aspects and dimensions. While watching from the sofa and following social media comments may reinforce old-fashioned dichotomies (see Coleman, 2008; Georgiou, 2008), travelling to attend the event and mixing with fans from other countries foster a greater sense of respect for other cultures.

It is clear that *fans* and *fandoms* play a key role in popular culture travel – and in particular in event-led travel. As we have seen above, relevant links can be drawn between ESC travel and international sport travel – in the sense that the audiences are predominantly made up of dedicated fans and fan communities – but it is also important to note that a major difference is the intimate nature of the ESC, where fan involvement exceeds traditional audience participation. As illustrated by the Stockholm 2016 event, the ESC is an event not only organized *for* fans but also in many respects an event organized *by* fans – thus adding a dimension to the connection between the travelling fans and the location(s) where the event takes place. The ESC fans are therefore seen not only as ambassadors for the event itself or the competition, but also for the *destination*. This implies that involving fans in the planning and management of large-scale events – instead of merely viewing them as spectators – may be a fruitful approach for destinations that wish to host memorable and successful events that lead to a positive tourism legacy.

Note

1 The responses were in Swedish and have been translated by the authors, Henrik and Sara Linden. The survey was kindly distributed online by Anders Ringqvist on 3 May 2017 via the Melodifestivalklubben member pages.

References

Baker, C. (2014). "The Gay World Cup"? The Eurovision Song Contest, LGBT Equality and Human Rights After the Cold War. *Wordpress*, 4 April. Retrieved from: https://bakercatherine.wordpress.com/2014/04/04/the-gay-world-cup-the-eurovision-song-contest-lgbt-equality-and-human-rights-after-the-cold-war/

Baker, C. (2017). Diversity, Family, and LGBT Rights: Watching Eurovision Across Borders. *ESC Insight*, 3 May. Retrieved from: http://escinsight.com/2017/05/03/diversity-family-lgbt-rights-eurovision/

Borjas, W. P. (2016). Getting Drunk and Hugging It Out With Eurovision Fans in Stockholm. *Vice*, 16 May. Retrieved from: www.vice.com/en_uk/article/partying-the-night-away-with-eurovision-fans-in-stockholm-124

British Embassy Kyiv (2017). Travel Advice on Eurovision 2017 in Ukraine. *Gov.uk*, 21 March (updated 4 May). Retrieved from: www.gov.uk/government/world-location-news/travel-advice-on-eurovision-2017-in-ukraine

Carniel, J. (2017). Welcome to Eurostralia: The Strategic Diversity of Australia at the Eurovision Song Contest. *Continuum: Journal of Media and Cultural Studies*, 31(1), 13–23. doi: 10.1080/10304312.2016.1262089

Cohen, S. (2010). Searching for Escape, Authenticity and Identity: Experiences of "Lifestyle Travellers". In M. Morgan, P. Lugosi & J. R. B. Ritchie (Eds.), *The Tourism and Leisure Experience: Consumer and Managerial Perspectives* (pp. 27–42). Bristol: Channel View Publications.

Coleman, S. (2008). Why Is the Eurovision Song Contest Ridiculous? Exploring a Spectacle of Embarrassment, Irony and Identity. *Popular Communication*, 6(3), 127–140.

Crawford, G. (2004). *Consuming Sport: Fans, Sport and Culture*. Abingdon: Routledge.

Crotti, R., & Misrahi, T. (2017). The Travel & Tourism Competitiveness Index: Travel & Tourism as an Enabler of Inclusive and Sustainable Growth. In R. Crotti & T. Misrahi (Eds.), *The Travel & Tourism Competitiveness Report 2017: Paving the Way for a More Sustainable and Inclusive Future* (pp. 3–29). Geneva: World Economic Forum.

Digance, J. (2006). Religious and Secular Pilgrimage: Journeys Redolent with Meaning. In D. J. Timothy & D. H. Olsen (Eds.), *Tourism, Religion and Spiritual Journeys* (pp. 36–48). Abingdon: Routledge.

Duffett, M. (2013). *Understanding Fandom: An Introduction to the Study of Media Fan Culture*. New York: Bloomsbury.

EBU (2017). Line Up Complete for 62nd Eurovision Song Contest Grand Final. *EBU News*, 11 May. Retrieved from: www.ebu.ch/contents/news/2017/05/line-up-complete-for-62nd-eurovision-song-contest-grand-final.html

EUROfiasco (2016). You've Been Waiting for This, Right? *EUROfiasco*. Retrieved from: www.eurofiasco.com/2016/

Eurovision (2017). *How Do the National Selections for the Eurovision Song Contest Work?* Retrieved from: https://eurovision.tv/about/in-depth/national-selections/

Evans, G. (2003). Hard Branding the Cultural City: From Prado to Prada. *International Journal of Urban and Regional Research*, 27, 417–440.

Ferdinand, N., & Shaw, S. (2012). Events in Our Changing World. In N. Ferdinand & P. J. Kitchin (Eds.), *Events Management: An International Approach* (pp. 5–22). London: Sage.

Florida, R. (2002). *The Rise of the Creative Class: And How It's Transforming Work, Leisure, Community and Everyday Life*. New York: Basic Books.

Fricker, K. (2013). "It's Just Not Funny Anymore": Terry Wogan, Melancholy Britain and the Eurovision Song Contest. In K. Fricker & M. Gluhovic (Eds.), *Performing the "New" Europe: Identities, Feelings, and Politics in the Eurovision Song Contest* (pp. 53–76). London: Palgrave Macmillan.

Gander, K. (2017). Eurovision 2017: Meet the LGBT Song Contest Fans Who Go Every Year. *Independent*, 12 May. Retrieved from: www.independent.co.uk/travel/europe/eurovision-2017-fans-lgbt-song-contest-kiev-baku-travel-ukraine-safety-a7732506.html

Georgiou, M. (2008). "In the End, Germany will Always Resort to Hot Pants": Watching Europe Singing, Constructing the Stereotype. *Popular Communication*, 6(3), 141–154.

Getz, D. (2013). *Event Tourism: Concepts, International Case Studies, and Research*. Putnam Valley, NY: Cognizant Communication Corporation.

Gold, J. R. & Gold, M. M. (2017). *Olympic Cities: City Agendas, Planning and the World's Games, 1896–2020* (3rd edition). London and New York: Routledge.

Graceland (2017). *Elvis at Graceland*. Retrieved from: www.graceland.com/elvis/elvisatgraceland.aspx

Guerrier, J. (2015). This Isn't Your Parents' Fandom. *Viacom International Insights*, 31 March. Retrieved from: http://internationalinsights.viacom.com/post/115140819087/

Hall, C. M. (2002). ANZAC Day and Secular Pilgrimage. *Tourism Recreation Research*, 27(2), 83–87.

Harrington, C. L. & Bielby, D. D. (2010). A Life Course Perspective on Fandom. *International Journal of Cultural Studies*, 13(5), 429–450.

Highfield, T., Harrington, S., & Bruns, A. (2013). Twitter as a Technology for Audiencing and Fandom: The #Eurovision Phenomenon. *Information, Communication & Society*, 16(3), 315–339.

Hills, M. (2002). *Fan Cultures*. London and New York: Routledge.

Iglesias, J. D. (2015). Eurovision Song Contest and Identity Crisis in Moldova. *Nationalities Papers: The Journal of Nationalism and Ethnicity*, 43(2), 233–247. doi: 10.1080/00905992.2014.993957.

IGLTA (n.d.). *About IGLTA: LGBT Travelers Are Welcome Here*. Retrieved from: www.iglta.org/about-iglta/

Institute of World Policy (2017). *What Did the Guests of Eurovision 2017 See in Ukraine? Results of the Opinion Poll*. Kyiv: Institute of World Policy.

Ismayilov, M. (2012). State, Identity, and the Politics of Music: Eurovision and Nation-Building in Azerbaijan. *Nationalities Papers: The Journal of Nationalism and Ethnicity*, 40(6), 833–851. doi: 10.1080/00905992.2012.742990.

Jamieson, L. M. & Orr, T. J. (2009). *Sport and Violence: A Critical Examination of Sport*. Oxford: Butterworth-Heinemann.

Jenkins, H. (2008). *Convergence Culture: Where Old and New Media Collide: Updated and with a New Afterword*. New York and London: New York University Press.

Jensen, J. (1992). Fandom as Pathology: The Consequences of Characterization. In L. A. Lewis (Ed.), *The Adoring Audience: Fan Culture and Popular Media* (pp. 9–29). London and New York: Routledge.

Jordan, P. (2014). *The Modern Fairy Tale: Nation Branding, National Identity and the Eurovision Song Contest in Estonia*. Tartu: University of Tartu Press.

Jordan, P. (2016). Eurovision 2016 to Be Broadcast in the United States. *Eurovision*, 2 May. Retrieved from: www.eurovision.tv/page/news?id=eurovision_2016_to_be_broadcast_in_the_united_states

Jordan, P. (2017). Eurovision 2017 Reaches Over 180 Million Viewers. *Eurovision*, 23 May. Retrieved from: https://eurovision.tv/story/Eurovision-2017-reaches-more-than-180-million

Landry, J. (2000). *The Creative City: A Toolkit for Urban Innovators*. London: Earthscan.

Linden, H. & Linden, S. (2017). *Fans and Fan Cultures: Tourism, Consumerism and Social Media*. London: Palgrave Macmillan.

Lugosi, P. (2014). Mobilizing Identity and Culture in Experience Co-Creation and Venue Operation. *Tourism Management*, 40, 165–179.

Malhotra, A. (2017). Interview, Stockholm, 27 March.

Morgan, M. (2006). Making Space for Experiences. *Journal of Retail and Leisure Property*, 5, 305–313.

Pearce, P. L. (2005). *Tourist Behaviour: Themes and Conceptual Schemes*. Clevedon: Channel View Publications.

Pike, S. (2016). *Destination Marketing: Essentials*. London and New York: Routledge.

Pine, B. J. & Gilmore, J. H. (1999). *The Experience Economy: Work Is Theatre and Every Business a Stage*. Boston: Harvard Business Review Press.

Qvist, B. (2016). How Eurovision Finally Cracked America. *Guardian*, 12 May. Retrieved from: www.theguardian.com/tv-and-radio/2016/may/12/how-eurovision-finally-cracked-america-justin-timberlake

Rahbar, A. (2017). Case Study 11: A Snapshot of Vienna, an Iconic Destination for LGBT tTavellers. In UNWTO, *Second Global Report on LGBT Tourism* (pp. 92–93). Madrid: UNWTO.

Rehberg, P. (2007). Winning Failure: Queer Nationality at the Eurovision Song Contest. *SQS – Suomen Queertutkimuksen Seuran lehti*, 2(2), 60–65.

Richards, G. (2011). The Festivalization of Society or the Socialization of Festivals? The Case of Catalunya. In G. Richards (Ed.), *Cultural Tourism: Global and Local Perspectives* (pp. 257–280). London: Routledge.

Richards, G. (2013). Tourism Development Trajectories: From Culture to Creativity? In M. Smith & G. Richards (Eds.), *The Routledge Handbook of Cultural Tourism* (pp. 297–303). London and New York: Routledge.

Rosén, L. (2017). Interview, Stockholm, 27 March.

Sandvoss, C. (2005). *Fans: The Mirror of Consumption*. Cambridge: Polity Press.

Sandvoss, C. (2008). On the Couch with Europe: The Eurovision Song Contest, the European Broadcast Union and Belonging on the Old Continent. *Popular Communication*, 6(3), 190–207.

Scott, N. (2015). Original Sin: A Lack of (Tourism) Knowledge (Tourism Is More Sinned Against than Sinning). In T. V. Singh (Ed.), *Challenges in Tourism Research* (pp. 201–206). Clevedon: Channel View Publications.

Stanfill, M. (2013). "They're Losers, But I Know Better": Intra-Fandom Stereotyping and the Normalization of the Fan Subject. *Critical Studies in Media Communication*, 30(2), 117–134.

Stockholms stad (2016). *Host City Summary Report: Eurovision Song Contest 2016*. Stockholm: Stockholms stad.

SVT (2016). USA-bloggaren om Eurovision: "Som en blandning av Idol och OS – fast bättre!" [excerpt from *Aktuellt*]. *SVT*, 4 May. Retrieved from: www.svt.se/kultur/som-en-blandning-av-idol-och-os-fast-battre

Szalai, G. & Roxborough, S. (2016). Oscars: How Many People Watch the Ceremony Worldwide? *Hollywood Reporter*, February 23. Retrieved from: www.hollywoodreporter.com/news/oscars-worldwide-tvaudience-867554

Taylor, J. & Woodward, I. (2014). Festival Spaces, Identity, Experience and Belonging. In A. Bennett, J. Taylor & I. Woodward, *The Festivalization of Culture* (pp. 11–25). Abingdon: Ashgate.

UNWTO (2017). *Second Global Report on LGBT Tourism*. Madrid: UNWTO.

VisitBritain (2017). *#OMGB – GREAT Britain – Home of Amazing Moments campaign*. Retrieved from: www.visitbritain.org/great-britain-home-amazing-moments-campaign

Visit London (2017). *Fans of London: Become a Fan of London this Spring*. Retrieved from: www.visitlondon.com/fans

Wren, A. (2017). This Is Kyiv: Transport and Travel in the Eurovision Host City. *ESC Insight*, 8 April. Retrieved from: http://escinsight.com/2017/04/08/kyiv-transport-travel-eurovision-host-city/

23

THE (PROMOTIONAL) VALUE OF PUBLIC-SPIRITEDNESS

Irish football fans at Euro 2016

Neil O'Boyle

Setting the scene

In this chapter, I reflect on the relationship between tourism and popular culture generally, and sport and nation branding specifically. Sport has long played a central role in nation building (and more recently, branding), and national myth-making through sport is common across all continents and wholly reliant on the media. Indeed, Rowe et al. (1998, p. 133) argue that 'there is surely no cultural force more equal to the task of creating an imaginary national unity than the international sports-media complex'. In this chapter I examine the media lionizing of Irish football fans attending the 2016 UEFA European Championship in France (hereafter 'Euro 2016') and reflect on the implications of this for Ireland as a tourist destination and nation brand. In both the domestic (Irish) and international news coverage of this tournament, Irish fans were applauded for their conscientious and affable behaviour while in France, with much of this news coverage focusing on video footage of Irish fans taken on smartphones and posted to the Internet (most likely by fans themselves). As the tournament progressed, therefore, Irish fans quickly became the 'feel good' story of Euro 2016, with many of their videos receiving millions of views online. Portugal emerged as the eventual winner of the tournament, but in nation brand terms, Ireland was arguably the real winner. Here, I examine the role of these travelling football fans as (unofficial) promotional subjects of the Irish nation brand. To begin, however, let us consider the relationship between tourism, popular culture and destination marketing.

Theoretical underpinnings: gazing, marketing and popular culture

Tourism, as is well known, is the world's largest commercial service sector industry. Yet, as a practice involving human interaction with places and artefacts – and with other humans, of course – tourism is fundamentally about *gazing*. 'Gazing', Urry and Larsen (2011, p. 2) tell us, 'is a performance that orders, shapes and classifies, rather than reflects the world'. In *The Tourist Gaze 3.0* (2011), Urry and Larsen explain that the tourist gaze is socially organized and systematized, and that it has been refined and developed over a long period of time and has involved the input of all sorts of tourist professionals, including writers, photographers, heritage guides, travel agents, tour operators and so on. These countless professionals are tasked with reproducing ever new objects of the tourist gaze, and in turn, destination marketing has evolved from merely showcasing the natural wonders of places to emphasizing their uniqueness within the broader experience economy. In his early reflections on the rise of the 'brand state', van Ham (2001, p. 3) suggested that nation branding was gradually supplanting traditional nationalism and that it lacked the deep-rooted and often antagonistic sense of national identity and uniqueness that can accompany nationalism. More recently, Jansen (2008, p. 121) has claimed that nation branding as a commercial practice emerged at the end of the Cold War as a means of repositioning nations within the master narrative of globalization. Jansen observes that nations have always used flags and anthems and other symbolic forms to mark their sovereignty, but she argues that nation branding differs in its more explicit commercial ambitions and in its greater dependency on experts in design, marketing, public relations and media production. She cites the following passage, taken from a brand consultancy, to illustrate the evolutionary relationship between nation branding and consumer goods branding:

> The new concept of the Brand-state, with its stress upon image and reputation, is becoming an essential element of the strategically well-managed government or community. Like a well-branded product or service such as Coca-Cola or American Express, the top leadership of state and civic entities is now challenged to think in imaginative ways about the brand of their realm, and the particulars of brand management, such as brand positioning, brand strategy, brand quality (quality of life), brand satisfaction (citizen satisfaction), and overall brand loyalty [. . .] Smart states are building powerful social brands around carefully crafted identities that are reflective of both what they stand for and who they wish to become.
>
> *(KLM, Inc. Management Consultation, 2003 in Jansen, 2008,*
> *pp. 126–127)*

The emphasis here on what Clancy (2009, p. 11) describes as 'showcasing the nation, its land, history, and people' tends in practice to have a reductive, essentializing effect, because nation brands (like any other kind of brand) must adhere to a limited set of values built around a core image. In this sense, nation branding signifies merely a more sophisticated and all-encompassing means of capturing the tourist gaze and promoting a view of nations as repositories of stability, continuity and uniqueness (Urry & Larsen, 2011). In a more critical vein, Jansen argues that nation branding 'is a monologic, hierarchical, reductive form of communication that is intended to privilege one message, require all voices of authority to speak in unison, and marginalize and silence dissenting voices' (2008, p. 134). However, it is important to note that new forms of communication made available via digital platforms have made the 'policing' of dissenting voices extremely difficult. Recognizing this, nation branders have made efforts to utilize the whole spectrum of new communication forms, including such things as social media, podcasts and blogs. Equally, they have become increasingly skilled at linking their promotional activities to popular culture and entertainment, giving rise to new concepts and practices, such as film-induced tourism. The hugely successful Braveheart, for example, proved a significant asset in helping to drive Scottish tourism, though the film itself has become notorious for its historical inaccuracies (Cobley, 2004). More generally, Horrigan (2009, p. 56) argues that when it comes to destination image, films offer tourism boards 'not only a big screen to showcase beautiful landscapes, but also the ability, with branded entertainment strategies, to develop more sophisticated strategies that are meant to protect and increase the integrity of their brand'.

John Fanning (2006, p. 235) observes that Ireland was among the early pioneers of nation branding, with state involvement in the branding of Ireland as a tourist destination dating back more than 50 years. In fact, Tourism Ireland, the body primarily responsible for marketing Ireland internationally, is in many respects exemplary of the new shift in destination marketing – and has been highly successful in its efforts. Currently, Ireland ranks third out of 136 countries in the World Economic Forum's most recent Travel and Tourism Competitiveness Report (WEF, 2017). In addition to having a presence on Twitter, Facebook and Instagram – along with posting original content on its own YouTube channel (which includes entertainment news, music videos and travel vlogs) – Tourism Ireland has made considerable efforts to capitalize on film and television production in Ireland. This entertainment orientation is evident in the use of actor Liam Neeson to narrate specially produced short films for online viewing (such as Tourism Ireland's 2016 #GoGreen4PatricksDay campaign) but also in content designed specifically to appeal to fans of film and television franchises, such as 'location maps' of Northern Ireland based on filming sites for *Game of Thrones*, or more recently, a specially commissioned 'behind the scenes' film about the making of *Star Wars: The Force Awakens* on the west of Ireland.

Like film- and television-inspired tourism, sport is a crucial vehicle for driving tourism. Hosting sporting events can yield significant economic returns for host nations, but tourists can also be drawn to places because of the uniqueness of the sports there (for example, bull fighting in Spain), or because they wish to see signature stadia like London's Wembley Stadium or Barcelona's Camp Nou, or to visit attractions like the Old Trafford Museum. Sports tourism is a significant growth area in Ireland and the country has a strong record of hosting international sporting events, such as the Ryder Cup (2006), the Solheim Cup (2011), and the Heineken Cup (2013). Just as significant, however, is the number of visitors who partake in non-competitive sporting activities, as acknowledged by Ireland's Department of Transport, Tourism and Sport:

> The sports tourism industry is worth an estimated €450bn globally and is the fastest growing tourism sector. During 2014, overseas activity/sport tourism was worth €900m to Ireland. Tourists engaged in a range of non-competitive sporting activities such as cycling, golf, hiking, walking, angling and water based pursuits. Ireland's strong position as a destination for these outdoor activities assists in the regional diversification of tourism, and supports Ireland's overall reputation as a clean, green country . . . Sports Tourism is a high yield sector with the adventure or sports traveller spending on average 40% higher than the average overseas holiday maker.
>
> *(DTTS, 2016, p. 43)*

Sports tourists are often keen to participate in live events and visit physical sites of sport, but it is important to recognize that the vast majority of people will experience international sporting contests far away from the playing field, as members of a widely dispersed global media audience. The 2016 Olympic Games in Rio, for example, were witnessed and shared by a vast global audience and broke previous records set by London 2012 for media coverage and digital engagement. Hence, why events of this magnitude carry such ideological importance and why they play such an important role in the realm of cultural representation.

As already noted, staging international sporting events like the Olympics or the World Cup offer a powerful means of promoting the nation brand and encouraging tourism. Such events can be used in different ways by different nations. For some, staging such events can be used to suggest that the host nation has 'arrived' on the global stage and has joined an exclusive 'club' of nations (Rowe, 2012, p. 2232). For others, such events can be used as 'rebranding' opportunities, perhaps to soften the nation's international image and reputation (Dart, 2016) or to recast its colonial past (Branston, 2012). However, sporting events *overseas* can also provide marketing opportunities, and can be used to significantly enhance nation brand equity. Once again, this is an area in which Tourism Ireland has excelled, with the organization proving especially adept at capitalizing on public relations opportunities overseas to generate positive coverage for Ireland in the international media. In 2013, Siobhán McManamy, Tourism Ireland's Head of Cooperative Marketing, commented: 'Tourism Ireland aims to keep the island of Ireland in the news around the world, through a constant, steady flow of good news stories about Ireland' (Tourism Ireland, 2013). In the section that follows, I examine laudatory news coverage of Irish football fans at Euro 2016 – as exemplary a 'good news' story for Ireland as there ever was.

The Irish at Euro 2016

Like any form of news coverage, coverage of international sporting events will vary depending on the outlet and the audience, and such news will be 'read' across the world through a complex prism of social categories, including nation, gender, race and class (Rowe et al., 1998, p. 124). Nevertheless, the need to capture the 'liveness' of international sporting events and the (still relatively new) pressure to provide multiplatform updates, increases the tendency towards standardization in coverage of such events. To this, we must add that sports journalists aim to produce coverage that is interesting, attractive and exciting for audiences – an aim that is helped by the raw material of their trade. As Poulton and Roderick (2008, p. xviii) observe, 'sport offers everything a good story should have: heroes and villains, triumph and disaster, achievement and despair, tension and drama'. In this section, I examine how Irish fans quickly became a central story within the international news coverage of Euro 2016. In the section that follows it, I attempt to locate Euro 2016 in terms of our wider discussion of tourism, popular culture and nation branding.

Euro 2016 kicked off in Paris in June 2016, with Portugal eventually emerging as the overall winner of the Henri Delaunay Trophy. As the tournament progressed, the public-spirited behaviour of Irish fans quickly became a central news story, fuelled by video footage of Irish fans uploaded to the Internet (in many cases by Irish fans themselves). To date, many of these videos have been viewed several million times. In one such video, Irish fans sing lullabies to a baby on a Bordeaux train as the child's bemused parents look on. In another video, Irish fans serenade a young French woman who appears both embarrassed and delighted at this mass attention. In yet another video, Irish fans sing cheerfully as they clean up beer cans and bottles as evening falls in Bordeaux. And just when onlookers might have been satisfied that the kind-heartedness of Irish fans was surely exhausted, a new video appeared showing some of them changing a tyre for an elderly couple in Paris! 'Vive L'Irlande!' the grateful elderly Frenchman says to the camera.

News media quickly picked up on this unfolding story. Across the world, diverse news outlets such as Sky News and the BBC, *Le Monde* and Aljazeera, Fox News and the *Washington Post*, celebrated the behaviour of Irish fans, with some such as Sky News, ESPN and Aljazeera going so far as to produce video montages of the most memorable (Irish fan) moments of Euro 2016. 'Republic of Ireland fans are the best thing about Euro 2016', the UK Mirror announced in a headline, while CNN declared online that Irish fans were 'out of control at Euro 2016 – in the best possible way'. French sports newspaper *L'Equipe* described how fans from both the north and south of Ireland had 'sung, drunk, danced, and left leaving smiles on all faces', while Fox News reported that 'social media is full of examples of Irish kindness' and that 'that Irish wit has been a fixture at the tournament'. A headline for NPR declared, 'And as if they could not be adorable enough, in a quiet moment, Irish fans sang on a French train to help lull a baby to sleep.' For Stephan Reich, journalist with German sports magazine *11Freunde*, the qualification of the Irish was 'a godsend. The Boys in Green can celebrate like no other nation, always peaceful, always sympathetic and emphatic, with an infectious, childlike joy.'

Here, we are reminded that media personnel play a crucial role in constructing images of nations and nationness, and that their constructions are imbued with ideological meaning. It is the job of these professionals to naturalize events for audiences, and to encourage feelings of interest, identification and attachment; their aim is to add colour, entertainment and a sense of atmosphere. 'It is not surprising that what emerges is a distorted and packaged representation of reality rather than a neutral, objective and natural presentation' (Stead, 2008, p. 195). Anais Bordages's article for Buzzfeed in June 2016, titled 'Here is proof that Irish fans have already won Euro 2016', sums up the media glorification of Irish fans at this tournament. The subtitle of the article, 'While other fans start fights, the Irish are here to have a good time', highlights how news media at the time also frequently drew stark contrasts between the Irish and other fans, notably English and Russian fans. Indeed, it is noteworthy that viewer comments posted below many of the aforementioned videos on Youtube continue this oppositional framing. For example, under the video 'Irish Fans help French couple change flat tyre' (posted on Youtube by Newstalk, an Irish radio news broadcaster), one viewer commented, 'english (sic) fans slashed the tyre', while another added, 'english (sic) fans were busy flipping coins at kids and laughing at them'. In direct contrast, comments about Irish fans were generally effusive in their praise. 'Irish people nicest people in world by far. They always happy just amazing people', commented one viewer. 'Irish fans restored my faith in humanity', commented another.

Towards the very end of the tournament, Irish fans received official commendation for their behaviour in the form of the Medal of the City of Paris, awarded to them by the city's mayor, Anne Hidalgo. Back home in Ireland, President Michael D. Higgins proclaimed that 'Ireland could not wish for better ambassadors abroad.' In all of this coverage – both at home and abroad – the goodness, friendliness and helpfulness of the Irish were emphasized, with fans depicted as 'plenipotentiaries of national character' (Rowe et al., 1998, p. 123).

In recent decades, there has been much scholarly reflection about transformations in Irish identity. Tom Inglis (2008, p. 38), for example, argues that there has been 'an explosion in varieties of Irishness', and suggests that global flows of ideas and people are creating 'new ways of being Irish'. Similarly, Natasha Casey (2006, p. 84) argues that Irishness now exists 'in a myriad of forms' and that it 'continues to adapt, accommodate, and appeal to remarkably diverse audiences'. And yet despite profound social, economic and cultural change in Ireland during the past several decades, global representations of Ireland and Irishness still conform largely to a touristic image, which reveals not only the immense success of Irish tourism marketing, but also its close relationship with other industries, notably the film industry. In his *Screening Ireland*, for example, Pettitt highlights that upon its release, *The Quiet Man* 'became an international advert for Ireland just months before the state's new tourism agency, Bord Fáilte came into existence in July' (2000, p. 64). Ireland's peripherality and remoteness, its landscape and cultural richness – and its smallness – have all been central to how Ireland has been constructed internationally. For Clancy, the Irish are known for their charm and sociability; in his words, they are seen internationally as 'simple, clever and friendly folk' (2009, p. 98). Negra goes further to suggest that Irishness is imagined as an innocent identity and a salve for the afflictions of modern life:

> Virtually every form of popular culture has in one way or another, presented Irishness as a moral antidote to contemporary ills ranging from globalisation to post-modern alienation, from crises over the meaning and practice of family values to environmental destruction.
>
> *(Negra, 2006, p. 3)*

Of course, this image of small, happy-go-lucky people keeping their native traditions alive in the face of oppressive modernizing pressures rubs up against the reality of Ireland as an intensely globalized country, and as a hub of international trade and software capital. Yet the popularity of such representations of Irishness also reflects the fact that national identity is shaped without as well as within; in the Irish case, diasporic definitions of Ireland and Irishness have proven particularly important (see McLoone, 2000).

Dominant tropes of Irishness, such as happy-go-luckiness, are very much evident in the news coverage of Irish fans attending Euro 2016, but we cannot ignore the crucial role played by Irish fans themselves. However, the question of 'agency' here is a difficult one. In a sense, we can think of Irish fans and the media as engaged in overlapping representational projects. Yet, the extent to which these fans were subjects or objects is unclear; were they proactively shaping news narratives or merely 'performing' in expected ways for an international audience? Whether intentional or not, the all-singing, all-dancing embodied performances of these fans were rich in news values, and were made available to the media in the form of short, packaged and entertaining video clips. This video footage also had a serial or diary-like quality to it, which meant that the ongoing antics of the Irish fans became a parallel 'feel good' story to the unfolding events on the playing fields. The Irish, it seems, were 'storying' their participation at Euro 2016 in daily video entries, and we can think of this footage as performing a kind of identity work on their behalf. A cynical reading, of course, might suggest that the ostensibly spontaneous and authentic displays of nationness and affective unity in the videos were entirely contrived, staged and knowingly performative (Cronin, 2016). However, the more important point, for our purposes here, is that fan footage and news coverage were in a sense co-constitutive, and worked not only to make Irishness public for international audiences, but to perpetuate and reinforce a globally attractive image of Ireland and Irish people.

The (promotional) value of public-spiritedness

Media coverage of Euro 2016 (discussed above) enables us to conceptualize travelling sports fans in a number of ways. Firstly, we can think of such fans as tourists. The sea of largely pale-skinned, green-clad Irish fans who visited France in the summer of 2016 were obviously there to watch football, but they clearly did more than just that; they ate and drank, interacted with locals, visited unfamiliar places and likely bought souvenirs. And they also *gazed* at their French hosts, who gazed back at them. As Urry and Larsen (2011, p. 17) remind us, the tourist gaze as a social practice implicates 'both the *gazer* and the *gazee* in an ongoing and systematic set of social and physical relations'. This mutual gazing is evident in the videos discussed above, with the faces of French locals displaying various emotions in response to the antics of Irish fans (such as bemusement on the faces of the new parents on the Bordeaux train, or playful embarrassment by the girl being serenaded).

A second way of thinking about travelling sports fans is that they function as cultural ambassadors (or 'fanbassadors'). Here, it is useful to think of fans as engaged in a kind of unofficial 'citizen diplomacy': 'Citizen diplomacy, broadly defined, refers to contact between ordinary citizens of different nations, in such contexts as sports, education, tourism, and business' (Kessler, 2009, p. 38). The importance of these 'unscripted encounters' is that they offer opportunities for positive and meaningful cultural relations. Again, this notion is strongly evident in news coverage of the Irish at Euro 2016, and in the Irish President's explicit praise of their behaviour while in France. What is crucially important in such instances of citizen diplomacy (and why they are so valuable to nation branders) is that 'ordinary' people – or in our case, ordinary *Irish* people – are endowed with special status as promotional subjects. ('These are the very people you'll encounter when you visit Ireland', the nation branders are effectively telling us).

Sports exchanges and international competitions provide perhaps the greatest single opportunity for people-to-people contact and communication – more so even than music or art because with sports, the fans – the people – tend to be so much more actively involved in the creative athletic achievements. Witness the impact that thousands of cheering fans have upon the performances of athletes and teams receiving such adulation.

(Edwards, 1998 in Kessler, 2009, p. 40)

In his examination of citizen diplomacy in US–Iranian relations, Kessler (2009) found that when successful, citizen diplomacy can help challenge and even dismantle harmful stereotypes. As he writes (almost as if penned specifically about Euro 2016): 'If orchestrated well, a simple soccer match can thereby fulfil the diplomat's seemingly lofty wish, by allowing a newly-formed, positive impression of his country to permeate a very large audience' (ibid., p. 40). However, when such instances of citizen diplomacy are framed by the media as 'quintessentially' Irish (or American, or Iranian, etc.) this can clearly deepen cultural stereotypes – which brings us to a final way of thinking about travelling sports fans. Above all, perhaps, we can think of such fans – for better or worse – as cultural signs. Beyond acting and behaving like tourists, or even as cultural ambassadors, fans carry meanings that transcend these specific categories and feed into much wider understandings of people and places. In the case of Irish fans, our primary concern here, their physicality, their clothing, their costumes and banners, their language style, their style of singing and dancing, their drink-fuelled bonhomie – all of these function as signifiers of Irish identity, carried to us by the media. It is for this reason that Urry and Larsen (2011, p. 116) suggest that the tourist gaze and media gaze often overlap and reinforce each other. Again, 'gazing' is not just a matter of seeing; it 'involves cognitive work of interpreting, evaluating, drawing comparisons and making mental connections between signs and their referents' (ibid., p. 17). It can be suggested that 'spontaneous goodwill' emerged as the dominant signifier of Irishness in the news coverage of Euro 2016. (The complete absence of any oppositional discourse or framing of Irishness is also noteworthy). A potential concern for more critical observers, of course, is that this thin-coated glorification is not so very far from more historically one-dimensional (and less flattering) representations of Irishness rooted in colonialist caricatures. Yet, for our purposes here, such representations demonstrate that 'the "scripts" of national identity' tend to be comparatively stable (Aronczyk, 2017, p. 115). More specifically, the case of the Irish at Euro 2016 highlights how a whole range of actors – including elected officials, destination marketers, journalists, online commenters and of course fans – are implicated in promotionalism. 'Here what matters most is not "meaning" per se, or "truth" or "reason" [. . .] but "winning" – attention, emotional allegiance, and market share' (Hearn, 2008, p. 201). For the Irish nation brand, the unanimously positive coverage of Irish fans at Euro 2016 was a clear 'win'; not only did it amount to free publicity, it generated massive conversation – 'that most sought after of promotional phenomena' (Cobley, 2004, p. 207) – both online and offline. Moreover, it provided confirmation that Irishness continues to be a most valuable identity currency (see Negra, 2006). More generally, however, it reminds us that beyond players and teams and match statistics, there is a 'cultural economy of sport', in which 'information, images, ideas and rhetorics are exchanged, where symbolic value is added, where metaphorical (and sometimes literal, in the case of publicly listed sports clubs) stocks rise and fall' (Rowe, 2004, p. 24).

One final point. In as much as Irish fan behaviour at Euro 2016 conformed with generally positive tropes about Irishness and helped buttress the efforts of marketing bodies like Tourism Ireland, fans can be somewhat unpredictable and sometimes risky promotional subjects, and these individuals do not always behave in their various roles (as tourists, cultural ambassadors and signs) as nation branders would like. Equally, the participatory culture brought about by Web 2.0 also means that tourism industries are now less able to 'control' information flows. 'Place branding and star reviewing is no longer in the hands of the tourism industries; tourists are now part of that place-making and experience evaluating process' (Urry & Larsen, 2011, p. 60). In the case of Euro 2016, Irish fan footage – and the thousands of viewer comments accompanying it online – can be compared to tourist reviews on TripAdvisor or Virtualtourist insofar as they function to 'recommend' Ireland. However, the beatific image of the Irish at this tournament clashes with damming reports about the behaviour of some Irish emigrants in the United States and Australia (see Gibney, 2012). This offers a reminder that in promotional culture, losses can come as easily as victories, and – where nations are involved – it is impossible to keep a 'clean sheet' indefinitely.

Implications for popular culture tourism

As with other forms of nationness, Irishness is made meaningful across myriad texts in a representational ecology that spans movies, plays and novels, advertising and sport, news reports, tourist brochures, online blogs, social media posts, reviews on travel and reservation websites and so on. In light of this increasingly complex mesh of texts – and ever mindful of the global public stage that has recently emerged and on which virtually all nations 'have to appear, to compete, to mobilise themselves as spectacle and to attract large numbers of visitors' (Urry & Larsen, 2011, p. 147) – nation branders attempt to carve out distinctive promotional messages, mixing enduring myths with emerging cultural phenomena. Here, I focused on sport as one of the most tangible manifestations of national identity in the modern world, and as a growing element of the global tourism industry.

In this chapter, I examined the media lionizing of Irish football fans at Euro 2016 in the context of a broader reflection on the relationship between tourism and popular culture. The chapter demonstrates how tourism as a discourse interacts and overlaps with other forms of discourse (such as news), and – in the case of media coverage of Euro 2016 – highlights how the benevolent behaviour of Irish fans became part of a larger narrative relating to national identity. Indeed, the mediated performances of Irish fans attending this tournament transcended sporting identification and even idealized fan behaviour, with fans emerging as plenipotentiaries of Irish national character. Rowe et al. (1998, p. 133) point out that sports media play a crucial role in rendering nations to themselves and in classifying citizens and their actions:

> The task ahead is not to tell the sports media to desist from speaking of the nation – which would be futile – but to encourage the cultural brokers of the sports media to re-cast their regimented images of sporting citizens and represent them in all their chaotic, hybridic diversity.

Little 'hybridic diversity' was evident in news coverage of Irish fans at Euro 2016, yet these performative bodies were nonetheless spectacular boons to 'Brand Ireland'.

The multifaceted persons who came to the attention of the world's media during the summer of 2016 in their capacity as 'Irish' football fans were (and are) clearly more than football fans. Yet, when it came to media coverage of the tournament, it was the Irishness of these fans that was all important, and was used to explain their seemingly spontaneous and instinctive behaviour. In this, I suggest, we witness an intermingling of the tourist gaze and media gaze.

Just as the inhospitable, jagged cliffs of Skellig Michael (used in the filming of *Star Wars*) help preserve the myth of Ireland as a premodern twilight place at the edge of the world, the mediated performances of Irish fans at Euro 2016 help keep alive a vision of a warm and friendly people. These happy-go-lucky bodies, draped in green and dispensing goodwill on every French boulevard, are uncomplicated in their Irishness and are posterchildren of citizen diplomacy. Ireland is promoted as a land of perfect hosts – a land of 'a hundred thousand welcomes' (*céad míle fáilte*). But in news coverage of Euro 2016, we are presented with a vision of the Irish as perfect guests: they are humble, helpful and always joyful – more 'hospitable' even than their appreciative French hosts. And in this mediated instance of geography meeting choreography, we witness the (promotional) value of public-spiritedness.

References

Aronczyk, M. (2017). Portal or police? The limits of promotional paratexts. *Critical Studies in Media Communication*, 34(2), 111–119. doi:10.1080/15295036.2017.1289545.

Branston, G. (2012). Spectacle, dominance, and 'London 2012'. https://orca.cf.ac.uk/64586/1/branston_spectacle.pdf.

Casey, N. (2006). The best kept secret in retail: Selling Irishness in contemporary America. In D. Negra (ed.) *The Irish in Us: Irishness, Performativity, and Popular Culture* (pp. 84–109). Durham and London: Duke University Press.

Clancy, M. (2009). *Brand New Ireland: Tourism, Development and National Identity in the Irish Republic*. Surrey and Vermont: Ashgate.

Cobley, P. (2004). Marketing the 'glocal' in narratives of national identity. *Semiotica*, 150(1/4), 197–225.

Cronin, M. (2016). Serenading nuns: Irish soccer fandom as performance. *Post-Celtic Tiger Irishness Symposium*. Friday, 25 November, 2016, Trinity College Dublin.

Dart, J. (2016). Brand Israel: Hasbara and Israeli sport. *Sport in Society*, 19(10), 1402–1418. doi: 10.1080/17430437.2015.1133595.

Department of Transport, Tourism and Sport. (2016). *National Sports Policy Framework: Public Consultation Paper*. Dublin: DTTS. Available at: www.dttas.ie/sites/default/files/publications/sport/english/national-sports-policy-framework-public-consultation/public-consultation-document_2.pdf.

Edwards, H. (1998). 'Let's play': On Iran, U.S. sports exchanges. *The Iranian*, 15 May.

Fanning, J. (2006). *The Importance of Being Branded*. Dublin: Liffey Press.

Gibney, C. (2012). 'The bad behaviour of some young emigrants makes me ashamed.' *Irish Times*, 29 August. Available at: www.irishtimes.com/blogs/generationemigration/2012/08/29/bad-behaviour/

Hearn, A. (2008). Meat, mask, burden: Probing the contours of the branded self. *Journal of Consumer Culture*, 8(2), 197–218.

Horrigan, D. (2009). Branded content: A new model for driving tourism via film and branding strategies. *Tourismos: An International Multidisciplinary Journal of Tourism*, 4(3), pp. 51–65.

Inglis, T. (2008). *Global Ireland: Same Difference*. New York and London: Routledge.

Jansen, S. C. (2008). Designer nations: Neo-liberal nation branding – brand Estonia. *Social Identities* 14(1), 121–142.

Kessler, D. (2009). The citizens' affair: Sports and tourism in post-1998 United States–Iran relations. *Stanford Journal of International Relations*, Fall, 38–49. Available at: https://web.stanford.edu/group/sjir/pdf/Iran_11.1.pdf

McLoone, M. (2000). *Irish Film: The Emergence of a Contemporary Cinema*. London: British Film Institute.

Negra, D. (2006). *The Irish in Us*. Durham, NC: Duke University Press.

Pettitt, L. (2000). *Screening Ireland*. Manchester: Manchester City Press.

Poulton, E. & Roderick, M. (2008). *Sport in Films*. London: Routledge.

Rowe, D. (2004). *Sport, Culture and the Media: The Unruly Trinity* (2nd edition). Berkshire: Open University Press.

Rowe, D. (2012). Mediating the Asian Olympics: The summer games – image projection and gaze reception, *International Journal of the History of Sport*, 29(16), 2231–2243. doi: 10.1080/09523367.2012.744519.

Rowe, D., McKay, J. & Miller, T. (1998). Come together: Sport, nationalism and the media image. In L. A. Wenner (ed.) *Mediasport* (pp. 119–133). London: Routledge.

Stead, D. (2008). Sport and the media. In B. Houlihan (ed.) *Sport and Society: A Student Introduction* (pp. 328–347). London: Sage.

Tourism Ireland (2013). Press release: Tourism enterprises attend innovative workshop. Available at: www.tourismireland.com/Press-Releases/2013/November/Tourism-enterprises-attend-innovative-workshop

Urry, J. & Larsen J. (2011). *The Tourist Gaze 3.0.* London: Sage.

van Ham, P. (2001). The rise of the brand state. *Foreign Affairs*, 80(5), 2–6.

World Economic Forum (2017). *The Travel and Tourism Competitiveness Report*. Available at: www3.weforum.org/docs/WEF_TTCR_2017_web_0401.pdf

PART IV

Getting on the map

Popular culture tourism and place-making

24

#LITERARYME

The legacy of the Bloomsbury Group on London's literary village

Melanie Ramdarshan Bold

Setting the scene

The area of Bloomsbury, in London, has been a firmly established literary district ever since it became the meeting place for a coterie of writers, artists, and intellectuals in the early twentieth century. The collective gathered at the home of Virginia Woolf and her sister, in Gordon Square, to discuss political, sexual, artistic, and social issues. The set soon became known as the Bloomsbury Group and included notable core members such as writers Virginia and Leonard Woolf, art critic Clive and his artist wife Vanessa Bell (sister of Virginia Woolf), and writer E. M. Forster (Bell, 1990). Other writers and poets, such as Aldous Huxley and T. S. Eliot, were also associated with the group. There have been many studies about the history and development of the Bloomsbury Group, particularly their influence on and contribution to art and culture, their unconventional lifestyles, and the social dynamics of the assemblage; however, there have been no studies exploring the impact of the Group on cultural and literary tourism, and the creative industries, in Bloomsbury today (Spalding, 2013; Rosenbaum, 2014; Licence, 2015).

Although the ethos of the Bloomsbury Group was very multidisciplinary in its approach – members of the group included Economist, John Maynard Keynes, Biographer, Lytton Strachey, and Journalist, Desmond MacCarthy, in addition to the aforementioned writers, poets, critic, and artist – this chapter will focus on the group's literary endeavors and thus literary tourism, and organizations, in the area (Goodwin, 2011). The interwar period, between 1905 and 1930, was particularly fruitful for literary activity, by the Bloomsbury Group: for example, the Woolfs establishing Hogarth Press, in 1917, which published the works of Virginia Woolf and T. S. Eliot.[1] Since then, Bloomsbury has become a center for publishing in the UK with internationally renowned publishers – such as Faber and Faber (founded in 1929), The Folio Society (founded in 1947), Persephone Books (founded in 1998), and, of course, Bloomsbury Publishing (founded in 1986 and famous for publishing *Harry Potter*) – and a plethora of smaller publishers, literary agencies, and other literary organizations, residing in the area. Freeman (2010) identified that creative companies tend to cluster together, more than other sectors, so the establishment of the Bloomsbury Group, and subsequently Hogarth Press, in the area could account for this growth in the literature industry. At this juncture it can be noted that Bloomsbury Group member, T. S. Eliot, was an editor at Faber and Faber where his work is also published. Additionally Persephone Books publish work by Virginia Woolf and use artwork by another Group member, Duncan Grant, for their endpapers. Although the Group is clearly still very much embedded in the area, and within some of the organizations that have been established since, is evident that Bloomsbury has transformed into a literary village that offers more to visitors than the Bloomsbury Group.

The findings of this research help us understand Bloomsbury as a literary tourism destination, what the characteristics of a literary village are, and how influential the Bloomsbury Group are on literary tourism in Bloomsbury today, particularly for a new generation of social media savvy tourists. Although this research focuses on Bloomsbury, it could have practical applications for the development of other literary villages.

Disciplinary and theoretical underpinnings

Tourism linked to popular culture and fandom is being increasingly recognized by tourism organizations, tourists, and academics. In particular, places associated with literary figures are notably abundant because, as Ousby (1990) argues, their legacy endures with the author's writing. Literary tourism occurs when a writer, or novel, becomes so popular that fans of the writer or novel want to visit places associated with the writer or described in the novel (Busby & Klug, 2001). What Squire (1994, p. 104) describes as "places celebrated for associations with books or authors." As Robinson and Anderson (2002) note, literary tourism is a not a new phenomenon; however, Lundberg and Lexhagen (2014) explain that it has grown in popularity as content is fostered across different platforms (in particular through film). If we take the Bloomsbury Group as an example, it has been estimated that a BBC drama *Life in Squares*, about the group, shown in 2015, would ignite a rush of group-related tourism in Bloomsbury and in other parts of the country where the group gathered (Thorpe, 2015). It is now easier than ever before to visit literary tourism sites, without the aid of a guided tour, and in the UK literary tourism has grown into a significant occurrence (Watson, 2006).

Various scholars have explored different aspects of cultural tourism, for example the intersection between literary tourism, cultural heritage, and regional and national identity (Ousby, 1990; Abram, Waldren, & Macleod; 1997, Macleod, 2004; Palmer, 2005). In particular, and most relevant to this study, Rekom and Go (2006) explore how literary tourism contributes to the strengthening of the cultural identity of a group, which in turn are the markers of tourism attraction. Through situating the Bloomsbury Group firmly within the area, and thus ensuring that it is a literary tourist destination, other literary organizations, or landmarks, in the area can be considered part of the literary village by proximity or association to the Group. As such, literary tourism, in this area, could appeal to both types of literary tourists: literary pilgrims and more general heritage tourists (Herbert, 2001). Scholars have identified two types of places for literary tourists: (1) real-life places connected to the writer's life (e.g. their house/s, grave, birthplaces, etc.) or (2) imagined places that appear in, or are associated with, a writer's book/series (Herbert, 2001; Robinson & Andersen, 2002; Herbert, 2003; Watson, 2006). This study focuses on both types of places, and also looks at the other places/organizations (such as publishers, libraries, and bookshops) that are connected to literary production and have, by being in the area, become tourist attractions in themselves (Darnton, 1982).

Six different types of literary tourism have been identified: Butler (1986) developed the first four and Busby and Klug (2001) added a further two. These are as follows:

1. A homage, and/or pilgrimage, to particular locations: related to the author (e.g. where an author lived) (Butler, 1986).
2. A location of significance within a literary work/s: concerned solely with the book and not with the author (Butler, 1986).

3. A location that is/was favored by a literary figure/group of literary figures (Butler, 1986). This type of literary tourism is more niche (Busby & George, 2004), however, it is particularly relevant to this study since Bloomsbury is an area that appealed to a broad range of notable, literary and cultural figures.
4. A location that becomes a tourist destination in its own right as a result of the popularity of the author and/or a literary work/body of literary work (Butler, 1986).
5. Locations, and notable people associated with those locations, which are communicated to a wider audience through travel writing (Busby & Klug, 2001).
6. Film-induced literary tourism: where the film-adaptation of a book prompts the tourist to read the original work and thus visit as a result of this (Busby & Klug, 2001).

The results of the empirical research fall neatly into the first four categories, as discussed below, although some types are more popular than others (in the context of this study).

Using Lundberg and Lexhagen's (2014) 'Pop Culture Research Model Elements,' this chapter identifies how the three areas of fans and culture, technology developments, and innovation in destination and attractions have transformed Bloomsbury into a literary tourism destination, grounded in its Bloomsbury Group roots. While some companies have capitalized upon the popularity of literary tourism – for example, World Travel offer a six-day 'Virginia Woolf' tour for £1,090 while VoiceMap have developed a GPS audio walking tour app for 1.99 USD – there is also an abundance of free guides, reviews, and recommendations online (through various websites, blogs, or social media platforms). Walking tours – whether they are writers' trails, setting trails, or memory trails – are particularly popular in Bloomsbury, particularly those managed through smartphones or other digital devices (Herbert, 2001). This chapter also explores literary tourism as cultural capital as displayed through social media, and investigates the implications for literary tourism destinations (Bourdieu, 1986).

Methodology

A case study of Bloomsbury, as a literary village, was used for this research. Herbert (2001) argues that literary tourist attractions have to be located near other tourist attractions, with various facilities and amenities, because people that visit these attractions out of curiosity still outnumber those who visit on a literary pilgrimage. The Bloomsbury area, in the center of London, meets this criteria because not only is it close to general tourist attractions but there are also a number of literary attractions – relevant to different fans and fandoms – in the area and its surrounds.

The case study is comprised of a compilation and analysis of a sample of literary tourism activities circulated online (free and paid-for) and was compared to an analysis of the #literaryme hashtag (details below). Online guides enable tourists to research their potential destinations in a more efficient way, while user-generated content demonstrates the popularity of a destination: this study looks at both (Lundberg & Lexhagen, 2014). A convenience sample of self-identifying, bibliophile participants – i.e. those who would be most likely to participate in literary tourism – was used for this research. In October 2015, 61 students were tasked with exploring the literary landmarks (e.g. publishers, bookshops, statues, authors' houses, etc.) of the Bloomsbury area, and its surrounds, and were asked to tweet photographs of their favorite landmarks. The students were then asked to tweet this photograph with the hashtag #literaryme. This resulted in 111 tweets, which have been analyzed for this chapter. Through a content analysis of the #literaryme hashtag on Twitter, this chapter investigates and details the key landmarks literary tourists in Bloomsbury and surrounding areas visit and compares this to paid-for and free guides online.[2]

It must be noted that the sample for this study is not representative of the general population: the participants fall within the Millennial Generation/Generation Y i.e. those born between the early 1980s and the mid-1990s/early 2000s (Howe & Strauss, 2000; PwC, 2013). According to Generational Theory, different generations each have traits, values, skills, and expectations that are easy to foretell (Mannheim, 1952; Howe & Strauss, 2000; Scott, 2000; Huntley, 2006). As such, looking at literary tourism through this generational lens can help the tourism industry to understand and connect with the newest entrants into the tourism market (Pendergast, 2010). Benckendorf, Moscardo, and Pendergast (2010) assert that, by 2020, this generational group will be key consumers of tourism experiences.

To give a brief breakdown of the participants: 10 percent were male; 90 percent were female; 39 percent were from the UK or Ireland; 25 percent were from mainland Europe; 16 percent were from North America; 7 percent were from Asia; and the remaining 13 percent were from Eurasia, South America, Australasia, and South Africa. All of the students were educated to at least undergraduate level and expressed a strong interest in books and literary culture. The participants in this research, therefore, fall under the categories of genuine literary pilgrims and/or well-educated tourists, described by Herbert (2001, p. 313) as "versed in the classics and with the cultural capital to appreciate and understand this form of heritage."

Findings

The literary landmarks, represented through the #literaryme hashtag, covered a much wider range of literary interests than just the Bloomsbury Group. These ranged from the traditional (e.g. the Charles Dickens museum) to the niche (e.g. Gay's the Word bookshop) to the cult (e.g. Senate House Library, the building that inspired George Orwell's *1984*) to the contemporary (e.g. Platform 9¾ at King's Cross train station). The most popular literary landmarks were bookshops, libraries, blue plaques/architecture, museums, publishers/literary institutions, and pubs where literary figures frequented. In comparison, the sample of online itineraries had a more traditional focus with a preference towards places associated with the Bloomsbury Group. For example, all of the online guides included Gordon Square – and the buildings where various members of the Bloomsbury Group lived[3] – as part of their tours while only two tweets, and adjoining photos, referred to this historic square. Overall, the literary 'landmarks' displayed in the tweets painted a broader literary landscape than the more traditional, historically-focused, guides and did not rely on historical buildings, authors, or the famous literary group.

In fact, only 15 tweets (14 percent of overall tweets), and 13 different people, explicitly referred to the Bloomsbury Group in their tweets. Over half of the Bloomsbury Group specific tweets referred to Virginia Woolf (the most prominent group member): five of these tweets were photos of, including selfies with, the bust of Virginia Woolf, which is situated in Tavistock Square (see Figure 24.1). Tavistock Square was an important place for Woolf, not only did she live at numbers 46 and 52, the area also inspired her writing, as evidenced in Woolf's unfinished memoire: "Then one day walking round Tavistock Square I made up, as I sometimes make up my books, *To The Lighthouse*; in a great apparently involuntary, rush" (Woolf, 1978, p. 94). This fits within Hoppen, Brown, and Fyall's (2014) and Watson's (2006) assertions that,

> nowadays, it is possible to visit a large range of literary tourism sites, ranging from places where "your favourite author was born, grew up, courted, lived or died" over those where "your favourite books were written," to those places "where they are set."
>
> *(Watson 2006, cited in Hoppen et al., 2014, p. 37)*

Figure 24.1   Virginia Woolf Bust, Tavistock Square, London.

Blue-plaque hunting, however, was popular with both the more traditional online guides and the social media participants. London's famous blue plaques, which commemorate locations associated with people of cultural, historical, or literary significance, are dotted on walls of build-ings across the city. This not only highlights the historical richness of London but, with over 900 plaques to be discovered, also provides a dominion for literary tourism. The blue plaques have been run by English Heritage since 1986 – previous custodians include the Society of Arts (1867–1901), the London County Council (1901–1965), and the Greater London Council (1965–1986) – and celebrated their 150th year anniversary in 2016 (English Heritage, 2016; Spencer, n.d). This anniversary was marked with a number of special, guided walks, a series of talks, a new app, a new book, new merchandise, and the unveiling of a number of new blue plaques (English Heritage, 2016). Bloomsbury is a particularly popular area for blue-plaque hunting, especially for those interested in literary tourism, because former residents include, to name a few, members of the Bloomsbury Group and the Hogarth Press, Charles Dickens, Charles Darwin, Percy Bysshe and Mary Shelley, Dame Millicent Fawcett, Raja Ram Mohun Roy, E. M. Forster, and Sir William Empson. There were 23 tweets and photos with blue plaques in this study: this is possibly because of the new app, and the fact that the blue plaques are constantly being updated and newer figures (across the arts) are now being represented, which might appeal to this younger generation of tourists.

The most popular literary landmarks in this study were bookshops, with 42 tweets (38 percent of all tweets) referring to a mix of conglomerate, independent, and antiquarian bookshops.[4] These included Gower Street Waterstones (chain bookshop), Gay's the Word (independent, speciality bookshop: LGBTQIA+), Judd Books (independent, secondhand, mainly academic bookshop), Jarndyce Books (independent, antiquarian bookshop), Persephone Books (independent, speciality bookshop: women writers), Souvenir Bookshop (independent, rare and secondhand bookshop), London Review Bookshop (independent bookshop), and the bookshops at the British Museum and the British Library. Hoppen et al. (2014, p. 42) assert that, "bookshop tourism tends to be the domain of independent, often small book retailers, which might specialize in certain literature genres." While bookshop tourism can promote independent bookshops, particularly those of a specialist nature, Waterstones (Gower Street) attracted the most twitter traffic from the participants. A number of factors could contribute to this: the location, in the heart of Bloomsbury; the iconic, Grade II listed building (see Figure 24.2); the history of the shop and the building (it first became a bookshop, Dillons, in 1956); or the three stories of books (including new, secondhand, and antiquarian). It is clear that Bloomsbury is an area that supports a collection of different bookshops

Figure 24.2 Waterstones, Gower Street, London.

(conglomerate, historical, academic, independent, secondhand, antiquarian, specialist). This endorses Bloomsbury's reputation as a literary village since literary tourism often occurs in towns, precincts, and areas with a cluster of bookshops (Seaton, 1999).

A number of other non-traditional literary landmarks featured on the #literaryme hashtag. Among these, libraries and book publishers were particularly popular. The British Library featured prominently: 17 tweets referred to libraries and 14 of these referred to the British Library. The most popular tweets about the British Library were 'selfies' with the smoked glass wall of the King's Library (4), photos with the various 'pop-up' exhibitions[5] (4), photos outside the building (3), and photos with the book bench (see Figure 24.3) (3). Typically, book publishers are not recognizable brands, even with the most voracious book buyers; however, 14 tweets referred to the publishers Faber and Faber and Bloomsbury Publishing (Clark & Phillips, 2014). This could be because of Faber and Faber's association with the Bloomsbury Group and Bloomsbury Publishing's association with *Harry Potter*. It is clear that literary tourism is no longer solely connected to authors of classic literature, or classic literature itself: the popularity of *Harry Potter* tours is testament to this (Herbert, 2001; Hoppen et al., 2014). However, literary tourism can now also include non-traditional associations to authors and literature, such as libraries and publishers.

All of the literary landmarks, showcased in this study, fell into the established four categories for literary tourism, despite being a mix of traditional and non-traditional tourist attractions

Figure 24.3   Book bench, the British Library.

(Butler, 1986). The homage to location (both fiction and author related) included tweets about Gordon Square, previous home to Virginia Woolf, and the very popular Platform 9¾ at King's Cross Station, where Harry Potter and his peers set off to Hogwarts, featuring a luggage trolley embedded in the wall for photo opportunities (see Figure 24.4). The location of significance within a literary work/s included tweets about, and photographs of, the art deco monolith Senate House (see Figure 24.5), which was the inspiration for George Orwell's Ministry of Truth in *1984* (based on its role as the Ministry of Information during World War II). The location that is/was favored by a literary figure/group of literary figures was, of course, Bloomsbury in general: an area that was frequented and enjoyed by a number of literary figures, not least the Bloomsbury Group. The Lamb Pub, which featured in a number of tweets, is a location that becomes a tourist destination in its own rights as a result of the popularity of the author and/or a literary work/body of literary work: this Grade II listed pub was a favorite haunt of Charles Dickens and saw the early courtship of Ted Hughes and Sylvia Plath. Fewer tweets fitted so neatly into Busby and Klug's (2001) two additional categories (the *Harry Potter* example,

Figure 24.4 Platform 9¾, Kings Cross Station.

Figure 24.5 Senate House, University of London.

provided above, did feature in the films), however, a number of landmarks in Bloomsbury could be placed within these e.g. Senate House, mentioned above, was featured in *Batman Begins* and *The Dark Knight* as Gotham City Courthouse.

The evolution of digital and social technologies has acted as a catalyst to the proliferation of fan culture: this extends to literary tourism, based on various fandoms (Lundberg & Lexhagen, 2014). As can be expected, with the emergence and development of technologies: literary tourism is now ubiquitous online, on social media, and on digital applications (e.g. apps, podcasts, e-books). This can be through free or paid for, guides, marketing and promotional material, reviews, and, as this study found, 'selfies' with various literary landmarks on social media. Selfies are now an established and commonplace part of tourism (Lo & McKercher, 2015). They are a way for tourists to evidence, to their networks and beyond, the extent of their travels, and to ensure that an intangible cultural experience is commemorated in a tangible form (Stylianou-Lambert, 2012). Such user-generated content is also a way for literary tourists (or potential literary tourists) to search for, or discover, popular destinations based on their fannish interests (Lundberg & Lexhagen, 2014). Of the 111 photographs, posted on Twitter for this study: 39 (35 percent of all photos) were selfies. Instead of self-objectification, the selfies in this study objectified literary tourism experiences and allowed the participants to demonstrate their cultural capital through photographs of themselves with their favorite books and next to literary landmarks (Bourdieu, 1986; Tiggemann, 2005). This type of user-generated content, shared across different social media platforms with specific hashtags, can help literary tourism destinations, and associated organizations, raise their visibility. Consequently, organizations can consider how to implement this into their marketing strategies. For example, the humorous chalkboard signs outside of Waterstones (see Figure 24.6) appeared frequently in the tweets for this study and beyond: this type of viral marketing is inexpensive yet highly beneficial for companies engaging in it (Lin & Huang, 2006; Litvin, Goldsmith, & Pan, 2008). The opportunities are even greater for organizations that are connected (even tentatively) to fandoms: for example, Platform 9¾ at King's Cross, which has a connecting shop selling *Harry Potter* merchandising, is already a popular tourism destination for *Harry Potter* fans; however, in terms of literary tourism, Bloomsbury Publishing is yet to capitalize on their association to

Figure 24.6 Bookshop chalkboard, Waterstones, Gower Street, London.

the book series and author (Roesch, 2009; Lundberg & Lexhagen, 2014). Social media, and the opportunity to share experience, makes tourism more interactive and networked: this is especially appealing to a younger generation of (digital native) tourists.

Implications for popular culture tourism

While this study focused on Bloomsbury as a literary village, and the impact of the Bloomsbury Group on literary tourism in the area, it also brought up many issues that could have implications for popular culture tourism. As discussed earlier literary tourism is no longer the domain of the canon of classic authors. This study found that while the Bloomsbury Group are, perhaps, the most notable former residents of Bloomsbury – and their associated landmarks are the ones that travel guides tend to focus on – the sample group of tourists had a more expansive, and bespoke, literary tourism experience that included visits to a more eclectic places. As such, literary tourism can focus on a wider range of both historical and contemporary literary figures, titles, landmarks, events, and associations available in particular locations. This means literary tourism, and cultural tourism in general, can be more egalitarian, appeal to a broader audience, and also raise visibility of, and footfall to, other cultural places in the vicinity.

For example, in terms of appealing to a broader audience, the participants in this study were part of Generation Y: thus this study can help us learn more about how to engage with this new generation of tourists (literary or otherwise). Pendergast (2010) asserts that Generation Y are currently the hero generation[6] and thus more likely to be interested in "brands, friends, fun, and digital future" (Pendergast, 2010, p. 6). Additionally, Generation Y are digital natives, and enabled digital and social technologies have larger networks than previous generations and are thus more likely to be influenced by their friends and peers (Sheperdson, 2000; Prensky, 2006; Pendergast, 2010). Consequently, they are more responsive to word-of-mouth communications through their networks and less likely to be directed by guidebooks and structured activities: something that this study confirms (Gardyn, 2002; Smith & Richards, 2013). As such, literary and cultural organizations may look to social media to promote themselves and/or their landmarks to appeal to this demographic in a more interactive way (Leask & Barron, 2013; Lundberg & Lexhagen, 2014). In particular, highly visual landmarks, that offer potential for selfies, could raise the visibility of the landmark/organization/area across different social platforms (see Figures 24.3 and 24.4 for examples of this).

Finally, as discussed in this study, the area of Bloomsbury houses a plethora of literary 'landmarks' (in the broadest sense) that appeals to both the traditional and the more contemporary literary visitor. These exceptional qualities (e.g. places linked to an author or associated settings in novels) coupled with the more general qualities of the area (e.g. the architecture, historic buildings, independent shops and restaurants, the proximity to other museums, cultural organizations, and other tourist attractions, etc.), as described by Herbert (2001), ensure that there are many opportunities for both guided and bespoke experiential destination development to attract the widest range of tourists possible. These can focus on a specific group or author, such as the Bloomsbury Group, or book series, such as *Harry Potter*. However, this research found that literary tourism does not need to focus on a particular author, their body of work, or on a single book; it can also include visiting places of literary interest such as bookshops, publishers, libraries, etc.: Bloomsbury offers the opportunity for a more extensive experience. These opportunities, and Bloomsbury's status as a literary village, could be augmented by the collaboration between various literary organizations in the area, including some mentioned in this study (e.g. the British Library, Waterstones and other local bookshops, Faber and Faber, etc.), as first postulated by Watson (2006) and cemented by Lundberg & Lexhagen (2014), and by interaction with different social platforms. This mix of exceptional and general qualities, and the opportunity for collaborative strategies, engenders a place's image to be "exploited for marketing purposes" (Hoppen et al., 2014, p. 43). Many private and public tourist agencies have capitalized on the popularity of the Bloomsbury Group to create group-specific literary tours; however, there is now scope to extend these tours to include the other landmarks, mentioned in this study, and/or for these organizations to develop marketing strategies based on their literary tourism capacities. Bloomsbury has the potential to develop itself into a strong literary brand, and market itself as a literary village, that not only has the historical connections to the Bloomsbury Group, but also can also extend and connect to contemporary popular culture now and into the future.

Notes

1 What is left of the Hogarth imprint is now part of Penguin Random House.
2 The five top online guides, on Google, which showed a detailed itinerary, were used for comparison. These were: Context Travel's 'Literary London: The Garden Squares of Bloomsbury: A Guided Tour of Literary London in Bloomsbury'; Voicemap's 'Bohemian Bloomsbury – Literary London'; London for Free's 'Writers Walk'; Authentic London Tours' 'Literary London Walking Tour (Bloomsbury)'; and World Travels' 'Bloomsbury Group Tour.'
3 Virginia Woolf, Vanessa Bell, and Adrian and Thoby Stephen lived at 46 Gordon Square; Lytton Strachey lived at 51 Gordon Square; James Strachey lived at 41 Gordon Square; and Vanessa Bell eventually moved to 50 Gordon Square with her husband Clive Bell (Rosenbaum, 2014).
4 A number of tweets were selfies of particular books, within various bookshops, but did not refer to the specific bookshops themselves.
5 The Alice in Wonderland exhibition, celebrating 150 years of the book, was there at the time of this study.
6 According to Howe and Strauss (2000), there are four different types of generational types, which follow a repetitious cycle in the following order: idealist, reactive, hero, and artist.

References

Abram, S., Waldren, J., & Macleod, D. V. L. (1997). *Tourists and Tourism Identifying with People and Places.* Oxford: Berg.
Bell, Q. (1990). *Bloomsbury.* London: Weidenfeld and Nicholson.
Benckendorff, P., Moscardo, G., & Pendergast, D. (Eds.) *Tourism and Generation Y.* Oxfordshire: CABI.
Bourdieu, P. (1986). The forms of capital. In Richardson, J. (Ed.) *Handbook of Theory and Research for the Sociology of Education* (pp. 241–258). New York: Greenwood.
Busby, G. & George, J. (2004). The tailor of Gloucester: Potter meets Potter – literary tourism in a cathedral city. In Robinson, M. & Picard, D. (Eds.) *Conference Proceedings Tourism and Literature: Travel, Imagination and Myth, 22–26 July.* Harrogate: Sheffield: Centre for Tourism and Cultural Change.
Busby, G. & Klug, J. (2001). Movie-induced tourism: The challenge of measurement and other issues. *Journal of Vacation Marketing* 7 (4): 316–332.
Butler, R. (1986). Literature as an influence in shaping the image of tourist destinations: A review and case study. In Marsh, J. (Ed.) *Canadian Studies of Parks, Recreation and Foreign Lands* (pp. 111–132). Trent, ON: Trent University.
Clark, G. & Phillips, A. (2014). *Inside Book Publishing.* 5th edition. London: Routledge.
Darnton, R. (1982). What is the history of books? *Daedalus* 111 (3): 65–83.
English Heritage (2016, February 25). English Heritage reveals anniversary plans for Blue Plaques scheme. *English Heritage.* Retrieved from www.english-heritage.org.uk/about-us/search-news/2016-blue-plaque-anniversary-plans
Freeman, A. (2010). London's creative workforce: 2009 update. *GLA Economics Working Paper Series*, 40. London: GLA Economics. Retrieved from www.london.gov.uk/sites/default/files/gla_migrate_files_destination/archives/mayor-economic_unit-docs-wp40.pdf

Gardyn, R. (2002). Educated consumers. *American Demographics* 24 (10): 18–19.

Goodwin, C. (2011). The Bloomsbury Group as creative community. *History of Political Economy* 43 (1): 59–82.

Herbert, D. (2001). Literary places, tourism and the heritage experience. *Annals of Tourism Management* 28 (2): 312–333.

Herbert, D. (2003). Literary places and tourism. In Macleod, D. V. (Ed.) *Niche Tourism in Question* (pp. 53–67). Dumfries: University of Glasgow Crichton Publications.

Hoppen, A., Brown, L., & Fyall, A. (2014). Literary tourism: Opportunities and challenges for the market-ing and branding of destinations? *Journal of Destination Marketing and Management* 3 (1): 37–47.

Howe, N. & Strauss, B. (2000). *Millennials Rising: The Next Great Generation.* London: Vintage Books.

Huntly, R. (2006). *The World According to Y.* Crow's Nest, Australia: Allen and Unwin.

Leask, A. & Barron, P. (2013). Engaging with Generation Y at museums. In Smith, M. & Richards, G. (Eds.) *Routledge Handbook of Cultural Tourism* (pp. 396–402). Oxford: Routledge.

Licence, A. (2015). *Living in Squares, Loving in Triangles: The Lives and Loves of Virginia Woolf & the Bloomsbury Group.* Stroud: Amberley.

Lin, Y. S. & Huang, J. Y. (2006). Internet blogs as a tourism marketing medium: A case study. *Journal of Business Research* 59 (10): 1201–1205.

Litvin, S. W., Goldsmith, R. E., & Pan, B. (2008). Electronic word-of-mouth in hospitality and tourism management. *Tourism Management* 29 (3): 458–468.

Lo, I. S. & McKercher, B. (2015). Ideal image in process: Online tourist photography and impression management. *Annals of Tourism Research* 52: 104–116.

Lundberg, C. & Lexhagen, M. (2014). Pop culture tourism: A research model. In Chauvel, A., Lamerichs, N., & Seymour, J. (Eds.) *Fan Studies: Researching Popular Audiences* (pp. 13–34). Oxford: Inter-Disciplinary Press.

Macleod, D. V. L. (2004). *Tourism, Globalization and Cultural Change: An Island Community Perspective.* Clevedon: Channel View Publications.

Mannheim, K. (1952). *Essays on the Sociology of Knowledge.* London: Routledge.

Ousby, I. (1990). *The Englishman's England: Taste, Travel and the Rise of Tourism.* Cambridge: Cambridge University Press.

Palmer, C. (2005). An ethnography of Englishness, Experiencing identity through tourism. *Annals of Tourism Research* 32: 7–27.

Pendergast, D. (2010). Getting to know the Y Generation. In Benckendorff, P., Moscardo, G., & Pendergast, D. (Eds.) *Tourism and Generation Y* (pp. 1–15). Oxford: CABI.

Prensky, M. (2006). Listen to the natives. *Educational Leadership* 63 (4): 8–13.

PwC (2013). *PwC's NextGen: A Global Generational Study.* PwC. Retrieved from www.pwc.com/gx/en/hr-management-services/pdf/pwc-nextgen-study-2013.pdf

Rekom, J. V. & Go, F. (2006). Being discovered, a blessing to local identities. *Annals of Tourism Research* 33: 767–784.

Robinson, M. & Andersen, H.C. (Eds.) (2002). *Literature and Tourism: Reading and Writing Tourism Texts.* London: Continuum.

Roesch, S. (2009). *The Experiences of Film Location Tourists (Aspects of Tourism).* Clevedon: Channel View Publications.

Rosenbaum, S. P. (2014). *The Bloomsbury Group Memoir Club.* London: Palgrave Macmillan.

Scott, J. (2000). Is it a different world to when you were growing up? Generational effects on social representations and child-rearing values. *British Journal of Sociology* 51: 355–376.

Seaton, T. (1999). Book towns as tourism developments in peripheral areas. *International Journal of Tourism Research* 1: 389–399.

Smith, M. & Richards, G. (Eds.) (2013). *Routledge Handbook of Cultural Tourism* (pp. 396–402). Oxford: Routledge.

Spalding, F. (2013). *The Bloomsbury Group.* 2nd edition. London: National Portrait Gallery.

Spencer, H. (n.d). The commemoration of historians under the blue plaque scheme in London. *Making History.* Retrieved from www.history.ac.uk/makinghistory/resources/articles/blue_plaques.html#1.

Squire, S. J. (1994). The cultural values of literary tourism. *Annals of Tourism Research* 21: 103–120.

Stylianou-Lambert, T. (2012). Tourists with cameras: Reproducing or producing? *Annals of Tourism Research* 39 (4): 1817–1838.

Thorpe, V. (2015, July 25). TV drama set to spark a tourist rush on the trail of the Bloomsbury Group. *Guardian*. Available at: www.theguardian.com/tv-and-radio/2015/jul/25/bloomsbury-group-vanessa-bell-life-in-squares

Tiggemann, M. (2005). Television and adolescent body image: The role of program content and viewing motivation. *Journal of Social and Clinical Psychology* 24 (3): 361–381.

Watson, N. J. (2006). *The Literary Tourist*. Basingstoke: Palgrave Macmillan.

Woolf, V. (1978). *Moments of Being: Unpublished Autobiographical Writings*. New York: Harcourt Brace Jovanovich.

25

"I WENT TO INDIA TO FIND MYSELF"

Tracing world cinema's neoliberal orientalisms

Rukmini Pande

Setting the scene

When the British television channel BBC 2 announced early in 2016 that it was about to produce a reality show based on the very successful movie franchise, *The Best Exotic Marigold Hotel*—in which a number of older celebrities would stay in a mansion in Jaipur, India in order to test out the possibility of retiring there—it was a remarkable demonstration of the ways in which the forces of Western cinematic representation, revitalized neo-orientalism, neoliberal capitalism, and the voyeuristic impulses of reality television are converging in the contemporary moment. In a write-up on the show in the *Huffington Post*, it was also detailed that, "viewers will see them [the celebrities] participating in activities such as practicing Yoga for the first time, and meeting Jaipur's royal family" (McGarth, 2016). Kim Shillinglaw, the controller of programming for the channel has also hailed it as kicking off a season of "entertaining new programmes with real purpose" (McGarth, 2016). What the purpose of this "social experiment" was with regard to the actual people of Jaipur was not touched upon.

Neither was this aspect reflected upon in the coverage of the first episode, with reviewers concentrating on the dynamics within the cast of characters and recommending it as entertaining television. A sampling of the "experiences" on offer to the viewers of the show included discovering that a busy market was like a "war zone" and that the available toilets were in a similarly distressing condition, as well as the spectacle of a participant asking a member of the royal family of Jaipur, "What do high society do for hobbies?" The implication being of course that some suitably quaint activities might be offered up in response. Another participant was optimistic that the trip would benefit her mental equilibrium, stating, "India is the perfect place to reflect and explore the spiritualism inside me. I'm hoping I'll have more time to meditate and improve myself" (Postans, 2016).

While India as a destination to "find" oneself is not a particularly new one for white, Western audiences, these framings today reflect much more complex negotiations with both the nation's efforts to "rebrand" itself as an economic and geopolitical powerhouse, and the changing cinematic depictions of it in recent Western English-language cinema than has so far been reflected in the literature around popular cultural tourism. These two trajectories might seem to be divergent at first glance. After all, films like *Slumdog Millionaire* (2008) and *The Best*

Exotic Marigold Hotel (2011) that will form the focus of this chapter spend significant amounts of time dwelling on the problems that beset the "real India" as opposed to the shining visions of inclusive economic growth and cultural harmony that are promoted by the Indian State. However, a closer analysis reveals both narratives to be drawing from a common lexicon; a lexicon that comprises primarily of an "exotic" and "exciting" otherness that nonetheless remains nonthreatening and knowable.

In this context there has been some debate over the precise form of "India" that currently has cachet in its cinematic representations for foreign viewer-tourists. For writers like Salman Rushdie, there is a distinction to be made between the sepia-tinged nostalgia for the colonial era that was evident in series such as the *Merchant Ivory* films, and the literal excrement-stained "realism" of *Slumdog Millionaire*. He noted in response to the spectacular success of the latter that, "'If the earlier films were raj tourism, maharajah-tourism, then we, today, have slum tourism instead" (quoted in Mendes, 2010, p. 477) Building on this, scholars like Mendes (2010, p. 478) posit that, "With eight Academy Awards of its own, including one for Best Picture, Boyle's *Slumdog Millionaire* demonstrates that not only the Raj period but also the idea of a Spiritual India have lost their exotic cachet in the twenty-first century."

It is my argument that this view is too simplistic and does not take into account the interplay between the multiple representations—both cinematic and advertorial—that form the mediascape that signifies "India" for the potential foreign tourist in the contemporary moment. This encapsulates varying shades and forms of exoticism, ranging from obscenely expensive luxury train travel packages that draw on colonial "raj" nostalgia, to the commodification of spiritual practices like yoga, to slum tourism that plays on the interconnected impulses of both voyeurism and white-saviorism. It is therefore vital, in any analysis of popular culture tourism in an Indian context, to ground the analysis in a recognition of the fact that *all* these portrayals continue to have a direct material effect on the ways in which Western travelers approach India and the ways in which Indian destinations fashion themselves. It is this dialectical relationship that will form the focus of this chapter.

I will now move on to detailing my theoretical lens, which utilizes a postcolonial framework. Indeed, this is an obvious choice as critical tourism studies has long been aware of the ways in which colonial imaginations influence the very act of tourism in the context of "third world" countries. At different times, theorists have pointed to the colonial power encapsulated in the "tourist gaze" (Urry, 2002), the problematic assumptions that drive Western tourists to search for "cultural authenticity" in the context of exoticized cultures (Boorstin, 1964; Cohen, 1972; MacCannell, 1973), and the similar structures of searching for spiritual salvation and transformative experiences that shape the regimes of independent tourism (Tickell, 2001). However, a specifically situated analysis of the ways in which both official promotional material produced by the Indian state and cinematic representations of "real India" intersect in the same regimes of colonialist and neo-colonialist power has so far not been attempted. This chapter will go some way in filling that gap, examining the filmic texts of *The Exotic Marigold Hotel* and *Slumdog Millionaire* in specific relation to the highly successful "Incredible India!" advertising campaign to demonstrate how these narratives continue to inform one another.

Theoretical underpinnings

As I have argued above, it is inaccurate to maintain that the "old" colonial imaginaries of India—as a repository of both Raj nostalgia and spiritual salvation—no longer hold considerable power for the potential tourist to the country. As I will demonstrate in close reading of the "Incredible India!" campaign in the next section, the central positioning of the practice of yoga as a (Hindu-allied) globally accessible path towards self-transformation was key to its overarching exercise of "nation branding" (Kerrigan, Shivanandan, & Hede, 2012) In the context of the popular culture texts under examination as well, *The Best Exotic Marigold Hotel* is very specific in its mobilization of the (once again Hindu) spiritual aspect of the country even as it seemingly concentrates on the "realities" of everyday life.

This drawing power of "sacred" tourism in India, which has been fuelled by popular culture depictions of it as associated with spiritual salvation has also been an area for tourism scholars. For instance, Sharpley and Sundaram (2005) have investigated how "ashram tourists" often come to certain sites located within the country in search of deep spiritual knowledge. In this pursuit they are of course following in the footsteps of celebrities like the Beatles. The band most famously visited the ashram of Maharishi Mahesh Yogi in the northern town of Rishikesh in 1968. Significantly for my argument in this chapter, the site is now referred to as the "Beatles Ashram" on the popular tourism review site Tripadvisor, therefore functioning as an almost too-perfect metaphor for the intermingling of the representational regimes of spirituality and popular culture for Western tourists within the site.

In another example of such impulses behind travel, Collins-Kreiner and Tueta Sagi's (2011) study of Western tourists visiting Dharamsala (the home of the Dalai Llama and the Tibetan government-in-exile after the hostile takeover of the nation by China in 1950) traces how these individuals are motivated to seek, "durable benefits such as self-expression, self-enrichment, recreation or renewal of self, self-expression, social interaction and a sense of belonging; they also seek lasting physical products of the activity, including education and learning" (p. 133). The association of Dharamsala with benefits to the individual visitor, rather than it being a focal point of the "Free Tibet" campaign or the conservation of Tibetan history and culture in exile is striking.

While critics like Rushdie and Mendes see the *Slumdog Millionaire* model of voyeuristic poverty tours as fundamentally different from the above examples of popular culture-based tourism, I would argue that they remain very much linked in their pursuit of a unique and transformational "experience." Much in the same way as the tourists studied above self-consciously model themselves as individuals seeking truth and knowledge rather than mere visitors; those that seek out Mumbai's famous slum of Dharavi articulate their motivations in very similar rhetoric—as rooted primarily in philanthropic impulses. As Dyson (2012) points out, the tours themselves employ the rhetoric of showcasing the "reality" of slum life ostensibly to counteract the "negative" images of them in mainstream media, but equally they must produce enough "authentic" examples of poverty and struggle in order to satisfy their customers.

In light of these commonalities therefore, it is my contention that these processes must be seen to be working in concert, rather than as disconnected and conflicting articulations of the idea of "India" for the foreign tourist who is, after all, exposed to *all* these narratives in different contexts. It is my contention that Graham Huggan's conceptualization of the "postcolonial exotic" offers a productive theoretical framework to analyze these sometimes divergent trajectories. As he argues in *The Postcolonial Exotic* (2001), the operations of globalization and neoliberal capitalism have led to a new articulation of the "exotic" in terms of postcolonial nations. He argues that while exoticism is an "aestheticizing process through which the cultural other is translated, relayed back through the familiar" (p. 14) it is also very much a political act that works to hide the power relations that fix marginalized groups into certain essentialized categories. This is also a process whereby cultural difference is fetishized and "valued" in monetary terms by the dominant culture. The end result is that "the marginalised other can be apprehended and described in familiar terms" (p. 24). This process has, however, been transformed by the entrance of the cultural broker, a figure that can mediate this global commodification of "difference" that is nonetheless non-threatening. It is only different enough to promise the viewer/reader/tourist/buyer a transformational "experience" that will enrich their own lives rather than lead to any deeper mutual cross-cultural exchange.

This mediation leads to the creation of a new category, the "postcolonial exotic," which is produced by competing "regimes of value" (Huggan, 2001, p. 5). Huggan differentiates these regimes into "postcolonialism" (which is a site of struggle and resistance against neo-colonising operations) and "postcoloniality" (which is a profit driven enterprise that seeks to monetize "difference") (p. 264). Crucially, however, he also argues that these competing regimes, though overtly oppositional, are fundamentally enmeshed in each other. This is because of the "inextricable connection between the production of the postcolonial and the globalization of consumer society" (p. 263). The "postcolonial exotic" is therefore a product of the friction between these two "contending systems" and results in "a series of exotically hybridised . . . products" (pp. 263–264).

While Huggan's primary focus is the commodification and circulation of the category of postcolonial writing in the neoliberal marketplace, it is quite productive to use the analytical category of the "postcolonial exotic" to see how the competing regimes of value as showcased in both officially sanctioned and independent popular culture narratives of "India" are intertwined as well. The cultural mediators in this case are both the filmmakers who produce specific narratives of discovery utilizing various familiar tropes that are rooted in essentialist notions, as well as the marketing teams hired by the Indian government to "rebrand" India as an attractive leisure destination for the high-end Western tourist. As I will demonstrate, both these narratives work within the aestheticization and fetishization of certain aspects of Indian culture to produce carefully calibrated "experiences" of knowable and valued "otherness" that nonetheless remain at a safe remove.

While it might be speculated that it would be difficult to find direct parallels between such theoretical critiques and officially authorized marketing campaigns that are attempting to reposition India within the global imaginary as a dynamic, exciting, and modern nation state confident in its own identity, striking similarities are almost immediately evident when the "Incredible India!" advertising campaign is examined. To summarize the campaign briefly, it ran from 2002–2010 in various phases and marked the first time that a project of such a scale was handed over to the private sector. The campaign was also almost exclusively outward-facing with most of the expenditure earmarked for making an impact in foreign markets including eye-catching spreads in magazines like the *National Geographic* and online competitions to generate further excitement. It also targeted large-scale tourism expos such as the Internationale Tourismus Bourse (ITB) in Berlin in March 2007. Greary (2013, p. 44) notes that the campaign was touted to be a great success and was credited with a 28.8 percent increase in foreign tourists in the subsequent years. The campaign also received a number of prestigious awards in prominent publications such as *Condé Nast Traveller* and *Lonely Planet*.

The most striking resonance between my critical arguments and the advertising campaign is found in the marketing team's explicit identification of the saleability of an "experience economy." As Greary (2013, pp. 40–41) also points out, this aspect was spelt out explicitly: "As part of the changing travel trends discussed by Amitabh Kant (2009), the marketing team wanted to capitalize on an 'experience economy' rather than a 'purchase economy' by focusing on those travelers seeking an 'experience beyond words.'" As I will detail in the next section, this description aligns the campaign serendipitously with the aspirational ethos of both films under consideration, even as it attempts to gloss over the more unsightly aspects of India's growing urbanization and much-hyped economic growth that they focus on. Also significantly, this framing also highlights the common visual lexicon of an "experience economy" that reflects across the various artifacts under consideration. The "Incredible India!" campaign after all draws from its power by projecting India as simultaneously a modern, accessible, and safe destination for Western tourists while continuing to underline its exoticism and "otherness" through tropes drawn from orientalist stereotypes, this time deployed in splashy videos and ad campaigns. In a globalized world where commodity culture encompasses all aspects of cultural production, it is vital to examine how these spaces are constructed as appealing to the wealthy Western tourist.

Methodology and discussion

I now turn my attention to a close reading of certain motifs and narratives embedded in the advertisements of the "Incredible India!" campaign that I will then trace in both *Slumdog Millionaire* and *The Best Exotic Marigold Hotel*. While the two films seem to mobilize completely different narratives on the surface, I will demonstrate how they are engaged in very similar projects of constructing neo-colonial imaginaries of the "real India." Further, I will highlight the fact that even though both films also seem opposed to the glossy and overblown claims of "modern India" as showcased in the advertising campaign, they nonetheless traffic in the same aspirational narratives of hope and second chances in a "new" world. I will also track the different ways in which the films construct an "authentic India" as other, through a "realism" that still relies heavily on colonialist stereotypes.

The first motif I wish to highlight is the primacy of yoga in the campaign as a spiritual pathway to personal transformation and "wellness." Indeed, this focus is not unique to only the "Incredible India!" campaign with the present Narendra Modi-lead government having pushed very strongly to create a global "International Yoga Day" in 2015. The launch of the "day" had the entire force of the governmental machinery behind it and the media blitz produced as a result was quite remarkable. Given its continued primacy in India's "branding," it is vital to unpack the deployment of this motif further. To return to the "Incredible India!" campaign, the 2003–2004 phase released promotional posters that placed depictions of various yoga positions or *asanas* against gorgeous natural backdrops. One such example can be seen in Figure 25.1.

As Greary (2013, p. 44) observes, this juxtaposition had the effect of "moving beyond the physical attributes" of India as a destination to emphasize,

> a journey of enlightenment with the aim of transcending distinctions of self and other—a place where one can find their "center" through a direct experience of India's ancient wisdom. This favorable and romanticized view of India as a treasure trove of ancient wisdom has a long history with the European and North American encounter with India, certainly since the eighteenth and nineteenth century.

Apart from these resonances, it is also vital to note that in both these government-backed efforts at "nation branding," yoga becomes the perfect motif to enforce the association of the "spiritual" soul of the nation as primarily Hindu in character while also distancing itself from the increasingly violent right-wing manifestations of Hindutva as an ideology. This is a delicate line to tread, as the increasing polarization along religious lines within the country is increasingly threatening to disrupt India's projection of itself as harmoniously secular nation.

However, as yoga has already crossed over into the West as primarily a fitness-aid and comfortingly vague spiritual practice (Alter, 2004; Strauss, 2005), it can still be leveraged with some flexibility to suit both the economic and ideological needs of an increasingly Hindutva ruling establishment. A later stage of the advertising campaign, unveiled in 2008–2009 took the yoga motif still further, now framing it as primarily a pathway to economic rebirth for older foreign

Figure 25.1 Depiction of yoga position against natural backdrop.

Source: Ministry of Tourism (2004).

tourists looking to retire. The campaign focused on certain individuals who had come to India as tourists but had stayed on for various reasons. One narrative highlighted thus can be seen in the Figure 25.2, where a (white) American woman is shown to have leveraged her interest in yoga into a successful business. As I will now demonstrate, the shift from India as tourist destination to India as a retirement possibility is something that *The Best Exotic Marigold Hotel* also accomplishes using a remarkably similar rhetorical strategy.

While it is not my intention to focus on the plots of the films themselves, a short summary at this juncture will be useful to contextualize my larger arguments. In the case of *The Best Exotic Marigold Hotel*, the film follows the journey of seven white British pensioners who come to Jaipur in order to try out retirement in what is promised to be in the luxurious surroundings of an old palace. Of course, when they get to India they are faced with the "reality" of the situation, which is that the palace is crumbling rather than luxurious, and the heat, noise, food, and dust of the country is overwhelming, even causing one of the characters—Jean Ainslie (Penelope Winton)— to declare the entire exercise a "grotesque fantasy" by people "playing at being young." India is mainly located pictorially in Jaipur and seen as dusty, grimy, and immensely crowded. A "war zone" full of noisy, colorful, yet strangely inarticulate figures as most of the speaking lines are focused on the white characters. The screentime that is given to the Indian characters is also devoted to conversations conducted in English. These interventions can be seen to be acting as "cultural mediators" to draw on Huggan (2001) once again, purporting to show viewers the "real India" while simultaneously "translating" it into a familiar idiom.

There is even an example of a "failure" of translation, once again through the character of Jean. Within the narrative she attempts (unsuccessfully) to understand why her other companions are adapting to the difficult conditions much more easily than her. "How can you bear this country? What do you see, that I don't?" She asks one of her companions, Graham Dashwood (Tom Wilkinson). He replies, "The light, colors, smiles; it teaches me something."

COUNTRY OF BIRTH ▶ USA
MOTHERLAND ▶ INDIA

Julie Martin was born near Hollywood in L.A.
A keen interest in yoga brought her to India, and
almost at once she felt a kinship, an overwhelming
sense of belonging. She studied and mastered
yoga and is now a leading exponent of this ancient
Indian tradition. She lives in India and continues
to be enthralled and amazed every day. If you are
looking for a spiritual and magical journey unlike
any other, visit India. Like Julie, you will find
that your search ends here.

Incredible !ndia

Figure 25.2 Framing yoga as a pathway to economic rebirth for older foreign tourists.

Source: Ministry of Tourism (2009).

Jean is the only one of the seven characters who returns to England, not having been able "get over" her disgust at the overt "grotesqueness" of life in India. For the others however, as the narrative shows, the reward for being able to look past the overt grime, poverty, and chaos is the discovery of love, professional success, and new relationships in the autumn of their lives. The aspirational bent of the chronicle is clear and the "realities" of life in India are reconfigured to become educational and indeed transformational rites of passage for the white characters that, once endured, allow them entrance into a much richer life than before. The underlying similarities between the cinematic and the marketing scripts that I have been tracing are brought into particular focus when the film's main Indian character, the hotel owner Sonny (Dev Patel), proclaims that he has "outsourced old age" uncannily reproducing the invitation that is used on the "Incredible India!" posters.

The second motif that I'd like to highlight from the campaign is articulated by the literature around its conceptualization that emphasized that modern visitors are increasingly seeking an immersive experiential form of tourism that manages to position itself as unique. Hudson and Ritchie (2009) note that marketers are increasingly employing the language of affect and passion rather than utility or "benefit" to attract such individuals to their products. Greary (2013, p. 39) notes that,

> Building on the concept of an "experience economy era," first formulated by Pine and Gilmore (1998), experiential marketing recognizes that consumers are not interested in purely functional benefits but want to have "special experiences and unforgettable memories" . . . Thus, in order to promote an unrivaled tourism experience, marketing campaigns also look to capitalize on the emotions of potential travelers and "bring brands to life" through a powerful aesthetic engagement.

While the "experiences" that are showcased on the "Incredible India!" posters underline the qualities of India as modern nation state they also offer up the possibility of "controlled chaos." As opposed to the yoga-focused part of the campaign, images like the one shown in Figure 25.3 evoke a sense of drama and the expectation of a uniquely immersive and "larger than life" experience. In this iteration, India's less overtly marketable qualities are refigured in order to project the possibility of an exotic adventure of another kind compared to the more "sanitized" ones available at other destinations.

Building from this, I would argue that though slum tourism would certainly not be part of the Indian government's plan for showcasing its soft power, much of the same rhetoric around immersive experientiality is reflected in the "grittiness" of *Slumdog Millionaire*'s frenetic tour of India's "underbelly." To summarize the plot of the film briefly once again, it is on the surface a completely different narrative to *The Best Exotic Marigold Hotel* as it follows an Indian protagonist—Jamal Mallik—on an extremely improbable journey from rags to riches through the dramatic device of a game show (modelled on "Who Wants to be A Millionaire") where his particular personal history allows him to win an enormous amount of money. Again while, *The Best Exotic Marigold Hotel* for the most part concentrates on the minutae of life in Jaipur, *Slumdog Millionaire* seems to wish to recreate the experience of a new visitor's headlong rush through the pages of *Lonely Planet*; from the slums of Dharavi to the iconic Taj Mahal as Jamal struggles to survive a tumultuous life. As opposed to the directly identificatory positions offered by the former movie, in *Slumdog Millionaire* the figure of the Western tourist is repeatedly interpolated into the narrative primarily as a dupe as Jamal is engaged in various "cons" to relieve the naïve of their money. At one point he even mocks two freshly hoodwinked patrons as having delivered an experience of the "real India" to them as promised.

Figure 25.3 Representing the expectation of a uniquely immersive experience.

Source: Ministry of Tourism (2007).

While the overt stance of the film seems to indicate a self-conscious position regarding both the glittering projections of "modern India" and the foreign tourist who bumbles about attempting to find the "real India," it must also be noted that, much like the slum tour referenced earlier, the film must (re)produce certain ossified images to satisfy its viewers. In his critique of the colonialist underpinnings of so-called "self-conscious" narratives of independent tourism Tickell (2001) points out that even irony is not deployed without motive in these contexts. He notes that even as such travelogues "employ types of structural irony in their representation of independent travel . . . we should remain aware that this use of irony serves to both question and reinstate a European cultural genealogy of representations of the Other" (pp. 44–45). By placing the viewers in a position of supremacy over the "dupes" in the narrative itself, the film covertly assures them of their position as "different" from those who would blunder in to these "dangerous" locales without proper preparation. In the same frame, however, these viewers are allowed to immerse themselves in the life of the slum as unseen voyeurs. As Mendes (2010) notes, this immersive effect was achieved by Danny Boyle (the director) instructing his crew to "sneak through crowds and shoot a large part of the film on digital video with handheld cameras that made them look more like tourists than film crew" (p. 475). This last passage perhaps sums up best the seeming inextricability of the tourist and the filmmaker.

The "tourism" of *The Best Exotic Marigold Hotel* and *Slumdog Millionaire* is then deployed at two levels; first on the level of the filmic texts themselves, as mobilizing the various motifs and metaphors of the "postcolonial exotic" that I have already discussed; and second by affecting actual tourist behaviors in the spaces that they frame in these narrative logics. While the vision of retiring in India is a very different one in the reality show, *The Real Exotic Marigold Hotel* from the carefully curated image presented in the advertisement in Figure 25.1, both are underpinned by the same aspirational narratives that position India's "bountiful" cultural heritage as a monetizable resource for older (white) tourists to retire in style.

Similarly, while the "realism" of poverty, violence, corruption, and crime highlighted in *Slumdog Millionaire* is certainly opposed to the "brand" of modern India as potential economic superpower that the "Incredible India!" campaign attempts to build, both texts share a common underlying logic of India as an "experience." Within this framing the actual and very real problems faced by the common Indian individual are mediatized and used for "shock value" to titillate both viewers and the tourists who then sign up for slum tours to see the "real" Dharavi (Meschkank, 2010). Ironically, of course, the film was not "really" shot in Dharavi at all, foregrounding the problematics of such representational politics. It is therefore vital to keep in mind the material connections between such popular culture place- and myth-making operations and actual destination management by local tour operators and other interested parties.

Implications for popular culture tourism

It is clear from the above analysis that the implications for popular culture tourism within a post and neo-colonial setting are manifold, and force a further consideration of how (neo-)colonialist frameworks continue to inform destination management and tourism locale construction in contemporary culture. As I have demonstrated, this is particularly key in the case of cultures like India, which have been subject to a long history of construction of otherness and exoticism through Western popular culture products. As opposed to theorists who wish to see clear demarcations between the effects of such historical influences and more modern manifestations, however, I have argued that these logics continue to influence the self-fashioning of certain destinations (and government-backed initiatives). The powerful imperative for these destinations to continue to fit into these orientalizing narratives must be seen as part of the continuing impact of the interlinked forces of capitalism and globalization.

This analysis has been framed in opposition to the many contemporary analyzes of popular culture tourism, which theorize the relationship between text and locale as one of celebration and subversive meaning-making. This is seen particularly in cases of fan-based tourism, such as that inspired by the *Harry Potter* franchise (Iwashita, 2006; Lee, 2012), as well as sports-fan tourism, where particular sites such as stadiums gain prominence due to their association with a particular event (Kurtzman & Zauhar, 1997; Weed & Bull, 2012). However, it is equally important to examine cases in which the relationship between popular culture text, tourist, and site is affected by historical and cultural forces that work in less celebratory ways. Even within fan tourism in Western media contexts such as *Harry Potter* it is vital to remain aware of potential power differentials. For instance, as J. K. Rowling prepares to expand her magical world to North America, there are growing concerns about her appropriation of Native American mythos as fuel for her own (now very lucrative) empire. As Adrienn (2015, para. 7–8), a Native American scholar-blogger points out,

> But we're not magical creatures, we're contemporary peoples who are still here, and still practice our spiritual traditions, traditions that are not akin to a completely imaginary wizarding world (as badass as that wizarding world is). In a fact I quote often on this blog, it wasn't until 1978 that we as Native peoples were even legally allowed to practice our religious beliefs or possess sacred objects like eagle feathers. Up until that point, there was a coordinated effort through assimilation policies, missionary systems, and cultural genocide to stamp out these traditions, and with them, our existence as Indigenous peoples. We've fought and worked incredibly hard to maintain these practices and pass them on.
>
> So I get worried thinking about the message it sends to have "indigenous magic" suddenly be associated with the *Harry Potter* brand and world. Because the other piece I deal with on this blog is the constant commodification of our spiritual practices too. There is an entire industry of plastic shamans selling ceremonies, or places like Urban Outfitters selling "smudge kits" and fake eagle feathers. As someone who owns a genuine time-turner, I know that marketing around *Harry Potter* is a billion dollar enterprise, and so I get nervous thinking about the marketing piece. American fans are going to be super stoked at the existence of a wizarding school on this side of the pond, and I'm sure will want to snatch up anything related to it—which I really hope doesn't include Native-inspired anything.

Since the writing of this response it has been revealed that the proposed magical system in North America does include decontextualized artifacts from Native American cultures and so it is probable that the associated merchandise will enact Adrienne's (2015) worst fears. It is therefore more vital than ever to engage with the more fraught intersections of popular culture tourism with issues of historical, economic, and racial marginalization especially as they remain embedded in (often beloved) popular culture texts.

Questions such as "Who has access to these sites and in what way is this access framed?" and "What are the effects of such tourism in real material ways on local populations?" are therefore of great import to these explorations. In this chapter, through my close reading of both promotional materials and ostensibly "realist" filmic texts, I hope to have demonstrated this importance as well as elucidated the ways in which seemingly disparate texts are influenced by common logics of producing the "postcolonial exotic." Further research, with a greater number of texts, will surely continue to expand on these theoretical pathways.

References

Adrienne, K. (2015). Dear JK Rowling, I'm Concerned About the American Wizarding School. Native Appropriations. http://nativeappropriations.com/2015/06/dear-jk-rowling-im-concerned-about-the-american-wizarding-school.html, accessed April 2, 2016.

Alter, J. S. (2004). *Yoga in Modern India: The Body Between Science and Philosophy.* Princeton, NJ: Princeton University Press.

Boorstin, Daniel J. (1964). *The Image: A Guide to Pseudo-Events in America.* New York: Harper.

Cohen, E. (1972). Toward a Sociology of International Tourism. *Social Research, 39*(1), 164–189.

Collins-Kreiner, Noga, & Keren Tueta Sagi. (2011). Tourism to India as Popular Culture: A Cultural, Educational and Religious Experience at Dharamsala. *South Asian Popular Culture* 9 (July): 131–145. doi: 10.1080/14746681003798078.

Dyson, Peter. (2012). Slum Tourism: Representing and Interpreting "Reality" in Dharavi, Mumbai. *Tourism Geographies* 14 (May): 254–274. doi: 10.1080/14616688.2011.609900.

Geary, D. (2013). Incredible India in a Global Age: The Cultural Politics of Image Branding in Tourism. *Tourist Studies* 13 (January). doi: 10.1177/1468797612471105.

Hudson, Simon, & Ritchie, J. R. Brent. (2009). Branding a Memorable Destination Experience: The Case of "Brand Canada." *International Journal of Tourism Research*, 11 (2): 217–228. https://doi.org/10.1002/jtr.720.

Huggan, G. (2001). *The Postcolonial Exotic: Marketing the Margins.* London and New York: Routledge.

Iwashita, C. (2006). Media Representation of the UK as a Destination for Japanese Tourists, Popular Culture and Tourism. *Tourist Studies* 6 (1): 59–77.

Kerrigan, F., J. Shivanandan, & A.-M. Hede. (2012). Nation Branding: A Critical Appraisal of Incredible India. *Journal of Macromarketing* 32 (May). doi: 10.1177/0276146712445788.

Kurtzman, J. & Zauhar, J. (1997). A Wave in Time: The Sports Tourism Phenomena. *Journal of Sport Tourism* 4 (2): 7–24.

Lee, C. (2012). "Have Magic, Will Travel": Tourism and Harry Potter's United (Magical) Kingdom. *Tourist Studies* 12 (1): 52–69.

MacCannell, D. (1973). Staged Authenticity: Arrangements of Social Space in Tourist Settings. *American Sociological Review* 79: 589–603.

McGarth, Rachel. (2016). *The Best Exotic Marigold Hotel*: Inspired Reality TV Show Coming To BBC Two. *Huffington Post*, January 7. www.huffingtonpost.co.uk/2016/01/07/marigold-hotel-bbc2-reality-tv-show_n_8928448.html.

Mendes, Ana Cristina. (2010). Showcasing India Unshining: Film Tourism in Danny Boyle's *Slumdog Millionaire. Third Text* 24 (July): 471–479. doi:10.1080/09528822.2010.491379.

Meschkank, Julia. (2010). Investigations into Slum Tourism in Mumbai: Poverty Tourism and the Tensions between Different Constructions of Reality. *GeoJournal* 76 (December). doi: 10.1007/s10708-010-9401-7.

Ministry of Tourism. (2004). http://incredibleindiacampaign.com/ campaign2004.html.

Ministry of Tourism. (2007). http://incredibleindiacampaign.com/campaign2007.html.

Ministry of Tourism. (2009). http://incredibleindiacampaign.com/campaign2009.html.

Postans, Adam. (2016). *The Real Marigold Hotel* Is Brilliant as Oldies Show CBB How to Do a Celebrity Show. *Mirror*, January 30. www.mirror.co.uk/tv/tv-news/real-marigold-hotel-brilliant-oldies-7276421.

Sharpley, Richard & Priya Sundaram. (2005). Tourism: A Sacred Journey? The Case of Ashram Tourism, India. *International Journal of Tourism Research* 7 (May). doi: 10.1002/jtr.522.

Strauss, S. (2005). *Positioning Yoga: Balancing Acts across Cultures.* Oxford: Berg.

Tickell, Alex. (2001). Footprints on The Beach: Traces of Colonial Adventure in Narratives of Independent Tourism." *Postcolonial Studies* 4 (April): 39–54. doi: 10.1080/13688790120046861.

Urry, John. (2002). *The Tourist Gaze.* Sage: London.

Weed, M. & Bull, C. (2012). *Sports Tourism: Participants, Policy and Providers.* Abingdon: Routledge.

26

THE FORCE MEETS THE KITTIWAKE

Shooting *Star Wars* on Skellig Michael

Ruth Barton

The concluding sequence of *Star Wars: Episode VII The Force Awakens* (directed by J. J. Abrams, 2015) was both a pay-off for the millions of fans of the series and a teaser. Following years of warfare and clandestine operations, the Resistance finally learns of the hiding place of the last Jedi. Rey (Daisy Ridley) flies off to meet with him on her own, heading to the blue, almost entirely water-bound planet where he is hiding out. She lands on a sparse rocky habitation sticking out of the waters, and ascends the narrow stairs to the top. There she finds herself looking at the back of a man in hooded, monastic garb, who is staring out over the sea. She reaches out the lightsaber to him as he turns and reveals himself to be Luke Skywalker (Mark Hamill). Before they can exchange words, the image disappears and the closing credits play. The audience is primed for *Episode VIII*.

Setting the scene

The Skellig islands – Skellig Michael (or the Great Skellig) and Small Skellig – lie off County Kerry. Skellig Michael is a UNESCO world heritage centre and houses a well-preserved monastic outpost of the Early Christian period. As the World Heritage Ireland website describes it:

> Located at the western edge of the European landmass, Skellig Michael was the chosen destination for a small group of ascetic monks who, in their pursuit of greater union with God, withdrew from civilisation to this remote and inaccessible place. Some time between the sixth and eight centuries, a monastery was founded on this precipitous rock giving rise to one of the most dramatic examples of the extremes of Christian monasticism.
>
> *(World Heritage Ireland, n.d.)*

Both islands are important bird sanctuaries and home to gannets, puffins, the Arctic tern, the black guillemot, the black-legged kittiwake and other Atlantic birds. Visitors are ferried to the island by local boatmen who are allowed access between mid-May and September. Visitors are only permitted ashore if official guides are present. Numbers are restricted and weather conditions determine whether the journey can be made or not. The climb to the top is steep and the Office of Public Works (OPW) issues numerous warnings to potential visitors about what the trip entails. This has been particularly important following two tourist deaths on the island. The decision to locate this segment of the shoot on the island was therefore contentious. On the other hand, the potential for enhanced tourism was widely promoted. As a spokesman for Fáilte Ireland (the National Tourism Development Authority) explained to the media: "The reach of a global brand such as *Star Wars* is just phenomenal. It's absolutely priceless in terms of raising Ireland's profile abroad" (in Gleeson, 2015, p. 5).

In this chapter, I want to look at the intersection between tourism and the location chosen for this final sequence. In particular, I want to focus on the negotiations between the *Star Wars* production team, the Irish Film Board (IFB) and the OPW over the use of Skellig Michael as a location and the immediate responses to it. In order to do this, I placed Freedom of Information (FOI) requests with the IFB and the OPW and will be drawing on those in what follows. I will also be taking into account discourses of Celticism, spirituality and peripherality that informed the decision to shoot in this remote location and the ensuing responses to it.

Theoretical and disciplinary underpinnings

The neoliberal argument:

From the beginning, it is clear that the IFB was much more enthusiastic about the proposed shoot than the OPW was. Emails from Naoise Barry, then Film Commissioner of the IFB, indicate that he was pushing for access to the islands for the location scouts from 2013. He was repeatedly frustrated by restrictions on the use of boats to ferry visitors and Atlantic weather conditions. High winds and turbulent seas prevented travel on numerous occasions. He was also inhibited by the need to keep the negotiations a secret. This extended to a confidentiality agreement that Barry, Niall Ó Donnchú (Assistant Secretary-General of the Department of Arts, Heritage and Gaeltacht) and others had to sign (email from Naoise Barry to Niall Ó Donnchú, 13 February 2014). In the end, the initial reconnaissance trip didn't take place until midweek of 1 and 2 April 2014. At the same time, Barry was able to confirm (email of 3 April 2014) that the *Star Wars* production team would qualify for a tax rebate of up to 22 per cent under Ireland's production tax incentive (Section 481). The assumption was that a film shoot would commence in September 2014. September is significant in what was to follow as the nesting season would be nearly over.

In an email of 4 June 2014, Naoise Barry outlined what they would be looking for in return for allowing the *Star Wars* production to use the location: "the Skellig be credited as a location in the movie, and also a request in the movies [*sic*] end-credits for our 3 Government Agencies [OPW, Department of Arts and Heritage and IFB]". In what was later to become contentious, the film's producers did not pay a location fee. In another email (9 July 2014), Barry spells out the reasons for attracting the shoot:

> The Irish Film Board has spent the last 18 months working to convince the films [*sic*] producers, [REDACTED] to bring this high profile project to Ireland, for the future benefit of Irish tourism, the Irish film industry, and the wider Irish economy. Improvements to Ireland's tax incentive for feature film & TV drama, mean we expect to attract more of these large productions to Ireland.

The OPW was unconvinced by the economic argument and as late as 6 June 2014 the Principal Officer of the Heritage Section of the OPW, Frank Shalvey, was emailing Edmund Samson, one of the location managers, suggesting alternative locations in Kerry. On 24 June, Shalvey confided to his colleagues in the OPW that, "At this stage, there are elements of the project emerging more clearly; some of them, frankly, are a bit scary." The scary part was that they [the production team]:

> wanted to "take down" a wall that appeared to them to be a modern construction, rebuilding it afterward. [. . .] I responded fairly strongly negatively to this – I would hope they realise that this is not on, but we'll see if they repeat this or similar.
>
> *(Email from Frank Shalvey to John Cahill, Grellan Rourke,*
> *OPW, 24 June 2014)*

The OPW by now seems to have been out of step with the mood music coming not just from the IFB but also from other official bodies. In an email (11 July 2014), the location manager [name redacted throughout but probably Edmund Sampson or Unit Production Manager, Martin Joy] confirms that:

> The support from everyone in last weeks [*sic*] meeting including that of the Minister and all the senior department heads coupled with their understanding of the importance of this type of project to Ireland economically in terms of tourism, culturally and as an advertisement for your new film initiatives is unprecedented and we need to capitalize on that to make this project the first of many.

The major outstanding concern was the effect of the shoot on seabirds. Up to this point, filming on Skellig Michael was only permitted for teams of up to eight people using battery-operated equipment. The exception had been Werner Herzog's notorious *Heart of Glass* (*Herz aus Glas*, 1976), which ends in a very similar manner on the Skellig. So similar are these two finales that one suspects an homage. However, the Herzog film was never mentioned in correspondence and, given that it would have served as a precedent, it seems that none of the participants in the debate was aware of it. The production approached private operators to fly them out to the island but was turned down. In the end, it emerged that the Air Corps had already flown to the island to assist with repair works to the settlement. They then became involved in the plans, presumably with the consent of the government. To aid the IFB's case Naoise Barry was able to forward a report dated 16 July 2014 by an ecological consultant (whose identity is redacted but OPW correspondence suggests that it was Simon Nobes) that backed up with appropriate academic studies the argument that the proposed helicopter use would have minimal effect on Skellig Michael's species. Although the consultant was hired by the producers, all sides expressed their respect for him. The OPW in fact was not responsible for wildlife conservation (this was the preserve of the National Parks and Wildlife Service [NPWS]) but found itself in the position of answering for all conservation on the island. It is also unclear to what extent other potential interested parties were being consulted; later it was claimed that they were not. The OPW was under extreme pressure at this stage as plans for filming had been brought forward from September to the end of July. Requests were changing fast.

Having observed the initial preparations, Claire O'Halloran, an OPW guide on the island, emailed Frank Shalvey expressing extreme concerns about the timing of the activity and its extent: "I am now certain that what is proposed is so appallingly out of scale, so completely inappropriate for this location in several ways that I actually find it almost impossible to believe that anyone is approving it" (email from Claire O'Halloran to Frank Shalvey, 8 July 2014). Later O'Halloran would go public with her concerns but only when she was out of contract with the OPW.

On 7 July 2014, Skellig Michael guide, Robert [Bob] Harris emailed Frank Shalvey:

I just want to add here [. . .] that I am in complete agreement with Claire [O'Halloran] when she expresses most serious reservations about the proposed project, particularly when it comes to the dangers proposed to wildlife on the island. I expressed identical concerns to you last week, and since then I have become aware of the much greater scope of the proposed project. Given the internationally protected status of the habitat, I wonder whether there is not an actual legal impediment to what is proposed.

Problems over the seabirds continued to threaten the shoot. An email from Frank Shalvey following a major meeting of all parties held on 15 July confirmed:

The discussion yesterday was very intense, as you can appreciate, and very focussed on bird etc. issues. NM [National Monument] issues are, surprisingly for once, quite OK by comparison. If it wasn't for our feathered friends, this might even be termed a dawdle.

(email from Frank Shalvey to Frank Shalvey, cc Edward Bourke, Grellan Rourke,
17 July 2014)

Frank Shalvey (email of 14 July 2014 to John McMahon et al.) was already feeling tetchy about the pressure that was being exerted on them to sign a location contract:

My problems with this Agreement are many but, in general, I would simply express it as being much too laden in favour of the Film Company. [. . .] In my view, we should simply decline to sign the Agreement and say that they'll have our full cooperation as we promised, but that we simply aren't in a position to agree to these clauses [around confidentiality in particular]. They are constantly saying to us that we should trust them – maybe its [sic] time to turn that around: if they want to get access to Skellig, they'll just have to do it without a legal Agreement in place and trust us. It might be interesting to see how far that particular suggestion will get us.

An email of 18 July 2014 [name redacted, probably the location manager] suggests that the lengthy negotiations might well be running out of time:

We are having to readjust our shoot to a sea based (minimal helicopter approach) to deal with an ecological issue around the nesting birds on the island. The work put in by Niall O'Donochu [sic], James Hickey [CEO of the Irish Film Board] and Naoise as [sic] been incredible, earlier this week we were faced with the very real possibility of not being able to shoot on the island at all but they have worked with us to turn this around.

On the same day the location manager was emailing Barry that, "It's not a no but it is a reconsider."

Through July, the OPW continued to stress the need to restrict activities and do nothing that would cause damage to the dry stone walling and other buildings. Further documentation shows a highly pared-down shoot. This was considered acceptable by the location manager as: "Much of the appeal of the location comes from its stark, Spartan beauty and its ancient, mystical ambience" ("Props", section 2.4.1, document dated 17 July 2014, name of author redacted).

A helicopter reconnaissance trip went ahead and Clare O'Halloran reportedly witnessed about 20 fledglings disappearing from Cross Cove (email from Edward Bourke [Senior Archaeogist,

National Monuments Service] to Grellan Rourke and Frank Shalvey, 16 July 2014). Some debate followed as to whether this could alternatively be as a result of the father guillemot teaching the chicks to fly. Later versions of the story (Siggins, 2015) described the chicks as kittiwakes. An eyewitness report contradicted the figure of 20, saying that they had only seen one chick in the water and another being eaten by a gull (email from Edmund Sampson to Niall O Donnchu et al., 16 July 2014). Still, it seems that following the kittiwake incident all further helicopter trips were abandoned and the island was only approached by water. What is not logged in the available correspondence is what exactly persuaded Frank Shalvey and the OPW that the shoot should go ahead, but at this mid-July point, with a frantic IFB on their backs and what seems like full support for the filming from the Department of Arts, Heritage and the Gaeltacht, the OPW gave their consent.

By 25 July the story had been leaked to the media. On that day, following newspaper coverage of the shoot, UNESCO contacted the government to enquire about the reports it had been reading (email from Kerstin Mainz [UNESCO] to Terry Allen [Department of Arts, Heritage and the Gaeltacht], Catherine Desmond [Department of Arts, Heritage and the Gaeltacht], and Grellan Rourke, 25 July 2014). Later the government justified its decision not to inform UNESCO on the grounds that the proposals to film did not constitute, "major restorations or new constructions which may affect the outstanding universal value of the property" and therefore did not require advance notification to the World Heritage Committee (letter from Terry Allen, Principal Officer National Monuments Service to Petya Totcharova, UNESCO World Heritage Centre, 2 September 2015). An exclusion zone was established around Skellig Michael to prevent sightseers and reporters from approaching the island to observe the filming.

Filming took place on 28 July and concluded on 30 July. *Star Wars: Episode VII The Force Awakens* was released in cinemas worldwide in mid-December 2015.

The neoliberal argument refuted:

> What we can conclude from this selection of exchanges between the various bodies is a three-way division of Irish responses to the request to film on Skellig Michael. One is the unsurprising support of the Film Board, who promoted the shoot on the grounds of tourism, but also saw it as strengthening their hand in an increasingly competitive environment for attracting overseas productions. This competitive environment also includes Northern Ireland, currently enjoying extraordinary success for hosting *Game of Thrones*. The other response was that of the government agencies, notably the then Department of Arts, Heritage and the Gaeltacht [Irish-speaking regions] and the OPW. The latter in particular expressed some major concerns about the shoot but, reading between the lines, were under strong pressure from the IFB to accede to the request. The final element of the equation was that of the OPW guides on Skellig Michael whose strenuous opposition to the shoot was a foretaste of the public response to come.

Bord Fáilte (the Irish Tourist Board) was swift to exploit the use of Skellig Michael in the film. It released a local advertising campaign that ran in cinemas before each screening aimed at reminding viewers that this was just one of numerous such locations that they could visit on the Wild Atlantic Way, a successful branding exercise that guides tourists along the Atlantic Coast of Ireland. Capitalizing on the release globally was facilitated by a pre-existing discourse that conceptualized Ireland as a peripheral location infused with Celtic spirituality and other pre-modern attributes. Indeed, early news items about the film suggested that Bord Fáilte need do little more than print its logo on publicity materials and sit back and watch the tourist bookings flow in.

In early December 2015, a *New York Times* article sounded an appropriate note of mysticism and awe in describing a trip to the site. The author, a seasoned Skellig Michael visitor, had travelled out to the island during one of the last visits permitted before the end of the season. Her boatman had been part of the filming and had signed a non-disclosure agreement regarding details of the shoot. However:

> you'd sooner keep a Wookiee [*sic*] from roaring than an Irishman from regaling a willing audience, and soon Mr. O'Driscoll was dishing away. "A bunch of us boatmen were standing around, and Mark Hamill came over," he recalled. "He said, 'Any advice for climbing the stairs?' We told him, 'Just pace yourself, and don't ever, ever look down.'"
>
> *(Hahn, 2015)*

The journalist climbed the 618 steps to the monastery and reported that:

> The views over the Atlantic were endless, and gulls and gannets soared and dived, their cries echoing with either anguished loneliness or triumphant salvation, possibly a bit of both. No wonder George Bernard Shaw, following a visit in 1910, described Skellig Michael this way: "I hardly feel real again . . . I tell you, the thing does not belong to any world that you and I have lived and worked in: It is part of our dream world."
>
> *(Hahn, 2015)*

Hahn's observations draw on the same discursive tropes as those promoted by Bord Fáilte. Aside from the invocation of the literary heritage and the elision of the natural and the human, she introduces the garrulous boatman, a familiar voice not just from travel writing on Ireland over the generations, but also from colonial and postcolonial constructions of Irish Otherness. As Mark McGovern (2003, p. 84) writes:

> the image of "garrulous paddy" has a long lineage and is deeply embedded in dominant representations of the Irish throughout modern history. An almost invariably alcohol-centred "stage Irish" persona is reflected in early travel writing on Ireland from at least the late 18th century onward helping to establish a series of easily recognisable and historicised symbols and cultural reference points for contemporary external visions of Ireland.

There are several further points to add to McGovern's analysis. The garrulous Paddy is not just an external construction. The figure may have been initially disseminated through British colonial writings and as stage entertainment, but, as many writers have argued, the indigenous Irish soon realized the potential in appropriating the stereotype for their own purposes. In the nineteenth century Paddy became a wily trickster, one of whose functions was to puncture British colonial superiority (Gibbons, 1987, pp. 210–21). One needs therefore to understand the contemporary garrulous Paddy as part of that tradition, as performing the stereotype rather than necessarily embodying it. The second point is that within Irish discourse, the Kerryman is a subversive figure. With his thick accent, rural ways and disdain for authority, he is at once the butt of the joke and its progenitor. Lastly, as this chapter will discuss below, the stereotype has its roots in a reality that may not chime with cosmopolitan expectations of the tourist experience. In this manner, the garrulous boatman is a performance (for the American journalist) and a reality, a member of a peripheral community whose identity is predicated on disdain for the centre's authority and (here) feelings of superiority to the cosmopolitan Other, Mark Hamill.

Michael Clancy (2009, pp. 81–82) has argued that:

> the content of the Irish brand continues to emphasize the Ireland of old rather than that of a modern, cosmopolitan society. To be sure, part of the message is for Ireland to be all things to all people, but more dominant traditional themes of Ireland as outside of modernity, a mystical and magical place that fosters personal transformation, simultaneously speak to the nation as one more consumer good at the same time that they offer a quaint throwback picture of the Irish nation to its own citizens during a period of rapid social change.

Celticism and peripherality can be leveraged as equally for commerce, therefore, as for identity formation. Their appropriation by the *Star Wars* "universe" is a reminder that under globalization national attributes can be freely purchased in the cultural marketplace. It is this feature of postmodernity and neoliberalism that helps to understand why it is was so important to *Star Wars* to shoot a sequence that had (obviously) no Irish content on a circa sixth-century monastic site. A promotional video featuring interviews with the makers and stars of *The Force Awakens* spells this out. Over shots of a ferry leaving the harbour in warm sunshine, Martin Joy explains: "We wanted to find somewhere completely from another time and place. Skellig Michael, an island off the Irish coast – we were just blown away by it. It certainly fed into our *Star Wars* universe" (Discover Ireland, 2016). Although this echoes content from the production cited above ("Much of the appeal of the location comes from its stark, Spartan beauty and its ancient, mystical ambience"), in fact this promotional video was funded by Tourism Ireland, the body tasked with marketing Ireland overseas. This funding and the similarities between the wording underline the common interests of two of the sides in the contentious decision to shoot on Skellig Michael. Despite the fact that the *Star Wars* series is science fiction and set in a "galaxy far, far away", the use of this specific location acted as a guarantor of authenticity. The spirituality associated with the monastic settlement is tonally consistent with the series' borrowings from world religions and its themes of good versus evil, sacrifice and rebirth. Visually, computer-generated imagery (CGI) still cannot render scenery in as realistic a manner as can location shooting and the final scene looks "real" in a way many of the battle and other galactic sequences do not (although this is not the only scene in the film shot on location). The *New York Times* article further reinforces this global understanding of Skellig Michael as a signifier of values the *Star Wars* series aspired to convey.

So far, so good, one might say. However, while the reservations of the OPW, and particularly of its guides, seemed to have been silenced by the greater force of the production, the Film Board, and the Department of Arts, Heritage and the Gaeltacht, matters turned out otherwise. Even before the film's release in December 2015, the use of Skellig Michael as the setting for the film's finale became increasingly controversial. Claire O'Halloran went public with her comments. Academics, writers, conservationists and others agreed. Suggestions of a cover-up emerged. The excitement that followed the leaked news of the shoot was soon replaced by outrage, with the broadsheets, notably the *Irish Times*, running a series of highly critical articles. Complaints focused on the damage to wildlife and the island's ecosystem, damage to UNESCO-protected structures, use of the navy to police the shoot and lack of consultation. These criticisms were in turn picked up by the global media, appearing in newspapers in Australia, Malta, New Zealand, the UK, and the USA, as well as on a number of websites. It was left to regular *Irish Times* columnist and cultural commentator, Fintan O'Toole (2015), to draw out the connections between the *Star Wars* shoot and the globalizing of Ireland. Opening his column with a discussion of the spiritual history of Skellig Michael and the importance of its remoteness as a reminder that there are limits to humanity's boundaries, he argued that:

> Once Skellig Michael becomes [. . .] Luke Skywalker's refuge, it ceases to be our refuge from the endless, voracious insistence on knowing the price of everything and the value of nothing. It ceases to be the edge of the world and becomes one of the world's quotidian commodities. It ceases to be "beyond". And in collaborating with this process, the Government is making it clear that, for contemporary Ireland, there is no "beyond" at all. There's nothing we won't sell, no line we won't cross, no aspect of our heritage that is not available for exploitation.
>
> *(O'Toole, 2015, p. 12)*

A consistent critic of Ireland's embrace of neoliberalism, O'Toole was articulating a position that lies behind many of the concerns expressed around the shoot. In a country struggling to come to terms with the cycle of boom/bust/boom that has become familiar from the Celtic Tiger, through the recession and on to the economic recovery, the identification of "national values" has become increasingly complicated. Inevitably, part of the response to this cycle has been a questioning of what Irishness stands for, even if it has not, at least yet, resulted in the embrace of the far-right nationalism that has emerged under similar conditions in other territories. Thus, one needs to see the concerns expressed around the archaeology and ecology of Skellig Michael as being rooted in a profound distaste for neoliberalism and its effects. If there are two identifiable remainders of an essential Irishness, however constructed that is, they might well be its ancient spirituality and its closeness to nature.

The boatman's revenge

Local tourism to Kerry experienced a huge influx of visitors arriving on the back of having seen Skellig Michael (or possibly heard about it) in *The Force Awakens*. In what follows, the garrulous boatman makes a second appearance, on this occasion inducting the tourist into an experience whose authenticity, for some, became excessive. There is no need here to rehearse the ongoing debates around the concept of authenticity within tourist discourse; or the overlaps between acts of pilgrimage and of tourism; however, it is worth noting that, in this specific case, tourists and fans alike were travelling to a pre-existing site of pilgrimage or "sacred site" (McCannell, 1976). Reports of visits to the islands describe a mix of traditional tourists/pilgrims and lightsaber-wielding *Star Wars* devotees, many in costume. Within this specific discourse, journeying to a peripheral location can be understood both as a visit to a simulacrum or reminder of the pro-filmic event and to a "real" spiritual site. The pre-existing tourism infrastructure for conveying pilgrims to the Skelligs found itself suddenly under interrogation as the dangers of taking the journey emerged.

RTÉ radio's "Liveline" program is a consumer complaints forum usually hosted by Joe Duffy. In the episode under discussion here, aired on 13 July 2016, Duffy was on summer vacation, and Philip Boucher-Hayes had taken his place. A caller, PJ, contacted the show to complain about his experience of the ferry journey out to Skellig Michael. He had been motivated to travel for spiritual reasons but his two younger companions were with him because of the *Star Wars* connection. As he told it, hardly were they out to sea but a swell hit the boat, causing his two travelling companions to throw up, one repeatedly. Later he realized that the boatman had not supplied them with lifejackets, not were any of the other passengers wearing them.

He had been, he conceded, prepared for a "hairy" trip, but not one as hairy as this. In the UK, he told Boucher-Hayes, no boat could travel if the passengers were not supplied with lifejackets. A medley of callers followed PJ, some with favourable comments on their experience of an Atlantic journey by local boat, others swearing they would never go again. Boucher-Hayes reminded his callers that it was unrealistic to make such a journey without expecting to be sick, wet and uncomfortable and that the climb to the top, which several had found themselves unable to undertake, was tough. Following these, Dermot, the skipper of the boat PJ had travelled on, came on air to explain his position, notably that if you always handed out lifejackets, they would get shabby and that there had never been an accident in the years he had been skippering a ferry. In further response to the complaints he added:

> There's nobody catching you by the ears and pulling you down the pier into boats. Besides, we are advertised. You should look into it. Did you see the video inside in Valentia [an island off County Kerry] on the Skelligs experience? It showed the conditions around the rock.

PJ pressed him further: "Dermot, what about if there is a freak wave, and the boat is overturned? What happens to the people on board the boat?" The reply was indignant: "You know something? When that happens get back on to me. These men are going out to the Skelligs having a lifetime of experience in these waters" (Boucher-Hayes, 2016).

In this instance, the garrulous boatman's disdain for controls and standardization rips through the conventions of the sanitized tourist offering. His logic is not that of the centre, but of a defiant peripherality. While an exchange on-air such as this might sound like Bord Fáilte's worst nightmare (and may have been received as such), in fact it is equally possible to argue that it enhanced the region's desirability as a destination. Most theorists of tourism agree that independent travel has become a popular alternative to the homogenization of the packaged tourist experience. "Despite the difficulties of accessing film locations," Stefan Roesch (2009, p. 79) writes, "many examples illustrate the devotion of film fans who will travel to even the remotest locations." Anyone preparing for a visit to Skellig Michael will encounter numerous on-line warnings about travel conditions (though not about safety) and may already consider themselves to be setting out on an adventure/quest rather than pre-purchasing a package. It is unfortunate that no *Star Wars* fans spoke on the broadcast though one may guess that they were not part of its listenership. Indeed throughout the multiple debates on the Skellig Michael shoot, they were more spoken for than speaking, emerging from the "Letters to the Editor" section of the *Irish Times* in a startlingly clichéd manner:

> The argument that Skellig Michael's inclusion then, and for the future, has merit on the premise that it will generate more tourism is belied by ignorance of the typical US Star Wars fan – a badly ageing character without a passport and whose range of movement consists of an assisted toddle no further than from the couch to the car.
>
> *(Broin, 2015)*

Implications for popular culture tourism

Although at first sight commonalities exist between the use of New Zealand as a location for Peter Jackson's *Lord of the Rings* (*LOTR*) (2001, 2002, 2003) and *Hobbit* (2012, 2013, 2014) films and the setting of the finale of *The Force Awakens* on Skellig Michael, it is in fact the distinctions between the two national experiences that makes them of interest and enable us to draw some conclusions about the latter. Rodanthi Tzanelli (2015, p.10) has analyzed the process whereby Peter Jackson and his creative team transformed *LOTR* and *The Hobbit* into national products so that, "European cultural patterns of suffering as well as their primary metaphysical binarisms (good vs. evil) persisted – or, rather, were reinterpreted in compatible native (Maori) contexts." Evidently, the scale of the location shoot is quite different, with only a fragment of *The Force Awakens* being filmed in Ireland whereas the Tolkien adaptations have become closely associated with New Zealand, not least because of Jackson's identity as a New Zealander. Nor is he just any New Zealander. As Deborah Jones (2008, p. 97) argues:

> Jackson's love for New Zealand and, specifically, his hometown of Wellington identifies him as a patriot who puts his country first, bringing a potential creative industries gold rush to all his compatriots. Eschewing the traditional path of talented New Zealander filmmakers to Hollywood, Jackson has made it clear that he wants to stay based here.

By contrast, in Ireland what emerged, particularly in the press coverage, was a failure to identify nationally with the Irish-set sequence or its makers. Even more than that, the use of Skellig Michael by the *Star Wars* production and the part played in securing this by the Film Board and various government agencies came to stand in for a loss of national values. If these concerns were sparked by the commercialization of Ireland's natural and spiritual heritage, at a local level, these globalizing tendencies were, at least to some extent, resisted by workers within the tourist industry who saw their traditional practices (of ferrying passengers) come under unreasonable expectations of conformity to international standards of water safety. Throughout this multi-voiced argument, tradition, tourism, conservation and commerce have repeatedly clashed in a manner that reflects not just this one incident but much of the discourse of contemporary Ireland. The Skellig Michael shoot above all demonstrates a general public and regional distrust of neoliberal, centrist policies.

Although there is no record of the *Star Wars* position in the controversy, they must take some of the blame for the public relations failure of the enterprise at the local level. Their insistence on secrecy bred distrust, particularly when it seemed they could "buy" any government agency they wanted. The fact that no fee changed hands made this slight even worse. Despite or because (depending on your position) of all of this, the Minister for Heritage, Heather Humphreys, gave permission for the production to return for an extended shoot, which it did in September of 2015. This time, they included mainland Kerry and Donegal, as well as the Skelligs. This time, too, the *Star Wars* team launched a major PR assault on the Irish public with Chewbacca visiting local children in their Kerry classroom and the production team making themselves available for interview. We may interpret this as an attempt to placate or out-manoeuvre the vocal archaeological and ecological critics of the venture, as was the decision to film in less contentious regions. In this they were considerably more successful than on their first visit. All this suggests that 20 Kittiwake chicks did (or did not) perish in vain.

References

Boucher-Hayes, P. (Host). (2016, 13 July). *Liveline*. RTÉ Radio.

Broin, U. (2015, 24 December). *Star Wars* and Skellig Michael [Letter to the Editor]. *Irish Times*, p. 15.

Clancy, M. (2009). *Brand New Ireland? Tourism, Development and National Identity in the Irish Republic*. Farnham: Ashgate.

Discover Ireland. (2016, April 15). *Star Wars: The Force Awakens – Behind the Scenes in Ireland*. [Video File]. Retrieved from: www.youtube.com/watch?v=i9f2y4jUYq8.

Gibbons, L. (1987). Romanticism, Realism and Irish Cinema. In K. Rockett, L. Gibbons, & J. Hill. *Cinema and Ireland* (pp. 194–257). Kent and New South Wales: Croom Helm.

Gleeson, C. (2015, 9 December). "Star Wars" Permitted to Film on Skellig. *Irish Times*, p. 5.

Hahn, L. (2015, 6 December). A Force from the Future Visits an Ancient Isle. *New York Times*, TR 5.

Jones, D. (2008). "Ring Leader": Peter Jackson as "Creative Industries" Hero. In H. Margolis, S. Cubitt, B. King, & T. Jutel (Eds.), *Studying the Event Film: The Lord of the Rings* (pp. 9–99). Manchester and New York: Manchester University Press.

MacCannell, D. (1976). *The Tourist: A New Theory of the Leisure Class*. London: Macmillan (1999 reprint).

McGovern, M. (2003). "The Cracked Pint Glass of the Servant": The Irish Pub, Irish Identity and the Tourist Eye. In M. Cronin & B. O'Connor (Eds.), *Irish Tourism: Image, Culture and Identity* (pp. 83–103). Clevedon, Buffalo, Toronto, Sydney: Channel View Publications.

O'Toole, F. (2015, 1 September). Beyond Belief – Why Did We Grant Disney's Skelligs wish? *Irish Times*, p. 12.

Roesch, S. (2009). *The Experiences of Film Location Tourists*. Bristol: Channel View.

Siggins, L. (2015, 1 August). Return of the Jedi: *Star Wars* Goes Back to the Skellig. *Irish Times*, p. B5.

Tzanelli, R. (2016). Heritage Entropy in New Zealand: *The Hobbit* (2010) Protests, Film-Work, and Post-Colonial Cosmology. *Global Studies Journal*, 9 (1), 1–14.

World Heritage Ireland. (n.d.). Skellig Michael. Retrieved from www.worldheritageireland.ie/skellig-michael.

27

THE NARRATIVE CAPITAL OF THE PLACE

How the *Millennium* narratives generate place-related values and attract tourists to Sweden

Joakim Lind and Bengt Kristensson Uggla

Setting the scene: *Millennium* popular culture as tourist industry

Between 2008 and 2016 at least 60,000 tourists have taken the official *Millennium* Walking Tour arranged by the Stockholm City Museum. In addition to this, 15,000 *Millennium* maps have been sold, and a couple of thousand more have been given away to city guests (for example, in welcome packages to delegations to the city). An estimated 70,000–90,000 visitors have taken the official *Millennium* tour, following the footsteps of Lisbeth Salander and Michael Blomkvist, either with a guide or with the *Millennium* map (this estimation is based on two people typically sharing a map). For the city of Stockholm, the tour and the map have reached a combined turnover of more than one million euros.[1]

A survey of *Millennium* tour foreign tourists taken in Spring 2010 (from Italy, Britain, Spain, Germany, Sweden, France, and ten other countries) revealed that the *Millennium* trilogy was the "main reason" for visiting Stockholm for 6 percent of these tourists (Lind, 2011, p. 2). Others stated that *Millennium* gave them another reason for choosing Stockholm as their destination, and many more refer to *Millennium* as an important (popular) cultural reference that was at the top of their minds when making their travel choice. Additionally, a considerable proportion of the people attending the tours are locals interested in experiencing their hometown through the *Millennium* lens.[2] This local effect is perhaps one of the most significant results of the *Millennium* stories, the increased quality of life, the pride of the citizens, together with how this attracts other people to move their home and businesses to the city. It seems that most visitors are simply satisfied to be in the *Millennium* environment, film-inspired tourists as well as film-location tourists (i.e. those who want to visit the precise filming spots). From 15 personal interviews of what were mainly international leisure tourists from Australia, Taiwan, Belgium, the UK, Spain, and Italy, conducted at the Stockholm Tourist Centre in January 2010, all had heard of both Stieg Larsson and the *Millennium* trilogy. Moreover, for several respondents, the *Millennium* stories were important in making the decision (if not the deciding factor) to travel to Stockholm.[3]

Even in 2017, more than ten years since the success of *Millennium* began, Stieg Larsson's narrative continues to bring people to Stockholm. And the show seems to go on. How is this industry possible? How is it that all these tourists are visiting places associated with stories and fictional people that never actually existed? And why are all those people so eager to revisit places where nothing from the story has actually taken place? These are serious questions when encountering popular culture and the tourist industry, as well as when examining the cultural economy of our time.

In order to understand the *Millennium*-induced tourism phenomenon, we need to remind ourselves that the *Millennium* tours are only a small part of a much bigger picture—an economy with global reach. In 2010, Stieg Larsson rose to number six on the *Forbes Magazine* list of Top Earning Dead Celebrities (Rose, 2010). During the following decade, the books sold 80 million copies, and have been published in more than 50 languages. Everything started with this three-volume work delivered to the publisher just before the author himself passed away due to a heart attack in 2004.

The bestsellers (2005, 2006, 2007), the movie-adaptions, taken together with several biographies, and a growing meta-literature (see Burnstein, 2011; Rosenberg, 2011) are to be considered as the creative core of the *Millennium* economy. The *Millennium* narrative legacy has also got a new life by David Lagercrantz, who so far has written a fourth and fifth book: *The Girl With the Spider's Web* (Lagercrantz, 2015) and *The Man who Chased his Shadow* (Lagercrantz, 2017).

The narratives have been further developed and extended in the hundreds of thousands of articles in press (Lind, 2012a), and the trilogy has inspired artists, writers, musicians, filmmakers, designers, and trendsetters in many countries. Let us note some financials at hand: Swedish journalist Jonas Leijonhufvud estimates the total turnover from the books to be approximately 420 million euros for the publishing house (Leijonhufvud, 2015). It has even been said that the *Millennium* series saved the Swedish publishing house Norstedts for many years.[4] For Moggliden, the company that owns the copyrights to Stieg Larsson's legacy (owned by Stieg Larssons family), the *Millennium* trilogy has an estimated total turnover of approximately 50 million euros gathered from copyrights from books, movies, audio books, and comic books (Johansson, 2014). The budget for the Swedish and US film productions based on *Millennium* was more than 80 million euros. The American adaptation of *The Girl With the Dragon Tattoo* has, according to Box Office Mojo, a worldwide lifetime gross of 207 million euros.

The original Swedish film trilogy, together with the American movie version of the first book, has attracted approximately 1 billion viewers. And in 2016, Hollywood is considering adopting David Lagercrantz' independent fourth sequel (Lagercrantz, 2015). *Millennium* is an excellent example of how narratives may be developed and reconfigured, re-contextualized, and transformed, generating a cultural economy long after the creator has died.

As such, there is no exaggeration in saying that Stieg Larsson's stories have attracted considerable global interest and attention. The media output has reached at least a hundred thousand articles written about the *Millennium* trilogy and its author so far—texts that have reached billions of people. Thus, different audiences have not only encountered the narratives themselves, but have also been introduced to, and become involved in, a sort of meta-culture and wider body produced through merchandising, articles, blog posts, fan sites, non-fiction books, and biographies, not to mention the series' influence on theater, artists, fashion designers, musicians, filmmakers, and writers all around the world. The stories that originate from the *Millennium* are a multifaceted narrative telling a story about Sweden. *Millennium* narratives are based not only on the texts of the trilogy, for the narratives also tell the story about Stieg Larsson, the struggle for his legacy, the business itself and the story about his own country—Sweden. Indeed, the stories seem to be involved in a dialectical process reflecting how we see ourselves, our culture, and our location.

In 2011, H&M launched a design collection by Trish Summerville, costume designer on David Fincher's version of *The Girl With the Dragon Tattoo*. The *New York Times'* Ruth La Ferla claims that Lisbeth Salander has helped to create or strengthen trends among young people, and that it has become increasingly popular for women to have a tattoo:

> The Salander style, a subversive mélange of goth, punk, classic rock and fetish-wear, has a spate of off-screen counterparts. They include the battle-ready black-on-black uniforms adopted by fashion insiders like the Elle editor Kate Lanphear; and the outlier get-ups of the rap rave group Die Antwoord, whose waxy pallor, gaunt frames and choppy hair call to mind extra-terrestrials. [. . .] Tattoo artists are cashing in. "What Salander has done is inspire women to go under the needle with their own message in mind," said Mr. Rakovic of Inked.
>
> *(La Ferla, 2012)*

It is ironic that the Socialist Stieg Larsson's character and alter ego Lisbeth's fictional representation of a well-established fashion trend (black-clad pierced goths were a trend in Sweden during the years of the millennium, when the author wrote his books) has, ten years later, been established as a new trend—one interesting enough to become a clothing collection of one of the world's largest clothing chains. The trend and representation of society has made a home run. It is *the spectacle society* at its finest, to paraphrase Guy Debord (1977/1967).

The full financial picture of the *Millennium* trilogy reaches far beyond the direct economy of the original books, for it has to be related to the different formats (books and movies), which makes the image of our subject both complex and multidimensional. The stories are fiction, but despite this—or perhaps because of it—they give rise to significant cultural economic values. How do the mechanisms behind these location narratives create financial value? And, how can these fiction narratives generate a capital of the place?

The *Millennium* trilogy is, in some ways, a dramatization of twenty-first-century Swedish society. Indeed, the image of Sweden in the *Millennium* books differs from the stereotypical image that sometimes haunts Sweden, as being a quiet, predictable country on the cusp of the Arctic Ocean, and far from being subject to big adventures. To its remarkably large international audience, Stieg Larsson's *Millennium*—coupled with the site-specific nature of the books—provides a fuller and more complex image of Sweden for those already familiar with the basics. For those with no previous understanding of Sweden, the story seems to make the readers more curious, attracted, and better informed too.

The destination promotion authority Visit Sweden and other official Sweden promoters have used Stieg Larsson and the trilogy extensively in their international communications for promoting Sweden. The campaign *Sweden Beyond the Fiction* was originally named *Sweden Beyond the Millennium* or *Sweden Beyond Stieg Larsson*. In September 2016, Visit Sweden released a feature article with David Lagercrantz, author of the fourth book, *The Girl With the Spider's Web* (Visit Sweden, 2016). It is widely recognized that the *Millennium* narratives, in their different formats, reach out as the best promoter, not only for tourists, but also for the place branding of Stockholm, the nation-branding of Sweden, and for Swedish writers and the Swedish film industry too (although the intensity might have dampened somewhat lately).

Theoretical underpinnings: the narrative capital of the place

In this chapter we intend to inscribe the phenomenon of *Millennium* tourism within a broader picture and to outline how we may interpret different parts of the ecosystem of popularized fiction. Our aim is to explore how narratives can refigure places, and thus function as driving forces contributing to the creation of economic value stimulated by *Millennium* through generating a narrative capital. In order to cope with the logic of the *Millennium* industry, we need to develop a theoretical framework that can help explain the meaning of what we have named *the narrative capital of the place*.[5]

There are at least five necessary theoretical elements in this framework: First, as a prerequisite for a more complex understanding of places, we need to learn more from *the place production dialectics* developed by Henri Lefebvre (1991), together with the framework for how the place narratives are transformed, according to David Harvey (1982, 1985, 2012). Second, from Paul Ricoeur we may learn about the strategic power of *fiction* for the interface between people and their world. Within his reflections on the mimesis process, the narrative *configuration* (mimesis II) is both considered as *prefigured* in the daily life of human action and suffering (mimesis I), and also attributed a capacity to *reconfigure* (mimesis III) "the world *in front of* the text," thus transforming our interpretation of reality (Ricoeur, 1984, pp. 52–82; 1988, pp. 157–179). Later, Ricoeur developed reflections on how the dialectic of our experience of lived time and cosmic time in the constitution of *historical time* responds to the dialectic of lived space and geometrical space in the constitution of an *inhabited* space (Ricoeur, 2004).

These much more robust conceptualizations of time and space make it possible to ground our discussion in realities that take us beyond an arbitrary idealism and make it possible to connect our understanding of space and place to financial capitals and economic realities. This theoretical framework is necessary if we want to understand how Stieg Larsson's epic has generated a new capital of the place.

Third, in order to provide such a framework, we need to move on to an element borrowed from Pierre Bourdieu—so as to be able to consider the conditions for the formation of cultural *capital*, and the processes of transformation between economic and cultural capitals (Bourdieu, 2011). This is necessary if we are to be able to constructively conceptualize the narrative capital of the place and both understand and explain our findings.

Fourth, to understand how the *Millennium* industry has generated a narrative capital of the place, we also need to redirect our theoretical focus from *value chains* to *value stars*, i.e. non-linear, multidimensional models for value-creation, according to theoretical frameworks developed by scholars such as Michael Porter (1998) and Richard Normann (2001).

During the last decades, cities and regions around the world show increased interest in the economic value and economic contribution from culture and the creative sector (Bille & Schulze, 2006; Scott, 1997, 2000; Throsby, 2001, 2010). This industry, where creative artistic elements are of crucial importance, is considered to have great importance and potential for growth in our part of the world (Johnson, 2009, p. 8ff).

Fifth, Pier Luigi Sacco has called for a new framework of models for value-creation based on culture (Sacco, 2011; Sacco et al. 2008). Sacco not only highlights the significant size of the *cultural industries*, what he finds even more important is *cultural participation*, which he recognizes as being a key factor for the exchange between social and economic sectors. The strong correlation between cultural participation and innovation capacity when comparing different European countries indicates that place-related narratives create values for those who live and work there, and for those who visit the site.

The *Millennium* case illustrates how popular culture narratives generate considerable values and how these stories are being developed, re-contextualized, and reconfigured in a complex web of interactions on several levels. Books, movies, and media coverage are major engines in an impressive popular culture economy—and this takes us far beyond standard instructions given in business studies textbooks.

Short methodological remarks

The empirical basis of this investigation consists of interviews with tourists and people from the community associated with *Millennium* and Stieg Larsson. Text and materials associated with media attention, from the press, and from broadcasts, have been used and analyzed.[6] The interviews were recorded between 2010 and 2016 (mostly during the period 2010–2012). Included are 8 representatives from the publishing houses; 9 Swedish Cultural affairs representatives from official prioritized markets; directors of *Visit Stockholm* and the Swedish institute; 4 business owners of businesses made known by *Millennium*; and interviews (semi-conducted) with 20 tourists attending the *Millennium* walk.

Tourists in the foot prints of *Millennium*

In his three-volume work, Stieg Larsson guides the reader through fictional narratives located in real environments that were familiar to him, including many addresses where he himself had lived and was part of his daily life. That the *Millennium* narrative is woven together with Stieg Larsson's life story seems to strengthen the interest in the writer and his real life. Reality and fiction are woven together, and the boundaries between them seem to be diffuse. In his books, Larsson develops an intrigue in which fictional characters live their lives in an ordinary reality in which the author has himself spent his daily life—Stockholm. The *Millennium* films strengthen this focus on particular places through their format, because they are also recorded "on location." Many articles depict stories where the writer reports from a journey in the footsteps of the story. All these activities activate the interest in the different locations and also directly communicate Swedish culture and qualities.

In the years after the films were released, Stockholm has been explored by French, British and American, but also Italian and Spanish, tourists—who have been guided through Stockholm in the footsteps of Mikael Blomkvist and Lisbeth Salander. The organized sightseeing tours have frequently been monitored by the press, inviting for color pictures of Stockholm and Södermalm's most beautiful environments. The *Mail on Sunday*'s Frank Barrett comments on this:

> What makes the books so interesting for visitors to Stockholm is that the characters are very clearly identified with the Södermalm area of the city. On a *Millennium* Tour you can see where these characters live, the restaurants they visit, the cafés they hang out at, even their favourite 7-Eleven store where they buy frozen pizza. [. . .] We climb from the City Museum to Monteliusvägen. From here we have a glorious view over the Stockholm waterfront from City Hall up to the Court House. It is here that the first book opens with Blomkvist's conviction for libel. [. . .] The places he [Stieg Larsson] included in the books are the places he frequented, the Mellqvist coffee bar, for example, where Lisbeth decides to break up with Mikael after seeing him kiss his on-off lover Erika. [. . .] The most impressive of the residences is the one that Lisbeth buys with her ill-gotten gains, a 21-room apartment on the top floor of Fiskargatan 9.
>
> *(Barrett, 2009)*

The stories themselves, supported by the publicity across all travel media, work as the best guides to specific addresses, particularly in Stockholm.[7] Regional and national tourist promoters have used *Millennium* in their marketing campaigns. Travel agencies, tour and sightseeing operators have offered *Millennium*-themed tours and cooperate with the city museum for the *Millennium* walking tours.[8] The City Museum hired extra English-speaking personnel in connection with the increased interest of the *Millennium* tours in 2010–2011. The Stockholm Sheraton Hotel has offered *Millennium* weekend trips including guided tours, with stops at the cafés and restaurants mentioned in the story.

Owners and personnel from all the places in the story can give witness to the *Millennium* effect. The Lebanese tavern *Tabbouli* at Tavastgatan 22 served as inspiration for Larsson's fictional Bosnian restaurant *Samir's Cauldron*, where a shoot-out takes place in the third book, *The Girl Who Kicked the Hornets' Nest*. Restaurant *Kvarnen*, is where Lisbeth Salander often met with members of the girl band *Evil Fingers*, but was also the main character Mikael Blomkvist's favorite coffee shop, *Mellqvist Kaffebar*, have profited from the *Millennium*:

> We have definitely noticed an increased interest. Every day it will feed 5–10 people and asking about the films. After we participated in a documentary on German television channel ZDF 100 people (Movie tourists) turned up in three weeks. Even the US NBC had an element and after there appeared a lot of Americans. Most it looks enough like a fun thing and just want to check out environment. But we believe in a new boost in association with the American films premiered. I feel that it is mainly Germans, but also Americans and other nationalities that are coming.
>
> *(Interview with Anders Persson,* Mellqvist Kaffebar,
> *March 2011 in Lind, 2011)*

The most obvious effects on the tourism industry are the approximately 90,000 tourists who have followed the guided tour organized by the City Museum, or bought the map. Between 2011 and 2015, tourism to Stockholm grew by 6.5 percent, and in 2015, Stockholm had 12.9 million guests staying the night (Stockholm Business Region, 2016). Stockholm is a popular destination for international tourists in general, thus how much impact *Millennium* has had on such international tourism in general is hard to measure exactly. Yet, the *Millennium* factor cannot be neglected. As a popular culture phenomenon, *Millennium* has become an integral part of the place narrative of both Sweden and Stockholm. It is likely that to most visitors to Stockholm *Millennium* is one of their cultural and literary references, both when planning their trip and once they have arrived. The particular group of visitors who have chosen their trip to Stockholm with *Millennium* as their prime motivation are certainly among those who walk the tour or buy the map. For most visitors, however, *Millennium* is probably just one in a series of reasons motivating them to choose this specific destination.

The district in Stockholm that is most associated with *Millennium*, Södermalm, is hip and has increased in popularity during last 10–20 years. This particular district of Stockholm has, over the years, undergone a gentrification that has increased house prices. Many shops, restaurants, and cafés are very popular. This transformation of Södermalm is of course mirrored in *Millennium*. Many of the addresses from *Millennium* are popular among people in Stockholm as well as tourists. One of Södermalm's most popular shopping streets is Götgatan—which is also the walking street between Samir's Cauldron and restaurant Kvarnen, where we find *Millennium*'s fictional editorial office. Thus today, the *Millennium* trilogy may be considered as part of an already well-established narrative reconfiguring Södermalm, Stockholm, and Sweden.

Figure 27.1 Elisabeth Daude, one of the experienced guides of the popular *Millennium* tour, shows some of the narrative hotspots from Monteliusvägen, with a view over Riddarfjärden and the City Hall.

Source: photo by Joakim Lind.

Millennium as multi-dimensional place branding

One strong contributing reason behind the *Millennium* series' success, at least domestically, is that the configuration of narratives and characters are poignantly influenced by previous narratives in Swedish literature. The geography of Larsson's narrative may in a certain sense be apprehended as a modern retelling of *The Wonderful Adventures of Nils Holgersson* by Selma Lagerlöf—a book that for decades was a popular fictional story about Sweden's history and geography, used in Swedish schools from early 1900. In a similar way, Lisbeth Salander may appear as a kind of postmodern Pippi Longstocking, a world-famous character of Astrid Lindgren and one of Stieg Larsson's role models and inspirations, a well-known fact to the main audience (Lind, 2012a). In the *Sydney Morning Herald*, Stephanie Bunbury associates *Millennium* with this Swedish tradition:

> It was what Pippi did next, in fact, that gave it life. As a fiction writer, Larsson was much more like Dan Brown than Tolstoy. In Lisbeth Salander, however, he invented a character who does as much as any Strindberg or Bergman heroine to put Sweden on the map.
>
> *(Bunbury, 2011)*

Everything points to the fact that Sweden is a central part of the plot. For that reason, most translators have also chosen to keep Swedish names and place names. Furthermore, Stieg Larsson guides the reader through a real-world environment where he lived his own life. Sweden is the place where everything happens, but the country is reconfigured, because it is received by the readers, viewers, and visitors through the filter of a fictional thriller.

The opening night of David Fincher's film version of *The Girl With the Dragon Tattoo* in December 2011 was covered by hundreds of journalists from all over the world (Gentele, 2011). In association with the premiere, City of Stockholm used the opportunity to promote Stockholm and Sweden by producing *Millennium*-themed press texts about the Stockholm region. This successfully resulted in several articles that went beyond the place-related narrative of *Millennium*, generating coverage about Stockholm and Sweden in general as a business region and tourist destination. Thus, the narrative does not seem to be free-floating, but rather closely linked to the particular place, as CNN's Mark Rabinowitz argues:

> The country of Sweden ought to get lead billing. As Fincher has said, this film could not have been transferred to a North American city and the smartest decision the producers made was to not only shoot it in Sweden but to make a very Swedish film. Considering how important the location is to the story, to move it anywhere else or to tone down the Scandinavian nature of the film would have been crippling.
>
> *(Rabinowitz, 2011)*

The *Millennium* series is also full of political and social perspectives, that are closely associated with Swedish contemporary history, and the books are littered with parallels to real events and people. This means that the popular interest in *Millennium* and Stieg Larsson, and the situations portrayed in the trilogy, create a deeper relationship and understanding of the historical realities in Sweden during the twentieth century.[9]

Together with other Swedish narratives and cultural phenomenon, *Millennium* probably contributes more to the image of Sweden than any destination branding campaign. As such, it is no coincidence that authorities like the Swedish Institute and Visit Sweden have addressed the values from literature and film in their communications and campaigns and have contributed to crime and noir-themed education material, such as *Sweden Beyond the Millennium*. The series was conducted in cooperation with universities that have Swedish and Scandinavian institutions and teacher network Swedish Association of Teachers and Researchers in America (ASTRA). The series provides an updated image of Sweden in the wake of the popularity of *Millennium* and aims at strengthening the existing cooperation between the Embassy and the universities by serving as a role model for future cooperation.[10]

Altered contexts

To the roster of literary death zones, one can now add an entire country: Sweden. According to the current wave of Scandinavian crime writers "hitting British book-stores with the ferocity of a Viking invasion," as Boris Johnson put it, the hitherto innocuous home of Saab, Sven-Göran Eriksson and stuff that requires an Allen key for assembly is one almighty killing field, its pine forests a veritable repository for body parts, those scenic small towns seething cauldrons of murderous malice.

(Dawson, 2012)

Sweden wants to be seen as an egalitarian society. But *Millennium* tells the opposite story, about huge differences between the wealthy and the most vulnerable. The country sees itself as neutral on the chess board of foreign policy. Larsson points at an influential and dangerous extreme political right, and at the appeal that Nazism had during World War II. Above all, the author reveals how the most powerful exploit and abuse their privileges in this supposed model society.

(Blumenfeld, 2011)

Sweden may have attained heights of gender equality only dreamed of in other parts of the world but, if we're to believe Larsson, that apparent moral superiority is merely cosmetic, concealing pervasive misogyny at every level of society.

(MacDougall, 2010)

The story of Sweden over the last 50 years has been one of a steady loss of exceptionalism. In some ways the outside world has grown more "Swedish"—we all wear seat-belts, drink less, and believe in gender equality. At the same time, Sweden has grown much more worldly—it drinks more, works and earns less, and struggles with the assimilation of immigrants. The Swedes themselves no longer believe in a Swedish model, or, when they do, it's very different from the heavily regulated "people's home" of myth.

(Brown, 2010)

Above are some quotes from established journalists in well-known media reflecting upon Sweden after their reading of the *Millennium* and the Stieg Larsson discourse. However, a crime novel telling a dramatized fictional story, which takes place in Sweden is no obvious recipe to success in and of itself. The *Millennium* narrative brings something else.

Steven Murray, who translated the trilogy into English, says that Larsson's stories would have been perceived as outstanding, even if he were still alive. What fascinates Murray most is how Larsson manages to keep the action alive, even in the midst of arcane digressions around a topic. In the books, Larsson mixes mythical dimensions with social, political, and economic realities. As Tonkin has highlighted:

The novels as a whole mix this near-mythical dimension with a hothouse domestic atmosphere among tight-knit cliques. Larsson has made the literary moods of saga and soap opera converge—with suspense as the adhesive. And, behind the quick-fire action, those great chords of moral and political witness continue to resonate. Long after the entertainment factor has faded, I predict that readers will remember some of Stieg's serious concerns. And if that isn't a mark of real literature, I don't know what is.

(Tonkin, 2009)

The mixture of literary quality and credible characters, coupled with a basic dramaturgy borrowed from mythology and contexts from the real world, may explain why the stories of Stieg Larsson have become universal, having such appeal to large audiences. The intrigue and its societal context also deal with general social issues that most people, regardless of where they live, can identify with: corruption, abuse of power, and injustice. These social issues raise universal questions about identity and the societies we are building.

The fact that *Millennium* addresses contemporary issues important to people all over the world is probably an important part of its great success in attracting such a big audience. It effectively tells the story about societal challenges on several levels. In these fictitious intrigues, Sweden serves as the example, the scene that mirrors the challenges. The *Jakarta Globe*-columnist, Karim Raslan, commented on these universal qualities, asking "This makes one wonder: does Indonesia need its own Lisbeth Salander?" (Raslan, 2012).

What has happened, in effect, is that Stieg Larsson has read our time at the turn of the millennium through his own lenses. In this way, the books make use of *prefigurations* from the ordinary world of human action and suffering, from which he then creates *configurations* in terms of intrigues and narratives. When these representations are then read (and viewed on screens), the result is a *refiguration* of Swedish history and society (cf. Ricoeur, 1984). Some people also create their own narrative. All these narratives add value to the cultural and symbolic value of the *Millennium*. Through the various media, these narratives reach the target groups that other phenomena could only dream of. By established media—like *n+1, Foreign Policy, Le Monde*, the *New York Times*, the *Guardian*, etc.—the story is being transformed, but it reaches out to people even if they do not read the books or see the movie, because such media make Stieg Larsson's stories and messages much more broadly accessible. Popular culture performs its magic, and the place seems to be reconfigured!

Millennium merges with the real-life story of Stieg Larsson himself, which further fuels interest in the author, his novels, and Sweden. Reality and fiction blend. The border becomes diffuse and the stories tickle the curiosity of audiences by their "no smoke without fire" logic. References to actual places and people create the illusion that the events have actually occurred, or at least *could have* occurred. The journalist Stieg Larsson fills fiction with verifiable references and stylistic tricks making his fiction accountable and realistic. The *Millennium* series serves as the media through which we read and interpret, and establish an emotional relationship to, the perception of a country or a region. Such a clear contemporary critique as *Millennium*, and the media stories about the author's contemporary context, influence people's perception and reading far beyond the related cultural phenomena.

Simon Anholt (2006) has developed the Nation Brand Hexagon and the Nation Brands Index. This is an index based on a survey taken from tens of thousands of people, in some 20 countries, who are asked to respond to their *perception* of 50 other countries. These perceptions relate to six categories: business, population, governance, tourism, culture, and the country's ability to attract talent for study, research, and work. Through the profound impact and reach of the *Millennium*, supported by the great international media coverage interpreting actual societal issues and challenges, it is likely that the *Millennium* has directly or indirectly contributed to the perception of Sweden with regards to Simon Anholt's six categories above. As a popular culture narrative that affects not only the variable cultures and heritages, it is also likely to have the capacity to contribute to other dimensions as well.

It is with this multi-dimensional narrative, disseminated through a complex media landscape, that the image of Sweden is being developed. Sweden as a destination is being communicated and actualized. Although the story only contributes to a small percentage of the large audience, the *Millennium* is a great contributor for place branding internationally.

Implications for popular culture tourism

One of the practical implications of this chapter relates to the conditions for the production of the creative core of popular culture tourism. What does it mean for the business model of this industry that the narrative capital of the place—in one of the biggest popular culture phenomena in Scandinavian history—was written by a left-wing, anti-capitalistic socialist with a not-for-profit focus?

Through Stieg Larsson's narrative, Sweden becomes a manageable imaginative arena for reflections on matters such as power structures, gender roles, sexuality, and equality. The *Millennium* narrative not only contains universal themes and addresses current social issues, its intrigue creates links to real locations and addresses, providing an excellent starting point for popular culture as a tourism phenomenon. The narrative configuration of the place, strongly influenced by the pre-figuration of ordinary life experiences, contributed to the reconfiguration of the place, thus making value-creation possible by increasing the capital of the place. But the creative core of these business processes is not generated in accordance with the standard models from textbooks associated with the incentives of *economic man*, but originates from a left-wing journalist. This means that we also need to reconsider the business models that describe the cultural economy.

Indeed, creativity is necessary for cultivating a cultural economy. But, creativity is not generated automatically by utility maximization, and creativity cannot survive and prevail in isolation. The *Millennium* industry provides an excellent example of the need to manage the complexity associated with how we go about linking cultural creativity with different value-creating networks (Normann, 2001). From this perspective, it would be much more relevant to reflect upon how literature, films, and other popular culture texts affect how we interpret and understand the world, and to identify the movements and migration patterns that can be tracked to popular culture and the mediatized culture in its different formats. Tourism is only one of many movements that can be tracked to popular culture and the narratives related to a phenomenon.

Millennium narratives, and how they are being developed through various formats—books, movies, film productions, and media—contribute to the image of the place on several levels as well as contributing to how these narrative fields create value and equity for different fields. The creative industries' development, the *Millennium* films sets, and the groups of film promoters are, in our presentation, to be credited with contributing to the success of the Swedish film industry, filmmakers, and actors. Tourists are coming to Stockholm, and other parts of Sweden, with *Millennium* as a prime motivation. The Swedish Institute and Visit Sweden used *Millennium* to develop the image of Sweden abroad and in marketing campaigns. We can now see how the fictional *Millennium* narrative works to arise curiosity about Sweden and Swedish society. Popular culture has become a platform for understanding our contemporaries.

The *Millennium* stories contribute to a billion-euro industry—considerably larger than the economy that can be measured solely in sales from the book and the film industry. The *Millennium* phenomenon, and how this narrative has created big business, also raises questions about the wide range of values created for a place reconfigured by narratives in terms of tourists, local and global cultural industries. Our hope is to recognize the *Millennium* tourism ecosystem, its timeline, and outline as a Gaussian-like curve, but also to elaborate on some of the more long-term effects on the collective literary story of Stockholm and Sweden—i.e. *city* as well as *nation branding*.

Thus, the *Millennium* narratives provide us with an example of how popular culture stories generate values, on micro, meso, and macro levels. We, furthermore, gain some important ideas about how the narratives help to create site-specific values, and how this value creation develops as an interplay between these different levels, where the popular story is disseminated in different formats, contributing to values that mutually reinforce each other within a framework of an extensive economic value-chain—or, in order to stress the non-linear character of this economy, we may use the term value-star.

Epilogue: the narrative capital relocated to a new place?

In 2015, Swedish author David Lagercrantz took over the legacy and the fourth part in the series was published. Destination promoters keep their fingers crossed that this book's publication will turn into a successful film too, one that can revitalize the *Millennium*-induced tourism. In the original narrative, Stieg Larsson made the district of Södermalm the focal point of the story. This is also a central area in the trilogy and where the guided tours take place.

In the new book, Lagercrantz has relocated the major action of the plot to another part of Stockholm, the district of Vasastan and the streets in the area of Vasaparken (which is also the territory where David Lagercrantz himself happens to live). This is also the district where world-famous author Astrid Lindgren lived most of her life, with view over the park Vasaparken at Dalagatan 46.

If we consider the fact that Stieg Larsson used Astrid Lindgren's character Pippi Longstocking as a prefiguration of Lisbeth Salander, it does seem that this figure has now returned "home" to her roots. How will the fiction tourist industry surrounding Lisbeth Salander and *Millennium* continue to be rewritten and cross-fertilize with Pippi Longstocking in this new area? Providing an answer to this question will be the starting point of new business opportunities for the tourist industry.

In September 2017, at the same time that we wrote the final lines of this chapter, the fifth installment of the *Millennium* series, and the second title by David Lagercrantz—*The Girl Who Takes an Eye for an Eye*—was published (Lagercrantz, 2017). The *Millennium* narratives generate new stories—and the industry is growing further. How far can the *Millennium* narratives travel? What kind of additional values and movements can these narratives create and contribute to? In this chapter, it seems like we have so far only scratched the traceable surface of the resources the *Millennium* trilogy provides for the creation of the narrative capital of the place.

Notes

1 Lind (2011). Figures and estimates are based on information from Sara Claesson, Head of Communications at the Stockholm City Museum September 15, 2016.
2 Noted by Elisabeth Daude, a guide at the Stockholm City Museum during an interview September 9, 2014.
3 Survey was made by Stockholm City Museum spring 2010 with 125 tourists attending the *Millennium* tour (Lind, 2011).
4 Obviously, this was not enough, in June 2016 the old publishing house Norstedts was sold to the young start-up Storytel, which specializes in audio- and e-books, and sold for less than 16 million euros (Ström, 2016).
5 *The Narrative Capital of the Place* is also the title of a PhD project being prepared by Joakim Lind.
6 In 2012, Joakim Lind conducted a media analysis where he read through a large amount of articles from a number of countries (Lind, 2012a, 2012b).
7 For example, Coldwell 2016.
8 The Stockholm City Museum has exclusive rights for using Millennium in guided tours and maps.
9 See also Dickson (2011) and Fraser (2009).
10 From an interview with Britt-Marie Forslund, coordinator, Department for Press, Culture and Information, Embassy of Sweden in Washington, DC, March 2013.

References

Anholt, S. (2006). *Competitive Identity*. London: Palgrave Macmillan.
Barrett, F. (2009). Stockholm, Stieg Larsson's *Millennium* and the city at the centre of a literary phenomenon. *Mail on Sunday*, July 19. www.dailymail.co.uk/travel/article-1200678/Stockholm-Stieg-Larssons-Millennium-city-centre-literary-phenomenon.html#ixzz1n2eAHCDw (Retrieved 9/7/2016).
Bille, T. & Schulze, G. (2006). Culture in urban and regional development. In D. Throsby and V. Ginsburgh (Eds.), *Handbook on the Economics of Arts and Culture* (1052–1099). North-Holland: Elsevier Science.
Blumenfeld, Samuel. (2011). "Millénium" + Fincher, le casting parfait. October 7. www.lemonde.fr/m-styles/article/2012/01/17/millenium-fincher-le-casting-parfait_1583331_4497319.html (Retrieved 10/03/2016).
Bourdieu, Pierre. (2011). The forms of capital (1986). In Imre Szeman & Timothy Kapocy (Eds.), *Cultural Theory: An Anthology* (81–91). Chichester, UK: Wiley-Blackwell.
Brown, Andrew. (2010). We're all Swedes now: How the world caught up with Stieg Larsson. *Foreign Policy*. May, 26. http://foreignpolicy.com/2010/05/26/were-all-swedes-now/ (Retrieved 9/25/2016).
Bunbury, Stephanie. (2011). In Swedish footsteps. *Sydney Morning Herald*, 31 December. www.smh.com.au/entertainment/movies/in-swedish-footsteps-20111229-1pdr7.html (Retrieved 9/6/2016).

Burnstein, D. (Ed.). (2011). *The Tattooed Girl: The Enigma of Stieg Larsson and the Secrets Behind the Most Compelling Thrillers of Our Time*. New York: St. Martin's Griffin.

Coldwell, W. (2016). 10 of the best alternative city tours in Europe. *Guardian*, August 1. www.theguardian. com/travel/2016/aug/01/10-best-alternative-city-tours-europe-warsaw-reykjavik-barcelona (Retrieved 9/25/2016).

Dawson, J. (2012). Meet the girl with the dragon tattoo. *Sunday Times*, February 14. www.thesundaytimes. co.uk/sto/culture/film_and_tv/film/article197281.ece (Retrieved 10/03/2016).

Debord, G. (1977/1967). *The Society of the Spectacle*. Translated by Fredy Perlman and Jon Supak. Detroit: Black & Red.

Dickson, D. (2011). "Dragon Tattoo" film paints Sweden in darkest shades. *Reuters*, December 14. www. reuters.com/article/us-dragontattoo-stockholm-idUSTRE7BD0TP20111214 (Retrieved 9/6/2016).

Fraser, N. (2009). Understand Swedish society through Stieg Larsson's popular fiction. *Independent*, October 1. www.independent.co.uk/news/world/europe/understanding-swedish-society-through-stieg-larssons-popular-fiction-1796052.html (Retrieved 10/1/2016)

Gentele, J. (2011). Hollywood fick komma till Stockholm. *Svenska Dagbladet*, November 22. www.svd.se/hollywood-fick-komma-till-stockholm (Retrieved 9/6/2016)

Harvey, D. (1982/1999/2006). *The Limits to Capital*. Oxford: Blackwell

Harvey, D. (1985). *The Urbanization of Capital: Studies in the History and Theory of Capitalist Urbanization 2*. Oxford: Blackwell.

Harvey, D. (2012). *Rebel Cities: From the Right to the City to the Urban Revolution*. London: Verso.

Johansson, R. (2014). Arvet efter *Millennium*: Mer än en halv miljard. *Expressen*, November 18. www.expressen.se/nyheter/arvet-efter-millennium-mer-an-en-halv-miljard/ (Retrieved 9/7/2016).

Johnson, L. C. (2009). *Cultural Capitals: Revaluating the Arts Remaking Urban Spaces*. London: Routledge.

La Ferla, R. (2012). Wonder women, highly metallic. *New York Times*, February 1. www.nytimes. com/2012/02/02/fashion/lisbeth-salander-bringing-back-leather-and-spikes.html?_r=0 (Retrieved 9/27/2016).

Lagercrantz, D. (2015). *Det som inte dödar oss [The Girl in the Spider's Web]*. Stockholm: Norstedts förlag.

Lagercrantz, D. (2017). *Mannen som sökte sin skugga [The Girl Who Takes an Eye for an Eye]*. Stockholm: Norstedts förlag..

Larsson, S. (2005). *Män som hatar kvinnor [The Girl with the Dragon Tattoo]*. Stockholm: Norstedts förlag.

Larsson, S. (2006). *Flickan som lekte med elden [The Girl Who Played with Fire]*. Stockholm: Norstedts förlag.

Larsson, S. (2007). *Luftslottet som sprängdes [The Girl Who Kicked the Hornets' Nest]*. Stockholm: Norstedts förlag.

Lefebvre, H. (1991). *The Production of Space*. Oxford: Blackwell.

Leijonhufvud, Jonas. (2015). Miljoner hägrar när ny Millenniumbok släpps. *Dagens Industri*, April 7. www.di.se/artiklar/2015/4/1/miljoner-hagrar-nar-ny-millenniumbok-slapps/ (Retrieved 9/7/2016).

Lind, J. (2011). *Millenniumrapporten: Ekonomiska effekter och exponeringsvärdet av Stockholmsregionen i de svenska Millenniumfilmer. Analys genomförd av Cloudberry Communications*. Stockholm: Filmregion Stockholm Mälardalen, Regionförbundet Sörmland, Film i Sörmland och Stockholm Business Region Development.

Lind, J. (2012a). *Mediebilden av Sverige efter Stieg Larsson och Millennium*. Stockholm: Cloudberry Communications AB, Svenska institutet.

Lind, J. (2012b). *Sweden Beyond the Millennium and Stieg Larsson*. Stockholm: Swedish institute.

MacDougall, I. (2010). The man who blew up the welfare state. *n+1magazine*. February 27. https://nplusonemag.com/online-only/book-review/man-who-blew-up-welfare-state/ (Retrieved 10/03/2016).

Normann, R. (2001). *Reframing Business: When the Map Changes the Landscape*. Chichester: John Wiley & Sons.

Porter, M. E. (1998). *Competitive Advantage of Nations*. New York: The Free Press.

Rabinowitz. M. (2011). Review: "The Girl with the Dragon Tattoo" is a measured and suspenseful thriller. *CNN*, December, 20. http://edition.cnn.com/2011/12/20/showbiz/movies/review-the-girl-with-the-dragon-tattoo/ (Retrieved 9/6/2016).

Raslan, K. (2012). In search of Lisbeth. *Jakarta Globe*, March 29. http://jakartaglobe.beritasatu.com/archive/karim-raslan-in-search-of-lisbeth/ (Retrieved 9/7/2016).

Ricoeur, P. (1984). *Time and Narrative*, Vol. 1. Translated by Katheleen Blamey & David Pellauer. Chicago: University of Chicago Press.

Ricoeur, P. (1988). *Time and Narrative*, Vol. 3. Translated by Katheleen Blamey & David Pellauer. Chicago: University of Chicago Press.

Ricoeur, P. (2004). *Memory, History, Forgetting.* Translated by Katheleen Blamey & David Pellauer. Chicago: University of Chicago Press.

Rose, L. (2010). Top-earning dead celebrities. *Forbes*, October 25. www.forbes.com/2010/10/21/ michael-jackson-elvis-presley-tolkien-business-entertainment-dead-celebs-10-intro.html (Retrieved 6/9/2016).

Rosenberg, R. S. (Ed.) (2011). *The Psychology of the Girl with the Dragon Tattoo: Understanding Lisbeth Salander and Stieg Larsson's Millennium Trilogy.* Robin S. Rosenberg (Editor, Contributor), Shannon O'Neill (Editor). Dallas: Ben Bella Books.

Sacco, P. (2011). *Culture 3.0: A New Perspective for the EU 2014–2020 Structural Funds Programming, Produced for the OMC Working Group on Cultural and Creative Industries.* Brussels: European Expert Network on Culture.

Sacco P., Ferilli G., & Pedrini S (2008). System-wide cultural districts: An introduction from the Italian viewpoint. In S. Kagan & V. Kirchberg (Eds.), *Sustainability: A New Frontier for the Arts and Cultures* (400–460). Frankfurt a. M: VAS Verlag.

Scott, A. J. (1997). The cultural economy of cities. *International Journal of Urban and Regional Research* 21: 323–339.

Scott, A. J. (2000). *The Cultural Economy of Cities: Essays on the Geography of Image-Producing Industries.* London: Sage.

Stockholm Business Region. (2016). *Facts About Stockholm's Tourism Industry Statistics for 2015.* Stockholm: Stockholm Business Region.

Ström, V. (2016). Storytel köper Norstedts—aktien rusar. *Dagens Industri*, June 22. http://digital.di.se/ artikel/storytel-koper-norstedts--aktien-rusar (Retrieved 06/30/2017).

Throsby, C. D. (2001). *Economics and Culture.* Cambridge: Cambridge University Press.

Throsby, D. (2010). *The Economics of Cultural Policy.* Cambridge: Cambridge University Press.

Tonkin, B. (2009). What was the secret of Stieg Larsson's extraordinary success. *Independent*, October 2. www.independent.co.uk/arts-entertainment/books/features/what-was-the-secret-of-stieg-larssons-extraordinary-success-1796021.html (Retrieved 7/9/2016).

Visit Sweden. (2016). *Sweden: Beyond the fiction New Millennium author David Lagercrantz talks about The Girl In the Spider's Web.* www.visitsweden.com/sweden/Featured/Sweden-Beyond/Swedish-Litterature/ Interview-with-David-Lagercrantz/ (Retrieved 9/25/2016).

28

A 'TOURISTED LANDSCAPE'

Speculations about 'consuming history', using a case study of an Australian folk hero

Michael Fagence

Setting the scene: engaging with history and heritage

History is a set of stories and a range of discursive practices that have been borrowed liberally by popular culture.

(de Groot, 2009, p. 1)

In many, many places, there is a huge appetite for the past, which needs to be understood and respected in its myriad forms. It is met by displays of 'history' and by ways of approaching the past that are not narrowly academic, but are more akin to tourism.

(Jordanova, 2006, p. 132)

The act of 'borrowing' stories from history and the presentation of them through different expressions of popular culture, including history-linked and heritage-based tourism, has drawn a diversity of interesting commentaries and speculations. For example, this action has been described as 'consuming history' (de Groot, 2009), as 'engaging the past' (Landsberg, 2015), as engaging with 'usable pasts' (Jordanova, 2006), and as 'encounters with popular pasts' (Robinson & Silverman, 2015). This chapter uses speculations such as these to create a platform on which to construct a means of bringing some spatial and semiotic order to the aggregation and presentation of stories from history in that special communication space where popular culture and tourism converge: the 'touristed landscape'.

In a commentary that specifically targets the telling of stories from history through the mediums of film and television Sobchack (1996) has observed that "popular audiences have become involved in and understand the stakes in historical representation, recognize 'history in the making', and see themselves not only as spectators of history but also as participants in and adjudicators of it" (p. 7). There is a distinct concordance here with history-linked tourism, especially as it performs the twin functions of informing and entertaining (Coles & Armstrong, 2007), as it appeals across a spectrum of consumers (Kerstetter et al., 2001), and as it meets with the assertion of Lippard's (1999) assertion that "a whiff of the past rather than a history course is all that most of us want or have time to take in" (p. 10). Among other commentaries about the levels of popular interest in history and heritage is Lowenthal's (1996, p. ix) observation that

> All at once heritage is everywhere . . . the chief focus of patriotism and a prime lure of tourism. One can barely move without bumping into a heritage site . . . To neglect heritage is a cardinal sin, to invoke it a national duty.

One outcome of this growth of popular interest has been to cause dispute between professional historians (Smith, 2006; Tosh, 2015) and various sectors of burgeoning popular culture (de Groot, 2009; Jensen, 2009; Jordanova, 2000). In this dispute the contention most often refers to the transformation of the stories of history into commodities across a range of cultural forms; and the criticisms have been levelled at what is claimed to be the sanitization of the stories so as to render them suitable for popular consumption, to 'dumbing down' the stories by retreating from authentic 'historic truth', and to transforming history into 'a genre of entertainment' (Coles & Armstrong, 2007; Lowenthal, 1996; Shepherd, 2002; Smith, 2006). Even if the basic dispute between the polarized viewpoints may not be fully resolvable, there are two possible bridging points. One of these is derived from the research of Kerstetter and her colleagues (2001). From an empirical investigation they fashioned a structure that makes provision for those interested in history and heritage to extend along a continuum from a 'full-fledged history buff' to a 'history green-horn'. A second bridging point is offered by Landsberg (2004) with her reference to 'prosthetic memories'. These are conjured at a personally determined 'point' (along the indefinite and imaginary continuum)

> at the interface between a person and a historical narrative about the past . . . In this moment of contact an experience occurs through which the person sutures himself or herself into a larger history . . . [and] takes on a more personal, deeply felt memory of a past event through which he or she did not live.
>
> *(Landsberg, 2004, p. 2)*

This is the point of personal satisfaction and empathy with the story. It may not be fully coincident with the point of 'historic truth', but it is likely to be a 'point' at which history-linked and heritage-based tourism can become intellectually and emotionally as well as commercially satisfactory and validated.

The conceptualization of a 'touristed landscape' fits well with this situation. It is used here to demonstrate how the symbolic importance of place, space and 'text' binds the past with the present (de Groot, 2009, pp. 239–240), how it can become the focal point of displayed history (Jordanova, 2006), how it can contribute to individually formed 'prosthetic memories' (Landsberg, 2004) and how it can become the core and consuming interest in history-linked and heritage-based tourism. It also reaches out to Jordanova's (2000) challenge for engagement with "all means, deliberate and otherwise, through which those who are not professional historians acquire their sense of the past" (p. 20). In the sections that follow there is, first, a brief commentary on the disciplinary underpinnings of this study and on the formulation of the spatial framework of the 'touristed landscape'. Then, this framework is applied to a case study of the story of the Australian bushranger-cum-outlaw-cum-folk hero Edward (Ned) Kelly, with most consideration directed at matters caught in the investigative cross-wires of geography, heritage, history and semiotics as they contribute to a Kelly-relevant 'touristed landscape'. In the concluding section the commentary will focus on the usefulness and versatility of the 'touristed landscape' as a 'hyper-real layering, place-making and sense-making' tool (Gyimothy et al., 2015) contributing to an improved level of understanding at the interface of tourism, popular culture and history.

Disciplinary underpinnings: towards a 'touristed landscape' framework

We no longer have to divide reality into water-tight compartments or mere super-imposed stages corresponding to the apparent boundaries of our scientific disci-plines. On the contrary, we are compelled to look for interactions and common mechanisms.

(Piaget quoted in Darbellay, 2016, p. 363)

This section and the next (the case study) form the core of this chapter. In this section the task is to set the groundwork for the construction of the idea of the 'touristed landscape', the concep-tual tool that is used later to present the evidence of a history-linked and heritage-based tourism product based on the story of the Australian bushranger Ned Kelly. There are four steps: in the first there is a brief commentary about 'thinking across disciplines', a process that is highlighted in the Piaget statement at the head of this section. In the second there is an explanation of the heuristic methodology used to 'explicate meanings and patterns' from the discovered evidence, and of the framework approach used as the organizational tool. Then, in the third, the broad context of 'seeing, reading and interpreting' cultural landscapes is used as the lead to the concep-tualizations of 'themescapes'. In the fourth and final stage attention is focused on the translation of the idea of 'themescapes' into 'touristed landscapes'.

Thinking across disciplines

Piaget's quotation at the head of this section acknowledges the changes that have taken hold of studies across the social sciences and humanities in recent decades. A particularized chal-lenge was set for studies in heritage and tourism by Jamal and Kim (2005). The conduct of this study has been, in part, shaped by those challenges. As it progressed the study here was exposed to a research issue that faced research problems, knowledge systems, knowledge spaces, force-fields and networks that have their own complexity and inter-relatedness. The response for this study was to settle into a 'comfort zone' that leaned towards the disciplines of geography and history, and added in companionable elements from the toolkits from culture, heritage, semiotics and tourism. Intellectual support for this process was drawn par-ticularly from Darbellay's (2016) recent commentaries about thinking across disciplines and 'the gift of interdisciplinarity', and from the commentary of Gyimothy and her colleagues (2015), which argued in favour of taking up the advantage of "a wider social science agenda, which acknowledges cross-disciplinary synergies" (p. 15). Similar advocacies can be found in Belhassen and Caton (2009), Coles et al. (2006), Lundberg and Lexhagen (2013), and Tribe and Liburd (2016).

Methodology

A straightforward heuristic research approach was used in this study. It follows the Moustakas (1990) advocacy to use an approach and methods able to 'explicate meanings and patterns . . . rel-evant to the question' (p. 44). The method-crafting process used here has drawn on some of the cross-disciplinary advocacies listed previously. These have been woven into an investigative and interpretive framework. This approach was favoured because of its capacity to:

reveal where gaps lie, suggest questions for future research in a more directed fashion, . . . show how particular studies contribute to our understanding . . . bring together conceptual and methodological dimensions . . . [and can be used] as building blocks to draw together more effectively the diverse studies.

(Pearce and Butler, 2010, p. 233)

Other benefits of using the framework approach include its potential to provide a structure for a common set of relevant variables and the disaggregation of them into subcomponents, the design of any necessary data collection instruments, the conduct of fieldwork and the analysis of findings (Ostrom, 2009). Its usefulness as a framing device to 'discover', record and marshal the attributes of place distinctiveness (Urry, 1992, 2002) also helps with the interpretation of 'themescapes' (Rodaway, 1994), and this is a stepping-stone towards sense-making about places (Gyimothy et al., 2015), and to the formalization of 'touristed landscapes' (Cartier, 2005a).

Reading cultural landscapes

The significance of 'reading' the landscape is encapsulated in an observation by Smith (2006): the importance of landscape, she says, lies in offering both "a vista wherein a range of histories, chronologies, events and meanings may be viewed and displayed" (p. 168) and in its symbolism "of the social and political ideologies . . . which are embodied within the landscape through human action" (p. 78). Marquee sources about cultural landscapes have been referenced in, for example, Meinig and Jackson (1979) and Minca (2007). A common thread in these is a belief that landscape is 'a text' that draws together tangible and intangible features to reveal different layers of 'meaning' and heritage motifs and contributions to 'tourist imaginaries'. One line of development from the idea of 'cultural landscape as text' has been Rodaway's (1994) notion of a 'themescape'. It is his view that a 'themescape' is "a themed environment, and specifically a space or place which is identified by a single coherent theme or idea" (p. 165). In his model, a 'themescape' is most often expressed geographically as an enclosed and 'thematically controlled' space or district. Within such a district the evidence of history may include original resources, but the likelihood is that the presentations will be resemblances or copies, and may include re-enactments. The crucial points are that in a 'themescape' there should be a coherence of theme (Rodaway, 1994, pp. 164–166), legibility (Lynch, 1960) and distinctiveness (Urry, 2002).

'Touristed landscapes'

It is at this point that a number of elements of the previous discussion can be brought together and fused into a conceptual frame of reference. The original conceptualization of the 'touristed landscape' was by Cartier (2005a) who generated it to fit with a research project that, among other things, was exploring questions 'at the crossroads of contemporary issues in cultural studies of travel' (p. 2). Essentially, Cartier refers to a 'landscape' that has been affected by tourism – hence a 'tourist*ed* landscape':

we use 'touristed' to signal that tourists significantly patronize these landscapes . . . touristed landscapes, and as places, represent an array of experiences and goals acted out by diverse people in locales that are subject to tourism but which are also places of historic and integral meaning.

(2005a, p. 2)

Using that as a starting point, this study has moved tangentially towards the idea of the 'touristed landscape' as a target, with a theme capable of being used at a number of scales, and in situations where the subject matter – in this study, commoditized heritage – is dynamic, contested, symbolic and representative. This means that the subject matter has distinctiveness as it contributes to (and is/has been influenced by) a complex interaction of cultural, economic, political and social changes, both in past periods (that is, the history and heritage linkages) and in the present (that is, as it presents the stories of the past in current expressions of popular culture, including tourism). For the purposes of this study the controlling factors are geographical, historical and semiotic, and the focus is firmly on tangible resources.

Drawing down on the commentaries about 'reading cultural landscapes', then adding in the commentaries of Cartier (2005a, 2005b) and elements from the case studies in Cartier and Lew (2005), and engaging with the loose framework of 'themescapes' (Rodaway, 1994), it is possible to construct a profile of a 'touristed landscape', which extends across nine 'factors of influence' (see Figure 28.1). In summary, these 'factors of influence' may be assembled in three groups as follows:

- factors that influence what is included: 'physical and material reality', 'texts' and 'things', re-presentations and re-positioned presentations;
- factors that influence arrangements: configurations, hierarchies, defining frameworks; and
- factors that influence how the resources may be interpreted: perspectives, experiences, interpretations.

In essence, a 'touristed landscape' is a contrived landscape, an aggregation of items and symbols, some of which may be in their original position and state, and others that may be remnants or refurbishments, or might have been repositioned (even moved off-site). It is a formalized landscape, shaped to accommodate circumstances from a past period as they are manifest in the present, and created to suit the interests and expectations of consumers, or providers or guardian agencies. The guardian agencies may be governments responding to local, national or even international protocols and regulations, or commercial or not-for-profit organizations. Any touristed landscape is likely to be impacted by speculations fuelled by fact, fantasy and imagination as it, and the resultant cultural heritage resources, are fashioned into a determinable space that can be separately identified because of its association with a place, an event, a person, or 'text'/'thing' (building, document, monument, panorama, performance, space, structure). Cartier has suggested tourist visits to such landscapes are generated particularly as responses to what the destination promises, and that once there, tourists are 'seduced' by encounters with spectacles, with symbols, with mythic images and with 'meanings' that are self-constructed or thath may be contrived and 'managed' by whichever agencies are responsible for providing access to and for sustaining the evidence linked to its story (2005b, p. 301; see also the previous reference to the idea of 'prosthetic memories' raised by Landsberg, 2004). Many of these matters will be drawn into the case study.

Case study: the 'touristed landscape' of the Ned Kelly story

The Ned Kelly story is used here as an example of the interactions between matters of history, tourism and popular culture, and especially how those interactions contribute to the creation of a distinctive 'themescape' and 'touristed landscape'. After a brief introductory section that presents a summary of important elements of the story, there is a brief commentary on some of the principal symbols associated with that story. That is followed by a description of the

FACTORS OF INFLUENCE

What is included	How it is arranged	How it is interpreted
Physical and material reality: • Places, spaces, sites • Tracks, trails, routes • Domestic buildings • Public buildings • Structures • Townships • Monuments • Archaeological remnants • Safe havens, lookouts	**Perspectives:** • Foreground • Middle-ground • Background	**Configurations:** • Linear • Radial, concentric • 'Spot' • Loose • Regional
'Texts', 'things': • Artefacts • Armour, weapons • Diaries, correspondence • Official public records • Documents, photographs • Newspaper and magazine reports	**Hierarchies:** according to: • Location • Organizational structure • Accessibility	**Experiences:** • Education • Information • Entertainment (exotica, novelty) • Identity • Ideology
Re-presentations, re-positioned presentations: Items from the previous categories relocated to: • Exhibitions, galleries, libraries, museums, monuments memorials, cemeteries, plaques • Ceremonies • Re-enactments	**Defining frameworks:** according to: • Natural environment • Cultural legend, folktale, myth • Presentation practices • Ordinances	**Interpretations:** according to: • Ethnicity, race, nationality • Social group (class) • Gender • Education

Figure 28.1   Factors of influence.

geographical patterns that were born through the period of the Kelly activities and that continue to give shape to the current pattern of Kelly story-related 'touristed landscapes'.

The Ned Kelly story

Ned Kelly's story is the timeless tale of the hero, the man who transcends the often brutal or mundane realities of his existence to become a symbol of something larger than himself.

To understand Ned Kelly's unique staying power in the Australian consciousness we will need to know about some of the important elements of the Kelly saga and its ongoing mythology. These elements are Ned himself, the oral outlaw tradition to which he was heir, and the popular media industry that has proliferated around his image.

(Seal, 1980, p. 1)

At its simplest level the story is an account of one family's responses to the economic, political and social circumstances and challenges prevailing in the north-eastern districts of the Australian State of Victoria in the late 1800s, and of the choices made by that particular family in the face of those challenges (Jones, 2008; McQuilton, 1979). The background circumstances include a pervasive prescriptive and discriminatory land and settlement legislation, widespread Anglo-Irish competition and animosity, rural poverty linked to poor farming choices and practices, bushranging and larrikinism linked to activities of family and district clans and gangs, and intimidation by the police and oppressive judicial sentencing. What sets the Kelly family story apart from others, and gives it its degree of distinctiveness, is the family's responses to and involvement in a number of dramatic events. Some of these were simply the outcome of happenstance, while others were deliberate and engineered by family members and sympathizers. The catalogue of these dramatic events, extending over the short period 1878–1880, includes, for example, the formation and outlawing of the Kelly Gang, two bank robberies, two sieges (in one of which three policemen were killed), an attempt to derail a train, frequent confrontations with the police, the judiciary and government, the murder of a police informer, cross-country pursuits by the police, bushranging activities (especially horse stealing), the fostering of a group of sympathizers and the production of two so-called political manifestos. Kelly's story has both factual and imagined components, and although it is largely verifiable from public records of various kinds and from information in the public domain (from newspapers, magazines, photographs, diaries, government and police reports and so on), it is accompanied by embellished commentaries in legends, folktales, poems, doggerels, songs, rhymes, even some artworks and by various interpretations in both fiction and non-fiction literature, in music, in film, in drama and art, and, in recent years, popularization through tourism. The traction of the story in many forms of popular culture has remained constant since Kelly's execution in November 1880, and this has been aided and abetted by its linkages with the broadly configured 'outlaw legend' (Seal, 1996, 2011), and by what has claimed it to be: "a compelling example of the potency of the outlaw hero tradition . . . the closest thing Australia has to a national hero" (Seal, 1996 p. 145).

Symbolism of the Kelly story

Although the story has a substantial factual basis, it is the symbolism of some of the components of the story that underpins much of its significance and its sustained presence in various forms of popular culture. That symbolism is derived in part from the story fitting what Serle (1971) has described as "the last expression of the lawless frontier . . . the last protest of the mighty bush" (p. 11). Embedded in the story are three sets of symbols, one of which is indicative of a general cultural situation, a second set is linked specifically to happenings in the story, and the third set is indicative of both past and present geographical distinctiveness. There is a consistent 'message' through the symbolism, and it refers to attitudes of defiance towards authority, independence, fearlessness and bravery. It is these characterizations, and the emotional attachments to them, which sustain the fascination of the story for both scholarship and popular culture, and that underpin the formation of the various 'touristed landscapes'.

Of the three sets of symbols, one encompasses the general circumstances prevailing in the Kelly region of Victoria in the late 1800s. Notable among these were an Irish–Catholic connection, families drifting from one rural holding to another, frequent altercations with the agencies of law and order, commitments to bushranging and petty crime, larrikinism and 'grand-standing' with horse racing and bare knuckle fighting and the formation of district and family-based clans and gangs. These are the loose strands through the 'touristed landscapes'. A second set of symbols has particular linkages with the events of the final dramatic phase of the Kelly story. Within this set is the physical evidence of the police holding cells, the police barracks, the gaols, the courthouses and the remnant sites of abandoned homesteads, the hillside caves and remnant camp sites. Also within this set are the two draft so-called political manifestos (the Cameron and Jerilderie Letters), which air the family's grievances and make a case for regional independent government for north-east Victoria. The third set of symbols is tightly linked to those in the second set. In addition to various totems and plaques, it is the four suits of armour fashioned by the Kelly Gang for use at the final siege (Glenrowan), which have become one of Australia's most recognized symbols. The armour is often depicted in a stylized form for commercial products, collectibles, souvenirs and road signs (in the Kelly district). A stylized form of the helmet used by Sidney Nolan for his series of paintings has become an internationally recognized symbol, and it was incorporated into one of the episodes in the opening ceremony of the Sydney Olympic Games in 2000.

An Australian journalist captured the essence of this three-set symbolism with his comment: "What makes Ned a legend is not that everyone sees him the same – it's that everyone sees him" (Flanagan, 2013, p. 16), and it is the variations in nature, type, form and associated story among the symbols that enliven the significance of the separate 'touristed landscapes'.

The geographical dimension

A simple description of the geographical circumstances would be that the Ned Kelly story was played out across a region in the north-east of the Australian State of Victoria in a loosely configured corridor of approximately 100 km wide (north-west to south-east) by 300 km (south-west to north-east) (Figure 28.2). Its positional parameters include a frame formed by three small ranges of hills, an extensive plain crossed by a number of major water courses and alignment astride a main transport (road and rail) route linking Melbourne with Sydney. Within this corridor there is a loose arrangement of small nodal townships, small population clusters and outliers of homesteads and remnant township sites linked to river-crossing points and to former gold mining activities and to forestry. This patchwork pattern of places, spaces, settings, buildings and other structures has persisted from the nineteenth into the twenty-first century. Some of the formerly significant townships have declined to be now little more than remnants, while others have grown into more important roles. An outcome has been that the regional pattern associated with the Ned Kelly story has a loosely developed pattern of nodes. Each of these

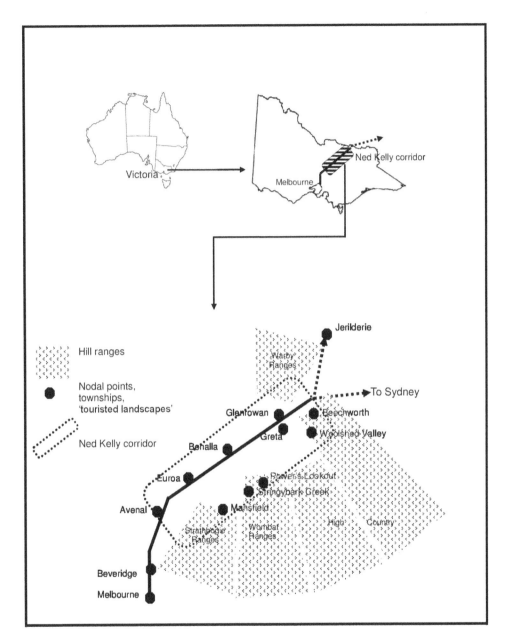

Figure 28.2 Location map.

boasts a separate identity based on its particular critical mass of story-related evidence including its peculiar set of 'imaginaries' and meanings', its 'seductive encounter' with facts, folktales, legends and myths, its distinctive complement of symbols and its significance as an anchor point for at least a part of the story. What exists at this time may be characterized as a loose pattern of co-existing, interlocking and in some cases overlapping nodes of story-related evidence – and a diversity of 'touristed landscapes'.

The 'touristed landscape' of the Kelly story

It is necessary to be aware that 'touristed landscapes' are contrived, impacted variously by sets of influences, composed of different combinations of elements and contribute in a particularized way to the structure, 'meanings' and the telling of the Ned Kelly story. There are no markers 'on the ground' to indicate the existence and boundaries of any particular 'touristed landscape'. Any judgement that a particular landscape unit exists is dependent upon judgements made on the basis of the resources *in situ*, the configuration of them, and the interpretive perspective which is applied (see Figure 28.1). In the following paragraphs there is a summary interpretation of some of the most significant tangible evidence of the Ned Kelly story linked to estimable 'touristed landscapes'. This commentary is supported by Figure 28.3 and Figure 28.4 captures, as an example, the distribution of attraction elements in the Beechworth 'touristed landscape'.

There is only a small-scale 'touristed landscape' at Beveridge; it includes what is considered to be the earliest significant homestead of the growing Kelly family. The 'touristed landscape' at Avenal is loosely configured. It includes the sites of the homesteads and farms worked by the Kelly family, the gravesite of Kelly's father, the bridge over Hughes Creek where Ned Kelly effected the rescue of a drowning boy and the few public and commercial buildings significant at the time the Kelly family lived in the township. A similarly loose configuration is at Greta. All that remains of the story there are sites of three remnant Kelly homesteads and the unmarked family gravesites in the cemetery. Benalla, which might well have been the epicentre of the family's business, legal and social activities, persists as a focal point of the Kelly story. Public records show it was a focal point of police action and court cases involving the Kelly family, and many of the important buildings in use in the Kelly period though the use of them has changed. Direct evidence of the Kelly period is to be found in the folk museum, gravesites in the town cemetery and artworks in the art gallery. This small township has a multi-nodal 'touristed landscape' form.

It is the drama of the later phases of the Kelly story that bestows on other townships and places in the loosely drawn corridor. For example, the small township of Euroa is important in the story principally because it was there that the first of the two bank robberies took place; the Cameron letter was composed at a nearby homestead. Mansfield's significance is heightened by being the host site of the graves of the three policemen killed in the ambush at Stringybark Creek (which, with German's and Bullock Creeks, form a trio of bush settings that fit within a loose touristed landscape form), and the police memorial in the centre of the township. Nearby is the small nodal site of bushranger Harry Power's Lookout. There is only one record of the Kelly Gang crossing the Murray River into the adjoining state of New South Wales; the purpose was to rob the bank at Jerilderie. While at this small town, the Jerilderie Letter was composed. Escalation to the levels of confrontation between the Victorian police and the Kelly Gang significantly shaped the future tourism potential of Glenrowan and Beechworth. At the first of these – Glenrowan – the siege was the climax of the confrontations; it became the site of 'the last stand of the Kelly Gang'. Despite the potential, the 'touristed landscape' is mainly ideational, symbolic and atmospheric because there is only remnant evidence of the events of the siege, with important sites marked by totems, a trail and supported by small-scale museum collections. Some sites have been the subject of archaeological digs but the evidence recovered by Heritage Victoria has been moved and is stored offsite in Melbourne. By far the most seriously tourism-influenced landscape in the region is at Beechworth (see Figure 28.4), which, with the adjoining Woolshed Valley, marks a significant collection of Kelly-period public buildings, many of which are situated within a historic precinct. In addition, and beyond the confines of

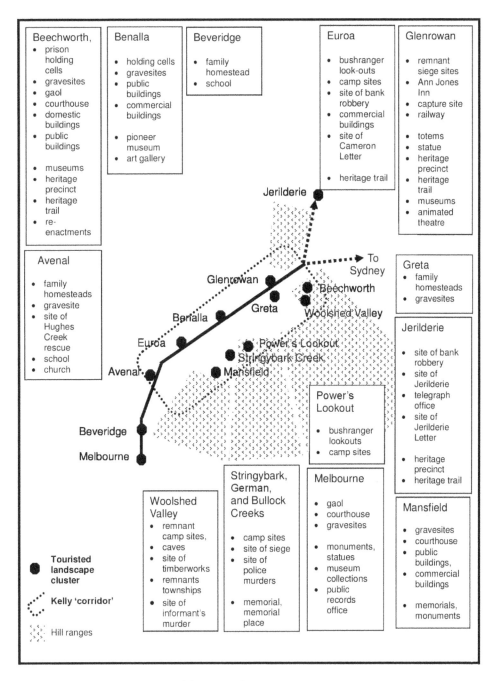

Figure 28.3 'Touristed landscapes' of the Ned Kelly story.

the precinct, are the gaol, a number of significant private residences and beyond the township bush sites that contributed significantly to the unfolding story. For many years there has been a Ned Kelly commemorative weekend with re-enactment scenes. The final 'touristed landscape' is centred on Melbourne, where Kelly was finally sentenced and executed (November 1880),

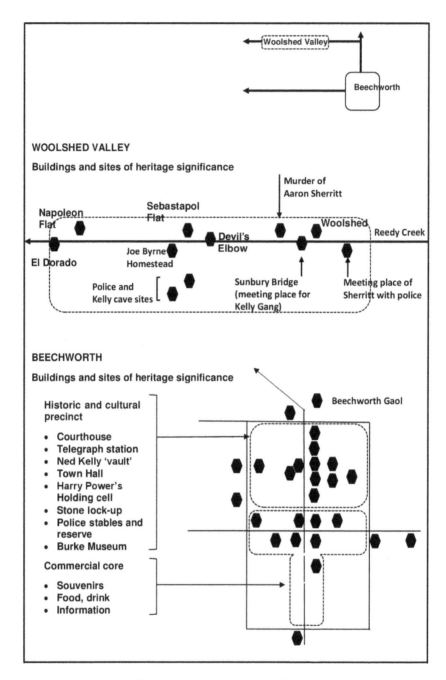

Figure 28.4 Indicative 'touristed lanscapes' – Beechworth and Woolshed Valley.

but few of the sites and buildings are sufficiently contiguous for a cohesive unit to be drawn. Artefacts recovered from the siege site at Glenrowan, the Cameron and Jerilderie Letters, three of the four suits of Kelly Gang armour and much of the 'official' documentation about the Kelly Outbreak are deposited in the Police Museum, the State Library and the Public Records Office.

A number of interpretive points can be made about the 'touristed landscapes' described in this section. Among them are that:

- they vary in configuration, in content, in contribution to the unfolding story, in critical mass and in scale;
- they are different in their degree of significance to the original story and to the circumstances of their 'conversion' into a tourism product;
- while some 'touristed landscapes' maintain prominence, others have become remnants, particularly as their physical fabric has deteriorated;
- and finally, they have experienced different degrees of interest and attention from agencies concerned with commodification, entrepreneurial exploitation, conservation, governance and with scholarship.

As some commentators have suggested, the Ned Kelly Story has a diversity of meanings, different messages for different people, and it is this controversy, coupled with its presentation in so many expressions of popular culture, that continues to sustain its high profile in Australian history, and maintains the levels of interest in it as a resource for tourism. Although there are many small rural townships and isolated 'special places' in the region that have associations with the story and have their own stories, legends, myths and folktales, it is their share in and contribution to the overarching story that captures and sustains popular attention and interest, and it is the consolidation of this into a number of distinctive 'touristed landscapes' that has been considered here. The Ned Kelly story has not been well co-ordinated across the region; the potential for an integrated and consolidated set of 'touristed landscapes' remains.

Implications for popular culture tourism

It has been the purpose of this chapter to examine a point at which popular culture, tourism and the telling of stories from history interconnect and become a significant presence in the process of 'consuming history'. This point is referred to here as a 'touristed landscape'. It is a contrived phenomenon with the potential to be used as a particularly crafted lens with which to discover and expose information about a historical event and many of the resources associated with it, and to assemble, sort and communicate that information in ways that are different from those used in other mediums of popular culture. Further, it may be used to expose levels of detail, degrees of focus and emphasis and expressions of spatial configurations that boast an attractiveness for tourism across a wide spectrum of touristic interest. A 'touristed landscape' may be considered as a core component of history-linked and heritage-based tourism.

A number of ideas and perspectives have been fused here to help with the challenge of communicating matters of history through tourism. This study has been particularly and deliberately nuanced in the burgeoning domain of 'consuming history', of 'engaging with the past'. It is a specially nuanced component of popular culture in that, while being part of the general expansive and penetrative thrust of tourism, it draws selectively on matters of history as it meets the twin challenges of education and entertainment. Although matters of history have their own attraction, for them to be attractive for the purposes of public culture, and especially for tourism, they need to be accessible, not only physically and spatially but also intellectually, emotionally and economically, and they need to be memorable. It is in these matters that the commentaries of Sobchack (1996) and Landsberg (2004) have resonance for tourism. To paraphrase, and combine Sobchack with Landsberg, their observations are that popular 'audiences' seek to become involved in the stories of history as spectators, as participants and as adjudicators, and what they 'take away' from their encounters with history are surrogate or 'prosthetic memories'. The process used here was to open up the basic concept of 'touristed landscape', to expose significant groups of influencing factors and then to consider their contribution in a narrative about the Australian bushranger Ned Kelly.

There have been ideas and processes used here that, while being tuned appropriately to serve the needs of the chosen case study, also have potential for careful transfer – after suitable adaptation, of course – to other forms of popular culture and to other expressions of popular culture tourism. What is offered here is a conspectus of opportunities. The implications of four key elements are isolated for consideration.

One of these key elements has been the elaboration of the 'touristed landscape' device first conceptualized by Cartier (2005a). In its first-stated and most general form it had a potential usefulness across most areas of the study of popular culture tourism. It is essentially a communication device that provides a frame for a story by focusing attention on matters of place-making and sensemaking, possibly culminating in an identifiable 'themescape'. Its usefulness for nuanced or narrowly defined tourism activities was demonstrated in the case study with its special focus on a story from history. Closely linked to the circumstances of the conceptual device is the need to be able to operate across disciplinary boundaries in order to unpack satisfactorily information and interpretations that lie within the scope of different subject areas. This is the second key element, and it involves the opportunity and capacity to think and work across disciplinary boundaries and to develop a particularized and custom-built 'comfort zone' for researching the problem, for engaging with a complexity of knowledge fields and spaces, and for dealing with the force fields and networks that influence them. In the case study in this chapter an operational 'comfort zone' was created by drawing together what were described in an earlier section as 'companionable elements from the toolkits of culture, geography, heritage and history, semiotics and tourism'. The challenges here were subject relevance, disciplinary relevance and cross-disciplinary compatibility. There is a third key element: responsiveness to the dictates of any particular case. In this chapter, the challenge of responsiveness was to matters of geography, chronology, symbolism and to visitor-spectrum. Whereas in respect of the first three of these the basic literature that focuses on the interface of tourism with geography, heritage and semiotics is generally adequate, for the operationalization of tourism through the spatial framework of the 'touristed landscape' and to meet the expectations of the consumers of the tourism attraction/product more specific guidance is likely to be necessary. The fourth key element is the most general, but also the most particular. This study was tied into the burgeoning domain of 'consuming history' (de Groot, 2009). It is an example of a contribution to popular culture in general and to history-linked and heritage-based tourism in particular where the subject matter of history becomes presented for public consumption through the agencies of popular culture and tourism. It reveals the special nuances embedded in geography, heritage, history, semiotics and tourism, and their linkage through tourism attraction, and the need to engineer these linkages through a custom-designed cross-disciplinary investigative and interpretive strategy.

References

Belhassen, Y. & Caton, K. (2009). Advancing understandings: a linguistic approach to tourism epistemology. *Annals of Tourism Research*, 36 (2), 335–352.

Cartier, C. (2005a). Introduction: touristed landscapes/seductions of place. In C. Cartier & A. Lew (Eds.), *Seductions of place: geographical perspectives on globalization and touristed landscapes* (pp. 1–16). London: Routledge.

Cartier, C. (2005b). San Francisco and the left coast. In C. Cartier & A. Lew (Eds.), *Seductions of place: geographical perspectives on globalization and touristed landscape* (pp. 134–152). London: Routledge.

Cartier, C. & Lew, A. (Eds.) (2005). *Seductions of place: geographical perspectives on globalization and touristed landscape*. London: Routledge.

Coles, J. & Armstrong, P. (2007). Dumbing down history through popular culture: communities of interest or learning as consumption? Retrieved from www.leeds.ac.uk/educol/documents/163834.html (accessed 27/6/2013).

Coles, T., Hall, C. & Duval, D. (2006). Tourism and post-disciplinary enquiry. *Current Issues in Tourism*, 9 (4–5), 293–319.

Darbellay, F. (2016). From disciplinarity to postdisciplinarity: tourism studies dedisciplined. *Tourism Analysis*, 21, 363–372.

De Groot, J. (2009). *Consuming history: historians and heritage in contemporary popular culture*. London: Routledge.

Flanagan, M. (2013, 30 March). Rebels who knew the end was coming, but stood up anyway, *The Age* (Melbourne), Insight Section, p. 16.

Gyimothy, S., Lundberg, C., Lindstrom, K., Lexhagen, M. & Larson, M. (2015). Popculture tourism: a research manifest. In D. Chambers & Rakic, T. (Eds.), *Tourism research frontiers: beyond the boundaries of knowledge* (pp. 13–27). Bingley, UK: Emerald.

Jamal, T. & Kim, H. (2005). Bridging in the interdisciplinary divide: towards an integrated framework for heritage tourism research. *Tourist Studies*, 5 (1), 55–83.

Jensen, B. (2009). Usable pasts: comparing approaches to popular and public history. In P. Ashton & H. Kean. (Eds.) *People and their pasts: public history today* (pp. 42–56). Basingstoke, UK: Palgrave Macmillan.

Jones, I. (2008). *Ned Kelly: a short life*. Port Melbourne: Lothian Books.

Jordanova, L. (2000). Public history. *History Today*, 50 (5), 20–21.

Jordanova, L. (2006) *History in Practice* (2nd ed.). London: Hodder Arnold.

Kerstetter, D., Confer, J. & Graefe, A. (2001). An exploration of the specialization concept within the context of heritage tourism. *Journal of Travel Research*, 39, 267–274.

Landsberg, A. (2004). *Prosthetic memory: the transformation of American remembrance in the age of mass culture*. New York: Columbia University Press.

Landsberg, A. (2015). *Engaging the past*. New York: Columbia University Press.

Lippard, L. (1999). *On the beaten track: tourism art and place*. New York: The New Press.

Lowenthal, D. (1996). *The heritage crusade and the spoils of history*. London: Viking.

Lundberg, C. & Lexhagen, M. (2013). Pop culture tourism: a research model. In A. Chauvel, N. Lamerichs & Seymour, J. (Eds.) *Fan studies: researching popular audiences* (pp. 1–22). Freeland, Oxford: Inter-Disciplinary Press.

Lynch, K. (1960). *The image of the city*, Cambridge, MA: MIT Press.

McQuilton, J. (1979). *The Kelly Outbreak: the geographical dimensions of social banditry*. Carlton, VA: Melbourne University Press.

Meinig, D. & Jackson, J (Eds.) (1979). *The interpretation of ordinary landscapes*, New York: Oxford University Press.

Minca, C. (2007). The tourist landscape paradox. *Social and Cultural Geography*, 8 (3), 433–453.

Moustakas, C. (1990). *Heuristic research: design, methodology, and applications*. Newbury Park: Sage.

Ostrom, E. (2009). A general framework for analysing sustainability of socio-ecological systems. *Science*, 325 (July 24), 419–422.

Pearce, D. & Butler, R. (Eds.) (2010). *Tourism research: a 20-20 vision*. Oxford: Goodfellow.

Robinson, M. & Silverman, H. (Eds.) (2015). *Encounters with popular pasts: cultural heritage and popular culture*. London: Springer.

Rodaway, P. (1994). *Sensuous geographies*. London: Routledge.

Seal, G. (1980). *Ned Kelly in popular tradition*. Melbourne: Hyland House.

Seal, G. (1996). *The outlaw legend*. Cambridge: Cambridge University Press.

Seal, G. (2011). *Outlaw heroes in myth and history*. London: Anthem Press

Serle, G. (1971). *The rush to be rich: a history of the colony of Victoria, 1883–1889*. Melbourne: Melbourne University Press.

Shepherd, R. (2002). Commodification, culture and tourism. *Tourist Studies*, 2 (2), 183–201.

Smith, L. (2006). *Uses of heritage*. London: Routledge

Sobchack, V. (1996). *The persistence of history*. New York: Routledge.

Tosh, J. (2015). *The pursuit of history*. London: Routledge.

Tribe, J. & Liburd, J. (2016). The tourism knowledge system. *Annals of Tourism Research*, 57, 44–61.

Urry, J. (1992). The tourist gaze 'revisited'. *American Behavioural Scientist*, 36 (2), 172–186.

Urry, J. (2002). *The tourist gaze* (2nd ed.). London: Sage.

29

SPAIN AS THE SCENERY OF MASS TOURISM PHENOMENA – BETWEEN ELITE TOURISM AND POPULAR TOURISM

The image of the country through cinema and photography

*Maria-Josep Mulet Gutiérrez, Joan Carles Oliver Torelló
and María Sebastián Sebastián*

Setting the scene: pervivence of tourism boom iconography

The image of Spain as a tourist destination from an iconographic perspective, reflected on public photography, graphic guides, postcards, and cinema, has been pieced together and historically transformed according to the different institutional politics and the reaction to previous models. The numerous studies analyzing this adopt a socio-cultural and ideological vision that mostly attends to enduring cultural or psychological topics without impinging on the visual specific component or in what it supposes, from a historical-artistic approach, the survival of iconic and representative traditions. In the touristic figuration field, the transposition of media language strategies (Dorfles, 1973) and the quotes and counter-discourse to the previous imagery, which are still present in the new touristic modality linked to the popular culture tourism, have played a key role.

In the tourist studies area, the polysemic nature of the term *image* has been useful to bind together appreciations occurring in the "performance" sphere: value judgment, opinions, feelings, etc., to synthesize a complex reality, build a media meaning or positioning a *mark* in a positive value ranking around the media projection of a certain territory.

In the Spanish case, the tension between the reality and the international projection through the image built has some peculiar characteristics that are currently in a changing process, with the intention to avoid part of the influential iconography of the touristic "boom" of 1960. This iconography associated with the Hispanic arises within the picturesque and the illustrated and romantic tradition, seeing consolidation with the start of the tourism masses. The image that Spain has adopted in the representations of popular culture tourism owes its configuration to an eminently historical buildup that had in its own "iconic" nature and visual and graphic history a constant example upon which settle.

Given the high number of publications that analyze specific aspects of the repetition of stereotypes, topics, and constant visual discourse in the postal and cinematographic image from the tourist studies perspective, we consider it necessary to restrict our scope to two fundamental nuclei: the transformations suffered in the patrimonial, monumental, and picturesque image, and those taking place in the strictly touristic one. These could be divided in turn into more accurate facets that, in the Spanish case, deal with the usual dichotomy between modernity and tradition: the image of comfort versus rural and pauperism, the industrialized and changing urban scenario versus the immutable, monumental, or patrimonial historical space, the new democratic and tolerant European or American visitor versus the authoritarian and conservative resident. These tensions between opposites were taken to the limit in the touristic boom iconography, and currently continue, reorganizing its basic components and recovering previous models to propose new dualities: the monumental and architectural heritage, disassociated from its historical value, versus the static monotony of the contemporary city's industrialized architecture; the passionate and intuitive local character versus the moderated and distant foreign character, to name a few examples. In a period of true eclecticism in the concentration of components of touristic attraction, the iconic alternatives react against the coloristic, dynamic, and excessive language of the trivialized and massively increased tourism of the 1960s and 1970s, showing a return to natural and idyllic scenarios as an antonym of a business world and of the main centers of economic power, opting for less saturated tonalities and static arrangements. The willpower of modernity projection (used by Franco's regime governing Spain in those days, as a tourist attraction) mollifies, so that the hotel architecture is displaced by the author architecture and that of theme parks and transport and communication infrastructures, by mega shopping complexes.

To analyze both axes we will focus on two types of mass media that have provided the specific image of Spain and Spanish consolidation: photography (in the form of postcards) and cinema, which we combine aesthetically and discursively. We use the name "audio-visual postcard" to refer to a group of formal and conceptual interactions between the postcard (and its synthetic and stereotyped weight) and cinema (only the "advertising-cinema" and "strategy-cinema" willpower), which act under an influential institutional umbrella (Riego, 2010, 2011; Barón & Ordóñez, 2011). There is a specific bibliography on this topic that allows the tackling of the tourists' representation as well as how to perform an iconic selection of characteristic milestones of the country image. Our study framework mainly covers the 1960s and the early 1970s, as it is within this period where a change in relation to the previous iconic models is evidently revealed, although we are also interested in studying the present popular culture tourism as a survival and institutional contrast to this model. We are not going to deal with certain manifestations that have opened a new vision in the definition of a popular culture tourism in Spain (as the recent visits associated with famous television sagas such as *Game of Thrones*, since 2011, or *Penny Dreadful*, 2014–2016), nor are we going to associate the Spanish cinematographic scenarios to a determined way of understanding mass tourism.

Spain as a tourist destination became an institutional matter in 1905 when the National Commission was created, the nucleus of the following "Comisaría Regia" (1911) and the National Tourism Board (1928). During the Francoist regime, after the Spanish Civil War (1936–1939), the Ministry of Information and Tourism (1951) promoted the first tourism recovering attempts until the expansion period arrived (1962–1973), triggering the so-called process of touristic "boom" and configuring the more effective visual identity of "sun and beach" tourism. This remained in the 1980s with the creation of organizations like the National Institute for Tourism Promotion (1984), later called the Spanish Tourism Institute (1991). The continuous institutional changes happening within the different democratic political periods – Socialist Government (1982–1996) and conservative or Popular Party (1996–2004) – have not resulted in significant changes of the conception of this touristic model. A panoramic view of the advertising campaign during the last few years of the twentieth century and the beginning of the twenty-first century reflects alternation between basic components of previous models of advertising (e.g. *Spain: Everything under the Sun*, 1984–1990; *Bravo Spain*, 1998–2001; *Smile! You Are in Spain*, 2004–2009) and proposals of an alternative nature (a bit more recent) towards the excess of sun and beach tourism, and related to emerging markets (*Spain By*, 1995–1997; *Spain Marks*, 2002–2003; *I Need Spain*, 2010).

Disciplinary underpinnings: from local to general approximations to the photographic and cinematographic visual discourses

In the cinematographic field – and slightly less in the photographic – studies related to the touristic influence of *developmentalist* cinema were produced during the 1960s and 1970s, during the last period of the Franco's government, when liberalizing institutional willingness was more evident and the change in the nation's institutional projection had begun. In this regard, contributions of Antonia del Rey Reguillo (2007), Antonio Martínez Puche (2012), or Rafael Gómez Alonso (2006) are indispensable, as well as those related to the study of specific cases, whether they are of a regional nature (Sandoval, 1998; Hernández, 2008; Campo & Fraiz, 2010; Zamarreño, 2010; Aguiló & Mulet, 2011; Jiménez, 2012) or related to the analysis of a particular piece of work (Afinoguénova, 2012; Sánchez-Biosca, 1997). Here we must also highlight the bibliographic impulse generated by Woody Allen's film *Vicky Cristina Barcelona* (2008) in the field of tourist studies associated with cinematography (Navarrete, 2005; Calvo, 2008; Merino, 2008; Elduque, 2009; Aertsen, 2011; Rodríguez, Fraiz Brea, & Alén González, 2012; Osácar, 2016). As regards the analysis of the postcard and photography of a touristic nature from the first decades of mass tourism in Spain, it is worth mentioning the environmental remarks from Bernardo Riego (2011), Alicia Fuentes' (2015) specific remarks related to the mass tourism iconography, those of a local nature (Mulet & Seguí, 2005), and those establishing direct links between environmental photography, from a general point of view, and the touristic practices (Vega, 2011; Velasco, 2011).

The proliferation of studies about the capability of a particular film production in order to attract visitors, the so-called *movie-induced tourism* (Riley, Baker, & Van Doren, 1998), has implied the emergence of the film commissions, offices specialized in the management and publicity of certain locations susceptible to being used by cinematographic producers, however, analysis and quantification of the phenomenon is only very recent (González, Araujo, & Rodríguez, 2015). The use of the frame in which the action occurs in a film to promote a particular destiny began much earlier. The localizations form part of the storyline of the film, as a component that becomes another "touristic view" (Nieto, Del Rey Reguillo, & Afiguenova, 2015) and as such, is heir to the iconographic tradition that we are discussing. The changes in monumental, landscape, and individual touristic vision affects the photographic and cinematographic representation that will influence the tourist in deciding to visit a certain location induced by their attachment to a television or cinematographic production.

Methodology: Spanish modernity, monumental and natural patrimony, and the image of the tourist through cinema and postcards

From this historiographic combination, we deduce a thematic axis that influences the actual touristic representations derived from the mass media; this deals with the tension and dichotomy between modernity and tradition in the image of Spain. The appearance of the tourist in Spanish territories, frequently represented on postcards since the 1960s, as well as the reconversion of patrimonial and monumental collections from a romantic heritage in a new iconographic combination connected to the modern hotels and leisure infrastructures, are inspired by this willingness of harmonious transition between the traditional (political, ideological, and social) and the incipient desire of mercantile incorporation without the loss of ethical values connected to a country of dictatorial roots. The intense institutional ambition to broaden the reconciliation between modern and traditional resulted in new iconography that had as one of its agents a new vision of the "topics of new acquisition" (Navarrete, 2005), which equalized the image of Spain under an umbrella of "Spain is different": sun and beach tourism broke through between monuments, history, and folklore images, sometimes bringing them together or simply substituting them (Crumbaugh, 2010). In this way the institutions developed an enormous tourist industry of low cost, centered on what were considered the "modern" requirements of the tourists (Pack, 2009).

Both in the cinematography of the so-called Spanish folklore associated with the dissemination of customary expressions that gained sense from the presence of antagonists (with the arrival of the new opposing the traditional), and in the graphic publicity and photography of the touristic character (and among them, especially, the postcard), some strongly consolidated iconic connotations were acquired, which shaped a strong impression of the Spanish. As an example, the first minutes of the film *Verano 70* (Pedro Lazaga, 1969) presented a true confrontation between touristic models in a form of successive fixed images, to introduce, in a jocose tone, a comparison between the previous touristic models of the consumer society and those of sun and beach, where the vision of the national and foreign tourist, their routines, their objectives, preferences, and way of life, had acquired such a high degree of localness that it was taken almost to parody.

The same modern versus traditional dichotomy is noticeable in the storyline of some films from the same director, such as *El turismo es un gran invento* (Pedro Lazaga, 1968). During the initial conversation between the actors, Paco Martinez Soria and J. L. Lopez Vazquez, in a completely rural setting, the first to speak represents the modernity and opportunistic mercantilism: "everything should be changed and brought up to date"; meanwhile the second speaker personifies conservatism by talking of the value of historic patrimony and monuments in terms of historic and religious authority: "But we have the parish church which is a romantic jewel from medieval times! Which was used once by Charles III to confess!" The change in the understanding of the historical monuments and its gradual integration into the picture of the beach scene can be extrapolated perfectly to the postcard sphere. The postcards of significant monuments practically disappeared and, if registered, they were in the core of the so-called "multi-views" or local folklore customs, under the same ethnographic perspective of the regional dress and the local popular dances (see Figure 29.1). It pacified the patrimonial and landscape pre-eminence deposited in films of the 1920s–1930s, for example, in *El secreto de la pedriza* (Francesc Aquilo, 1926) or *Flor de Espino* (Jaime Ferrer, 1925) where the storyline is mainly a pretext to show the scenery. Considering the survival of this discussion, which can be described as displacement of monumental values as a way of giving an impression of a nation through leisure centers, it is obvious, but by no means less problematic, that the reconsideration and valuation of the most iconic monumental and architectural patrimony of mass tourism should go through an integration with the "Spanish way of life" and experience both emotional and intellectual patrimony. Such is the tone that patrimony and monuments acquire as a backdrop in the film *Vicky Cristina Barcelona* (Woody Allen, 2008) where the initial motivation of one of the main characters (Cristina) is precisely to get to know the architecture of Gaudi to be able to complete their PHD thesis on the Catalan Identity. In contrast, in *L'auberge espagnol* (Cedric Klapish, 2002), the

Figure 29.1 Casa Planas, typical costumes. Agrupación folclórica Revetlla. Postcard. Mallorca, Spain, 1967.

Source: courtesy of the Josep Planas Family.

same scenes with the Catalan architect merge into less idealist scenes of the city, although they become, once again, the place of emotionally dense scenes (observe the contrast with *En construccion*, 2002, from Jose Luis Guerin, or *Biutiful*, 2010, from Alejandro González Iñárritu). The recent images of the architecture of Gaudi in the ultimate campaign promoted by the Ministry of Industry, Energy and Tourism, *I Need Spain* (2010) follow the same storyline, establishing as a living back ground and even sporting, of a couple who take an undetermined route by bicycle with the Sagrada Familia in the background.

The process of iconographic construction is well known and precedes the notion of the "touristic gaze" (Urry & Larsen, 2012) at the start of sun and beach tourism: the photography densified and united a preexisting set of scenes and descriptions that, since the end of the eighteenth century, connected the Spanish territories with exotic romanticist imaginary of Arabic and flamenco together with the diffusion of patrimonial monumental elements. The union between the reductionist customs and national typologies and the iconic consolidation of its historic and artistic landmarks had some counterpoints in the images of modernization associated with photographers such as C. Clifford, J. Laurent, or W. Atkinson. However, the generalization of topics associated with the local customs of Andalucía, or cultural and ethnographic uniformity in Spanish territory, show in this period, and especially in the last decades of the nineteenth century, a splendid moment derived from the boom of the commercialization and popularity of collecting the postcard. Family traditionalism, the environments close to the bucolic scenarios and religious conservatism, together with the clichés associated with virile, passionate, or crafty masculinity, were exploited as the national identity during the Franco years (1939–1975) until they hoped to make a change in the 1960s by means of promoting iconography of rest and progression. The earlier international projection (not official) of poverty, illustrated by photographic reports such as the famous *Spanish Village* by W. Eugene Smith (1951) or the film *Surcos* (Jose Antonio Nieves Conde, 1951) had its counterpart in the luxury coastal resorts, while the efforts of the institutions to reconcile the arrival of new forms of conduct and thinking of the foreigner with the immovable Spanish values or religiosity and morality (e.g. the concept "modern . . . but Spanish" portrayed by the singer and actor Manolo Escobar in the film *En un lugar de la Manga*, directed by Mariano Ozores in 1970) included its audio-visual and graphic promotion.

This image acquired through contraposition helps us to understand how a great number of tourist expressions connected to popular media, such as sports, gastronomy, festivals, and other elements instigating tourist destinations, have been shaped. Many of the scenes on postcards from the last years of the 1960s to the beginning of the 1970s are plentiful in the necessity to combine tradition and modernization (trendiness), sometimes under the notion of well-being and tourist leisure, other times reflecting the new urban industries and communication, but always over a background of sun and beach (see Figures 29.2 and 29.3). One of the examples where you can clearly observe the idea of "trendiness" associated with the new tourist architecture and the comfort of the infrastructures in the sector is the film *Amor a la Española* (Fernando Merino, 1966), which was considered one of the first full-length feature films that directly reflects the phenomenon of sun and beach tourism. The combination between Andalusian folklore as an element valued by the tourist, adapted to the new appearance of the feminine model and to scenarios of modernity, are manifested in the film *Búsqueme esa chica* (Fernando Palacios, George Sherman, 1964), based in Mallorca and with a plot that incorporates some dance sequences in front of the hotel Mediterráneo, an example of the architectural restorations associated with the new conception of comfort and frequent scenarios on postcards.

The second axis relates to the monumental and natural patrimony in the images connected to popular culture tourism in Spain. The pre-eminence of images associated with pauperistic connotations in the two decades preceding the tourist boom were much more significant in Spain than in the rest of Europe. Similarly to what happened with the new vision of the patrimonial landmarks, the institutional effort to counteract the image of a rural and economically backward country transmitting an international projection related to modernization and economic well-being, transformed the paradise-like images associated with models of the territory. The valuation of the natural, climatic, and landscape elements is not an invention from the 1960s tourism, but took advantage of the dynamic of a previous tradition associated with *Mediterraneanismo* and to the escapist search of non-industrialized scenes, especially significant in the elite tourism of the 1960s in areas like the Balearics and Canary Islands. When institutional speeches popularize and spread these scenarios, they turn into a place that combines landscape and climate benefits with new touristic facilities. The view of the natural landscape visited by the tourist during the first years of mass tourism alternates the celebratory and festive tone of the beach scenes with casual relaxing and leisure in the surroundings of new touristic complexes. On the other hand, it seems interesting to observe that some international cinema examples in 2000–2010, in the

Figure 29.2 García Garrabella y Cia, Torremolinos. Beauties of the city. Postcard. Spain, *c.*1970.

Figure 29.3 Casa Planas, Hotel Playa Cala Millor. Postcard. Mallorca, Spain, 1971.

Source: courtesy of Josep Planas Family.

search of localizations away from the touristic overcrowding and globalization, have resorted to Spanish scenery returning to an image close to the pre-touristic landscapes, but not necessarily making explicit reference to the place where they have been filmed. As an example, in the film *The Stranger Within* (Adam Neutzky-Wullf, 2012) the Tramuntana mountain range, the mountain chain in the north of island of Mallorca, is projected as a pretty natural landscape where vernacular architecture is aesthetically integrated in the surroundings and constitutes a bucolic counterpoint to the cosmopolitan and urban attitude of the New York couple while on holiday on the island. Likewise, in *Sexy Beast* (Jonathan Glazer, 2000), Andalucía and Costa del Sol appear again like elite tourism landscapes, despite the fact that the argumentative connotations are different from the aforementioned case.

In a recent study carried out by the Elcano Royal Institute (Francescutti, 2015), 15 films without any Spanish co-production were analyzed, reaching the correct conclusion that, together with the association of Spain with crime and as a romantic place, the image of the country as a tourist destination and allusions to Hispanic stereotypes generated in previous periods clearly still survive. However, we should differentiate between particular allusions to landscapes and natural environment from those scenes where "the specifically touristic" become an authentic audio-visual postcard, where the stereotypes emerge within the touristic sphere, without escaping from the intrinsic of its logic. An example would be the film *Zindagi Na Milegi Dobara* (India, Zoya Akhtar, 2011), a musical sequence of prototypical landscapes seen through the eyes of the naïve and passionate traveler. This film provides perfect examples of the consequences of the homogenization and symbolic and cultural nationalization process suffered in the national territory as a result of the will to maintain modest and unified visual identity. The postcard image of the autochthon particularities in mass tourism welcomes the milestones of its previous iconographic tradition, but this time is immersed in the *kitschification* process (Figueroa, 2000) and the setting of its folkloric facets. As in this type of cinema, which pretends to show mass tourism scenes, in the touristic photography and postcards we need to synthesize, just a single image or small film sequence can create cultural associations that transcend the mere iconographic stereotypes of Spain and appeal to certain traveler perceptions of knowing the "real" character of the area.

Provided that the image of Spain created in the postcards tends to associate with negative touristic connotations, the recent institutional campaigns promote confronting strategies where they try to "eliminate" the iconic, emphasizing the experience of Spain, rather than the visual identity created by mass tourism. The image incited in *I need Spain*, the last institutional campaign mentioned, chooses elements from the mass tourism visual character to counteract the fact that touristic consolidation in Spanish territory is associated with the excess of sun and beach tourism: the traveler replaces the postcard by a straight visit to the Prado Museum or the monument image by the tourist observing it and *living* it.

Monumental heritage and landscape fluctuate between its integration in the scenes of sun and beach and its positioning as part of vital and urban modernity, half way between its connection to the scenes of *all-inclusive* and the presence of new backgrounds associated with an *idyllic tourist area* (Nieto, Rey-Reguillo, & Afiguenova, 2015). The auto reference of the tourist iconography generated with the postcard, the fact that its images possibly inhabit an iconosphere parallel to the socio-cultural reality that is diffused in it (Osborne, 2000) leads us to believe that its authors use preceding iconography motives to renew or modify the *touristic memory* according to the mentality and the interests of each period.

The last axis is the appearance of the tourist. Together with the view of the landscape and the monumental landmarks, another of the thematic axis to which we refer is the representation of the tourist himself. The view of the contemporary visitor is conditioned by their experience and own life lessons, essential factors *to approach a comprehension of the visited area* (Vega, 2011) but is also the reason that it has been considered as a *contaminated* opinion. The photography of the mass tourist taking photographs has been transformed into a spectacle and enormous topic, looking for a value unconnected of its own configuration, a *touristic value* (Brucculeri, 2009). The staging of the tourist as an advertisement, a constant in the images of the postcards from the beginning of the 1960s until the most recent promotional tourist films, signifies to direct the attention of the actual tourist in that which *really* they have come to find in the area, through which they may establish a long-lasting bond, maybe because it fulfills their previous expectations before their visit or they may identify with the more picturesque qualities of the country. Postcards of a typical Mallorca photographed by the tourist would include nineteenth-century clothing, folklore crafts, and cuisine. Other caricatured graphic postcards show the male and female tourist equipped with a camera in completely rural surroundings, unconnected and separated from its natural and open urbanism. The camera is their method of observing looking for the picturesque and pure, illustrating the distinctiveness manifested between model and photographer, a resource that accentuates still further the distance between characters (see Figure 29.4). In *Vicky Cristina Barcelona* the tourist photographer appears again looking for the artistic and exotic, at the same time native, of their surroundings, marveling at the succession of photographs that offer architectural, monumental, and vital reality to her stroll through Barcelona and Oviedo.

The representation of the tourist within cinematography has been addressed by Rey Reguillo (2013). One of his principal contributions is the recognition of the change suffered by this figure since the 1970s and up to the present day, from the models of the tourist confronted with the

Figure 29.4   Ediciones Bohigas, Typical Mallorca. Postcard. Mallorca, Spain, *c*.1965.

local mentality to the profile of the tourist with cultural unease. As iconography coincides in the area of the cinema and postcards we find that principally the representation of the tourist is as an erotic attraction, with a happy pose, dynamic and young, photogenic, and with connotations close to cinema "nudity" illustrated by plays like *Three Swedish for three Rodriguez* (Pedro Lazaga, 1975) a clear example of the so-called "landism" (in reference to Alfredo Landa, one of its main actors) in the 1970s (Del Rey, 2013).

On the other hand, and in a very different general sense, the images of common of groups of tourists in summer style and leisure gastronomic scenes or night parties are very common. It is not difficult to find figurative examples close to this representation of groups of jolly tourists in a celebratory pose in the postcards of the 1960s and 1970s, as in the present day, as is manifested in the maritime quarrels in the short film *Vale* (Alejandro Amenábar, 2015), a publicity promotion assignment filmed in the Balearic Islands for a beer company, in which they eradicate the references to large-scale tourism and place the characters in an ideal setting.

Implications for popular culture tourism: persistence and transformation of an established tourist iconography

The crisis of 1973 represented a break in the accelerated growth in the arrival on a large scale of tourists and the beginning of a certain reflection on the tourist model of "sun and beach" dominant up to this time. After the recuperation at the end of the 1970s, the tourist model began to change with a greater diversification and branching out, coinciding with the beginning of environmental awareness and the appearance of rural tourism in the 1990s, which continued to be emphasized in successive decades. In spite of this, the demand for "sun and beach" has been maintained until today in alternative manifestations of popular culture tourism, in the same way that reminiscences of the iconography of mass tourism still survive.

The strong influence of this figurative tradition and the provoked reaction in the generation of the actual tourist image has one of its principal symptoms in the numerous line up of artists who use in their images a subversive tone and some critical elements and topics that have been present since 1960s. Their approach moves away from publicity to create a reflection on the stereotypes of tourism as a globalized activity. Proposals like *Brunchcity* by Andrea G. Portoles and Bea Crespo use gastronomy as the identifying element, creating outlines that reproduce relevant monuments from urban districts like Madrid and Barcelona on a base defined by typical food from each place. More commonly are the real settings, beaches, and venues dedicated to leisure, the places where artistic tasks are developed. The Balearic Islands have been chosen by English artists like Martin Parr who focuses on tourist social behavior. His project *Bored Couples* (1980–1990) included images taken in Mallorca, the island that he returned to in 2009, focusing on the beaches of Magaluf. Also, the Italian Fernando Scianna focused on coastal areas full of tourists, exactly the reverse to the Catalan Jordi Bernadó, who, in the publication *Mallorca Boom*, beyond some prototypical images, analyzed the transformation of the island territory and landscape under constructive pressure derived from large-scale tourism through a series of views of natural or artificial areas uninhabited areas. Some comparative images from the photographer Jaume Gual created with the intention to be more documental and topographic, evidence the visual clash between historic representations and the coastal scenarios of large-scale tourism in the Balearics (see Figure 29.5). Pilar Albarracín works on topics that have been promoted on the image of Spain in popular culture tourism in the series *Flamencas* (2009), manipulating postcards using photomontages, and Agustí Torres reflects on new antagonisms on the impact of global tourism and the rituals of the photographic shot associated with the image of the tourist in mosaic series like *I Wish I Were Here* (2011) (see Figure 29.6). The construction was also

Figure 29.5 Jaume Gual, Torrent de Pareis, Escorca, Majorca, Spain, 2013.

Source: comparative photography based on an image by Bartomeu Reus Bordoy, decade of 1930. Courtesy of Jaume Gual and Bartomeu Reus family.

Figure 29.6 Agustí Torres, *I Wish I Were Here*, Pessoa, 70 x 120 cm. Color photography, 2002.

Source: courtesy of the author.

the principal motive in the series *Vacaciones en el Mar* from Amparo Garrido, which through the main plans of the facades of tourist accommodation would reflect on the economic and architectonic motives that gave form and dimension to the establishments. The most excessive facet of sun and beach tourism is its association with sex and alcohol. In the play by Mariona Obrador, the characteristic forms of language of the multi-view postcards, commonly associated with the combination of picturesque scenes, landscapes, monuments, and ethnography are converted here in combinations of situations and snapshots of uncontrolled and wild nights (*Mallorca Paradise: The Dump of the European Shit*, 2016). Along the same lines, Javier Izquierdo tours Magaluf, one of the most conflictive zones of Mallorca and known worldwide as the area of uncontrolled drinking, with the title "Passion for Magaluf" paraphrasing the campaign by the Balearic Government "Passion for Palma De Mallorca" and changing its luxurious and sophisticate atmospheres (Yachts, Golf courses) for nightly scenes plagued with drunken youths.

The language of large-scale tourism in the hands of contemporary art illustrate to which point its iconographic strategies are still currently valid. The cinema and the postcard, when they are shown as concrete elements of tourist publicity, shape two interrelated routes of diffusion of a "Spanish imaginary," which today we perceive in the full process of transformation: between the intense influence of the image of sun and beach tourism and the projection of an emotional world far from the economic and ideological problems of the Western world.

Acknowledgment

This chapter is part of the research project I+D: HAR2016-77135-P. Programa Estatal de Fomento de la Investigación Científica de Excelencia (Ministerio de Economía, Industria y Competitividad. Gobierno de España).

Bibliography

Aertsen, Víctor U. (2011). El cine como inductor del turismo. La experiencia turística en Vicky, Cristina, Barcelona. *Razón y palabra*, 77. Retrieved from www.razonypalabra.org.mx/varia/77%204a%20 parte/54_Aersten_V77.pdf.

Afinoguénova, E. (2012). La España negra en color: El desarrollismo turístico, la auto-etnografía y España insólita by Javier Aguirre, 1965. *Archivos de la filmoteca: Revista de estudios históricos sobre la imagen*, 69, 38–57.

Aguiló, C., & Mulet, M. J. (2011). El fenómeno del turismo de masas a través del cine de ficción: Mallorca como escenario. *I Congreso Internacional Historia, literatura y arte en el cine en español y portugués*. Salamanca: Centro de Estudios Brasileños, Universidad de Salamanca, 1369–1389.

Barón, M. S., & Ordóñez, C. A. (2011). Postales audiovisuales. Exotismo, turismo y Pa' Colombia. *Calle 14: revista de investigación en el campo del arte*, 5(7), 78–92.

Brucculeri, M. C. (2009). *Semiotica per il turismo*. Roma: Carocci.

Calvo, A. G. (2008). Postales imposibles. *Dirigido por . . . Revista de cine*, 381, 40–41.

Camprubí, R., Guia, J., & Comas, J. (2009) La formación de la imagen turística inducida: un modelo conceptual. *Pasos. Revista de Turismo y Patrimonio Cultural*, 7(2), 255–270.

Crumbaugh, J. (2010). *Destination Dictatorship: The Spectacle of Spain's Tourist Boom and the Reinvention of Difference*. Albany: State University of New York Press.

Del Rey Reguillo, A. (Ed.) (2007). *Cine, imaginario y turismo: estrategias de seducción*. Valencia: Tirant Lo Blanch.

Del Rey Reguillo, A. (2013). *Turistas de película*. Madrid: Biblioteca Nueva.

Dorfles, G. (1973). *El Kitsch. Antología del mal gusto*. Barcelona: Editorial Lumen.

Elduque, A. (2009). Vicky Cristina Barcelona: fotos y pasión en la ciudad condal. *Filmhistoria online*, 1(1).

Figueroa, M. (2000). La Kitschificación. *Artyco*, 9, 37–40.

Francescutti, P. (2015). Un paraíso turístico entre la tradición, la modernidad y el crimen organizado: España vista por el cine extranjero. *ARI*, 30. Retrieved from www.realinstitutoelcano.org/wps/portal/rielcano_ es/contenido?WCM_GLOBAL_CONTEXT=/elcano/elcano_es/observatoriomarcaespana/ari30-2015-espana-vista-cine-extranjero.

Fuentes, A. (2015). *Aportaciones al estudio visual del turismo: la iconografía del boom de España, 1950–1970*. Doctoral thesis, Universidad Complutense de Madrid, Madrid.

Garlik, S. (2002). Revealing the unseen: tourism, art and photography. *Cultural Studies*, 16(2), 289–305.

Garrod, B. (2009). Understanding the relationship between tourism destination imagery and tourist photography. *Journal of Travel Research*, 47(3), 346–358.

Gómez Alonso, R. (2006). El turismo no es un gran invento: aperturismo y recepción del ocio y consumo a través del cine español de los 60. *Área abierta*, 15, 4–10.

González, A., Araujo N., & Rodríguez, L. (2015). Turismo cinematográfico: La conquista online de nuevos mercados. *Rotur, Revista de Ocio y Turismo*, 9, 17–34.

Hernández, J. (2008). *La imagen de Andalucía en el turismo*. Sevilla: Fundación Centro de Estudios Andaluces.

Jiménez García, E. M. (2012) *Turismo inducido a través del cine: génesis del imaginario romántico de Córdoba en el contexto cinematográfico español (1920–1930)*. Doctoral thesis. Universidad Carlos III, Madrid.

Martínez Puche, A. M. (2012). *Territorios de cine: desarrollo local, tipologías turísticas y promoción*. Alicante: Universidad de Alicante.

Mulet, M. J., & Seguí, M. (2005). *Fotografia i turisme. Josep Planas i Montanyà*. Barcelona: Lunwerg editors.

Navarrete, L. (2005). La españolada en el cine. In Poyato, P. *Historia(s), motivos y formas del cine español*. Córdoba: Plurabelle, 23–31.

Nieto, J. J., Del Rey-Reguillo, A., & Afiguenova, E. (2015). Narración, espacio y emplazamiento turístico en el cine español de ficción (1951–1977). *Revista Latina de Comunicación Social*, 70, 584–610.

Osácar Marzal, E. (2016). La imagen turística de Barcelona a través de las películas internacionales. Pasos. *Revista de Turismo y Patrimonio Cultural*, 14(4), 843–858.

Osborne, P. (2000). *Travelling Light: Photography, Travel and Visual Culture*. Manchester, New York: Manchester University Press.

Pack, Sasha D. (2009). *La invasión pacífica. Los turistas y la España de Franco*. Madrid: Turner.

Ren, C., Pritchard, A., & Morgan, N. (2009). Constructing tourism research: a critical inquiry. *Annals of Tourism Research*, 37(4), 885–904.

Riego, B. (2010). *España en la tarjeta postal. Un siglo de imágenes*. Barcelona: Lunwerg Editores.

Riego, B. (2011). Una revisión del valor cultural de la tarjeta postal ilustrada en el tiempo de las redes sociales. *Fotocinema. Revista científica de cine y fotografía*, 2, 2, 3–18.

Riley, R., Baker, D., & Van Doren, C. S. (1998). Movie induced tourism. *Annals of Tourism Research*, 25(4), 783–987.

Rodríguez Campo, L., & Fraiz Brea, J. A. (2010). Consideraciones estratégicas para la promoción del turismo en Galicia a través del cine. *Revista Galega de Economía*, 19(2), 155–164.

Rodríguez Campo, L., Fraiz Brea, J. A., & Alén González, E. (2012). La trama y las imágenes en el cine como promoción turística de un destino. Evaluación del caso Vicky, Cristina, Barcelona. *Papers de Turisme*, 51, 133–147.

Sánchez-Biosca, V. (1997). Un realismo a la española: El Verdugo, entre humor negro y modernidad. *Co-textes*, 36, 79–90.

Sandoval Martín, M. T. (1998). Promoción turística a través del sector audiovisual: el caso de Canarias. *Revista Latina de comunicación social*, 9. Retrieved from www.ull.es/publicaciones/latina/a/37san.htm.

Santillán, L. (2011). Fotografía, turismo y consumo. Bases conceptuales para el análisis de la imagen fotográfica comercial turística. *Reflexión Académica en Diseño y Comunicación*, XII(16), 140–144.

Stenberg, E. (1997). The iconography of the tourism experience. *Annals of Tourism Research*, 24(4), 951–969.

Urry, J., & Larsen, J. (2012). *The Tourist Gaze 3.0*. Thousand Oaks, CA: Sage.

Vega, C. (2011). *Lógicas turísticas de la fotografía*. Madrid: Cátedra.

Velasco, I. (2011). El papel de las tarjetas postales en la conformación de la imagen del destino turístico: El caso de la ciudad de Segovia. In *Espacios y destinos turísticos en tiempos de globalización y crisis*. Vol. II. Madrid: AGE, 49–63.

Zamarreño, G. (2010). Cine y turismo en la Costa del Sol. Retrato de unos colonizados. In *Usos, costumbres y esencias territoriales*. Madrid: Ministerio de Ciencia e Innovación, Universidad de Málaga, 581–598f.

30

PLAYING AT HOME

Popular culture tourism and place-making in Japan

Paul Mason and Gregory L. Rohe

Setting the scene

When it comes to tourism, the concept of the ludic looms large in Japan. Play is translated in Japanese as *asobi*, although this word is used in a far wider sense than its English equivalent. University students in the West would hesitate to use the term "play" outside of contexts involving sport or games, and yet in Japan *asobi* covers that activity of spending time with friends that we clumsily label "hanging out." It also covers the salaryman engaged in an evening's entertainment in the less salubrious part of town. And it certainly applies to leisure travel. We trace these ludic impulses from their antecedents in history, through to the fan practices that have become inextricably associated with popular culture tourism and place-making in Japan.

Considering tourism through the lens of play has been used by many to open up tourism to understandings based on the deeper roles it can fulfill in society. In the context of Japanese attitudes to play, Daliot-Bul (2014) cites a number of researchers (Winnicot, 1971; Sutton-Smith, 1980; Turner, 1974; Sutton-Smith & Kelly-Byrne, 1984) to suggest that play functions as a potential site of cultural experimentation and critique because it is free from "external constraints and consequences" (Daliot-Bul, 2014, p. 50).

If we accept the argument that play is indeed such a "liminoid" zone (Turner, 1974), then tourism fits the bill perfectly. Turner's suggestion that in post-agrarian societies play is supplanting rituals as a marker of rites of passage is supported in the case of tourism generally by Cohen (2004) and especially so in the case of Japan by the phenomenon of *shūgakuryokō*: in which educational mileposts are marked by group trips, whether to cultural highlights such as Kyoto or, increasingly, to Disneyland (Oedewald, 2009). "[P]lay has become idealized in postmodernity because it allows some control over the constantly shifting natures of identity, social relations, and space, and over the expansion of reality into multiple physical and virtual realities" (Daliot-Bul, 2014, pp. xxxiii–xxxiv). Such an activity will be subject to an interplay of forces, and we can therefore invoke de Certeau's (1984) "petty tactics," whereby the strict hierarchical meaning of a situation is repurposed by those involved in it to suit their own ends.

In addition to the historical context, we will consider issues based on fan theory. One fan-generated distinction, which has been picked up by fan scholars, is that of affirmational vs transformational fandom (obsession_inc, 2009). Simply put, this is the distinction between those who *consume* (as an audience) something, and those who *play with* something. This contrast

353

between a receptive and ludic orientation is a useful way of looking at characteristics of the Japanese situation.

Historical context and theoretical underpinnings

While there were a number of socio-cultural and political restrictions impeding mobility in Japan during the ancient and feudal periods, the Japanese were nonetheless remarkably intrepid. Indeed, the decades prior to the imposition of *sakoku* (the official policy of enforced isolation) saw Japanese Christian missions to Europe and Central America, as well as an active trade (both with and without governmental sanction) across Asia, belying popular notions of Japanese insularity. Domestic travel was at least a possibility for most Japanese as well. The German physician Engelbert Kaempfer, who made the trip between Nagasaki and Edo (now Tokyo) several times in the late seventeenth century, marveled at the sheer number of travelers along the Tōkaidō, observing that, "It is scarce credible what numbers of people daily travel on the roads in this country," adding that the Tōkaidō Road was, "upon some days more crowded than the public streets in any (of) the most populous town(s) in Europe" (Kaempfer, 1906, p. 330). More than a century later, Philipp Franz von Siebold, another German physician working for the Dutch, made the same trip, commenting not only on the number of travelers, but moreover their socio-economic diversity (Funck, 2013a, p. 12).

Although by no means commonplace, throughout its history, travel in Japan has had a prominent place in the popular imagination, and therefore has been inextricably linked to essential aspects of popular culture, be it text, performance, or visual representation. As Traganou (2004) has pointed out, one of the earliest examples of the dynamics between text and travel would be the ancient practice of *kunimi* (viewing the country) in which the Emperor and his retinue would travel to officially sanctioned *meisho* (famous places) and compose panegyrics extolling the aesthetic significance of the terrain, and sanctifying it as a critical and representative space within the Yamato realm. This official place-making was at once literary – many of the compositions being collected in poetic anthologies like *Man'yōshū*, in the eighth century, and *Kokin Wakashū*, over a century later – as well as sacred, in that the text was believed to be imbued with *kotodama*, the spiritual power of the Emperor to affirm and reaffirm possession of the place and to pacify its local gods (*kami*) (Traganou, 2004, p. 69). Subsequent evocation of these *meisho* became as integral to Japanese literary creation as seasonal references to indigenous flora and fauna, and points to a long-standing and exuberant dynamic in Japan between travel, text, and place-making.

With the establishment of *sakoku* in the early seventeenth century, international travel to and from Japan became heavily curtailed; domestic travel, conversely, flourished, resulting in what has been described as a "travel boom" (Traganou, 2004, p. 68) during the early modern (Edo) period. Prohibitions on mobility were undoubtedly legislated and enforced, but there are a number of examples of travelers negotiating around these prohibitions or, in some cases, disregarding them entirely. Furthermore, many restrictions on domestic travel were enforced with varying degrees of severity depending on the time and place, leading Vaporis (1994) to suggest that, "Countless persons from all social ranks defied governmental authority by traveling without official permission despite the volumes of legislation intended to regulate or restrict movement" (Vaporis, 1994, p. 5). A useful paradigm to consider here is de Certeau's (1984) non-oppositional binary of strategies (methods of authoritarian control) and tactics (ways in which individuals living within an authoritarian structure manipulate and circumvent that structure to their advantage in their everyday lives). The pilgrimage, one of the few travel activities condoned by the Edo-period authorities, is a pertinent example. Official restrictions on who could go on a pilgrimage, when and how they could travel, where they could stay, along with the overall taxation of such activities, all point to a rigid governmental strategy designed to maintain authoritarian control. An abundance of contemporary textural and visual material related to the pilgrimage, however, including maps, guidebooks, literary texts, and popular woodcut prints, indicate that while visiting a sacred site or sites was the ultimate goal of many pilgrims, the pilgrimage itself could also function as a pretext (or tactic) to sightsee, consume, and simply experience the affirmational joy of travel. The abundance of this material highlights an ever-expanding list of *meisho* to be seen and experienced, and a widening selection of locally produced *meibutsu* (famous things) available for popular consumption. The antics of Yaji and Kita, Jippensha Ikku's fictional pilgrims in the Edo-period bestseller *Tōkaidōchū Hizakurige* (1802–1809) as they navigated the officially designated route to the Grand Shrine at Ise, suggest that, as later critics have maintained, for many Japanese of the time the distinction between the sacred and the profane was tentative, if not completely non-existent. Graburn (1983), in his seminal article on the subject, points to the dynamic exchange between the pilgrimage, the ludic, and a flourishing consumer culture.

Governmental prohibitions on mobility did not apply, or were enforced less rigorously on some occupational travelers like *geinin* (performers), who could travel with relative ease (Vaporis, 1994). Perhaps this tradition of itinerancy is one of the reasons that the theme of travel and travelers often plays such a central role in the performing arts of Japan. A common structure in the Japanese Noh drama, for example, involves a traveler (often a Buddhist priest) who encounters a mysterious figure on the road who turns out to be an unsettled spirit, unable to resolve its connection to the physical world (Komparu, 1983). After re-enacting some critical event in the character's life, the figure is able (with the priest's benediction) to break its attachment to this world and travel to the afterlife. Here, then, the physical journey of the first part of the play is echoed by the spiritual journey at its closing, and indeed in many Noh plays the physical journey can be seen as a metaphor for the spiritual journey of life. *Rakugo*, the more light-hearted traditional art of comic storytelling, has a separate subgenre known as *tabibanashi* (travel stories), which provide the listener the opportunity for both outward and inward exploration. According to Shores (2008), these tales of travelers and their humorous encounters on the road helped to inform the listener of the wider world and their place in it.

Travel has always been a critical element in Japanese visual culture. In the Suma chapter of Murasaki Shikibu's eleventh-century classic *The Tale of Genji*, the protagonist, Prince Genji, having been temporarily exiled to the Suma coast (now in the city of Kobe), stops at the well-known shore and reflects: "He had once heard a description of this sea and these mountains and had imagined them from afar; and now that they were before him, he painted a set of incomparable views of an exceptionally lovely shore" ("Murasaki Shikibu," 2001, p. 244). Genji's reaction to the *meisho* spread out before him is a common one to travelers throughout history and around the world: Through visual representation, he endeavors to capture and preserve its memory. When he finally returns to the capital, Genji's depiction of his travels wins him acclaim at the court and plays a role in the eventual rehabilitation of his reputation.

Visual representation is central to the interplay between travel and culture in Japan. For example, illustrated travel diaries, either in the form of *e-nikki* (picture diaries, illustrated by the writer) or *nikki-e* (diary pictures, illustrated by artists other than the writer) were prevalent during the Heian period and beyond. Although today we have no extant versions of the earliest *e-nikki*, we do have, like the *Genji* passage above, textural references to the practice. A more common convention was the illustration of *nikki-e*, a number of prominent examples of which, like the *Ise Monogatari Emaki* (*The Tale of Ise Picture Scroll*), survive today (Plutschow, 1973, pp. 101–102). Moreover, these texts have served as inspiration for later artists, preserving and extending the *meisho* place-making dynamic. Depictions inspired by *The Tale of Ise*, particularly the poem written by Ariwara no Narihira (825–880) at Yatsuhashi ("eight bridges," in what is now Aichi Prefecture), are instructive. Ogata Korin's early eighteenth-century folding screens, *Irises at Yatsuhashi*, for example, operate on a number of aesthetic levels: They at once reference the bridges and irises of the *meisho* itself (representation), Narihira's poem (text), and the act of the poem's creation (performance), all of which in turn reiterate the cultural significance of the place.

When considering visual representation during the Edo period, perhaps no other form of popular culture was more widely disseminated than the woodblock print, often referred to as *ukiyoe* (floating [or transitory] world pictures). Few of these are more evocative of travelers and traveling than the *meisho* series of Katsushika Hokusai (1760–1849) and Ando Hiroshige (1797–1858), which function not only as paeans to specific sites on the *meisho* circuit, but to the very experience of travel itself. The attire of many of the travelers in these prints often betrays their purpose on the road, pointing to the notion that travel can be transformational.

The pilgrimage was, above all, a transformational experience, the distinctive garb of the pilgrim simply an outward indicator that allowed him or her to pass official checkpoints unmolested by the authorities. There are instances, however, of the pilgrims' transformation becoming a truly subversive expression of resistance to that authority, as with the frenzied, quasi-millennial *okage-mairi* and *ee ja nai ka* ("It's OK!") movements, which used mass pilgrimages at the end of the Edo period as springboards for genuine civil disobedience (Traganou, 2014, p. 74; Wilson, 1992, pp. 95–122). Yet it is important not to lose sight of the role of pleasure – of playful experience – in Japanese travel. In modern Japan, as in so many other parts of the world, this is epitomized by the theme park, and its most notorious exponent: Disney.

Theme park Japan

Following Giddens's (1990) suggestion that modernity is a Western project, Lee and Fung (2013, p. 42) argue that Disney theme parks "provide symbols for Asians to experience the West as an imaginary concept." A similar argument is made by Hendry (2009): that Tokyo Disneyland is offering an experience that differs from that sought by European or American visitors: where they want the thrilling rides, the Japanese visitor wants a fantasy trip to the US. We will consider a little later whether this idea still holds. Meanwhile, let us consider the background.

In Japan's reconstruction after the Second World War, the West was identified with modernity; Asia with the past (Iwabuchi, 2002). However, it was not quite so simple. For one thing, the past in Japan is not all it seems. The famed "Japanese tradition" is not the simple historical fact that it appears. As the authors of *Mirror of Modernity* make clear (Vlastos, 1998), many of the trappings of traditional Japan are recent constructs: one might almost describe them as symbols for Japanese to experience the past as an imaginary concept.

Giddens associates modernity with a radical anxiety, and we can see that the fabrication of tradition entails a means of coping with that anxiety. From this point of view, Disney theme parks would perform a similar function with regard to the West, marking it as simultaneously "other" and "safe." However, while this may have been true of Disneyland after its introduction, and during the economic boom years, it is much more difficult to see evidence for it in contemporary Japan. Anecdotal evidence from thousands of Japanese students over the last two decades suggests that for them the twin appeals of Disneyland are the thrilling rides (as with their American counterparts), and the Disney characters. Even as early as 2001, Yoshimi (2001) was arguing that Japanese people now viewed Disneyland as a part of their own culture: a position supported by its use as a destination for rite-of-passage school *shūgakuryokō* trips (Oedewald, 2009), as well as coming-of-age ceremonies (AFP, 2017).

Disneyland is far being from the only theme park in Japan derived from foreign culture. Universal Studios Japan (USJ) (Universal Studios Japan, 2017) is more unambiguously foreign, presenting an experience based primarily on Hollywood movies. However, since its content is mainly science fiction or fantasy franchises it would be hard to argue that USJ has supplanted Disney as a means of experiencing the West. There are some more curious cases. Huis Ten Bosch (Huis Ten Bosch Inc, n.d) is a theme park based on a recreated Dutch town, while Parque España (Welcome to Shima Spain Village, 2015) is based on Spain. If Disney's Main Street USA was the most obvious candidate for its role as "symbol of the West," then these two would seem to be following in its footsteps. The problem is that it is hard to argue for either of these as representatives of the West, much less modernity. Both evoke the past rather than even the present. In the case of Parque España, the feel is far closer to Disney, with "characters" based on animal versions of Don Quixote and Sancho Panza, among others, interacting with attendees.

It is easy to see these elaborate constructs as simulacra *à la* Baudrillard. However Hendry (2009) rejects postmodern interpretations, feeling that they are better viewed as museums. She supports this with the attention to detail with which they are constructed. And while it may seem difficult to view a cartoon animal Sancho Panza as a museum exhibit, a glance at how museums all over the world are introducing interactive and entertaining – more playful – experiences makes the suggestion less jarring. Moreover, Japan contains other, similar, attractions that are clearly museums. Meiji Mura (Museum Meijimura, 2013) is a museum of real buildings from historical Japan, mainly the Meiji period, brought to a site north of Nagoya and reconstructed. It has attractions and activities, but is evidently a museum. Interestingly enough, the word *mura* used in its name is also used for the Japanese name of Parque España: "Spain Mura." It means village, and is closely associated in the Japanese imagination with the (constructed) traditional (Vlastos, 1998).

As noted above, the traditional in Japan is presented in symbolic form, as an imaginary concept, and thus there are numerous theme parks that, like Meiji Mura, enable modern Japanese to experience their past, or aspects of their culture. While the majority of Japanese live in the built-up strip running from Tokyo along the coast to Osaka (the route of the Tokaido), the rural areas of the remainder of the country are regarded as the "real" Japan even though, as suggested earlier, this authenticity rests on a constructed tradition. Theme parks or museums in the rural areas range from ninja villages to the birthplace of celebrated manga artist Mizuki Shigeru, and offer excuses for urban Japanese to venture into the more sparsely populated regions of Japan for something other than hot spring, golf, or ski resorts. When this form of place-making takes the form of the "branding" of traditional locations, it allows Japanese dwelling in the "Modern" to return to a symbolic "Home."

These sites also appeal to foreign tourists. This form of "self-orientalization" (Tobin, 1992, p. 30) is also expressed in the many television shows about foreigners experiencing interesting things about Japan (for example, *This Doesn't Make Sense, Japanese People!; Cool Japan; Why Did You Come To Japan?* etc).

The rise of the *otaku*

If the theme park was indeed originally a response to the radical anxiety of modernism then we can look for other ways in which popular culture has been employed. One of the most celebrated features of modern Japan is the fan/geek identity construct, the *otaku*. The word itself originated in 1984 as a derogatory term, akin to "nerd" or "geek" (Galbraith, 2015). It achieved notoriety when it was attached to a mass murderer in 1989, and was associated with a moral panic about the behavior and sexual inadequacies of young fans (Kamm, 2015). Over the subsequent years, however, its connotations have mellowed, and it is now used in common discourse in much the same way as "fan" is in the West.

Otaku is here used to refer to those males or females who are actively involved in an inter-related nest of media including, but not limited to, manga, animé, plastic models, collectibles, face-to-face and computer gaming, cosplay, and certain areas of the music industry. The term is also useful precisely because it has been adopted by non-Japanese: Indeed, a significant number of fans of manga and animé outside Japan have taken to referring to themselves as *otaku* (see Jenkins, 2006 for an analysis of this). The *otaku* contribution to Japanese tourism arises from their role in place-making. Two major trends will be considered: fan scene sites and fan pilgrimages.

Fan scene sites

A fan "scene" is a collective term for a virtual community of fans with shared interests (Gosling & Crawford, 2011). By "fan scene site," we refer here to those physical locations that are invested with significance to fans as a result of fan activity. In the case of Japan, specific examples include Harajuku and, especially, Akihabara. Harajuku became a fan scene site as a result of its pedestrianization and prevalence of fashion shops. From the 1980s onwards, numbers of "cos-players" started to treat the streets of Harajuku as the place to show off their creations, dressing up as fictional characters. Although the word cosplay (in Japanese *kosupure*) is a Japanese coinage, short for "costume play," it is not a Japanese creation. Such costuming events have been a part of Western science fiction fandom for decades (Culp, 2016). The coining of the term, however, stimulated a surge in its popularity in Japan, coinciding with the start of the global expansion of popularity of Japanese media, which led many around the world to see cosplay as a Japanese phenomenon. Notably, the word "play" was introduced to the activity by a Japanese observer (Ashcraft & Plunkett, 2014). Huizinga (1949) comments that dressing up is the best expression of the "otherness" of play.

Cosplay is distinctively linked to Japanese popular (*otaku*) culture, but it does have an analog in the world of the constructed traditional. Visitors to Kyoto often take photographs of the young girls dressed as *maiko*, or geisha-in-training, who are to be seen walking its streets. In doing so they are consuming an image of Japanese tradition associated with Kyoto, now one of the world's most popular tourist destinations. Yet some of the *maiko* on the streets of Kyoto are, in the terms of foreign tourists, frauds. They are not geisha-in-training, but young women (from all over Japan) who are enjoying dressing up as *maiko* and experiencing the tradition and romance – the "otherness" – of the city themselves. Although the term is not used, these women are effectively cosplayers.

Harajuku cosplayers, while also mainly women, are expressing themselves as famous manga and animé characters. Although cosplay in Harajuku is much reduced from its peak of popular-ity, this transformational fan practice is still a defining characteristic of the location. It represents an informal mechanism of place-making; in this it contrasts with the World Cosplay Summit held in the city of Nagoya, at which cosplay is an international commercial tool. The Summit in turn draws our attention to a specific fan scene site: the convention. Lamerichs (2014) describes Japanese popular culture-themed conventions in The Netherlands, noting how they become affective spaces. The same is true of Japanese conventions such as Comiket.

A little way across the city from Harajuku, Akihabara became the *otaku* mecca in a similarly informal manner, through its former association with electronics shops and the appeal they had for the original *otaku*. It subsequently attracted formal attention as a "place-brand," becoming a destination for *otaku* tourists, drawn not by electronics, but by a commercial district that plays up to an *otaku* identity (Kikuchi, 2015). This commercial imperative means that the *cosplay* of Akihabara differs from that of Harajuku. The former is represented by maid cafés, where the cosplay element is a deliberate commercial invocation of *moe*, the sense of yearning that characterizes *otaku* (Azuma, 2012). Cosplay is employed as a commercial practice to attract fans, not only of specific media franchises, but of the more nebulous world of *otaku* fandom itself.

Maid cafés emerged from computer gaming: they started as cosplay reenactments of their computer game originals, held as special events at conventions. They became very popular, and, although associated with Akihabara, have spread all over Japan and even to other countries (Sharp, 2014). Regular users of maid cafés report a sense of "home" associated with them (Galbraith, 2011). Although there are different varieties, the defining feature of the maid café is, of course, the maids themselves, who wear cosplay-style maid costumes and serve customers "home-cooked" treats, accompanied by light conversation and other activities. Despite its origins in mildly erotic computer games, it is overwhelmingly a non-overtly sexual activity (Galbraith, 2011). The maids strive to be *kawaii*, the Japanese word meaning "cute" that has acquired cult-like significance.

Akihabara, the home of maid cafés, is also home to AKB48, a music ensemble that closely resembles maid cafés in the costumes worn by members, and the way in which fans are encouraged to participate. Providing a physical location associated with a musical act, where concerts and events are held, and that fans are encouraged to visit, is a clever commercial strategy, which also makes use of the fan pilgrimage, to which we now turn.

Fan pilgrimages

Cohen (2004) in attempting a phenomenology of tourist experiences, describes two forms of tourism that are relevant to us here. The first is *experiential tourism*, in which the tourist seeks to vicariously experience (or we could say museumize) some authentic concept in which they believe, but do not necessarily have in their own life. The second is *recreational tourism*, in which the concept is recognized as non-existent. It is "'nostalgic,' a playful pilgrimage to a by now fictive Center, experienced both joyfully and sadly as if it were real" (Cohen, 2004, p. 91).

In the case of the fan pilgrimage, one variety described by Brooker (2007) and Sandvoss (2005) is the "virtual" pilgrimage – a way of describing the act of media consumption. While the notion of pilgrimage is metaphorical, there is unquestionably a "fictive Center." Significantly, Brooker describes this experience in terms of "homecoming," a term that resonates, for example, with descriptions by fans of visiting fan scene sites such as Akihabara or fan conventions (see, for example Nakajima, 2008; Lamerichs, 2014). Hills (2002), on the other hand, stresses the physicality of locations, or "cult geographies." They reinforce the affective experience of the fan with a material dimension. Sandvoss picks up the pilgrimage analogy, though wrestles with the religious connection. As already discussed, it is considerably less problematic in Japan, which has a less absolutist, and arguably more "playful" religious tradition – one that makes it easier for us to follow Hills and focus on the "affective-interpretive process." Sandvoss suggests that sites generate a feeling of *Heimat*: "Places of media fandom are of such particular importance to fans, then, because they offer the rare opportunity to relocate in place a profound sense of belonging which has otherwise shifted into the textual space of media consumption" (Sandvoss, 2005, p. 64). Pilgrimages are not just to the fan scene sites described above, however. Indeed, the above writers, coming from the specific field of media fandom, are thinking more in terms of visits to locations and studios connected with media properties.

Couldry defines media pilgrimages as not only involving the physical act of traveling to a film location, but also the symbolic act of temporarily crossing the boundary from one's ordinary everyday life into the special world of media. However, Couldry argues that this play between worlds never threatens the integrity of the boundary between these worlds. Rather, these media pilgrimages reinforce the separation of these two worlds and validate the specialness and magic of the media world.

(Norris, 2013, para 2.2)

Norris is writing in connection with a bakery in Tasmania that attracts tourists, especially Japanese tourists, on account of its perceived (and exploited) similarity to a location in the Ghibli animé *Kiki's Delivery Service*. He points out that such media pilgrimages can occur in parallel to more "traditional" tourist motivations. This reminds us of the traditional Japanese pilgrimage, in which a religious transformation and an entertaining journey are not considered incompatible. While it can coincide with more traditional sightseeing, a media pilgrimage can be a transformational experience, transforming the self by adopting a new role. "Dressing up" does not always involve clothing.

While the above site was in Tasmania, Japan has its share of such locations, such as Yakushima and Tomonoura, which attract recreational tourists for their connections with the Ghibli movies *Princess Mononoke* and *Ponyo* respectively (Funck, 2013b). Modern pilgrims to such locations are developing their own tourist experiences. As suggested by Cohen (2004), they are searching for an authentic-feeling experience even though it derives from fiction. As with the artificial environments of Huis Ten Bosch and Parque España, it is not that visitors do not care about authenticity; rather it is the nature of the authenticity they care about. Hills (2002), following Eco (1998), critiques this idea by pointing to the chimeric nature of the "reality" that is taken as the basis for the authentic. As already noted, Disney is offering an experience perceived as authentic. For many Japanese visitors, what matters is that the experience feels *kawaii* and authentically "Disney": thus that it coincides with their existing affective relationship towards the brand. Similarly, the *otaku* arriving in Akihabara or Ikebukuro can feel satisfied; can feel that they are "home" insofar as Akihabara or Ikebukuro successfully fulfills that affective relationship. This is not a given, of course; the negative comments of some Japanese visitors to the Tasmanian bakery on issues such as differences with the movie or the owner's commercial motivations (Norris, 2013) demonstrate that there is a critical engagement with a concept of authenticity.

Yamamura (2009) contrasts these forms of fan tourism with mass tourism, linking them to the capacity for individualized emotional networking offered by the Internet. On the other hand, while such fan tourism does emerge from processes outside the industry, there is no doubt that it is rapidly exploited by the industry and moreover, as the next section will consider, by the government.

Implications of government intervention for popular culture tourism

Cool Japan

Iwabuchi (2002) asserts that the spread of Japanese popular culture throughout the world has been assisted by the absence of a specifically Japanese character to that culture: "what is appreciated, unlike American popular culture, is still not an image or idea of Japan but simply a materialistic consumer commodity" (Iwabuchi, 2002, p. 34). It is arguable whether or not this was a valid point when Iwabuchi was writing, and the testimony of American animé fans –

however imperfect their actual grasp of Japanese culture – in sources such as Allison (2009) suggests otherwise. The promotion of Japan as a source of popular culture is something that both fans all over the world, as well as the international media, have been doing since the 1990s (see Daliot-Bul, 2014; H.-K. Lee, 2014). The Japanese government's Cool Japan initiative was explicitly designed to exploit Japan's popular culture on a global level both as a source of income in its own right, and to stimulate inbound and domestic tourism (METI, 2014). Ironically, of course, government endorsement is rarely seen as "cool," and the whole program has been subject to criticism, not only from fans, but from prominent artists such as Takashi Murakami (Banyan, 2014). Nevertheless, attempts by government and government-sponsored organizations to hitch their wagon to *otaku* culture have persisted. In 2008, for example, the minister of foreign affairs posed for a photo with animé character Doraemon, a Japan National Tourism Organization (JNTO)-produced video included animé and manga material, as well as maid cafés, and more recently even Prime Minister Abe cosplayed Super Mario for the handover ceremony at the 2016 Rio Olympics.

Funck (2013b) reports 2007 data from JNTO about motivations for foreigners visiting Japan from which she concludes that "[f]or all groups, modern Japanese culture like manga and animé is becoming more popular, even though the percentage of those interested is still low" (p. 182). For Western tourists to Japan, this coincides with a decline in numbers motivated by culture and history. There has certainly been an upsurge in incoming popular culture tourism to Japan (along with an overall increase), but the extent to which this has derived from the Cool Japan initiative is highly ambiguous. Akihabara offers a case study of some of the contradictions involved here.

The tourist information that greets the casual visitor to Tokyo stresses the identity of Akihabara as a commercial technological hub. There is little to suggest its identity as the heart of *otaku* culture. For this, it is necessary to have prior knowledge, or to have researched in more detail. Material aimed at the Western *otaku* includes books such as Macias and Machiyama (2004) or Nakajima (2008), though these quickly date and are, in any case, completely independent of government initiatives. The Japan National Tourist Organization, while devoting most of its web pages to Japan's natural beauty and traditional culture, does have a section that specifically refers to Akihabara as the *otaku* Mecca (Immersing Yourself in Japanese Anime & Comics, n.d.), carrying several pages of detail about Akihabara, and *otaku* locations in Tokyo in general. However, a somewhat half-hearted attitude is conveyed by the occasional weaknesses in translation, and the paucity of links. JNTO's regular page on Akihabara is noticeably more professionally produced, and does not contain the word "*otaku*." Even the promotional video on the page, presented by a Singaporean animé fan in maid costume, is more interested in the linguistic skills of the area's electronic store clerks than its appeal as a fan destination (Akihabara area, n.d). This is remarkable given that Akihabara is, for foreign visitors, *the otaku* destination.

Conclusion

Text, performance, and visual representation – the essential elements of Japanese popular culture – have been informed by, and indeed are largely inextricable from, issues of travel and mobility in Japan. While packaged, "affirmational" tourism has dominated in Japan for many decades, the emphasis on the ludic in Japanese society has spawned more playful, "transformational" alternatives, which appear to be gaining ground. These echo historical antecedents, though of course this does not suggest some essentialist Japanese character, so much as a characteristic of the ludic to be found anywhere in the world.

While these forms of tourism, and the places that are made by them, are playful, this does not mean that they are not serious. The government certainly views them seriously, though its perspective appears to be contested by those more closely and informally involved those whose connected derives from affect. We have suggested that the draw of traditional Kyoto is based on the same recreational forms of affect as pilgrimage sites based on *otaku* favorites: both pull towards a fictive center. As with the pilgrimages of old, there is an experience of transformation that may be profound – or may just be a bit of fun, dressing up, playing around a bit. In a rootless world, the fictive center to which this play leads is a sense of home.

References

AFP. (2017, January 9). Hair today, hungover tomorrow as young Japanese come of age. *Japan Times*. Retrieved from www.japantimes.co.jp/news/2017/01/09/national/hair-today-hung-tomorrow-young-japanese-come-age/#.WS94FD20mdQ.

Allison, B. (2009). Interviews with adolescent animé fans. In M. I. West (Ed.), *The Japanification of children's popular culture: From Godzilla to Miyazaki* (pp. 119–146). Lanham, MD: Scarecrow Press.

Ashcraft, B., & Plunkett, L. (2014). *Cosplay world*. New York: Prestel.

Azuma, H. (2012). Database animals. In M. Ito, D. Okabe, & I. Tsuji (Eds.), *Fandom unbound: Otaku culture in a connected world* (pp. 30–67). New Haven: Yale University Press.

Banyan. (2014, June 16). Squaring the cool. *The Economist*. Retrieved from www.economist.com/blogs/banyan/2014/06/japans-soft-power.

Brooker, W. (2007). A sort of homecoming: Fan viewing and symbolic pilgrimage. In J. Gray, C. Sandvoss, & C. L. Harrington (Eds.), *Fandom: Identities and communities in a mediated world* (pp. 149–164). New York: New York University Press.

Cohen, E. (2004). *Contemporary tourism: Diversity and change*. Amsterdam: Elsevier.

Culp, J. (2016, May 9). Meet the woman who invented cosplay. *Racked*. Retrieved from www.racked.com/2016/5/9/11451408/cosplay-inventor-morojo-myrtle-r-douglas

Daliot-Bul, M. (2014). *License to play: The ludic in Japanese culture*. Honolulu: University of Hawaii Press.

De Certeau, M. (1984). *The practice of everyday life*. Berkeley: University of California Press.

Eco, U. (1998). Travels in hyperreality. In U. Eco, *Faith in fakes: Travels in hyperreality* (pp. 1–58). London: Vintage.

Funck, C. (2013a). The roots of Japanese travel culture. In C. Funck & M. Cooper (Eds.), *Japanese tourism: Spaces, places and structures* (pp. 10–39). New York: Berghahn Books.

Funck, C. (2013b). Welcome to Japan. In C. Funck & M. Cooper (Eds.), *Japanese tourism: Spaces, places and structures* (pp. 160–186). New York: Berghahn Books.

Galbraith, P. W. (2011, February). Maid in Japan: An ethnographic account of alternative intimacy. *Intersections: Gender and Sexuality in Asia and the Pacific* (25). Retrieved from http://intersections.anu.edu.au/issue25/galbraith.htm.

Galbraith, P. W. (2015). "'Otaku' research" and anxiety about failed men. In P. W. Galbraith, T. H. Kam, & B.-O. Kamm (Eds.), *Debating otaku in contemporary Japan* (pp. 21–34). London: Bloomsbury.

Giddens, A. (1990). *The consequences of modernity*. Cambridge, UK: Polity Press.

Gosling, V. K., & Crawford, G. (2011). Game scenes: Theorizing digital game .audiences. *Games and Culture* 6(2), 135–154. doi:10.1177/1555412010364979.

Graburn, N. (1983). *To pray, pay and play: The cultural structure of Japanese domestic tourism*. Aix-en-Province: Centre des Hautes Etudes Touristiques.

Hendry, J. (2009). Fantasy travel in time and space: A new Japanese phenomenon? In S. Guichard-Anguis & O. Moon (Eds.), *Japanese tourism and travel culture* (pp. 129–144). Abingdon, UK: Routledge.

Hills, M. (2002). *Fan cultures*. Abingdon: Routledge.

Huis Ten Bosch Inc. (n.d.). *Huis Ten Bosch*. Retrieved from Huis Ten Bosch: http://english.huistenbosch.co.jp.

Huizinga, J. (1949). *Homo ludens: A study of the play element in culture*. London: Routledge and Kegan Paul.

Iwabuchi, K. (2002). *Recentering globalization: Japanese culture and transnationalism*. Durham, NC: Duke University Press.

Japan National Tourism Organization. (n.d.). *Akihabara area*. Retrieved from Japan: The official guide: www.jnto.go.jp/eng/regional/tokyo/akihabara.html.

Japan National Tourist Organization. (n.d.). *Immersing yourself in Japanese anime & comics*. Retrieved from Japan: The official guide: www.jnto.go.jp/eng/indepth/exotic/animation/index.html.

Jenkins, H. (2006). Pop cosmopolitanism: Mapping cultural flows in an age of media convergence. In H. Jenkins, *Fans, bloggers and gamers: Exploring participatory culture* (pp. 152–172). New York: New York University Press.

Kaempfer, E. (1906). *The history of Japan: Together with a description of the Kingdom of Siam 1690–92* (Vol. 3). (J. G. Scheuchzer, Trans.) Glasgow: James MacLehose ans Sons.

Kamm, B.-O. (2015). Opening the black box of the 1989 otaku discourse. In P. W. Galbraith, T. H. Kam, & B.-O. Kamm (Eds.), *Debating otaku in contemporary Japan* (pp. 51–70). London: Bloomsbury.

Kikuchi, S. (2015). The transformation and diffusion of "otaku" stereotypes and the establishment of "Akihabara" as a place-brand. In P. W. Galbraith, T. H. Kam, & B.-O. Kamm (Eds.), *Debating Otaku in contemporary Japan* (pp. 147–161). London: Bloomsbury.

Komparu, K. (1983). *The Noh theatre: Principles and perspectives*. Tokyo: Weatherhill.

Lamerichs, N. (2014). Embodied fantasy: The affective space of anime conventions. In L. Duits, Z. Koos, & S. Reijnders (Eds.), *The Ashgate research companion to fan cultures* (pp. 263–274). Farnham, UK: Ashgate.

Lee, H.-K. (2014). Transnational cultural fandom. In *The Ashgate research companion to fan cultures* (pp. 195–207). Franham, UK: Ashgate.

Lee, M., & Fung, A. Y. (2013). One region, two modernities: Disneyland in Tokyo and Hong Kong. In A. Y. Fung (Ed.), *Asian popular culture: The global (dis)continuity*. Abingdon, Oxon: Routledge.

Macias, P., & Machiyama, T. (2004). *Cruising the anime city: An otaku guide to Neo Tokyo*. Berkeley. CA: Stone Bridge.

METI. (2014). *Cool Japan initiative*. Tokyo, Japan: Ministry of Economy, Trade, and Industry, Japan. Retrieved from www.meti.go.jp/policy/mono_info_service/mono/creative/file/1406CoolJapan Initiative.pdf.

"Murasaki Shikibu." (2001). *The tale of Genji* (R. Tyler, Trans.) New York: Penguin.

Museum Meijimura. (2013). *The Museum Meiji-Mura*. Retrieved from The Museum Meiji-Mura: www. meijimura.com/english.

Nakajima, M. (2008). *The Akiba: A manga guide to Akihabara*. Tokyo: Japan Publications Trading.

Norris, C. (2013). A Japanese media pilgrimage to a Tasmanian bakery. *Transformative Works and Cultures 14*. Retrieved from http://dx.doi.org/10.3983/twc.2013.0470.

obsession_inc. (2009, June 1). *Affirmational vs transformational fandom*. Retrieved from Obsession_inc web log: http://obsession-inc.dreamwidth.org/82589.html.

Oedewald, M. (2009). Meanings of tradition in contemporary Japanese domestic tourism. In S. Guichard-Anguis & O. Moon (Eds.), *Japanese tourism and travel culture* (pp. 105–128). Abingdon: Routledge.

Plutschow, H. E. (1973). *Japanese travel diaries of the middle ages*. (Doctoral dissertation, Columbia University, New York). Retrieved from http://oriens-extremus.org/wp-content/uploads/2016/08/ OE-29-1.pdf.

Sandvoss, C. (2005). *Fans: The mirror of consumption*. Cambridge, UK: Polity Press.

Sharp, L. (2014). The heterogeneity of maid cafés: Exploring object-oriented fandom in Japan. *Transformative Works and Cultures 16*. Retrieved from http://dx.doi.org/10.3983/twc.014.0505.

Shores, M. (2008). Travel and tabibanashi in the early modern period: Forming Japanese geographic identity. *Asian Theatre Journal* 25(1), 101–121.

Sutton-Smith, B. (1980). A sportive theory of play. In H. B. Schwartzman (Ed.), *Play and culture* (pp. 10–19). West Point, NY: Association for the Anthropological Study of Play.

Sutton-Smith, B., & Kelly-Byrne, D. (1984). The idealization of play. In P. K. Smith (Ed.), *Play in animals and humans* (pp. 305–322). Oxford: Blackwell.

Tobin, J. J. (1992). Introduction: Domesticating the West. In J. J. Tobin (Ed.), *Remade in Japan: Everyday life and consumer taste in a changing society* (pp. 1–41). New Haven, CT: Yale University Press.

Traganou, J. (2004). *The Tokaido road: Travelling and representation in Edo and Meiji Japan*. Abingdon, UK: Routledge.

Turner, V. (1974). Liminal to liminoid in play, flow, and ritual: An essay in comparative symbology. *Rice University Studies* 60(3), 53–92.

Universal Studios Japan. (2017). *Universal Studios Japan*. Retrieved from Universal Studios Japan: www. usj.co.jp/e/.

Vaporis, C. (1994). *Breaking barriers: Travel and the state in early modern Japan*. Cambridge: Harvard University Press.

Vlastos, S. (Ed.). (1998). *Mirror of modernity: Invented traditions of modern Japan*. Berkeley, CA: University of California Press.

Welcome to Shima Spain Village. (2015). Retrieved from Shima Spain Mura: www.parque-net.com/foreign/english/.

Wilson, G. (1992). *Patriots and redeemers in Japan: Motives in the Meiji restoration.* Chicago: University of Chicago Press.

Winnicot, D. W. (1971). *Playing and reality.* London: Tavistock.

Yamamura, T. (2009, February). Kanko joho kakumei to bunka soshutsugata kanko no kanosei: Anime seichi junrei ni miru jisedai tsurizumu no hoga [Revolution in tourist information and possibilities of creative tourism]. *Chiikikaihatsu* 533.

Yoshimi, S. (2001). Japan: America in Japan/Japan in Disneyfication: The Disney image and the transformation of "America" in contemporary Japan. In J. Wasko, M. Phillips, & E. R. Meehan (Eds.), *Dazzled by Disney? The global Disney audiences project* (pp. 160–181). London: Leicester University Press.

31

TRAVELING TO ICONS OR ICONS ON TRAVEL

Displacement and representation of places in movies

Burcu Kaya and Medet Yolal

I believe our culture is indeed postmodern in this oxymoron like manner as it transcends the notion of present. It reaches back to the past and forward to the future trying to synthesise these two "imaginary places" in narrative fashion.

(Degli-Esposti, 1998, p. 4)

Setting the scene: the *Troy* movie

Popular culture has long been conversant with the *Iliad* and the *Odyssey*. Thus, the Trojan War myth found different reflections on the screen. The most recent version is *Troy* (2004). *Troy* was written by a young American screenwriter, David Benioff, and produced by Warner Bros at a cost of about 180 million dollars (Winkler, 2007, p. 3). Although the movie narrates the myth of Troy, which has its roots and ruins in Canakkale, Turkey, the producers preferred to build the city of Troy on the Mediterranean island of Malta (Flynn, 2004). Therefore, this movie represents a suitable example for the notion of displacement – which is also known as *runaway production*. The atmosphere created in the movie leaves no trace of the actual Troy. Besides, it epitomizes postmodern storytelling and turns into a distinct representation of an authentic myth.

Although *Troy* is just one example of displacement among others, it is a well-rounded version in film tourism owing to its iconic nature as well. The movie depicts the gigantic Trojan Horse of the myth elaborately. Even though the movie was shot in locations different from the original site, the Horse used in the movie was placed in the city center of Canakkale as a representative figure after the movie. Moreover, the archaeological site of Troy, which is also in Canakkale, hosts another version of the Horse, which was built by a Turkish architect in 1975. We will refer to the filmic Horse as the Trojan Horse, and the one in the archaeological site as "Horse in situ." The Horse in situ is the carrier of the traditional myth while the Trojan Horse embodies an altered popular culture version of the narrative. The Horse in situ provides an embodied experience that enables visitors to hide inside just like the soldiers in the myth. It offers tourists an imaginary historical glimpse and emerges as the most salient and idiosyncratic part of the myth as an icon.

These two iconic Horses reveal the interesting modality of the postmodern era in which authenticity and simulacra co-occur. As representative figures and the narrative holders, these are important tools for marketing of the destination (Yılmaz & Yolal, 2008). This significant competence was also demonstrated by the 73 percent increase in tourist arrivals followed by the release of the movie (Hudson & Ritchie, 2006, p. 389). It can also be noted that these elements are so close to being fetishized by their nature as they turn into powerful actors that reinforce the imagination of spectators and function as fictional identity carriers built by fans. In the same vein, film induced tourism has also been associated with pilgrimage, owing to this sacred and fantastic attribute of places where the movies are shot (Beeton, 2005, p. 35).

In this chapter, our aim is to reveal the conditions that have enabled the iconic Trojan Horse to travel to Canakkale, Turkey, and place-making of this tourism imaginary on its current location where it also represents a postmodern narrative. We grasp the film and Trojan Horse as tourism imageries, which also points out to the socially constructive power of the Horse on the site. By the social construction of space, we mean "the actual transformation of space through people's social exchanges, memories, images, and daily use of the material setting-into scenes and actions that convey symbolic meaning" (Low, 1996, p. 862).

Bolan, Boy, and Bell (2011) grasp displacement just as a form of change in the depicted location. Nevertheless, drawing on the conceptualization of imaginaries, we believe that we should reveal the conditions of this conceptualization in order to shed light on not only local–global connections but also ideological, economic, and technological agendas in this process (Salazar & Graburn, 2014). Thus, we argue that the discussion of displacement should incorporate more than authenticity and tourist motivation issues. This holistic discussion seeks to develop a fruitful base for a critical point of view regarding the displacement notion. It also facilitates concretization of tourism imageries and postmodern place-making theories, which are rare to be deciphered through apparent examples in tourism studies. We begin by offering a short overview of the main frameworks that we use in shaping our conceptualization. We then proceed to describe some possible approaches that shape our evaluations, and this is followed by an examination of the postmodern place-making process of the Trojan Horse as a tourism imagery from a critical point of view.

Theoretical underpinnings

Icons

Iconography was first coined by Erwin Panofsky, a prominent art historian. Panofsky argued that iconography can also be applied to the popular cinema ([1934] 1997). Yet the notion of iconography was first adopted to the realm of cinema by Lawrence Alloway (Neale, 2000, p. 11). Alloway (1963) claims that symbols represented in films exceed the contextual meaning of the artwork itself. Icons are evaluated to be second-order symbols. The symbolic meaning of these symbols may be rooted in the previous similar texts, and they may carry multiple meanings apart from the individual text (Grant, 2007, p. 12). Icons may appear as objects, archetypal characters, and specific actors in films. Western movies are striking incidences of this kind of iconic representation: "the cowboy who dresses all in black and wears two guns, holster tied to either thigh, is invariably a villainous gunfighter. This is the iconographic wardrobe of a generic type, bearing little relation to historical reality" (Grant, 2007, p. 13). While such a stereotypical icon can be further followed by other filmmakers in the same genre, this may demonstrate a rupture with historical reality. Nevertheless, the icons still have cultural backgrounds and meanings.

The meaningful experience and visual pleasure derived from films may easily be interpreted in the same vein with Urry's (2002, p. 3) discussions of the tourist gaze "which is constructed through signs." Therefore, it is not a coincidence that evaluation of films through *the signifier* and *the signified* is much common in literature. The *sign* corresponds to the physical form of the sign such as the image or photograph while the *signified* coincides with the mental conceptualization of the physical form (Turner, 1999). Moreover, these two forms of experience are already intertwined. Leotta (2011) argues that the technological innovations have altered the subjectivity of the traveler. The gaze in cinema that provides a displacement without a physical mobility, presents portrayals of imaginaries to the spectators (Leotta, 2011, p. 14). In this view, the film viewer is evaluated as a form of immobile *flânerie*. Tourists and film viewers are likened since they are perceived as "seekers of established features" (Zimmerman & Reeves, 2009, p. 156). Yet we believe this point of view again accepts the film viewer – and the tourist as well – as passive receivers whose imageries are not included in the whole process, even though they are valuable elements for on-site consumption of movie-induced tourists (Riley, Baker, & Van Doren, 1998).

Imaginaries

One of the powerful elements that play a crucial role in the tourist fantasies is popular culture such as the visual and textual content of documentaries and fiction movies (Salazar, 2010, p. 44). Cinema and imagination apparently interpenetrate. Cinema gains its power from taking the audience to a world that persuades them about the reality of the imaginary. Further, the film diminishes the gap between dream and the existence of a certain impression of reality (Metz, 1982, p. 101). These blurring boundaries between the imaginary and the real create the essence of filmic experience (Turner, 1999, p. 28).

By stressing the strong relation between imagining and the vacation, Salazar (2012) deployed the term of imaginary to the realm of tourism. Imaginaries are conceptualized by Salazar (2012, p. 864) as "socially transmitted representational assemblages that interact with people's personal imaginings and are used as meaning-making and world-shaping devices." Similarly, Di Giovine (2014, p. 149) argues that "there are many tourist imaginaries as there are tourists." By pointing out this broad range of experiences, Salazar and Graburn (2014) underline the agency inscribed into the individuals. Even though imaginaries are alienating after rupturing and taking an independent, institutional(ized) life such as in religion or politics, it is still the individuals who imagine, not societies. Yet imaginaries owe their power to their socially shared attributes, and circulation across the globe (Salazar & Graburn, 2014, p. 3). Moreover, Leite (2014, p. 274) argues that "at its best, the anthropological study of tourism imaginaries combines processual analysis of the relationship between representation, practice, and experience with careful attention to political-economic conditions and effects."

Social imaginaries are ways of understanding the social while becoming social entities themselves that mediate collective life (Gaonkar, 2002, p. 4). Salazar and Graburn (2014) argue that the sources of imaginaries include more general resources such as parental and family milieu; early worldviews; and early prototypes of self and alterity established through family interactions, stories, and attitudes. The authors also underline the importance of setting apart these background sources from the normally cited proximate channels such as modern media. These channels further play upon already internalized worldviews, directing them to specific destinations. In this regard, the worldwide advertising industry as a media that uses imaginaries is a good example of these mediated messages that create interest towards tourist destinations.

Displacement

It can be argued that in movies, the replacement of real places with fictitious ones becomes possible again by virtue of human imagination. The case that movies are shot in one location in reality but represent somewhere else is known as displacement (Bolan et al., 2011). Although films play a crucial role in motivating tourists to visit particular places, these blurring boundaries between real and imaginary worlds would end up with disappointment due to the inauthentic character of destinations compared to ones depicted in films. Therefore, while looking for an authentic film experience, the film tourist may be disappointed to discover the displacement (Roesch, 2009, p. 76) as their expectations can be different from the site that has historical accuracy. On the other hand, filmic places gain their power by the imagery of the spectator. They can play a crucial role and serve to memorize fictional events that never took place in history (Reijnders, 2010, p. 44). Therefore, it is also difficult to suggest that today's post-tourists are solely in search of 'authentic experiences' in places they visit (Bolan et al., 2011, p. 105). At first glance, elements that may be considered to be entirely inauthentic would be "quite" real for the post-tourist (Beeton, 2005, p. 174) owing to their imagination as an integral element in this process. Just like differences exist in society, not all film-induced tourists are the same (Beeton, 2005, p. 105). While some of the film-induced tourists may be in search of particular images, others may seek the authentic images and experiences that the film promised (Jewell & McKinnon, 2014, p. 108).

In juxtaposing these two locations, as depicted and set, one of the most common questions that come to mind is which one would be chosen by visitors – the site where the film was set or the one where the film was shot? About the backstage experiences, Beeton (2005) argues that even though film viewers are familiar with the process of filmmaking (Beeton, 2005, p. 105), some of them may not "wish to go so far in stripping away the effects of the fantasy" (Beeton, 2005, p. 194). Drawing upon this argument, we argue that instead of visiting a place that will "strip" the filmmaking process and cause the imagery of the film to wither, tourists may wish to visit the historical place as a reinforcement of their imagination, which has no undertone about the filmmaking process.

Then which place will benefit from the film? Frost's (2006) response to this question is the actual location that has a historical accuracy (p. 251). O'Connor and Kim (2016) argue that even though both places can take the advantage of the film to different degrees, these two places cannot equally benefit from displacement (p. 19). In any case, the exact answer of this question is not clear in the literature yet. But it is for sure that spectators should be well-informed about the displacement (Bolan et al., 2011, p. 113).

Some possible approaches

One of the possible approaches that can be used in the examination of the place-making process of the Trojan Horse is Foucault's (1986) notion of "heterotopia." Foucault (1986) employs heterotopia to deduce the intertwining of the real and utopic places and the blurring boundaries between them. In his well-known article "Of other spaces," Foucault distinguishes the discontinuity that appears on the sites as *utopias* and *heterotopias*. As such, "utopias are sites with no real place" (Foucault, 1986, p. 24). They exist in perfect model forms and function as a gate that leads to heterotopias. In contrast to utopias, heterotopias are located in reality (p. 24). In the article, Foucault is interested in sites "that have the curious property of being in relation with all the other sites, but in such a way as to suspect, neutralize, or invert the set of relations that they happen to designate, mirror, or reflect" (p. 24). Therefore, heterotopology could be described "as a sort of simultaneously mythic and real contestation of the space in which we live in" (p. 24).

One of the tools that Foucault employs to define the discontinued sites that disrupt the reality is the "mirror" metaphor. Foucault indicates the location of heterotopias through the mirror that provides mixed and joint experiences. The mirror is a channel that links the real space with the unreal one. The mirror itself is a utopia since it demonstrates just an illusion or reflection of reality. Yet Foucault (1986, p. 24) evaluates it also as "a heterotopia in so far as the mirror does exist in reality, where it exerts a sort of counteraction on the position" the subject occupies. Therefore, Foucault points to not only the reality of the space rooted in unreality that is being perceived by passing through the virtual but also to the controversy that occurs in this process.

Contrary to Foucault, Soja adopts a critical approach that balances socially constructed attributes of places and their empiric features. Soja's approach enables us "to capture what is actually a constantly shifting and changing milieu of ideas, events, appearances, and meanings" (1996, p. 2). For this purpose, Soja uses *thirdspace* in order to underline the oxymoronic attribute of spaces. Soja builds on Lefebvre and points out three types of spaces as perceived space, conceived space, and spaces of representation. While the first two types include real and imagined spaces, the last one "contains all other real and imagined spaces simultaneously" (p. 69). Moreover, Soja frequently emphasizes that none of these three spaces can be shown as privileging to the other: "The three moments of the ontological trialectic thus contain each other; they cannot successfully be understood in isolation or epistemologically privileged separately" (p. 72). Therefore, contrary to Foucault, Soja includes all types of spaces at once. Representational space is grasped as a dynamic, "living" and "speaking" entity. Since spaces of representation combine the real and the imagined at once without privileging one over the other, they also emerge as "'counter spaces,' spaces of resistance to the dominant order arising precisely from their subordinate, peripheral or marginalized positioning." This also approximates what Soja defines as *thirdspace* (p. 68).

Soja describes his point of view on spatialized ontology in his book, *Postmodern Geographies* (1989). He argues that the distinct evaluation of this ontological trialectic could not provide an efficient conceptualization. Although "physical and psychological processes and forms can be theorized independently with regard to their spatial dimensions and attributes," these conceptualizations provide blurred borderlines among three interrelated spaces (Soja, 1989, p. 120). He grasps spatiality as something unfixed and affected by social tensions and contradictions that are always in transformation (p. 122). He not only provides a dynamic point of view that includes different layers of spaces' social production but also points to the rhetorical and methodological obstacles to reveal "deeper social origins of social spatiality, [. . .] its contextualization of politics, power and ideology," (p. 124) which are intrinsic to this process.

Case study: dream ride of the Trojan Horse

The nature of the Trojan Horse's place-making process is varied. The Horse oscillates between a blend of narratives and meanings that reveal themselves in four layers. First, the Horse converts the city center to a form of *thirdspace* in Soja's terms. It combines the perceived (real) and conceived (imagined) space at once. It currently stands just in the middle of the "reality," yet, it is a tourism imagery that successfully reproduces a popular narrative, too. Moreover, it creates a dialogue between the histories of Turkey and Europe. European people find themselves in the story that includes Greeks (Melotti, 2011, p. 203). And third, owing its own reality to being a filmic icon, the Horse connects the spectators to the film. As the last trait, it intertextually refers to the Horse in situ as creating another link. The Horse in situ and the Trojan Horse stand for sustaining the narratives that are already interlaced. Barnes and Duncan (2006, p. 8) unfold the interplay as following:

> Places are intertextual sites because various texts and discursive practices based on previous texts are deeply inscribed in their landscapes and institutions. We construct both the world and our actions towards it from texts that speak of who we are or wish to be. Such "texts in the world" then recursively act back on the previous texts that shaped them.

Figure 31.1 The Horse in situ (top) and the Trojan Horse (bottom).

Source: photo by authors.

This also reveals that "the local can by no means (be) assumed to be locked forever in place. On the contrary, the boundaries of place [. . .] are porous and open to traffic in both ways" (Zhang, 2013, p. 324). Thus, those places also allow multiple narratives to operate. While multiple narratives remain, their changing effect on the places is always there too. As emphasizing the ever-changing process of tourist sites, Edensor (1998, p. 8) asserts that "tourist sites are themselves not static entities. Their material shape, symbolic importance and the ways in which they are perceived, represented and narrated change over time."

The Horse in situ is both a symbol and the holder of the historical myth. Yet this narrative was radically changed in the film (Winkler, 2015, p. 2). Thus, the Trojan Horse is the holder of the postmodern version of the narrative that is produced by the movie. These Horses produce a postmodern space. Since Foucault's perspective informs both the illusionary and the counter spaces (other sites), the site in Canakkale where the filmic icon is situated can be considered as a heterotopia. The Trojan Horse not only inverts the place but also embodies a counter position to the ancient Horse. It can be argued that in the daily life of the city, it creates a place outside the ordinary, which is situated in the midst of the ordinary. The Trojan Horse may be explained through the mirror metaphor as being a reflection of the historical Horse and exerting a counter action to it by embodying narratives different from the historical ones. Even though the heterotopology, "as a set of simultaneously mythic and real contestation of the space in which we live" (Foucault, 1986, p. 24), seems to provide a fertile ground for the evaluation of the Trojan Horse, the Horse cannot be considered just as a reflection. As a popular cultural entity, it has its own roots in popular culture narratives as a filmic icon with its own fame. Thus, the filmic Trojan Horse is also real/authentic, beyond being a sole reflection. It is converting the traditional myth as an element of popular culture that is constructed by the film and maintained in the popular realm by the spectators. We witness the Trojan Horse causing a discontinuity in the space of the city, and produce a counter narrative to the historical one. Two different sites are being produced simultaneously. Although Foucault (1986, p. 27) demonstrates that these sites can operate in such ways too, he grasps these attributes as being "*two extreme poles*" and implies that they cannot be both at once:

> The last trait of heterotopias is that they have a function in relation to all the space that remains. This function unfolds between two extreme poles. Either their role is to create a space of illusion that exposes every real space [. . .]. Or else, on the contrary, their role is to create a space that is other, another real space, as perfect, as meticulous, as well arranged as ours is messy, ill constructed, and jumbled. This latter type would be the heterotopia, not of illusion, but of compensation.

Here we shift to Soja's approach in demonstrating the oxymoronic attitudes of Trojan Horse. Reading Troy through Soja (1996) enables us to evaluate the place-making process of the Trojan Horse simultaneously in two layers as real and imagined spaces. We aim to put forth a complete portrayal of the case of Trojan Horse by demonstrating all fragmented pieces of material and illusionary features of it as a tourism imagery as well. Soja (1989, p. 120) grasps spatiality as a concept that "socially produces and . . . exists . . . as a set of relations between individuals and groups, an 'embodiment' and medium of social life itself." This point of view is in the same vein that we grasp the Trojan Horse as a tourism imagery in order to highlight the Horse's valuation and social construction.

Soja's "thirdspace" framework also allows us to examine the place-making process of Trojan Horse from a critical point of view. In his capitalism critique, Soja (1989) warns against the illusion of opaqueness, or the empiricist myopia in other words. He deems it problematical to approach epistemology of spatiality directly through the geographical appearances (p. 123). This point of view avoids social conflict and social agency since the spatial organization is demonstrated as socially inert (pp. 123–124). Since "the imagination is now central to all forms of agency, is itself a social fact, and the key component of the new global order" (Appadurai, 1996, p. 31), we need to separate the layers that different agencies are involved in. It is not possible to consider these two notions of agency and imaginary separately.

In the past, we witnessed the narrative reality to be changed and adapted to the time and context in which it is re-told. This ended up with "hybrid forms that do not correspond exclusively with the historical reality of any single period" (Özveren, 2007, p. 631). According to Özveren, *One Thousand and One Nights* is a good example of this. Yet, the contemporary situation is more complicated. The catalyst for the narrative transformation is not limited to the time elapsed. Therefore, as an old narrative, Troy does not only carry multi-epochal traits but also adopts the narration of different agencies at once in a contemporary era. Apart from the society, narratives of Troy are retold and reshaped by different agents such as popular culture entities. Thus, narratives appear in multiform simultaneously and the multiform spaces come to life accordingly.

Then, from a critical point of view, how should we evaluate the movies as an agent of change while scrutinizing the constructions of tourist spaces that incorporate multiple agencies? We can consider them simply as social products (Turner, 1999) and contemporary story-tellers (Hirschman, 2000). Yet, the narratives and the iconic attributes ascribed to movies inevitably have an ideological feature that is closely linked to the social imagery (Berezhnaya & Schmitt, 2013, p. 15). Thus, films' construction of ideologically charged places and evaluation of the place in the context of tourism is just a partial dimension of films' role in the social realm. The Trojan Horse as a tourism imaginary creates a thirdspace that includes abstract and concrete dimensions. The abstract dimension of Troy and Canakkale, which is constructed by the narratives and the movies, is the part where commodification starts long before the actual visit (Shaw & Williams, 2004, p. 184). Moreover, the initial version of the Trojan Horse imagery, which was constructed through social narratives, provides a base for its popular culture version. Thus, the Trojan Horse imagery exactly creates a "capitalist space" that "serves multiple functions. It is at once, a means of production, an object of consumption, and a property of relation" (Deutche, 1996, p. 75). In the nexus of these close relations, it is clear that "the commodification of the tourist site involves an ideological as well as a financial investment. Returns on one are dependent on the flourishing of the other" (Jewesbury, 2003, p. 228). Consequently, the narrative is created repeatedly in order to nourish this circle.

The context of an old narrative to be re-told and its links with the process of commodification, have been dealt frequently in the postmodern literature. In his prominent essay, Jameson (1991) scrutinizes "the random cannibalization of all the styles of the past," while criticizing postmodern culture's way of recreating the past again and again as an element of so-called nostalgia, instead of creating a unique style. For Jameson, the pursuit of unique styles has reached its final point with "the collapse of the high-modernist ideology of style." Now, "the producers of culture have nowhere to turn but to the past, the imitation of dead styles, speech through all the masks and voices stored up in the imaginary museum of a now global culture" (pp. 16–17). This is an argument that may also point out to the different versions of Troy films. While different narratives rooted in the same historical myth appear in films over the course of time, they may not take the historical one as a point of reference. Instead, these films may exceed the historical myth, and represent a specific genre or a subject matter by creating their own dialogue. Yet, even in this domino effect, the image would retain its power and persist to infiltrate the social sphere "naturally." In his critique of simulacrum, Jameson further argues that "the culture of the simulacrum comes to life in a society [. . .] of which Guy Debord has observed, [. . .] that in it 'the image has become the final form of commodity reification'" (p. 17). This critique also sheds light on the process of conversion of a film into a meaningful social dynamic. Promotional materials such as talk shows, magazine articles, and behind-the-scenes views are utilized in this continuum to extend the film into the social sphere. As this whole process of commodification procures the film a more profound value in the society, these attempts can be followed by the fetishization of the film as well (Klinger, 1989, pp. 11–12).

In the context of retelling an old narrative by popular culture, the effects on tourism spaces emerge in different ways. The film can contribute to the existing destination image rather than creating a new one (Frost, 2006, p. 253). In the construction of popular culture narrative as in the case of Troy, a novelty can be sought in an old or forgotten one. Several factors such as industrial and economic ones may motivate the filmmakers to adapt popular novels or historical narratives rather than creating an original screenplay (Turner, 1993, p. 105). An educated eye can realize the difference between two versions. The new narrative can nourish and arouse curiosity about the previous one or can totally overshadow it. Moreover, this narrative can be especially created for turning a place into a tourist attraction by highlighting distinctive qualities of the destination and guaranteeing a dream holiday (O'Connor & Kim, 2016, p. 25). This process also indicates popular culture narratives that are used in the process of commodification of places. Alternatively, destinations can benefit from the extant film for luring tourists, although they are not produced directly for a destination. Yet when the film incorporates displacement, the situation becomes more complicated: one may wonder the exact place that the narrative belongs. Therefore, placing one-minute long promotional films showing the antique city of Troy and its remains prior to the film screenings in European cinemas (Roesch, 2009, p. 33) was a proper move for the Turkish Tourism Ministry to overcome disadvantages of displacement, and inform the spectators. Moreover, in the opening of the movie *Troy*, a historical map indicating the site reinforces the impact of the promotional efforts of Turkey.

While contradictions of the agency and the social construction of Troy comprise an important part, we need to acknowledge the other angle of the big picture too: the circulation of the Trojan Horse as a tourism imagery. As Salazar (2010) points out, we need to acknowledge the socio-cultural structures and mechanisms that enable such displacements (p. 9). We live in a world, as Castells (2000) observes, in which "space of flows" unfolds and is "made of territories, physical places, whose functional or symbolic meaning depends on their connection to a network, rather than on its specific localities" (p. 696). Moreover, impactful globalization, pervasive tourism practices, and imaginative mobility seem to maintain their exponential growth. The fluidity of tourism imageries and porous borders of spaces nourish each other. The Trojan Horse's multidimensional spatial construction that comprises displacement and physical mobility reveals itself as a perfect archetype that imaginaries "moving in global 'rounds,' not strictly circular, reaching new horizons, and periodically feeding back their places of departure" (Salazar, 2010, p. 9). This can be the reason why the Horse is currently situated in Canakkale even though it is rooted in an altered narrative. The myth inspires the popular culture and evokes alternative imageries without a total rupture of its locus.

Implications for popular culture tourism

In this chapter, we sought to demonstrate the iconic Trojan Horse's travel as a tourism imaginary and place-making process in its current location. Movies, intrinsically having imaginative elements, have a global playground for creating places that never exist or turning authentic places into a totally different one. Displacement is one of the crucial frameworks to uncover these distinct representations of places induced by movies. Moreover, it causes stochastic consequences that create direct relationships among diverse locations. These consequences raise new questions regarding sites of the agency as well, since multiple places that popular culture triggers do not derive from displacement only. Multiple narratives, produced by society and popular culture simultaneously, cause multiple constructions of places to unfold at once. When it is an old narrative that is adapted as a tourism imaginary, this may not be a process that is totally innocent due to its close relationship with the commodification of sites. Moreover, beyond simply being commoditized representations with a symbolic content, "they often propagate historically inherited stereotypes that are based on the myths and fantasies" (Salazar, 2012, p. 871).

Displacement gives important clues for the conceptualization of tourism imaginaries that point out the need to unravel the mechanisms created by popular culture. Together, these two concepts are powerful elements for the examination of ideational and material levels of popular culture's construction of places, and have the power to uncover political and economic circumstances. This is vital since spaces of representation comprise real and imagined at once, laden with politics and ideology (Soja, 1996, p. 68). Therefore, we need to adopt a holistic approach for rigorous scrutiny of the process and the results. Moreover, local narratives are also very important in the process of circulation of tourism imaginaries and confounding hegemonic representations of space that is reinforced by popular culture. Likewise, local and oral histories have a capacity to challenge commodified versions (Edensor, 1998, p. 17). Therefore, we argue that we need to grasp the roots and routes together.

In this chapter, we attempted to contribute to the literature by bringing a different approach to the notion of displacement and concretizing tourism imageries as well as postmodern place-making theories, which are rare to be deciphered through apparent incidences in the tourism studies. Nevertheless, we are still in need of empirical studies that can reflect local trajectories as well. Further, icons in tourism and tourism imaginaries are rarely empirically studied. As Hottola (2013, p. 219) comments on this issue; "this is regrettable because we do not only see, but we also imagine."

References

Alloway, L. (1963). On the iconography of the movies. *Movie Reader, 7*, 16–18.

Appadurai, A. (1996). *Modernity at large: Cultural dimensions of globalization.* Minneapolis: University of Minnesota Press.

Barnes, T. J., & Duncan, J. S. (2006). *Writing worlds: Discourse, text and metaphor in the representation of landscape.* New York: Routledge.

Beeton, S. (2005). *Film-induced tourism.* Clevedon: Channel View Publications.

Berezhnaya, L., & Schmitt, C. (Eds.) (2013). *Iconic turns, nation and religion in Eastern European cinema since 1989.* Leiden: Brill.

Bolan, P., Boy, S., & Bell, J. (2011). "We've seen it in the movies, let's see if it's true": Authenticity and displacement in film-induced tourism. *Worldwide Hospitality and Tourism Themes, 3*(2), 102–116.

Castells, M. (2000). Toward a sociology of the network society. *Contemporary Sociology, 29*(5), 693–699.

Degli-Esposti, C. (1998). *Postmodernism in the cinema.* New York: Berghahn Books.

Deutsche, R. (1996). *Evictions: Art and spatial politics.* Cambridge, MA: MIT Press.

Di Giovine, M. A. (2014). The imaginaire dialectic and the refashioning of pietrelcina. In N. B. Salazar & N. H. Graburn, (Eds.), *Tourism imaginaries: Anthropological approaches* (pp. 147–171). New York: Berghahn Books.

Edensor, T. (1998). *Tourists at the Taj: Performance and meaning at a symbolic site.* New York: Routledge.

Flynn, G. (2016, February 14). The battle of making Troy. *Entertainment Weekly.* Retrieved from http://ew.com/article/2004/05/14/battle-making-troy/

Foucault, M. (1986). Of other spaces. *Diacritics, 16*(1), 22–27.

Frost, W. (2006). Braveheart-ed Ned Kelly: Historic films, heritage tourism and destination image. *Tourism Management, 27*(2), 247–254.

Gaonkar, D. P. (2002). Toward new imaginaries: An introduction. *Public Culture, 14*(1), 1–19.

Grant, B. K. (2007). *Film genre: From iconography to ideology.* London: Wallflower Press.

Hirschman, E. (2000). *Heroes, monsters & messiahs: Movies and television shows as the mythology of American culture.* Kansas City, MO: Andrews McMeel.

Hottola, P. (2013). Real-and-imagined women: Goddess America meets the world. In O. Moufakkir & Y. Reisinger (Eds), *The host gaze in global tourism* (pp. 219–231). Cambridge, MA: CABI.

Hudson, S., & Ritchie, J. B. (2006). Promoting destinations via film tourism: An empirical identification of supporting marketing initiatives. *Journal of Travel Research, 44*(4), 387–396.

Jameson, F. (1991). *Postmodernism, or, the cultural logic of late capitalism.* Durham, NC: Duke University Press.

Jewell, B., & McKinnon, S. (2014). The commercial and dream landscape cultures of films. In M. Roe & K. Taylor (Eds.), *New cultural landscapes* (pp. 99–117). London: Routledge.

Jewesbury, D. (2003). Tourist: Pioneer: Hybrid: London Bridge, the mirage in the Arizona Desert. In D. Crouch & N. Lübbern (Eds.), *Visual culture and tourism* (pp. 223–239). Oxford: Berg.

Klinger, B. (1989). Digressions at the cinema: Reception and mass culture. *Cinema Journal, 28*(4), 3–19.

Leite, N. (2014). Locating imaginaries in the anthropology of tourism. In N. B. Salazar & N. H. Graburn (Eds.), *Tourism imaginaries: Anthropological approaches* (pp. 260–277). New York: Berghahn Books.

Leotta, A. (2011). *Touring the screen: Tourism and New Zealand film geographies.* Bristol: Intellect Books.

Low, S. M. (1996). Spatializing culture: The social production and social construction of public space in Costa Rica. *American Ethnologist, 23*(4), 861–879.

Melotti, M. (2011). *The plastic Venuses: Archaeological tourism in post-modern society.* Cambridge: Cambridge Scholars.

Metz, C. (1982). *The imaginary signifier: Psychoanalysis and the cinema.* Indiana: Indiana University Press.

Neale, S. (2000). *Genre and Hollywood.* London: Routledge.

O'Connor, N., & Kim, S. (2016). Media-related tourism phenomena: A review of the key issues. In J.-A. Lester & C. Scarles (Eds.), *Mediating the tourist experience: From brochures to virtual encounters* (pp. 13–32). New York: Routledge.

Özveren, E. (2007). Bazaars of the thousand and one nights. *European Journal of the History of Economic Thought, 14*(4), 629–655.

Panofsky, E. (1934/1997). Style and medium in the motion picture. In L. Irving (Ed.), *Three Essays on Style* (pp. 91–128).Cambridge, MA: MIT Press.

Reijnders, S. (2010). Places of the imagination: An ethnography of the TV detective tour. *Cultural Geographies, 17*(1), 37–52.

Riley, R., Baker, D., & Van Doren, C. S. (1998). Movie induced tourism. *Annals of Tourism Research, 25*(4), 919–935.

Roesch, S. (2009). *The experiences of film location tourists.* Clevedon: Channel View Publications.

Salazar, N. B. (2010). *Envisioning Eden: Mobilizing imaginaries in tourism and beyond.* New York: Berghahn Books.

Salazar, N. B. (2012). Tourism imaginaries: A conceptual approach. *Annals of Tourism research, 39*(2), 863–882.

Salazar, N. B., & Graburn, N. H. (Eds.) (2014). *Tourism imaginaries: Anthropological approaches.* New York: Berghahn Books.

Shaw, G., & Williams, A. M. (2004). *Tourism and tourism spaces.* London: Sage.

Soja, E. W. (1989). *Postmodern geographies: The reassertion of space in critical social theory.* London: Verso.

Soja, E. W. (1996). *Thirdspace: Journeys to Los Angeles and other real-and-imagined places.* Oxford: Blackwell.

Turner, G. (1993). The genres are American: Australian narrative, Australian film, and the problems of genre. *Literature/Film Quarterly, 21*(2), 102.

Turner, G. (1999). *Film as social practice.* New York: Routledge.

Urry, J. (2002). *The tourist gaze.* London: Sage.

Winkler, M. M. (2007). *Troy: From Homer's Iliad to Hollywood.* Oxford: Blackwell.

Winkler, M. M. (2015). *Return to Troy: New essays on the Hollywood Epic.* Danvers: Brill.

Yılmaz, H., & Yolal, M. (2008). Film turizmi, destinasyonların pazarlanmasında filmlerin rolü (Movie tourism, the role of movies in destination marketing). *Anadolu Üniversitesi Sosyal Bilimler Dergisi, 8*(1), 175–192.

Zhang, Y. (2013). Thirdspace between flows and places: Chinese independent documentary and social theories of space and locality. In C. Rojas & E. Chow (Eds.), *The Oxford handbook of Chinese cinemas* (pp. 320–342). New York: Oxford University Press.

Zimmermann, S., & Reeves, T. (2009). Film tourism: Locations are the new stars. In R. Conrady & M. Buck (Eds.), *Trends and issues in global tourism 2009* (pp. 155–162). Berlin: Springer.

32

THE INDIANIZATION OF SWITZERLAND

Destination transformations in the wake of Bollywood films

Szilvia Gyimóthy

I was so much looking forward to today, because we are going to see snow in Switzerland. It was very-very high on my agenda. The movies have painted a very colorful picture and now I am very happy that I decided to take up o Jungfraujoch. We are going to see such beautiful mountains, I mean . . .. this is like DDLJ[1] revisited.
(Mumbai male tourist, field notes, Glacier Express, Grindelwald, 2017)

Setting the scene

Traveling in the wake of films, literature, TV series, and music is not solely a Western phenomenon. In the last 50 years, Swiss locations featured in more than 200 Indian motion pictures, which positively affected tourist flows from Asia to Switzerland. According to the Swiss Tourism Statistics (FSO, 2013), the number of tourist arrivals from the subcontinent increased almost sevenfold in the past ten years, with annual growth rates of 3–4 percent. In 2014, over 400,000 Indians visited this Alpine country, only overhauled by the UK and France as the most popular holiday destination in Europe (ETC, 2014).

A holiday in Europe is a matter of prestige among affluent Asian middle-class families and Switzerland tops the list of the most romantic honeymoon destinations in the world among Indian visitors (Euroscreen, 2015; Mittal & Anjaneyaswamy, 2013). As the opening excerpt illustrates, snowcapped mountains are key attractions, recalling nostalgic memories of romantic Bollywood productions shot in the Alps. Productions of the late director, Yash Chopra, were especially influential in branding Switzerland as a utopian landscape of love. *Silsila* (1981), *Chandni* (1989), *Dilwale Dulhaniya Le Jayenge* (1995), and later *Neal n Nikki* (2005) as well as *Bachna Ae Haseeno* (2008) fashioned consistent visual aesthetics, musical tropes, and narratives of romantic love that successfully addressed both resident and global Indian audiences (Bandyopadhyay, 2008; Mukherjee, 2012; Schaefer & Karan, 2012).

It is noteworthy that the plots of all Chopra's films revolve around international travel, which can be understood through the concept of hypermediatization (Jensen & Waade, 2009). Hypermediatization stands for how sense-making processes in communication (in our case popular cultural representations) are altering material and physical aspects of space. The lead characters in Chopra's films would embark on an escapist journey to Europe (honeymoon, Interrailing, stag parties) in the quest for forbidden pleasures, such as adventure, romance, freedom, or luxurious leisure experiences (Dudrah, 2012). Recently, film commissions and tourism boards in Austria, Italy, England, Holland, and Spain have attempted to capitalize on the Bollywood bandwagon, offering attractive financial incentives to shoot romantic feature films in their country. However, as Switzerland was the only European mountain destination Indian audiences have been exposed to since the late 1960s, its brand equity remains the strongest in terms of destination awareness and location choice (Gyimóthy, 2015). As an act of gratitude, Switzerland offered honorary citizenships to Yash Chopra for his cultural ambassadorship and erected a statue of him in central Interlaken. Equally significantly, Bollywood films contributed to the shaping of new place identities, enabling the development of new tourism products:

> The classic HLGR tour offers a unique train ride through the Alps with the Golden pass, snow fun activities and exclusive shopping on Glacier 3000-Peak Walk and an optional visit to Chillon Castle. In the evening, a gala dinner awaits you on the top of Mt. Kuklos, serving delicious Indian curry and Bollywood music.
>
> *(Highlights of the Lake Geneva Region, sales promotion material)*

The "highlights" integral to such offers are at odds with the traditional logic of tourism packages, typically aiming at opening a specific sensory window, with authentic local experiences for the tourist. However, Bollywood discotheques or curry dinners have nothing to do with Swiss cultural history or traditions; still they are becoming more and more ordinary parts of the destination landscape.

Scope and goal of the chapter

The implications of non-Western popular cultural phenomena and Asian leisure mobility for Alpine destinations are not well understood. Studies on the topic of Bollywood-induced mobilities focus primarily on its demand; entailing as diaspora tourism studies (Monteneiro, 2014), qualifying transnational identity constructions (Mukherjee, 2012), or quantifying destination awareness and choice (Josiam et al., 2014, 2015). However, we must also consider the palpable consequences and challenges of non-Western mediatization of European space on location and see how destinations are transforming under the pressures of large numbers of Asian travelers. Hence this chapter will address the questions: How are Swiss destinations changing in the wake of Bollywood-productions and visitors? How are traditional Alpine imaginaries augmented and/or challenged? What new tourism practices emerge? How are Asian and (Western) European tourism performances diversifying, let alone crossbreed and accumulate new narrative layers?

In order to explore Bollywood-induced destination transformations, the concept of texture (Jansson, 2007) is invoked. Textural analysis (Jansson, 2014) is based on Lefebvre's (1991) threefold spatiality, distinguishing between lived space, conceived space, and perceived space. The approach has therefore the potential to combine the analysis of material performances and communicative representations converging in the process of production/consumption of tourism spaces. The chapter opens with a review of the rise of Bollywood-in-the-Alps, followed by a theoretical exploration of mediatized mobility and the concept of texture. Second, the chapter offers methodological deliberations on adapting textural analysis to a Swiss context. Third, the findings are presented along two dimensions of Bollywood-induced destination transformations; i.e. representations (capturing the changing role of two Swiss destinations in communication) and textures (capturing disruptive tourist performances). The chapter concludes with a reflection on the consequences of popular cultural place-making in the Alps and discusses the likely challenges and conflicts that may emerge from catering for tourist segments yearning for fundamentally different mountain experiences.

Theoretical underpinnings: mediatized tourism and textures

Media geographers and tourism scholars have long acknowledged the role of media in producing social space and the intimate linkages between mediatization and socio-spatial transformations (Couldry & McCarthy, 2004; Falkheimer & Jansson, 2006; Hjarvard, 2008; Jansson, 2007). Regarding tourism as an embodied performance, not only is it shaped by mediatized narratives, but it also shapes and reconfigures the narrative layers of a place (Frost, 2009; Gyimóthy et al., 2015; Larson, Lexhagen, & Lundberg, 2013; Lundberg & Lexhagen, 2012; Månsson & Eskilsson, 2013). Hence, mediatized mobility blurs the distinctions between texts and contexts; between symbolic and material spaces, and renders media production and consumption increasingly fluid (Jansson, 2013). For instance, the Swiss *Lungerer See* has been renamed to *Lake Chopra* and the top of *La Berneuse* is now known as Mt. Cox & Kings by Asian operators. These new topographies aptly demonstrate the transformations in socio-spatial textures (Jansson, 2007) including the amalgamation of various practices shaping and shaped by Hindi popular cultural expressions.

Mediatized mobility and the entangled production/consumption of tourism spaces can be studied along Jansson's notion of texture (Jansson, 2007). Textural analysis offers an approach that combines the analysis of material performances and communicative representations. Derived from the Latin *textere* (to weave), texture refers to the communicative fabric of space (p. 194) or the spatial materialization of culture (p. 195), that can be both observed and sensed. Texture analysts may thus capture place auras, atmospheres and moods "sitting in the walls." The relationships between people and places, material objects, sounds, smells, light, and colors contribute to a peculiar ambience; hence it is possible to trace them as they emerge in a dialogue between bodies, things, technologies, feelings, sensory impressions and fantasies. In other words: "communication is producing and becoming space and space is producing and becoming communication" (p. 195).

Textural analysis simultaneously considers the material, symbolic, and imaginary realms/processes of place-making, and as such, is grounded in Lefebvre's (1991) trialectics of spatial production. Lefebvre's threefold spatiality acknowledges (1) spatial practices, i.e. activities and material conditions of lived space; (2) representations or conceived space (e.g. maps, drawings, films, or promotional brochures); and (3) perceived space (capturing imagination, myths, and ideologies). As texture is produced in time and space, textural analysis requires not only the recording of scenes, rituals, and performances, but also temporal regularities (timing, tempo, repetition), and shifts in moods and ambiances. As such, it does not make too much sense to describe or distinguish among smellscapes, soundscapes, or other scapes occupied by a single sense. Lived space emerges as a mix of auditory, visual, olfactory, or haptic impressions, creating intensive synergies or disharmonies as our sensual impressions are counterbalancing or offsetting each other. Hence the analytical process may focus on capturing pulsating and vibrant textures by linking patterned visitor flows, timing, and tempo with sensory and affective dimensions.

Textural analysis may also chronicle spatial transformations and the historicity of a destination, as it (similar to archeological investigations) enables us to chart the sediments of past spatial and communicative practices (representations and conceived space). Multimodal recordings will expose meaningful spatial structures and scripted patterns of tourist performances contributing to the texturation of space. Tourist destinations may be likened to the texture of a colorful patchwork: made up of diverse "scraps of interwoven communicative threads" (Adams & Jansson, 2012), including strategic and organic promotion, fictive representations, and digitally augmented tourist messages.

As Jansson (2007) contends, texture is the site of ideological spatial reproduction, where meanings are ordered, negotiated, and contested. Patterns of practices and flows emerge according to signifying practices, which in turn, reproduce structural characteristics. The scripted and staged nature of tourist practices is well documented by Larsen and Meged (2013) among others. For instance, similar individual practices of tourist photography (e.g. selfies in front of an attraction) may mature into collective patterns signifying mass tourism practices in a destination, and thus, become taken for granted. Hence, texture may first become visible, when it is destabilized by new rhythms or rituals – for instance, by conspicuous wedding proposals in public space. The task is then to find an analytical strategy that challenges taken-for-granted, mundane readings of the destination. Elm and Löfgren (2016) offers several useful analytical ideas. Considering that destination space is constituted of interwoven practices, rules, rhythms, traditions, and affects, routines and rhythms become central. Routines (originating from the French *routin* or small path) are performative, tangible manifestations of mundane mobilities and relationships, which, owing to their repetitive nature become invisible and taken for granted. For instance, there are many routines that are reflected in the practices of summer excursionists in the Alps. They would know what to wear, how to tread, protect themselves against the sun, etc. Taken together, these small routines constitute a disciplining and ordering logic, differentiating between the experienced and newcomer guest on the mountain. Another useful analytical concept is rhythm or rhythmscapes (Jensen, Scarles, & Cohen, 2015). Public spaces, such as train stations, transit zones, or tourist destinations have a pulsating circadian rhythm, as the movements of individuals dissolve into a coordinated mass flow and changing tempo during the course of the day. Hence textures can also be described across these circadian shifts of the communicative fabric, along densities and intensities, regularities and inconsistencies (Jansson 2007, p. 195), in the non-random street ballet of a given locality.

Methodology

To delimit scoping the study of Bollywood-induced destination transformations in Switzerland, the three most visited destinations of the Swiss grand tour were selected (Mount Titlis, Glacier3000, and Jungfraujoch. Data collection was designed to map textural transformations in these particular places and thus, also noted dominant, practice-scripting cinematic, and touristic representations of these destinations. Diverse modalities of data were collected over a longer period of time, entailing various promotional, documentary, and statistical materials, Yash Chopra's films featuring Swiss locations as well as a field trip to Luzern-Engelberg (Mount Titlis), Interlaken, Jungfraujoch, Gstaad, and Glacier3000. The fieldwork focused on a multi-sited participant observation, but also yielded snapshot interviews with Indian guests and tourism actors as well as vast audiovisual material (photographs, videos, miniature films, and 15 audio files).

As elaborated above, texture refers to the spatial materialization of culture, a patterned performance that is accumulating singular practices. Textural analysis thus explores enactments and negotiation of communicative patterns in various places. Inspired by Billy Ehn and Orvar Löfgren's cultural analytical approach of the inconspicuous (Ehn & Löfgren, 2016), an eclectic analytical toolkit was opened to problematize cliché-ridden tourist rituals and inexplicable touristic performances. In this way, it was possible to make sense of new, signifying tourist practices that challenge or co-exist with established ones. The analysis is divided into three parts, going from the generic to the particular (or from macro to micro aspects of textures). First, we will address mediatized paths and trajectories that shape and were shaped by Asian visitor flows. Second, the new spatial ordering logics of the three mountain destinations will be introduced. Third, we will discuss disruptive tourist performances and communicative/spatial responses to accommodate them.

Transforming trajectories: the emergent beaten track of Bollywood-in-the Alps

The birth of Bollywood-in-the-Alps can be dated around the 1960s, where Indian filmmakers started to shoot in foreign international locations (Dwyer, 2002). In the same period, military tension in Kashmir forced Indian film crews to look for new exotic sites for romantic productions (Schneider, 2002; SRF, 2000). The first Indian film in Switzerland was Raj Kapoor's *Sangam* [*Confluence*] (1964) featuring a story about a honeymoon to Europe. *Sangam* triggered the interest of India's film industry for snowcapped and safe Swiss sites, and became the favorite shooting location for Yash Chopra (who himself spent his honeymoon in the Alps). As noted earlier, Yash Chopra pioneered and refined a particular cinematic genre framing romance within leisure consumerist practices (travel, fashion, and dance) showcasing the spectacular lifestyle of the super-rich (Dwyer, 2002). His choice of locations was strongly inspired by the itinerary of his own honeymoon, and he returned to shoot to Interlaken, Gstaad, and Zweisimmen several times.

The landscapes and sights featured in Chopra's Bollywood films are indistinctive and in general are not among Switzerland's biggest attractions. DDLJ's key locations (Zweisimmen's train station, the church and bridge in Saanen, or the confectionary shop in Gstaad as well as the green meadows around) are typical for the Swiss countryside, but have no iconicity or specific recognition value. As Schneider (2009) explains, the fantastical situations and the Swiss setting function solely as an imaginary space for the love-play of the protagonists. Bollywood produces escapist cinema, which projects dreams on utopian, foreign locations. With its snowy peaks, pastoral idyll, and peaceful meadows, Switzerland is an ideal, liminal setting replacing the traditional Hindi landscapes of romance (Dwyer, 2002). An iconic, recognizable site is thus pointless. For Asian audiences, the Swiss mountains represent an imaginary Disneyland of Love (Shedde, 2002), a pastiche-like paradise standing in stark contrast to the mundane realities of the Indian countryside, often represented as a space of poverty, labor, and unrest. The comparison with the Himalayas was reiterated by the Indian tourists on the field trip, praising Switzerland for their cleanliness, safety, and organization.

Today, two main Swiss towns, Luzern and Interlaken, skim most of Asian tourism flows across European space, offering them a short-stay package (combining a high-altitude experience, luxury shopping, and optional historical visit) on the route between Milan/Paris and London. Some smaller operators provide specialized Bollywood tours for FITs, but groups are always offered Bollywood-themed dinner parties during their 2–3 days in Switzerland. When tour operators started to capitalize on the huge success of DDLJ, they were looking at an optimal location to expand the length of stay in the country. As the films lacked recognizable icons, these could in principle be placed anywhere in Switzerland. The choice fell on Engelberg/Mt. Titlis in Cental Switzerland, which, paradoxically, does not feature in any Bollywood films. In an interview, the CEO of Glacier3000 (Berner Oberland), Gstaad laments:

> We could have been the first reach in Switzerland because 20 years ago SOTC and Kuoni together chose Villars as the main resort for Club Med and to build up the Indian village in the summertime. But for some reason they decided to build up in

Engelberg the Hotel Terrace. This was the big decision then if they have chosen us; perhaps we would have been the Titlis of Switzerland instead of them.

Before 2008, Glacier3000 was not on the tour circuit, despite its vicinity to Gstaad and Saanen. In order to change the flow of visitors, the destination managers invested massively into the high alpine infrastructure to change the attractivity of the product, entailing, among others, an alpine roller coaster, snow buses, a watch and souvenir shop, and a peak to peak suspension bridge. The real turn came in 2008, when Yash Chopra returned to Gstaad to shoot his new film. The opportunity was seized immediately to change the representational flows:

> I read the newspapers that they [Yash Chopra's film crew] were coming to the region to shoot the films and I thought that this big actor was playing there so I contacted the local authorities hear where they would be shooting [. . .]. So I went there and I said; "listen, I am from Glacier 3000, a great location on a snow mountain – do you have 5 minutes to see a snow location and come shooting?" He said yes, so I had the helicopter waiting for us, and I showed him around and 2–3 days later they came to shoot, including both a husky dog sledge and the roller coaster in one of the songs. This story surely had a big impact [. . .]. But Bachna Ae Haseeno was seen by millions of people and they would ask where to find those places and experiences.
>
> *(CEO Glacier 3000, interview)*

DDLJ had a powerful impact on Indian popular culture and tourist imaginaries, and after 20 years, it is still running in Indian cinemas. The film *Bachna Ae Hasseno (BAH)* [*Watch Out Girls*] from 2008, made several intertextual references to *DDLJ* and reused some of its locations in the Berner Oberland. But BAH also imitated the mediatized anticipation of Swiss romance for generations growing up on DDLJ, creating a plausible narrative of a contemporary Sikh girl embarking on Eurail in the hope of finding true love. DDLJ has also left its trace on the marketing communication of Switzerland Tourismus (2012) and the Indian operators would include its locations in their packages. The Newly Swissed website even features an interactive map of Bollywood shooting locations, thereby reconfiguring conceived space along non-Western imaginaries. Yash Chopra's productions provide a normative frame of reference for the aspirational Indian traveler, by depicting the touristic practices and appearances of well-off, cosmopolitan consumers, in which Switzerland is framed as a theme park of love and romance (see Figure 32.1).

New spatial ordering logic: "Las Vegas in the Alps"

The fieldwork observations and interviews further emphasize the texturation of contemporary Switzerland as a romantic theme park – reduced to a postmodern, post-industrial consumption arena. The spatial design of Jungfraujoch, Titlis, and Glacier3000 all offer modulized, easy to consume "real mountain experiences" that do not require particular physical or psychological fitness. Conceived space is communicated similar to theme parks or malls, numbering the various stops and playful opportunities to engage with the exotic world of snow and ice. The outdoor snow fun parks are complemented with indoor walks (glacier walk, history walk) to compensate for bad weather. Inside the tunnels of Jungfraujoch, one could have a multimax projection of the glacier, and pass by an oversized glass bowl with snowflakes, sporting all the major Swiss brands. Furthermore, in a room decorated by sparkling Edelweiss flowers, visitors would take a selfie with life-size figures signifying Swissness (cows, peasants, mountaineers).

Figure 32.1   Reenacting the love-play of Bollywood films.

These "free" experiences were complemented by exclusive shopping arenas, including Europe's highest watch and chocolate shops, calibrated to accommodate the pressure from larger groups. Clearly, these high-altitude commercial spaces are bearing more similarities more with Asian casinos and indoor malls than with the unspoilt Alpine wilderness Switzerland stands for in the eyes of European tourists (Figure 32.2).

Textural changes also manifest themselves in diversifying and creolized gastronomic offerings in Swiss destinations. For instance, all mountain destinations had a Bollywood restaurant

Figure 32.2   The Altitude Mall experience.

offering Indian style buffets cooked by a specially recruited Indian chef. Local operators consider Indians groups to be disinclined towards local tastes. Although Swiss gastronomic highlights (rösti, sausages, and fondue) still feature on the menus, they do so in company of masala chai, vegetarian samosas, or noodle soups. As one hotelier in Interlaken lamented:

> Interlaken changed incredibly a lot. The shops . . . The good thing is that you can find every watch on earth, the choice is big, you can find every fast food cuisine from the world, but one thing for sure, it has changed a lot. It's no more the typical traditional small bakery or the small Swiss restaurant what comes in sight, so it is sad.
>
> *(Receptionist, Hotel Weisses Kreuz, IInterlaken, interview)*

These textural transformations signal how Switzerland (yet again) is repositioning itself to accommodate the consumer tastes of the affluent global traveler. Pastoral or natural Swiss landscapes are mostly valued as a commodified backdrop to underscore ritualized romantic spectacles and position identities on the dating market. For instance, a young Korean woman visiting Jungfraujoch took hours to pose (alone) for the perfect wedding photograph on the Aletsch Glacier. Such egocentric performances echo Eva Illouz' assertion of an emerging, new kind of romance among the middle classes, which is tied to consumerism and manipulated by the mass media (Illouz as in Dwyer, 2002).

Disruptive performances

Thin-soled shoes skid across the ice. Snowballs fly. Delighted squeals can be heard as soon as the furrowed slopes upon which it is possible to slide down a few meters into the snow have been discovered. Saris flap in the wind, camera phones and video cameras are set up (Frank, 2016, p. 206)

The colorful crowd of tourists frolicking in the snow is a ubiquitous sight on the top of Mount Titlis or Jungfraujoch. As Frank (2016) observes, Indian tourists are disrupting (and disordering) the spatial-communicative fabric of Swiss destinations in creative ways. As one of the waitresses claimed: "you see them from afar on the looks, you hear them and they are very loud." Many Indian groups would wear identical, bright blue sunglasses accompanied by colorful garments (saris and kurtas), warm blankets and flip-flops; a combination that is vastly different from layered outdoor clothing appropriate for high-altitude visits. For many, it was their first time of seeing snow, let alone, taking a cable car to 3,000 meters, which sometimes prompted remarkable collective responses. On several occasions of cable car departures, I experienced entire groups breaking out in an impulsive chant in Hindi, praying for a safe trip.

Upon arrival to the top, Asian (Korean, Chinese, and Indian) tourists would instantaneously start scurrying around in the winter theme park "wonderland." This would often entail exploring the snow in playful, tactile, and haptic ways, for instance, tasting it, making snowballs, snowmen lying "snow angels" in the snow. Honeymoon couples take selfies, often asking a third party to throw snow on them while the marriage proposal is reenacted (Figure 32.3). As Dwyer (2002, 2014) contends, honeymoons in Switzerland are a consumerist spectacle of the emergent Indian middle classes, which are enacted along a list of compulsory rituals, paraphrasing the love-play scenes from diverse Bollywood films.

Besides, the fieldwork provided many odd events illustrating visitors' aspirations of internalizing mountain practices. For instance, when noticing the skis carefully stored in racks at Mt Titlis, Indian tourists would pick a pair of skis to strike a pose with bent knees for the camera. Most of the time, they stepped on the skis with the tail in front and left them on the snow

Figure 32.3 Playing and posing in the snow.

after the picture was taken. These disruptions were not left unresponded. An older Swiss skier approached them with a firm voice, "Put the skis back!" At other occasions, signs in English and Chinese instructed tourists how to use the selective waste system, or asking them *not* to waste food, *not* to picnic, *not* to climb up on installations. In most cases, such written instructions had little effect, leaving the front line personnel (lift operators, waitresses, janitors, and train conductors) fighting a daily battle to discipline the crowds. As Frank (2016) notes, such "domestication" efforts are often condescending towards the "primitive" or "uncivilized" Other. However, there were also instances of more compassionate approaches, as that of head waiter of Glacier 3000 restaurant:

> The Indian guests have no idea how to behave on a mountain like this or how to take the chair lift. Even for us, who are used to take the chairlift with skis, it is a challenge; "ooh it's a bit strange" . . ., just imagine for them. So the staff has to be really careful, and think of the security aspect as well they have to be switched on all the time.
>
> *(Head waiter, Glacier3000, interview)*

At other occasions, Indian tourists demonstrated creative new ways through which the indoor spaces of Jungfraujoch could be used. Tired after hours of playing in the snow under the sun (and perhaps having altitude sickness as well), many of them decided to take a nap on the station floor (or even the window sills) until their train departed. This resulted in a chaotic situation, where other tourists heading for their trains were unable to leave because of the "human obstacles" in the full width of the corridor (Figure 32.4).

Conclusions: implications for popular culture tourism

This chapter captured the Indianization of Switzerland, that is, the processes shaping emerging destination textures that are at once cosmopolitan and transcultural. The representational and

Figure 32.4 Taking a nap on the mountain station floor.

textural analyzes unveiled spatial ambiguities, emerging along ruptures of new topographies and materialities, new mapping practices, the entanglements of new and old imaginaries, and diversifying tourist performances. As such, non-Western popular cultural tourism in Switzerland has significantly contributed to regional development dynamics and further strengthened the competitiveness of Central Switzerland and the Berner Oberland. The chapter demonstrates that Yash Chopra's consistent romantic representations of Switzerland (and subsequent intertextual articulations of these) are turning Swiss mountain tops into liminal consumption arenas or altitude theme parks. Indirectly, Bollywood films established new cross-sectoral synergies between the global fashion, travel and entertainment industry, and local tourism and retail operators, and spurred experience innovations augmenting Swiss landscapes with new cultural meanings. Cultural contraflows may present new opportunities for the strategic repositioning of nation branding and destination marketing in theme park Europe.

Nevertheless, the ever increasing number of Asian tourists and the "Indianization of Switzerland" challenge in some aspects the established textures of Alpine travel spaces. Local operators are concerned about the disruptive performances of new travelers and often use the tactics of spatial and gastronomic segregation in servicing them. Consequently, Asian visitors move across Switzerland without ever leaving the ultra-commodified tourist enclave – very similar to the managerial approaches to Scandinavian tourists in Mediterranean destinations in the early 1980s. Such conformist approaches have proven highly unsustainable, and it is relevant to ask whether Swiss destination planners and operators are prepared for the next stage of internationalization with even larger tourist arrivals.

Taking a look at the destination promotional materials, Asian guests are seldom represented. Websites and brochures are still dominated by white, middle-class couples and families, and traditional tourism performances, while other tourist preferences are largely ignored. Very few marketers have exploited the opportunities residing in new experience concepts, entailing not only brief visual consumption of Bollywood landscapes, but allowing for more sensuous and playful engagements with the natural environment and building collective narratives with a more cosmopolitan flair. Seen from a destination planning perspective, non-Western popular cultural place-making marks the dawn of new, extroverted commodification strategies, which may be combined with endogenous, community-based initiatives. Managing the balance between the emergent, cosmopolitanized Alpine destination textures may present vast challenges for destinations embarking on popular culture induced tourism trajectories. The governance perspective of non-Western place-making presents a promising research avenue for the future.

Note

1 DDLJ or *Dilwale Dulhaniya Le Jayenge* [*The Bravehearted Will Take the Bride*] (1995) is a cult film epitomizing Bollywood romance set in Switzerland. It has been running in Indian cinemas for the last 20 years and had a global reach.

References

Adams, P. C. & Jansson, A. (2012). Communication geography: a bridge between disciplines. *Communication Theory*, 22 (3) 2999–3018.
Bandyopadhyay, R. (2008). Nostalgia, identity and tourism: Bollywood in the Indian diaspora. *Journal of Tourism and Cultural Change*, 6 (2), 79–100.
Couldry, N. & McCarthy, A. (2004). *Mediaspace: Place, Scale and Culture in a Media Age*. London: Routledge.
Dudrah, R. (2012). *Bollywood Travels: Culture Diaspora and Border Crossings in Popular Hindi Cinema*. Abingdon: Routledge.
Dwyer, R. (2002). Love in Switzerland: the Indian middle classes, romance and consumerism. In Schneider, A. (Ed.) *Bollywood: The Indian Cinema and Switzerland*. English version. Zürich: Museum for Gestaltung und Kunst, pp. 25–27.
Dwyer, R. (2014). *Bollywood's India: Hindi Cinema as a Guide to Contemporary India*. London/Chicago: Reaktion Books.
Ehn, B. & Löfgren, O. (2016). At analysere det oversete. In Andersen, S. T. & Jacobsen, M. H. (Eds.), *Kultursociologi og kulturanalyse*. København: Hans Reitzels Forlag, pp. 137–165.
European Travel Commission (ETC) (2014). *Market Insights India*. Retrieved from www.etc-corporate. org/reports/market-insights-india.
Euroscreen (2015). *Bollywood in Europe: A Case Study*. Report commissioned by Film London
Falkheimer, J. & Jansson, A. (2006). *Geographies of Communication: The Spatial Turn in Media Studies*. Göteborg: Nordicom.
Federal Statistical Office (FSO) (2013). *Swiss Tourism Statistics 2012*. Neuchâtel, Switzerland: FSO.
Frank, S. (2016). Dwelling-in-motion: Indian Bollywood tourists and their hosts in the Swiss Alps. *Cultural Studies*, 30 (3), 506–531.
Frost, W. (2009). From backcloth to runaway production: exploring location and authenticity in film-induced tourism. *Tourism Review International*, 13 (2), 85–92.
Gyimóthy, S. (2015). Bollywood-in-the-Alps: popular culture place-making in tourism. In A. Lorentzen, K. Topsøe Larsen, & L. Schrøder, *Spatial Dynamics in the Experience Economy*. Abingdon: Taylor & Francis, pp. 158–174.
Gyimóthy, S., Lundberg, C., Lindström, K., Lexhagen, M., & Larson, M. (2015). Popculture tourism: a research manifesto. In D. Chambers (Ed.), *Tourism Social Science Series Tourism Research Frontiers*. Bingley, UK: Emerald, pp. 13–27.
Hjarvard, S. (2008). *En verden af medier*. København: Samfundslitteratur.
Jansson, A. (2007). Texture. *European Journal of Cultural Studies*, 10 (2), 185–202.
Jansson, A. (2013). Mediatization and social space: reconstruction mediatization for the transmedia age. *Communication Theory*, 23 (1) 279–296.
Jansson, A. (2014). Reconstruction mediatization for the transmedia age. *Communication Theory*, 23, 279–296.
Jensen, J. L. & Waade, A. M. (2009). *Medier og Turisme*. Århus: Academica.
Jensen, M. T., Scarles, C., & Cohen, S. (2015). A multisensory phenomenology of InterRail mobilities. *Annals of Tourism Research*, 53, 61–76.

Josiam, B. M., Spears, D. L., Dutta, K., Pookulangara, S. A., Dutta, K., Kinley, T., & Duncan (2015). Using structural equation modeling to understand the impact of Bollywood movies on destination image, tourist activity, and purchasing behavior of Indians. *Journal of Vacation Marketing*, 21(3), 251–261.

Josiam, B. M., Spears, D. L., Dutta, K., Pookulangara, S. A., & Kinley, T. (2014). "Namastey London": Bollywood Movies and their impact on how Indians perceive European destinations. *Hospitality Review*, 31 (4), 1–22.

Larsen, J. & Meged, J. W. (2013). Tourists co-producing guided tours. *Scandinavian Journal of Hospitality and Tourism*, 13 (2), 88–102.

Larson, M., Lexhagen, M., & Lundberg, C. (2013). Thirsting for vampire tourism: developing pop culture destinations. *Journal of Destination Marketing and Management*, 2 (2) 74–84.

Lefebvre, H. (1991). *The Production of Space*. Oxford: Blackwell.

Löfgren, O. & Ehn, B. (2001). *Kulturanalyser*. Gleerups Utbildning AB.

Lundberg, C. & Lexhagen, M. (2012). Bitten by the *Twilight Saga*: from pop culture consumer to pop culture tourist. In R. Sharpley & P. R. Stone (Eds.), *The Contemporary Tourist Experience: Concepts and Consequences*. Abingdon: Routledge, pp. 147–164.

Månsson, M. & Eskilsson, L. (2013). *The Attraction of Screen Destinations*. Report commissioned by Film London and the Euroscreen Partnership, Rzeczow, Poland.

Mittal, N. & Anjaneyaswamy, G. (2013). Film induced tourism: a study in Indian outbound tourism. *Atna, Journal of Tourism Studies*, 8 (2), 37–54 doi: 10.12727/ajts.10.337.

Monteneiro, S. (2014). Back to Bollystan: imagined space and diasporic identity in contemporary Hindi cinema. *Quarterly Review of Film and Video*, 31 (5), 435–451.

Mukherjee, M. (2012). Mustard fields, exotic tropes and travels through meandering pathways: reframing the Yash Raj trajectory. In A. G. Roy & C. G. Huat (Eds.), *Travels of Bollywood Cinema*. Oxford: Oxford University Press, pp. 34–53.

Schaefer, D. & Karan, K., (2012). *Bollywood and Globalization: The Global Power of Popular Hindi Cinema*. Singapore: Taylor & Francis.

Schneider, A. (2002). *Bollywood: The Indian Cinema and Switzerland*. English version. Zürich: Museum for Gestaltung und Kunst.

Schneider, A. (2009). Theme park Europe: transmission and transcultural images in popular Hindi cinema. In A. Schneider & B. Meissmann (Eds), *Transmission Image: Visual Translation and Cultural Agency*. Newcastle upon Tyne: Cambridge Scholars, pp. 86–107.

Schweizer Radio und Fernsehen (SRF) (2000). *Bollywood im Alpenrausch – Indische Filmemacher erobern die Schweiz* [*Bollywood Conquers the Alps*]. Documentary by Christian Frei.

Shedde, M. (2002). Switzerland is a Disneyland of love. In A. Schneider (Ed.), *Bollywood: The Indian Cinema and Switzerland*. English version. Zürich: Museum for Gestaltung und Kunst, pp. 4–6.

Switzerland Tourismus (2012). *Switzerland for Movie Stars*. Luzern: Schweiz Turismus.

PART V

Establishing a common ground

Popular culture tourism and destination management

33

FILM TOURISM STAKEHOLDERS AND IMPACTS

W. Glen Croy, Marieke Kersten, Audrey Mélinon and David Bowen

Setting the scene

Film tourism has been heralded as a positive outcome by destinations featuring in film and television; further emphasizing a film industry, while promoting awareness of a destination (Beeton, 2005; Croy & Walker, 2003; Cynthia & Beeton, 2009; Hudson, 2011; Karpovich, 2010; Rittichainuwat & Rattanaphinanchai, 2015; Tuclea & Nistoreanu, 2011). The result has been widely recognized as stimulating tourist demand to the featured destination (Busby & Klug, 2001; Hudson & Ritchie, 2006; O'Connor, Flanagan, & Gilbert, 2008; Riley, Baker, & Van Doren, 1998), even though great increases in tourist numbers may generally be an exceptional expectation (Croy, 2011). Due to the perceived success of inducing tourists, authors have claimed films as marketing and promotional tools, enhancing a destination image with minimal cost involvement from the tourism industry (Bolan & Williams, 2008; Croy, 2010; Croy & Walker, 2003; Hudson, 2011; Hudson & Ritchie, 2006; Tooke & Baker, 1996). In this chapter, 'film' refers to popular culture mediums including movies and television, whereby people may be exposed to incidental destination images. Furthermore, film tourism applies "to visitation to sites where movies and TV programs have been filmed [and set], as well as to tours to production studios, including film-related theme parks" (Beeton, 2005, p. 11).

Increasingly however, there is an awareness of the true cost of film-induced tourism. Authors are noting impacts that film tourism may bring to stakeholders of a destination (Beeton, 2005, 2006; Heitmann, 2010). Particularly impacted upon is the community based at the film site, or where the film is perceived to be set (Beeton, 2006; Chen & Mele, 2017). Key impacts include job opportunities, congestion, infrastructure development, noise, economic change, environmental damage, and limited access to public land (Beeton, 2008; Busby & Klug, 2001; Mason & Cheyne, 2000; Riley et al., 1998). While evidence continues to indicate that destinations featured in films have received high levels of tourist visitation, authors are concurrently suggesting methods to manage impacts that film tourists are producing. Suggestions include increased communication between the Destination Management Organizations (DMOs) and the film industry in order to promote a cohesive destination image (Bolan & Williams, 2008; Cynthia & Beeton, 2009; O'Connor et al., 2008; Wray & Croy, 2015), and the community's increased awareness of tourist expectations to avoid a disappointing experience for the tourist (Connell & Meyer, 2009). Unfortunately, these suggestions are unlikely to effectively target the impacts.

The film industry is not often concerned with the image of the destination, but rather focused upon the film they would like to make (Wray & Croy, 2015). Furthermore, catering to tourists' wants may directly oppose the community's wishes and further exacerbate the issues.

Community wants and needs for their ideal destination has been a growing focus in film tourism, and the importance of satisfying all stakeholders (Beeton, 2001, 2004, 2005, 2006; Croy, 2010; Heitmann, 2010). Nonetheless, there is limited discussion about avoiding the impacts on community before film tourism arrives, as compared to reacting to problems after they occur (Chen & Mele, 2017; Croy & Buchmann, 2009). Ideally, potential film tourism impacts need to be managed in a proactive manner, primarily focusing upon reducing negative impacts on the community and enhancing the community benefits derived from tourism.

Within this context, this chapter aims to review issues for film tourism stakeholders, and provide indicative considerations to manage film impacts through the image generated. First, stakeholders of film tourism are identified and outlined. Second, a review of film tourism impacts to the identified stakeholder groups is presented. Third, a discussion of DMOs management implications are presented, before conclusions are noted.

Disciplinary underpinnings

Stakeholder theory, pioneered by Freeman (1984, p. 46), defines stakeholders as "any group or individual who can affect or is affected by the achievement of the organization's objectives." Like in business, both researchers and practitioners have identified that "without the support of stakeholders, tourism would not be successful in the long term" (Beeton, 2006, p. 39). Ryan (2002) has further outlined that the identification of stakeholders, and the issues affecting them, is necessary for sustaining socially responsible and successful tourism development. He adds, importantly, that there is the need to develop communication relationships between stakeholders to increase the collective understanding of these issues.

Many film tourism studies have not explicitly listed stakeholders. The term 'stakeholder' is often generically used in discussions regarding aspects of film tourism (Connell, 2005a; O'Connor et al., 2008). Alternatively, studies target a specific stakeholder group to discuss, such as a grassroots community group. As a base, Heitmann (2010) has identified four prominent stakeholder groups: the film industry, tourists, DMOs, and the community.

Heitmann's (2010) four categories of stakeholders are by no means an exhaustive list, and are relatively inclusive. To exemplify the inclusivity, and potential dangers of generalization, previous studies highlight distinctions within each of these stakeholder groups. When acknowledged, tourist stakeholders have been further detailed in film tourism studies. Beeton (2004), for example, makes a distinction between the holidaymaker and film tourist in Barwon Heads, used in the Australian television series *Sea Change*. Similarly, Busby and O'Neill (2006) distinguish between literary tourists and film tourists to Cephallonia, Greece, comparing the influence of book and film *Captain Corelli's Mandolin*. Mordue (2001) determines that residents perceive attitude and behavioral differences between 'traditional' tourists and the new 'film' tourists, in turn treating the tourist types with differing levels of respect. His findings were that the traditional tourist was perceived as more responsible and sustainable, but is being replaced by the contrasting film tourist. Therefore, 'tourists' as a homogenous stakeholder group does not allow for the distinction between, perceived or actual, attitudes and behaviors of different tourist types.

Communities are another category made up of many individuals and smaller groups with differing interests and motives. Beeton (2006, p. 61) highlighted that "communities are complex entities comprising many different groups or stakeholders." Furthermore, the private sector of the tourism industry is often confusingly classed under the community category.

Residents with a commercial stake in the tourism business sometimes overlap as locals and private business operators (Connell, 2005a). Added to the community complexity is the role of the public government tourism sector, at times aligned with or contrastingly pitted against the private sector (Connell, 2005a). The government tourism sector will be discussed as part of the DMO category.

Community members are often portrayed as individualistic and lack a common goal. This was witnessed in community meetings regarding the impacts of *Heartbeat* (Goathland, England), whereby community members held no clear vision, resulting in feelings of nothing getting resolved (see Mordue, 2001). All the same, grassroots community groups may emerge with similar aims. For example, the Friends of the Lake District expressing concern over perceived "negative social and environmental impacts" following the release of *Pride and Prejudice* (Beeton, 2001, p. 18). Beeton (2001, 2006) also drew attention to impacts of film tourism to neighboring communities, as well as indigenous people and disadvantaged people, who may otherwise be overlooked as community stakeholders.

A DMO, in this chapter, refers to Destination Management Organization, and is a purposeful move from a DMO focused specifically on 'M'arketing, reflecting discussions by Buhalis (2000) and Heitmann (2010). This purposeful move is a response to the growing recognition that tourism does generate a number of impacts, positive and negative, and management has a greater inherent emphasis on the destination, as compared to marketing with an inherent emphasis on the tourist. DMOs ideally aim to consider the management of a destination and the destinations' image in a holistic and inclusive manner. Although marketing is a large role for DMOs, the facilitation of community involvement is being increasingly recognized (Beeton, 2006). In part, this may be driven by DMOs tending to be part of the local, regional, or national government and have political, legislative, and financial responsibilities to their communities, and the means to meet the responsibilities (Buhalis, 2000; Wray & Croy, 2015).

The underlying contest appears to be between the DMO and the tourism industry. While at a surface level the stakeholders appear to have similar interests, DMOs are expected to maintain a long-term sustainable vision for the destination, often pitted against the private tourism sector, accused of predominantly focusing on short-term profitable goals. In this contest for long-term sustainability and short-term profit, Beeton (2006) warns that private industry contributions to destination management are leading to an inappropriate share of power.

The film industry has been arguably simpler to define than the other stakeholder groups. The film industry comprises of those involved in the making of films, including actors, directors, sound engineers, and the film company. The film industry may recognize their stake in ensuring relations with the community are kept amicable (Beeton, 2008; Cynthia & Beeton, 2009; Wray & Croy, 2015), to augment further concessions and incentives for the film company to film in a town. Yet the attitude of the film industry is reported as unenthusiastic and uninterested in collaborating with other film tourism stakeholders, their goal being to make a film or television series and be long gone before tourists discover the site (Heitmann, 2010).

Within film tourism research, the above stakeholders have been assessed as having differing levels of power and interest. The DMO is often given the role to include and manage the differing stakeholders and the issues they face. Previous literature has placed the tourism industry, and the (film) tourist as having high power and interest due to destinations becoming more dependent upon tourism (Mason & Cheyne, 2000). The film industry has also been identified as having high power as a powerful disseminator of destination image (Beeton, 2004), though low interest in using that power. Film tourism studies are now identifying the increasing power and active interest of the local community, as their quality of life is affected by the 'success' of film tourism and tourists (Chen & Mele, 2017; Connell, 2005b; Mordue, 2009). Furthermore, the tourist experience is also affected by the reaction of the local community, negative or positive, to contact with tourists in their community place (or space) (Beeton, 2005; Busby & O'Neill, 2006; Mordue, 2001). Of course, "ideally, consideration should be given to each stakeholder (group), irrespective of the level of interest and/or power held" (Heitmann, 2010, p. 37), and the destination be managed for its best outcomes.

Impacts

A number of film-tourism impacts and the stakeholders impacted have been reported in previous studies. Impacts can be positive or negative, largely dependent upon the stakeholders' perspective (Beeton, 2006). Each stakeholder group has a different yet not exclusive list of impacts affecting them. Many of the impacts described are similar to general tourism impacts (Heitmann, 2010). Nonetheless, this chapter notes film tourism specific impacts, or rather, the specific predilection that film tourism stakeholders may have to a particular impact. Of increasing note, the relationship between film and tourism can generate direct, indirect, and cumulative impacts, some immediately evident, and others working through tourism systems over an extended time before being demonstrated.

Table 33.1 presents an overview of the impacts discussed in film tourism studies. Impacts are categorized by the stakeholder predominantly affected: community, tourist, DMO, and film industry. There are three notes for the interpretation of the table. First, there is a diversity of perspectives and goals within these inclusive stakeholder groups. Second, stakeholders are not exclusively affected by an impact, and thus may appear more than once, potentially with a different perspective on the impact. Third, most film tourism studies have been destination case studies, and thus the generalizability of the impacts is indicative, not conclusive. The impacts are not distinguished as negative or positive, yet where authors have identified a strong bias this is reflected in the description column of Table 33.1. The prominent authors presenting each stakeholder impact are also noted.

Table 33.1 Film tourism stakeholder impacts

Stakeholder impacts	Description	Selected references
Community impacts		
Economic	People perceive a change in the local economy wealth Often seen as positive if receiving direct benefits, often seen as negative if not receiving direct benefits	Basáñez & Ingram, 2013; Beeton, 2001, 2005, 2008; Chen & Mele, 2017; Chiang & Yeh, 2011; Connell, 2005b; Hao & Ryan, 2013; Heitmann, 2010; Hudson & Ritchie, 2006; Kim et al., 2007; Martin-Jones, 2014; O'Connor, 2011; Riley et al., 1998; Schofield, 1996; Shao et al., 2016; Tooke & Baker, 1996; Tuclea and Nistoreanu, 2011
Congestion and overcrowding	Increased visitation to a community or area	Beeton, 2001, 2004, 2008; Busby & Klug, 2001; Chen & Mele, 2017; Chiang & Yeh, 2011; Connell, 2005b; Croy & Buchmann, 2009; Hudson & Ritchie, 2006; Larson, Lundberg, & Lexhagen, 2013; Mordue, 2009; Tooke & Baker, 1996; Tuclea & Nistoreanu, 2011; Riley et al., 1998; Zhang, Ryan, & Cave, 2016

Environmental	Tourism often occurs in fragile environments that can be impacted upon	Beeton, 2001; Buchmann, Moore & Fisher, 2010; Chiang & Yeh, 2011; Connell, 2005b; Hudson & Ritchie, 2006; Martin-Jones, 2014; Tooke & Baker, 1996; 2012; Tuclea & Nistoreanu, 2011; Zhang et al., 2016;
Infrastructure & facility development	Infrastructure and facility changes in response to tourism increases, including aesthetic changes in the community	Beeton, 2001, 2004, 2005, 2010; Chiang & Yeh, 2011; Croy & Walker, 2003; Heitmann, 2010; Kim et al., 2007; Mordue, 2001
Employment	Increased employment opportunities through tourism	Beeton, 2005, 2008; Chiang & Yeh, 2011; Croy & Walker, 2003; Heitmann, 2010; Karpovick, 2010; O'Connor, 2011
Inflation	Land, goods and services value increase due to increased local economy, opportunities, and demand	Beeton, 2001, 2005; Heitmann, 2010; Kim et al., 2007; Riley et al., 1998; Tuclea & Nistoreanu, 2011; Zhang et al., 2016
Cultural revitalization	An increase in arts, crafts, and local culture being promoted	Beeton, 2005; Croy & Walker, 2003; Hao & Ryan, 2013; Kim et al., 2007; O'Connor et al., 2008; Schofield, 1996
Privacy	Loss of privacy for locals, particularly private land where filming was located	Beeton, 2001, 2004, 2008; Chiang & Yeh, 2011; Kim et al., 2007; Tuclea & Nistoreanu, 2011
Noise	Increased noise, often due to increased traffic and tourist numbers	Beeton, 2008; Chiang & Yeh, 2011; Croy & Buchmann, 2009;
Cultural commodification	Culture commodified and changing for the benefit of tourists	Beeton, 2005; Connell, 2012; Croy & Buchmann, 2009; Heitmann, 2010; Mordue, 2001
Cross-cultural interaction	Cross-cultural communication occurring between tourist and host community	Beeton, 2005; Kim et al., 2007; Larson et al., 2013; Mordue, 2001; Zhang et al., 2016;
Contact avoidance	Host community avoiding or acting aggressive towards tourists	Beeton, 2005; Connell, 2005a, 2012; Heitmann, 2010; Larson et al., 2013; Mordue, 2009
Community division	Division of those who have/do not have a relationship with tourists	Beeton, 2005; Chiang & Yeh, 2011; Connell, 2005a; Heitmann, 2010
Crime	Outsiders bringing crime into an area, or an evident wealth divide inciting theft in locals	Beeton, 2005; Riley et al., 1998
Neighboring affect	Neighboring town affected by tourism (predominantly economic benefits)	Beeton, 2001

More specific to film-tourism

Tourist type change	Tourist typology changing as a new film tourist type emerges	Beeton, 2001; Connell, 2005b; Croy & Buchmann, 2009; Mestre, del Rey, & Stanishevski, 2008; Mordue, 2001, 2009

(continued)

Table 33.1 (continued)

Stakeholder impacts	Description	Selected references
Stereotyping	Community being perceived stereotypically as a result of media images. Alternatively, tourists being perceived stereotypically due to a lack of communication between host and tourist	Croy & Buchmann, 2009; Mercille, 2005; Mordue, 2000, 2009; Iwashita, 2006; O'Connor et al., 2008
Community representations	Film and film tourism overriding local history and stories	Chen & Mele, 2017; Croy & Buchmann, 2009; Wray & Croy, 2015
Short tourist boost	Reliance on film tourism that may only be for a short duration	Connell, 2005a, 2005b; Croy & Walker, 2003
Limiting access	Access to the destination limited due to film-site overuse	Beeton, 2001; Croy & Buchmann, 2009

Tourist impacts

Cross-cultural interaction	Cross-cultural communication occurring between tourist and host community	Beeton, 2005; Kim et al., 2007; Mordue, 2001; Zhang et al., 2016

More specific to film tourism

Authenticity	Tourists seeking authenticity within destinations Alternatively, tourists may be seeking myths due to the media representation of place	Buchmann, Moore, & Fisher, 2010; Busby & Klug, 2001; Croy & Buchmann, 2009; Frost, 2006; Riley et al., 1998; Schofield, 1996
Displacement	Film tourists overcrowding a destination and overrunning the existing tourist base	Beeton, 2001, 2005; Connell, 2005a; Larson et al., 2013; Loureiro & Barbosa de Araujo, 2015; Mestre et al., 2008
Inflationary prices	Existing tourist base unable to afford holidays in the area due to film tourists	Beeton, 2001, 2005; Kim et al., 2007; Mordue, 2001; Tuclea & Nistoreanu, 2011; Zhang et al., 2016
Image dissonance	The destination image, portrayed by the media, different to the real destination image and creating confusion	Beeton, 2004; Karpovich, 2010; Riley et al. 1998
Expectations not met	Disappointment, often due to evidence of film no longer being visible	Beeton, 2008; Carl, Kindon & Smith, 2007; Mordue, 2001
Limiting access	Access to certain areas of a destination being limited, interfering with planned holiday	Beeton, 2001; Croy & Buchmann, 2009
Privacy	The privacy of the existing tourist base being compromised by film tourists	Beeton, 2005

DMO impacts

Superficial representations	Representing historical events superficially. For example, avoiding representing poverty in historical tourism	Beeton, 2004; Chen & Mele, 2017; Connell, 2012; Frost, 2006; Riley et al., 1998; Schofield, 1996

Overcrowding/ overuse	Needing to manage destination overuse by fencing off or limiting access to certain areas	Beeton, 2001

More specific to film tourism

Image dissonance	The destination image portrayed by film conflicting with the ideal destination image	Beeton, 2004; Chen & Mele, 2017; Connell, 2012; Croy, 2010; Croy & Buchmann, 2009; Larson et al., 2013
Sudden increase	Lack of preparedness Lack of a commercial tourism industry	Hudson, 2011; Riley et al., 1998; Wray & Croy, 2015
Short-term tourism	Reliance on tourism that is of short-term duration	Connell, 2005a, 2005b; Croy & Walker, 2003
Crime	Icon hunters stealing from location	Beeton, 2005; Riley et al., 1998
Localized impact	Not all regions witness an increase in tourism visitation after a film	Croy & Walker, 2003

Film industry impacts

Relationship building	Creating an ongoing relationship with other destination stakeholders in order to continue usage of the destination	Beeton, 2008; Croy & Walker, 2003; Cynthia & Beeton, 2009
Concessions	Benefits perceived by the community and DMO can lead to concessions and benefits for the film crew (including extra parking, cheaper accommodation)	Beeton, 2008; Cynthia & Beeton, 2009
Corporate social responsibility profile	To be perceived as benefiting a community through film tourism, the film company is adding to its community social responsibility profile rather than simply seen as seeking financial gain	Beeton, 2008; Mercille, 2005
Economic impact	Direct impact from the production on location	Connell, 2012

Previous studies have noted a diverse range of film tourism effects on the local community. The number and diversity of impacts are increasing community awareness, interest, and encouraging the use of their latent power as a tourism stakeholder, after all "it is their home, and they will be feeling the immediate and cumulative impacts" (Croy & Heitmann, 2011, p. 198). Therefore, the local community's wants and needs must be catered for within the management of tourism impacts, and film tourism more specifically. Four key community impacts are stereotyping, the short-term boost in tourism, tourist type changing, and limiting access to previously public land.

Film representations are powerful influences in seeing places and people in particular stereotypical ways, and are often biased and selective (Connell, 2012; Iwashita, 2006; Hao & Ryan,

2013; Rejinders, 2011). The community can be perceived stereotypically according to the images presented of them through film or television. Alternatively, the community can often stereotype tourists according to the behavior and actions of a few, or a lack of awareness regarding tourists (Mordue, 2009). Films can positively influence a destination's visitation numbers, providing the local economy with a tourism boost (Connell & Meyer, 2009; Croy & Walker, 2003). However, increased visitation can be within a short time period (Connell, 2005b), and the reliance on an industry that is often not able to support the immediate numbers or maintain the enthusiasm into the longer term would affect the local economy and tourism business owners. In this visitor number change, it has also been identified that there is also a change in tourist type, often shifting from family-orientated tourists towards film tourists (Beeton, 2001). For example, residents of Goathland "set up a clear dichotomy between two tourist types: the countryside 'appreciating' tourists and *Heartbeat* tourists" accepting the former tourist type while commonly rejecting the latter (Mordue, 2001, p. 244). Another prominent film impact upon the local community stakeholder is limited access to certain areas in the destination due to either filming or overuse by film tourists (Beeton, 2001; Croy & Buchmann, 2009).

For the tourist stakeholder, impacts were largely felt by the pre-film segments beset by film tourists. Impacts of film tourism for pre-existing tourists included inflationary pricing of tourist goods resulting in not being able to afford their usual holiday (Beeton, 2001). Further impacts included reduced privacy of the tourists, particularly where their activities or accommodation coincided with filmed features (Beeton, 2005). Furthermore, film tourism was also found to overcrowd and congest destinations, displacing the pre-existing tourists. Issues for the film tourists include location authenticity, as often the destination is unable to match the representation or myth of the media to fulfil the tourist desire (Croy & Buchmann, 2009; Schofield, 1996). Image dissonance, is another tourist impact, where the media-portrayed image differs from the image portrayed by the DMO and community, leading to tourist confusion and loss of tourist opportunity (Beeton, 2004). A final tourist impact is when expectations are not met, as film evidence is no longer visible or indicated.

DMO impacts are similar to community impacts, though more focused upon the management of these issues. Two general impacts related to film tourism include first the overcrowding and overuse of specific areas, leading to the fencing off and limitation of access (Beeton, 2001), and second, superficial, or even sanitized, representations of historical local events depicted within the media and tourism image of an area (Connell, 2012). More specific to film tourism, impacts include image dissonance, in that the image portrayed by film conflicts with the community's self-image (Chen & Mele, 2017). Another prominent impact is the lack of one; not all destinations featured in films and television receive a tourist boost. Therefore, DMOs must manage unfulfilled expectations of an increase in visitation (Croy & Walker, 2003; Wray & Croy, 2015). Furthermore, an increase in tourists and the DMO's reliance on film may have a short-term duration, and a destination may be unprepared and miss the opportunity. Finally, studies have noted souvenir taking at film sites, and other related increases in crime that may affect destination icons (Beeton, 2005).

The film tourism impacts are generally a consequence of the film industry, rather than on the film industry. Nevertheless, there have been destination efforts to purposefully create relationships with film production organizations (Cynthia & Beeton, 2009; Hudson, 2011; Wray & Croy, 2015). It also appears that the film industry has engaged these relationships for favorable future concessions, especially in the case of television series productions. Additionally, the film industry may also engage these relationships due to increased potential community resistance to filming due to noted tourism impacts on the community, and raise their corporate social responsibility profile (Beeton, 2008).

As Table 33.1 and the discussion have indicated, there are impacts upon various stakeholder groups that can affect them in different ways. The nature of the impact appears to be dependent upon each stakeholder's role in the community, the type of tourist, the destination management organization's handling of an issue, and the intentions of the film company featuring the destination. Overall, the origin of these film tourism impacts is in the image created, and how it continues to resonate with audiences (Croy, 2010; Loureiro & Barbosa de Araujo, 2015). The image sparks and enhances motivations and desires to visit places, potentially for expected experiences that are unachievable. More importantly, the expected tourist experiences may not align with the community's desires or self-image, and further magnify the impacts for the community (Beeton, 2005, 2006; Chen & Mele, 2017). With the awareness of the influential role of film image, there needs to be an active focus on managing the desired, perceived, and promoted destination image (Croy, 2010).

Implications for popular culture tourism: destination management organization

Proactive management of the many film tourism impacts can result in successful and sustainable tourism for the destination and community (Beeton, 2006; Croy, 2010). The stakeholder group most suitable to accomplish such success is the DMO for a number of reasons, including its resource capacity (Buhalis, 2000), potential for cohesion in approach, high influence, and interest level in destination image (Heitmann, 2010), and extensive networks (Wray & Croy, 2015).

As previously noted, the emphasis is on the *management* of the destination's tourism, and a core means is to manage expectations and experiences specifically through the destination image portrayed in the community and perceived by tourists. Hudson and Ritchie (2006) provide a plethora of suggestions to increase the film tourist base of a destination, advising DMOs to lobby for tax breaks for the filming stakeholders and actively promote their destination to the film industry. These are not negative suggestions, particularly if the increase in tourism is beneficial for the community, but the focus is largely on attracting tourists, with an underlying assumption that filmed places desire more tourism. Of course, not all types of tourists benefit all types of communities, and more tourism is not always beneficial. Alternatively, this chapter supports the community-aligned management of a destination, even minimizing the tourist visitation number in order to maximize community benefits from tourism (Beeton, 2006). The destination image, through proactive management, can be an advantageous tool utilized to improve the tourist destination and experience of all stakeholders (Croy, 2010; Hudson, 2011; Hudson & Ritchie, 2006; Wray & Croy, 2015). In this context, DMOs need to be aware of the range of stakeholders, their perspectives, and the potential impacts that film could have on them (Croy, 2010; Heitmann, 2010). As such, the first implication for DMOs is a need to actively assess their destination stakeholder environment and the collective community's self-image.

Crucial in this approach, is that the community also has a full understanding of the consequences of their desires, and that a stop on film tourism, may actually be a stop on film and tourism, including their integrated and multiplying connections. The ideal community self-image is likely to be attractive to tourists, and the DMO has the most powerful, yet still limited role in controlling the tourists that are attracted (Beeton, 2005; Croy, 2010). Importantly, and the second implication, is that the DMO will need to educate the community of the consequences of their self-image, and the role they can play in managing tourism alignment.

The impacts noted have mainly arisen due to the message transmitted between the film and tourist about the destination. The tourist has formed their impression of a destination from the film, and other available sources (Cherifi et al., 2014; Schofield, 1996), and this is "a principal component of tourists' decision-making process" to visit the destination (Croy, 2010, p. 22). Additionally, the message transmitted between destination and tourist will contribute towards creating expectations of the destination and an awareness of appropriate behavior while visiting the destination. Unfortunately for the DMO, as the images received by tourists are often not generated by the DMO, they have limited influence over the type of image portrayed of the destination. Being aware of the image presented of the destination by the film industry is crucial, but is by no means the sole strategy a DMO should undertake. DMOs increasingly need to adapt and harmonize the image relayed to tourists (Croy, 2010; Hudson, 2011).

Importantly, the harmonization of the portrayed image should be aligned to the community's self-image as a happy community can lead to an appreciation of the tourism industry and negate reported hostility towards tourists (Chen & Mele, 2017; Connell & Meyer, 2009; Hao & Ryan, 2013; Larson et al., 2013; Mordue, 2009). The first point of collaboration should therefore be with the local community, understanding the objectives for their place.

It is necessary for DMOs to focus upon advantageous components of film tourism (Croy, 2010; Hudson, 2011; Iwashita, 2006), while simultaneously reducing or mitigating the potential negative impacts of the image. Beeton (2006, p. 136) discusses 'demarketing' as a means to manage a destination image before people visit, "the stage when images and expectations are created and decisions on destinations made." Furthermore, she discusses educating potential visitors regarding appropriate behavior, discouraging or encouraging certain tourist markets through the style and information of promotional material, and re-imaging the destination.

Consequently, the third implication for DMOs is to actively manage and modify the destination's image to align with the community's desired image. In the image management, DMOs need to be especially inclusive of film, and other media images, rather than a single focus on the controlled and less credible images (Wray & Croy, 2015). If the image portrayed by film is opposed to the community's self-image, there are methods available to manage impact (Beeton, 2006; Croy, 2010; Hudson, 2011; Hudson & Ritchie, 2006). In this image management, the focus needs to be on the tourist decision-making process, in their pre-visit information sourcing. For example, reduce the impact of the film image by portraying the opposing self-image. Within this image promotion, educate tourists to ensure expectations and behavior are better matched with the destination. Furthermore, incorporating the film image into what the local community wants, using the film reputation to create awareness of an area yet injecting local community desires. As DMOs have very limited control over the image portrayed in film, it is advantageous to utilize the higher profile representation to manage the destination image.

Future research and conclusion

Further research needs to be undertaken in two areas. The first area is to identify and assess the stakeholders' perspectives of film tourism impacts and the generalizability of perspectives. This chapter has highlighted the diversity within stakeholder groups, indicating multiple perspectives, desires, and responses to film tourism. Film tourism studies are beginning to further investigate these points, though more detailed research is needed. The second area is the DMOs actual management of destination image. Papers have provided strategic frameworks (Croy, 2010; Wray & Croy, 2015), and the image management methods (Beeton, 2006; Hudson, 2011; Hudson & Ritchie, 2006), though there are very limited examples of implementation of film-destination image management.

In conclusion, film is identified as a means to promote destinations and generate further tourist visitation. Unfortunately, the increased visitation often also brings film tourism impacts. To manage the impacts, a focus on the film production or tourists' desires may have limited effectiveness. Film tourism affects a range of community, tourist, film industry, and DMO stakeholders. Importantly, each of these stakeholders is inclusive of internal diversity and perspectives, complicating the management of film tourism impacts. The impacts themselves are often similar to general tourism impacts, though magnified by the film's profile in the community and potential tourist audience. The positivity of film tourism impacts is dependent on the stakeholder's perspective, and each stakeholder is likely to face positive and negative impacts. The film tourism impacts originate in part from the image perceived by the potential tourists, and the variance in the perceived image compared to the inclusive community's self-image. If the image perceived by potential tourists is different from the community's, then the tourists' expectations, experiences, and behaviors of the destination will also vary. These image variations were identified as a source of film tourism impacts.

Importantly, DMOs are presented as the stakeholder in the best position to understand and manage film tourism, and especially the destination image. The management needs to be community aligned, and the inclusive community needs to understand the consequences of their vision. The image management is to provide benefits for the community, while educating potential tourists of the actual experiences available at the destination. In this, three implications for DMOs have been presented: (1) to assess the stakeholders' ideal image; (2) to educate the community of the image consequences; and (3) to actively manage the image, inclusive of the organic images representing the destination. In the image management, the DMO should utilize the film images.

Overall, of crucial importance is the recognition that tourism can benefit a community, particularly rural communities often used for film settings. Yet, DMOs must cater for community needs rather than simply promote their destination based on a film image. A promoted image not aligned with the community's would likely attract an unwelcome type or number of tourists, leading to an unhappy community, and missing opportunities available now and in the future.

References

Basáñez, R. P., & Ingram, H. (2013). Film and tourism: the imagined place and the place of the imagined. *Worldwide Hospitality and Tourism Themes*, *5*(1), 39–54.

Beeton, S. (2001). Smiling for the camera: the influence of film audiences on a budget tourism destination. *Tourism, Culture and Communication*, *3*(1), 15–26.

Beeton, S. (2004). Rural tourism in Australia: has the gaze altered? Tracking rural images through film and tourism promotion. *International Journal of Tourism Research*, *6*(3), 125–135.

Beeton, S. (2005). *Film-induced tourism*. Clevedon: Channel View Publications.

Beeton, S. (2006). *Community development through tourism*. Collingwood: Landmarks Press.

Beeton, S. (2008). Location, location, location: film corporations' social responsibilities. *Journal of Travel and Tourism Marketing*, *24*(2), 107–114.

Beeton, S. (2010). The advance of film tourism. *Tourism and Hospitality Planning & Development*, *7*(1), 1–6.

Bolan, P., & Williams, L. (2008). The role of image in service promotion: focusing on the influence of film on consumer choice within tourism. *International Journal of Consumer Studies*, *32*(4), 382–390.

Buchmann, A., Moore, K., & Fisher, D. (2010). Experiencing film tourism: authenticity and fellowship. *Annals of Tourism Research*, *37*(1), 229–248.

Buhalis, D. (2000). Marketing the competitive destination of the future. *Tourism Management*, *21*(1), 97–116.

Busby, G., & Klug, J. (2001). Movie-induced tourism: the challenge of measurement and other issues. *Journal of Vacation Marketing*, *7*(4), 316–332.

Busby, G., & O'Neill, K. (2006). Cephallonia and *Captain Corelli's Mandolin*: the influence of literature and film on British visitors. *Acta Turistica*, *18*(1), 30–51.

Carl, D., Kindon, S., & Smith, K. (2007). Tourists' experiences of film locations: New Zealand as 'Middle-earth.' *Tourism Geographies*, *9*(1), 49–63

Chen, F., & Mele, C. (2017). Film-induced pilgrimage and contested heritage space in Taipei City. *City, Culture and Society, 9*, 31–38.

Cherifi, B., Smith, A., Maitland, R., & Stevenson, N. (2014). Destination images of non-visitors. *Annals of Tourism Research, 49*, 190–202.

Chiang, Y.-J., & Yeh, S.-S. (2011). The examination of factors influencing residents' perceptions and attitudes towards film-induced tourism. *African Journal of Business Management, 5*(13), 5371–5377.

Connell, J. (2005a). Toddlers, tourism and Tobermory: destination marketing issues and TV-induced tourism. *Tourism Management, 26*(3), 763–776.

Connell, J. (2005b). "What's the story in Balamory?": the impacts of a children's TV programme on small tourism enterprises on the Isle of Mull, Scotland. *Journal of Sustainable Tourism, 13*(2), 228–255.

Connell, J. (2012). Film tourism: evolution, progress and prospects. *Tourism Management, 33*(5), 1007–1029.

Connell, J., & Meyer, D. (2009). Balamory revisited: an evaluation of the screen tourism destination-tourist nexus. *Tourism Management, 30*(2), 194–207.

Croy, G., & Heitmann, S. (2011). Tourism and film. In Robinson, P. Heitmann, S., & Dieke, P. (Eds), *Research themes for tourism* (pp. 188–204). Oxon: CABI.

Croy, W. G. (2010). Planning for film tourism: active destination image management. *Tourism and Hospitality Planning and Development, 7*(1), 21–30.

Croy, W. G. (2011). Film tourism: sustained economic contributions to destinations. *Worldwide Hospitality and Tourism Themes, 3*(2), 159–164.

Croy, W. G., & Buchmann, A. (2009). Film-induced tourism in the high country: recreation and tourism contest. *Tourism Review International, 13*(2), 147–155.

Croy, W. G., & Walker, R. (2003). Rural tourism and film: issues for strategic regional development. In Hall, D., Roberts, L., & Mitchell, M. (Eds), *New directions in rural tourism* (pp. 115–133). Aldershot: Ashgate.

Cynthia, D., & Beeton, S. (2009). Supporting independent film production through tourism collaboration. *Tourism Review International, 13*(2), 113–120.

Freeman, R. E. (1984). *Strategic management: a stakeholder approach*. Boston: Pitman.

Frost, W. (2006). Braveheart-ed Ned Kelly: historic films, heritage tourism and destination image. *Tourism Management, 27*(2), 247–254.

Hao, X., & Ryan, C. (2013). Interpretation, film language and tourist destinations: a case study of Hisbiscus Town, China. *Annals of Tourism Research, 42*, 334–358.

Heitmann, S. (2010). Film tourism planning and development: questioning the role of stakeholders and sustainability. *Tourism and Hospitality Planning and Development, 7*(1), 31–46.

Hudson, S. (2011). Working together to leverage film tourism: collaboration between the film and tourism industries. *Worldwide Hospitality and Tourism Themes, 3*(2), 165–172.

Hudson, S., & Ritchie, J. R. B. (2006). Promoting destinations via film tourism: an empirical identification of supporting marketing initiatives. *Journal of Travel Research, 44*(3), 387–396.

Iwashita, C. (2006). Media representation of the UK as a destination for Japanese tourists: popular culture and tourism. *Tourist Studies, 6*(1), 59–77.

Karpovich, A. I. (2010). Theoretical approaches to film-motivated tourism. *Tourism and Hospitality Planning and Development, 7*(1), 7–20.

Kim, S. S., Agrusa, J., Lee, H., & Chon, K. (2007). Effects of Korean television dramas on the flow of Japanese tourists. *Tourism Management, 28*(5), 1340–1353.

Larson, M., Lundberg, C., & Lexhagen, M. (2013). Thirsting for vampire tourism: developing pop culture destinations. *Journal of Destination Marketing and Management, 2*(2), 74–84.

Loureiro, S. M. C., & Barbosa de Araujo, A. (2015). Negative film plot and tourists' image and intentions: the case of *City of God*. *Journal of Travel & Tourism Marketing, 32*(4), 352–365.

Martin-Jones, D. (2014). Film tourism as heritage tourism: Scotland, diaspora and *The Da Vinci Code* (2006). *New Review of Film and Television Studies, 12*(2), 156–177.

Mason, P., & Cheyne, J. (2000). Residents' attitudes to proposed tourism development. *Annals of Tourism Research, 27*(2), 391–411.

Mercille, J. (2005). Media effects on image: the case of Tibet. *Annals of Tourism Research, 32*(4), 1039–1055.

Mestre, R., del Rey, A., & Stanishevski, K. (2008). The image of Spain as tourist destination built through fictional cinema. *Journal of Travel and Tourism Marketing, 24*(2), 185–194.

Mordue, T. (2001). Performing and directing resident-tourist cultures in *Heartbeat* country. *Tourist Studies, 1*(3), 233–252.

Mordue, T. (2009). Television, tourism and rural life. *Journal of Travel and Tourism Research, 47*(3), 332–345.

O'Connor, N. (2011). How can the film-induced tourism phenomenon be sustainably managed? *Worldwide Hospitality and Tourism Themes, 3*(2), 87–90.

O'Connor, N., Flanagan, S., & Gilbert, D. (2008). The integration of film-induced tourism and destination branding in Yorkshire, UK. *International Journal of Tourism Research, 10*(5), 423–437.

Rejinders, S. (2011). *Places of the imagination: media, tourism, culture.* Farnham and Burlington: Ashgate.

Riley, R. W., Baker, D., & Van Doren, C. S. (1998). Movie induced tourism. *Annals of Tourism Research, 25*(4), 919–935.

Rittichainuwat, B., & Rattanaphinanchai, S. (2015). Applying a mixed method of quantitative and qualitative design in explaining the travel motivation of film tourists in visiting a film-shooting destination. *Tourism Management, 46*, 136–147.

Ryan, C. (2002). Equity, management, power sharing and sustainability-issues of the new tourism. *Tourism Management, 23*(1), 17–26.

Schofield, P. (1996). Cinematographic images of a city: alternative heritage tourism in Manchester. *Tourism Management, 17*(5), 333–340.

Shao, J., Li, X., Morrisson, A. M., & Wu, B. (2016). Social media micro-film marketing by Chinese destinations: the case of Shaoxing. *Tourism Management, 54*, 439–451.

Tooke, N., & Baker, M. (1996). Seeing is believing: the effect of film on visitor numbers to screened locations. *Tourism Management, 17*(2), 87–94.

Tuclea, C.-E., & Nistoreanu, P. (2011). How film and television programs can promote tourism and increase the competitiveness of tourist destination. *Cactus Tourism Journal, 2*(2), 25–30.

Wray, M., & Croy, W. G. (2015). Film tourism: integrated strategic tourism and regional economic development planning. *Tourism Analysis, 20*(3), 313–326.

Zhang, X., Ryan, C., & Cave, J. (2016). Residents, their use of a tourist facility and contribution to tourist ambience: narratives from a film tourism site in Beijing. *Tourism Management, 52*, 416–429.

34

FILM TOURISM COLLABORATIONS

A critical analysis of INTERREG destination development projects

Lena Eskilsson and Maria Månsson

Setting the scene: film tourism as a destination development tool

The popular culture tourism phenomenon that is in focus in this chapter is film tourism. The concept of film tourism relates to tourism induced directly or indirectly by a tourist destination being viewed on film or TV. It attracts people who are interested in audio visual media and who respond to the opportunity to visit a production location and to find more information about it whether actual or fictional (Eskilsson & Månsson, 2015). For the tourist it can either be the primary driver for visiting a destination or something that gives added value to a region or place (see for instance Beeton, 2016; Connell, 2012; Hudson & Ritchie, 2006; Månsson, 2011, 2015). The potential of film products for attracting tourists visiting a destination seen on screen is evident in well-known productions like *The Sound of Music* (1965) in Salzburg, *Notting Hill* (1999) in London, or the film and TV series *Wallander* in Ystad, but also in more recent productions such as *Downton Abbey*, *Harry Potter*, and *The Bridge*. During the last years, there has been a growing interest in attracting film productions to different places, regions, and countries for economic purposes.

Films, film products, and following film tourism are all examples of popular culture as well as being phenomena related to culture in general. They are also increasingly connected to regional economic growth. The reason for this is that "culture" is more and more presented by politicians and other public actors as a solution for social and economic development. However, research has shown that evaluating especially the economic impact of culture is not an easy task (see Lindqvist, 2013). Even though there are difficulties in evaluating the outcomes of these projects there is still a "hype" among destination developers to search for local film products to exploit for touristic purposes. The hope is that these projects will create an economic growth at the destination. There has therefore been a growth in the number of different projects and collaborations that tries to harness the potential that films and film tourism might have on a place. A type of film tourism project that has emerged are EU-funded INTERREG projects, with the focus of regional development. During the last decade, tourism has clearly become an integrated element in several regional development projects and strategies supported by the EU. The tourism sector is now in this context seen as an important contributor to regional economies, by increasing incomes and offering job opportunities (Nilsson, Eskilsson, & Ek, 2010).

Film tourism is known in research and by practitioners but the knowledge when it comes to different stakeholders' actual work with these issues is less established. Destination development is complex work, characterized by different agendas and interests. The question then is who are the different stakeholders that take part in these film tourism development projects, how do they actually collaborate, and what is actually possible to achieve? The aim of this chapter is therefore to critically analyze film tourism development projects, especially the selection of stakeholders, the project process, and outcomes in EU-funded INTERREG projects.

Disciplinary underpinnings: film tourism stakeholders

In this section stakeholder theory will be approached in relation to destination development projects and more specifically film tourism development projects and its stakeholders. One of the seminal texts about stakeholder theory was written by Freeman in 1984. In this book Freeman discussed from a strategic management perspective, organizations with different stakeholders. He concluded that a stakeholder to an organization is a group or individual who can affect or is affected by the achievement of the organization's objectives (Freeman, 2010, p. 46). Freeman had a firm perspective and in his case stakeholders were, for example, customers, owners, competitors, government, and suppliers to mention just a few. Some of these are obviously also relevant when exploring destination development stakeholders. According to Freeman, it is first, important to identify who the relevant stakeholders are and what they add to this particular case. Second, different processes to handle the relationship with the different stakeholders must be in place and, finally, a discussion of what all the different stakeholders add to the process must be negotiated (Freeman, 2010).

The organization-centric perspective has later been expanded to also include, for example, destinations. Sautter and Leissen (1999) as well as Ryan (2002) applied stakeholder theory to tourism in order to discuss the different stakeholders that are in play for tourism planning of the development of a destination. Instead of the firm as in Freeman's case, Sautter and Leissen (1999) put *tourism planners* in focus. They argue therefore that "tourism planners need to have a full appreciation of all the persons or groups who have interests in the planning, processes, delivery and/or outcomes of the tourism service" (Sautter & Leissen, 1999, p. 315). From a tourism planners' perspective, they identified the following stakeholders: local businesses, residents, activist groups, tourists, national business chains, competitors, government, and employees. Line and Wang (2016) addressed stakeholders in tourism from a multi-stakeholder approach. They identified similar groups with each of their own subgroup of stakeholders: community entities, tourists, local industry, competitors, and intermediaries. In many cases the similar stakeholders are identified for the process.

Even though there are many different stakeholders addressed, it is often regarded to be the destination management organization (DMO) that is in charge of the planning and marketing of a destination. It is the DMO that is considered to have the power as well as the resources to drive the process of tourism development and marketing (Buhalis, 2000, p. 98). However, Touhino and Konu (2014) argue that, on the other hand, it is not necessarily the DMO that is in charge of the development of a destination. They found in their research that it is highly connected to the context and can vary from place to place. For instance, they showed that some destinations might not even have a DMO and it was in these cases the public sector, such as different governmental organizations, that drove the process. So, all development processes are dependent on the context, which is important for identifying the stakeholders. It is therefore vital from a tourism planning perspective to identify on a destination level who all these different stakeholders are. Moreover, it is important to also keep in mind, according to Komppula

(2016), that organizations consist of people and the outcome of a tourism planning project is affected by these different individuals within organizations. That is to say, peoples' individual skills and knowledge within these organizations are vital as they have great impact on the process. So when various stakeholders create a network, a key aspect of a successful destination development (Haugland, Ness, Grønseth, & Aarstad, 2011), it is also important to have the different individuals within each stakeholder in mind.

So far, stakeholders have been discussed in general for tourism development but what happens when stakeholders in film tourism development projects are in focus? Many different stakeholders need to collaborate in the making of films and other media products as well as in developing and marketing the destination. Heitman (2010) considered the following five partners as crucial for destination development focusing on film tourism: the destination management organization (DMO), tourism businesses, film industry, tourists, and community. Thus, most of the stakeholders are the same as the ones mentioned before in other tourism development planning projects. However, for film tourism projects a whole new sector is added and that is the film industry. Out of the five stakeholders, Heitman (2010) points out DMOs, community, tourists, and film industry as the key stakeholders. The DMO is important since they are managing the different stakeholders in marketing of destinations, the community since they are affected by tourist activities, the tourists with their motivations and expectations, and, finally the film industry who are in charge of putting the destination on screen in a film or TV production. This is a disparate group of stakeholders and having the film industry as a stakeholder is complicated since they are often not particularly interested in tourism planning and development. For them the destination is a location in which to make a film and not a tourism destination, which means that the aims and goals for the different stakeholders vary (cf. Heitman, 2010). However, it is stressed that DMOs and the film industry need to collaborate in order to create sustainable tourism planning. But that it is easier said than done because even if different collaborations are needed between stakeholders in order to create fruitful collaborations for destination development, this is not always obvious for all stakeholders in play. For example, some tourism organizations are still unfamiliar with focusing on film as a potential destination marketing activity. It was revealed in a study about the work of European destination marketing organizations that although 67 percent had access to film products in their region only 38 percent exploited these opportunities (Di Cesare, Salandra, & Craparotta, 2012). Furthermore, this study showed that uncertainty of who should be doing what and a lack of knowledge of the film sector from a tourism perspective had a negative impact on potential collaborations. Thus, there is a need to enhance the understanding of different sectors in order to create meaningful collaborations among stakeholders.

In the discussion so far, it is a single destination that has been in focus, but in our case study it is rather multiple destinations that collaborate in a tourism development project, namely an INTERREG project. These types of development projects are interesting as the funding works as a catalyst for bringing different stakeholders together from both private and public organization on both a local, national, and international level (Lemmetyinen, 2010). Although this is a rather common type of project there is limited research about these EU-funded tourism development projects. Lemmetyinen (2010) explored the value that different stakeholders got from being part of an INTERREG project. She concluded that the closer the cooperation was among the different partners in the project, the better were the possibilities for learning and knowledge exchange within the project. Moreover, the key value for the stakeholders were the sharing of expertise, know-how, and other resources, which then could improve the competitiveness of small and micro-sized enterprises (Lemmetyinen, 2010). Nilsson et al. (2010) analyzed tourism development in cross-border regions in the Baltic Sea area. One of the conclusions was that the visions and goals of most tourism-related INTERREG programs share the "classical" themes known from regional development elsewhere, such as economic development, prosperity, and improved employment. Furthermore, like in many tourism-related visions they are clearly growth oriented, with aims related to measuring and increased visibility (Nilsson et al., 2010).

Next, the different stakeholders as discussed in this section will be critically analyzed in our case study with regards to stakeholder selection, work process, and outcomes.

Methodology

Case study context

In this chapter we critically analyze a film tourism INTERREG project, one of several EU-funded projects, with its different collaborations and motivations. The empirical material has been collected in liaison with an INTERREG IVC-project called *EuroScreen*. The financing came from the European Union's Regional Development Fund, which has as an overarching aim to help regions of Europe work together to share experiences and good practice in areas of innovation and the knowledge economy. The objective of the INTERREG IVC program was to improve the effectiveness of regional policies and instruments. The main idea was to create an exchange of experiences among partners who then implement this knowledge locally to develop their own local and regional policies (INTERREG IVC, 2016).

EuroScreen was a three-year project (2012–2014) with the aim to align policies between the screen sector and the tourism industry. The *EuroScreen* partnership consisted of nine organizations across eight regions all over Europe. The different collaborating organizations represented film commissions (organizations that attract and support film productions to regions), municipalities, regional development agencies, and Lund University as an academic partner. The authors of this chapter represented Lund University and had as academic experts a slightly different role in the project. The role of Lund University was more of a partner than a stakeholder since the university had no agenda of their own when it came to tourism development and policy-making.

Methodological approach

Our methodology has a qualitative approach and different methods were applied during the empirical work. The material consists of cases, policies, and practices, which were collected through questionnaires and interviews with the organizations and their stakeholders from the participating regions as well as participatory observations from meetings within the partnership.

At the very start of the project, questionnaires with semi-structured questions were sent to all partners in order to gather the organizations' and their stakeholders' experiences within the field. The questionnaire was divided into four parts: (1) overview of the organization's experience of screen tourism activities with a special focus on marketing and co-operation activities; (2) examples of campaigns, methods, and techniques used to measure screen tourism effects; (3) wider examples of campaigns with partner countries; as well as (4) interesting worldwide examples. After analyzing the questionnaires, complementary interviews with the different stakeholders identified by the organizations took place (see also Månsson & Eskilsson, 2013). The questionnaires and following interviews revealed existing cases, practices, and policies within the field which we could explore and analyze further.

During the three years *EuroScreen* was running, the partnership had two annual meetings, each lasting two to three days and hosted by the different participating organizations. These meetings consisted of discussions, workshops, and presentations by participating organizations as well as by local practitioners and stakeholders. At these meetings, we took the role as participatory observers, following the discussions and taking detailed meeting process notes.

Our participatory observations focused mainly on three aspects: (1) the film tourism arguments put forward by the different stakeholders; (2) input regarding impact and measurability for destinations from the different stakeholders; and (3) collaborations, policies, and practices. We especially focused on how the discussions went, who was active, and what was important/not important to the attending stakeholders. The notes taken contained both tacit and explicit information, as is common in participant observations (DeWalt & DeWalt, 2002; Silverman, 2001). In the qualitative thematic analysis of the meetings, our unofficial notes were complemented by the official meeting minutes.

In the final year of the project, consultancy firms were engaged to develop more practitioner-oriented outcomes in the form of a film tourism impact measurement tool and a "good practice" handbook. We then took part as participatory and interactive observers in the whole process starting from the call, bidding and selection process, work in progress, and presentation at the *EuroScreen* final conference in London 2014.

Implications for popular culture tourism

Stakeholders in an INTERREG film tourism development project

The *EuroScreen* project that is critically analyzed in this chapter had a range of different stakeholders, as mentioned above (for more details see Månsson & Eskilsson, 2013). One group of stakeholders came from the film sector, namely *film commissions*. The lead partner was Film London, which is the UK capital's film and media agency. Their aim is to work with all the screen industries to sustain, promote, and develop London as a major international production and film cultural capital. Another film commission was also involved in the project and that was Apulia Film Commission situated in south-east Italy, they play a central role in their local audio visual sector.

The next groups of stakeholders were four different regional *development agencies* from Bucharest, Maribor, Rzeszow, and Malaga. Bucharest-Ilfov Regional Development Agency from Rumania is an intermediate body for the implementation of the Regional Operational Programme for Regional Development in their region. Maribor Development Agency in Slovenia is a similar organization, which is also responsible for the co-ordination of regional development activities in their region. Rzeszow Regional Development Agency from south-east Poland is an organization that supports the development of the Podkarpackie province, and is responsible for economic development policy and implementation. The final development agency in this project was Promalaga, which is also a public company. Promalaga has strong expertise of both tourism and film sectors and works with development in these areas.

The three final stakeholders in the *EuroScreen* project had different backgrounds. They were Fondazzjoni Temi Zammi from Malta, a not-for-profit foundation that operates in the field of, for example, skills development relating to tourism and audio visual sectors. Then there was the municipality of Ystad, a small local public authority situated in the very south of Sweden. Ystad City Council has been developing activities that link film and tourism for several years. Finally, there was one academic partner, Lund University, also from the south of Sweden. These above mentioned stakeholders were in some sense the official partners in the *EuroScreen* project; however, there were also other partners involved. The actual writing of the application for bidding for the project was done by two private partner organizations who later became involved in the project as consultants, contracted to be in charge of the administration and financial side of the project. It was in many cases also these two organizations who recruited the different stakeholders for the project, which has implications for the selection criteria and the process of the project. It is then interesting to wonder about the choice of stakeholders. The consultancy firms had contacts in the culture and media sector as well as great experience of EU-funded projects. However, what is obvious in the selection of stakeholders in this project is a lack of organizations directly involved in tourism and especially destination marketing organizations. This is interesting because DMOs are seen as in the forefront of tourism development planning (cf. Buhalis, 2000) and still they are absent as a stakeholder in project *EuroScreen*. This project was therefore not a tourism led destination development project. The consultancy firms had a strong position in the first two years of the project in a leadership role, although formally the film commission Film London was the led partner. During the project phase these roles altered and Film London became both the formal and informal leader. The presence of film commissions for tourism development projects is also present in another INTERREG project dealing with film tourism; however, in this case both film commissions and tourism organizations were involved (Filmby Arhus, 2012).

The leading role of a film commission in *EuroScreen* is in line with a current trend with film commissions' involvement in tourism planning and development. Film commissions used to have a production-specific focus, mainly trying to attract film productions and neglecting the effect a film production could have on a region in a more touristic context (Hudson, 2011). However, that has now changed and besides a focus on impact on jobs created, growth in local tax revenue, new business activities, and expenditure along the way while making the film, film commissions are now actively involved with film tourism as it is seen as having a long-term economic benefit (cf. Cynthia & Beeton, 2009).

There are roughly 300 film commissions globally who are members of The Association of Film Commissioners International (Afci, 2013). It is estimated that twice as many exist, since not all film commissions are members of this organization. The numbers of film production hubs are also growing and they all aim at attracting film productions to their specific region (Becheri & Maggiore, 2013). The number of film commissions has grown rapidly in the last two decades. For example, in the late 1990s there were three film commissions in Italy and since then another 27 have emerged (Becheri & Maggiore, 2013). Since they are all aiming at attracting film productions to their specific region, the competition is fierce (see Månsson & Eskilsson, 2013). Worth noting is also the growing interest for film tourism by film commissionaires as seen in the *EuroScreen* project but also by the Cineposium (yearly film commission conference) organized by the Association of Film Commissioners International in 2015 focusing purely on film tourism (Afci, 2015). The interest by film commissions and other stakeholders in film tourism is due to film being seen as a fast-growing creative industry that will generate revenue and growth to the local economies. The film commission is therefore to some extent a new partner in the tourism destination development as they are becoming more and more involved in film tourism development projects and their role as a stakeholder thus needs to be more strongly emphasized. Heitman (2010) addressed the film sector but not the film commission as a separate group of stakeholders in film tourism development projects.

One conclusion is that the model by Heitman (2010) needs to be complemented with a film commission as a new and active stakeholder in film tourism development projects (see Figure 34.1). What can be concluded is that film commissions had a driving role in the *EuroScreen* project. The film focus was also strong for many of the other stakeholders in the project. For example, for the municipality of Ystad it was people with film focus who attended project meetings and

Figure 34.1 Film tourism stakeholders for destination development.

not those working with tourism. This rather unbalanced mix of stakeholders had an impact on the process of the project as will be further discussed below.

Critical factors for process and outcomes in an INTERREG film tourism development project

One of the main findings in this chapter is the different and often conflicting starting points and agendas from the different stakeholders in these projects. A reason for this is, for example, the diverse knowledge base that causes a prolonged initiation phase. In project *EuroScreen* there was, for example, a selection criterion for the different stakeholders based on their existing experience of film tourism. A few regions were considered as being in the forefront of film tourism (Apulia, London, and Ystad). However, that all depends on how film tourism experience is defined. In this case, experience of attracting film productions were highly regarded as film tourism experience. The second category of stakeholders had some film tourism experience (Malaga and Malta) and then there were three less advanced regions in terms of film tourism (Bucharest, Maribor, and Rzeszow). It is important that a diverse range of stakeholders collaborate in film tourism development projects, however organizations' sometimes weak knowledge of the phenomenon in play as well as of each other's work created problems in the beginning. Since there was no tourism organization included as stakeholder there was a lack of understanding of tourism, the tourists and what they search for, and about destination marketing and development among the stakeholders. At the same time, there was a weak understanding among some of the partners of what film commissioners are and the work they do. Moreover, the disparate understanding of film tourism was highly visible in the answers to the questionnaires that were sent out to all stakeholders in the beginning. In one of the questions regarding films and media products from the regions that could be used for touristic purposes, a response from one of the stakeholders was the commercials they had made themselves to promote their region. As it turned out another stakeholder did not even have the necessary resources of films and TV productions made in the region to develop tourism with. Thus, in the beginning a substantial amount of time was spent on getting everybody involved and to some extent create a common understanding. This became evident in the report that was written, which showed how initially the aim was a short introduction to film tourism but the project had to grow to create a common knowledge ground. It can therefore be concluded that when stakeholders in projects are on very different learning levels it has a profound impact on the project, especially when it comes to time spent to get everybody on the same level.

It was not just the different levels of experience that had an initial restricting factor to the project. An integral part of INTERREG projects is learning and knowledge exchange. According to Lemmetyinen (2010), it is important that there is a flow of information and knowledge within the project. The information and knowledge exchange in project *EuroScreen* was rather one-sided to begin with due to the disparate knowledge. Moreover, the more knowledgeable partners had to share knowledge with the other partners. The value for each stakeholder is also dependent on the leaders of the project. In this project, it was a film commission that was the lead partner. It therefore became a natural focus on films and film production and locations although the aim of the project was to develop tourism of already existing products. Thus, the mix of stakeholders also has an impact on the focus of the project since they all had different agendas for participating. Although there was a prolonged initiation phase, a network was created: a key aspect of successful destination development (Haugland et al., 2011). Thus, the project had to overcome many hurdles to begin with in order get everybody to work in the same direction.

The idea of *measurability* is another critical complicating factor since there are conflicting understandings of what is possible to measure within the collaborating organizations. The lack of DMOs and other stakeholders with knowledge of tourism was striking in the discussions about how to measure tourism effects. Especially interesting in this context was the work with one of the two promised final outcomes of the project, the construction of an "impact development tool" for measuring film tourism. In the end this task was finally redefined as "assessing the impact of screen productions on tourism and brand value." In the following external call for proposals the task was further narrowed down to developing and testing a quantitative methodology that could allow regions and cities to quantify the "location placement value" of productions filming in the destination beyond the primary production spent and the return on investment/media value generated.

Eight organizations took part in the bidding process, and after a ranking process, a consultancy firm won the bid. The different stakeholders in *EuroScreen* were, however, not united in this decision, with the not-for-profit organization and academic partner ranking the applying academic organizations with more research-oriented methodological approaches, before the consultancy firms with more product-oriented outcomes. It was, however, clearly stated by the lead partner and private partner organizations that they wanted a sellable product that could be used for quantitative measuring. The appointed consultancy firm developed a location placement value formula based on a methodology that analyzed a social media dataset of user-generated, location-based commentary. It was presented in terms of the minimum equivalent online advertising spend generated by 12 productions filmed at four *EuroScreen* locations (London, Malta, Apulia, and Ystad). The dataset used did not, however, say anything about actual visiting or travelling to the destinations as a result of film productions. In many cases, there was no connection at all between writing about a movie and being a film tourist and travelling to the destination as a result of this, as in the following examples of quotes from the dataset: "*I am Kurt Wallander*" (retrieved from Flickr, destination Ystad) and "Wait, they shot in Mdina? Damn! I was back there in October and never even knew they filmed in Malta" (retrieved from reddit, destination Malta). The question is what the location placement value formula can actually say about measuring film *tourism*. It might, however, to some extent "measure" *destination awareness* as a result of film productions.

In film tourism projects contexts there is also a *search for best cases* that can be used as role models for destinations. The other promised final outcome of the *EuroScreen* project, a handbook in the form of a manual, is a publication that collates and presents examples of best practice with the aim of sharing best practice and insight with other EU regions. This raises questions of *transferability*; to what extent can one best practice be duplicated to another place with different local characteristics. Another interesting aspect is that the *EuroScreen* manual has as a main aim to serve as a valuable resource for screen tourism to be utilized by development agencies, film commissions, municipalities, policy makers, and NGOs wishing to maximize the economic and cultural benefits resulting from screen tourism. This reflects once again the absence of DMOs in the whole project process.

Concluding remarks

This chapter has contributed to enhanced knowledge, from a theoretical point of view, about the different stakeholders in film tourism development projects. By exploring the INTERREG project *EuroScreen*, it is evident that there is a new stakeholder that has emerged in film tourism development projects and that is film commissions. It is a stakeholder with great knowledge of film and TV series in a region, a knowledge that could be turned into a resource for development by tourism organizations. Thus, when looking at stakeholders in play for film tourism development, film commissions are an integral part of the process. However, the different and often conflicting starting points and agendas from the different stakeholders in these projects might cause a prolonged initiation phase. A reason for this is, for example, the diverse knowledge base and a lack of understanding for each other's work. Thus, it is important that a diverse range of partners collaborate in film tourism development projects, but organizations' sometimes weak knowledge of the phenomenon in play as well as of each other's work creates problems in the beginning. For those working with film tourism it is therefore vital to carefully select the different stakeholders in a project including the individuals in them because it might have a restricting factor on things being able to be accomplished within a certain time frame. The idea of measurability is another complicating factor since there are conflicting understandings of what is possible to measure within collaborating organizations. There is also a search for best cases that can be used as role models, which totally neglects local characteristics. This raises questions of transferability; to what extent can one best practice be duplicated to another place. Thus, there are many issues that have an impact on a film tourism development project such as *EuroScreen* that can be critically discussed. However, what can be concluded is that projects such as these can make a difference to single destinations even though there are to begin with limited knowledge and conflicting agendas with, for example, new policies being developed, local and international networks created, and possibilities for new tourism development.

References

Association of Film Commissioners International (Afci). (2013). Retrieved from www.afci.org/about-afci/history.
Association of Film Commissioners International (Afci). (2015). Retrieved from www.afci.org/news/afci-awards-cineposium-2015-barcelona.

Becheri, E., & Maggiore, G. (2013). *XVIII edizione Rapporto Sul Turismo Italiano 2011–2012*. Milan, Italy: FrancoAngell.

Beeton, S. (2016). *Film-induced tourism* (2nd ed.). Clevedon, Buffalo, Toronto: Channel View Publications.

Buhalis, D. (2000). Marketing the competitive destination of the future. *Tourism Management, 21*(1), 97–116.

Connell, J. (2012). Film tourism: Evolution, progress and prospects. *Tourism Management, 33*(5), 1007–1029.

Cynthia, D., & Beeton, S. (2009). Supporting independent film production through tourism collaboration. *Tourism Review International, 13*(2), 113–119.

DeWalt, K. M., & DeWalt, B. R. (2002). *Participant observation: a guide for fieldworkers*. Walnut Creek, CA: AltaMira Press.

Di Cesare, F., Salandra, A., & Craparotta, E. (2012). Films and audiovisual potentiality in tourism destination promotion: A European perspective. *Tourism Review International, 16*(2), 101–111.

Eskilsson, L., & Månsson, M. (2015). Film tourism and literature tourism. In S. M. Dahlgaard Park (Eds.), *The SAGE encyclopedia of quality and the service economy* (pp. 236–238). Thousand Oaks, CA: Sage.

Filmby Aarhus. (2012). *Experience films in real life: A handbook on film tourism*. Retrieved from www.north seascreen.eu/production-news.cfm.

Freeman, R. E. (2010). *Strategic management: A stakeholder approach*. Cambridge: Cambridge University Press.

Haugland, S., Ness, H., Grønseth, B.-O., & Aarstad, J. (2011). Development of tourism destinations: An integrated multilevel perspective. *Annals of Tourism Research, 38*(1), 268–290.

Heitmann, S. (2010). Film tourism planning and development: Questioning the role of stakeholders and sustainability. *Tourism and Hospitality Planning & Development, 7*(1), 31–46.

Hudson, S. (2011). Working together to leverage film tourism: Collaboration between the film and tourism industries. *Worldwide Hospitality and Tourism Themes, 3*(2), 165–172.

Hudson, S., & Ritchie, B. (2006). Promoting destinations via film tourism: An empirical identification of supporting marketing initiatives. *Journal of Travel Research, 44*(4), 387–396.

INTERREG IVC. (2016). Retrieved from www.interreg4c.eu/programme/index.html, 20160924.

Komppula, R. (2016). The role of different stakeholders in destination development. *Tourism Review, 71*(1), 67–76.

Lemmetyinen, A. (2010). The role of the DMO in creating value in EU-funded tourism projects. *Scandinavian Journal of Hospitality and Tourism, 10*(2), 129–152.

Lindqvist, K. (2013). Making sense of financial incentive as a policy tool for the independent arts sector. *Public Policy and Administration, 28*(4), 404–422.

Line, N. D., & Wang, Y. (2016). A multi-stakeholder market oriented approach to destination marketing. *Journal of Destination Marketing & Management*, http://dx.doi.org/10.1016/j.jdmm.2016.03.003i.

Månsson, M. (2011). Mediatized tourism. *Annals of Tourism Research, 38*(4), 1634–1652.

Månsson, M. (2015). *Mediatized tourism: The convergence of media and tourism performances*. PhD dissertation. Lund University: Lund.

Månsson, M., & Eskilsson, L. (2013). *EuroScreen: The attraction of screen destinations. Baseline report assessing best practice*. Rzeszów, Poland.

Nilsson, J. H., Eskilsson, L., & Ek, R. (2010). Creating cross-border destinations: Interreg programmes and regionalisation in the Baltic Sea area. *Scandinavian Journal of Hospitality and Tourism, 19*(2), 153–172.

Ryan, C. (2002). Equity, management, power sharing and sustainability: Issues of the "new tourism." *Tourism Management, 23*(1), 17–26.

Sautter, E. T., & Leissen, B. (1999). Managing stakeholders: A tourism planning model. *Annals of Tourism Research, 26*(2), 312–328.

Silverman, D. (2001). *Interpreting qualitative data: Methods for analyzing talk, text and interaction*. London: Sage.

Touhino, A., & Konu, H. (2014). Local stakeholders' view about destination management: Who are leading tourism development? *Tourism Review, 69*(3), 202–215.

35

GROWING COMPETITION FOR SCREEN TOURISTS ACTIVATES NEW DESTINATION MARKETING TACTICS

Valeriya Radomskaya

Setting the scene

Contemporary tourism is very diverse. Tourists are encouraged to explore the most incredible places on, under, or even above the earth (Lemelin et al., 2013). The opportunities provided by modern technologies push the boundaries of the travel market further each year, helping the market expand its product range (Rifai, 2015). As it expands, the travel sector interacts with other industries. A good example of such expansion is the giant entertainment industry, which has developed rapidly with the help of communication media. PwC's *Cities of Opportunity* report from 2015 shows that 30 big urban cities alone are estimated to spend a staggering $184 billion on the entertainment and related media by 2018 with employment at 6.3 million people. Tourists are among the increasing numbers of those in the entertainment and media-driven audiences. Such travel is triggered not only by the real-world images but also by the images from the imaginary worlds (Reijnders, 2011; Shandley, Jamal, & Tanase, 2006). Strange though it may sound, people travelling to such locations are willing to enter the imaginary places of fiction through real places. Jean Baudrillard (1994), to a certain extent, has explained this paradox between reality and simulacra in his work on simulacra and simulation, which speaks of relationships among reality, symbols, and modern society. This paradox in turn has created a phenomenon such as popular culture tourism.

Popular culture tourism started to evolve in the early 1930s, with films causing tourists to rush to different film locations (Roesch, 2009, p. 8). The potential of popular culture to attract tourists was recognized not only by the tourism industry. The American entrepreneur Walter Elias Disney opened his first Disneyland in 1955. It all started with a desire to build a tourist attraction to entertain fans who wished to visit his production studios in Burbank. Inspired by his many screen fans, and his daughter, Walt Disney created a symbol of modern popular culture – Disneyland, the world's most famous theme park. The symbiosis between early popular culture and tourism was well described by Ritzer and Liska (1997), and Shaw and Williams (2004) in their works about McDisneyfication and tourism.

Academic studies that concentrate entirely on on-screen tourism have a shorter history, emerging in the early 1990s (Connell, 2012). As the connection between popular culture and tourism strengthens with every blockbuster and bestseller released, more research papers have appeared. Works explaining a variety of phenomena, such as on-screen tourism (Beeton, 2010; Chua & Iwabuchi, 2008; Larson, Lundberg, & Lexhagen, 2013; Roesch, 2009), literary tourism (Fawcett & Cormack, 2001; Hoppen, Brown, & Fyall, 2014), and music tourism (Gibson & Connell, 2005, 2007a) have attracted the attention of numerous tourism stakeholders. It is hardly surprising to find destination marketing organizations all around the world becoming increasingly interested in the subject of popular culture tourism. Despite being a relatively new element of tourism activity, high-profile DMOs utilize screen tours in inbound marketing campaigns, most notably, as Connell (2012) points out, the UK, USA, Australia, New Zealand, and Korea. While DMOs through trial and error are trying to come up with the best marketing solutions to secure their destination's attractiveness, researchers are identifying different marketing strategies (Croy, 2010; Hudson & Ritchie, 2006; Riley & Van Doren, 1992).

Aims

Hudson and Ritchie's (2006) study of DMOs revealed that nearly all destinations could be more proactive with on-screen tourism. With new movies, TV shows, and animation being released every year, many in tourism find themselves involved and busy in their development: travellers are busy discovering new destinations or re-discovering old ones, while tourism stakeholders are busy ensuring customer satisfaction. Given the relatively short longevity of most screen tours, the DMOs battle for every customer, to ensure that maximum profits are obtained. The growing competition for screen tourists activates new destination marketing tactics.

The study presented here is part of a research program on the popular culture phenomenon. It explores a variety of new marketing tools used by DMOs to attract screen tourists, with special attention paid to marketing tools that come with advanced media technologies. The focus is on the actions of the public organizations responsible for tourism development at the destination: what new strategies do they adopt and how do they balance the place identity with the destination image constructed by the movies and TV shows.

Methodology

Which strategy can be adopted depends on the unique character of the place. To make the research more comprehensive, a map of a representative range of DMOs was constructed to show a geochart of the study. For more details, please refer to the "findings" section of the study, below.

Using the purposive sampling technique, ten DMOs were selected, ranging from big state-run organizations to more local entities. The chosen sampling technique is a type of non-probability sampling method that is most effective when one needs to study certain units or cases "based on a specific purpose rather than randomly" (Tashakkori & Teddlie, 2003, p. 713). The purposive sample is designed "to pick a small number of cases that will yield the most information about a particular phenomenon" (Teddlie & Yu, 2007, p. 83). In this case, the researcher was looking at active public organization responsible for tourism development whose marketing strategy utilized on-screen tourism. Among these organizations, only the DMOs capable of illustrating the use of advanced destination marketing techniques were chosen to participate in the study.

The methodology used in this study places a strong emphasis on non-reactive data collection techniques. The non-reactive data collection procedures are especially suitable for collecting data from large pre-existing databases in order to generate new information. Luckily, the Internet provides an ocean of opportunities for non-reactive data collection. Therefore, to obtain data on the destination marketing techniques, a specific type of online research method (ORM) has been used. ORMs are most efficient when dealing with non-reactive data collection. Kozinets (2009) describes the ORM as a natural observational technique used to gain an unbiased point of view. Online content analysis was the main type of ORM used in this study. Online content analysis or online textual analysis is a specific type of online research technique that is used to describe and make inferences about online material through systematic coding, classification, and interpretation. Online content analysis is, in most cases, a non-reactive and unobtrusive method of data collection.

Fielding, Lee, and Blank (2008, p. 8), reflecting on how we continuously leave more digital traces behind as we communicate, note that the world "is increasingly becoming self-documenting and self-archiving." Most public sector organizations keep their action plans accessible to the public by posting them online. By analyzing these posts, the researcher can obtain a valuable insight into the recent advances and potential marketing activities of the DMOs. To find these posts, the researcher methodically examined several types of online sources: corporate websites, government websites and digital archives, major news organizations' websites, web-based tourism discussion boards, news blogs, social media, journal papers, and other research materials.

Findings

In a highly competitive environment such as the tourism market, tourism stakeholders lead a relentless battle for clients. Every season they are forced to come up with new business strategies to win back old customers and bring in new ones. To achieve this, DMOs use a variety of marketing techniques. The variety of marketing strategies and ideas is a principle most successful businesses adopt in order to succeed. Variety is crucial to understanding consumer markets, which are diverse and multicultural (Thomas, 2004). Variety in marketing approaches provides organizations with necessary tools to address current consumer demands (Torres & Murray, 2000). Understanding customers' needs and improving one's tourism business strategy based on that knowledge, gives an organization an advantage over its competitors.

There are many interesting techniques to choose from in tourism marketing, especially when it comes to promoting a film location. There exists an ample number of studies on location marketing describing all kinds of marketing approaches (Beeton, 2005, 2008; Croy, 2010; Hudson & Ritchie, 2006; Lee, Scott, & Kim 2008; Vagionis & Loumioti, 2011). By reviewing academic papers and analyzing strategies that utilize on-screen tourism, a list of most commonly used marketing methods was created. More than 20 destination marketing websites have been analyzed

Table 35.1 Traditional destination marketing methods

- Joining film commissions that help with location scouting
- Offering grants and tax credits, as well as other incentives to encourage studios to use the location
- Mastering tourism product placement
- Engaging the film's stars to promote the film location
- Inviting travel specialists, travel writers, and other media to the film location
- Selling film memorabilia and maintaining film icons/sites/scenes/sets to maintain authenticity
- Making film festivals
- Promoting film tours and film walks, and creating film and site maps for tourists

to ensure that these methods have a practical application. The same approach was later used to identify the advanced destination marketing tactics. The created list is presented in Table 35.1. This information served as a baseline for future comparisons when identifying the advanced marketing methods.

Traditional destination marketing methods are widely used by all levels of DMOs. These methods have a stable reputation for attracting a certain number of tourists. The marketing budget based on this approach does not take long to prepare, and the costs are well known. While it is not always a budget-friendly approach, the risk factor is relatively low, as opposed to risks that come with new marketing tactics that are yet to prove effective.

While many DMOs rely heavily on traditional marketing methods, some adopt new approaches. The new marketing methods do not necessarily substitute the existing ones, but rather add depth to an existing marketing campaign by targeting new audiences (Table 35.2). Unfortunately, it is beyond the scope of this study to cover all newly applied marketing techniques, instead, the focus of this study is on five advanced destination marketing tactics inspired by growing on-screen tourism.

DMOs engage in a variety of marketing activities both before and after release of a film (Hudson & Ritchie, 2006). That is why the selected advanced tactics cover all three stages of film production. Every chosen tactic complies with following criteria, as shown in Figure 35.1.

Using the purposive sampling method, 10 DMOs were selected to illustrate the use of advanced destination marketing tactics (Table 35.3). This sample meets the following requirements:

- it ranges from big state-run organizations to more local entities;
- it represents different parts of the world; and
- all DMOs in the sample use on-screen tourism-inspired tactics in their current marketing policy.

Table 35.2 Advanced destination marketing tactics

Tactics	Stages		
	pre-production	Production	Post-production
• Using digital travel content and computer-generated environments for location promotion	+		+
• Focusing on user-generated content	+	+	+
• Making films on filmmaking at a destination		+	+
• Mastering collaborative marketing	+	+	+
• Creating "camera-ready" communities	+		+

Figure 35.1 The three stages of film production.

Table 35.3 List of 10 DMOs

1. Visit Britain and Visit England	www.visitbritain.com, www.visitbritain.org
2. The Columbus Convention and Visitors Bureau	Official website: http://visitcolumbusga.com/ and http://columbus.locationshub.com/search_results.aspx
3. TEXAS Convention and Visitors Bureaus	The Film Friendly Texas (FFTX) Website: http://gov.texas.gov/
4. I amsterdam	Official portal website of the City of Amsterdam: www.iamsterdam.com
5. Turespaña	Official website: www.tourspain.es
6. The Bermuda Tourism Authority	Official website: www.gotobermuda.com
7. Tourism New Zealand	Official website: www.tourismnewzealand.com
8. The City of Sydney	In collaboration with Screen NSW, www.screen.nsw.gov.au/. Official website: www.cityofsydney.nsw.gov.au
9. The Ministry of Tourism, Government of India	In collaboration with the LA India Film Council, www.laindiafilmcouncil.org. Official website: http://tourism.gov.in/
10. NYC & Company	Official website: www.nycgo.com/

The geochart in Figure 35.2 shows that the selection represents different parts of the world (Americas, Europe, Asia, and Oceania), thus maintaining the principle of geographic diversity.

Implications for popular culture tourism

This section gives a more detailed description of the advanced destination marketing tactics and provides examples of practical application. Implications for destination marketers are also discussed.

Figure 35.2 The geochart of the study.

Tactic N 1: using digital travel content and computer-generated environments for location promotion

The use of digital travel content, such as destination guide applications for location promotion, is a recent marketing technique used by Visit Britain and I Amsterdam (ArrivalGuide: Free Guide to Amsterdam, 2016). Destination applications like PXCom's in-flight entertainment applications and ArrivalGuides are a great example of smart use of digital destination-related content. Company PXCom uses inflight entertainment systems to provide the passengers with multimedia destination-related information. While ArrivalGuides is a destination content provider with a vast network of high-quality and up-to-date destination information and city guides. Their strategic partnership in September 2014 unveiled a new era of destination guide applications: "With the new apps, airlines can provide their passengers with a rich selection of multimedia and interactive content. While flying, passengers are now able to access large quantities of updated destination information for their trip planning" (Nedog, 2015). This is good news for many screen tourists that prefer flying to their destination. ArrivalGuides with the help of PXCom's in-flight applications can deliver an assortment of information on everything from film tours and walks, to film and site maps for tourists (see Figure 35.3).

These destination guide applications offer a new take on traditional marketing approaches to information delivery. DMOs, such as VisitBritain.com and VisitLondon.com, share their content with ArrivalGuides to offer any tourist all available information on their object of interest. Christian Rose-Day, the Editor at Visit London, ensures that the content on the ArrivalGuides tourist information site stays up to date with the information displayed on the official tourist portal (Rose-Day, n.d.).

Computer-generated environments like virtual reality (VR) and augmented reality (AR) are becoming powerful marketing tools (Bulearca & Tamarjan, 2010; Lui, Piccoli, & Ives, 2007). These computer-generated environments are created with the help of a technology that combines elements of the real world with virtual elements, allowing interaction between objects

Figure 35.3 A screenshot of *Harry Potter* tour on ArrivalGuides website.

both real and virtual in real time. While many marketing organizations are only just beginning to discover VR and AR, some players are ahead of the game (Pereira, Silva, Abreu, & Pinto, 2014). The potential of VR in future tourism marketing practice has been recognized in recent tourism literature (Huang, Backman, Backman, & Chang, 2016). Huang et al.'s (2016) study results show that the VR touristic environment leads to higher travel intention because of greater perception of autonomy, competence, and relatedness of the users. A good example of VR-inspired marketing strategy is the collaboration between Screen NSW and The City of Sydney (the local tourism government authority for central Sydney and surrounds). Screen NSW is part of the New South Wales government initiative that was established to "assist, promote and strengthen the screen industry in NSW . . . encourage employment in all aspects of screen production, encourage investment in the industry, enhance the industry's export potential" (ScreenNSW: Who We Are, n.d.). Their new project "360 Vision" is Australia's first ever virtual reality development initiative. "360 Vision," along with other projects run by Screen NSW and the City of Sydney, aims to: (1) "encourage more international film production in Sydney for the economic benefit of Sydney economy"; and (2) "promote the enjoyment of screen culture by Sydneysiders and tourists for cultural and economic benefit" (About Sydney City of Film, n.d.)

Since Sydney's appointment as "UNESCO Creative City of Film" in 2010 (Judge, 2010), Australian state New South Wales became a location for high levels of local and international production, including feature films, such as *The Wolverine*, *The Great Gatsby*, *Felony*, *The LEGO Movie*, *The Sapphires*, *Mad Max: Fury Road*, and Angelina Jolie's *Unbroken*, as well as many Australian TV dramas. Projects like "360 Vision" are part of the competitive strategy used by the state to secure its leading position in on-screen tourism marketing.

AR, though not as widely used as VR, already sets marketing trends in the tourism and hospitality field (Qiu, 2016). The success of the mobile game Pokémon Go released in 2016 demonstrates the power of AR technology. Only three days after the release of the game, the number of daily active users was already approximate to that of Twitter (Skrebels, 2016). Today, it is common to see large numbers of people gathering around local landmarks to collect pokémon. Pokémon Go Sydney Walk that got together 2,000 players at the Sydney Opera House is only one of the events of this theme (Rossignol, 2016). In August 2016 writer Patrick Ness, creator of science fiction TV series *Class* (a spin-off of *Doctor Who*), tweeted that Cardiff Bay is becoming a heavy, heavy Pokémon area (Ness, 2016). Cardiff bay is a popular *Doctor Who* experience location. AR may not be a full-fledged tourism marketing tool yet, but obviously sets the trend.

Tactic N 2: focusing on user-generated content

User-generated content (UGC) is re-shaping the way people process news, gossip, and even research. UGC websites are "creating new viewing patterns and social interactions" by encouraging users to be more creative, and businesses to seek new business opportunities (Cha, Kwak, Rodriguez, Ahn, & Moon, 2007, p. 1). While not being new to tourism marketing in general, UGC is still relatively new to on-screen tourism. Yet in its current campaigns, Visit Britain places an emphasis on user-generated content when targeting screen tourists. A campaign known as "#OMGB moment" is a true example of a UGC-derived marketing. The initial campaign launched on January 14, 2016, #OMGB GREAT Britain – Home of Amazing Moments was "an evolution of our [VisitBritain/VisitEngland] previous marketing campaigns and a new overarching proposition in promoting tourism to Britain" ("#OMGB – GREAT Britain," 2016).

Designed for tourists seeking firsthand experiences, the #OMGB website is an ideal tool for searching, planning, and choosing film tours. The idea behind the campaign is very simple: it encourages people to upload images of their own memorable moments using the hashtag #OMGB. These moments and experiences will then be showcased through digital, TV, print, and outdoor marketing activity. If a tourist is seeking a first-hand experience of a British film location or willing to share his or her own experiences, #OMGB might be a good way to start. The #OMGB campaign is going global and has already been launched in Australia and China on September 2016.

Tactic N 3: making films on filmmaking at a destination

Making films on filmmaking is a strategy that can target both film producers and screen tourists. Usually created by film commissions, these short films tell stories about filming locations. "Shooting in Spain" is a project that includes a series of films on filmmaking at a destination run by Spain Film Commission – a non-profit association and a founding member of the European Film Commission Network (EUFCN). Spain Film Commission works in collaboration with Spanish audiovisual, trade, and tourism institutions and is supported by the local government (Ministerio de Educacion, Cultura y Deporte). "Shooting in Spain" was created to facilitate "International promotion of Spain . . . by conveying the vision of a modern, diverse and fully competitive country on an international level" (Spain Film Commission, n.d.). Apart from short films, "Shooting in Spain" offers 360° views – virtual tours and spherical photographs of shooting locations in Spain (360° VIEW, n.d.). The project's media library provides links to documentaries featuring Spain, while the filmography section contains a list of "Directors that Have Shot in Spain" (Shooting in Spain, n.d.). Another DMO that runs a similar project is the Bermuda Tourism Authority. "Filming in Bermuda" follows the same business and marketing principles as "Shooting in Spain," though the project is still in its development stage. Making films on filmmaking is a budget-friendly marketing tactic with high visual appeal and a clear message that can target a wide audience.

Tactic N 4: mastering collaborative marketing

Tourism destination marketing involves many stakeholders and a complex product offer. Complexity and interdependency among stakeholders created many local tourism marketing alliances (Palmer & Bejou, 1995). Gray (1989, p. 227) refers to collaboration as "a process of joint decision making among key stakeholders of a problem domain about the future of that domain." Collaboration is "seen to take place at individual, organizational, national, regional and international levels, all geared towards addressing common issues" (Hill & Lewis, 2015, p. 76). Collaborative efforts are encouraged at each of these levels as they foster a greater degree of consensus and joint decision-making (Okazaki, 2008).

Collaboration is particularly important in destination marketing efforts due to the complex nature of tourism industry. Relevant studies suggest that collaborative marketing is a practical solution to various challenges in destination marketing (Wang & Xiang, 2007) and is effective in building consistent brand identity and offering competitive value proposition (Park, Cai, & Lehto, 2009). This study has already touched upon several examples of marketing collaborations in the tourism field, yet few were carried out on international collaborations in on-screen tourism. A good example of an international level of collaboration is the Thailand–India cine connect project.

The objective of the Thailand–India cine connect project is to connect Thai and Indian people in film businesses together as well as to explore the business opportunities, particularly in the areas of promoting Thailand as a film shooting location.

(Koumelis, 2016)

Another collaboration, this time between the the Ministry of Tourism, Government of India, and State DMOs in 2012, illustrates a national level of collaboration in tourism. In 2012 the Ministry of Tourism of India instituted a National Tourism Award, "Most Film Promotion Friendly State/UT," to encourage the state DMOs, Governments, and Union Territories to facilitate filming in their state or territory. Two years later the Press Information Bureau, Government of India, released a document titled "Potential for Film Tourism in the Country," which "recognizes films as a powerful tool for promotion of tourism destinations and locations" in India (Press Information Bureau, 2014, p. 1).

On an organizational level, a collaboration between stakeholders can sometimes be of a less explicit nature. For example, Tourism New Zealand offers tourism stakeholders and travel media cross-marketing opportunities together with free access to its visual library. This library contains a collection of images and footage about New Zealand that can be used in the promotion of New Zealand as a tourist destination. Ever since the first *Lord of the Rings* movie, New Zealand has been known as a film location (Jones & Smith, 2005). In attempt to further capitalize on screen exposure, Tourism New Zealand offers many informative resources and free sales tools for tourism stakeholders to help "visualise the New Zealand experience" (100% Pure New Zealand, n.d.). The latest sales tools include film location maps and videos on Disney's family film *Pete's Dragon*.

We think there is a great opportunity for you to showcase your vacation product to New Zealand and we've included some tools that can help you do just that . . . we think the content we're sharing with you can be used to promote all of new New Zealand.

(Disney's Pete's Dragon*, n.d.)*

Such collaborations enable organizations to absorb innovations (Powell, Koput, & Smith-Doerr, 1996), which ultimately leads to higher survival rates (Zach, 2012). Another recent example of an organizational marketing collaboration inspired by on-screen tourism is the 2016 Family Ambassador Campaign launched in New York. NYC & Company, the city's destination marketing organization, teamed up with Nickelodeon, an American television network, to promote New York as a family-friendly location. Their project "Discover NYC with Team Turtles" uses the Teenage Mutant Ninja Turtles to guide families around New York and help them experience the most family-friendly things to do and see throughout the five boroughs.

The multigenerational appeal was key with our selection of the Teenage Mutant Ninja Turtles . . . People traditionally haven't thought of New York City as a family destination but that is changing. With this campaign, we're relinquishing full control of the brand and letting the turtles tell their story about the city.

(Peltier, 2016)

DMO collaboration with partners has long been recognized as essential to creating cohesive tourism products and thus competitive tourism destinations (Jamal & Getz, 1995).

Tactic N 5: creating "camera-ready" communities

A recent tendency in destination marketing is to create camera-ready communities by encouraging communities to streamline permitting processes that would allow film productions. In Georgia, the Camera Ready Communities program connects film and TV productions with county liaisons across the state to provide local expertise and support.

Georgia's Convention and Visitors bureaus (CVBs) have long realized the benefits of community involvement. The Camera Ready Communities program was launched early in 2010 to train and certify Georgia counties to work effectively with production companies and provide one-on-one assistance in every aspect of production, from location scouting and film permits to traffic control, catering and lodging. Among the first camera-ready communities was Columbus, Georgia's second-largest city.

The Columbus area is not new to on-screen tourism: from *The Green Berets* being filmed locally by movie legend John Wayne in 1960s, to *Tank*, a comedy featuring James Garner and Shirley Jones in the 1980s, to Mel Gibson's *We Were Soldiers* in 2002. Closer to modern history was the filming of the *Need for Speed* movie in 2013. Given the history, The Columbus Convention and Visitors Bureau's Camera Ready Community has enough strength to help Georgia become a tourism destination capable of attracting considerable numbers of screen tourists.

Another example of a camera-ready community is Texas. The Film Friendly Texas (FFTX) program run by the Texas Film Commission aims to connect filmmakers to locations across the state. The communities are encouraged to streamline permitting processes that would allow a film production to close streets for filming scenes. The FFTX program also provides ongoing training and guidance to help communities effectively accommodate on-location filming and market their communities as filming destinations.

Conclusions

This chapter highlights several techniques, five of which are identified as dominant, used by DMOs for taking advantage of on-screen tourism. If we follow the history of destination marketing development, we will find that most recent marketing techniques are highly influenced by modern technologies and are a result of a collaboration between tourism stakeholders and other entities. The results obtained support this statement.

On-screen tourism is a growing phenomenon worldwide. However, many tourism organizations have been slow to adopt new marketing techniques and tap the potential benefits of on-screen tourism. It could be due to a lack of knowledge or evidence that explains the potential behind the advanced marketing tactics. At this stage, more research is required. A cost–benefit analysis to evaluate the advanced marketing tactics might be a good direction for future research.

The new technologies that maximize access to vivid representations of places on-screen facilitate greater public contact with destinations of tourism appeal. The ways in which these new links may be used in tourism destination management is of interest in the continuing pursuit of innovation in tourism.

References

100% Pure New Zealand (n.d.). Retrieved from http://traveltrade.newzealand.com/en-us/sales-tools/.
360° VIEW (n.d.). Retrieved from www.shootinginspain.info/index.php/en/360-view.html.
About Sydney City of Film (n.d.). Retrieved from www.screen.nsw.gov.au/page/about-sydney-city-of-film.
ArrivalGuide: Free Guide to Amsterdam (2016). Retrieved from www.iamsterdam.com/en/visiting/plan-your-trip/products/arrival-guide.

Baudrillard, J. (1994). *Simulacra and simulation*. Ann Arbor: University of Michigan Press.

Beeton, S. (2005). *Film-induced tourism* (Vol. 25). Clevedon: Channel View Publications.

Beeton, S. (2008). Location, location, location: Film corporations' social responsibilities. *Journal of Travel & Tourism Marketing*, 24(2–3), 107–114.

Beeton, S. (2010). The advance of film tourism. *Tourism and Hospitality Planning & Development*, 7(1), 1–6. doi: 10.1080/14790530903522572.

Bulearca, M., & Tamarjan, D. (2010). Augmented reality: A sustainable marketing tool. *Global Business and Management Research: An International Journal*, 2(2), 237–252.

Cha, M., Kwak, H., Rodriguez, P., Ahn, Y., & Moon, S. (2007). I tube, you tube, everybody tubes: Analyzing the world's largest user generated content video system. Proceedings of the 7th ACM SIGCOMM conference on Internet measurement. San Diego, California, ACM: 1–14.

Chua, B. H., & Iwabuchi, K. (2008). *East Asian pop culture: Analysing the Korean wave*. Hong Kong: Hong Kong University Press.

Connell, J. (2012). Film tourism: Evolution, progress and prospects. *Tourism Management*, 33(5), 1007–1029. doi: 10.1016/j.tourman.2012.02.0084.

Croy, W. G. (2010). Planning for film tourism: Active destination image management. *Tourism and Hospitality Planning & Development*, 7(1), 21–30. doi: 10.1080/14790530903522598.

Disney's *Pete's Dragon* (n.d.) Retrieved from http://traveltrade.newzealand.com/en-us/sales-tools/disney-s-pete-s-dragon/.

Fawcett, C., & Cormack, P. (2001). Guarding authenticity at literary tourism sites. *Annals of Tourism Research*, 28(3), 686–704. doi: 10.1016/S0160-7383(00)00062-1.

Fielding, N., Lee, R. M., & Blank, G. (Eds.) (2008). *The SAGE handbook of online research methods*. London: Sage.

Gibson, C., & Connell, J. (2005). *Music and tourism: On the road again*. Clevedon: Channel View Publications.

Gibson, C., & Connell, J. (2007). Music, tourism and the transformation of Memphis. *Tourism Geographies*, 9(2), 160–190. doi: 10.1080/14616680701278505.

Gray, B. (1989). *Collaborating: Finding common ground for multi-party problems*. San Francisco, CA: Jossey-Bass.

GREAT Britain – Home of Amazing Moments campaign (n.d.). Retrieved from www.visitbritain.org/great-britain-home-amazing-moments-campaign.

Hill, N. S., & Lewis, A. (2015). An assessment of the caribbean tourism organization's collaborative marketing efforts: A member nation perspective. *Journal of Vacation Marketing*, 21(1), 75–85.

Hoppen, A., Brown, L., & Fryall, A. (2014). Literary tourism: Opportunities and challenges for the marketing and branding of destinations. *Journal of Destination Marketing & Management*, 3(1), 37–47. doi: 10.1016/j.jdmm.2013.12.009.

Huang, Y. C., Backman, K. F., Backman, S. J., & Chang, L. L. (2016). Exploring the Implications of virtual reality technology in tourism marketing: An integrated research framework. *International Journal of Tourism Research*, 18(2), 116–128.

Hudson, S., & Ritchie, J. R. B. (2006). Promoting destinations via film tourism: An empirical identification of supporting marketing initiatives. *Journal of Travel Research*, 44, 387–396. doi: 10.1177/0047287506286720.

Jamal, T. B., & Getz, D. (1995). Collaboration theory and community tourism planning. *Annals of Tourism Research*, 22(1), 186–204.

Jones, D., & Smith, K. (2005). Middle–earth meets New Zealand: Authenticity and location in the making of *The Lord of the Rings*. *Journal of Management Studies*, 42(5), 923–945.

Judge, V. (2010). Sydney crowned UNESCO City of Film. Retrieved from http://screen.nsw.gov.au/data/publish/578/101209_SydneyNamedUNESCOCityOfFilm.pdf.

Koumelis, T. (2016). Thailand–India cine connect: Exploring potentials to bridge their film industries. *Travel Daily News*. Retrieved from www.traveldailynews.asia/news/article/61997/thailand-india-cine-connect-exploring-potentials.

Kozinets, R. V. (2009). *Netnography: Doing ethnographic research online*. London: Sage.

Larson, M., Lundberg, C., & Lexhagen, M. (2013). Thirsting for vampire tourism: Developing pop culture destinations. *Journal of Destination Marketing & Management* 2(2), 74–84. doi: 10.1016/j.jdmm.2013.03.004.

Lee, S., Scott, D., & Kim, H. (2008). Celebrity fan involvement and destination perceptions. *Annals of Tourism Research*, 35(3), 809–832.

Lemelin, R. H., Dawson, J., & Stewart, E. (2013). *Last chance tourism: Adapting tourism opportunities in a changing world*. Oxford: Routledge.

Lui, T. W., Piccoli, G., & Ives, B. (2007). Marketing strategies in virtual worlds. *ACM SIGMIS Database*, 38(4), 77–80.

Nedog, K. (2015). PXCom & ArrivalGuides unveil a strategic partnership. Press Release. Retrieved from http://arrivalguides.biz/press-releases/pxcom-arrivalguides-unveil-a-strategic-partnership/.

Ness, P. (2016, August 10). Cardiff Bay is a heavy, heavy Pokémon area. [Tweet]. Retrieved from https://twitter.com/Patrick_Ness/status/763425514388422656?ref_src=twsrc%5Etfw.

Okazaki, E. (2008). A community-based tourism model: Its conception and use. *Journal of Sustainable Tourism*, 16(5), 511–529.

#OMGB – GREAT Britain (2016). Home of Amazing Moments campaign. Retrieved from www.visit britain.org/great-britain-home-amazing-moments-campaign.

Palmer, A., & Bejou. D. (1995). Tourism destination marketing alliances. *Annals of Tourism Research*, 22(3), 616–629.

Park, O., Cai, L. A., & Lehto, X. (2009). Collaborative destination branding. In L. A. Cai, W. C. Gartner, & A. M. Munar (Eds.) *Tourism branding: Communities in action* (pp. 75–86). Bingley, UK: Emerald.

Peltier, D. (2016). New York turns to Ninja Turtles for this year's family tourism push. *Skift*. Retrieved from https://skift.com/2016/04/20/new-york-turns-to-ninja-turtles-for-this-years-family-tourism-push/.

Pereira, F., Silva, D. C., Abreu, P., & Pinto, A. (2014). Augmented reality mobile tourism application. In F. B. Tan and A. M. Correia (Eds.), *New perspectives in information systems and technologies* (vol. 2, pp. 175–185). New York: Springer International.

Powell, W. W., Koput, K. W., & Smith-Doerr, L. (1996). Interorganizational collaboration and the locus of innovation: Networks of learning in biotechnology. *Administrative Science Quarterly*, 41(1), 116–145.

Press Information Bureau (2014). Potential for film tourism in the country (released by the Ministry of Tourism Press Information Bureau). Retrieved from http://pib.nic.in/newsite/mbErel.aspx?relid=103694.

PwC (2015, February). *Cities of opportunity: The urban rhythm of entertainment and media* [Report]. Retrieved from www.pwc.com/us/en/industry/entertainment-media/publications/assets/pwc-cities-of-opportunity.pdf.

Qiu, S. (2016). Five influential marketing trends in the tourism and hospitality field. Retrieved from www.hospitalitynet.org/news/4077724.html.

Reijnders, S. (2011). Stalking the Count: Dracula, fandom and tourism. *Annals of Tourism Research*, 38(1), 231–248. doi: 10.1016/j.annals.2010.08.006.

Rifai, T. (2015). The travel and technological revolutions: UNWTO Secretary-General at ITB 2015. Retrieved from http://media.unwto.org/press-release/2015-03-03/travel-and-technological-revolutions-unwto-secretary-general-itb-2015.

Riley, R. W., & Van Doren, C. S. (1992). Movies as tourism promotion: A "pull" factor in a "push" location. *Tourism management*, 13(3), 267–274.

Ritzer, G., & Liska, A. (1997). McDisneyization" and "post-tourism": Complementary perspectives on contemporary tourism. In C. Rojek & J. Urry (Eds.), *Touring cultures: Transformations of travel and theory* (pp. 96–109). London: Routledge.

Roesch, S. (2009). *The experiences of film location tourists*. Clevedon: Channel View Publications.

Rose-Day, Christian (n.d.). LinkedIn profile information. Retrieved from https://uk.linkedin.com/in/christianroseday.

Rossignol, D. (2016). Pokémon Go brought 2,000 players together at the Sydney Opera House. Nerdist. Retrieved from http://nerdist.com/pokemon-go-brought-2000-players-together-at-the-sydney-opera-house/.

ScreenNSW: Who We Are (n.d.). Retrieved from www.screen.nsw.gov.au/page/who-we-are.

Shandley, R., Jamal, T., & Tanase, A. (2006). Location shooting and the filmic destination: Transylvanian myths and the post-colonial tourism enterprise. *Journal of Tourism and Cultural Change*, 4(3), 137–158. doi: 10.2167/jtcc056.0.

Shaw, G., & Williams, A. M. (2004). *Tourism and tourism spaces*. London: SSGR Publications.

Shooting in Spain (n.d.). Retrieved from www.shootinginspain.info.

Skrebels, J. (2016). Pokémon Go about to overtake Twitter's daily active users on android. IGN News. Retrieved from www.ign.com/articles/2016/07/11/pokemon-go-about-to-overtake-twitters-daily-active-users-on-android.

Spain Film Commission (n.d.). Retrieved from www.shootinginspain.info/index.php/en/spain-film-commission-uk.html.

Tashakkori, A., & Teddlie, C. (2003). *Handbook of mixed methods in social & behavioral research*. London: Sage.

Teddlie, C., & Yu, F. (2007). Mixed methods sampling. *Journal of Mixed Methods Research*, 1(1), 77–100. doi: doi:10.1177/2345678906292430.

Thomas, D. (2004). Diversity as strategy. *Harvard Business Review, Human Resource Management*. Retrieved from https://hbr.org/2004/09/diversity-as-strategy.

Torres, A. M., & Murray, J. A. (2000). Diversity and marketing practice. *Irish Marketing Review*, 13(2), 3.

Vagionis, N., & Loumioti, M. (2011). Movies as a tool of modern tourist marketing. *Tourismos: An International Multidisciplinary Journal of Tourism*, 6(2), 353–362.

Wang, Y., & Xiang, Z. (2007). Toward a theoretical framework of collaborative destination marketing. *Journal of Travel Research*, 46(1), 75–85.

Zach, F. (2012). Partners and innovation in American destination marketing organizations. *Journal of Travel Research*, 51(4), 412–425. doi:10.1177/0047287511426340#OMGB.

36

(G)A(I)MING AT THE THRONE

Social media and the use of visitor-generated content in destination marketing

Tina Šegota

Setting the scene

Popular culture's influence by way of increasing tourism visitations has long been debated (Beeton, 2005, 2010), with film-induced tourism placed at the forefront. Film-induced tourism is a unique form of tourism motivating visitors to experience on- and off-location sites featured in popular movies and TV series (Beeton, 2005; Hudson & Ritchie, 2006). In recent years, film-induced tourism has developed into a growing worldwide phenomenon and its benefits have increasingly been perceived because it "offers something for everyone" (Hudson & Ritchie, 2006, p. 387). Film-induced tourism not only provides the tourist with a chance to experience unique sites featured in their favorite movies and/or TV series, but as a result these sites very often gain the status of an icon (Riley, Baker, & Van Doren, 1998), depending on their special qualities, characteristics, and their role in films, which can be further exploited in destination marketing strategies (Hahm & Wang, 2011; Hudson & Ritchie, 2006; O'Connor, Flanagan, & Gilbert, 2008). Larson, Lundberg, and Lexhagen (2013) showed that tourists' consumption of popular culture sites may be beneficial if destination management organizations (hereinafter DMOs) wish to capitalize on it in their tourism developmental strategies. However, these strategies are not only reserved for the real world where experiences of tourists' engagement with the attraction are created, but are nowadays transferred to the online world where the *world*-of-mouth (Hays, Page, & Buhalis, 2013; Qualman, 2009) is experienced with the help of social media.

Nowadays, social media are perceived as highly significant for tourists' destination choice due to their widespread accessibility and popularity (Chung & Buhalis, 2008; Gretzel, 2006; Gretzel, Yuan, & Fesenmaier, 2000; Hays et al., 2013). Moreover, it is user-generated content that is fundamental to social media, offering an additional glance at how places and landscapes are consumed by tourists. Therefore, with a little creativity and a well-thought-out social media strategy, DMOs can benefit from the user-generated content and exploit it to engage with their prospective tourists, increasing destination brand awareness and creating a positive destination image attitude (Hays et al., 2013; Tuten, 2008). However, limited attention has been paid to these practices in relation to popular culture, in particular to film-induced tourism. This chapter addresses this gap by examining DMOs' practices concerning Instagram activities in connection to the popular series *Game of Thrones*. The purpose of this study is to identify how the *Game of*

Thrones phenomenon was embedded in Instagram activities of the national DMOs in countries where the filming took place, and to further report on Croatia, which is argued to have excelled in the aforementioned practice. This chapter will start with a review of the relevant literature on the role of popular culture in destination marketing, describe the interrelatedness of social media and destination image, and then present an analysis of the influence of *Game of Thrones* on national DMOs' Instagram activities. The final section will discuss the implications for destination marketing in relation to social media and popular culture tourism.

Theoretical underpinnings: popular culture tourism and destination marketing

Popular culture has become an important topic of broad discussion in tourism and the related marketing field and, more recently, has attracted growing interest of those attempting to understand the benefits of destination marketing activities in connection with literature and film tourism (Beeton, 2010; Larson et al., 2013). In this latter case, Bolan and Williams (2008) argue that when we talk about the benefits of film tourism we usually consider film as a medium with the potential to reach and touch markets that are unreachable through traditional marketing activities. First, a destination's exposure in a film, especially if it is a commercially successful movie or TV series, may generate a wider market reach otherwise unaffordable and unachievable for most tourism promotion bodies. In this sense, film generates awareness of a destination among those viewers who may not be addressed by other marketing tools. Second, film has been shown to play an important role in the process of forming a destination image, which, on the other hand, is acknowledged as the most important aspect of a tourist's decision-making process. In this case, film as an autonomous image-formation agent provides substantial information to people within a very limited time, while people are more likely to evaluate this information as more objective and unbiased since autonomous agents are considered as independent information sources (that is, not influenced by official destination representatives). Finally, film imagery, which includes on-screen virtual characters, an appealing storyline, memorable music, and remarkable landscapes, helps to build relationships that may seem impersonal, intangible, and inaccessible until the destination is actually visited. In that sense, the bond imaginatively created between the audience and the film characters materializes itself at the moment tourists visit the destination and recreate similar experiences as those on-screen performances. For those tourists who consider themselves true fans of the film, these landscapes might represent the pull factors for film-site visits (Riley & Van Doren, 1992). On the other hand, for general tourists these landscapes might influence the propensity to visit a destination, but its effect would be difficult to measure (Young & Young, 2008). This is because the majority of film tourism is incidental and the consumption is influenced by the place and time of what is to be consumed (Connell, 2012). However, it is undeniable that, to some extent, film emphasizes the extraordinariness of these authentic landscapes, places, and sites, which would otherwise be considered an 'ordinary' object of tourist consumption.

As Bolan and Williams (2008) also note, many destination promotion activities in relation to the benefits of film are actively pursued by DMOs soon after the film is released and not before. In that sense, these early-stage benefits are most certainly lost and not exploited enough by destination marketers. Exceptions to this are the practices of New Zealand and its relationship with the trilogy *The Lord of the Rings*, and that of Forks, USA and the Italian towns Volterra and Montepulciano connected to the *Twilight Saga* phenomenon. With the former, as explored and reported by Croy (2010), tourism representatives and government officials were actively involved in developing and creating marketing activities through which the movie audience has been addressed and encouraged to pay a visit to the so-called Middle-earth. The Middle-earth is a challenging environment with a significant role in the movie since its landscapes and scenery strongly support the elements of the story. New Zealand tourism representatives were reported to have recognized the movie's important role in destination image and thus to have taken an active role in connecting the trilogy with stories about the country. In the case of the *Twilight Saga* phenomenon, Larson and colleagues (2013) reported that both Italian and US destination representatives also adopted an active role in developing *Twilight*-related tourism, but not all fully maximized the benefits. Here, it is interesting to note that both examples of 'good practice' relate to two popular culture franchises filmed and screened over several years and thus their influence on tourism-related activities is easier to examine and isolate. However, *The Lord of the Rings* and the *Twilight Saga* are not the sole examples of commercially successful popular culture franchises in the interest of academic researchers, some additional ones are presented in Table 36.1.

Many authors also argue that destination managers and those responsible for tourism promotion have not completely capitalized on the positive influence film has on destination image and on generating higher visitor numbers to destinations (Bolan & Williams, 2008; Croy, 2010; Larson et al., 2013; Wray & Croy, 2015). In most cases, film-induced tourism benefits were not maximally utilized because destination managers assessed that the already established destination image, place authenticity, or place qualities would be challenged by this particular form of tourism. In this context, pre-established place identities generate distinctiveness and uniqueness of how a "resident from a specific place (such as a city or town) has an association with this

Table 36.1 Selected franchised movies and TV series

Film franchise	Destination(s)	Author(s)
Harry Potter (7 movies; 2001–2011)	UK	Grihault (2003, 2007)
The Lord of the Rings (movie trilogy; 2001–2003) The Hobbit (movie trilogy, 2012–2014)	New Zealand	Beaton (2015); Buchmann (2006, 2010); Buchmann, Moore, & Fisher (2010); Carl, Kindon, & Smith (2007); Croy (2010); Li, Li, Song, Lundberg, & Shen (2017); Mitchell & Stewart (2012); Moses Peaslee (2010); Piggott, Morgan, & Pritchard (2004); Singh & Best (2004)
The Twilight Saga (4 movies; 2009–2012)	USA, Italy, Canada	Larson et al. (2013); Lexhagen, Larson, & Lundberg (2014); Lundberg & Lexhagen (2012); Lundberg, Lexhagen, & Mattsson (2012)
Mad Max (4 movies; 1979, 1981, 1985, 2015)*	Australia	Frost (2010); Wray & Croy (2015)
Downton Abbey (6 seasons; 2011–2016)*	UK	Baena & Byker (2015); Bagnoli (2015)
Game of Thrones (6 seasons; 2011–2016)*	Croatia, Iceland, Malta, Morocco, Northern Ireland, Spain, USA	Murray (2017); Tzanelli (2016)

* Filming is said to be continuing.

place, and this bond enables the resident to differentiate himself/herself from people from other places" (Chen & Šegota, 2015, p. 148). And it is these that are challenged by the film imagery, especially if the destination is negatively portrayed in the film (Beeton, 2005; Larson et al., 2013; Light, 2007). As Beeton (2005, p. 163) suggested, when residents are dissatisfied with how film-induced tourism imposes meanings and an identity of the place they live in, DMOs ought to address the issue by "re-imaging the destination by demarketing," which could be a lengthy and costly process. Therefore, in some cases, there is simply no strategy that would tie the destination's marketing activities to a particular popular culture phenomenon, and hence those activities continue 'as usual.' Accordingly, the literature shows that tourism destinations have developed various strategies in order to preserve, manage, or re-establish place identity and authenticity in relation to popular culture phenomena.

Strategies on film-induced tourism

What then are these strategies for managing film-induced tourism? Larson and colleagues (2013) define them as: fabricating place authenticity, guarding place authenticity, and no strategy.

First, fabricating place authenticity strategy is all about subalterning, in the majority, tourism development of the destination to experiences related to a popular culture phenomenon, that is to fictionally constructed realities (Larson et al., 2013). A film's key role in creating images of a place, and consequently its memorability, awareness, familiarity, and expectations, is perceived as crucial for enhancing the influx to a destination tourism (Croy, 2010). However, this subalterning is not only reserved for the development of tourism products and services, but also stretches to destinations' marketing activities. As previously mentioned, a consumer's sensitivity to destination image can be influenced by a film, which "can therefore help to make intangible tangible and [. . .] can further aid in promotion destinations to the tourist in a more accessible and unbiased way" (Bolan & Williams, 2008, p. 388).

Second, the strategy on guarding place authenticity, on the other hand, involves the DMOs' interest to develop tourism related to the popular culture phenomenon, although the latter is kept to a minimum. Therefore, the guarding place authenticity strategy refers to prioritizing tourism development so as to give prominence to the qualities of the place and its authenticity with very little emphasis on the popular culture phenomenon (Larson et al., 2013). In this context, attributes associated with popular culture may be integrated into the destination's existing marketing activities in order to stimulate the influx of tourists to a destination without disrupting the destination's core values and existing experiences (Bolan & Williams, 2008; Croy, 2010; Neville, 2014).

Finally, no strategy for the case where destination representatives have shown no interest in the popular culture phenomenon and that priority is given to the established place identity and authenticity over the (potential) benefits of this type of tourism (Larson et al., 2013). In this case, it has been evaluated that tourism development connected to satisfying the needs of film-induced market segments would only bring short-term or no benefits to the existing tourism and/or that the destination's unique character is 'better off' not creating experiences that would distort the identity of the place and its community.

All these strategies therefore underpin destinations' development directions with a particular emphasis given to destination marketing activities and on-location experiences in order to attract tourists and satisfy their needs. As noted in the introduction, this chapter is especially concerned with how these strategies on place authenticity in relation to popular culture phenomena have been pursued by DMOs in their communication with (prospective) tourists on social media, with a focus on Instagram. To better explore these practices, it is necessary to understand the general role of social media and why it is important for destination marketing.

The role of social media in co-creating destination image

When social media are mentioned, one cannot but think about what not long ago were unimaginable, whole new experiences and developments of different forms of communications brought by technological advancements. According to Safko and Brake (2009, p. 6):

> social media refers to activities, practices, and behaviours among communities of people who gather online to share information, knowledge, and opinions using conversational media. Conversational media are Web-based applications that make it possible to create and easily transmit content in the form of words, pictures, videos, and audios.

It is the content of social media and its creators that both have a significant role in the destination image formation process. First, it is pictures and videos posted on social media that make the 'intangible tangible': that is, they transform intangible, perishable, and variable places of the tourist gaze into "graspable objects" (Urry & Larsen, 2011, p. 180) by eternalizing and materializing their *in situ* experiences, memories, and emotions with the destination in pictures or video. Second, when shared online, these pictures and videos of one's gaze have the propensity to be instantly consumed (i.e. generate attraction and reaction) by others and thus ignite their desires for the same experiences, memories, and emotions. Moreover, it is about pictures and videos having the ultimate power to give evidence of a destination's unique characteristics that are passed from person to person. Thus, tourists become creators and consequently advocates of the destination's image independently of tourism officials, for whom social media are perceived as a trustworthy and independent information medium. And it is the latter that gives credibility to social media in shaping tourism-related choices and decisions (Cox, Burgess, Sellitto, & Buultjens, 2009; Xiang & Gretzel, 2010).

In this context, for Hays and colleagues (2013) social media are all about the participation, conversation, and fluidity of online communities that create the content and rely on it for their tourism-related decisions. According to Daugherty, Eastin, and Bright (2008, p. 16), "user-generated content refers to media content created or produced by the general public rather than by paid professionals and primarily distributed on the Internet." Such tourist-to-tourist communication makes DMOs "no longer the unrivalled experts on the attributes or quality of destinations and tourism services and products" (Hudson & Thal, 2013, p. 157). However, DMOs can benefit from the visitor-generated content[1] and exploit it in order to increase awareness of and develop loyalty to destinations (Hays et al., 2013; Hidalgo Alcazar, Silicila Pinero, & Ruiz de Maya, 2014; Tuten, 2008). In addition, visitor-generated content can be used to reassure the authenticity of a destination with DMOs' role as an intermediary in tourist-to-tourist communication. In this sense, DMOs usually have a large number of social media followers that, most of the time, willingly share their experiences in the form of pictures or videos with the place for various purposes. When given permission, DMOs can repost some of this content to engage in this 'peer-to-peer' interaction and hence create a much stronger sense of co-creation of the destination image.

This co-creation of destination image is even more important in the context of popular culture tourism. Social media not only enable a variety of word-of-mouth activities to take place, but its content guarantees that, to some extent, the 'popular culture tourist gaze' will be authentic, unique, and real, especially for those who consider themselves true fans and are eager to re-experience the authenticity of the destination where the filming happened. In search for this film-induced authenticity of the destination, tourists are nowadays much more present in the online world because their information search is more efficient in terms of both time and scope (Gretzel, 2006; Gretzel et al., 2000; Hays et al., 2013). However, the literature suggests that many DMOs struggle to keep up with new communication trends (Croy, 2010) and that very few national DMOs recognize social media as "a vital tool in marketing strategies" (Hays et al., 2013, p. 236).

Methodology

The general interest of the study presented in this chapter is in DMOs' utilization of the benefits of both popular culture-induced tourism and social media in destination image formation activities. More specifically, the purpose is to examine the complex relationship between: (1) the popular culture phenomenon of the *Game of Thrones*; (2) Instagram as a social media marketing tool; and (3) the destination marketing activities of official DMOs of destinations where the TV series was filmed.

Illustrations in this chapter draw upon the HBO TV series *Game of Thrones*, which became highly successful immediately after its first screening on April 17, 2011. The original series is based on George R. R. Martin's bestseller series of fantasy novels *A Song of Ice and Fire* that portray chronicles of violent dynastic struggles among noble families for the Iron Throne while more threats emerge from the north of the continent and from distant eastern lands. This record-setting TV series can command with a production budget of up to US\$ 10 million per episode (there are 10 episodes per season), an average of 20 million viewers per episode, and won a total of 38 Emmy awards, making it the most successful TV series in film history (HBO, 2016). In order to confirm these appraisals, it is noted that *Game of Thrones* is the Guinness two-times record holder for the most Emmy awards for a fictional series and a drama (Guiness World Records, 2016).

The primary reason for choosing Instagram as a social media platform to analyze for this study lies in its classification as a photo-sharing tool (Oliveira & Panyik, 2015). Instagram has more than 500 million active users who capture and share over 95 million photos every day (Instagram, 2016). Moreover, Instagram users can capture, edit, share, like, comment, and tag pictures and videos. It also enables the following of other Instagram users and/or user-generated content that are hashtagged (for example, @croatiafulloflife, #lovecroatia), which increases the visibility of posts.

Further, this study is exploratory in nature and both qualitative and quantitative research methods were utilized to examine in which ways DMOs employ Instagram as an image-focused social medium to complement their destinations' image with the commercially successful TV series *Game of Thrones*. First, Larson and colleagues' (2013) proposition of a three-strategy framework underpinned the research for this study. Therefore, three categories – fabricating destination image authenticity, guarding destination image authenticity, and no strategy – were set as the basis for further analysis. Second, data were collected from official Instagram profiles of DMOs where filming took place, with strong emphasis on allocating pictures accompanied by specific hashtags referencing the *Game of Thrones* (e.g. #gameofthrones, #got, #GOTterritory, etc.). This quantitative approach helped in benchmarking the social media activities across the three strategies for all destinations associated with the TV series from season one onwards. Here the emphasis is on all destinations, regardless of the number of screening seasons they featured in. Lastly, complementary to this analysis, we performed an interview with a representative of a national tourism organization in charge of social media marketing activities of the destination, for which it was shown to have capitalized the most from the visitor-generated content related to the TV series.

Table 36.2 Instagram statistics for the analyzed DMOs, data collected August 22, 2016

Country	Instagram profile	Official hashtags	First post	Followers (total)	Posts (total)	GoT filming seasons	GoT posts	GoT reposts
Croatia	@croatiafulloflife	#CroatiaFullOfLife; #Croatia; #lovecroatia	December 12, 2012	108,000	5,268	2–5	189	157
Iceland	@inspiredbyiceland	#IcelandAcademy	August 13, 2013	45,800	342	2–6	1	1
Malta	@visitmalta	#VisitMalta	June 11, 2013	27,000	216	1	1	1
Morocco	@wehavethisthingwithmorocco	—	December 9, 2015	33,300	156	pilot, 3	0	0
Northern Ireland	@discoverni	#DiscoverNI	June 12, 2012	20,500	599	1–6	37	7
Scotland	@visitscotland	#ScotSpirit; #LoveScotland; #VisitScotland	October 25, 2012	215,000	2,198	pilot	0	0
Spain	@spain	#visitspain	May 7, 2014	141,000	1,004	5–6	1	1

Note: GoT = *Game of Thrones.*

Instagraming for the rise on the throne

From the data analyzed from the DMOs' posts on Instagram, it is evident that the DMOs differ in their destination marketing strategies of associating their social media activities to the popular TV series *Game of Thrones* (see Table 36.2). For example, Malta, Morocco, and Spain, which were featured in a few seasons, or even without any screening series in respect of Scotland, have shown no interest in linking their destination image to the TV show through their Instagram profiles. The same goes for Iceland, with the exception that it has been an on-location setting for almost all filming and screenings of the series (the exception is season one). However, this, what Larson and colleagues (2013) refer to as no strategy, is surely an indication that these five DMOs opted to create visual imagery that emphasized the destination's unique character. It could be argued that with this 'no strategy' approach DMOs focused on existing tourism segments rather than attracting film-induced tourists.

In relation to popular culture phenomena, guarding place authenticity in social media activities can be observed for Northern Ireland. Northern Ireland was chosen for both on- and off-location filming and therefore holds huge potential for generating an influx of film-induced tourism. However, contrary to that presumption, Northern Ireland's DMO has been very cautious in aligning the destination's image with the commercially successful TV series. In most cases, Instagram pictures portrayed a natural environment accompanied by the hashtag #GOTterritory that indicates landscape and scenery (with the potential of) being featured in the TV series. Interestingly, a series of six postal stamps inspired by season six (i.e. the latter was screened in 2016) was issued. In this case, Instagram was used as an additional medium to advertise and market the stamp collection with captions like "Send a postcard from Winterfell with a limited edition #GOTterritory stamp. Be quick, a limited number is available at @visitbelfast. #NorthernIreland." On average, these ads generated 234 likes. In conclusion, the @DiscoverNI Instagram account showed that the official Northern Ireland DMOs guarded the authenticity of the place and thus decided to not fully exploit the benefits of *Game of Thrones*-induced tourism in their online marketing activities.

On the other hand, Croatia did just that: it seized the opportunities given by the filming of the *Game of Thrones* series in Dalmatia and decided to 'cash-in' on its worldwide popularity. In general, it was shown that Croatia's DMO has been very active in developing destination image and nurturing its presence on Instagram with a total of over 5,000 posts in less than four years. And with the changing of filming locations from Malta to Croatia in season one of the series, Croatia has become a synonym for King's Landing, the most crucial scenery of the series known for its Iron throne. The majority of the filming took place in Dubrovnik and at nearby tourist attractions (see Figure 36.1), giving Dubrovnik an additional reference to its unique attractiveness. Dubrovnik, included on the list of UNESCO World Heritage Sites in 1979, was already an established tourist destination in Croatia, however, soon after 2012 it "represented the pilgrimage destination for those real fans of the *Game of Thrones*" (Croatia Tourism, 2016). That consequently meant that more and more pictures would emerge of destinations recognized as filming sites by those tourists that visited the site urged by the popular culture tourist gaze and those incidental tourists for whom the series represented an extra motivation to visit the place. Regardless of the driving mechanism, visitor-generated content testifying to the place's authenticity has been emerging on Instagram hashtagged #gameofthrones, #kingslanding, and #croatia. And it is these that have been perceived as "a marketing niche based on the iconic TV series, and therefore beneficial to destination image" (Croatia Tourism, 2016). The @CroatiaFullOfLife Instagram account only has 3.5 percent of all its posts associated with the *Game of Thrones*, although it has by far the most posts hashtagged #gameofthrones compared to

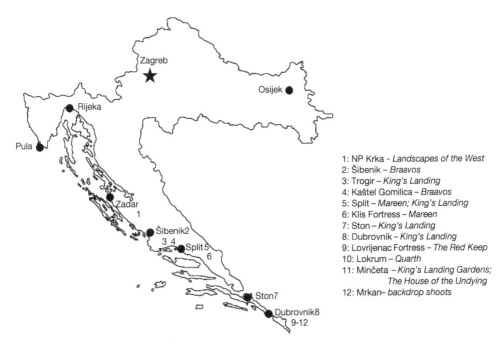

1: NP Krka - *Landscapes of the West*
2: Šibenik – *Braavos*
3: Trogir – *King's Landing*
4: Kaštel Gomilica – *Braavos*
5: Split – *Mareen; King's Landing*
6: Klis Fortress – *Mareen*
7: Ston – *King's Landing*
8: Dubrovnik – *King's Landing*
9: Lovrijenac Fortress – *The Red Keep*
10: Lokrum – *Quarth*
11: Minčeta – *King's Landing Gardens;*
The House of the Undying
12: Mrkan– *backdrop shoots*

Figure 36.1 Map of Croatia showing selected *Game of Thrones* film locations.

Source: World Atlas (2016), with *Game of Thrones* film locations inserted by the author.

other countries. Moreover, the majority of these are reposted (83 percent), of which 73 percent portray the landscape and scenery of micro-destinations (i.e. Dubrovnik, Split, Lokrum, etc.) whereas 17 percent also feature people recreating some scenes from the film. That is, these represent visitor-generated content that Croatia's DMO shared among its Instagram followers with the aim to "enhance the destination's organic image, which on the one hand already existed" (Croatia Tourism, 2016), but which has the propensity to create a much stronger sense of co-creation of the destination image among visitors. And it is the latter that should have represented the greatest benefit of film-induced tourism in social media activities since a fictionally constructed reality has just been materialized in reality via the eternalization of someone's experience (i.e. picture). It is interesting to note that Croatian tourism officials do not perceive repostings and #gameofthrones associations as a social media activity that would enhance the authenticity of the posts or that of the macro- or micro-destination image. They are primarily interested in "what interests their tourists, how active they are and how they have spent their holidays in Croatia" (Croatia Tourism, 2016). Regardless, Croatian DMO social media practices, intentional or accidental in their own right, embody the elements of fabricating place authenticity strategy.

Implications for popular culture tourism

Tourism is a very competitive industry for destinations whose consumers look for the image and extraordinariness of their tourism-related decisions (Pirnar & Gunlu, 2012). This is even more evident in the tourism-related decisions of those people mesmerized by popular culture phenomena who pursue visits to destinations 'tipped' to be on- and off-location settings of their favorite film. As Jones (in Figueroa, 2015) said, "for the *Game of Thrones'* fans out there, it all comes live in Dubrovnik. You will walk the same paths, touch the same walls and soak up the views you see on the show." The tourist gaze Jones referred to is reinforced by popular culture and "has resulted in a massive upward shift in the level of what is *ordinary* and hence what people view as *extraordinary*" (Urry & Larsen, 2011, p. 116). It is in this context that DMOs have seen the benefits of an influx of tourism driven by the desire to experience the authenticity of on-screen fabricated realities. However, this film-induced tourism was shown not to be warmly welcomed by the DMOs and their tourism developmental strategies, both offline and online.

This chapter aims to assist those responsible for tourism destination marketing in understanding the benefits of popular culture tourism for destination image. More specifically, with the new technologies and Web 2.0 tourists became co-creators of destination image by sharing, liking, and posting their experiences on social media. In particular they use Instagram, which is primarily based on the sharing of photos, known to be *worth a thousand words*. It is these visitor practices that generate the content 'that is out there' for DMOs to freely incorporate in their social media activities in order to develop destination images and enhance the authenticity of the place. And, for what it's worth, isn't it better that DMOs participate in tourist-to-tourist communication on social media by reposting and thus invisibly imposing control over the destination image, which would take place regardless of DMOs' willingness to participate?

Note

1 For the purpose of this chapter, user-generated content will be called visitor-generated content to emphasize the role of the tourist prior to that of the social media user.

References

Baena, R., & Byker, C. (2015). Dialects of Nostalgia: *Downton Abbey* and English Identity. *National Identities, 17*(3), 259–269. http://doi.org/10.1080/14608944.2014.942262.

Bagnoli, L. (2015). 'Downton Abbey' and the TV-induced Tourism. *Journal of Tourism, Culture and Territorial Development, 4*, 102–116.

Beaton, N. (2015). Magic of New Zealand's Middle-earth. *Australasian Leisure Management, 111*(July/Aug), 38–41.

Beeton, S. (2005). *Film-Induced Tourism.* Clevedon, UK: Channel View Publications.

Beeton, S. (2010). The Advance of Film Tourism. *Tourism and Hospitality Planning & Development, 7*(1), 1–6. http://doi.org/10.1080/14790530903522572.

Bolan, P., & Williams, L. (2008). The Role of Image in Service Promotion: Focusing on the Influence of Film on Consumer Choice within Tourism. *International Journal of Consumer Studies, 32*(4), 382–390. http://doi.org/10.1111/j.1470-6431.2008.00672.x.

Buchmann, A. (2006). From Erewhon to Edoras: Tourism and Myths in New Zealand. *Tourism Culture & Communication, 6*(3), 181–189. http://doi.org/10.3727/109830406778134090.

Buchmann, A. (2010). Planning and Development in Film Tourism: Insights into the Experience of *Lord of the Rings* Film Guides. *Tourism and Hospitality Planning & Development, 7*(1), 77–84. http://doi.org/10.1080/14790530903522648.

Buchmann, A., Moore, K., & Fisher, D. (2010). Experiencing Film Tourism: Authenticity and Fellowship. *Annals of Tourism Research, 37*(1), 229–248. http://doi.org/10.1016/j.annals.2009.09.005

Carl, D., Kindon, S., & Smith, K. (2007). Tourists' Experiences of Film Locations: New Zealand as 'Middle-earth.' *Tourism Geographies, 9*(1), 49–63. http://doi.org/10.1080/14616680601092881.

Chen, N., & Šegota, T. (2015). Resident Attitudes, Place Attachment and Destination Branding: A Research Framework. *Tourism and Hospitality Management, 21*(2), 145–158.

Chung, J. Y., & Buhalis, D. (2008). Information Needs in Online Social Networks. *Information Technology & Tourism, 10*(979), 267–281.

Connell, J. (2012). Film Tourism: Evolution, Progress and Prospects. *Tourism Management, 33*(5), 1007–1029. http://doi.org/10.1016/j.tourman.2012.02.008.

Cox, C., Burgess, S., Sellitto, C., & Buultjens, J. (2009). The Role of User-Generated Content in Tourists' Travel Planning Behavior. *Journal of Hospitality Marketing & Management, 18*(8), 742–764. http://doi.org/10.1080/19368620903235753.

Croatia Tourism (2016, September 23). Email interview with a representative from the organisation.

Croy, W. G. (2010). Planning for Film Tourism: Active Destination Image Management. *Tourism and Hospitality Planning & Development, 7*(1), 21–30. http://doi.org/10.1080/14790530903522598.

Daugherty, T., Eastin, M. S., & Bright, L. (2008). Exploring Consumer Motivations for Creating User-Generated Content. *Journal of Interactive Advertising, 8*(2), 16–25. http://doi.org/10.1080/15252019.2008.10722139.

Figueroa, A. (2015). *Croatia's Tourism Grows Thanks to Festivals and 'Game of Thrones.'* Retrieved from www.travelagentcentral.com/croatia/croatias-tourism-grows-thanks-festivals-and-game-thrones-52369.

Frost, W. (2010). Life Changing Experiences: Film and Tourists in the Australian Outback. *Annals of Tourism Research, 37*(3), 707–726. http://doi.org/10.1016/j.annals.2010.01.001.

Gretzel, U. (2006). Consumer Generated Content: Trends and Implications for Branding. *E- Review of Tourism Research, 4*(3), 9–11.

Gretzel, U., Yuan, Y.-L., & Fesenmaier, D. R. (2000). Preparing for the New Economy: Advertising Strategies and Change in Destination Marketing Organizations. *Journal of Travel Research, 39*(2), 146–156. http://doi.org/10.1177/004728750003900204.

Grihault, N. (2003). Film Tourism: The Global Picture. *Travel & Tourism Analyst, 5*, 1–22.

Grihault, N. (2007). Set-Jetting Tourism: International. *Travel & Tourism Analyst, 4*, 1–50.

Guiness World Records. (2016). Retrieved from www.guinnessworldrecords.com/news/2016/9/game-of-thrones-wins-three-emmys-and-breaks-two-world-records-444586.

Hahm, J., & Wang, Y. (2011). Film-Induced Tourism as a Vehicle for Destination Marketing: Is It Worth the Efforts? *Journal of Travel & Tourism Marketing, 28*(2), 165–179. http://doi.org/10.1080/10548408.2011.546209.

Hays, S., Page, S. J., & Buhalis, D. (2013). Social Media as a Destination Marketing Tool: Its Use by National Tourism Organisations. *Current Issues in Tourism, 16*(3), 211–239. http://doi.org/10.1080/13683500.2012.662215.

HBO. (2016). Retrieved September 20, 2016, from www.makinggameofthrones.com/production-diary/game-of-thrones-triumphs-2016-emmys.

Hidalgo Alcazar, C., Silicila Pinero, M., & Ruiz de Maya, S. (2014). The Effect of User-Generated Content on Tourist Behavior: The Mediating Role of Destination Image. *Tourism & Management Studies, 10*(Special Issue), 158–164.

Hudson, S., & Ritchie, J. R. B. (2006). Promoting Destinations via Film Tourism: An Empirical Identification of Supporting Marketing Initiatives. *Journal of Travel Research, 44*(4), 387–396. http://doi.org/10.1177/0047287506286720.

Hudson, S., & Thal, K. (2013). The Impact of Social Media on the Consumer Decision Process: Implications for Tourism Marketing. *Journal of Travel & Tourism Marketing, 30*(1–2), 156–160. http://doi.org/10.1080/10548408.2013.751276.

Instagram. (2016). Retrieved August 25, 2016, from www.instagram.com/about/us/.

Larson, M., Lundberg, C., & Lexhagen, M. (2013). Thirsting for Vampire Tourism: Developing Pop Culture Destinations. *Journal of Destination Marketing and Management, 2*(2), 74–84. http://doi.org/10.1016/j.jdmm.2013.03.004.

Lexhagen, M., Larson, M., & Lundberg, C. (2014). The Virtual Fan(G) Community: Social Media and Pop Culture Tourism. In A. M. Munar, S. Gyimothi, & L. Cai (Eds.), *Tourism Social Media: Transformations in Identity, Community and Culture* (pp. 133–157). Bingley, UK: Emerald. http://doi.org/10.1108/S1571-5043(2013)0000018010.

Li, S., Li, H., Song, H., Lundberg, C., & Shen, S. (2017). The Economic Impact of On-Screen Tourism: The Case of *The Lord of the Rings* and *The Hobbit. Tourism Management, 60*, 177–187. http://dx.doi.org/10.1016/j.tourman.2016.11.0232016.11.023.

Light, D. (2007). Dracula Tourism in Romania Cultural Identity and the State. *Annals of Tourism Research, 34*(3), 746–765. http://doi.org/10.1016/j.annals.2007.03.004.

Lundberg, C., & Lexhagen, M. (2012). Bitten by the *Twilight Saga*: From Pop Culture Consumer to Pop Culture Tourist. In R. Sharpley & P. Stone (Eds.), *Contemporary Tourist Experience: Concepts and Consequences* (pp. 147–164). Abingdon: Routledge.

Lundberg, C., Lexhagen, M., & Mattsson, S. (2012). *Twication: The Twilight Saga Travel Experience.* Östersund: Jengel Forlag AB.

Mitchell, H., & Stewart, M. F. (2012). Movies and Holidays: The Empirical Relationship Between Movies and Tourism. *Applied Economics Letters*, *19*(15), 1437–1440. http://doi.org/10.1080/13504851.2011. 631888.

Moses Peaslee, R. (2010). "The Man from New Line Knocked on the Door": Tourism, Media Power, and Hobbiton/Matamata as Boundaried Space. *Tourist Studies*, *10*(1), 57–73. http://doi.org/10. 1177/1468797610390993.

Murray, N. M. (2017). GoT Belfast? How a Television Epic about a War-Torn Land was Employed to Rebrand Northern Ireland. In A. Bayraktar & C. Uslay (Eds.), *Global Place Branding Campaigns across Cities, Regions, and Nations* (pp. 1–24). Hershey, PA: IGI Global. http://doi.org/10.4018/978-1-5225-0576-1.ch001.

Neville, A. (2014). Tourism Social Media: Transformations in Identity, Community, and Culture. *Journal of Tourism and Cultural Change*, *12*(1), 88–90. https://doi.org/10.1080/14766825.2013.873385.

O'Connor, N., Flanagan, S., & Gilbert, D. (2008). The Integration of Film-Induced Tourism and Destination Branding in Yorkshire, UK. *International Journal of Tourism Research*, *10*(5), 423–437. http://doi.org/10.1002/jtr.676.

Oliveira, E., & Panyik, E. (2015). Content, Context and Co-Creation: Digital Challenges in Destination Branding with References to Portugal as a Tourist Destination. *Journal of Vacation Marketing*, *21*(1), 53–74. http://doi.org/10.1177/1356766714544235.

Piggott, R., Morgan, N. J., & Pritchard, A. (2004). New Zealand and *The Lord of the Rings*: Leveraging Public and Media Relations. In N. J. Morgan, A. Pritchard, & R. Pride (Eds.), *Destination Branding* (2nd ed., pp. 207–225). Burlington, MA: Elsevier.

Pirnar, I., & Gunlu, E. (2012). Destination Management and Quality-of-Life. In M. Uysal, R. R. Perdue, & J. M. Sirgy (Eds.), *Handbook of Tourism and Quality-of-Life Research* (pp. 529–545). New York: Springer.

Qualman, E. (2009). *Socialnomics: How Social Media Transforms the Way We Live and Do Business.* Hoboken, NJ: John Wiley and Sons.

Riley, R. W., Baker, D., & Van Doren, C. S. (1998). Movie Induced Tourism. *Annals of Tourism Research*, *25*(4), 919–935. http://doi.org/10.1016/S0160-7383(98)00045-0.

Riley, R. W., & Van Doren, C. S. (1992). Movies as Tourism Promotion. *Tourism Management*, *13*(3), 267–274. http://doi.org/10.1016/0261-5177(92)90098-R.

Safko, L., & Brake, D. K. (2009). *The Social Media Bible: Tactics, Tools, and Strategies for Business Success.* Hoboken, NJ: John Wiley and Sons.

Singh, K., & Best, G. (2004). Film-Induced Tourism: Motivations of Visitors to the Hobbiton Movie Set as Features in *The Lord of the Rings*. In W. Frost, W. G. Croy, & S. Beeton (Eds.), *International Tourism and Media Conference Proceedings* (pp. 98–111). Melbourne: Tourism Research Unit, Monash University.

Tuten, T. (2008). *Social Media Marketing in a Web 2.0 World.* Westport, CT: Praeger.

Tzanelli, R. (2016). From *Game of Thrones* to Game of Sites/Sights: Reconfiguring a Transnational Cinematic Node in Ireland's e-Tourism. In K. Hannam, M. Mostafanezhad, & J. Ricky (Eds.), *Event Mobilities: Politics, Place and Performance* (pp. 52–67). Abingdon: Routledge.

Urry, J., & Larsen, J. (2011). *The Tourist Gaze 3.0* (3rd ed.). London: Sage.

World Atlas. (2016). Retrieved August 1, 2016, from www.worldatlas.com/webimage/countrys/europe/outline/hr.htm.

Wray, M., & Croy, W. G. (2015). Film Tourism: Integrated Strategic Tourism and Regional Economic Development Planning. *Tourism Analysis*, *20*(3), 313–326. http://doi.org/10.3727/108354215X143 56694891898.

Xiang, Z., & Gretzel, U. (2010). Role of Social Media in Online Travel Information Search. *Tourism Management*, *31*(2), 179–188. http://doi.org/10.1016/j.tourman.2009.02.016.

Young, A. F., & Young, R. (2008). Measuring the Effects of Film and Television on Tourism to Screen Locations: A Theoretical and Empirical Perspective. *Journal of Travel & Tourism Marketing*, *24*(2–3), 195–212. http://doi.org/10.1080/10548400802092742.

37

THE INFLUENCE OF CULINARY MOVIES AS A POPULAR CULTURE TOURISM PHENOMENON IN SHOOT DESTINATIONS

Sara Forgas-Serra, Joaquim Majó Fernández and Lluís Mundet i Cerdan

Setting the scene

Films contribute to our knowledge of spaces and the cultures reflected in them, thus forming an image of the destination shown in the film. As Kim and Richardson (2003, p. 217) said, "news coverage and popular culture (as in films, television programs, and literature) can provide substantial information about a place in a short period of time." When films presenting this knowledge and information generate mass media phenomena, they connect with a wave of popular culture tourism, as the audience want to visit the places shown in the film. This leads us to film-induced tourism, since, according to Hudson and Ritchie (2006a, p. 256), "film tourism – sometimes called movie-induced or film-induced tourism – is defined as tourist visits to a destination or attraction as a result of the destination being featured on television, video, DVD or the cinema screen." Riley, Baker, and Van Doren (1998, p. 919) reinforce this view, stating that "movies provide the objects and subjects for the gaze of many people, and for some people, movies induce them to travel to the locations where they were filmed."

The main objective of this chapter is to investigate how culinary films influence tourism flow in the places where they were filmed. Even if we take into account that not all of these kinds of films have a specific setting, they still create a culinary image of the destination. For instance, while the setting of *American Cuisine* (1999) is not important, the film constructs an image of French gastronomy and its restaurants. On the other hand, there are examples of films that "can also be used to direct attention towards geographical areas or draw attention to less known destinations. France, for instance, uses the film *Chocolat* (2000) to draw attention to Burgundy" (O'Connor, Flanagan, & Gilbert, 2008, p. 425); and we can recognize La Havana through the ice cream parlor *Coppelia* in *Fresa y Chocolate* (*Strawberry and Chocolate*); or learn more about Jutland (Denmark) from *Babette's Feast*.

"The media often claim that films and TV dramas have a positive impact on a specific destination, but there is often no method of calculating this effect" (Li, Li, Song, Lundberg, & Shen, 2017, p. 177). To explore part of this impact, our research focus was aimed at determining how destination marketing organizations (DMOs) of the places where films were shot take advantage of this. That is, do they promote the destination through the movie? How? And is that the main points they are promoting?

Theoretical underpinnings

Different authors have established the relationship between film-induced image and tourism and the process of image formation. Before films, this image was created through books and literature, but,

> in the 21st Century, fictional films (movies and TV series) have taken over from literature as the most influential form of popular media, creating strong emotional ties to areas and can present certain activities that visitors and recreationists desire to imitate or experience.
> *(Beeton, 2008, p. 39)*

Unlike books, where the created image comes from the reader's imagination, "films provide viewers with images, accounts, and stories of life that are often far removed from the viewer's experience. They also have the potential to influence consumer perception, which can become part of enduring mental and social representations" (Macionis & Sparks, 2009, p. 94).

According to Kim and Richardson (2003, p. 216), "image has emerged as a crucial market-ing concept in the tourism industry." Within the tourism industry, we could say that film-tourism forms a part of cultural tourism, as Hudson and Ritchie (2006b, p. 387) point out: "Falling loosely under the umbrella of cultural tourism, film tourism is a growing phenomenon worldwide, fueled by both the growth of the entertainment industry and the increase in inter-national travel." Indeed, "cultural tourism has several aspects, both tangible and intangible, such as works of art, language, gastronomy, art and music, architecture, historical sites and monu-ments, festivals and cultural events, religion, education, clothing, etc." (Moira, Mylonopoulos, & Kontoudaki, 2015, p. 136). As cinema is considered the seventh art, and tourists traveling for film motivations are visiting different aspects of cultural tourism, as they are shown in the film, we could add film tourism as a part of cultural tourism.

Jewell and McKinnon (2008, p. 153) state that "movie tourism can be seen as a new form of cultural landscape" and "the images the movie goer forms as a result of watching it provides responses of the location as a 'must see' destination" (Jewell & McKinnon, 2008, p. 160), which also leads us to include this type of tourism under the umbrella of cultural tourism. As Connell (2012) argues, film tourism could be understood from a cultural perspective, since it is related to literary tourism and cultural geography and "going to the cinema remains one of the most popu-lar cultural activities in many societies" (Connell, 2012, p. 1011). Moreover, "TV series-induced tourism" – and we could understand film tourism by extension – "is a type of new cultural tour-ism that has great potential to advance cultural exchange and understanding" (S. S. Kim, Agrusa, Lee, & Chon, 2007, p. 1351). Mestre, del Rey, and Stanishevski (2008, pp. 193–194) also refer to film tourists as cultural tourists, stating that "fictional cinema is a great creator of cultural images that travel all around the world and have a significant impact on audiences."

The fact is that landscape and culture are very important in building the image of a destina-tion in the mind of a tourist. For Riley and Van Doren (1992, p. 274),

> the key for the construction of a favorable destination impression appears to be a for-mula of idyllic or extraordinary landscape qualities, a unique social and cultural vantage point, and/or an image that tourists identify with and wish to explore or rediscover.

Furthermore, this created image will be long-lasting, because,

> film images persist for decades, provide publicity and create identities. The exposure a film gives a city, province or country is an advertisement viewed by potentially millions of people, an audience that could not be reached through specifically targeted tourism promotions.
>
> *(Hudson & Ritchie, 2006a, p. 258)*

Therefore, the fact of seeing a movie where a landscape or culture appear that we wish to know more about does not mean we have to go on the trip immediately, rather the idea can stay with us for a long time before we do so. When all is said and done, as Buchanan (2010, p. 81) suggests (concerning *The Lord of the Rings* and New Zealand), "for most film tourists it is precisely the connection between both scenery and film that makes the visit of a selected location so special." That is, as Riley et al. (1998, pp. 919–920) pointed out:

> Through movies, people are sometimes induced to visit what they have seen on the silver screen. If this gaze is directed at objects or features which are extraordinary and thus distinguish the "site/sight" of the gaze from others, then the properties of a movie location – whether scenic, historical, or literary – qualify as icons for tourists to gaze upon. That is, in the sense that people are seeking sights/sites seen on the silver screen, they become movie-induced tourists.

To sum up then, "the creation of a destination image stimulates information search behavior concerning that destination and this heightened interest level leads to potential travel behavior to visit the location" (Hahm & Wang, 2011, p. 167). What is more, destinations where films have been shot can benefit in diverse ways, and especially economically, because "additional businesses and services can be created through film tourism that in turn can encourage the extension and strengthening of the visitor season" (Hudson & Ritchie, 2006b, p. 387).

Although further theoretical underpinnings regarding touristic image were found, only a few related to the image of gastronomy shown through films or culinary shows, as, for example, Busby, Huang, and Jarman (2013) do regarding the celebrity chef Rick Stein and his restaurant in Padstow (Cornwall, England). In this case, according to Busby et al. (2013, pp. 570–571), "what does not seem to have been considered in the research are television portrayals of tourist destinations with local foods and chefs to the fore," when, in reality "the nexus between film, gastronomy and tourism centers on destination enhancement and awareness" (p. 572).

Concerning promotion by DMOs, Riley and Van Doren (1992, p. 268) expound "the case that motion pictures filmed in the USA for US and international markets have been influential in promoting US tourist destinations," stating that "strong support for the premise of increased tourism through identification of destinations in movies is enhanced by statistical case studies and anecdotal evidence gathered within the USA." But this phenomenon is not limited to the US, since it has become a global phenomenon, as Connell (2012, p. 1007) states:

> Despite being a relatively niche element of tourism activity, a marked uptake of film tourism initiatives by destination marketing organizations and economic development organizations, eager to capture additional promotion, visitor awareness and visitor numbers, is notable within an increasingly global context. A number of high-profile tourism destinations utilize film-related aspects in inbound marketing campaigns.

In this chapter we will focus on movies rated as gastronomic, those with a storyline about food, and their connection with tourism, as "research in recent years has indicated the importance of gastronomy in the tourism 'offer,' and clearly, destination image can be influenced by perceptions of local cuisine, which are, themselves, influenced by the television representations" (Busby et al., 2013, p. 579). Considering that, as Beeton (2006, p. 184) states, "many destinations have come to assume that having a movie or television series filmed in their region will automatically increase tourism, and that this will be to their advantage," we will analyze if these advantages are also taken into account in cooking movies filmed in France.

Methodology

Throughout this chapter, a content analysis of films and destination websites has been conducted. Kolbe and Burnett (1991, p. 243) define content analysis as "an observational research method that is used to systematically evaluate the symbolic content of all forms of recorded communications." Kassarjian (1977, p. 8) points out that "content analysis is the study of the message itself, and not the communicator or the audience." From this perspective, our study focuses on two messages: the message delivered through the selected movies and the one transferred by the official websites of the analyzed touristic destinations, in order to understand the relationship between the gastronomic movies and the DMOs where they have been filmed.

To initiate the content analysis, initial parameters have been established as a basis for the analysis to acquire the data that would provide the conclusions. As Paisley (1969, p. 133) states, content analysis is a research method defined as "a phase of information-processing in which communication content is transformed, through objective and systematic application of categorization rules, into data that can be summarized and compared." Kassarjian (1977, p. 9) adds that it has to be objective, since "each step in the research process must be carried out on the basis of explicitly formulated rules and procedures"; and systematic "is meant to eliminate partial or biased analysis in which only those elements in the content which fit the analyst's thesis are selected." In our case, initially, a list of culinary movies was obtained from different film websites such as Internet Movie Database (IMDb, 2016) (www.imdb.com) and Film Affinity (2016) (www.filmaffinity.com). As the study aims to research the culinary image portrayed of places in the films, the first filter for the film list was the condition of being related to gastronomy and used the following keywords: cooking, cook, chef, culinary arts, food, kitchen, and restaurant. This list was later compared to the gross lifetime rank in Box Office Mojo (2016) (www.box officemojo.com), in relation to the keyword "cooking."

From these databases, we took the first ten main culinary movies by box office, as this figure indicates which movies have been a mass media phenomenon and had a significant audience (Table 37.1). Year of production was not considered, as some of the oldest culinary films are still among the most viewed. Only films shot in France or talking about French cuisine were selected, which amounted to five of the ten mentioned above. The selected films were then analyzed using a set of questions designed to ascertain how gastronomy is presented in the movie (where the scene is mainly set, the relationship between the main character and food, food as the central or secondary subject, and so on). Results are shown in Table 37.2.

After determining where the movie was set, an analysis of the official tourism bureau website was carried out for the place in question (Table 37.3). A set of questions was designed to analyze whether the bureau considered the fact that a movie had been filmed there, and what it tells us about the gastronomy of the village/city, region, or nation.

Ultimately, we adopted a qualitative approach for the research methodology, since the film and the website analysis scrutinized the content following a deductive paradigm. A deductive approach in content analysis is useful when "the structure of analysis is operationalized on the basis of previous knowledge" (Elo & Kyngäs, 2008, p. 107).

Trustworthiness of findings was established since each author carried out the analysis separately, following previously established guidelines, and in the end a consensus on the most trustworthy results was achieved. As Elo and Kyngäs (2008) state, credibility is acquired with the simplification of the data in categories and the representation of this analysis through tables.

Findings

The list of films that talk about gastronomy is a long one. The different databases consulted order them by keywords, popularity, user rating, or box office. Some examples under the keywords chef, cooking, and cook in IMDb are: *Burnt, Ratatouille, Chef, The Hundred-Foot Journey, Julie & Julia, It's Complicated,* and *Today's Special.* In the same database, but by popularity: *Charlie and the Chocolate Factory, Ratatouille, Chocolat, Fried Green Tomatoes, Julie & Julia, No Reservations, Because I Said So, Delicatessen, Like Water for Chocolate, Food Inc,* and so on. On Film Affinity the best ranked in the "cooking" genre are, among others, *Babette's Feast; Eat Drink Man Woman; Ratatouille; The Cook, the Thief, His Wife and Her Lover; Tampopo; Estomago; Like Water for Chocolate; A Touch of Spice; Bella Martha; Chocolat;* and *An (Sweet Red Bean Paste).* As we can see, some are repeated on the different lists, and many others have not been mentioned due to the length of the list.

For our analysis, we took into account box office ranking according to Box Office Mojo, with *Ratatouille* (2007), *Julie & Julia* (2009), *Chocolat* (2000), *The Hundred-Foot Journey* (2014), *No Reservations* (2007), *Chef* (2014), *Como agua para chocolate* (*Like Water for Chocolate*) (1993), *Burnt* (2015), *Big Night* (1996), and *Yin shi nan nu* (*Eat Drink Man Woman*) (1994) as the highest ranking gastronomic films. Of these ten, five were based on somewhere in France and/or narrate stories related to French cuisine, even if they are set in other places of the world. Table 37.1 lists the films, their location, and whether they relate to French cuisine. Finally, *Ratatouille, Julie & Julia, Chocolat, The Hundred-Foot Journey,* and *Burnt* were chosen so as to use a reference destination that includes as many films as possible, in this case France and its cuisine.

Table 37.1 Relation between the selected films

Movie	Year	Location	French gastronomy
Ratatouille	2007	Paris (France)	Yes
Julie & Julia	2009	Paris, Rouen, Le Havre (France) Queens, NY (USA)	Yes
Chocolat	2000	Flavigny-sur-Ozerain (France)	No
The Hundred-Foot Journey	2014	Saint-Antonin-Noble-Val (France) Paris (France)	Yes
No Reservations	2007	Manhattan (USA)	No
Chef	2014	Los Angeles, Miami, New Orleans, Austin (USA)	No
Like Water for Chocolate	1992	Mexico	No
Burnt	2015	Paris (France) New Orleans (USA) London (UK)	Yes
Big Night	1996	New Jersey (USA)	No
Eat Drink Man Woman	1994	Taipei (Taiwan)	No

The five selected films, mentioned above, were analyzed for their responses to a series of questions regarding both gastronomy and the iconic features of the places where they were shot. Table 37.2 shows the results of this analysis. As we can see, a variety of places were identified with regard to where the story takes place, from a private home in the case of *Julie & Julia* or a shop in *Chocolat*, to a restaurant in *Ratatouille*, *The Hundred-Foot Journey*, and *Burnt*. In the case of *The Hundred-Foot Journey*, a one-star French restaurant, an Indian restaurant, and a culinary laboratory in Paris are displayed. Throughout the films we can sense the interests of the characters, from wanting to learn how to cook or improve their cooking techniques though classic French cook books, either from home or working at a restaurant, to trying to obtain a first, second, or third Michelin star. With the exception of *Chocolat*, where the story revolves around chocolate and its recipes, in the films we discover the great dishes of French cuisine such as ratatouille, bouillabaisse, partridge, or a variety of desserts, often repeated in different films, as well as their typical basic sauces (béchamel, velouté, espagnole, hollandaise, and tomato sauce). Regarding the iconic features of the places where the story unfolds, although these do usually appear at some point in the film, it is to a much lesser extent than images of the actual dishes. For example, even if some of the scenes from four of the five movies had been shot in Paris, the Eiffel Tower is displayed for a few minutes, compared to the time that dishes are displayed. This finding reveals how in this type of film the aim is to show the product, the food, the procedure that takes place to turn it into a dish, and the final result. It is worth noting that all of the movies include scenes where the dish is actually served, either at a restaurant or at a private household.

With regard to our analysis of the official websites, including both France in general and the places where the different films are set (Paris, Flavigny-sur-Ozerain, and Saint-Antonin-Noble-Val), as can be observed in Table 37.3, they all have a section dedicated to food, whether to display local products or restaurants and producers that can be visited. The French website offers recipes for French dishes and presents the cuisine of different regions. As for the local websites, only the Burgundy has a specific section on local products and typical dishes and desserts of the region. Paris and Tarn-et-Garonne have a section dedicated to restaurants and/or local producers, but do not specify the products on offer. Only two of the towns where a movie was filmed refer to it on their website, and merely in a very superficial way. A reference to the film *Chocolat* can be found at the end of the description of Flavigny-sur-Ozerain, explained as a curiosity of the place. As for *The Hundred-Foot Journey*, no specific reference is found in the information on Saint-Antonin-Noble-Val, although a search for *The Hundred-Foot Journey* on the website reveals a PDF file that, when presenting places to visit, mentions the movie filmed there and a related tour. In the case of the France website, a search for all of the films analyzed here only returns information on *Julie & Julia*, in relation to cooking classes available in the place where Julia Child learned how to cook, and *Ratatouille*, referring to the attraction at Disneyland Paris amusement park. The Paris website does not make any reference to any of the films analyzed, even though an iconic feature of the city appears in all of them except for *Burnt*.

Discussion

The main aim of this research was to observe whether the destination marketing organizations (DMOs) of places where films were shot take advantage of this fact. The study focused on France as a general destination due to its cuisine, and the villages of Flavigny-sur- Ozerain and Saint-Antonin-Noble-Val, and the city of Paris in particular. After analyzing the websites of these places, we observed that no specific promotion is done in connection with the films, except, and only superficially, in the case of *Julie & Julia* and *Ratatouile* in Paris, and *The*

Table 37.2 Culinary movie analysis

Movie	Setting	Character	Type of cuisine	Dishes/products mentioned	Iconic features
Ratatouille	Restaurant	Chef's apprentice	French	Ratatouille	Eiffel Tower (Paris)
Julie & Julia	Private household	Woman who wants to learn French cooking	French (Julia Child's book)	French dishes	Eiffel Tower, Versailles, Orsay (Paris)
Chocolat	Shop	Shopkeeper	Chocolate	Chocolate	Village square (Flavigny-sur-Ozerain)
The Hundred-Foot Journey	1-star French restaurant; Indian restaurant; culinary laboratory	Indian chef learning French cuisine 1-star restaurant owner	French (Jules Gouffré's book) and Indian	Five basic sauces: bechamel, veloute, Spanish, Dutch, and tomato, and French dishes	River and town (Saint-Antonin-Noble-Val) Eiffel Tower (Paris)
Burnt	Restaurant	2-star chef who wants a third	French	Bouillabaisse, partridge, and other French dishes	London Eye, London bus, and bridges

Table 37.3 Web analysis

Site	Culinary section?	Shows dishes/culinary products?	Make reference to a culinary film?	Suggest activities linked to the film?
France official site (France, 2016)	Yes, link on homepage. "Foodie heaven" in "Inspire me"	Yes. Recipes from different regions	No	Yes. Cooking classes (*Julie & Julia*); *Ratatouille* attraction at Disneyland Paris
Paris official convention and visitors bureau website (2016)	Yes, link on homepage. "Eating out." About restaurants	No	No	No
Burgundy official site (Designed by Burgundy, 2016)	Yes, link on homepage. "Gastronomy" in "Discover Burgundy"	Yes. "Typical products from Burgundy"	Not in culinary section In "Discover Burgundy Must see tourist attractions/Sites/Flavigny-sur-Ozerain" Yes: *Chocolat*	No
Official website for tourism in Tarn-et-Garonne (2016)	Yes, link on homepage. "Food & Drink." Restaurants and producers	No	No. And neither in "Visit/Classified cities and villages/Saint-Antonin-Noble-Val" Yes in the brochure "Tarn-et-Garonne, slow living and tourism"	Yes. Special guided tour following in the steps of the protagonist

Hundred-Foot Journey in Saint-Antonin-Noble-Val. We would therefore say that the DMOs are not building on the success of these films, which are the highest grossing culinary films to date. This may be because the cuisine of France is already well known, and it does not therefore have as great a need for promotion as other destinations. Be that as it may, "film tourism is potentially also threatened by stagnation, and the timing of publicity and the introduction of new attractions is vital to continue the rejuvenation" (Buchmann, 2010, p. 84) of destinations such as the ones concerned in this study. Always bearing in mind that, as some authors state (Beeton, 2006; Connell, 2012), in the case that DMOs enhance tourism, especially in small villages, both positive and negative impacts may come from it so it should therefore be controlled.

Returning to the question raised at the beginning of this chapter, it is now possible to state that the analyzed destinations are not promoting gastronomy as a main point, even though films related to gastronomy are shot there. Regarding the landscape and cultural icons shown in the selected films, we can conclude that culinary films do not usually show much landscape or many iconic tourist attractions, but rather relate emotions, usually perceived through food and particularly good food. Rather than showing cultural and landscapes icons, they show culinary ones, which comprise the most representative and typical dishes of French cuisine.

Finally, after conducting this study we conclude that dishes can be transported to other geographies other than those where they originated. The importance of cuisine is how the dish is prepared, the recipe and the ingredients, while the place may change. A good example of this can be found in the film *The Hundred-Foot Journey*, in which the Indian main character moves his kitchen to a remote village in France, where he seeks out ingredients to make his dishes. After all, "the value of gastronomy to tourism is multiplied many times by translation to the small screen" (Busby et al., 2013, p. 579).

Implications for popular culture tourism

To date, little research has been conducted on the subject presented in this chapter. Even though these are well-known movies that have had big audiences and achieved a significant number of followers, DMOs in the places where they were shot do not noticeably promote the location through the film. During the research, the authors have noted that films might not have a direct relevant relationship with an existing location, although there could be a close relationship between the culinary image projected in the film and the final image tourists have of a destination. In the case of France, it can be very complicated and maybe, unnecessary, since it is a much consolidated destination, partly thanks to its gastronomy. If we take notice of the villages where movies have been shot, such as Flavigny-sur-Ozerain and Saint-Antonin-Noble-Val, it is clear that the DMOs should use the fact that a high-impact blockbuster movie has been shot there in order to attract more tourists. They should initially promote themselves from the website of the destination, because as we have seen, all of them have one but they don't use it with that aim, they present themselves in a very superficial way in relation to the movie. If a good web design is done and they link the site to search engines so that people who look for information about the movie find their website, many users who are unaware of the fact that the movie has been shot there, may have a desire to visit that municipality.

In this study, we examined only five of the many culinary films in existence. In addition, we analyzed a country that already receives a large number of tourists for other reasons beyond the films that may be shot there. Therefore, it may be interesting to devote further studies to determining the relationship between these films and the promotion done by DMOs in the countries where they have been shot, or the type of cuisine they refer to. Furthermore, from a different perspective, an analysis could be conducted of whether the dishes that are shown in movies are offered in French restaurants and whether they promote that themselves, taking advantage of the fact that they are known to many people because of the big screen.

References

Beeton, S. (2006). Understanding film-induced tourism. *Tourism Analysis, 11*, 181–188. https://doi.org/10.3727/108354206778689808.

Beeton, S. (2008). From the screen to the field: The influence of film on tourism and recreation. *Tourism Recreation Research, 33*(1), 39–47. https://doi.org/10.1080/02508281.2008.11081288.

Box Office Mojo. (2016). Retrieved January 20, 2016, from www.boxofficemojo.com.

Buchmann, A. (2010). Planning and development in film tourism: Insights into the experience of *Lord of the Rings* film guides. *Tourism and Hospitality Planning & Development, 7*(1), 77–84. https://doi.org/10.1080/14790530903522648.

Busby, G., Huang, R., & Jarman, R. (2013). The Stein effect: An alternative film-induced tourism perspective. *International Journal of Tourism Research, 15*, 570–582. https://doi.org/10.1002/jtr.

Connell, J. (2012). Film tourism: Evolution, progress and prospects. *Tourism Management, 33*, 1007–1029. https://doi.org/10.1016/j.tourman.2012.02.008

Designed by Burgundy. (2016). Retrieved January 30, 2016, from www.bourgogne-tourisme.com/.

Elo, S., & Kyngäs, H. (2008). The qualitative content analysis process. *Journal of Advanced Nursing, 62*(1), 107–115. https://doi.org/10.1111/j.1365-2648.2007.04569.x.

Film Affinity. (2016). Retrieved January 20, 2016, from www.filmaffiniy.com.

France. (2016). Retrieved October 15, 2016, from uk.france.fr.

Hahm, J., & Wang, Y. (2011). Film-induced tourism as a vehicle for destination marketing: Is it worth the efforts? *Journal of Travel & Tourism Marketing, 28*(2), 165–179. https://doi.org/10.1080/10548408.2011.546209.

Hudson, S., & Ritchie, J. R. B. (2006a). Film tourism and destination marketing: The case of *Captain Corelli's Mandolin. Journal of Vacation Marketing, 12*(3), 256–268. https://doi.org/10.1177/1356766706064619.

Hudson, S., & Ritchie, J. R. B. (2006b). Promoting destinations via film tourism: An empirical identification of supporting marketing initiatives. *Journal of Travel Research, 44*, 387–396. https://doi.org/10.1177/0047287506286720.

Internet Movie Database (IMDb). (2016). Retrieved January 20, 2016, from www.imdb.com.

Jewell, B., & McKinnon, S. (2008). Movie tourism: A new form of cultural landscape? *Journal of Travel & Tourism Marketing, 24*(2–3), 153–162. https://doi.org/10.1080/10548400802092650.

Kassarjian, H. H. (1977). Content analysis in consumer research. *Journal of Consumer Research, 4*, 8–18. https://doi.org/10.1086/208674.

Kim, H., & Richardson, S. L. (2003). Motion picture impacts on destination images. *Annals of Tourism Research, 30*(1), 216–237. https://doi.org/10.1016/S0160-7383(02)00062-2.

Kim, S. S., Agrusa, J., Lee, H., & Chon, K. (2007). Effects of Korean television dramas on the flow of Japanese tourists. *Tourism Management, 28*, 1340–1353. https://doi.org/10.1016/j.tourman.2007.01.005.

Kolbe, R. H., & Burnett, M. S. (1991). Content-analysis research: An examination of applications with directives for improving research reliability and objectivity. *Journal of Consumer Research, 18*, 243–250.

Li, S., Li, H., Song, H., Lundberg, C., & Shen, S. (2017). The economic impact of on-screen tourism: The case of *The Lord of the Rings* and *The Hobbit. Tourism Management, 60*, 177–187. https://doi.org/10.1016/j.tourman.2016.11.023.

Macionis, N., & Sparks, B. (2009). Film-induced tourism: An incidental experience. *Tourism Review International, 13*, 93–101. https://doi.org/10.3727/154427209789604598.

Mestre, R., del Rey, A., & Stanishevski, K. (2008). The image of Spain as tourist destination built through fictional cinema. *Journal of Travel & Tourism Marketing, 24*(2–3), 185–194. https://doi.org/10.1080/10548400802092718.

Moira, P., Mylonopoulos, D., & Kontoudaki, A. (2015). Gastronomy as a form of cultural tourism: A Greek typology. *TIMS Acta, 9*, 135–148. https://doi.org/10.5937/TIMSACT9-8128.

O'Connor, N., Flanagan, S., & Gilbert, D. (2008). The integration of film-induced tourism and destination branding in Yorkshire, UK. *International Journal of Tourism Research, 10*, 423–437. https://doi.org/10.1002/jtr.676.

Official website for Tourism in Tarn-et-Garonne. (2016). Retrieved September 20, 2016, from www.tourisme-tarnetgaronne.fr/.

Paisley, W. J. (1969). Studying style as deviation from encoding norms. In G. Gerbner (Ed.), *The analysis of communications content: Developments in scientific theories and computer techniques* (pp. 133–146). New York: Wiley.

Paris. Official website of the convention and visitors bureau. (2016). Retrieved September 28, 2016, from en.parisinfo.com.

Riley, R. W., Baker, D., & Van Doren, C. S. (1998). Movie-induced tourism. *Annals of Tourism Research*, *25*(4), 919–935. https://doi.org/10.1016/S0160-7383(98)00045-0.

Riley, R. W., & Van Doren, C. S. (1992). Movies as tourism promotion: A "pull" factor in a "push" location. *Tourism Management*, *13*(3), 267–274. https://doi.org/10.1016/0261-5177(92)90098-R.

38

VISITOR EXPERIENCES OF POPULAR CULTURE MUSEUMS IN ISLANDS

A management and policy approach

Nikolaos Boukas and Myria Ioannou

Setting the scene

Much of the tourism activity worldwide is met on insular destinations (i.e. Mediterranean islands, the Caribbean, Indonesia, etc.). Indeed, the morphological character and idiosyncrasies of islands such as their remoteness, unique natural and cultural landscapes, authentic sceneries, and climate, makes them desirable destinations for millions of tourists (Carlsen & Butler, 2011; Lewis-Cameron & Roberts, 2010). Nonetheless, the majority of island destinations are mostly planned to satisfy mass tourism needs, while most of the tourist activities concentrate around the 3S model of development – sea, sand, and sun – which features in many southern insular places (Briguglio & Briguglio, 1996). As such, mass tourism dominates in many island destinations, including Cyprus.

The economic benefits of mass tourism for island economies are evident. Nevertheless, a series of negative impacts associated with mass tourism such as seasonality, unbalanced development, exceeded capacity, and commercialization threaten the islands' sensitive character and overshadow their genuine natural and cultural significance. However, the role of cultural heritage for islands is twofold: on the one hand, it could be the means to really diversify the destination's product/service mix, and hence help it escape from the conventional model of mass tourism development to a more specified one, (i.e. cultural tourism), and, on the other hand, it can more efficiently transfer to tourists the real meanings of islands as tourist attractions, through their culture. As such, popular culture as a significant element of tourism production and more specifically, popular culture museums as ambassadors of culture could help islands build a stronger identity and attachment with the tourists, and overall shape a basis for a more holistic and long-term tourist development.

This chapter studies the views of cultural heritage management and policy makers in Cyprus (as a representative island destination), in regards to the way/s visitor experiences of popular culture museums are shaped, and examines how culture helps or can help the overall marketing of insular destinations. Specifically, the chapter explores the role of popular culture tourism in Cyprus on the overall tourism development of the island and investigates the role of museums as promoters of cultural tourism. Moreover, the chapter analyzes the motives and expectations of popular culture visitors in Cypriot museums and explores the challenges and opportunities for popular culture tourism in Cyprus. Finally, the chapter proposes marketing strategies for establishing and projecting a popular culture tourism product through museums in island destinations, such as Cyprus.

Theoretical underpinnings

Islands and tourism: the need for diversification

Tourism is considered as an important vehicle for islands' economic development generating income to many stakeholders. This is even more evident for islands with good weather conditions and idyllic landscapes, such as in the Mediterranean, South Pacific, or the Caribbean (Butler, 2008). Characteristically, in the Mediterranean island of Cyprus (with approximately 840 million residents), 2,659,400 tourists arrived in 2015 generating €2,062.4 million revenue to the economy (Cyprus Tourism Organization, 2016). These figures have managed to place the island on the map of the world's important destinations. In this regard, for many islands, tourism comprises a significant (if not the only) economic activity that offers foreign income to them, an increase of their residents' quality of life, creation of jobs in the hospitality and recreation sector, and high multiplier effects.

Nonetheless, the injection of money to the islands' fragile economies is not enough for developing a healthy and balanced tourist activity. Indeed, in the literature of island tourism there are many negative phenomena that accompany islands' tourist activity, such as their over-dependence on mass tourism, foreign markets, and foreign investors, the over-utilization of their natural and cultural resources, the unplanned development, their susceptibility to local and global crises, and the overall unsustainable manner of developing and managing tourism (with) in them (Boukas & Ziakas, 2013, 2014; Carlsen & Butler, 2011; Lewis-Cameron & Roberts, 2010). Those phenomena create the conditions that threaten the sustainable stewardship of islands' limited resources (i.e. land, water, etc.) and alter their socio-cultural character in the long term.

Consequently, the over-dependence of island economies on tourism in a very competitive environment raises questions as to how island destinations can be efficiently developed and managed without significantly altering their socio-cultural and environmental deposits for their current and future state. Conventional forms of tourism that now dominate in many islands worldwide, such as mass tourism, despite the economic boost they bring, overexploit the natural and cultural resources of the islands (the main attraction for visiting them), while they harm their environment. Moreover, they bring a series of environmental and social complications to the destination, its residents, and the visitors (i.e. criminality, unregulated development, etc.) (Goeldner & Ritchie, 2012). In other words, while mass tourism is still evident and dominates the world tourism system, its impacts make island destinations not attractive and competitive anymore. As a result, potential mass tourists seek to find other 'purer' island destinations or 'lost paradises' in the world. Visiting in volumes however, once again brings problems for the destinations' fragile ecosystem and eventually damages their natural/cultural fabric.

The lost competitiveness of islands, especially compared to other continental destinations with many more and diverse resources, is one of the main problems that currently challenges islands' tourism policy, among them Cyprus (Boukas & Ziakas, 2013). It is evident that mass tourism may not work anymore and urgent solutions on innovative products may be the answer for islands' rejuvenation and long-term sustainability. While culture has been used frequently in the overall tourist development of many destinations in the cases where mass tourism dominates (i.e. the Greek islands), its role in the overall tourist product is mostly peripheral rather than central (Boukas, 2012). Moreover, even in the cases where culture does have a more fundamental role, emphasis is mostly given to high-culture attractions (i.e. archaeological visits) rather than popular culture ones. For instance, as Sdrali and Chazapi (2007) argue, the Greek island of Andros has mostly been developed as a cultural destination due to its antiquities, Byzantine and post-Byzantine monuments, castles, medieval towers, monasteries, and churches, even though as the authors mention, pre-industrial technology monuments, exhibition centers, and libraries are also evident. However, popular culture elements could facilitate the effort towards the construction and promotion of a more sustainable, harmonized, and diversified tourism product for islands.

The role of popular culture and museums to cultural tourism

Culture is a complex concept that is open to different interpretations. Jenks (1993, p. 9) argues that: "the dominant European linguistic convention equates 'culture' largely with the idea of 'civilization.'" According to Burns (1999), culture amalgamates a series of components, from religion, myths, values, ideologies, education, language, legal and political frameworks to economics, technology, material culture, social organizations, and kinship. Culture therefore, characterizes how a society lives, works, and/or plays (Goeldner & Ritchie, 2012). In tourism terms, all the aforementioned elements shape a destination's product/service mix, identity, and character, and facilitate to establish a strong and recognized brand as far as destination marketing is concerned. As Misiura (2006) argues, country branding incorporates a series of heritage elements including famous people, their role to events (i.e. art, dance, literature, etc.), major historical elements that can be celebrated, components of architecture, food and drink, people, and language, as well as folklore. Indeed, the magnitude of cultural tourism is great while culture is considered as one of the most important motives for traveling in international tourism (McKercher & duCros, 2012). As such, through cultural tourism, history becomes a commodity and cultural assets are transformed into tourist products. Considering that WTO and UNESCO characterize cultural tourism as a 'good' form of tourism that could help to encounter the 'bad' form of mass tourism (Richards, 2001) and its implications, the planning and promotion of more gentle forms of tourism, such as cultural tourism is, more than ever, essential, especially for island destinations.

Popular culture is also evident in tourism while popular culture characteristics can be important (re)presenters of a destination's socio-cultural fabric. Strinati (2004) argues that popular culture can be met in various societies and groups within them, while it also incorporates diverse historical periods, and that this is the reason that there is no strict and exclusive definition of it. Along the same lines, Heilbrun (1997) suggests that despite the categorization between high and popular culture, there are many other different types of culture such as architecture, photography, antiques, folk arts, home entertainment, and sound, which do not necessarily fit in to either of these two categories. Moreover, Edensor (2002, p. 14) claims that: "Popular culture itself has become a prime site for contestations of value embedded deep within fields such as television and film criticism, popular music and 'modern' art." In this regard, popular culture is an abstract concept embedded in several elements of our world. Therefore, popular culture or the culture consumed and accessed by a wide range of audiences including differing ages, races, and socio-economic backgrounds, incorporate several elements that could become tourist attractions (i.e. museums such as aquariums, arboretums, botanical gardens and observatories, nightlife such as comedy and dance clubs, dance studios, bands and orchestras, movie theaters and film festivals, costumes, commemorative artefacts, etc.) (Anadon, 2004; Edensor, 2002). Those elements can communicate the culture of a place to a large number of people, including tourists, and can help the creation of specific niche tourist products (i.e. event and festival tourism, gastronomic tourism, theme park tourism, transport tourism, etc.) (Novelli, 2005). As such, popular culture can enhance the enrichment and diversification of the tourist offering of a destination while simultaneously communicating in a more efficient way the real sense of the place, thus creating unique identities.

Nonetheless, when mentioning popular culture, we also need to appreciate its significance in comparison to high culture, especially when discussing cultural heritage tourism as a means for the diversification of islands' tourism product–service mix. Popular culture industries focus mostly on the expression of a society's way of life rather than the main strictly educational role (characterizing high culture) (Ivanovic, 2008), hence providing more democratized experiences for larger audiences of people. In cultural tourism terms and in a postmodern environment therefore, the role of high and popular culture has also shaped contemporary tourism products. As Richards (1996) argues, cultural experiences are an amalgamation of elements from both high and low culture. Richards' opposition is based on the fact that, on the one hand, there is not a clear distinction between culture, tourism, and our daily life; in this respect, the consumption of culture could be passive such as experiencing the atmosphere of a place or activity such as visiting a folk museum. On the other hand, the author argues that high culture does have – among others – a commercial character; in this regard, many strategies of heritage management emphasize the economic benefits of high culture rather than other more intrinsic ones (i.e. an archaeological museum organizes galas in its premises for increasing profitability). Based on this statement, in our globalized postmodern world, culture is not static; in contrast, it changes rapidly, it evolves and incorporates several characters from numerous places and for various audiences. As such, cultural tourist experiences are important components in the world liberal tourism trade and assets of popular culture are of great importance to their formation.

To this end, popular culture is a significant ambassador of many places while museums themselves are the best way by which to understand and interpret popular culture (Moore, 1997). Popular culture has a direct relationship to museums since as exhibitors of cultural elements, they are in a large part extensions of popular phenomena. Schoreder (1981) placed particular emphasis upon the popular culture in museums arguing that all museums function as cultural archives, research centers, but also as providers for the recreation, education, and inspiration of the public(s); the author also mentions the term 'populism' to explain museums' effort not only to preserve culture for future generations but also to serve the whole public of the present with respect and understanding. This is of great importance for tourism, since popular culture museums are open to a variety of publics – often international tourists – seeking to experience elements of the past and the presence of a destination, and therefore to learn, interpret, and be entertained.

In this regard, popular culture museums become the visitor centers for tourists and offer them holistic tourist involvement through leisure, entertainment, and community activities. In places where tourist development is evident, these museums facilitate to communicate the meanings of the destinations to a large variety of visitors. Therefore, they act as ambassadors of the destinations to tourists while in a large degree they depend financially on tourist activity. Consequently, popular culture museums could help the creation and/or enhancement of cultural tourism on island destinations while operating as producers of unique and diversified visitor experiences, generating significant income for their future sustainability.

Shaping museum visitor experience

Mapping and understanding the experience of customers has become, in recent decades, a central focus both for academics and practitioners. The first reference to customer experience was made in the early 1980s, by Hollbrook and Hirschmann (1982), who challenged current thinking, asserting that experiential aspects such as fantasies, feelings, and fun need to be incorporated in consumer behavior. Since then, a multitude of researchers have embraced customer experience as a key construct in their studies. Such studies, however, take different perspectives in examining customer experiences. Broadly speaking, many researchers approach customer experience from the institution's perspective, i.e. how customer experiences are delivered across various touchpoints (e.g. Pine & Gilmore, 1998; Verhoef et al., 2009), focusing on design and service elements. A broadened perspective is offered by the popular service-dominant logic (SDL; see, for example, Vargo & Lusch, 2004, 2016), which emphasizes the co-creation of the experience, while on the other hand, others (Heinonen et al., 2010; Heinonen & Tore, 2015) argue that experience is something that happens in customers' sphere, hence moving the focus away from the provider to understand how customers sense, relate, and act and how experience is co-created. A further point of difference pertains to whether the experience is viewed at a micro, meso or macro level (Akaka, Vargo, & Schau, 2015). Similarly, there is a lack of consensus on the elements that shape customer experience, which may largely be attributable to the different research streams (e.g. experiential marketing, retailing, services marketing). The most often cited factors are consumer factors (such as demographics, goals, attitudes), the environment and atmospherics, the role of service personnel, and the effect of other customers (Berry, Carbone, & Haeckel, 2002; Gentile, Spiller, & Noci, 2007; Parasuraman, Berry, & Zeithaml, 1991; Verhoef, Reinartz & Krafft, 2010). For Schmitt (1999), who has been highly influential in the field, customer experience can be described across the five dimensions of sensory experiences (sense); affective experiences (feel); creative cognitive experiences (think); physical experiences, behaviors and lifestyles (act); and social-identity experiences (relate). Hence, in spite of the increasing body of knowledge on the concept, there is to date no universally accepted definition of customer experience and the concept is ill-defined (Carù & Cova, 2003; Gentile et al., 2007).

Nevertheless, in spite of these conceptualization issues, customer experience is gaining increasing attention in services literature in general and in tourism literature. In particular, researchers in tourism have embraced the concept and coined a new term, experiential tourism. That is, experience constitutes a key theoretical construct in the tourism literature, where destinations are viewed as a series of experiences, delivered over time and resulting in lasting memories (Pine & Gilmore, 1998; Richards, 2001). Put differently, within this sphere, destinations are seen as enhancing the possibility that visitors can create their own memorable experience (Farber & Hall, 2007; Tung & Ritchie, 2011; Zimmerman & Kelly, 2010). To this end, particular emphasis has been placed on atmospherics, entertainment, and escapism (e.g. Bonn, Joseph-Matthews, Dai, Hayes, & Cave, 2007; Hosany & Witham, 2010). Therefore, experiential tourism prevails in the environment of museums; popular culture museums in this respect, should capitalize on experiential tourism in order for more holistic experience to be delivered to the visitors and a more concrete image about popular culture to be formed in museums visitors' travel ladder.

Methodology

To address the scope and objectives of the chapter, the study employed qualitative research techniques. The qualitative research approach was judged to be a significant method for giving an in-depth analysis of the issues under consideration (Malhotra, 2009; Yin, 2009), for discovering the visitor experiences of popular culture museums in Cyprus, from a management and tourism policy approach. Data collection incorporated semi-structured in-depth interviews with popular museums' managers and officials as well as tourism policy officials and review of archival material in regards to tourism and cultural policy matters of Cyprus. A purposive sampling method was judged to be an efficient way in order to derive insight from the most accurate sources. Specifically, different actors of the interaction were interviewed. From them, three people represented the tourism policy of the island and the remaining five were managers/owners and officials of popular museums. All those informants have a crucial position in the decision-making of management and cultural tourism policies in popular museums.

In regards to the popular culture museums that participated in the study, three museums from the capital city of Cyprus in Nicosia were selected to be studied: (a) Costas & Rita Severis Foundation, Centre of Visual Arts & Research (CVAR) (paintings, costumes and memorabilia related to Cyprus and its neighbors); (b) the Leventis Municipal Museum of Nicosia (folklore and modern heritage museum); and (c) the Loukia and Michael Zampelas Modern and Contemporary Art Museum. The fact that only museums from Nicosia were selected is justified mostly by two main purposes. First, as a city, Nicosia has a number of popular culture museums. Second, despite the fact that Nicosia is the capital city of Cyprus, it is not one of the main tourist attractions, mostly because it is located in the center of the island and not close to the beach. Considering that the dominant model of tourism in Cyprus is mass tourism this is explainable. However, Nicosia has all the qualities to become a popular culture tourism destination; it is characterized by a plethora of cultural traces, it is globalized and has several destination attributes that could contribute positively to a unique tourist product formation. The selection of the specific museums was made based on their position in the city (two of them are central and the third suburban) as well as their character.

The interviews took place in the interviewees' offices and museum premises and lasted on average 60–90 minutes. Two interviewers conducted and recorded the interviews. An interview guide was utilized to give a general direction to the interviews and bring to the surface important matters and themes. The main areas that the guide covered were related with: the role of popular culture in islands' tourist development and their identity; the perceptions of museum visitors and their experience; the challenges and opportunities for developing popular culture tourism in Cyprus; the environmental conditions and policy consideration for the successful and sustainable tourism development of the island utilizing popular culture. Finally, the interview transcripts were transcribed verbatim and then translated in to English and each author thoroughly examined the transcripts along with the archival material, underlining important sections to be considered in the analysis of the results. Ideas were compared and three main axes were derived to explain the aim of the chapter: the role of popular culture museums to cultural tourism development; motivational and experiential determinants of visitors to Cyprus' popular culture museums; and challenges and opportunities for popular culture tourism in Cyprus.

Implications for popular culture tourism

The role of popular culture museums for the cultural tourism development of Cyprus

A central pillar discussed in the interviews both with the tourism policy sector as well as with museum professionals was to conceptualize the role of popular culture overall and popular culture's museums to cultural tourism development of islands, focusing on the case of Cyprus. Respondents emphasized that cultural tourism in general and popular culture specifically, are elements met in the island, even though they do not receive the same levels of the market share met in other coastal areas. This underlines the dominance of mass tourism. As a respondent representing the tourism policy states:

> Culture [both high and popular] is spread all over the island. However, most of the tourists reside in the coastal levels and when visit[ing] places that have cultural elements such as Nicosia – even if the places possess rich culture – they have only some fixed hours available to look for it. Therefore, they do not have the time to appreciate all the cultural elements available in the destination, even if they have time to see most of them.

The above statement underlines the secondary character of culture in the formation of the Cypriot tourism product–service mix. Additionally, other interviewees focused on the nature of cultural tourism in Cyprus, as a respondent representing the museums claimed:

> Cyprus, since old times, has been identified with the nice beaches; steadily and slowly though, a form of cultural tourism started to be developed, but focused mostly on archaeology and lasted for many years . . . only recently there is some change and a new form of culture started to be presented . . . initiated by the Byzantine character and the Medieval aspects of Cypriot culture . . . though lately the recent history of Cyprus and the contemporary way of life represented through folklore museums and arts has been grown and interests more and more visitors.

Nonetheless, popular culture is evident in Cyprus and – in comparison to the past – it is now presented among other channels, through popular culture museums. As mentioned by a museum representative:

> In contrast to what exists mostly in Cyprus, our museum focuses on the recent history of Cyprus through paintings about Cyprus as seen by foreign painters, the evolution of the Cypriot costume, the various memorabilia that express the several periods and significant events of Cyprus, and a large research center that is open to the wide[r] public . . . through these elements someone can see how buildings have been changed, how the life of modern Cypriots has been evolved, the differences in the landscapes but also the symbiosis between the two communities [the Greek-Cypriot and Turkish-Cypriot].

Another respondent representing the tourism policy of the island mentioned that popular culture museums have started to play an important role in the travel itineraries of the travel agents that bring tourists to Nicosia. As the interviewee from the tourism policy side argued: "When someone is in Nicosia, there are not many things for him/her to do. Museums and most importantly popular culture museums are a very good option while you are in the city in order to see its character." Nonetheless, the respondent concluded that there are still so many other elements of popular culture to be exhibited by the museum and appreciated that there is more ground to be covered for the future development of cultural tourism. However, it was also mentioned that we need to examine the types of tourists that visit the cultural heritage museums as well as their motivation and travel behavior in order to fully value the potential of this type of tourist development.

Motivation and experiential determinants of visitors to Cyprus' popular culture museums

In line with extant literature that postulates that customer experience includes not only the experience during the consumption of the tourist product, but also prior to departure planning, the current study illustrates that the visitors' motives significantly affect their experience, where considerable differences between individual and group visitors have been underlined. Specifically, individual visitors tend to be more purposeful cultural tourists (McKercher & duCros, 2012) and as it was highlighted by museum officials: "they plan their experience in advance, do their research, and know which cultural places they want to visit" and "they come with a plan and are well informed of the museums they will visit." On the contrary, group visitors have less interest and are marginally informed about the museums they visit, since this experience is orchestrated by the travel agents, who are the ones that plan their visits and direct visitor flows to museums and cultural sites.

In line with the existing literature, the role of atmospherics has also been found to be salient. To this end, both the policy makers and the museums' management highlighted a series of atmospheric elements, including, museum layout, presentation of exhibits, and correct lighting to draw attention to exhibits. Some representative comments include:

> The museum is divided by different artists and themes . . . it is easier for visitors' to explore . . . We place great emphasis on layout and the colors used . . . Different lighting is used for different exhibits and different presentation techniques . . . some are shown in use.

To this effect, museums are largely aiming to 'give voice to exhibits' through various presentational efforts, trying to transform plain presentation into explanatory ones. Signage and audio guides are also seen as affecting the visitors' experience: "We try to use simple language in our signs . . . and to present all relevant information clearly."

In addition, the museums' management noted the critical role of employees in shaping visitors' experiences. In fact, one of the museums asserts that actively interacting with visitors constitutes a core part of their offering, arguing that: "We aim to walk through the museum with each customer or group, viewing and discussing the exhibits with visitors." It can therefore be argued that the findings implicitly address the importance of museum–visitor interaction, moving away from the myopic stance that visitor experiences are shaped and can be determined by the provider alone. In fact, the results suggest that museums are aware of this and they aim to engage visitors, co-create their experience, and shift it from merely viewing the exhibits to "helping them understand and interpret them."

In recognition of the importance of actively engaging visitors in the co-creation process, museums have also started to provide various educational programs and targeted events. Currently, it appears that the majority of educational programs are focusing primarily on the youth segment, which, according to the managers of the museums, is the most receptive segment; and a plethora of creative, extraordinary, and engaging educational programs are constantly designed. As Jenkins, Purushotma, Weigel, Clinton, and Robison (2009) suggest, museums are important providers of afterschool programs for children while educators should utilize these programs to expand youths' comprehension of the world. With respect to events, the manager of a museum explained how prior to the opening of the exhibition of a new topic/theme, a special event is organized in advance, which may include the presentation of a documentary, a lecture, relevant music, etc. and this is communicated to a particular mailing list.

It can therefore be argued that both the form and the level of interaction with the visitors surfaces as a key construct in shaping their experiences. Put differently, interactiveness engages visitors and through these interactive experiences, value is co-created and experiences are enhanced (Grönroos, 2011; Heinonen et al., 2010). Hence, contrary to a significant stream of research that adopts the firm-dominant perspective, the findings cast a serious doubt on the proposition that the firm shapes the experience for the customer alone, and suggest that value co-creation can better explain visitors' experience with popular culture museums. This experience needs to be an interactive and engaging process for such visitors.

Challenges and opportunities for popular culture tourism in Cyprus

According to the interviews, several challenges in regards to popular culture tourism as reflected by museums in Cyprus were raised. In this matter, the most important finding mentioned by all the respondents was – as mentioned earlier – the role of travel agencies in bringing tourism flows to popular culture museums. As a tourism policy official mentioned:

> Due to the fact that most hotels are located in coastal areas, tourists use travel agencies to visit Nicosia. However, they only have [a] few hours to see many things. Because of this the places that they take them are fixed. People are not free to walk around and look. Even a well-informed tourist that would like to see certain places will have to be limited to this fixed schedule. Of course, this applies mostly to group tourists; individual tourists form their own visits.

In line with the above argument another representative of the tourism policy sector claimed:

> We are at the disposal of travel organizers . . . these are those people that create the trips, bring visitors to museums, and control the client. We are trying through various seminars to educate the representatives of these organizers to give proper information to tourists about the elements that exist in the area . . . it is the responsibility of those agencies that guide tourists . . . nonetheless, what they do is to just take them to some pre-determined places according to their itinerary and only for a specific period of time.

This specific statement is one of the most important problems that popular culture museums face. As a respondent representing a museum demonstrates:

> Unfortunately, we don't have as many tourists as we would like to have. Travel agencies and tourist guides used to bring tourists to Nicosia only for half a day and they take them to the archaeological museum – the "Greekness" of the place – or to the Byzantine museum, and then let them free to the market for shopping. We have tried plenty of times to change this situation . . . we invite guides to the museums and tell them that we will take care of the guide in the premises in order for them to do the rest, we also invited tour agencies to show them the contribution of the museum to their programs, and we try through the Cypriot Tourism Organization.

Or another one from a museum:

> In cooperation with the tourism policy there is a bus that visits the museum every Monday and brings tourists that want to see contemporary Cypriot art. Every now and then there are also ad hoc visits but not on a stable basis. We would like to have more tourists though because we see there is an increasing interest by them.

Another challenge is the nature of museums on the island. As a museum official mentioned: "There are so many museums of different character and ownership that confuse visitors and tourists." In this argument, the tourism policy contends that they do promote museums but there is a problem of the status of museums overall in Cyprus:

> There are many private museums and many small collections on Cyprus in an excessive degree for the size of it. Cultural services tried to encourage local communities and individual people to operate museums but there are problems with their management and the perceived experience. Now, cultural services set standards in order to concentrate only on those museums that can offer a proper quality experience such as certain operation timetables, standards in regard to language used, etc.

The above arguments underline a difficult situation in terms of museums' efficient management not only by their owners but under a prism of cultural and tourism policy. Tourism policy representatives argued that even though they have a good relationship with cultural policy they would like to have more cooperation as far as tourist visitation is concerned.

A final remark on the challenges that popular culture museums face is their financial condition. All the museums are private organizations that depend on their profitable operation for their survival. This complicates the ways to efficiently expose themselves to tourists. As argued: "money that policy uses to finance and promote the museums is not enough in comparison to those invested in other tourism projects and activities." Therefore, popular culture museums not only face competition by other museums that traditionally benefit more from policy (i.e. public museums) but need to exist on their own means in an environment that does not support cultural tourism and in a very fragile economic time. Of course, the lack of financial support does not allow museums to enhance their provided experience by incorporating modern technologies and improving their amenities.

Nonetheless, what are the opportunities to develop and promote this specific form of tourism through museums? According to respondents, popular culture museums in Cyprus can, not only grow, but also comprise one of the main activities for tourists: "Islands are small territories, therefore visitors can go to several museums in a day and thus on some days they can have an overall good image about the popular culture of Cyprus." As another respondent from the tourism policy argued:

> Not all tourists are mass tourists. There are people that are really interested in Cypriot culture. The many museums that we have – many of them representing the popular character of the island – is an opportunity to bring tourists to places such as Nicosia. There are markets; we just need to stimulate them.

Another museum representative also mentioned the change of mentality of contemporary tourists. As suggested, culture is not something static. In contrast, it is something active and continuously changing. The respondent argued that visitors are more sophisticated than in the past and have different reference points to compare; not only they are happy with popular culture elements but they also seek them out. As the respondent suggested:

> Policy needs to radically change. We had enough with the archaeology on the island. Contemporary tourists want something visual that [they] can see and understand. Archaeology, presupposes knowledge, a guide and specific interest. Not all tourists are interested in it. I think we need to develop tourism in order to cover the whole history and life of Cyprus. They try but only solely, such as the wine of Cyprus, the carnival, or Venus of Cyprus – which again is archaeology. All these, are specific elements and not for all the year. There are so many things on popular culture that we can develop in order to bring more visitors in a constant pace.

In this regard, popular culture can become the main ingredient in the product modification and diversification of islands such as Cyprus. Unique experiences obtained through unique management techniques utilizing contemporary cultural elements such as those from popular culture could become a means for the rejuvenation of many islands.

Concluding remarks

Findings of the study indicate that chronically, not only is culture overall overshadowed by mass tourism in regards to Cyprus tourism development, but also that the role of popular culture has not been discovered and appreciated until very recently. This underlines the missed opportunities to develop a holistic cultural heritage tourism product on the island and express an overall new identity to visitors. Indeed, the dominance of high culture in Cyprus' cultural tourism has largely to do with political decisions. As Stylianou-Lambert, Boukas, and Bounia (2015) argue in their study on Cypriot museums, since the beginning of the new born state (the Republic of Cyprus in 1960s), attention by policy makers has been paid to the Greek-related character of Cyprus, expressed through the classical era and Christian world items. This attention aimed to connect the modern island to its ancient Greek past and Byzantine times. As a promoter of culture, tourism contributed towards this direction by incorporating high-culture elements to its tactical promotional activity. As such, popular culture elements have been systematically neglected by tourist authorities in the past, even though in recent years they have been incorporated into the exhibitions of Cypriot museums.

In order, therefore, to promote popular culture tourism through museums a series of actions are proposed. These actions need to be considered both by tourism policy and museum officials. Tourism policy need to have a more direct communication with cultural policy regarding not only the promotion of popular culture heritage museums in Cyprus but also their development (i.e. content, way/s of presentation, quality standards, etc.) and management, in order to create product dedicated to tourists. The synergy between cultural heritage management and cultural tourism is not a recent topic and it is true that sometimes their roles are contradictory. Nonetheless, as McKercher and duCros (2012) argue, there is a need to appreciate each other's role and contribution, since ultimately this synergy leads to mutual benefits. Thus, tourism needs to understand that cultural heritage management has a sacred duty to protect the exhibited asset, and cultural heritage management needs to be benefited by tourism and utilize beneficial management and effective strategies for the long-term sustainable development of popular culture tourism. In this vein, there is a need for a more direct control of the aspects of museums that incorporate the tourist experience such as a tighter control schemes on museum timetables that operate on the island and the quality of the exhibits as well as their presentation to tourists. On the other hand, tourism policy needs to stress to travel agents to bring tourists to museums and that popular culture is an integral part of the island's culture, and to consider in their itineraries visits to all popular culture museums and not just a selection of them. This can be managed through the provision of incentives to the travel agents (e.g. economic ones) and an effective communication structure that would stress the significance of popular culture museums along with those of high culture, to their future profitability by generating more demand. Finally, there is an urgent need for both tourism and cultural policy of islands to understand that culture is not only some elements of the past and a peripheral activity, but a dynamic component that still evolves and can act autonomously as a specialized tourist product.

On the other hand, popular culture museums need to incorporate management practices in their environment. Initially, they need to understand that by analyzing the situation they operate they have to face different levels of competition (Kotler, Kotler, & Kotler, 2008, p. 55): enterprise competitors that include other types of organizations that satisfy the needs of prospective visitors; desire competitors that are related to the array of desires that people may have; generic competitors that include the various types of organizations that potential consumers can use to satisfy their desires, and; form competitors that incorporate those competitors that could satisfy the specific type of leisure activity selected. The authors suggest that the most intense competition for museums happens at the desire and generic levels. In this regard, museums need to understand that as providers of experiences and under the prism of tourism they need to compete with other activities that for various reasons mentioned in this chapter are more dominant (i.e. other forms of tourism).

In this regard, popular culture museums need to operate on the desire level and explore those types of desires they would like to satisfy. If it is recreation (tight relationship with tourism), museums need to concentrate on elements that underline the recreational aspects in a museum environment, such as cultural heritage interpretation techniques (i.e. thematic panels, thematic routes in the museum, representation related to museum's exhibits, visitor participation through first-hand experience such as replicas, etc.) (Veverka, 1998). Similarly, on the generic level of competition, museums need to explore ways in order to provide an aesthetic experience. Towards this line, popular culture museums could adopt the argument of McKercher & duCros (2012) and offer exhibits that are 'spectacular/entertaining' with a 'touch of fantasy.' In contrast to high culture, popular culture is much more open towards this direction and it can be projected to more diversified audiences through various ways, as indicated in the findings.

Finally, popular culture museums need to understand that not all their visitors are cultural tourists (e.g. individual and group travelers or specific and general cultural tourists). As derived from the study, various segments of visitors understand, accept, and appreciate popular culture offered by islands' museums in a different manner. In this regard, there is a need for identifying target markets in cultural heritage museums, based on their motivational determinants and experiential characteristics (Boukas, 2014). Not all people react in the same way to the same stimulus. As such, segmentation techniques (psychographic, behavioral, etc.) could be applied for the better design and projection of the museums' contents and exhibits.

To conclude, therefore, popular culture museums need to comprehend which types of tourists and visitors they want to have, and then manage the presentation and promotion of their exhibits to satisfy their expectations. On the other hand, tourism policy needs to actively support museums through the provision of managerial tools such as better distribution of people to their premises, quality control mechanisms to keep high standards of operation, or financial incentives, in order to project further popular culture tourism on islands. Islands need to capitalize on popular culture museums in order to enhance and differentiate their overall mature tourist offering. In this respect, popular culture is not only an added ingredient to the existing product–service mix but an active pillar for the long-term sustainable development of insular destinations.

References

Akaka, M. A., Vargo, S. L., & Schau, H. J. (2015). The context of experience. *Journal of Service Management, 26*(2), 206–223.

Anadon I. 2004. *Greater Impact? High culture or popular culture: Consumption and employment analysis of elite and popular culture*. Chicago: University of Chicago Cultural Policy Center, Retrieved from http://culturalpolicy.uchicago.edu/emergingscholarsconf04/papers/anadon.pdf.

Berry, L. L., Carbone, L. P., & Haeckel, S. H. (2002). Managing the total customer experience. *MIT Sloan Management Review, 43*(3), 85–89.

Bonn, M. A., Joseph-Mathews, S. M., Dai, M., Hayes, S., & Cave, J. (2007). Heritage/cultural attraction atmospherics: Creating the right environment for the heritage/cultural visitor. *Journal of Travel Research, 45*(3), 345–354.

Boukas N. (2012). "Young faces in old places": Perceptions of young cultural visitors for the archaeological site of Delphi. *Journal of Cultural Heritage Management and Sustainable Development, 2*(2), 164–189.

Boukas, N. (2014). Segmenting youth tourists to cultural heritage destinations: Motivational determinants and experiential characteristics. *International Journal of Leisure and Tourism Marketing, 4*(1), 63–89.

Boukas N., & Ziakas V. (2013). Impacts of the global economic crisis on Cyprus tourism and policy responses. *International Journal of Tourism Research, 15*(4), 329–345.

Boukas N., & Ziakas V. (2014). A chaos theory perspective of destination crisis and sustainable tourism development in islands: The case of Cyprus. *Tourism Planning & Development, 11*(2), 191–209.

Briguglio, L., & Briguglio, M. (1996). A Sustainable transport policy for tourism on small islands: A case study of Malta. In L. Briguglio, W. L. Filho, R. Butler, & D. Harisson (Eds.), *Sustainable tourism in islands and small states: Case studies* (pp. 180–199). London: Thomson Learning.

Burns, P. (1999). An introduction to tourism and anthropology. London: Routledge.

Butler, R. (2008). Islands. In M. Lück (Ed.), *Encyclopedia of tourism and recreation in marine environments* (p. 254). CABI: Wallingford.

Carlsen, J., & Butler, R. (2011). Introducing sustainable perspectives of island tourism. In J. Carlsen, & R. Butler (Eds.). *Island tourism: Sustainable perspectives* (pp. 1–8). Oxford: CAB International.

Carù, A., & Cova, B. (2003). Revisiting consumption experience a more humble but complete view of the concept. *Marketing theory, 3*(2), 267–286.

Cyprus Tourism Organization (2016). *Cyprus tourism in figures 2010*. Nicosia: Cyprus Tourism Organization.

Edensor, T. (2002). *National identity, popular culture and everyday life*. Oxford: Bloomsbury.

Farber, M. E., & Hall, T. E. (2007). Emotion and environment: Visitors' extraordinary experiences along the Dalton Highway in Alaska. *Journal of Leisure Research, 39*(2), 248–270.

Gentile, C., Spiller, N., & Noci, G. (2007). How to sustain the customer experience: An overview of experience components that co-create value with the customer. *European Management Journal, 25*(5), 395–410.

Goeldner, C. R., & Ritchie, B. J. R. (2012). *Tourism, principles, practices, philosophies* (12th ed.). Princeton, NJ: John Wiley & Sons.

Grönroos, C. (2011). Value co-creation in service logic: A critical analysis. *Marketing Theory, 11* (3), 279–301.

Heilbrun, J. (1997). The competition between high culture and popular culture as seen in the *New York Times*. *Journal of Cultural Economics, 21*(1), 29–40.

Heinonen, K., Strandvik, T., Mickelsson, K. J., Edvardsson, B., Sundström, E., & Andersson, P. (2010). A customer dominant logic of service. *Journal of Service Management, 21*(4), 531–548.

Heinonen, K., & Tore, S. (2015). Customer-dominant logic: Foundations and implications. *Journal of Services Marketing, 29*(6/7), 472–484.

Hollbrook, M. B., & Hirschman, E.C. (1982). The experiential aspects of consumption: Consumer fantasies, feelings, and fun. *Journal of Consumer Research, 9*(2), 132–140.

Hosany, S., & Witham, M. (2010). Dimensions of cruisers' experiences, satisfaction, and intention to recommend. *Journal of Travel Research, 49*(3), 351–364.

Ivanovic M. (2008). *Cultural tourism*. Cape Town: Juta.

Jenkins, H., Purushotma, R., Weigel, M., Clinton, K., & Robison, A. J. (2009). *Confronting the challenges of participatory culture: Media education for the 21st century*. London: MIT Press.

Jenks, C. (1993). *Culture*. London: Routledge.

Kotler, N. G., Kotler, P., & Kotler, W. I. (2008). Museum marketing and strategy: Designing missions, building audiences, generating revenue and resources. San Francisco, CA: John Wiley & Sons.

Lewis-Cameron, A., & Roberts, S. (2010). Small island developing states: Issues and prospects. In A. Lewis-Cameron & S. Roberts (Eds.). *Marketing island destinations: Concepts and cases* (pp. 1–8). London: Elsevier.

McKercher, B., & duCros, H. (2012). *Cultural tourism: The partnership between tourism and cultural heritage management* (2nd ed.). Binghamton, NY: Haworth Hospitality Press.

Malhotra, N. K. (2009). Review of marketing research. In N. K. Malhotra (Ed.). *Review of marketing research* (vol. 5, pp. ix–xvi). Bingley, UK: Emerald.

Misiura, S. (2006). *Heritage marketing*. Oxford: Butterworth-Heinemann, Elsevier.

Moore, K. (1997). *Museums and popular culture*. London: Cassell.

Novelli, M. (2005). *Niche tourism: Contemporary issues, trends and cases*. Oxford: Butterworth-Heinemann, Elsevier.

Parasuraman, A., Berry, L. L., & Zeithaml, V. A. (1991). Understanding customer expectations of service. *Sloan Management Review, 32*(3), 39–48.

Pine, B. J. P., & Gilmore, J. H. (1999). *Experience economy: Work is theatre and every business a stage.* Cambridge, MA: Harvard business school press.

Richards, G. (1996). Production and consumption of European cultural tourism. *Annals of Tourism Research, 23*(2), 261–283.

Richards, G. (2001). *Cultural attractions and european tourism*. Oxford: CABI.

Schmitt, B. (1999). *Experiential marketing: How to get customers to sense, feel, think, act, relate to your company and brands*. New York: Free Press.

Schroeder, F. E. H. (1981). *Twentieth-century popular culture in museums and libraries*. Bowling Green, OH: Bowling Green University Popular Press.

Sdrali, D., & Chazapi, K. (2007). Cultural tourism in a Greek insular community: The residents' perspective. *TOURISMOS: An International Multidisciplinary Journal of Tourism, 2*(2), 61–75.

Strinati, D. (2004). *An introduction to theories of popular culture* (2nd ed.) London: Routledge.

Stylianou-Lambert, T., Boukas, N., & Bounia, A. (2015). Politics, tourism and cultural sustainability. In E. Auclair & G. Fairclough (Eds.). *Heritage and cultural sustainability* (pp. 176–189). New York: Routledge.

Tung, V. W. S., & Ritchie, J. B. (2011). Exploring the essence of memorable tourism experiences. *Annals of Tourism Research, 38*(4), 1367–1386.

Vargo, S. L., & Lusch, R. F. (2016). Institutions and axioms: An extension and update of service-dominant logic. *Journal of the Academy of Marketing Science, 44*(1), 5–23.

Verhoef, P. C., Lemon, K. N., Parasuraman, A., Roggeveen, A., Tsiros, M., & Schlesinger, L. A. (2009). Customer experience creation: Determinants, dynamics and management strategies. *Journal of Retailing, 85*(1), 31–41.

Verhoef, P. C., Reinartz, W. J., & Krafft, M. (2010). Customer engagement as a new perspective in customer management. *Journal of Service Research, 13*(3), 247–252.

Veverka, J. A. (1998). *Interpretive master planning*. Tustin, CA: Acorn Naturalists.

Yin, R. K. (2009). *Case study research: Design and methods* (4th ed.). Thousand Oaks, CA: Sage.

Zimmerman, C. A., & Kelley, C. M. (2010). "I'll remember this!": Effects of emotionality on memory predictions versus memory performance. *Journal of Memory and Language, 62*, 240–253.

39

LIFESTYLE TOURISM

Combining place attachment and involvement in a destination management approach

Michael J. Gross

Setting the scene: introduction

Tourism destinations have an ever-present imperative to create and sustain competitive advantage, which has led to increasingly large volumes of marketing appeals about a seemingly limitless range of destinations, all contending for the traveler's attention. Differentiation has become difficult to achieve since any number of destinations can now provide the benefits sought by any particular group of travelers, and destinations have become highly substitutable (Pike, 2002). It has become common in the postmodern world for destinations to conceive themselves as simulated places that have been created for consumption and within which consumption can occur (Urry, 1995), such as a Disney theme park or Las Vegas. This has happened in response to the much more open and fluid consumer culture ushered in by postmodernism, which has required a more adaptable and flexible consideration of the relationship between the tourism experience and the tourist (Hanefors & Mossberg, 1998). But are such simulated places the only possible competitive strategic option for destinations? What alternatives might exist for a destination that wishes to market itself in a different way? In their discussion of postmodern tourism, Oakes and Minca (2004) argue that the most revealing quality of tourism is the expression of postmodern subject formation as tourism occurs in actual places, and that tourism presents an enormous range of field sites for study. The present study engaged this challenge, and took the study of postmodern subjectivity out of the concept's textual home and into a living tourism environment where postmodern subjectivity could be empirically tested, the Australian tourism destination of the state of South Australia.

Increased competition to attract tourists has given rise to a wide range of destination marketing strategies. Typically, this will involve the promotion of scenic environments, iconic attractions, or events that appeal to specific target markets. In contrast, South Australia has pursued a strategy based on the attraction of the lifestyle offered within the state by attempting to achieve a position as a lifestyle tourism destination (SATC, 2002a). The strategy relies on a range of expressions of popular culture represented by the destination's lifestyle attributes, posing a unique comprehensive view of popular culture forms integrated and marketed with the concept of lifestyle. This offers a perspective on popular culture tourism suggesting that a destination may integrate and market its popular culture attributes, products, and experiences. An important implication of this approach is that the lifespan of popular culture tourism can be extended, or even become sustainable, since it is built on an array of long-lasting destination characteristics and assets. The study reported in this chapter sought to examine the likely effectiveness of this strategy with four considerations guiding the research design: (1) the selection of South Australia as the setting for the research, (2) the choice of 'tourism experience' as the attitude object, and the use of (3) involvement, and (4) place attachment as measures of visitor attitudes towards tourism experiences.

Lifestyle tourism is an emerging concept in the marketing of tourism destinations, as will be represented in the following discussion of South Australia. As lifestyle aspects of leisure travel become increasingly important and travelers continue to search for new experiences, the range of destination marketing opportunities increases (Kelly, 2002). In 1998, the Australian Local Government Association (2016) initiated the designation of lifestyle regions in a number of places in the country (Larcombe & Cole, 1998). Annual reports on the 'State of the Regions' provide a stock take of the economic well-being of Australia's regions and their prospects for economic development and employment growth. Lifestyle regions are one of six types of regions that form a framework for regional development, which also includes the five other types of knowledge-intensive, dispersed metro, independent city, resource-based, and rural regions. The characteristics of lifestyle regions are loosely defined and include such elements as coastal areas with low employment levels and high reliance on transfer payments, environments that have attracted retirees, tourists, holidaymakers, and people in the workforce choosing a non-metropolitan and coastal lifestyle, and are sometimes characterized by elements of popular culture such as reference to lifestyle regions as 'sea change' regions after a popular Australian television series (Beer, Maude, & Pritchard, 2003, p. 50)

Tourism destinations that lack an apparent competitive *raison d'être* are obliged to create one, and South Australia has undertaken a strategy of using the lifestyle of the state as a marketing tool. The SATC, the destination management organization for the state, considers that South Australia has a relaxing, enjoyable, high-quality lifestyle, and believes that the state contains the ingredients necessary to develop lifestyle tourism as a key strategic asset. The good living lifestyle brand promotes South Australia as offering: a clean and green destination with a Mediterranean climate conducive to outdoor dining, relaxation, fun, health, rejuvenation, an experience that can be challenging, intellectual, and innovative all at once. The main lifestyle tourism attributes of the state are considered to include expressions of popular culture such as: wine, food, events, nature-based/ecotourism experiences, coastal experiences, the capital city Adelaide as gateway to the Outback, induction center for Aboriginal tourism, arts, culture, history and heritage, sport, recreation, and adventure (SATC, 2009).

The lifestyle concept has featured in SATC's strategic planning since the early 2000's (SATC, 2002b) in a variety of contexts, indicating a focus that made the state an ideal location for the present study. Lifestyle is integrated in the destination marketing strategy from the perspective of vision, consumer trends, target markets, positioning, and branding. Specific strategies include encouraging special interest tourism, positioning South Australia as a destination in which one will find an authentic Australian experience, and providing experiences that reflect local lifestyles. The overall strategic direction for tourism in the state is towards providing a diverse range of activities and experiences.

It is in the tourism community's interest to explore to what extent the lifestyle offerings of a destination may be unique and distinctive, and how that knowledge might be developed into competitive advantage. While lifestyle has been used as a branding tool in the general marketing environment for a variety of products and services, such as consumer electronics, furniture, health care, magazines, real estate, and television programs (Pegler, 1996), the use of lifestyle as a branding tool for a tourism destination has had limited application or theoretical exploration, a fact that provides productive ground for the investigation of the use of lifestyle as a tourism destination branding tool both from the perspective of the tourist and that of the tourism professionals who are responsible for the implementation of marketing strategies and tactics. Therefore the purpose of this study was to determine what, if any, theoretical basis may exist to support the viability and utility of a lifestyle tourism strategy for the marketing of a destination.

Theoretical underpinnings

Lifestyle in a postmodern tourism context

In popular culture, lifestyle has come to mean that which is trendy and generally contributes to an attractive and comfortable existence (Chaney, 1996). Edensor (2002) suggested that a postmodern view of lifestyle includes recognition of increasing trends towards broader notions of sociality and consumer choice and taste, as well as reflexive, technically skilled, self-authoritative individuals who construct and reconstruct their identities and lifestyles. Among the central features associated with postmodernism are: the effacement of the boundary between high and mass/popular culture; a stylistic promiscuity favoring eclecticism and the mixing of codes; parody, pastiche, irony, playfulness, and the celebration of the surface 'depthlessness' of culture; the decline of the originality/genius of the artistic producer; and the assumption that art can only be repetition (Featherstone, 1991). The sociological discourse of postmodern tourism consists of two theoretical frameworks – the 'simulational' and the 'other' (Munt, 1994). The simulational line of scholarship has focused around the analysis of 'hyperreal' experiences, using simulated theme parks and other contrived attractions as manifestations of typical postmodern environments (Acland, 1998; Baudrillard, 1983; Belk, 1996; Johns & Gyimothy, 2003; Pretes, 1995; Ritzer & Liska, 1997). Conceptualizations of the 'other' postmodern tourism stress the search for the 'real' and point to the growing appeal of the natural environment as expressions of postmodernism (Galani-Moutafi, 2000; Goulding, 2000; Urry, 1990a). Uriely (1997) suggests that the two theoretical frameworks are not mutually exclusive, but are rather complementary, and reflect the 'both-and' nature of postmodern theories, whereby conceptualizations of postmodern tourism depart from the tendency of modernist theories to homogenize the tourism experience as a general type, and postmodern tourism is characterized by a multiplicity of motivations, experiences, and environments.

The postmodern tourism consumer may well remove the impetus from the standardization and globalization of tourism products. Such tourists will require more individualistic and highly developed products, likely demanding greater variety and choice of tourism products (Swarbrooke & Horner, 2007, p. 197). As Cohen (1979) has suggested, different kinds of people may desire different modes of touristic experiences; hence *the* tourist does not exist as a type. It is all about the individual and how meeting their personal preferences affirms their individuality. A postmodern counter-movement of consumers against the McDonaldization of consumer products as described by Belk (1996) has also been manifested in the tourism industry. An example of the operationalization of this phenomenon has been the introduction of boutique, or lifestyle hotels (Munsters & Freund de Klumbis, 2005), which operate as unique properties of 50–100 rooms, with attention to fine detail and individual decoration. Lifestyle hotels serve as an alternative to the traditional 'box' hotels, and target customers who seek a more customized hospitality experience with higher levels of personal service. They are predominantly non-chain operated, although traditional box hotel companies have entered the lifestyle hotel market, with Starwood launching the 'W' brand in 1998, and Intercontinental Hotels Group introducing the 'Hotel Indigo' brand in 2004. The entry of larger companies into this market suggests a recognition of increasing levels of demand from postmodern tourists seeking more customized and individualized tourism and hospitality experiences (Pizam, 2015).

In an investigation of lifestyle tourism it is important to move beyond the study of tourism as a commodity, and to recognize the experiential aspects of tourism. Sternberg (1997) has characterized the literature on tourism experience as a struggle between a camp that laments the passing of the genuine art of travel (Boorstin, 1963), and one that celebrates the deeper quest for authenticity (MacCannell, 1976). Critics of the latter camp reject the 'pseudo-event' quality of postmodern tourism, while critics of the former camp object to its elitist nature, and call for a more inclusive attitude about what constitutes the tourism experience. MacCannell (1976) is considered to have recognized the importance of the authenticity concept for tourism analysis, with authentic experiences characterized as the worthwhile and spontaneous experience of travel, and having the elements of spontaneity, worth, and genuineness (Pearce & Moscardo, 1986).

With the growth of knowledge of tourism consumer behavior (Swarbrooke & Horner, 2007), it is now more possible and realistic to conceptualize a lifestyle tourism experience, as our understanding and the tools available to examine the components of that construction are more available, deployable, accurate, and ultimately more useful. The research work done in the consumer literature in recent decades by such authors as Hirschman and Holbrook writing together (1982) and in combination with other authors (Hirschman & Stampfl, 1980; Holbrook, Chestnut, Oliva, & Greeneleaf, 1984; Holbrook, O'Shaughnessy, & Bell, 1990) has advanced the state of knowledge of experiential consumption and demonstrated the utility of such knowledge for practical application in industry. Consumption experience has also been conceptualized within the postmodern dialogue, sometimes viewed from a critical perspective on the commodification of experience (Holbrook, 2001).

Researching in the areas of tourist motivation and typologies, Prentice (2004) identified three sociological paradigms that described the purposes of tourism in terms of consumption experience. The first two, the romantic paradigm and the mass tourism paradigm, described tourism respectively as personal enlightenment, and as escape from the everyday tedium of work. Prentice described the third paradigm of lifestyle formation as 'becoming' rather than 'being' through tourism, whereby tourism activities are undertaken with the specific purpose of expressing an aspect or multiple aspects of lifestyle through the consumption of tourism experiences. He likened the lifestyle formation paradigm to a modular approach to the tourism experience, with a blurring of boundaries between producer and consumer, and with the construction of the experience increasingly shared between producer and consumer. This perspective was supported by Richards and Wilson (2006), who contended that many postmodern tourists are becoming tired of encountering the serial reproduction of culture in different destinations, and are searching for alternatives. In their conceptual paper, they offered lifestyle as an important component in considering the increasingly creative skilled consumption undertaken by tourists. They proposed that as tourists become increasingly creative in their search for tourism experiences that connect with their lifestyles, creative tourists are in essence 'prosumers,' engaged in a combination of skilled consumption and skilled production. They cited lifestyle entrepreneurs as examples of this, such as the avid surfer who either becomes a professional surfer, or else opens a surf-related business as a means of supporting a lifestyle preference.

Chaney (1996) provides an insightful summarizing thought to this discussion of lifestyle in a postmodern tourism context highlighting the simultaneous operation of conflicting forces sometimes present in the contradictory nature of postmodernism, and reinforcing Uriely's (1997) view that the 'simulational' and 'other' exist complementarily: "There is a necessary tension between a global rationality imposed by cultural corporations seeking economies of scale in the manufacture of taste, who are opposed by local knowledges which diffuse, subvert and appropriate commodities and services for 'irrational' styles" (p. 84). The present study examines these forces in a destination management context.

Combining involvement and place attachment

Consumer involvement can be defined as the perceived personal importance and/or interest consumers attach to the acquisition, consumption, and disposition of a good, service, or an idea (Mowen & Minor, 1998, p. 64). From the early conceptual work (Bloch & Bruce, 1984; Selin & Howard, 1988) linking leisure with involvement, most leisure involvement research has focused on activity contexts (Dimanche & Havitz, 1994). Specific tourism involvement studies have been less prevalent, and include grouped touristic activities (Dimanche, Havitz, & Howard, 1991); opinion leadership (Jamrozy, Backman, & Backman, 1996); travel motivation and destination selection (Josiam, Smeaton, & Clements, 1999); tourist profiles (Gursoy & Gavcar, 2003); destination branding (Ferns & Walls, 2012); backpacking (Akatay, Cakici, & Harman, 2013); and sport travel (Brown, Smith, & Assaker, 2016).

The reason for wide research interest in leisure involvement is that, relative to other products and services, touristic activities tend to engender high levels of both enduring and situational involvement (Havitz & Howard, 1995). In a paper reviewing 52 leisure involvement data sets over a ten-year period, Havitz and Dimanche (1999) concluded that involvement has proven to be a reasonably good variable for explaining and predicting leisure behavior. The same authors have also affirmed that the consumer involvement profile (CIP) multidimensional scale originally developed by Laurent and Kapferer (1985) has proved reliable and valid in touristic contexts (Dimanche & Havitz, 1994). Consistent with these findings, the CIP scale was selected for use in the present study, which examined the applicability of a modified version of the CIP scale, using the attitude object of tourism experiences to better understand the nature of tourists' involvement.

Place attachment is conceived as an affective bond or link between people and specific places (Hidalgo & Hernandez, 2001). Leisure researchers have studied place attachment primarily as a psychological element of recreation experiences (Williams, 2002). The place attachment construct has been defined as having two distinct dimensions: place identity, which refers to a symbolic or affective attachment to a place, and place dependence, which refers to a functional attachment to a place (Kajan, 2014; Loureiro, 2014; Suntikul & Jachna, 2016).

The study of involvement and place attachment in combination is an emerging stream in leisure and tourism research. There is growing evidence suggesting involvement with activities leads to attachment to settings (Kyle, Bricker, Graefe, & Wickham, 2004). The use of the place attachment and involvement constructs in combination has occurred only recently in leisure studies, and in the context of recreation. Moore and Graefe (1994) used the conceptual frameworks of activity specialization and place attachment to study recreation trail users, finding predictive relationships that were moderated by frequency of use. Bricker and Kerstetter (2000) studied whitewater recreationists, using involvement to measure levels of specialization and levels of place attachment to a particular river. A relationship was noted between dimension levels of specialization and place attachment. Moore and Scott (2003) used commitment and place attachment to study users of a trail in a park, and found predictive relationships between the dimensions. Kyle, Graefe, Manning, and Bacon (2003) investigated the relationship between activity involvement and place attachment through a study of hikers on a particular trail. A relationship was also noted between dimension levels of involvement and place attachment, along with some predictive properties of a proposed model. Their analysis of data gathered from hikers on the Appalachian Trail in the eastern United States has provided the basis for a number of studies along similar lines of enquiry, all of which have contributed insights into the underlying motivations for recreationists' engagement in specific leisure pursuits and visitation to specific recreation settings (Kyle, Graefe, Manning, & Bacon, 2004). Hwang, Lee, and Chen (2005) sampled groups of national park visitors in Taiwan, finding that both involvement and place attachment had positive effects on perceived service quality and satisfaction. These results suggested the value of combining involvement and place attachment as measures in the present study of tourism experiences. By combining examination of the dimensions of involvement with those of place attachment, the present study sought to assess the suitability of measuring both in a tourism context.

Study methodology and findings

The study research design consisted of two sequential mixed method phases. Phase 1 established the meaning of lifestyle tourism among members of the South Australia tourism industry, in order to ascertain to what extent the concept could offer a competitive advantage for the marketing of a tourism destination. This phase asked whether professionals in the tourism industry recognized lifestyle tourism as a concept, and what meaning, if any, lifestyle tourism had for them. Phase 2 considered the perceptions of the consumer, and was an examination of the dimensionality of lifestyle tourism with the aim of obtaining an understanding of how tourists in South Australia perceived the concept. The four research objectives of the study were to:

1. develop an understanding of the concept of lifestyle tourism;
2. develop a model representative of the proposed elements of lifestyle tourism;
3. develop a method for measuring lifestyle tourism;
4. test the measurement method using the model developed of lifestyle tourism.

The first research objective was pursued through qualitative methods in Phase 1, which was an exploratory analysis of lifestyle tourism. Phase 1 sought to examine whether industry practitioners understood and supported the concept of destination lifestyle and the extent to which they had participated in activities consistent with the aims of a marketing strategy based on lifestyle. A total of 25 respondents from the South Australia tourism industry participated in interviews and focus groups using a sampling strategy intended to assure sectoral balance, with professionals participating from across the state tourism industry.

The remaining three research objectives were pursued through quantitative methods in Phase 2, which was an examination of the dimensionality of lifestyle tourism. Phase 2 integrated the Phase 1 findings into an instrument that was used to survey visitors to South Australia. The personal experiences of the tourists, that is, their involvement in the destination, and their attachment to place were used as indicators by which to measure the degree to which lifestyle tourism is rooted in unique, place-specific experiences.

Exploratory factor analysis (EFA) was performed to check the dimensionality of the survey instrument before using confirmatory factor analysis (CFA) to establish a measurement model for the manner in which the instrument measured the constructs of tourists' involvement and place attachment in tourism experiences. Place attachment was conceptualized as a multidimensional construct consisting of place identity and place dependence. Tourism involvement was also conceptualized as a multidimensional construct consisting of centrality to lifestyle, attraction, and self expression. As South Australia markets itself using the food and wine aspects of the lifestyle of the destination as a point of difference, a lifestyle dimension was also included that attempted to measure tourists' attitudes of how food and wine feature in their tourism experiences in the state. Structural equation modeling (SEM) was then used to test the relationships between the involvement and place attachment constructs representing lifestyle tourism.

Three themes emerged from the Phase 1 findings:

1. lifestyle tourism as experience;
2. the role of food and wine in lifestyle tourism;
3. the importance of place attachment in lifestyle tourism.

Phase 1 findings were integrated into the quantitative methods for Phase 2, through a survey instrument formulated using the involvement and place attachment constructs. Following a pilot study to test the instrument, the main survey was conducted with tourists (n = 476) in five South Australian tourism regions from November 2004 through May 2005 that measured respondents' levels of involvement and place attachment for tourism experiences in South Australia.

EFA of the data generated six dimensions proposed to represent lifestyle tourism: *centrality to lifestyle, attraction, self-expression, food & wine, place dependence,* and *place identity.* CFA was used to develop and test a measurement model for the six dimensions contained within the constructs of involvement and place attachment, substantiating that the survey instrument resulted in a summated scale that reliably and validly measured separate dimensions of lifestyle tourism. SEM was then used to develop a structural model that was found to effectively measure the relationships between the constructs of involvement and place attachment representing lifestyle tourism (see Gross, Brien, & Brown, 2008; Gross & Brown, 2006, 2008). The structural model, showing coefficients in standardized form, is shown in Figure 39.1. The configuration of the latent constructs was of the involvement construct consisting of the four dimensions of *centrality to lifestyle* (8 items), *attraction* (6 items), *self expression* (6 items), *food & wine* (3 items), and the place attachment construct consisting of the two dimensions of *place dependence* (4 items), and *place identity* (4 items). The key structural model fit statistics are shown in Table 39.1.

Implications for popular culture tourism: conceptualizing lifestyle tourism

The findings of the study make a contribution to the body of popular culture tourism knowledge in both theory and practice. From a theoretical standpoint, the study validates the view that, in a South Australian context, a theoretical basis exists to support the viability and utility of a lifestyle tourism strategy for the marketing of a destination. It also recognizes the viability of combining involvement and place attachment in a tourism context. From a practical standpoint, the study provides a validated model that can be used by destination managers and operators to diagnose and measure the elements of lifestyle tourism that are relevant to their destination.

Table 39.1 Summary of structural model fit statistics

Model	Chi-square	DF	Chi-square/DF	P-Value	CFI	RMSEA	90% C.I. RMSEA
Final SEM	1177	414	2.843	.000	.912	.062	(.058, .066)

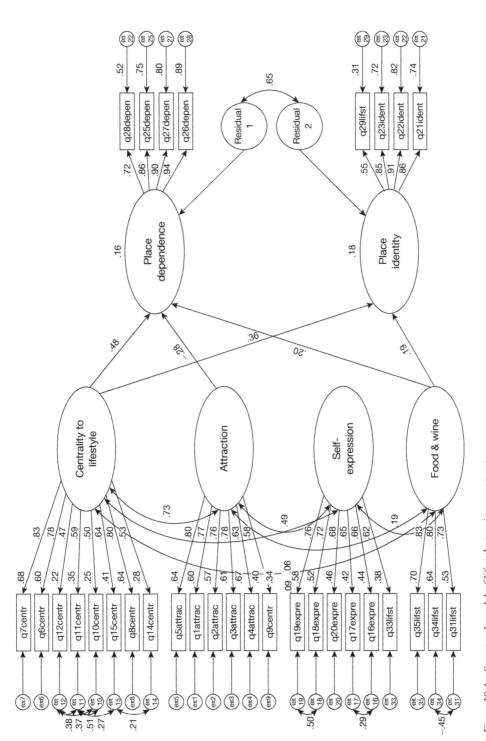

Figure 39.1 Structural model of lifestyle tourism constructs.

Lifestyle tourism is not theorized as a type of special interest/niche tourism, but rather as an umbrella concept that potentially includes a wide range of niches. This study is about the importance of tourism experiences in tourists' lifestyles, and how that importance relates to the places where the tourism experiences are consumed. Lifestyle tourism was conceived as the relationship between the levels of place attachment of tourists to a destination and their levels of involvement in tourism experiences in that destination. The essence of the conceptualization of lifestyle tourism in the present study is the relationship as revealed in the structural model between the involvement dimensions of *centrality to lifestyle* and *food & wine* and the place attachment dimensions of *place dependence* and *place identity*.

Thus, lifestyle tourism may be said to exist in those settings in which the key involvement dimension of *centrality to lifestyle* is observed to relate positively and significantly with the place attachment construct's dimensions of *place dependence* and *place identity*. 'Setting' in this usage denotes the simultaneous consideration of the relationship between the involvement and place attachment constructs as represented in the study's structural model. A key additional element of lifestyle tourism would be the particular involvement dimension(s) provided by the destination under study. In the present study, *food & wine* was such a dimension in a South Australian setting. It is expected, however, that different dimensions of popular culture are likely to emerge as significant in other destinations. While the postmodern debates around authenticity versus inauthenticity may inform the environment in which the concept of lifestyle tourism may be said to exist, those debates cannot completely account for the concept. There will be enough room in existing and emerging markets to accommodate MacCannell's (1976) tourists in search of authenticity and Urry's (1990b) post-tourists. Evidence for this is seen in the expansion of the Disney theme parks around the world (Tokyo in 1983, Paris in 1992, Hong Kong in 2005, Shanghai in 2016) occurring simultaneously with the growth of continually more inventive and esoteric forms of alternative tourism (Macbeth, 2000; Mason, 2000; McGehee & Norman, 2001). As Walter (1982) expressed, the opportunities for discovery abound, and there is no limit to what may be found. Existing and emerging markets will be sufficiently large to allow the coexistence of an increasing variety of niche markets, and the tourism industry will need to develop strategic visions and operational delivery skills that present a flexible menu approach to product and service provision to those markets.

As a practical matter, the tourism industry needs to bring operational order to the postmodern explosion of variety of consumer choice. The industry can no longer rely on a business model that considers demand to follow supply. Rather, the tourism industry will need to develop increasingly sophisticated skills in the supply and delivery of customized experiences that match the identified needs of consumers. The findings of the present study suggest a number of ways that lifestyle tourism may have utility in the marketing of tourism experiences in a state such as South Australia. First, lifestyle is among the most stable and enduring qualities of a destination (Hjalager, 2004), and may provide insulation from the often fleeting and volatile nature of consumer tastes and popular culture (Larson, Lundberg, & Lexhagen, 2013). Brands that are built on less enduring features appear less stable, and vulnerable to the boom or bust cycles that plague destinations that chase trendy, often transient images (Whang, Yong, & Ko, 2016). Many lifestyle destinations exhibit characteristics that allow them to adapt to changing circumstances without losing the integrity of their offerings, which renders the place less sensitive to the fleeting fashions and postmodern distractions of tourists' experience appetites (Richards & Wilson, 2006). When world or national events, such as the destruction of the World Trade Center in New York on September 11, 2001, produce rapid, massive, and long-lasting impacts on tourism behavior (Michman, Mazze, & Greco, 2003), lifestyle destinations may have a natural resilience because of the intrinsic value they offer tourists.

Second, a lifestyle brand is built on a range of tangible and intangible attractions and should therefore be more durable than a destination based primarily on a single attraction. As a state lacking an iconic attraction, South Australia has assembled a range of complementary features that are bundled under the umbrella term of lifestyle. Organizations that market, develop, and manage places are well advised to aim for some diversification in both their industries and their target markets (Kotler, Haider, & Rein, 1993), given that a range of attractions parceled under a unifying theme is likely to assist in the strategic placement of the destination.

Third, the concept of lifestyle operates along a spectrum comprehensive enough to make both the marketing of a narrowly focused single activity as meaningful as marketing an array of experiences. Even when a lifestyle attraction appeals primarily to one segment in the market, for example, divers attracted to a dive tourism destination, elements of the destination can also appeal in terms of a broad range of activities that fit the varied lifestyles of popular culture tourists.

Finally, marketers describe the need to live the brand (Bendapudi & Bendapudi, 2005; Gotsi & Wilson, 2001), which refers to the passion and authenticity with which brand champions advocate and model the values represented by their brand. The nature of lifestyle as a way of life (Veal, 2000) represents an ongoing opportunity to truly live the brand of the destination.

As the fields of popular culture tourism research and destination management develop, the directions and the methods used to pursue those directions will reach for and achieve increasingly high levels of creativity, complexity, and sophistication. The present study brings the fields a step closer in the search for understanding of the complex relationships between tourists and the places they visit. Like the broad notion of lifestyle itself, the range of possible destinations in which the concept of lifestyle tourism could be explored is extensive. This study contributes to that discourse and suggests a framework for the future development of a research agenda of this kind.

References

Acland, C. R. (1998). Imaxtechnology and the tourist gaze. *Cultural Studies, 12*(3), 429–445.

Akatay, A., Cakici, A. C., & Harman, S. (2013). Involvement with backpacking: a research on backpackers visiting Istanbul. *Tourism, 61*(4), 361–377.

Australian Local Government Association. (2016). State of the regions report. *Canberra.* Retrieved from http://alga.asn.au/?ID=165&Menu=50,95.

Baudrillard, J. (1983). *Simulations.* New York: Semiotext(e).

Beer, A., Maude, A., & Pritchard, B. (2003). *Developing Australia's regions: theory and practice.* Sydney: University of New South Wales Press.

Belk, R. (1996). Hyperreality and globalization: culture in the age of Ronald McDonald. *Journal of International Consumer Marketing, 8*(3/4), 23–37.

Bendapudi, N., & Bendapudi, V. (2005). Creating the living brand. *Harvard Business Review, 83*(5), 124–132.

Bloch, P. H., & Bruce, G. D. (1984). Product involvement as leisure behavior. *Advances in Consumer Research, 11*(1), 197–202.

Boorstin, D. (1963). From traveller to tourist: the lost art of travel. *The image: or what happened to the American dream* (pp. 86–125). Harmondsworth: Penguin Books.

Bricker, K. S., & Kerstetter, D. L. (2000). Level of specialization and place attachment: an exploratory study of whitewater recreationists. *Leisure Sciences, 22*(4), 233–257.

Brown, G., Smith, A., & Assaker, G. (2016). Revisiting the host city: an empirical examination of sport involvement, place attachment, event satisfaction and spectator intentions at the London Olympics. *Tourism Management, 55*(August), 16–172.

Chaney, D. (1996). *Lifestyles.* London: Routledge.

Cohen, E. (1979). A phenomenology of tourist experiences. *Sociology, 13*(2), 179–201.

Dimanche, F., & Havitz, M. E. (1994). Consumer behavior and tourism: review and extension of four study areas. *Journal of Travel & Tourism Marketing, 3*(3), 37–57.

Dimanche, F., Havitz, M. E., & Howard, D. R. (1991). Testing the Involvement Profile (IP) Scale in the context of selected recreational and touristic activities. *Journal of Leisure Research, 23*(1), 51–66.

Edensor, T. (2002). *National identity, popular culture and everyday life.* Oxford: Berg.

Featherstone, M. (1991). *Consumer culture & postmodernism.* London: Sage Publications.

Ferns, B. H., & Walls, A. (2012). Enduring travel involvement, destination brand equity, and travelers' visit intentions: a structural model analysis. *Journal of Destination Marketing & Management, 1*(1–2), 27–35.

Galani-Moutafi, V. (2000). The self and the other: traveler, ethnographer, tourist. *Annals of Tourism Research, 27*(1), 203–224.

Gotsi, M., & Wilson, A. (2001). Corporate reputation management: 'living the brand.' *Management Decision, 39*(2), 99–104.

Goulding, C. (2000). The commodification of the past, postmodern pastiche, and the search for authentic experiences at contemporary heritage attractions. *European Journal of Marketing, 34*(7), 835–853.

Gross, M. J., Brien, C., & Brown, G. (2008). Examining the dimensions of a lifestyle tourism destination. *International Journal of Culture, Tourism and Hospitality Research, 2*(1), 44–66.

Gross, M. J., & Brown, G. (2006). Tourism experiences in a lifestyle destination setting: the roles of involvement and place attachment. *Journal of Business Research, 59*(6), 696–700.

Gross, M. J., & Brown, G. (2008). An empirical structural model of tourists and places: progressing involvement and place attachment into tourism. *Tourism Management, 29*(6), 1141–1151.

Gursoy, D., & Gavcar, E. (2003). International leisure tourists' involvement profile. *Annals of Tourism Research, 30*(4), 906–926.

Hanefors, M., & Mossberg, L. L. (1998). The tourism and travel consumer. In M. Gabbott & G. Hogg (Eds.), *Consumers and services* (pp. 141–161). Chichester, UK: John Wiley & Sons.

Havitz, M. E., & Dimanche, F. (1999). Leisure involvement revisited: drive properties and paradoxes. *Journal of Leisure Research, 31*(2), 122–149.

Havitz, M. E., & Howard, D. R. (1995). How enduring is enduring involvement? A seasonal examination of three recreational activities. *Journal of Consumer Psychology, 4*(3), 255–276.

Hidalgo, M. C., & Hernandez, B. (2001). Place attachment: conceptual and empirical questions. *Journal of Environmental Psychology, 21*(3), 273–281.

Hirschman, E. C., & Holbrook, M. B. (1982). Hedonic consumption: emerging concepts, methods and propositions. *Journal of Marketing, 46*(3), 92–101.

Hirschman, E. C., & Stampfl, R. W. (1980). Roles of retailing in the diffusion of popular culture: micro-perspectives. *Journal of Retailing, 56*(1), 16–36.

Hjalager, A. M. (2004). Sustainable leisure life modes and rural welfare economy: the case of the Randers Fjord Area, Denmark. *International Journal of Tourism Research, 6*(3), 177–188.

Holbrook, M. B. (2001). Times Square, Disneyphobia, HegeMickey, the Ricky Principle, and the downside of the entertainment economy: it's fun-dumb-mental. *Marketing Theory, 1*(2), 139–163.

Holbrook, M. B., Chestnut, R. W., Oliva, T. A., & Greenleaf, E. A. (1984). Play as consumption experience: the roles of emotions, performance, and personality in the enjoyment of games. *Journal of Consumer Research, 11*(2), 728–739.

Holbrook, M. B., O'Shaughnessy, J., & Bell, S. (1990). Actions and reactions in the consumption experience: the complementary roles of reasons and emotions in consumer behavior. *Research in Consumer Behavior, 4*, 131–163.

Hwang, S. N., Lee, C., & Chen, H. J. (2005). The relationship among tourists' involvement, place attachment and interpretation satisfaction in Taiwan's national parks. *Tourism Management, 26*(2), 143–156.

Jamrozy, U., Backman, S. J., & Backman, K. F. (1996). Involvement and opinion leadership in tourism. *Annals of Tourism Research, 23*(4), 908–924.

Johns, N., & Gyimothy, S. (2003). Postmodern family tourism at Legoland. *Scandinavian Journal of Hospitality and Tourism, 3*(1), 3–23.

Josiam, B. M., Smeaton, G., & Clements, C. J. (1999). Involvement: travel motivation and destination selection. *Journal of Vacation Marketing, 5*(2), 167–175.

Kajan, E. (2014). Community perceptions to place attachment and tourism development in Finnish Lapland. *Tourism Geographies, 16*(3), 490–511.

Kelly, I. (Ed.). (2002). *Australian regional tourism handbook: industry solutions 2001.* Cooperative Research Centre for Sustainable Tourism.

Kotler, P., Haider, D. H., & Rein, I. (1993). *Marketing places: attracting investment, industry, and tourism to cities, states, and nations.* New York: The Free Press.

Kyle, G., Bricker, K., Graefe, A., & Wickham, T. (2004). An examination of recreationists' relationships with activities and settings. *Leisure Sciences, 26*(2), 123–142.

Kyle, G., Graefe, A., Manning, R., & Bacon, J. (2003). An examination of the relationships between leisure activity involvement and place attachment among hikers along the Appalachian Trail. *Journal of Leisure Research, 35*(3), 249–273.

Kyle, G., Graefe, A., Manning, R., & Bacon, J. (2004). Effect of activity involvement and place attachment on recreationists' perceptions of setting density. *Journal of Leisure Research, 36*(2), 209–231.

Larcombe, G., & Cole, M. (1998). Australian regional employment and growth trends, prospects and strategies. *National Economic Review, 40*(March), 13–39.

Larson, M., Lundberg, C., & Lexhagen, M. (2013). Thirsting for vampire tourism: developing pop culture destinations. *Journal of Destination Marketing & Management, 2*(2), 74–84.

Laurent, G., & Kapferer, J. N. (1985). Measuring consumer involvement profiles. *Journal of Marketing Research, 22*(1), 41–53.

Loureiro, S. M. C. (2014). The role of the rural tourism experience economy in place attachment and behavioral intentions. *International Journal of Hospitality Management, 40*(July), 1–9.

Macbeth, J. (2000). Utopian tourists: cruising is not just about sailing. *Current Issues in Tourism, 3*(1), 20–34.

MacCannell, D. (1976). *The tourist: a new theory of the leisure class.* London: Macmillan.

McGehee, N. G., & Norman, W. C. (2001). Alternative tourism as impetus for consciousness-raising. *Tourism Analysis, 6*(3/4), 239–251.

Mason, P. (2000). Neat trends: current issues in nature, eco- and adventure tourism. *International Journal of Tourism Research, 2*(6), 437–444.

Michman, R. D., Mazze, E. M., & Greco, A. J. (2003). *Lifestyle marketing: reaching the new American consumer.* Westport, CT: Praeger.

Moore, R. L., & Graefe, A. R. (1994). Attachments to recreation settings: the case of rail-trail users. *Leisure Sciences, 16*(1), 17–31.

Moore, R. L., & Scott, D. (2003). Place attachment and context: comparing a park and a trail within. *Forest Science, 49*(6), 877–884.

Mowen, J. C., & Minor, M. (1998). *Consumer behavior* (5th ed.). Upper Saddle River, NJ: Prentice-Hall.

Munsters, W., & Freund de Klumbis, D. (2005). Culture as a component of the hospitality product. In M. Sigala & D. Leslie (Eds.), *International cultural tourism: management, implications and cases* (pp. 26–39). Oxford: Elsevier Butterworth-Heinemann.

Munt, I. (1994). The 'other' postmodern tourism: culture, travel and the new middle classes. *Theory, Culture & Society, 11*(3), 101–123.

Oakes, T., & Minca, C. (2004). Tourism, modernity, and postmodernity. In A. A. Lew, C. M. Hall, & A. M. Williams (Eds.), *A companion to tourism* (pp. 280–290). Malden, MA: Blackwell.

Pearce, P., & Moscardo, G. (1986). The concept of authenticity in tourist experiences. *Australian and New Zealand Journal of Sociology, 22*(1), 121–132.

Pegler, M. M. (1996). *Lifestyle stores.* New York: PBC International.

Pike, S. (2002). ToMA as a measure of competitive advantage for short break holiday destinations. *Journal of Tourism Studies, 13*(1), 9–19.

Pizam, A. (2015). Lifestyle hotels: consistency and uniformity vs. individuality and personalization. *International Journal of Hospitality Management, 46*(April), 213–214.

Prentice, R. (2004). Tourist motivation and typologies. In A. A. Lew, C. M. Hall, & A. M. Williams (Eds.), *A companion to tourism* (pp. 261–279). Malden, MA: Blackwell.

Pretes, M. (1995). Postmodern tourism: the Santa Claus industry. *Annals of Tourism Research, 22*(1), 1–15.

Richards, G., & Wilson, J. (2006). Developing creativity in tourist experiences: a solution to the serial reproduction of culture? *Tourism Management, 27*(6), 1209–1223.

Ritzer, G., & Liska, A. (1997). McDisneyization and post-tourism: complementary perspectives on contemporary tourism. In C. Rojek & J. Urry (Eds.), *Touring cultures: transformations in travel and theory* (pp. 96–109). London: Routledge.

Selin, S. W., & Howard, D. R. (1988). Ego involvement and leisure behavior: a conceptual specification. *Journal of Leisure Research, 20*(3), 237–244.

South Australian Tourism Commission (SATC). (2002a). *Annual Report 2001/02.* Adelaide, South Australia.

South Australian Tourism Commission (SATC). (2002b). *South Australian Tourism Plan 2003–2008*. Adelaide, South Australia.

South Australian Tourism Commission (SATC). (2009). *South Australian Tourism Plan 2009–2014*. Adelaide, South Australia.

Sternberg, E. (1997). The iconography of the tourism experience. *Annals of Tourism Research*, *24*(4), 951–969.

Suntikul, W., & Jachna, T. (2016). The co-creation/place attachment nexus. *Tourism Management*, *52*(February), 276–286.

Swarbrooke, J., & Horner, S. (2007). *Consumer behaviour in tourism* (2nd ed.). Oxford: Butterworth-Heinemann.

Uriely, N. (1997). Theories of modern and postmodern tourism. *Annals of Tourism Research*, *24*(4), 982–985.

Urry, J. (1990a). The 'consumption' of tourism. *Sociology*, *24*(1), 23–35.

Urry, J. (1990b). *The tourist gaze*. London: Sage.

Urry, J. (1995). *Consuming places*. London: Routledge.

Veal, A. J. (2000). Leisure and lifestyle: a review and annotated bibliography. School of Leisure, Sport & Tourism, University of Technology Sydney. Retrieved from www.leisuresource.net/service3.aspx.

Walter, J. (1982). Social limits to tourism. *Leisure Studies*, *1*(3), 295–304.

Whang, H., Yong, S., & Ko, E. (2016). Pop culture, destination images, and visit intentions: theory and research on travel motivations of Chinese and Russian tourists. *Journal of Business Research*, *69*(2), 631–641.

Williams, D. R. (2002). Leisure identities, globalization, and the politics of place. *Journal of Leisure Research*, *34*(4), 351–367.

40

DESTINATION DEVELOPMENT IN THE WAKE OF POPULAR CULTURE TOURISM

Proposing a comprehensive analytic framework

Kristina N. Lindström

Setting the scene

Popular culture tourism: a booster for local development?

This chapter revolves around the notion of popular culture tourism as a potential booster and rejuvenation strategy for local economies (e.g. Connell, 2012; Richards, 2014). The fact that many regions in the industrialized world deal with a transformation from traditional industry to experience-based production calls for planning and development strategies adapted to this new place-making logic (Gyimóthy et al., 2015; Larsson & Lindström, 2013). A great number of studies prove the success of popular culture tourism as a booster for local economies (e.g. Beeton, 2001; Connell, 2012; Larson, Lundberg, & Lexhagen, 2013; Lee & Bai, 2016; Lexhagen, Larson, & Lundberg, 2014; Lundberg & Lexhagen, 2012), however often with a focus on short-term and tourist-centric impacts of this special interest tourism, i.e. number of tourists, tourist spending and image-making. Studies with a critical stance or with a broader regional development approach are more exceptional (Gyimóthy et al., 2015). Consequently, local community interests risk being neglected in favor of visitors' interests (Saarinen, 2006; Scott, 1997). As pointed out by Gyimóthy et al. (2015), research in the field focusing on long-term consequences and solutions of popular culture tourism demand is scarce. Hence, the key observation put forward and scrutinized is the observed contradiction between the main argument for paying attention to popular culture tourism, i.e. being a booster for regional development and, the narrow focus often applied in theory and practice. This gap, it is argued, leads to limited profound knowledge of the implications of this category of special interest tourism in the local community. Consequently, in-depth understanding of the causes and consequences of popular culture tourism in a local context tends to be weak, leading to a poor basis for policy-making and the like.

The aim of this chapter is to propose and elaborate a comprehensive analytic framework for the study of popular culture tourism in a local context. An evolutionary economic geography (EEG) approach is applied as an analytic lens and hence, a broad temporal and spatial contextualization of tourism development is stressed (e.g. Brouder et al., 2017). The potential of taking a broader social science approach in the study of popular culture tourism is highlighted by, for example, Gyimóthy et al. (2015), who stress, among other propositions, the crucial but poorly understood implications of popular culture tourism in regional policy and planning. The fact that popular culture tourism means new place-making logics, challenges existing regional processes and structures. Furthermore, a too narrow focus on tourism as an isolated discrete economic sub-system leads to missed opportunities to reveal obvious links between tourism and the wider society (Britton, 1991; Saarinen, 2006). Hence, it is argued that broader economic, environmental and social dimensions need to be addressed to create sustainable strategies in tourism and consequently to move beyond the narrow boundaries of the tourism business field towards a more critical approach (Tribe, 2008).

Following this introduction, in the next section the state-of-the-art literature in the field of popular culture tourism is briefly examined and theoretical knowledge gaps defined. Thereafter, an evolutionary economic approach is proposed as a fruitful theoretical framework to gain a holistic and critical understanding for place-making in the wake of popular culture tourism development. The EEG theoretical approach is further elaborated and a tentative and generic analytic framework is presented. In the final section of the chapter, theoretical and practical implications are summarized and discussed.

Disciplinary and theoretical underpinnings

State of the art and knowledge gaps

The phenomenon of popular culture tourism is increasingly gaining interest both in academia and in practice. A wide range of studies covering this topic have been published in tourism studies as well as in disciplines such as human geography, sociology, cultural studies, communication studies and media studies (Beeton, 2016; Connell, 2012; Heitmann, 2010; Richards, 2014). Furthermore, the vast majority of studies in the field of popular culture tourism (or one of its sub-categories, e.g. film tourism) are confined case studies, focused on the direct economic potential of popular culture induced tourist consumption and of supply and destination development. Hence, despite the obvious underlying argument of special interest tourism in the wake of film, TV series, literature and music as a booster for local development, it can be argued that few studies manage to explain the processes of local development through popular culture tourism (Gyimóthy et al., 2015). However, there are also a number of case studies in the field taking a more critical stance, scrutinizing impacts of popular culture tourism from a local perspective and revealing critical issues regarding the consequences of popular culture tourism investments in the local communities (e.g. Beeton, 2008; Croy, 2010; Heitmann, 2010).

Despite this, one key observation is that existing state-of-the-art literature fails to explain the complex processes behind special interest tourism such as popular culture tourism (Connell 2012; Gyimóthy et al., 2015; Heitmann, 2010). Consequently, despite efforts to scrutinize the consequences of popular culture tourism development in the local community, the lack of critical, systematic and holistic studies of this phenomenon as an integrated, local yet global production system raise several questions about the triggers and consequences of local development through popular cultural tourism development. In other words, the simplification of popular culture place-making calls for alternative theoretical perspectives highlighting tourist spaces as organic, dynamic, induced, socially and historically constructed meaning systems and practices (e.g. Gyimóthy et al., 2015; Saarinen, 2004).

As the interest for popular culture tourism as a cultural phenomenon and an economic activity is growing and its significance in local society develops, the need to understand popular culture tourism as a deeply rooted and integrated part of local development increases. However, despite a growing empirical interest in popular cultural tourism as a tool for local development, a limited number of studies embrace the phenomenon from a local perspective. Furthermore, as already stressed, these studies tend to be confined case studies (e.g. Heitmann, 2010) and more rarely integrated into analysis of broader regional structures and processes (cf. Hall, 2005; Saarinen, 2004). One fundamental limitation is the narrow understanding of space in tourism studies in general (including the field of popular culture tourism) and, more specifically the fact that space is often referred to as a tourist destination, i.e. a geographical area developed by tourism stakeholder for tourist consumption. However, as pointed out by Saarinen (2004), the notion of the tourist destination as the arena for tourism consumption and production is by nature problematic as it implies a homogenous, static and technical understanding of the local community. Consequently, the destination approach tends to offer a too shallow understanding of the society, favoring a tourist-centric approach (Saarinen, 2006), limiting deeper analysis of the impacts of popular culture tourism on society. With that said, a holistic and systematic understanding of space is proposed, including tourism and popular culture space of production (and consumption), as well as other relevant parts of the regional economic landscape (e.g. highlighting local perspectives of popular culture tourism).

Moreover, popular culture tourism development means new multi-scalar constellations of institutions and actors and new contextualization of tourism development, moving beyond traditional ways of organizing tourism. Hence, the fact that popular culture tourism constitutes a multi-sectoral "glocal" economic sector calls for alternative theoretical approaches, such as economic geographical theories of the production of tourism (cf. Ioannides & Debbage, 1998). Stakeholders' adaptability to internal and external influences and, the co-evolution of tourism with other domains of the economy has so far received scant attention, despite the fact that innovative tourism experiences are often created along the fault lines with, for example, traditional industry, fashion, gastronomy and popular culture (cf. Hall, 2005; Larsson & Lindström, 2013).

Introducing evolutionary economic geography

The knowledge gap addressed highlights the importance of describing, not only "what" is going on, but also a deeper temporal and contextualized understanding for "how" and "why" popular culture tourism evolves in and impacts communities. With that said, an evolutionary economic geographical theoretical and conceptual framework is proposed for the study of popular culture tourism. With such an approach, the relational ontology of place is addressed, acknowledging the social constructions of localities and the significance of historical evolution and multi-scalar and multi-sectoral interactions for local development (Brouder, 2014; Brouder et al., 2017).

> EEG concepts are creating a new framework to aid not only in understanding how destinations evolve over time, but also in interpreting the role of tourism as a way of accumulating capital in destinations and its implications in terms of the dynamics of economic variety, environmental (in)equity and social justice. EEG also highlights how transformations of destinations as places help them survive as communities.
>
> *(Brouder et al., 2017, p. 9)*

The study of tourism within the theoretical and conceptual framework of evolutionary economic geography is a relatively new phenomenon (for an overview see e.g. Brouder et al., 2017, p. 10ff; Brouder & Eriksson, 2013). However, the interest in destinations' evolution is not a new phenomenon, yet traditional evolutionary analysis (e.g. Butler's (2006) tourist area life cycle model) of tourist destinations consider the evolutionary process linear and hence, fails to contextualize and explain stakeholder relationships and collaboration on a deeper level and over time (Sanz-Ibáñez & Clavé, 2014).

The theoretical underpinnings of the EEG approach are threefold, building up an analytic framework based on the assumptions that local economies are complex multilayered systems, history matters and local development is shaped by interaction between agents and between agents and the landscape they are situated in (Boschma & Martin, 2010; Brouder & Eriksson, 2013). Hence, institutional and spatial complexity and evolution over time are considered crucial factors in the analysis of destination development. Consequently, the EEG conceptual framework offers opportunities to understand temporal and spatial drivers of change.

Local economies are complex multilayered systems

Complexity theory highlights the fact that local and regional economies are complex and multi-layered systems of interdependent environments and institutions operating on different geographical levels. To fully understand how these environments and institutions evolve and act, we need to embrace this complexity (Beinhocker, 2006; Martin & Sunley, 2015). Consequently, local, regional and global social, cultural, technological, institutional, industrial, etc. environments influence and determine tourism development through complex patterns of human relationships and institutional links (Martin & Sunley, 2015). As pointed out by Brouder et al. (2017), this stresses a shortcoming in tourism research, namely the tendency to deal with tourism with a single-sector approach (see also Smith et al., 1998) and, by doing so miss opportunities to scrutinize inter-sectorial dependencies between tourism and other sectors (Larsson & Lindström, 2013).

History matters

Path dependency or the general idea of "an inability to shake free from history" derives from evolutionary economics, however applied in various disciplines as a way to understand why and how institutions develop in certain ways (Arthur, 1989; David, 1985). In the field of evolutionary economic geography the concept was introduced by Martin and Sunley (2006) as a fundamental place-dependent explanatory principle of the evolution of the regional economic landscape and how individuals and organizations have a limited capacity to embrace change (Boschma & Frenken, 2006). Hence, the concept of path dependence stresses how the economic landscape shapes specific development paths over time and how these paths reveal crucial information about the performance of institutions within a tourist destination. By studying the trajectories of tourism development in a local economy, related theoretical concepts such as lock-in (David, 1985), path plasticity (Strambach, 2010) and path creation (Garud & Karnøe, 2001), bring nuances to the notion of path dependence. In the study of historical processes of regional development it is of great interest to understand dominant paths and how these are reproduced and possibly influence alternative development, as well as the occurrence of sudden shock that might lead to either crisis or the emergence of new paths (Henning et al., 2013).

Knowledge interaction and contextuality shapes local development

The notion of generalized Darwinism implies that local and regional development is determined by the principles of variety, novelty, selection and continuity, created by inter- and intra-regional competition (Boschma & Martin, 2010; Essletzbichler & Rigby, 2010). Consequently, growth through tourism in a local context is based on the notion of and interpretations of determinants of growth, sustainable development and/or innovation and the striving for an ideal combination of complementary economic activities. Here special attention needs to be paid to the recombination of knowledge, nature of knowledge transfer and accumulation of knowledge in low-technology sectors with a lot of informal network relations. In spite of less formal structures than in, for example, manufacturing industries, studies show how geographic proximity and intentional collaboration are important drivers of knowledge exchange in the tourism sector (Weidenfeldt et al., 2010). Brouder and Eriksson (2013) raise questions regarding the nature of tourism networks and the value of less formal volitional collaboration and the level of dissimilarities between network members without losing the ability to collaborate and to what extent geographic proximity can compensate for the lack of formal networks and dissimilarities.

To sum up the key contribution of evolutionary economic geography in the study of tourism development, it brings three theoretical tools to study evolution and complexity in tourism development. By doing so it opens up for a more holistic understanding of temporal and spatial drivers of change in tourism development. In the next section, an analytical framework, based on the three overlapping analytical layers will be introduced and adapted to popular culture tourism.

Methodology

In this section the theoretical framework presented above is further elaborated into a generic analytic model of key elements, specifically focusing on local development in the wake of popular culture tourism. The framework is based on the underlying assumption that an integrated and evolutionary approach to regional development provides "a heuristic device to guide the understanding of factors underlying change" (Gill & Williams, 2017, p. 48). Hence, it does not constitute a process model per see, but an analytical lens. Like previous research in the field of "evolutionary economic tourism geography" it is argued that the study of complex phenomena, such as popular culture tourism development, requires multi-method techniques. Hence, empirical data should include a combination of surveys, semi-structured interviews and document analysis of strategy and policy documents, trade reports, etc. (Gill & Williams, 2011; Larsson & Lindström, 2013). Furthermore, Gill and Williams (2017) suggest narrative case studies as an appropriate tool.

Despite the promising nature of evolutionary economic geography to bring new insights into the field of popular cultural tourism through its holistic focus on implications and consequences of place-making, critique of the EEG field and its applicability in empirical studies needs to be carefully scrutinized. Grabher (2009) offers a general overview of the critical debate of conceptual and empirical challenges of evolutionay economic geography and, for example, Brouder et al. (2017) and Sanz-Ibáñez and Clavé (2014) discuss the challenges of the EEG approach in a tourism context. According to them, the applicability in a tourism context lingers on how notions and concepts of the evolutionary economic geography are adapted to the specific circumstances of tourism (i.e. popular culture tourism) and the development of methods for data collection. With that said, a growing number of empirical studies prove the potential of evolutionary economic geography. A recent publication on "tourism destination evolution" (Brouder et al., 2017) offers several empirical examples of potential synergies of applying an EEG theoretical approach in tourism studies. The case studies presented in the volume show the richness of evolutionary economic geography, the variations in the applicability of the EEG theories to capture regional complexity, path dependency and general

Darwinism in tourism development. Despite the lack of popular culture tourism case studies, several relevant conceptual, methodological and empirical approaches can serve as inspiration. Furthermore, in a study by Larsson and Lindström (2013), intersectoral knowledge transfer was examined, revealing path dependency and lock-in moments and structures in the (lack of) regional collaboration between the tourism and traditional manufacturing sectors. In this study, as well as in the study by Gill and Williams (2011), the EEG approach was used as a "lens" through which to analyze the evolution of a tourist destination. Hence, the historical legacy is considered a key forming aspect, i.e. "history matters," rather than being a deterministic power (see also Hudson, 2005). Figure 40.1 provides a visualization of the three analytical dimensions proposed for the study of place-making in the wake of popular culture tourism.

The first analytic dimension highlights the complexity of the popular culture tourism production system (cf. Britton, 1991) and, hence popular culture tourism as a complex multi-layered and multi-scalar production system in the local economy. The repositioning along the experience economy logic significant in many local economies today, implies new and complex governance processes and stakeholder structures (Gyimóthy et al., 2015). In the case of popular culture tourism, the character of the cultural sector and the tourism sector and, how these are linked to each other, in a local context is a crucial starting point in the analysis. A study by Heitmann (2010) identifies key stakeholders in film tourism and points to the fact that various institutions such as the film industry, tourism businesses, the destination marketing organization, tourists and the community represent a very homogenous group of stakeholders. As pointed out in a study by Larsson and Lindström (2013), special interest tourism often calls for

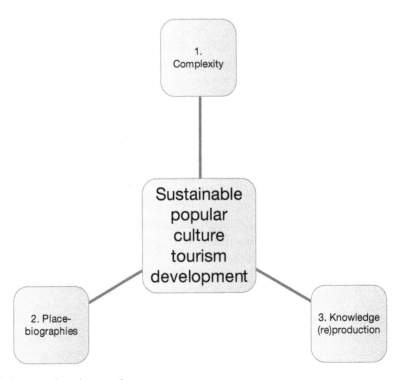

Figure 40.1 An analytic framework.

inter-sectoral collaboration between the tourism sector and other sectors of the local economy. Despite this, linkages to more established sectors tend to be weak (Hall, 2005, cf. Ioannides & Debbage, 1998). Furthermore, the level of sectoral convergence in the experience economy is of key interest (Gyimóthy et al., 2015). Insights into deeper understanding of the embedded relationships between public and private stakeholders in tourism and local producers of film, TV, literature and music, reveal knowledge about how local resources are utilized and processed in the popular culture tourism production system. For example, one important observation would be to what extent investments in popular culture tourism include a broad collaboration between local stakeholders or apply to more narrow collaborative arrangements concentrated around the local destination marketing organization. The argument here is the broader the collaboration is, the more inclusive the tourism development will be (cf. Bramwell & Lane, 2000). One crucial aspect is its multi-scalar character and the 'glocal' production system (Gyimóthy et al., 2015). For example, combined processes of Europeanization and regionalization in many countries in the EU mean that local planning and development are facing multi-level contexts. Consequently, opportunities for regional and EU actors to coordinate local initiatives, for example investments in the tourism sector and film production, separately or in combination emerge (cf. Månsson & Eskilsson, 2013).

The second analytic dimension forms an evolutionary layer of key relevance for the understanding of popular culture tourism development in a local context. That is, to map out and analyze key events, decisions and circumstances in the past and, by doing so gain better understanding for the current status of popular culture tourism and reveal clues for future development. As pointed out by Gyimóthy et al. (2015), little systematic research has been conducted with the purpose of capturing long-term effects of and solutions to changes in demand for popular culture tourism in a local context. Through the unpacking of popular culture tourism place-making biographies, a deeper understanding for how the phenomenon evolves and is organized in space and time will emerge. In some cases, a region's cultural sector and tourism sector have long, yet separated, histories and, in other cases one of the sectors is established in the regional economy whereas the other is emerging. In a pilot study, Lindström and Gyimóthy (2015) compared the trajectories of popular culture tourism in three European regions and highlighted that the legacy of the tourism sectors and cultural sectors (e.g. film production) in the regions varied a lot, indicating different conditions (financial resources and human capital) in the development of popular culture tourism.

The evolution of the popular culture tourism phenomenon provides information about path dependency and lock-in in the popular culture production system and hence, important information about, for example, the cultural sector's willingness to commercialize and past collaborations (or lack thereof due to lock-in) and knowledge-exchange. Interestingly enough, lock-in may cause both success and stagnation in the evolution of popular culture tourism development. One crucial aspect is how strategic regional inter-organizational collaborative partnerships (or lack thereof) between tourism stakeholders and stakeholders in the popular culture sector(s) evolve and establish over time. In accordance with the evolutionary perspective, the creation of "paths" in a local economy is dependent on the level of specialization. The more diversified the local business life is, the more likely it is that new special interest tourism will develop, i.e. new sectorial combinations (Brouder & Eriksson, 2013; Holm, Østergard, & Olsen, 2013). One example of negative lock-in is when tourism evolves from being a success story to becoming the dominating economic sector in a local community and, as such creates a one-sided, volatile and vulnerable economic landscape (see Brouder et al., 2017; Capo, Font, & Nadal, 2007).

The third analytic dimension is focused on how meaning and value of popular culture tourism is produced, reproduced and negotiated in the local context. Deeper analysis of how the notion of popular culture tourism triggers embedded relationships between previously distant actors is of specific interest, specifically how they link to each other and to the geographical space through knowledge transfer. The notion of related variety or complementarity are of key interest in this part of the analysis. That is, that the knowledge exchanged should be different and complementary, but not too different to trigger learning processes in the popular culture production system (Boschma, Eriksson, & Lindgren, 2009; Boschma & Iammarino, 2009; Frenken, Van Oortr, & Verburg, 2007). Consequently, collaboration between the sometimes very disparate actors in the culture and tourism sectors fails due to too different world views, interests and goals. Examples could be the view of profit-making, and stakeholders' engagement in responsibility for sustainable development (cf. Heitman, 2010). Often this leads to negative lock-in and blocks collaboration and joint learning in popular culture tourism. However, when analyzed and handled in a strategic way, joint learning processes can improve knowledge exchange and highlight local policy-making with a focus on sustainable development (Gyimóthy et al., 2015). Hence, it can be argued that long-term stability and the ability to rejuvenate as a tourist destination is dependent on a deep involvement of key stakeholders and the creation of shared visions and consensus among these.

The analytic framework presented above stress the production of popular culture tourism in a wider geographical context, stressing the embeddedness of popular culture tourism development in complex, evolutionary and complementary processes. In the final section of the chapter, the implications of such an approach for popular culture tourism are summarized and discussed.

Implications for popular culture tourism

Popular culture tourism is considered a booster for many local economies, yet little is known about the mechanisms enabling the (re)production of these contended successful development trajectories and hence the ability to understand and forecast sound planning of this praised special interest tourism is limited, mainly focusing on demand and tourist-centric perspectives (e.g. Gyimóthy et al., 2015).

The concept of popular culture tourism (i.e. the scope of this volume) is one important contribution to a more holistic understanding, reflecting the fact that the production and consumption of leisure activities converge in endless place-making circuits (cf. Ateljevic, 2000; Gyimóthy et al., 2015; Jenkins, 2004, 2006). With the intention to further develop the notion of complex and embedded place-making in the wake of popular culture tourism, the purpose of this chapter has been to propose and elaborate a contextualized and integrated approach. By doing so, new insights are brought to light, embracing the complex, path-dependent and knowledge-based local (and global) processes shaping the underlying conditions of popular culture tourism development. The fact that broader dimensions of collaborations and knowledge-exchange are addressed, promote sustainable strategies in tourism and consequently move beyond the narrow boundaries of the tourism business field towards a more critical approach (Tribe, 2008).

The study has both theoretical and practical implications of key relevance for sustainable popular culture tourism development. The fact that many regions in the world are going through a transformation towards an experience-based production, and often with investments in popular culture tourism, calls for planning and development strategies adapted to this new place-making logic. One key argument is the need to broaden the popular culture tourism knowledge base, moving away from policy-thinking bias based on short-term and demand-driven metrics.

In this chapter, evolutionary economic geography has been proposed as an appropriate analytic framework to gain in-depth understanding for the implications of popular culture tourism in the local economy and a comprehensive analytic framework is introduced. The hypothesis is that tourist regions' competitive situatedness within the creative economy is formed by path-dependent and multiple relationships among popular cultural stakeholders and tourism stakeholders, rather than place-bound attributes and commissioning strategies.

In terms of policy, the proposed analytic framework reveals policy complementaries and can serve as a tool for identification of important drivers assisting place-making through popular cultural tourism expressions. Broader collaborative arrangements between tourism stakeholders and stakeholders in the cultural sector is fundamental for successful and sustainable popular culture tourism development, however this is far from an easy task due to path-dependency and lock-in situations. Structured analysis and the identification of temporal and spatial drivers of change may give valuable insights into strengths and weaknesses of the popular culture economic landscape.

This chapter is an attempt to bring new perspectives into the field of popular culture tourism. Evolutionary economic geography, like most theoretical approaches, stress certain aspects of the real world at the expense of others (Essletzbichler & Rigby, 2010) and, hence alternative theories could provide valuable contributions to future work. The point to be made here is rather about the need to open up for debate new dimensions and perspectives addressing regional development and sustainability in the wake of popular culture tourism as a way forward for local economies.

References

Arthur, W. B. (1989). Competing technologies, increasing returns, and lock-in by historical events. *Economic Journal*, *99*(394), 116–131.

Ateljevic, I. (2000) Circuits of tourism: Stepping beyond the 'production/consumption dichotomy.' *Tourism Geographies*, *2*(4), 369–388.

Beeton, S. (2001). Lights, camera, re-action: How does film-induced tourism affect a country town? In M. F. Rogers & Y. M. J. Collins (Eds.), *The future of Australia's country towns*. Bendigo, VIC: Centre for Sustainable Regional Communities, La Trobe University, pp. 172–183.

Beeton, S. (2008). Location, location, location: Film corporations' social responsibilities. *Journal of Travel & Tourism Marketing*, *24*(2–3), 107–114.

Beeton, S. (2016). *Film-induced tourism* (Vol. 76). Clevedon: Channel View Publications.

Beinhocker, E. D. (2006). *The origin of wealth: Evolution, complexity, and the radical remaking of economics*. Cambridge, MA: Harvard Business Press.

Boschma, R., Eriksson, R. & Lindgren, U. (2009). How does labour mobility affect the performance of plants? The importance of relatedness and geographical proximity. *Journal of Economic Geography*, *9*(2), 169–190.

Boschma, R. A. & Frenken, K. (2006). Why is economic geography not an evolutionary science? Towards an evolutionary economic geography. *Journal of Economic Geography*, *6*(3), 273–302.

Boschma, R. & Iammarino, S. (2009). Related variety, trade linkages, and regional growth in Italy. *Journal of Economic Geography*, *85*(3), 289–311.

Boschma, R. & Martin, R. (2010). *The handbook of evolutionary economic geography*. Cheltenham: Edward Elgar.

Bramwell, B. & Lane, B. (Eds.). (2000). *Tourism collaboration and partnerships: Politics, practice and sustainability* (Vol. 2). Clevedon: Channel View Publications.

Britton, S. (1991). Tourism, capital, and place: Towards a critical geography of tourism. *Environment and Planning D: Society and Space*, *9*(4), 451–478.

Brouder, P. (2014). Evolutionary economic geography: A new path for tourism studies? *Tourism Geographies*, *16*(1), 2–7.

Brouder, P., Clavé, S. A., Gill, A. & Ioannides, D. (2017). Why is tourism not an evolutionary science? Understanding the past, present and future of destination evolution. In P. Brouder, S. A. Clavé, A. Gill & D. Ioannides (Eds.), *Tourism destination evolution*. Abingdon: Routledge, pp. 1–18.

Brouder, P. & Eriksson, R. H. (2013). Tourism evolution: On the synergies of tourism studies and evolutionary economic geography. *Annals of Tourism Research*, *43*, 370–389.

Butler, R. (Ed.). (2006). *The tourism area life cycle* (Vol. 1). Clevedon: Channel View Publications.

Capo, J., Font, A. R. & Nadal, J. R. (2007). Dutch disease in tourism economies: Evidence from the Balearics and the Canary Islands. *Journal of sustainable Tourism, 15*(6), 615–627.

Connell, J. (2012). *Film tourism: Evolution, progress and prospects.* Tourism Management, 33(5), 1007–1029.

Croy, W. G. (2010). Planning for film tourism: Active destination image management. *Tourism and Hospitality Planning & Development, 7*(1), 21–30.

David, P. A. (1985). Clio and the economics of QWERTY. *American Economic Review, 75*(2), 332–337.

Essletzbichler, J. & Rigby, D. L. (2010). Generalized Darwinism and evolutionary economic geography. In R. Boschma & R. Martin (Eds.), *The handbook of evolutionary economic geography.* Cheltenham: Edward Elgar, pp. 43–61.

Frenken, K., Van Oort, F. & Verburg, T. (2007). Related variety, unrelated variety and regional economic growth. *Regional Studies, 41*(5), 685–697.

Garud, R. & Karnøe, P. (2001). Path creation as a process of mindful deviation. In Garud, R. & Karnøe, P. (Eds)., *Path dependence and creation.* East Sussex: Psychology Press, pp. 1–40.

Gill, A. M. & Williams, P. W. (2011). Rethinking resort growth: Understanding evolving governance strategies in Whistler, British Columbia. *Journal of Sustainable Tourism, 19*(4–5), 629–648.

Gill, A. M. & Williams, P. W. (2017). Contested pathways towards tourism-destination sustainability in Whistler, British Columbia: An evolutionary governance model. In P. Brouder, S. A. Clavé, A. Gill & D. Ioannides (Eds.), *Tourism destination evolution.* Abingdon: Routledge, pp. 43–64.

Grabher, G. (2009). Yet another turn? The evolutionary project in economic geography. *Economic Geography, 85*(2), 119–127.

Gyimóthy, S., Lundberg, C., Lindström, K., Lexhagen, M. & Larson, M. (2015). Popculture tourism: A research manifesto. In D. Chambers & T. Rakić (Eds.), *Tourism research frontiers: Beyond the boundaries of knowledge* (Tourism Social Science Series, Vol. 20). Bingley: Emerald, pp. 13–26.

Hall, C. M. (2005). Rural wine and food tourism cluster and network development. In D. R. Hall, I. Kirkpatrick & M. Mitchell (Eds.), *Rural tourism and sustainable business* (Vol. 26). Clevedon: Channel View Publications, pp. 149–164.

Heitmann, S. (2010). Film tourism planning and development: Questioning the role of stakeholders and sustainability. *Tourism and Hospitality Planning & Development, 7*(1), 31–46.

Henning, M., Stam, E. & Wenting, R. (2013). Path dependence research in regional economic development: Cacophony or knowledge accumulation? *Regional Studies, 47*(8), 1348–1362.

Holm, J. R., Østergaard, C. R. & Olesen, T. R. (2013). Post exit knowledge diffusion in the aftermath of the Danish shipyards; and the lack of it. *The governance of a complex world.* Retrieved from: http://vbn.aau.dk/ws/files/71903116/HOLM_OSTERGAARD_OLESEN.pdf.

Hudson, R. (2005). Rethinking change in old industrial regions: Reflecting on the experiences of North East England. *Environment and Planning A, 37*(4), 581–596.

Ioannides, D. & Debbage, K. G. (1998). *The economic geography of the tourist industry: A supply-side analysis.* New York: Routledge.

Jenkins, H. (2004). The cultural logic of media convergence. *International Journal of Cultural Studies, 7*(1), 33–43.

Jenkins, H. (2006). *Convergence culture: Where old and new media collide.* New York: New York University Press.

Larson, M., Lundberg, C. & Lexhagen, M. (2013). Thirsting for vampire tourism: Developing pop culture destinations. *Journal of Destination Marketing & Management, 2*(2), 74–84.

Larsson, A. & Lindström, K. N. (2013). Bridging the knowledge-gap between the old and the new: Regional marine experience production in Orust, Västra Götaland, Sweden. *European Planning Studies, 8*, 1551–1568.

Lee, S. & Bai, B. (2016). Influence of popular culture on special interest tourists' destination image. *Tourism Management, 52*, 161–169.

Lexhagen, M., Larson, M. & Lundberg, C. (2014). The virtual fan (G) community: Social media and pop culture tourism. In A. M. Munar, S. Gyimóthy & L. Cai, (Eds.), *Tourism social media: Transformations in identity, community and culture.* Bingley, UK: Emerald, pp. 133–157.

Lindström, K. N. & S. Gyimóthy (2015). Film-induced tourism as regional development strategy: A critical assessment. Conference presentation, AAG Annual Meeting, Chicago.

Lundberg, C. & Lexhagen, M. (2012). Bitten by the *Twilight Saga*: From pop culture consumer to pop culture tourist. In R. Sharpley & P. R. Stone (Eds.), *The contemporary tourist experience: Concepts and consequences.* Abingdon: Routledge, pp. 147–164.

Månsson, M. & Eskilsson, L. (2013). *The attraction of screen destinations.* Report commissioned by Film London and the Euroscreen Partnership. Rzeczow, Poland.

Martin, R. & Sunley, P. (2006). Path dependence and regional economic evolution. *Journal of Economic Geography*, *6*(4), 395–437.

Martin, R. & Sunley, P. (2015). Towards a developmental turn in evolutionary economic geography? *Regional Studies*, *49*(5), 712–732.

Richards, G. (2014). Creativity and tourism in the city. *Current Issues in Tourism*, *17*(2), 119–144.

Saarinen, J. (2004). 'Destinations in change': The transformation process of tourist destinations. *Tourist Studies*, *4*(2), 161–179.

Saarinen, J. (2006). Traditions of sustainability in tourism studies. *Annals of Tourism Research*, *33*(4), 1121–1140.

Sanz-Ibáñez, C. & Anton Clavé, S. (2014). The evolution of destinations: Towards an evolutionary and relational economic geography approach. *Tourism Geographies*, *16*(4), 563–579.

Scott, A. J. (1997). The cultural economy of cities. *International Journal of Urban and Regional Research*, *21*(2), 323–339.

Smith, S. L., Ioannides, D. & Debbage, K. G. (1998). Tourism as an industry. In D. Ioannides & K. G. Debbage (Eds.), *The economic geography of the tourist industry: A supply-side analysis.* New York: Routledge, pp. 31–52.

Strambach, S. (2010). Knowledge commodification and new patterns of specialisation: Professionals and experts in knowledge-intensive business services (KIBS) (No. 04.10). *Working Papers on Innovation and Space.*

Tribe, J. (2008). Tourism: A critical business. *Journal of Travel Research*, *46*(3), 245–255.

Weidenfeld, A., Williams, A. M. & Butler, R. W. (2010). Knowledge transfer and innovation among attractions. *Annals of Tourism Research*, 37(3), 604–626.

CONCLUSION
Building a research agenda for popular culture tourism

Background: popular culture as a stage of tourism performances

The upsurge of different forms of popular culture (film, music, sports, video games, events, etc.) nowadays is inextricably linked to the post-modern production and commodification of cultural signs that are consumed by a range of global audiences (Debord, 1983/1967). These processes make popular culture a destination commodification apparatus. Simply put, the range of cultural meanings underpinning popular culture products is being marketed to induce tourism-related benefits for those destinations associated with them. This poses questions of how to incorporate popular culture associations into the overall destination product and service mix and which strategies should advance popular culture-based tourism development. To effectively answer these questions, there is a need to thoroughly examine the intersections between cultural production/consumption processes and the socio-economic and political conditions required for developing subsequent destination strategies. In this regard, an inter-disciplinary approach to investigating popular culture and tourism may be undertaken to incorporate disciplines such as cultural geography, psychology, marketing, film, media, fan, and tourism studies.

On this basis, academic research can shed light on the intertextuality of media-driven creation of cultural signs that feeds metaphorically the public discourse with interpretive perceptions and dialectical meanings about the conditions that make up the world around us. Specifically, the appeal of destinations connected with popular culture expressions to fans and tourists is attributed to the symbolic meanings of popular culture performances, which function as cultural significations. In particular, they bring forward signs and images laden with symbolic meanings, which are constantly (re)interpreted by residents and tourists, thereby rendering new meanings that reinforce affective or ideological attachments. This (re)creation of meaning among different actors in the tourism industry creates polysemic webs of significance (Geertz, 1973) that engender unexplored possibilities for understanding the contribution of popular culture tourism to social (re)ordering. In other words, the symbolic meaning of popular culture signs presents opportunities for people to (re)interpret the world around them (Turner, 1974). This is a process that can be understood through the dramatological perspective (Ziakas & Costa, 2012), which reveals the meanings of those symbolic representations extracted and (re)interpreted by locals and tourists. However, popular culture-induced tourism has not been systematically examined as a mode of symbolic action that exemplifies expressive and dramatic cultural dimensions that in turn shape social ordering (Schechner, 1985, 2003). An investigation of the cultural grounds of popular culture tourism can illuminate the interconnections between popular and expressive culture, explain the differences between popular culture tourism and other tourism forms, and identify destination place-making strategies to facilitate popular culture tourism development.

Fundamentally, popular culture forms are cultural expressions regarded as popular or mass culture, which is a cultural form clearly associated with entertainment and recreation and consumed by the majority of consumers of culture (Lindgren, 2005; Strinati, 2004). It is often described as a counterpart to 'fine culture' (Heilbrun, 1997). The majority of research on popular culture is rooted in cultural studies, sociology, media studies, and anthropology (Lindgren, 2005; Traube, 1996) and when tourism researchers have approached the topic they have usually applied a destination or a tourist perspective. Destination-oriented studies have employed concepts such as commoditization (MacCannell, 1973) and staged performance and authenticity (Cohen, 1988; Xie, Osumare, & Ibrahim, 2007), largely to explore the design and implementation of tourist experiences and the extent to which those experiences can be viewed as 'original.' Tourist-oriented research has also tended to focus on tourist experiences, for example examining the emotional ties between tourists and place stories/mythologies (Connell, 2004; Kim & Richardson, 2003; Philips, 2011; Watson, 2006), celebrity associations and destination perceptions (Lee, Scott, & Kim, 2008; McCartney & Pinto, 2014) and travel motives and perceived value (Earl, 2008; Lundberg & Lexhagen, 2012). However, no matter which perspective is taken, popular culture tourism is clearly more complex than traditional push–pull destination models suggest (Beeton, 2005).

The main challenges and complexities of popular culture tourism are outlined in Part I of the Handbook. The multiple definitions and meanings of popular culture as well as its many roles and impact on human society are discussed (Chapter 1 by Fedorak). Popular culture's relationship with tourism and its scholarship, socialization, and construction are further explored (Chapter 2 by Tzanelli). The characteristics and implications of synontological spaces (popular culture tourists' 'visits' in two ontological realms, fiction and reality) are further examined (Chapter 3 by Trauvitch). The challenges of how differing notions of popular culture, history and heritage, and modern forms of capital (tourism industry) come together to memorialize and commodify contrasting forms of popular culture and its implications are scrutinized in the case of Apocalypto and Mexico (Chapter 4 by Benavides), and narco-drama in Columbia (Chapter 5 by Naef).

Mapping the field

Although popular culture has been studied from a variety of disciplines and perspectives, the findings of these literatures are not yet integrated to provide a holistic assessment (based on an interdisciplinary analysis) of the nexus that ties popular culture and tourism. In mapping the diachronic and emergent relationships that enable popular culture to become a tourism medium, it is inevitable that traditions and trends struggle in an effort to prevail and establish their intellectual supremacy. This is well-evidenced in the birth and development of relatively new fields such as tourism, leisure, sport, and event studies. On the one hand, a critical perspective stands based on humanities and socio-cultural studies. On the other hand, a more instrumental approach evolves based on marketing and management disciplines. Where should be the middle line capable of synthesizing and balancing the inherent tensions that reflect wider socioeconomic changes and ideological battles? How can we set direction and priorities in order for 'constructing' a balanced account of popular culture and tourism?

In response, this Handbook generates essential theoretical and practical context in building a common ground. The chapters and subsequent composition of this volume reveal a number of issues and topical areas that concern the relationship between popular culture and tourism. Chapter contributions indicate the cogency of (cultural) expressive practices in the study of this phenomenon and the need for developing a comprehensive research framework to better appreciate and understand its nature, dynamics, and outcomes. A programmatic conceptual convergence of the core tenets that epitomize the intersection of popular culture and tourism can enable us to define the parameters, delineate the processes, and assess the outcomes of this emergent phenomenon. Such an integrative perspective warrants the development of popular culture tourism as an inter-disciplinary field of study.

In particular, the Handbook provides insights into important gaps in building a research agenda for the popular culture tourism field. First and foremost, it addresses the artistic versus physical divide exemplified in performances of arts and physical cultures. In essence, the Handbook has attempted to provide a comprehensive analysis of the range of popular culture forms that induce tourism. This endeavor aims to reconcile the inherent tension and division between artistic forms (cinema, music, literature) and physical cultures (sport, dance). Thus, while most chapters focus on the predominant forms of popular culture such as film and music, a number of contributions extend to examine the interplay of dance and football with national identity (Chapter 11 by Ana and Chapter 23 by O'Boyle), and the impact of technology adoption on cricket (Chapter 13 by Hassan). These inquiries reflect the multifaceted effects of mediatization on the evolving aestheticization and physicalization taking place across different popular culture expressions.

Second, two interlinked areas of importance identified are the *sense of place* and *branding*. The study of transition of destination image and its perception has been identified where the old and new live side by side (Chapter 32 by Gyimóthy). The local narratives and new representations of space reinforced by popular culture and their implications for tourism marketing have also been pinpointed as an important area of study (Chapter 31 by Kaya & Yolal, Chapter 29 by Mulet Gutiérrez, Oliver Torelló, & Sebastián Sebastián, Chapter 35 by Radomskaya). Linked to the dual narratives and place representations are the opposing senses of place (Chapter 16 by Palmer) in the context of neo-colonial frameworks, the postcolonial exotic, implemented by destination management for the purpose of creating attractive images of destinations (Chapter 25 by Pande). Other research identified destination marketing management failing to capitalize on the marketing potential of a destination's sense of place in the wake of popular culture and the need for a further exploration of this topic (Chapter 37 by Forgas-Serra, Majó Fernández, & Mundet i Cerdan). The soundscape of a place and how it reinforces a sense of place (Chapter 9 by Bolderman & Reijnders) along with how new behavior in the footsteps of popular culture shapes and changes the perception of place (Chapter 12 by Wieringa) have also been identified as important areas of research. The need for developing more knowledge on the different forms of popular culture expressions – as a function of mediatization – and their contribution to different perceptions of place for various stakeholders and its subsequent challenges has also been established (Chapter 27 by Lind & Kristensson Uggla).

Third, two other important areas for future research in popular culture tourism identified in the Handbook are *heritage* and *authenticity*. The new and old capitalizing on each other's existence at destinations has been further explored and pinpointed as important areas of future research in the case of popular culture in traditional museums (Chapter 38 by Boukas & Ioannou), literary landmarks (Chapter 24 by Ramdarshan Bold), and traditional music in contemporary settings (Chapter 10 by Henriques, Guerreiro, Mendes, & Ramos). The need for developing knowledge on how authentic heritage experiences rejuvenate and shape contemporary identities, such as medieval history and sites (Chapter 8 by Laing & Frost), dark travel in the form of cemetery tourism (Chapter 17 by Levitt), or royalty associations (Chapter 15 by Palmer & Long), was further established. These examples pinpoint the importance of history and heritage representations produced for authentic public consumption through the medium of popular culture expressions (Chapter 28 by Fagence). As such, the Handbook contributions corroborate epistemological elaborations on heritage interpretation (Uzzel, 1992), tourism 'worldmaking' processes in recreating social constructions (Hollinshead, 2009; Hollinshead, Ateljevic, & Ali, 2009), and tourism network hermeneutics (Tzanelli, 2007, 2013, 2015), shedding light on the role of popular culture in making, remaking, and unmaking places as tourist destinations. In this process the co-construction of meaning in place-making is pivotal by epitomizing its dialectical intertextuality with genres, symbols, and the media that shape cultural expressions and (re)interpretations as authenticity and heritage intermingle.

Socio-cultural underpinnings and place-making

The above chapter contributions highlight the importance of the socio-cultural grounds that underpin popular culture tourism. As explained, popular culture performances can be understood as expressive practices that, through their dramaturgical narratives and symbols and reinterpretation by fans and residents, invoke the fundamental characteristics of a host destination. From a dramatological perspective, popular culture performances can therefore be analyzed as texts conveying messages that promote the culture of a destination and its attractive characteristics to outsiders. In this regard, popular culture signs tied to a place constitute versions and interpretations of a community's fabric and may reinforce intended meanings via the strategic use of polysemic structures (i.e. narratives, symbols, and genres). Dramaturgy can also elucidate the construction process of tourism places and their identity formation as, by employing the metaphors of performance and performativity (Ziakas & Costa, 2012), tourism activity can be analyzed as a series of performances within places that are continuously created by the performances of tourists and hosts (Giovanardi, Lucarelli, & Decosta, 2014). As such, the making of a destination based on popular culture is the outcome of projected signs and their interactions with stakeholders stemming from the contextual environment of a place (human, social, cultural, physical, etc.). Subsequently, an orchestrated use of polysemic signs can foster cultural performance manifestations that negotiate and/or (re)create the symbolic meanings and conditions that make up a community's socio-cultural fabric by enabling metaphoric discourse between fans, tourists, and natives about issues of social concern or discord. From this perspective, the challenge is how the symbolic meanings of popular culture performances can be leveraged by a place to build a strong connection without forfeiting its authentic representation. Thus, the notion of authenticity raises questions about the making of place identity and its representation, while the role of local heritage in this process and who might construct it (Hollinshead, 1998, 1999) needs to be considered. Furthermore, as multiple interests, values, and meanings are met within popular culture tourism settings, the danger of conflict and/or exploitation exists. Consequently, there is an urging need to safeguard perceptions of authenticity so that processes of commodification, modernization, and cultural politics do not distort a destination's cultural fabric. Instead, it is essential that authenticity is rendered through enabling the impartial representation of symbolic existential elements that underpin a community's social order.

At the core of any discussion regarding the commodification and consumption of space, is the sense of place, which can be defined from the perspective of locals and visitors (Derrett, 2003). The former's sense of place consists of an emotional attachment to the place, its identity, and community, while the latter refers to the visitors' experience and consumption of the characteristics that a place exhibits. These along with reinterpretations of its cultural symbols may engender new meanings that embody its heritage and values. The reinterpretation of popular cultural heritage, hence, becomes part of a transformed and co-constructed sense of place that is readily commodified, and put together as a consumption practice. In this vein, the sense of place is redefined and validated by a wider diversity of people (both local insiders and outsiders), affording the possibility not only to authenticate the identity, image, and qualities of a destination to a broader audience but also to embed the destination into the global public sphere by explicating its relationship to the world. To do so, it is essential that destination assets be leveraged synergistically with the cultural significations (symbols, narratives, metaphors, etc.) engendered by popular culture performances. This can amplify the redefined sense of place through its reinterpretation within a co-construction process that looks at a destination's identity and renders it with meaning.

The conceptual framework the *Popcultural Placemaking Loop*, presented by Gyimóthy et al. (2015) showcases these co-creation and co-consumption processes of places in the form of performative negotiations between different stakeholders. It emphasizes the circular phases of negotiated reproduction including drivers and consequences for popular culture tourism. The transformation of place is at its center with processes of appropriation of place, dramaturgical performance, mediatization, perceptions of authenticity, and reinterpretation of cultural representations by audiences. The framework does not, however, explicitly pinpoint the importance of heritage in the development of popular culture tourism and its links to dramaturgy and authenticity. Thus, popular culture tourism development is a multi-dimensional, dynamic and complex process influenced by different factors, stakeholders, and operating on different levels. In order to advance understanding, the next section presents the destination management issues and requirements, which incorporate popular culture place-making processes.

Destination management and place-making

The Handbook contributions also established another two intertwined areas for research in building a future research agenda for the field from a destination perspective: *stakeholders* and *sustainability*. Central to a sustainable development of popular culture tourism is the understanding of proactive destination management including resource capacity management, networking, and image management for the benefit of the community (Chapter 33 by Croy, Kersten, Mélinon, & Bowen) as well as the exploration of different stakeholders' willingness to invest (Chapter 7 by Roesch), different competence and capacity (Chapter 34 by Eskilsson & Månsson), and conflicting agendas and power relations (Chapter 26 by Barton). In the case of film tourism, the phenomenon of displacement is analyzed where movies are filmed in one place but represent another one (Chapter 32 by Gyimóthy and Chapter 31 by Kaya & Yolal). The result may be that the visiting audience experiences significant dissonance when visiting the film location, as it may be hugely different from the film representation. From a broader marketing standpoint, lifestyle tourism has been recognized as a stable platform of popular culture expression resistant to the volatile nature of consumer preferences and therefore an important area for future research (Chapter 39 by Gross). A shift away from policy-thinking and development, based on short-term and demand-driven metrics, towards an evolutionary economic geography framework is proposed for building a future research agenda within the field (Chapter 40 by Lindström).

The above contributions address the nature of popular culture tourism being primarily demand-driven and often exhibiting a rapid initial growth that surprises destination stakeholders. This sometimes causes capacity problems at destinations unprepared for increased tourism demand.

Moreover, the media representation of a destination and its subsequent interpretation by tourists and fans can leave locals unsure as to how they should respond to the projection of their community. This can be exacerbated by reactive rather than proactive strategies, a lack of inter-agency collaboration (Bolan, Boy, & Bell, 2011; Long & Morpeth, 2016; Lundberg, Lexhagen, & Mattsson, 2012; Müller, 2006), and the ad hoc commodification of symbols and signs for consumption practice. If they are forced to employ a reactive strategy, destination stakeholders may not understand visitors' reinterpreted meaning of the place (Larson, Lundberg, & Lexhagen, 2013; Lundberg et al., 2012). Therefore, while destinations may gain significant (although often short-term) exposure, at the same time they become objects of worldwide public discourses, which are largely beyond their control.

A further challenge for popular culture tourism development is the lack of partnerships between the tourism and creative industries. This lack of partnership constrains the formulation of destination strategies. For example, the tourism industry is unable to create symbols for consumption practices and transformations of place (Larson et al., 2013). Instead, it follows later to embrace, adapt, or reject the media representation of a destination based on its perceived congruence with the culture, values, and heritage of a destination. Such reactions depend on tenable beliefs about the identity and self-image of a destination, which need to be reconfirmed, renewed, or reinvented. Thus, destination managers strive to render relevant meanings with significance by feeding metaphoric discourse about their local pertinence and amplifying the symbolic associations between a popular culture performance and the projected destination. This is both influenced by, and in turn influences, locals' esoteric understanding of their place and its relationship to the outside world.

Central to popular culture tourism is of course the fans. A typical association of a fan is a person with a deep relationship, involvement, knowledge about a popular culture phenomenon or expression such as a film, a TV show, a music band, or a celebrity. A popularized idea of a fan is an obsessed individual exhibiting an emotional fascination towards, for example, a celebrity. However, closer to the truth is that the majority of fans are highly knowledgeable individuals with a great passion for the object of their interest. There is no generally agreed upon definition of a fan or a fandom (i.e. the community) in academia. However, most definitions include descriptions of enthusiasts, identities, extensions of self, emotional investment or affect, communities, and purchase behavior (i.e. repeated consumption patterns) (Grossberg, 1992; Hills, 2002). In fact, the very common existence of fans and fandoms in current times is often pinpointed in literature: "fandom seems to have become a common and ordinary aspect of everyday life in the industrialized world" (Sandvoss, 2005, p. 3). One of the central research themes identified is the power relationship and resistance among and between groups of fans and the 'other.' This 'other' is represented by other fans or non-fans and the originator/copyright owner of the text (e.g. the author, film production company, and publisher) (Sandvoss, 2005). These social networks and its members' active participation and co-creation online and in real life are well documented in the literature (Hills, 2002; Jenkins, 2006; Sandvoss, 2005). One such example of fan productivity is the creation of travel-user generated content, by fans for other fans online (Lexhagen, Larson, & Lundberg, 2014). Fan travels to places associated with the object of interest has also been compared to pilgrimages with religious undertones (Aden, 1999; Hills, 2002; Sandvoss, 2005).

From this consumer perspective, the interlaced areas of *demand, social networks, co-creation*, and *identity* were also established by the Handbook contributions as central for further research in popular culture tourism. The urgency in understanding the complex demand and motivations for popular culture travel has been showcased in the Handbook (Chapter 6 by Kork) including both individual and social dimensions (Chapter 21 by Lexhagen), their link to fandoms

(Chapter 18 by Geraghty and Chapter 22 by Linden & Linden), celebrity associations (Chapter 19 by Yong Yeu Moy & Phongpanichanan) and cultural fantasies (Chapter 11 by Ana). The importance of understanding the social networks and co-creation processes that define fandoms was further emphasized such as when tourists become co-creators of marketing content on social media (Chapter 36 by Šegota) or when individual and collaborative adjustment processes allow artists and fans to engage in shared ventures (Chapter 20 by Schriever). Moreover, the Handbook contributions demonstrate the demand for further exploration of identifications in relation to popular culture tourism such as national identity (Chapter 23 by O'Boyle), and bring forward implicit links to dramaturgy of fans and place representations (Chapter 30 by Mason & Rohe and Chapter 14 by Lamerichs).

Epilogue

In conclusion, based on the Handbook's contributions that illustrate multitude theoretical foci as well as empirical insights, we argue for the following: it is imperative to establish an integrative mode of inquiry for studying popular culture tourism that encompasses different disciplinary approaches and expands the focus on identifying both conceptual and functional linkages among various forms of popular culture as they intersect with tourism. At the core of such inquiry is the search for experiential authenticity that fans and tourists embark on through their engagement in a type of popular culture. Such engagements reflect an existential urge of people to cross the borders between fiction and reality while re-interpreting and re-setting underlying social constructions. The processes and conduits that enable popular culture tourism to effectively play this part merit considerable research attention.

References

Aden, R. C. (1999). *Popular Stories and Promised Lands: Fan Culture and Symbolic Pilgrimages*. Tuscaloosa and London: University of Alabama Press.

Beeton S. (2005). *Film-Induced Tourism*. Clevedon: Channel View.

Bolan P., Boy, S., & Bell J. (2011). We've seen it in the movies, let's see if it's true: Authenticity and displacement in film-induced tourism. *Worldwide Hospitality and Tourism Themes, 3*(2), 102–116.

Cohen, E. (1988). Authenticity and commoditization in tourism. *Annals of Tourism Research, 15*(3), 371–386.

Connell, J. (2004). Toddlers, tourism and Tobermory: Destination marketing issues and television-induced tourism. *Tourism Management, 26*, 763–776.

Debord, G. (1983/1967). *Society of the Spectacle* (translated by K. Knabb from the French original of 1967). London: Rebel Books.

Derrett, R. (2003). Making sense of how festivals demonstrate a community's sense of place. *Event Management, 8*(1), 49–58.

Earl, B. (2008). Literary tourism: Constructions of value, celebrity and distinction. *International Journal of Cultural Studies, 11*(4), 401–417.

Geertz, C. (1973). *The Interpretation of Cultures*. New York: Basic Books.

Giovanardi, M., Lucarelli, A., & Decosta, P. (2014). Co-performing tourism places: The "Pink Night" festival. *Annals of Tourism Research, 44*, 102–115.

Grossberg, L. (1992). Is there a fan in the house? The affective sensibility of fandom. In L. A. Lewis (Ed.), *The Adoring Audience*. London: Routledge, pp. 581–590.

Gyimóthy, S., Lundberg, C., Lindström, K., Lexhagen, M., & Larson, M. (2015). Popculture tourism: A research manifesto. In D. Chambers & T. Rakic (Eds.), *Tourism Research Frontiers*. Bingley, UK: Emerald, pp. 13–26.

Heilbrun, J. (1997). The competition between high culture and popular culture as seen in the *New York Times*. *Journal of Cultural Economics, 21*, 29–40.

Hills, M. (2002). *Fan Cultures*. Abingdon: Routledge.

Hollinshead, K. (1998). Disney and commodity aesthetics: A critique of Fjellman's analysis of 'distory' and the 'historicide' of the past. *Current Issues in Tourism*, *1*(1), 58–119.

Hollinshead, K. (1999). Tourism as public culture: Horne's ideological commentary on the legerdemain of tourism. *International Journal of Tourism Research*, *1*(4), 267–292.

Hollinshead, K. (2009). The 'worldmaking' prodigy of tourism: The reach and power of tourism in the dynamics of change and transformation. *Tourism Analysis*, *14*(1), 139–152.

Hollinshead, K., Ateljevic, I., & Ali, N. (2009). Worldmaking agency-worldmaking authority: The sovereign constitutive role of tourism. *Tourism Geographies*, *11*(4), 427–443.

Jenkins, H. (2006). *Fans, Bloggers and Gamers: Exploring Participatory Culture*. New York: New York University Press.

Kim, H. & Richardson, S. (2003). Motion picture impacts on destination images. *Annals of Tourism Research*, *30*, 216–237.

Larson, M., Lundberg, C., & Lexhagen, M. (2013). Thirsting for vampire tourism: Developing pop culture destinations. *Journal of Destination Marketing & Management*, *2*(2), 74–84.

Lee, S., Scott, D., & Kim, H. (2008). Celebrity fan involvement and destination perceptions. *Annals of Tourism Research*, *35*, 809–832.

Lexhagen, M., Larson, M., & Lundberg, C. (2014). The virtual fan(G) community: Social media and pop culture tourism. In A. M. Munar, S. Gyimóthy, & C. Liping (Eds.), *Tourism Social Media: Transformations in Identity, Community and Culture* (Tourism Social Science Series, Vol. *18*). Bingley, UK: Emerald, pp. 133–157.

Lindgren, S. (2005). *Populärkultur: Teorier, Metoder och Analyser*. Malmö, Sweden: Liber.

Long, P. & Morpeth, N. D. (2016). *Tourism and the Creative Industries: Theories, Polices and Practice*. Abingdon: Routledge.

Lundberg, C. & Lexhagen, M. (2012). Bitten by the *Twilight Saga*: From pop culture consumer to pop culture tourist. In R. Sharpley & P. R. Stone (Eds.), *The Contemporary Tourist Experience: Concepts and Consequences*. Abingdon: Routledge, pp. 147–164.

Lundberg, C., Lexhagen, M., & Mattsson, S. (2012). *Twication: The Twilight Saga Travel Experience*. Östersund: Jengel Förlag AB.

MacCannell, D. (1973). Staged authenticity: Arrangements of social space in tourist settings. *American Journal of Sociology*, *79*(3), 589–603.

McCartney, G. & Pinto, J. (2014). Influencing Chinese travel decisions: The impact of celebrity endorsement advertising on the Chinese traveler to Macao. *Journal of Vacation Marketing*, *20*(3), 253–266.

Müller, D. (2006). Unplanned development of literary tourism in two municipalities in rural Sweden. *Scandinavian Journal of Hospitality and Tourism*, *6*(3), 214–228.

Philips, D. (2011). Mapping literary Britain: Tourist guides to literary landscapes 1951–2007. *Tourist Studies*, *11*(1), 21–35.

Sandvoss, C. (2005). *Fans*. Cambridge, UK: Polity Press.

Schechner, R. (1985). *Between Theater and Anthropology*. Philadelphia: University of Pennsylvania Press.

Schechner, R. (2003). *Performance Theory*. London: Routledge.

Strinati, D. (2004). *An Introduction to Theories of Popular Culture*. New York: Routledge.

Traube, E. G. (1996). 'The popular' in American culture. *Annual Review of Anthropology*, *25*, 127–151.

Turner, V. (1974). *Dramas, Fields and Metaphors: Symbolic Action in Human Society*. Ithaca: Cornell University Press.

Tzanelli, R. (2007). *The Cinematic Tourist: Explorations in Globalization, Culture and Resistance*. London: Routledge.

Tzanelli, R. (2013). *Heritage in the Digital Era: Cinematic Tourism and the Activist Cause*. London: Routledge.

Tzanelli, R. (2015). *Mobility, Modernity and the Slum: The Real and Virtual Journeys of Slumdog Millionaire*. New York & Abingdon: Routledge.

Uzzel, D. (Ed.). (1992). *Heritage Interpretation*. London: Bellhaven.

Watson, N. J. (2006). *The Literary Tourist: Readers and Places in Romantic and Victorian Britain*. Basingstoke, UK: Palgrave Macmillan.

Xie, P. F., Osumare, H., & Ibrahim, A. (2007). Gazing the hood: Hip-hop as tourism attraction. *Tourism Management*, *28*, 452–460.

Ziakas, V. & Costa, C. A. (2012). 'The show must go on': Event dramaturgy as consolidation of community. *Journal of Policy Research in Tourism, Leisure and Events*, *4*(1), 28–47.

INDEX